Fourth Edition

Diesel Engines and Fuel Systems

B.F. Wellington and A.F. Asmus

Barry Wellington & Alan Asmus

Diesel Engines and Fuel Systems

4th Edition

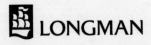LONGMAN

Addison Wesley Longman Australia Pty Limited
95 Coventry Street
South Melbourne 3205 Australia

Offices in Sydney, Brisbane and Perth and
associated companies throughout the world.

First published 1979
Reprinted 1981, 1982, 1984
Second edition 1988
Third edition 1991
Fourth edition 1995
Reprinted 1996

Illustrations by Jane Pennells, Marion Buckton and
Robert Milligan
Desk-top preparations by Christine Reynolds
Cover design by Rob Cowpe
Set in 11/13 Sabon
Printed in Australia by Australian Print Group

National Library of Australia
Cataloguing in Publication data

Wellington, B.F. (Barry F.).
    Diesel engines and fuel systems.

    4th ed.
    Includes index.
    ISBN 0 582 90987 2.

    1. Diesel motor. 2. Diesel motor – Fuel systems.
    I. Asmus, A.F. (Alan F.). II. Title.

621.436

In May 1992, Alan Asmus, one of the founding authors of *Diesel Engines and Fuel Systems* passed away. Since the book's inception, Alan was the principal driving force behind its constant updating and improvement. Without his technical knowledge and authorship, the book would not be of the high standard it is today.

Barry Wellington
June 1994

Contents

Acknowledgements

I would like to extend my sincere thanks to the following organisations which have assisted me with technical information, drawings and advice. Without such assistance, the task of preparing this book would have been impossible.

Australian Government Printing Service (AGPS)
Australian Institute of Petroleum Ltd
Bryce Berger Limited England
BTR Engineering (Australia) Limited
Castrol Australia
Caterpillar Inc. Australia
Consolidated Pneumatic Tool Co. Australia
    Pty Ltd

Cummins Diesel Australia
Detroit Diesel Australia
Deutz Australia Pty Ltd
Donaldson Australasia Pty Ltd
Dynamometers Australia
Federal Mogul Pty Ltd
Fiat Agri Australia
John Deere Limited
Loctite Australia Pty Ltd
Lab Volt Australia
Lucas CAV Limited England
Mack Trucks Australia Pty Ltd
Mazda Motors Pty Limited Australia
NS Komatsu Limited Australia
Perkins Engines Pty Limited England
Robert Bosch (Australia) Pty Ltd
Robert Bosch GmbH Germany
Scania Australia Pty Ltd
Society of Automotive Engineers-Australasia
Stanadyne Inc. USA
Toyota Motor Corporation Australia Limited
Volvo Australia Pty Ltd

I would like also to extend my sincere thanks to Bob Milligan for his invaluable technical expertise in drawing diagrams and proofreading the final draft. My thanks also to Mark Edwards for his technical assistance in proofreading the original draft copy.

Preface

The diesel engine has come a long way in the last ten years, especially with new developments in engine design, construction and the introduction of electronically controlled fuel injection systems. Therefore I have designed this fourth edition of *Diesel Engines and Fuel Systems* so that it stays abreast of these changes in order to keep readers informed of modern diesel engine technology.

There are now five new chapters which explain in detail the operation, construction and servicing of diesel engines. In addition to this new chapters on bearings and gaskets/seals have been included. For the first time, the book now illustrates and explains the complete workings of the diesel engine and its fuel injection systems.

The chapter on engine faultfinding and testing has been expanded to include information on where to connect test instruments to an engine and how to test an engine and draw up a performance graph. The chapters on in-line and distributor type fuel injection systems now include information on electronic fuel injection control and engine management. The chapter on Cummins Diesel fuel systems has also been updated, with a complete explanation of the Celect electronic fuel injection system.

Caterpillar are now using electronics on their unit-injected engines and this chapter now contains information on the electronically controlled 3176 engine. As a support to understanding electronic fuel injection systems, there is now a chapter on electronic system diagnosis which explains the ways in which faults within the system can be identified and repaired.

The chapter on Detroit Diesel fuel systems has been extended so as to illustrate and explain the operation of the various sensors used in the electronic engine management system.

Turbocompounding, how it works and why it is used on diesel engines now features in the chapter on turbochargers and blowers.

Finally, as emission controls are becoming stricter with diesel engines, some of the side-effects are starting to become apparent. These are discussed in the section on engine emission controls.

Once again, the response to requests for assistance from manufacturers, their agents, service people — in fact, the whole industry — has been both positive and prompt, and has made the compilation of this volume possible. The interpretation of the data has been my own, and is presented in the belief that it is accurate and correct.

Barry Wellington
Brisbane
1994

1

Some Important Terms

- **Inertia** is the resistance offered by a body to a change in its state of rest or uniform motion.
- **Force** is that which changes, or tends to change, a state of rest or uniform motion of a body.
- The **unit of force** is the newton, which is the force required to give a mass of 1 kilogram an acceleration of 1 metre per second squared (m/s^2); hence the force due to gravity acting on 1 kilogram is 9.80665 (usually accepted as 9.8) newtons.
- **Work** is done when a force overcomes resistance, and the point of application of the force moves. The **unit of work** is the **joule**, which is the work done when a force of 1 newton is applied and moves a body 1 metre in the direction of the application of the force. For example, if a jack lifts a mass of 1 kilogram through a distance of 1 metre, then 9.8 joules of work have been done — that is, 9.8 newtons (the force necessary to overcome gravity) multiplied by 1 metre (the distance) is equal to 9.8 joules.
- **Power** is the rate of doing work. The **unit of power** is the **watt**. When 1 joule of work is done in one second, 1 watt of power is consumed — for example, 9.8 watts are required to lift a mass of 1 kilogram through a distance of 1 metre in one second — again the 9.8 factor because the force due to gravity acting on 1 kilogram is 9.8 newtons.
- **Indicated mean effective pressure (IMEP)** is the average pressure in the engine cylinder during a complete engine cycle. Since the intake stroke pressure and the exhaust stroke pressure are close to atmospheric, they may be neglected, so that IMEP may be considered equal to the average pressure on the piston on the power stroke (which acts on the piston) minus the average pressure on the compression stroke (which represents work done by the piston).

  Note: In practice, IMEP is found by means of an indicator diagram (see Chapter 4).
- **Brake mean effective pressure (BMEP)** is that portion of IMEP that is converted to usable power. It is obvious that some of the IMEP must be consumed in overcoming internal engine friction. Therefore, only a portion of the IMEP is available to be converted to usable power at the flywheel.

  If friction could be eliminated, then IMEP would equal BMEP. However, friction exists inside an engine. Therefore

BMEP = IMEP – the pressure consumed in overcoming friction.

- **Indicated power** is the theoretical power of an engine, calculated from the indicated mean effective pressure.

If the indicated mean effective pressure is multiplied by the cross-sectional area of the piston, the total force acting on the piston may be found.

That is,

$$\text{force on piston} = P_M(\text{pascals}) \times A(\text{metres}^2)$$

where P_M is indicated mean effective pressure

and A is the cross-sectional area of the piston

But 1 pascal = 1 newton/metre²

Therefore:

force on piston

$$= P_M\left(\frac{\text{newtons}}{\text{metres}^2}\right) \times A(\text{metres}^2)$$

$$= P_M\left(\frac{\text{newtons}}{\text{metres}^2} \times \text{metres}^2\right)$$

$$= P_M \times A \text{ newtons}$$

Now, work done (joules) is equivalent to the applied force (newtons) multiplied by the distance through which it acts.

Therefore:

work done per working stroke
= force × length of stroke
= $P_M \times A$ (newtons) × L (metres)
where L is the length of stroke
= $P_M \times A \times L$ (newton metres)
But 1 newton metre = 1 joule

Therefore:

work done per working stroke
= $P_M \times A \times L$ joules
Now, power (work done per second)
= work done per working stroke × number of **working strokes per second**

$$= P_M \times A \frac{\text{joules}}{\text{strokes}} \times N \frac{\text{strokes}}{\text{second}}$$

where N is the number of **working strokes per second**

$$= P_M \times A \times L \times N \frac{\text{joules}}{\text{strokes}} \times \frac{\text{strokes}}{\text{second}}$$

$$= P_M \times A \times L \times N (\text{joules/second})$$

But 1 joule per second = 1 watt

Therefore:

Indicated power = $P_M \times A \times L \times N$ watts, which is usually written as:
Indicated power = $P_M LAN$

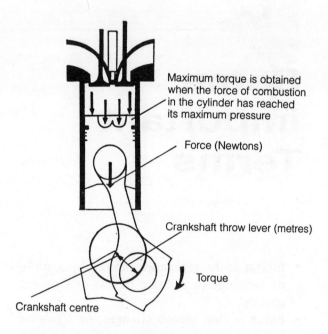

Maximum torque is obtained when the force of combustion in the cylinder has reached its maximum pressure

Force (Newtons)

Crankshaft throw lever (metres)

Torque

Crankshaft centre

Torque = Force × Distance
       = N × m
       = Nm

Fig 1.1   How an engine produces torque
Courtesy of Volvo

- **Brake power** is a measure of the engine power available, at the engine flywheel, to do work. It is less than **indicated power** by an amount equal to the power necessary to overcome the engine's internal friction.

The brake power of an engine is usually found by means of a dynamometer, which applies a braking force to the turning effort of the engine in question. The reaction causes a turning effort to be applied to the dynamometer, and this turning effort is measured. Its value, together with the engine's speed, is then substituted in a formula quoted by the manufacturer of the dynamometer for that particular dynamometer. The result is the brake power of the engine.

- **Torque** is turning effort. The crankshaft of an engine turns because of the force applied to the piston on the power stroke, which is transferred to the crankshaft via the connecting rod. At that engine speed at which the cylinder pressure is highest, the greatest turning effort is applied to the crankshaft. Usually, because of various inefficiencies at high speed, the maximum cylinder pressure does not occur at peak rpm, but at much lower speed. Therefore the maximum torque will occur at much less than peak rpm. Torque must not be confused with brake power, which involves a rate (or speed) factor. Thus, while torque will be less than maximum at peak rpm, the speed factor will result in brake power being maximum at or near peak revs.

- The **mechanical efficiency** of an engine is the ratio of its **brake power** to its **indicated power**. An engine that is mechanically efficient will not waste much power overcoming friction, and the brake power will not be much less than indicated power.

Mechanical efficiency

$$= \frac{\text{brake power}}{\text{indicated power}} \times 100\%$$

- **Indicated thermal efficiency** is the efficiency of an engine with regard to how efficiently it converts the chemical energy of the fuel to indicated power.

Indicated thermal efficiency

$$= \frac{\text{indicated power}}{\text{power available fuel used}} \times 100\%$$

- Every fuel contains a specific amount of heat energy, which is released when the fuel is burnt. This is known as the **calorific value** of the fuel, and is expressed in joules per kilogram of fuel. By measuring the amount of fuel used per minute or per hour, it is a simple matter to calculate the amount of heat energy supplied per second.

> Heat energy supplied (joules) per second
> = fuel used (kilograms) per second ×
>   calorific value of fuel (joules per
>   kilogram)
> But joules per second = watts

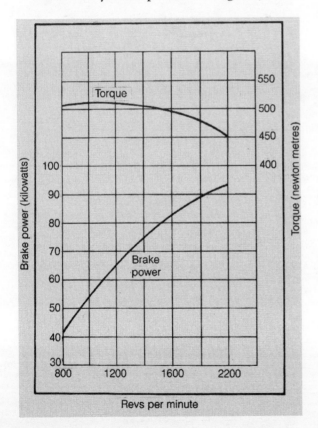

Fig 1.2 Typical brake power and torque curves for a large automotive diesel engine

Therefore:

Power available from fuel
= fuel used per second x calorific value of fuel

- **Brake thermal efficiency** is found by comparing the power output at the flywheel with the theoretical power available from the combustion of the fuel.

Brake thermal efficiency

$$= \frac{\text{brake power}}{\text{power available from fuel used}} \times 100\%$$

- The **volumetric efficiency** of a naturally aspirated engine is the ratio of the volume of air induced into the engine cylinder to the piston displacement — that is, how completely the cylinder fills with air (or air–fuel mixture). No unsupercharged engine has a volumetric efficiency of 100 per cent, and volumetric efficiency falls off at high rpm. The following factors influence volumetric efficiency:

- valve size and lift;
- port size;
- intake and exhaust manifold design;
- valve timing; and
- exhaust system restrictions.

- If an engine is supercharged, then the volumetric efficiency exceeds 100 per cent, since the air (or air–fuel mixture) is forced into the engine under pressure. If the quantity of air forced into the cylinder was allowed to regain normal pressure, then its volume would be greater than the piston displacement.

2 Comparing Petrol and Diesel Engines

Both petrol and diesel engines are internal combustion (IC) engines working on either the two- or four-stroke cycle. The basic design of both engines is similar, the main differences between the two being the method of introducing the fuel charge into the combustion chamber, and the means employed to ignite it. However, the engine features and performance characteristics may differ greatly. In Table 2.1, we have endeavoured to illustrate some of the differences between petrol and high-speed diesel engines of comparable size.

Admission of the fuel to the combustion chamber

In the diesel engine, air only is compressed on the compression stroke. The fuel charge required to produce the power stroke in each cylinder is accurately metered and pressurised by the fuel injection pump. It passes to the high-pressure injectors via pipes, and is sprayed into the combustion chamber, where it mixes with hot compressed air and is ignited.

In the petrol engine, fuel and air have traditionally been mixed in the throat of the carburettor, which is situated outside the engine cylinder. The air–fuel mixture then passes to the engine cylinder through the inlet manifold and the cylinder head inlet ports. Modern design has seen the introduction of fuel injection into the inlet ports of the cylinder head, with air only passing through the inlet manifold. However, in either case, the air–fuel mixture passes through the inlet ports into the combustion chamber of the engine, where it is ignited after being compressed.

Compression ratio

Before dealing with compression ratio, it is necessary to become familiar with the following terms:

- **Swept volume.** This is the volume of air displaced when the piston moves from bottom dead centre (BDC) to top dead centre (TDC) on its compression stroke.
- **Clearance volume.** This is the volume of air between the top of the piston and the cylinder head when the piston is at TDC at the end of the compression stroke.

Compression ratio is a comparison of the volume of air in the cylinder when the piston is at BDC with the volume of air present in the cylinder when the piston is at TDC. The volume of air in the cylinder when the piston is at BDC is equal to the swept volume plus the clearance volume, and the volume present when the piston is at TDC is equal to the clearance volume.

Therefore:

Compression ratio

$$= \frac{\text{swept volume} + \text{clearance volume}}{\text{clearance volume}}$$

It should be mentioned that the higher the compression ratio used, the hotter the gas being compressed will become.

Since the fuel and air are compressed in the cylinders of petrol engines, the maximum compression ratios used are limited, since high compression ratios, with their subsequent high air temperatures, would cause detonation of the mixture. Detonation is a dangerous condition which inflicts severe mechanical stress on engine components, as well as reducing engine performance.

However, diesel engines rely on the heat of the compressed air to ignite the fuel as quickly as possible when it is sprayed into the engine cylinders, so high compression ratios are very necessary. Thus diesel engines invariably have much higher compression ratios than petrol engines.

Ignition of the charge

It is well known that when air is compressed, heat is generated. Because of the high compression ratios used in diesel engines (14:1 to 24:1), the air taken into the engine cylinder is highly compressed (up to 3800 kPa). When the fuel charge is injected into and mixed with this highly compressed air at a predetermined point in the cycle, the heat in the air is sufficient to cause the fuel to ignite. This is called **compression ignition**.

With regard to the petrol engine, however, it must be remembered that the fuel and air are mixed external to the engine cylinder, and

Table 2.1 Comparison between diesel and petrol industrial engines

Feature	High-speed diesel engine	Petrol engine
Admission of fuel	Directly from fuel injector	From carburettor via the manifold, or injected into the inlet port
Compression ratio	From 14:1 to 24:1	From 7:1 to 10:1
Ignition	Heat due to compression	Electric spark
Torque	Varies little throughout the speed range	Varies greatly throughout the speed range
Brake thermal efficiency	35–43%	25–30%
Exhaust gases	Non-poisonous, but may cause suffocation	Poisonous
Engine construction	Robust	Relatively lighter than the diesel engine
Maximum crankshaft rpm	From 2500 to 5000 rpm	From 4000 to 6000 rpm
Compression pressure	Actual, 3100–3800 kPa Theoretical at 16:1 CR, 4254 kPa	Actual, 750–1400 kPa Theoretical at 8:1 CR, 1728 kPa
Compression temperature	Actual, 425–550°C Theoretical at 16:1 CR, 525°C	Actual, up to 230°C Theoretical at 8:1 CR, 375°C
Fuel used	Automotive distillate	Petrol

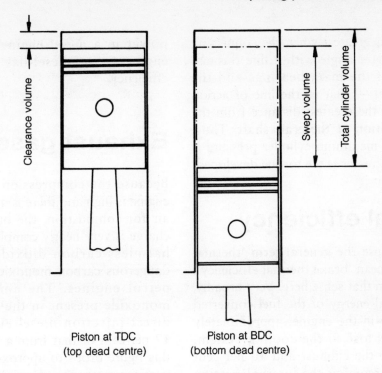

Fig 2.1   Comparing cylinder volume between top dead centre and bottom dead centre

the mixture is taken into the engine cylinder and compressed. This would make compression ignition, as used in the diesel engine, impractical, because the petrol vapour would ignite explosively during the compression stroke, causing very severe physical damage to engine components. It is therefore necessary to make use of lower compression ratios, and to ignite the air–fuel mixture in the combustion chamber by means of an electric spark at the desired point in the cycle.

Torque

Before studying this section, reference should be made to the definition of torque in Chapter 1. A diesel engine is said to have a 'high torque'. Broadly speaking, this means that the engine has good pulling power at all speeds, especially at low speeds. This is important when the diesel engine is used for automotive work, because it allows more work to be done in top gear and so eliminates the need for excessive gear changing.

With a petrol engine, the torque characteristic is not as constant as that of the diesel engine. As the speed of a petrol engine is reduced, so is its torque (and consequently its pulling power).

A petrol engine will not pull as well as a diesel engine at low speeds and is more inclined to stall than a diesel engine.

The difference in the torque characteristics of petrol and diesel engines may be directly linked to the combustion of the fuel charge. When combustion occurs in a petrol engine, maximum cylinder pressure exists for only a moment, at or near TDC, where the piston, connecting rod, big-end bearing and main bearings are generally 'in line'.

In a diesel engine, maximum cylinder pressure is sustained for a considerable time after the piston passes through the TDC position. As the crankshaft turns and the big-end journal moves past the 'in line' position, the force exerted on the piston by the gas pressure is transferred more effectively to the crankshaft via the connecting rod.

This effect is greatest when the connecting rod forms a right angle with a line through the centres of the main bearings and the big-end journal — that is, the line of action of the force is the greatest distance from the centre of rotation of the crankshaft. Thus, the longer the maximum cylinder pressure is sustained, the greater is the torque developed.

Thermal efficiency

It is usual to use the general term 'thermal efficiency' to mean 'brake thermal efficiency', and it is used in that sense here. Very broadly, of the chemical energy of the fuel converted to heat energy in the engine, approximately 20 per cent is lost to the cooling system, 27 per cent to the exhaust and 10 per cent is used in overcoming the internal friction of the engine, leaving about 43 per cent available to do useful work. This latter percentage is the (brake) thermal efficiency.

In an internal combustion engine, the more the air (or the air–fuel mixture) is compressed during the compression stroke, the greater the amount of power produced from combustion of the fuel, with a corresponding reduction in the amount of heat energy lost to the exhaust gases.

In petrol engines, compression ratios must be limited to prevent explosive ignition of the air–fuel mixture. Diesel engines, however, do not suffer this restraint and, indeed, need much higher compression ratios than petrol engines to achieve ignition of the fuel. Therefore, more of the heat energy of the fuel is converted to useful power, with less heat energy wasted as exhaust heat.

In addition, the compact, low-volume combustion chambers of diesel engines pemit less of the heat of combustion to be conducted to the cooling system than do the larger combustion chambers of petrol engines.

Therefore, of the energy supplied as fuel, a larger percentage is converted to usable power in a diesel engine than in a petrol engine — the diesel has a higher thermal efficiency.

Exhaust gases

Because the compression ratio of a diesel engine is high and there is more than adequate air for combustion, the burning of the fuel charge is very nearly complete. This results in harmless carbon dioxide instead of the dangerous carbon monoxide associated with petrol engines. The amount of carbon monoxide present in the exhaust gases of direct-injection diesel engines is around 17 per cent of that from a petrol engine, and this figure drops to approximately 5 per cent with some other combustion chamber designs.

The exhaust gases from a diesel engine also contain unburnt hydrocarbons (unburnt fuel), nitrogen oxides and oxides of sulphur. Although the exact cause of the characteristic diesel odour is not yet known, it has been found that engines with low hydrocarbon emissions do not usually have a strong exhaust odour. The oxides of nitrogen and sulphur combine with the water vapour resulting from combustion to form acids, which attack the cylinder liners and cause the lubricating oil to become acidic. This may lead to lung irritation.

Because the compression ratio of a petrol engine is considerably less than that of a diesel engine, the fuel charge does not burn with the same efficiency. This causes a greater percentage of lethal carbon monoxide to be present in the petrol engine exhaust gases — approximately 7 per cent at normal operation, but higher when idling in some instances. It is for this reason that diesel engines should be used in preference to petrol engines for mines, tunnels or any other undertakings where ventilation is inadequate.

Engine construction

Due to the high compression ratios and the combustion process employed in diesel engines, a diesel engine has much higher cylinder pressures than a petrol engine of similar power. This means that the internal stresses set up in the diesel engine components will be greater than those in a petrol engine. Consequently, the crankshaft, bearings, pistons, connecting rods and so on must be made stronger to withstand these stresses, and so enable the engine to function efficiently. With rapid advances being made in metallurgy, however, the weight of the modern diesel compares favourably with that of a petrol engine of similar power.

Crankshaft rpm

To understand why the crankshaft revolutions of a diesel engine are lower than those of a petrol engine of comparable size, it is necessary to understand the term 'inertia' (see Chapter 1). A force has to act on a body to overcome its inertia and so cause it to move or, if the body is in motion, to cause it to accelerate or decelerate. Now, if the body decelerates or comes to a complete stop, it is obvious that the force exerted by the inertia of the body must be overcome.

The piston of an IC engine must be brought to rest at both TDC and BDC pistons before its direction of motion is changed. This means that the inertia force exerted by the piston and connecting rod must be absorbed by these and other engine components. As the pistons and connecting rods used in a diesel are of heavier construction than those used in a petrol engine, the inertia force acting in a diesel engine is greater than that in a petrol engine doing the same number of rpm. The major components of a diesel engine, such as connecting rods, connecting rod 'big-end' bolts and crankshaft, must therefore be subjected to greater stresses. Mechanical failures such as broken connecting rod 'big-end' bolts and broken connecting rods may result from high inertia forces. In order to minimise these stresses, the crankshaft revolutions of a diesel engine are kept below those of a petrol engine.

Compression pressure

Compression pressure may be defined as the maximum air pressure created in the cylinder of an IC engine on the compression stroke. When the compression pressure in an engine cylinder is being checked, action should be taken to ensure that combustion does not occur. The actual compression pressure of the air in the cylinder of an engine is dependent on a number of factors, such as engine rpm, cylinder wear, ring wear and valve condition, but the theoretical compression depends on three factors:

1 the pressure of the air in the cylinder before it is compressed;
2 the compression ratio used; and
3 the gas constant for the pressure–volume relationship of the air under the conditions existing in the engine. (As pressure increases, so the volume decreases; the mathematical relationship of the two for a particular gas is known as the **gas constant**.)

The theoretical compression pressure of an engine is found by using the formula:

$$P_2 = P_1 r^n$$

where P_1 pressure of the air in the cylinder before compression;
P_2 = theoretical compression pressure;
r = compression ratio; and
n = the characteristic gas constant.

As has been stated previously, a petrol engine has a lower compression ratio than a diesel engine. Also, when the air–fuel mixture enters the cylinder of a petrol engine, it is cooled to a certain extent as the petrol vaporises. This improves the pressure–volume relationship, and so the value for n is slightly higher for a petrol engine than for a diesel. Because of the lower compression ratio used and the higher value for n, it should be obvious that the theoretical compression pressure in the cylinder of a petrol engine is much lower than that in the cylinder of a diesel engine.

Compression temperature

When a mass of air is compressed, the speed of the molecules in the air is increased, heat is generated, and so the temperature of the mass of air rises. Compression temperature may be defined as the temperature attained by the air which is compressed in the cylinder of an IC engine on the compression stroke. It should be noted here that compression temperature is the temperature attained by the air due to compression in the cylinder, and is not the temperature of the gases in the cylinder when combustion is in progress.

The actual compression temperature of the air in the cylinder of an IC engine is mainly dependent on the compression pressure, which is, in turn, dependent on the compression ratio and the mechanical fitness of the engine. An increase in engine rpm, however, will increase the compression pressure and subsequent compression temperature.

The theoretical compression temperature of the air in the cylinder of an IC engine depends on three factors:

1 the temperature of the air entering the cylinder before it is compressed;

2 the compression ratio used; and
3 the value of the characteristic gas constant, air being the gas used.

The theoretical compression temperature of an engine may be found by using the following formula:

$$T_2 = T_1 r^{n-1}$$

where T_1 = temperature of the air in the cylinder before compression begins. (In the above formula, absolute temperature must be used; this is found by adding 273 to the Celsius temperature.);

T_2 = theoretical compression temperature;

r = compression ratio;

n = the characteristic gas constant.

As has been discussed previously, petrol engines have a much lower compression ratio than diesel engines, while the value of n is slightly higher than for a diesel. Calculations based on typical values show that the theoretical compression temperature of the air in the cylinder of a diesel engine with a compression ratio of 16:1 is approximately 40 per cent higher than that of a petrol engine with an 8:1 compression ratio.

Note: It must be stressed here that the theoretical compression pressure and the theoretical compression temperature of the air that is compressed in the cylinder of an IC engine are influenced by such things as engine rpm, altitude, pressure–volume relationship and climatic conditions. Also, the theoretical figures are considerably higher than the actual compression pressure and compression temperature found in the engine working under normal conditions. This is due to such things as valve overlap, faulty engine valves, piston and ring wear, liner wear and loss of heat to the cooling system via the cylinder head and liners.

Fuel used

The fuels used in both high-speed diesel engines and petrol engines are refined from petroleum. Automotive distillate is most commonly used in modern, high-speed diesel engines and petrol is used in petrol engines. Although the cost of producing distillate and petrol is approximately the same, some governments choose to subsidise distillate production, making it a cheaper fuel for consumers.

Distillate has a higher flashpoint than petrol, so there is less fire risk involved with a diesel engine. It cannot be too highly stressed that petrol must never be used in a diesel engine. Petrol is more volatile than distillate, and if it were injected into the combustion chamber of a diesel engine and burnt, a high pressure rise would result. Extremely severe knocking would follow, and bearing failure, crushed pistons and broken connecting rods would probably result.

Some advantages of the diesel engine

- Because the thermal efficiency of a diesel engine is high, it uses less fuel than a petrol engine of comparable size, and is therefore more economical to operate.
- The diesel is more suitable for marine work because it does not use spark ignition, and consequently does not require electrical equipment, which may be damaged by water.
- Diesel fuel may be handled and stored with a greater degree of safety than petrol, as it has a higher flashpoint and there is, therefore, less risk of explosion or fire.

- The torque characteristic of a diesel engine does not vary greatly at either high or low speeds. This means that diesel engines, when used for automotive applications, will pull better in top gear.
- Diesel engines can be used underground in mines and tunnels with comparative safety, whereas a petrol engine cannot. The reason for this is that the amount of carbon monoxide present in the exhaust gas from a petrol engine is much greater than that present in the exhaust gas from a diesel, and could prove fatal for persons working in the vicinity.

Some disadvantages of the diesel engine

- A diesel engine was once harder to start in cold weather than a petrol engine. However, direct injection and the use of thermostat devices have improved the cold starting ability of the diesel to the point where it is equal to, or better than, the petrol engine in this regard.
- As the working stresses in a diesel engine are greater than those in a petrol engine, the construction of a diesel is generally heavier than that of a petrol engine of comparable output.
- The initial cost of a diesel engine is greater than that of a petrol engine of similar size. However, substantial savings in operating costs more than offset this.
- Because of the high operating pressures and the efficiency and precision required of the fuel injection system, the system is extremely sensitive to dirt and water and the fuel must be kept scrupulously clean.

3
The Mechanical Cycles

Although they range from minis to monsters in size, almost all reciprocating piston IC engines work on one of two mechanical cycles — the four-stroke cycle or the two-stroke (Clerk) cycle. These cycles designate, in correct sequence, the mechanical actions by which:

- the fuel and air gain access to the engine cylinder;
- the gas pressure (due to combustion) is converted to power; and
- the burnt gas is expelled from the engine cylinder.

There has been considerable contention regarding the Otto cycle, which is generally considered synonymous with the four-stroke cycle. More correctly, the Otto cycle is a four-stroke cycle with combustion occurring at constant volume (see Chapter 4).

The basic four-stroke cycle diesel engine

From the name, it is fairly obvious that there are four strokes in one complete engine cycle. A stroke is the movement of the piston through the full length of the cylinder and, since one such movement causes the crankshaft to rotate half a turn, it follows that there are two crankshaft revolutions in one complete engine cycle. The four strokes, in correct order, are as follows:

1 **The inlet stroke.** With the inlet valve open and the exhaust valve closed, the piston moves from TDC to BDC, creating a low-pressure area in the cylinder. Clean, filtered air rushes through the open inlet valve to relieve this low-pressure area, and the cylinder fills with air.
2 **The compression stroke.** With both valves closed, the piston moves from BDC to TDC, compressing the air. During this stroke, the air becomes heated to a temperature sufficiently high to ignite the fuel.
3 **The power stroke.** At approximately TDC, the fuel is injected, or sprayed, into the hot, compressed air, where it ignites, burns and expands. Both valves remain closed, and the pressure acts on the piston crown, forcing it down the cylinder from TDC to BDC.
4 **The exhaust stroke.** At approximately BDC, the exhaust valve opens and the piston starts to move from BDC to TDC, driving the burnt gas from the cylinder through the open exhaust valve.

At the completion of the exhaust stroke, the exhaust valve closes, the inlet valve opens and the piston moves down the cylinder on the next inlet stroke. Since there are three non-working strokes to one working stroke, some means of keeping the engine turning over must be provided, particularly in single-cylinder engines. It is for this reason, and to ensure smooth running, that a heavy flywheel is fitted to the crankshaft.

Scavenging the four-stroke cycle diesel engine

It is necessary, since efficient combustion is desired, to completely clear the burnt gas

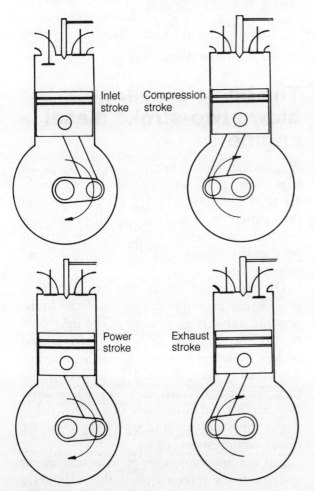

Inlet stroke   Compression stroke

Power stroke   Exhaust stroke

Fig 3.1   The four strokes

from the cylinder on the exhaust stroke, so providing a full cylinder of fresh air by the completion of the inlet stroke. Air that has burned with fuel has had almost all of its oxygen consumed, and cannot be used again. The clearing of the exhaust gas from the cylinder of an internal combustion engine is known as **scavenging**.

Both the upward movement of the piston on the exhaust stroke and the valve timing contribute to the scavenging of the burnt gas in the four-stroke engine.

It is usual for the exhaust valve to be opened before BDC, thus allowing a puff of high-pressure gas to escape at high velocity through the exhaust system. The upward movement of the piston ensures that the burnt gas continues this high-speed movement.

At the end of the exhaust stroke, the gas will continue to move through the exhaust system simply because of its momentum. This continued movement will cause a low-pressure area to develop behind the fast-moving exhaust gas, and this can be used to draw fresh air into the cylinder if the inlet valve opens at the instant the low-pressure area develops.

In practice, it is found that good scavenging can be achieved by opening the inlet valve just before TDC, and closing the exhaust valve just after TDC, thus allowing the exhaust gas to 'draw' fresh air into the cylinder before the inlet stroke actually begins.

The period of crankshaft rotation when both valves are open together is known as **valve overlap**, and occurs only at TDC.

Suitable positioning of the valves, usually one at each side of the combustion chamber, helps to guide the gases on their correct paths, and assists in achieving complete scavenging.

It is worthwhile to note at this stage that supercharged engines usually have more valve overlap than naturally aspirated engines.

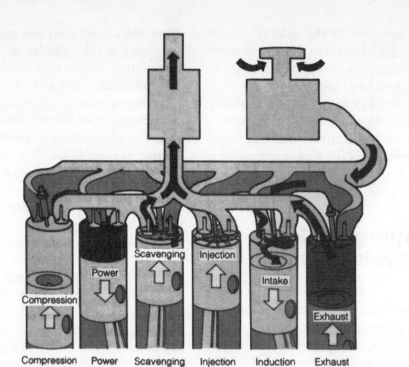

Fig 3.2 Stages of operation of a six-cylinder, naturally aspirated diesel engine

The two-stroke (Clerk) cycle diesel engine

In engines of this type, there are obviously only two strokes, or one crankshaft revolution, to one complete engine cycle. This means that there are twice as many working strokes per minute in a two-stroke diesel as there are in a comparable four-stroke, working at the same engine speed. Theoretically, then, the two-stroke engine should develop twice the power of a four-stroke of similar bore and stroke and the same number of cylinders but, due to scavenging difficulties, the power output is in the vicinity of one-and-a-half times that of a comparable four-stroke.

Two-stroke diesels may operate on either the scavenge blown principle or the crankcase compression principle. However, crankcase compression two-strokes are rarely seen and only scavenge blown two-strokes will be discussed here.

The basic scavenge blown two-stroke diesel engine

A scavenge blown engine makes use of an engine-driven air pump, or blower, to supply air to the engine cylinder. An inlet port in the cylinder wall is used instead of an inlet valve, in conjunction with either an exhaust port in the engine cylinder or an overhead exhaust valve.

On the power stroke, the exhaust valve or exhaust port opens first, and the high-pressure exhaust gas escapes. The inlet port then opens, allowing air (at between 15 and 60 kPa pressure) to sweep through the cylinder, clearing the exhaust gas and recharging the cylinder with fresh air. It is usual to close the exhaust valve or port first, allowing a slight pressure to build up in the cylinder before compression begins.

It is not uncommon for all loop scavenging systems to be referred to as the 'Schnuerle loop'.

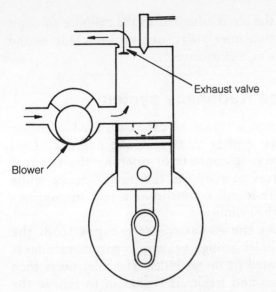

Fig 3.3 The scavenge blown two-stroke diesel engine (schematic diagram)

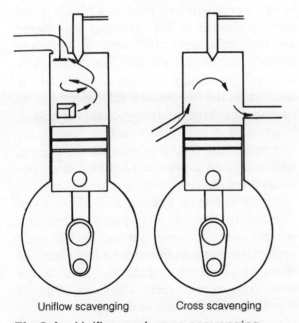

Uniflow scavenging   Cross scavenging

Fig 3.4 Uniflow and cross scavenging

It is general practice to have a number of inlet ports machined in the cylinder liner. These are cut at an angle or tangent to the cylinder liner, to give the incoming air a spiralling action, and are known as tangential ports. A large air jacket, called an air box, usually surrounds the outside of the ports and acts as an air reservoir, ensuring a good supply of air to all ports at all times.

Scavenging methods used in two-stroke diesels

Once the fresh air charge has entered the engine cylinder, it may act in one of three ways as it sweeps towards the exhaust port (or valve), driving the burnt gas ahead of it. The path within the engine cylinder through which the air sweeps as it drives out the exhaust gas classifies the scavenging system as one of the following three:

1 **Cross scavenging.** This is the simplest system, and is used on many small petrol engines. However, due to its relative inefficiency with regard to scavenging, it is becoming increasingly rare in modern diesel engines.

Scavenging is achieved by situating the inlet and exhaust ports on opposite sides of the engine cylinder. The piston, reciprocating in the cylinder, opens or closes these ports. In some cases, the piston crown is specially shaped to deflect the incoming air upwards throughout the cylinder, in an attempt to obtain complete scavenging.

2 **Uniflow scavenging.** Uniflow scavenging is considered the most efficient system of all, since the incoming air enters at one end of the cylinder and spirals throughout the entire length of the cylinder, to pass out through the exhaust port or the exhaust valve (depending on the design of the particular engine).

Mechanically operated exhaust valves in the cylinder head are usually used with this system, although opposed piston engines use one piston to control the exhaust ports and one to control the inlet ports. Again, the inlet ports are specially shaped to direct the incoming air in the required direction, and are known as tangential ports.

Because of its efficiency, the uniflow scavenging system is used on an extremely wide range of engines, from small high-speed engines such as the Rootes opposed-piston automotive engine and small Detroit Diesel engines, to large marine engines up to and exceeding 15000 kW.

3 **Loop scavenging.** There are a number of loop-scavenging systems, but the scavenge air paths are basically the same in all cases. Loop scavenging is more efficient than cross scavenging, since the incoming air moves from the inlet port to the top of the cylinder, and down to the exhaust port, driving out the burnt gas.

Piston-controlled ports are used, the exhaust port (or ports) being the upper. The inlet port (or ports) may be directly beneath the exhaust, or may be some distance around the cylinder liner. Regardless of their actual position in relation to the exhaust ports, the inlet ports are so shaped that they direct the incoming air upwards, thus ensuring complete scavenging in the form of a loop.

It is not uncommon for all loop scavenging systems to be referred to as the 'Schnuerle loop'. However, the Schnuerle loop system is a specific system in which

the air is admitted to the cylinder through two inlet ports, one on each side of the single exhaust port.

The Kadenacy system

This is a system of exhaust pulse scavenging that applies to two-stroke engines of all types. It consists of opening the exhaust valves or ports on the power stroke while there is still a pressure of a few atmospheres in the cylinder.

As the exhaust gas escapes from the cylinder at high velocity, a partial vacuum is created in the cylinder. The inlet ports then open and fresh air rushes in to relieve the low-pressure area thus created.

Engines using this system may either be blown (the partial vacuum and blower pressure combining to give efficient scavenging and high volumetric efficiency), or be dependent on the partial vacuum alone to induce the fresh air charge into the cylinder. In the latter case, the system can only be applied to engines working at fairly constant speed. When used in conjunction with a blower, the system is claimed to give efficient scavenging, with increased power and better fuel economy as a result.

The Kadenacy system has often been likened to the exhaust-pipe scavenging systems used on four-stroke engines. Correctly applied, the name indicates a far less sustained effect, the induction of the fresh-air charge occurring immediately after the exhaust impulse bursts from the exhaust port.

Uniflow two-stroke diesels

The Detroit Diesel engine has been mentioned previously and is so extensively used that it should be examined a little more closely. The Detroit Diesel engine is manufactured in a large number of variations and

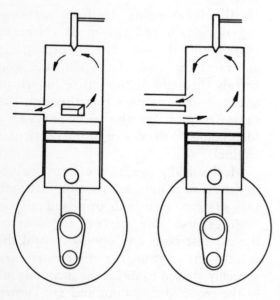

Fig 3.5 Loop scavenging

sizes, which power a diversity of equipment ranging from automotive vehicles to locomotives, boats to bulldozers.

Although it is a two-stroke engine, the operation of the Detroit Diesel is considered in four stages:

1 **Scavenging**. With the exhaust valves in the head open, and the piston crown below the ports, air from the blower passes into the cylinder and swirls towards the exhaust ports, driving out the burnt gases and leaving the cylinder filled with clean air.
2 **Compression**. As the piston begins to move towards TDC, the exhaust valvesclose and the piston then covers the

inlet ports. The air trapped in the cylinder is increasingly compressed as the piston rises.

3 **Power**. Just before TDC during compression, the fuel charge is sprayed into the intensely hot air and ignites. The resultant pressure rise drives the piston towards BDC, but before reaching this point, the exhaust valves open and the cylinder pressure is lost, ending the power stroke.
4 **Exhaust**. As soon as the exhaust valves open, burnt gases pass through the exhaust ports into the exhaust system. Once the piston opens the inlet ports, scavenging begins, to completely clear the cylinder of burnt gases.

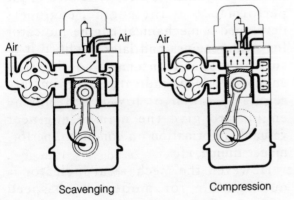
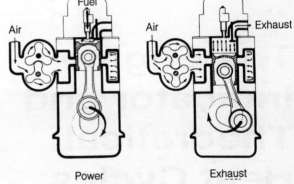

Scavenging   Compression   Power   Exhaust

Fig 3.6 **Detroit Diesel operation**

4

The Engine Indicator and Theoretical Heat Cycles

A heat cycle may be described simply as a sequence of pressure conditions necessary in the cylinder of an IC engine to efficiently convert the chemical energy in the fuel to mechanical energy available at the engine flywheel. A mechanical cycle, either four-stroke or two-stroke, is used to create the necessary pressures in the engine cylinder to fulfil the requirements of the heat cycle.

The cycles are presented pictorially as a graph of the pressure–volume relationship inside the cylinder of the working engine. This graph is termed a heat cycle diagram or indicator diagram, from a device called an engine indicator used to create the graph. Based on the concept of a perfect engine, engineers developed theoretical heat cycles termed **ideal heat cycles**. In practice, the actual heat cycle of real engines varies considerably from the theoretical.

The engine indicator

Because the pressure–volume relationship inside the cylinder is directly related to the performance of the engine, engineers developed a mechanical engine indicator for steam engines and later modified it to suit low-speed internal combustion engines. Indeed, indicator diagrams are regularly taken of low-speed marine engines to give the marine engineer valuable information on condition, performance timing, etc.

However, the mechanical indicator is not suitable for modern high-speed engines, where electronic indicators are used. These would seldom be seen outside manufacturers' engine-testing laboratories.

The indicator diagram

A heat-cycle diagram, whether theoretical or produced on an engine by an engine indicator, relates cylinder pressures to atmospheric pressure. A line to represent atmospheric pressure — the atmospheric line — is a feature of any indicator diagram.

In Fig 4.1a, the first stage of the development of an indicator diagram is shown. Line AL is the atmospheric line and line AB represents the partial vacuum created as the piston moves from TDC to BDC on the intake stroke.

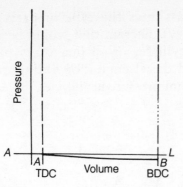

Fig 4.1a

As the piston moves toward TDC on compression stroke, the pressure rise is shown by line BC in Fig 4.1b.

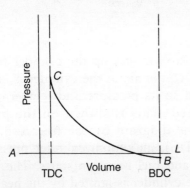

Fig 4.1b

In this example, combustion is considered to begin at TDC and maintain the pressure in the engine cylinder as the piston begins the power stroke (line CD in Fig 4.1c).

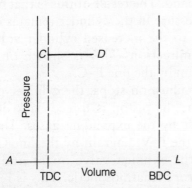

Fig 4.1c

Line DE (Fig 4.1d) represents the fall in cylinder pressure from the end of combustion to BDC. At BDC, the cylinder pressure is slightly above atmosphere.

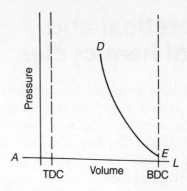

Fig 4.1d

The pressure during the exhaust stroke is shown by the line EA in Fig 4.1e as the piston moves from BDC to TDC.

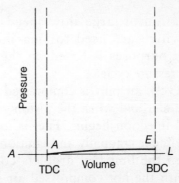

Fig 4.1e

The complete indicator diagram is, of course, a continuous graph, not a series of separate lines. The complete diagram is shown in Fig 4.2, and is clearly the combination of the stages described in relation to Fig 4.1. In practice, the lines representing the pressures on intake and exhaust strokes are usually omitted.

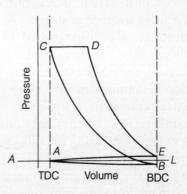

Fig 4.2

Theoretical and actual heat cycles

Engineers have proposed a number of theoretical heat cycles for internal combustion engines, the most notable being the constant pressure cycle by Dr Rudolf Diesel and the constant volume cycle, which was first successfully applied to an IC engine by Dr A.N. Otto.

The constant-pressure cycle

The operation of large slow-speed diesel engines which are used for marine and stationary purposes is based on the ideal constant-pressure cycle.

In this cycle, air only is compressed in the engine cylinder and when the piston reaches TDC, fuel injection begins. Fuel is injected into the cylinder gradually and ignition takes place when the first fuel droplets come in contact with the hot compressed air in the cylinder. As the fuel charge enters the cylinder, it burns at a controlled rate and so produces a steady expansion of the gases in the cylinder. As this expansion takes place, the piston — which has passed through TDC — moves down the cylinder, thereby increasing the enclosed cylinder volume.

Thus, by controlling the rate of admission of the fuel, the pressure neither rises nor drops as combustion continues, but is constant for a large number of degrees of crankshaft rotation. Combustion of the fuel charge, therefore, is said to take place at constant pressure, the constant pressure during combustion being the same as the pressure at the end of the compression stroke.

As combustion occurs at constant pressure, engines operating on this cycle can use higher compression ratios than those operating on the constant-volume cycle, without damage to engine components.

Fig 4.3a shows the type of pressure–volume (P–V) diagram that would be taken from the cylinder of an imaginary perfect slow-speed diesel engine operating on the ideal constant pressure heat cycle.

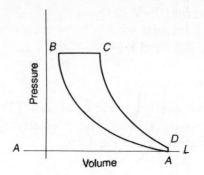

Fig 4.3a

As the piston moves up the cylinder from BDC to TDC, the air in the cylinder is compressed and so its pressure and temperature are increased. This is shown on the pressure–volume diagram by the line A–B. At point B (TDC), maximum cylinder pressure is attained and fuel injection starts. The fuel entering the cylinder is ignited by the heat of the compressed air and combustion begins. Combustion of the fuel charge progresses as the piston is forced back down the cylinder from the TDC position, so the pressurised gases created by combustion of the fuel are able to expand. The result of this is that combustion pressure in the cylinder remains constant, due to the increased cylinder volume during combustion. This is shown on the P–V diagram by the line B–C.

Once combustion stops, the cylinder pressure falls as the piston is forced back down the cylinder by the expanding gases. This is shown on the P–V diagram by the line C–D. At BDC, the exhaust valve opens and the pressure drops to atmospheric. This is represented by the line D–A.

The P–V diagram shown in Fig 4.3b has been taken from the cylinder of an actual slow-speed diesel engine operating on the constant-pressure cycle. Because such things as valve timing and fuel injection timing have been altered to suit actual engines, the P–V diagram from an actual engine differs from that of a theoretical engine. The mechanical condition of the engine and the quality of the fuel used also affect the shape of the actual P–V diagram. Note that the inlet and exhaust strokes have been omitted from Fig 4.3a and Fig 4.3b.

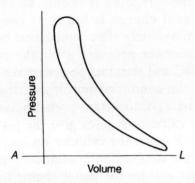

Fig 4.3b

The constant-volume cycle

This cycle was proposed by Beau de Rochas in 1862, and it was successfully applied to an IC engine by Dr A.N. Otto in 1876.

The operation of the petrol engine, which compresses an air–fuel mixture in its cylinders, is based on the constant-volume cycle. In the ideal constant-volume cycle, instantaneous and complete combustion of the fuel charge is assumed to take place when the piston has completed its compression stroke and is stationary at TDC. This means that the complete fuel charge is burnt while the clearance volume on the top of the piston is constant or unaltered. Although a sharp rise in pressure results from the instantaneous combustion of the fuel charge, this pressure is not sustained.

The sudden and rapid rise in pressure that occurs in the constant-volume cycle limits the compression ratio that can be used in an engine operating on this cycle. If the compression ratio used is too high, the pressure

rise in the cylinder during combustion is excessive and damage to engine components is possible.

Figure 4.4a shows the P–V diagram that would be taken from the cylinder of an imaginary perfect petrol engine operating on this ideal constant-volume heat cycle.

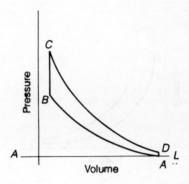

Fig 4.4a

As the piston moves up the cylinder from BDC to TDC, the air–fuel mixture is compressed and its pressure is increased. This is shown by the line A–B on the P–V diagram. At point B (TDC) the air–fuel mixture is ignited by an electric spark and instantaneous combustion occurs. A sharp but unsustained pressure rise results, and this is represented by the line B–C on the P–V diagram. Note carefully that, as pressure rises from B to C as a result of combustion, the volume does not change — it is constant during the combustion period. Due to the sharp pressure rise that occurs at TDC, the piston is forced down the cylinder on its power stroke and the cylinder pressure falls (line C–D).

At the bottom of the power stroke, the exhaust valve opens and the pressure drops to atmospheric. This pressure drop is shown on the diagram as the line D–A.

Note: Before the start of the next compression stroke, the piston must execute the exhaust and intake strokes. These are not shown. At the completion of the intake stroke, the pressure will once again be atmospheric and the compression stroke will again begin at A.

A P–V diagram taken from the cylinder of an actual petrol engine is shown in Fig 4.4b. Factors such as valve and ignition timing and engine condition cause this diagram to differ from the ideal diagram shown in Fig 4.4a. Again, the inlet and exhaust strokes have been omitted from the P–V diagrams shown in Fig 4.4.

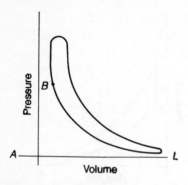

Fig 4.4b

The mixed cycle

The operation of modern high-speed diesel engines is based on what is known as a mixed cycle. This is actually a combination of the constant-volume cycle and the constant-pressure cycle and has some of the features of each.

Before discussing this cycle, the reader must realise that as the piston speed of a diesel engine is increased, the time available for injecting and burning the fuel charge is reduced. If fuel injection began at TDC in a high-speed diesel, the piston would be well down the cylinder before combustion started. In order to remedy this undesirable situation, the fuel injection timing must be advanced when high piston speeds are used.

In the mixed cycle, air only is compressed in the engine cylinder. Fuel injection must commence before the piston reaches TDC to overcome ignition lag and, after ignition occurs, combustion continues until just after fuel injection ceases. There is a sharp increase in cylinder pressure as the first droplets of the injected fuel are burnt and the constant-volume characteristic of the cycle is

evident. When the piston passes through TDC and begins to move down the cylinder, the fuel charge is still being burnt. However, due to the increasing cylinder volume on top of the descending piston, the gas expansion resulting from combustion does not create a pressure rise. This enables the cylinder pressure to remain constant, thus illustrating the constant-pressure characteristic of the cycle.

From the foregoing it should be evident that the fuel charge is burnt at constant volume immediately after combustion begins, and at constant pressure after the piston passes TDC and starts its power stroke. As a result of the continued burning of the fuel charge after TDC (constant-pressure combustion), the expanding gases give the piston a steady push down the cylinder on its power stroke while combustion continues. It is this action that enables the diesel engine to pull well at low speeds, and to have a near-constant torque characteristic at all speeds.

Fig 4.5a shows the P–V diagram that could be expected from the cylinder of an imaginary perfect high-speed diesel engine operating on an ideal mixed pressure heat cycle. As the piston moves up the cylinder from BDC to TDC, the air in the cylinder is compressed and so its pressure and temperature increase. This compression stage is shown on the diagram by the curved line A–B. Although fuel injection begins some considerable time before the piston reaches TDC (approximately $30°–15°$), the fuel charge does not start to burn until just before

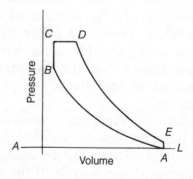

Fig 4.5a

TDC (approximately 6°–3°) because of ignition lag. As regards the ideal P–V diagram for this heat cycle shown in Fig 4.5a, it is assumed that combustion commences at TDC, so that the constant-volume phase of combustion may be clearly defined.

Fuel injection starts at point B, and for the case of the ideal P–V diagram it is assumed that combustion is instantaneous, although in actual practice this is not so. Due to combustion, there is an instantaneous pressure rise, which is shown on the ideal-cycle diagram by the line B–C. This phase of combustion is at constant volume.

As the piston moves down the cylinder from TDC, the remainder of the fuel charge is burnt and the pressurised gases created by combustion expand into the increasing cylinder volume on top of the descending piston. As a result, the cylinder pressure remains constant and is represented by the line C–D on the P–V diagram. This second phase of combustion is at constant pressure.

Once combustion ceases, the cylinder pressure slowly falls as the piston is forced further down the cylinder by the expanding gases. This is shown on the P–V diagram by the line D–E. At BDC, the pressure drops to atmospheric (line E–A). The shape of the actual P–V diagram that would be recorded from the cylinder of a high-speed diesel engine operating on the mixed cycle is shown

in Fig 4.5b. Note from this diagram that injection begins before TDC, and that combustion of the fuel injected during the ignition lag period is not instantaneous as in the ideal cycle. Since this combustion takes some time, the piston moves from a few degrees before TDC to a few degrees after TDC during the subsequent pressure rise. This results in the curved line B–C in Fig 4.5b.

Once combustion of the fuel injected during the ignition lag period has ceased, the fuel burns as it is injected. The piston moves down the cylinder as this combustion continues, and the cylinder pressure is maintained fairly constant (line C–D in Fig 4.5b).

The shape of remainder of the P–V diagram is dependent on engine characteristics. As is usual practice, the inlet and exhaust strokes have been omitted from Figs 4.5a and 4.5b

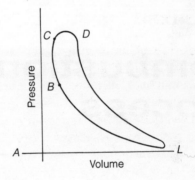

Fig 4.5b

5
The
Combustion
Process

In a compression ignition engine, the fuel is introduced into the combustion chamber by the injector, which breaks the fuel up into very small droplets that spread through the compressed air. As soon as the cool fuel comes in contact with the hot air, it takes heat from the air and an envelope of vapour forms around the droplets. The air that has cooled has to regain its heat from the main body of air and, as it does, the vapour also becomes hotter until it ignites. As soon as this occurs, the heat of combustion supplies the necessary heat to completely vaporise the fuel.

If the air is stationary in the combustion chamber, the burnt gas from the first combustion will surround each burning droplet, 'suffocating' it. If, on the other hand, the air is continuously moving, the burnt gas will move away from each fuel particle and fresh air will take its place, ensuring a plentiful supply of oxygen for continued combustion.

The time during which the fuel vaporises and ignites is dependent on three factors:

1 **The difference between the air temperature and the self-ignition temperature of the fuel.** If the air temperature is much higher than the fuel self-ignition temperature, the fuel will vaporise and ignite quickly — the greater the difference, the quicker will be the vaporisation, and the sooner ignition will occur.
2 **The pressure in the combustion chamber.** The greater the pressure, the more intimate the contact between the cold fuel and the hot air will be. The closer the contact between these two, the greater will be the rate of heat transfer from one to the other, again giving more rapid vaporisation and ignition.
3 **The fineness of the fuel particles.** If the fuel could be broken up into fine enough particles, the vaporisation required for combustion would be practically negligible and ignition would start almost immediately. However, the mass of the fuel particles under these conditions would not be sufficient to carry the particles far from the injector nozzle, and complete combustion would not occur. For complete combustion, good depth of penetration of the fuel particles into the combustion chamber is necessary, and the particles must have sufficient mass to carry them deep into the compressed air.

Again, if the particles are very fine, the total surface area presented to the compressed air will be large, and a great amount of fuel will be vaporised almost immediately. Once combustion begins, all the vaporised fuel will be burnt rapidly, and a very quick and high pressure rise will occur in the combustion chamber.

The stages of combustion

Combustion in the diesel engine may be divided into four distinct stages or phases:

1 **Delay period.** This is the period of crank-shaft rotation between the start of injection and the first ignition of the fuel charge. During this time, fuel is being injected continuously.
2 **Uncontrolled combustion.** Once ignition of the fuel in the combustion chamber begins, all the fuel that has accumulated during the delay period burns very rapidly, giving a sudden pressure rise. This stage usually occurs from a few degrees before TDC to a few degrees after TDC, giving a high cylinder pressure at the beginning of the power stroke. Obviously, the fuel injected during the uncontrolled combustion period burns as soon as it is injected.

3 **Controlled combustion.** When the uncontrolled combustion stops, the fuel burns as it is injected into the combustion chamber, the rate of admission of the fuel giving accurate control of the cylinder pressure. Immediate combustion of the fuel as it is injected during the controlled combustion period is ensured by the heat and pressure generated during the uncontrolled combustion period.

At large throttle openings, the injection and the controlled combustion periods are longer than at small throttle openings, the rate of admission of the fuel being constant for the period during which it lasts. This means that the maximum cylinder pressure (as a result of combustion) for a particular engine is the same regardless of the throttle opening, the extra power being derived from the longer combustion period.

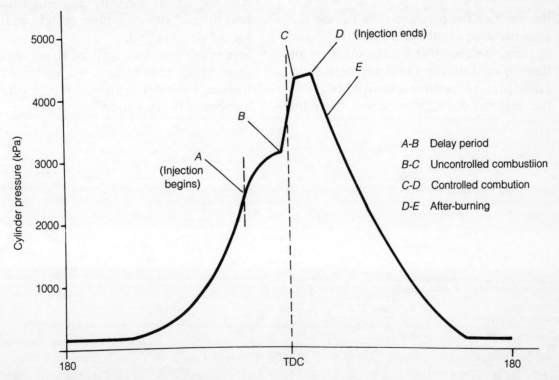

Fig 5.1   The stages of combustion

4 After-burning. During the controlled combustion period, almost all the fuel burns. However, some fuel particles fail to find the necessary air for combustion during this stage of combustion and these particles burn after injection has ceased. Again, some of the particles of fuel that settled on the combustion chamber walls during injection evaporate and burn during this final stage — 'after-burning'.

Diesel knock

The sudden pressure rise during the uncontrolled combustion period causes a shock wave to spread throughout the combustion chamber. When this wave strikes the metal of the cylinder head or piston crown, a characteristic metallic knock is audible, this being known as **diesel knock**.

The strength of the shock wave, and hence the intensity of the diesel knock, is influenced by the following:

- the amount the pressure rises during the uncontrolled combustion period. This, in turn, is dependent on the quantity of fuel injected during the delay period. In an effort to reduce the quantity of fuel injected during this period, the **pilot** **injection** system was developed. With this arrangement, injection begins at a steady rate, and once the delay period is over, injection increases to the normal rate. The **delay pintle** nozzle is another method of reducing the quantity of fuel injected initially. This nozzle allows only limited injection at first, thus reducing diesel knock, and then it opens fully to give normal injection.

- the time the pressure takes to build up. If the pressure rise is slower, the 'shock' effect will be less and diesel knock will be reduced. Many combustion chambers have been designed to achieve this end (see Chapter 6).

- the temperature, pressure and atomisation, as discussed earlier in this chapter;

- the engine speed. Diesel knock and rough running are usually more pronounced at low engine speed. Increasing the engine rpm creates greater air turbulence in the combustion chamber, which results in more vigorous mixing of the fuel particles with the air. As a result, the fuel particles heat up and vaporise more quickly, reducing the delay period.

- Some fuels are more inclined to encourage diesel knock than others. The tendency for fuels to knock is expressed as the **cetane number** of the fuel (see Chapter 15).

6

Combustion Chambers

The combustion chamber is that part of the engine where the fuel charge is burned. In some diesel engines, the combustion chamber is formed in the cylinder head, while in others it is formed in the crown of the piston. Regardless of where it is situated, the combustion chamber must be designed so that it is capable of producing maximum turbulence, not only during injection, but also when combustion is in progress.

This high degree of turbulence is necessary for three reasons:

1 to ensure complete mixing of the fuel and air;
2 to provide a continuous supply of air to the burning fuel particles (see Chapter 5);
3 to sweep burnt gas from the injection area so that, as more fuel is injected, it meets fresh air.

With regard to the mixing of the fuel and air, it must be remembered that the fuel charge is not injected into the combustion chamber until the piston is between 30 and 15 degrees of crankshaft rotation from TDC. Suppose the speed of the engine is 1900 rpm; the time available for the fuel to be injected, mixed with the air and burnt is approximately 1/500th of a second. It should be obvious that high air turbulence is necessary to mix the air and fuel thoroughly and quickly.

In Chapter 5, the 'delay period' in the combustion cycle was discussed. The duration of this period is largely dependent on the efficient mixing of the fuel and air in the combustion chamber. If mixing is quick and efficient, the delay period will be greatly reduced and this in turn reduces diesel knock. On the other hand, if mixing is slow and inefficient, a longer delay period will result and diesel knock will become more severe.

If the supply of fresh air required to prevent 'suffocation' of the burning fuel particles (and to sweep burnt gas from the injection area) is not continuous, complete combustion cannot take place. If combustion is incomplete, thermal efficiency must drop, with a corresponding increase in fuel consumption and a loss of power.

Complete combustion must also be achieved if a condition known as 'crankcase dilution' is to be avoided. This condition is caused by unburnt fuel passing the rings and mixing with the lubricating oil in the crankcase. As a result of this contamination, the lubricating properties of the oil are greatly reduced and severe engine wear results.

The paramount aim of combustion chamber design, therefore, must be to create very high turbulence so that the atomised fuel and air are thoroughly mixed and complete combustion is achieved.

Due to the amount of research carried out over the years, many types of combustion chamber have been developed. These are generally divided into two categories:

1 direct injection combustion chambers; and
2 indirect injection combustion chambers.

However, engines are usually classified as either 'direct injection' or 'indirect injection', the words 'combustion chamber' being dropped.

The main types of combustion chamber in use today have been classified as follows:

- open combustion chamber (direct injection);
- precombustion chamber (indirect injection);
- compression swirl combustion chamber (indirect injection);
- air cell or energy cell combustion chamber (indirect injection).

The choice of the combustion chamber design for a particular engine depends largely on its rpm, its principle of operation (two- or four-stroke), the size of the engine and the purpose for which it is to be used.

The open combustion chamber (direct injection)

The trend in modern high-speed diesel engines is towards the open combustion chamber. This system has developed from a small combustion chamber in the cylinder head to the modern system, which makes use of a flat cylinder head and a specially shaped cavity in the piston crown. It is usual for the piston to protrude slightly above the block surface, giving minimum clearance between the piston crown and the head, thus ensuring good turbulence and combustion **within** the piston cavity. Almost all two-stroke diesels use this system because of the ease of scavenging.

A multi-hole-type injector with a wide spray angle is located directly above the piston cavity, and sprays into this cavity where, since there is very little clearance between the piston crown and the head, almost all the compressed air is concentrated. High injection pressures (175–185 atmospheres approximately, for naturally aspirated engines) are needed to ensure droplet penetration and efficient air–fuel mixing.

Piston cavities and 'squish'

Piston cavities are cast in the piston crown, and take many different forms. The most common type is the toroidal piston cavity — a circular cavity, usually symmetrical about the piston

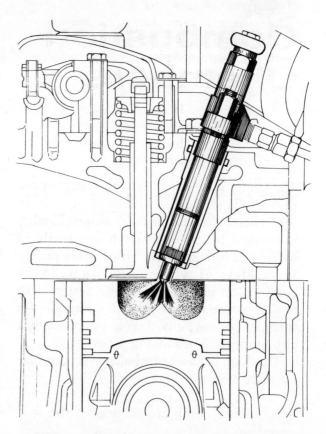

Fig 6.1 Direct injection combustion chamber
Courtesy of Volvo

axis, with a small cone projecting upwards from the bottom of the cavity towards the cylinder head. Some manufacturers favour a simple hemispherical cavity while others use a dished piston crown, although the latter is fairly rare. Yet another manufacturer uses a simple deep cylindrical cavity, which is almost flat on the bottom.

It is important to realise that each cavity must be used in conjunction with a particular injector nozzle, and the fitting of a nozzle with a slightly different spray angle can result in holes being burnt in the piston crown.

Regardless of the piston cavity design, the turbulence in the cylinder is created in the same way. As the piston approaches TDC on the compression stroke, the major portion of the air in the cylinder is compressed into the piston cavity. Because of the 'squish' effect, a high velocity is imparted to the air when it moves towards the piston cavity, thus causing a high degree of rotational turbulence in the piston cavity itself. The fuel injector is positioned above the piston so that fuel is injected directly into the turbulent air in the piston cavity, promoting efficient air–fuel mixing. It should be mentioned here that some engine manufacturers, such as Perkins, have the toroidal cavity in the piston slightly offset to promote swirl in a predetermined direction.

Squish may be defined as the rapid movement of the air being compressed in the cylinder of an open combustion chamber engine, from the cylinder walls towards the centre of the combustion chamber. It is most effectively created by using either a toroidal cavity piston or a plain cavity piston, the crown of which has only the necessary mechanical clearance from the cylinder head when it is at TDC.

As the piston approaches TDC on the compression stroke, the air trapped between the squish band on the piston periphery and the cylinder head is forced inwards, at high velocity, into the cavity in the piston crown. At or near the centre of the cavity, air meeting air causes mutual deflection towards the bottom of the piston cavity, beginning the circular turbulence shown in Fig 6.3. The degree of squish produced is largely dependent on the width of the squish band formed on the piston crown, with maximum squish velocity occurring at approximately 8° before TDC.

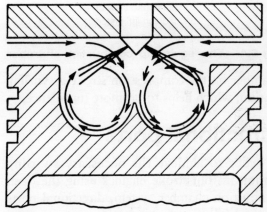

Fig 6.3   The 'squish' effect

Another design of combustion chamber utilising squish to cause turbulence is shown in Fig 6.4. Known as a 'squish lip', it has a much larger squish band than the conventional toroidal cavity piston, and because of this increased area, the air flow velocity is increased, improving combustion.

Usually some means of imparting a swirling motion to the air as it enters the cylinder on the induction stroke is used, giving the air moving towards the centre of the combustion

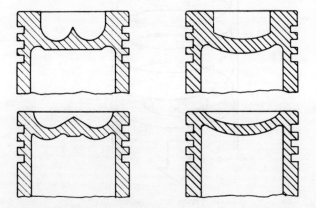

Fig 6.2   Typical piston cavities

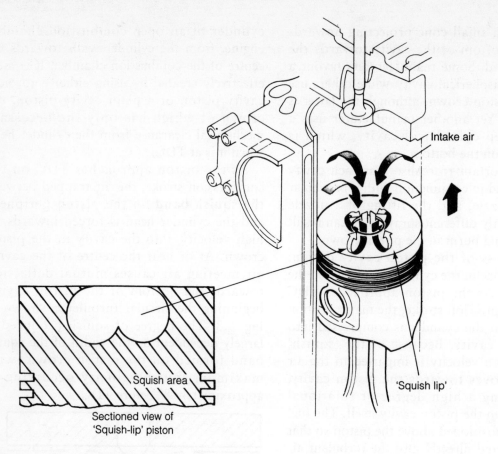

Intake air

'Squish lip'

Squish area

Sectioned view of
'Squish-lip' piston

Fig 6.4   The 'squish lip' combustion chamber   *Courtesy of Mazda*

chamber on the compression stroke a swirling motion, which helps to promote turbulence.

Directional ports

In order to achieve the necessary swirling motion in four-stroke engines using the open combustion chamber system, **directional ports** are used. These curved induction ports impart a spiralling motion to the incoming air, which not only continues during the compression stroke, but is intensified. Almost all manufacturers use the combination of spiralling intake air and piston-induced squish to achieve effective turbulence in direct-injection engines.

The shape and position of the inlet port are directly responsible for the swirl characteristics of the incoming air, and a normal type of inlet valve is used for admitting the air to the cylinder. Some of the larger diesels use two directional ports and, of course, two inlet

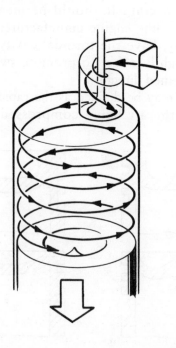

Fig 6.5   Air flow due to directional inlet port

valves to admit the air charge. Engines designed for automotive work, however, use only one directional port and one or two inlet valves per cylinder.

In earlier designs, masked valves were used to induce a directional swirl into the incoming air charge. The 'mask' consisted of a curved deflecting shield located between the valve seat and the stem. In operation, the masked valve had to be prevented from rotating to ensure mask alignment and subsequent correct air deflection. Because of the restriction this design imposed on incoming air flow, manufacturers have discontinued its use in modern diesel engines.

Tangential ports

Tangential inlet ports are used in two-stroke diesel engines to create air turbulence. These ports are situated in the lower half of the cylinder liner and are machined at a tangent to the liner walls as shown in Fig 6.6. The reason for this is to impart a rotary swirl to the air entering the cylinder. Tangential ports used in some large

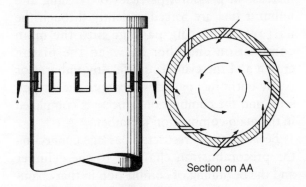

Section on AA

Fig 6.6 **Tangential ports**

two-stroke diesels are designed in such a way that the incoming air is deflected towards the top of the cylinder. This gives the air a swirling motion in the form of a spiral as it enters the cylinder, helping to achieve efficient cylinder scavenging as well as promoting turbulence. This cyclonic turbulence given to the incoming air by the tangential ports not only continues,

but is accelerated as the air is compressed on the compression stroke. This ensures good mixing of the air and the injected fuel, with the result that the fuel charge is burnt efficiently.

Almost all manufacturers of uniflow scavenged diesel two-strokes incorporate tangential ports in their design, the Detroit Diesel diesel and the Rootes opposed-piston diesel being typical examples.

Claimed advantages of open combustion chambers

- Due to its compact form, the surface area of the combustion chamber is small, resulting in a relatively low heat loss to the cooling system, thus giving high thermal efficiency.

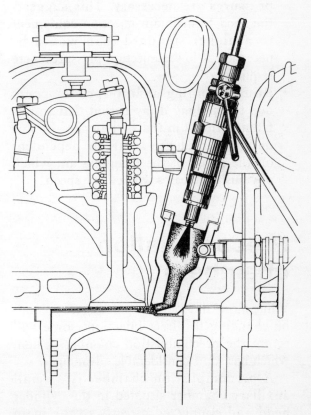

Fig 6.7 **Typical precombustion chamber**
Courtesy of Volvo

- Because of the low heat loss, the compressed air loses very little heat, giving good cold starting ability without the need for heater plugs (see Chapter 14).
- Again because of low heat loss, low compression ratios may be employed, while still giving good starting and efficient combustion.

Claimed disadvantages of open combustion chambers

- Since a number of small holes are used in the injector nozzle, instead of one large hole, blocking by carbon deposits is fairly common.
- To ensure penetration of the fuel particles into the compressed air, high injection pressures are necessary. This suggests the need to maintain injection equipment to a higher standard than would be necessary if lower injection pressures were required.
- Rough running at low speeds occurs due to the long delay period that results from rather limited turbulence. In this design, turbulence is largely dependent on the speed of the incoming air, which obviously increases with engine speed.

Precombustion chambers

While more and more manufacturers seem to be changing to direct injection, some still retain the precombustion chamber design, which has some considerable advantages.

A precombustion chamber is a small auxiliary chamber situated in the cylinder head and connected directly to the main combustion chamber by a small passage. In some designs, the precombustion chamber is separated from the main combustion chamber by a perforated plate made from heat-resistent alloy.

When the piston is at TDC on compression stroke, the major portion of the air charge has been forced through the connecting passage into the precombustion chamber. The remainder of the air is contained in the main chamber between the piston crown and the cylinder head. Some engine manufacturers (e.g. Caterpillar) use a piston with a dish-shaped cavity in the crown, while others use a piston with a flat crown in conjunction with a precombustion chamber. When a dished piston is used, between 35 and 40 per cent of the air is displaced from the cylinder on the compression stroke and is forced into the precombustion chamber, the remainder being left in the main combustion chamber.

When injection takes place (during the compression stroke), the fuel charge is injected into the hot compressed air in the precombustion chamber and ignition occurs. The subsequent burning of the fuel charge produces a substantial pressure rise in the confined space of the precombustion chamber and, owing to this increase in pressure, particles of burning and unburnt fuel are forced violently through the narrow connecting passage into the main combustion chamber between the piston crown and the cylinder head. Any unburnt or partly burnt fuel particles mix with the air present, and the combustion process is completed in the main combustion chamber.

Because of the restricted passage connecting the precombustion chamber to the cylinder and the beginning of combustion in that chamber, the sudden pressure rise from the uncontrolled combustion occurs largely within the chamber with minimal effect in the engine cylinder. Thus high cylinder pressures are eliminated, keeping diesel knock to a minimum and reducing internal stresses in the engine.

Caterpillar used precombustion chambers in its first diesel engines and is still using them, to a lesser extent, in its heavy-duty engines. The design is uncommon in that the precombustion chamber is not cast or machined in the head, but is a separate 'screw-in' unit into which the injector is directly fitted. The engine pistons have a heat-resistant insert fitted into the piston crown directly below the outlet from the precombustion chamber. This protects the alloy piston crown from the burning fuel particles, which are ejected at high velocity from the precombustion chamber, and which would eventually burn right through the piston crown.

Because of the combustion characteristics, the degree of atomisation of the fuel charge need not be as great as with direct injection engines, so that low injection pressures and pintle-type injector nozzles are usually employed. Caterpillar engines are a notable exception to the rule, using a single-hole nozzle of the firm's own design, featuring a very large orifice.

Claimed advantages of precombustion chambers

- The pintle-type nozzle usually used in conjunction with precombustion chambers has a relatively large orifice, plus a moving pintle, so that blockage due to carbon deposits is practically eliminated.
- The fuel does not have to be as finely atomised as for direct-injection engines, and consequently injection pressures are lower.
- Because of high turbulence and efficient mixing of the fuel and air, the fuel quality does not have to be as high as with other types of combustion chamber.
- Engine operation is smooth because maximum cylinder pressure during combustion is low.

Claimed disadvantages of precombustion chambers

- In almost all types, heater plugs must be used when starting the engine in cold weather, because of the heat lost from the compressed air to the relatively large combustion-chamber wall area.

- The heat lost from the compressed air to the walls and at the throat of the precombustion chamber is considerable, and generally engines using this system have relatively low thermal efficiency and high fuel consumption.
- Because of the heat loss to the combustion chamber, high compression ratios must be employed to achieve the necessary compressed air temperatures for efficient ignition.

Compression swirl combustion chamber

Although the trend appears to be towards direct injection, the compression swirl system is still very popular in the smaller automotive engines. A basic swirl chamber consists of an approximately spherical chamber in the cylinder head connected to the cylinder by a small passage. The passage joins to the side of the chamber at a tangent. This ensures that the air

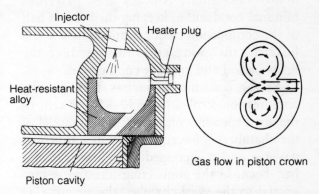

Section through combustion chamber

Fig 6.8   A typical swirl chamber

entering the chamber through the passage on the compression stroke swirls around inside the spherical chamber. The fuel is injected at a right angle to the swirling air, ensuring complete mixing. As soon as the pressure rise due to combustion is sufficient, a mixture of burnt, burning and unburnt fuel is ejected violently into the main chamber in the piston crown.

The most popular compression swirl chamber used in modern high-speed diesel engines would appear to be based on Sir Harry Ricardo's 'Comet' design, of which there are many variants. This compression swirl combustion chamber consists of a basic spherical chamber and tangential passage, but in addition the top of the piston has a figure-8 depression in its crown, which acts as part of the combustion chamber when the piston is at TDC, only very slight clearance being allowed between the flat of the piston crown and the head.

The swirl chamber itself is made in two parts. As it is formed in the cylinder head, the top half of the chamber is indirectly cooled by the engine's cooling system, but the bottom half is made of special heat-resisting alloy steel, or in some cases stellite, and is not cooled in any way. An air space is used to insulate the bottom half of the combustion chamber from the cylinder head, the only contact being a small area of the mounting flange that touches the cylinder head. This small contact area provides minimal conduction, keeping the bottom half of the combustion chamber hot so that it will heat the incoming air, and so reduce the delay period and improve combustion.

As the piston approaches TDC on the compression stroke, from 50–85 per cent of the air (depending on the particular model of the chamber) is forced through the tangential passage and compressed in the swirl chamber. Because the connecting passage is tangential to the swirl chamber, the air entering the chamber is given a rapid circular swirling motion. The velocity of the swirling air is dependent on the engine rpm, so as the engine speed is increased and the air velocity increases, greater turbulence results.

The fuel injector is positioned in such a way that when injection occurs, fuel is sprayed across, and at right angles to, the swirling air. When combustion begins, a pressure rise occurs in the swirl chamber and when the pressure in the chamber becomes greater than that of the incoming air, burning and partly burnt fuel particles are ejected at high velocity from the swirl chamber into the air remaining in the cavity in the piston crown. A figure-8 turbulence results, so that air in the cavity and the burning fuel particles are thoroughly mixed, completing combustion of the fuel charge.

Because of the heat lost to the large surface area of the swirl chamber — particularly the upper part — on compression stroke, cold-starting devices are generally needed to allow easy starting in cold weather. However, the Pintaux injector nozzle developed by CAV and Ricardo ensures good starting in swirl chambers under normal conditions without the use of such devices. Under colder conditions, however, a cold-starting aid may still be necessary with this compression swirl chamber, even where a Pintaux nozzle has been used.

The compression swirl combustion chamber may easily be confused with the precombustion chamber, since they are both separate chambers in the cylinder head in which the fuel is injected and combustion starts. It is here that the similarity ends. The passage connecting the swirl chamber to the engine cylinder is of much larger diameter than the passage connecting the precombustion chamber to the engine cylinder. Again the air enters the swirl chamber at a tangent and has the fuel sprayed across it, while air entering the precombustion chamber does so centrally and has the fuel sprayed directly into it.

Low injection pressures are used with compression swirl chambers, since thorough mixing and penetration are accomplished once combustion begins, making fine atomisation unnecessary. For the same reason, pintle injector nozzles are generally used, and these are, of course, self-cleaning. But Pintaux nozzles have one very fine hole in addition to the pintle hole, and this hole becomes choked with carbon very easily.

Claimed advantages of compression swirl combustion chambers

- Because of high turbulence and near-perfect combustion, the odour-producing exhaust gas emissions are minimised.
- Relatively low injection pressures can be used.
- Because of the high turbulence and good air–fuel mixing, the delay period is reduced and diesel knock is practically eliminated.

Claimed disadvantages of compression swirl combustion chambers

- Due to losses in thermal and mechanical efficiency, slightly more fuel is used than in direct injection engines.
- The heat lost by the compressed air to the top of the swirl chamber is considerable, causing cold-weather starting problems.
- Owing to the design of the compression swirl chamber, efficient scavenging of the burnt gas is a problem.

Air cell or energy cell combustion chambers

Over the years, many types of air cell have been developed, the most successful of these being the 'Lanova' energy cell. The most common version of this combustion chamber consists of a cell located in the cylinder head directly opposite the fuel injection nozzle. The energy cell is usually a removable unit screwed into the head, and consists of two differently sized and shaped cells in series, connected by a venturi choke. The cells are permanently in communication with the combustion chamber, through another venturi at the inner end of the inner cell.

The Lanova energy cell

To achieve certain desirable results, the combustion chamber over each cylinder is of figure-8 form. The valves open into the two recesses of the figure-8, between which is the narrower portion, or throat, of the chamber. On one side of the throat is the injection nozzle, which is positioned to spray the fuel directly across the throat towards the small orifice of the energy cell on the opposite side.

The bottom surface of the cylinder head has only gasket clearance over the flat portion of the piston surface, the combustion chamber recesses containing practically the entire volume. The tops of the pistons are also of figure-8 form, the height of the lobes being determined by the required compression space.

In operation, beginning with the induction stroke, the air enters through the inlet valve

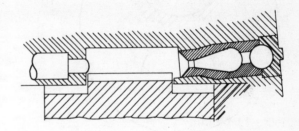

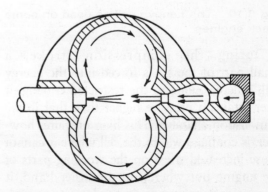

Fig 6.9   The Lanova cell (common type)

in one of the two recesses and, because of its offset position with respect to the cylinder axis, is given an initial swirling motion. On the compression stroke, this air is compressed into the confined space of the '8'-shaped combustion chamber, continuing the swirling motion. When the top of the compression stroke is approached, the air above the flat portions of the piston crown is rapidly displaced into the chamber recesses, attaining both high velocity and high temperature.

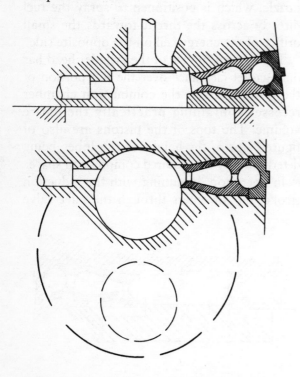

Fig 6.10   The Lanova cell as used on some Mack engines

During the compression stroke, a small part of the air is forced into the energy cell, where, owing to the restricted cooling, it later attains a pressure higher than that in the combustion chamber. This high pressure, however, is confined within the cell where it cannot cause increased stress on the working parts of the engine but where, on the other hand, it serves a definite purpose in combustion control.

At the proper instant, the fuel is sprayed by the nozzle directly across the chamber throat, the main body of the stream entering the energy cell and those portions near the edges being swept around the circular recesses in opposite directions, thus accelerating the already swirling air therein. As the fuel reaches the energy cell, it ignites instantaneously and a rapid combustion takes place. However, since the volume of air within the cell is small, only a small part of the fuel is thus consumed and the balance, the major portion, is blown violently back against the continuing stream from the injection nozzle. It is divided by the form of the throat into two streams of highly atomised fuel and hot air in the process of combustion, to swirl actively in opposite directions in two recesses. In doing so, these streams oppose the direction of rotation of the air already there so that air and fuel are most intimately mixed.

It is the relative volumes of the two cavities of the energy cell and the scientifically developed venturi that provide the control of combustion, a most valuable advantage of the system. They operate to control the rate at which the mixture of fuel and air is fed back to the combustion chamber, so that combustion is consequently controlled in such a way that the pressure rise occurs slightly after TDC, and continues at a moderate rate over a considerable number of degrees of crankshaft rotation, thus giving an expansion without the rapid and stress-inducing rise to excessive pressures that is characteristic of some combustion systems.

So efficiently does this principle operate that the peak pressures are little higher than those occuring in many petrol engines, while the more sustained combustion results in exceptionally high brake mean effective pressure. In addition, since the turbulence is being induced by thermal expansion, it is virtually independent of the engine speed and thorough and smooth combustion over a wide range of speeds is attained.

As a high degree of atomisation is not essential, the fuel injector nozzle used in conjunction with the Lanova energy cell is of the pintle type. The fuel injection pressure usually ranges from 110–120 atmospheres.

Although it may seem to have many advantages over other combustion chamber systems, the Lanova system has today almost vanished from the high-speed diesel engine scene.

Claimed advantages of air cell combustion chambers

- There is minimal shock loading on working components due to a high degree of controlled combustion.
- A clean exhaust is possible over a fairly wide range of speeds, because the turbulence in the combustion chamber is induced by thermal expansion and is virtually independent of the engine speed.
- Relatively low fuel injection pressures may be used because a high degree of atomisation is not required.

Claimed disadvantages of air cell combustion chambers

- There are starting difficulties when cold, due to the high loss of compressed air heat to the very large combustion chamber wall area.
- Efficient scavenging of the energy cell is difficult to achieve.
- The cylinder head is expensive because of the complicated moulding and machining involved in its manufacture.

7
Cylinder Head and Valves

The cylinder head is constructed of cast iron and is bolted to the cylinder block by means of high-tensile bolts. The cylinder head forms the upper part of the combustion chamber, together with the piston and cylinder walls. Inlet and outlet ports are provided in the cylinder head for the intake of air and the expulsion of exhaust gas. Passages are also provided in the cylinder head for circulation of coolant in order to ensure cooling of the high-temperature areas around the valves and combustion chamber. Located in the cylinder head above each cylinder is the injector and the intake and exhaust valve mechanism. A gasket is installed between the cylinder head and the cylinder block to seal the combustion chamber and all water and oil passages between the two components.

The conventional cylinder head has intake and exhaust ports on the one side, whereas some cylinder heads are constructed with the inlet ports on one side and the exhaust on the other. This is called a cross-flow head and is designed to improve the efficiency of the air flow in and out of the engine. Cylinder heads come in a variety of sizes: some engines use the one cylinder head to cover four or six cylinders; others use a pair of cylinder heads to cover four cylinders. On larger engines and air cooled engines, there is only one head per cylinder.

Intake and exhaust valves

The intake and exhaust valves are made of special alloy steel. They appear similar in shape and construction, with some intake valves having a larger head which provides a greater opening for less restricted air flow into the engine. Valves can be ground at either of two angles, 30° or 45°, depending on their application. Valves which are ground at a 45° angle have approximately 25 per cent more seating force than the 30° angle valves, resulting in a more efficient cleaning and sealing action at the valve seat. Most exhaust valves are ground at an angle of 45°. Valves which are ground at an angle of 30° create less restriction to air flow and are generally used in the air intake system, where they help improve engine breathing.

Some manufacturers stamp the head of their exhaust valves with an 'EX' and their inlet valves with an 'I' so as to identify them when head sizes are the same. Figure 7.2 shows a typical engine valve group assembly with all relevant parts named.

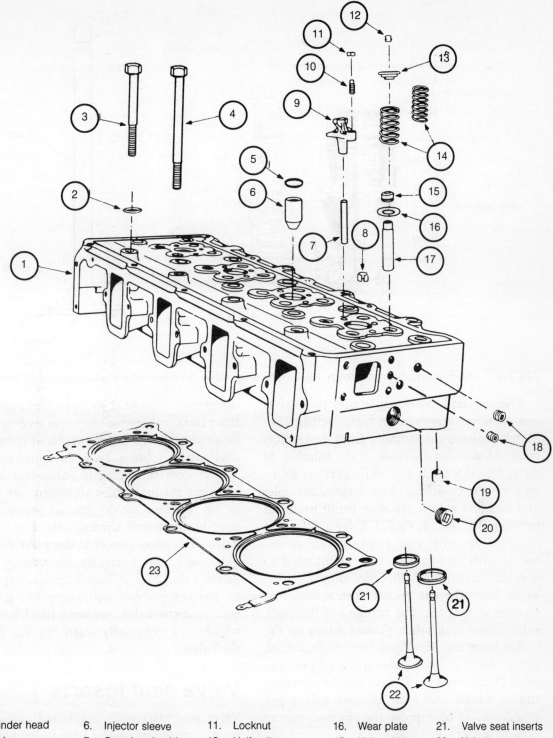

1.	Cylinder head	6.	Injector sleeve	11.	Locknut	16.	Wear plate	21.	Valve seat inserts
2.	Washer	7.	Crosshead guide	12.	Half collets	17.	Valve guide	22.	Valves
3.	Capscrew – short	8.	Split Ring dowel	13.	Spring retainer	18.	Pipe plugs	23.	Head gasket
4.	Capscrew – long	9.	Cross head	14.	Valve springs	19.	Ring dowel		
5.	O–ring	10.	Adjusting screw	15.	Valve seal	20.	Pipe plug		

Fig 7.1   **Exploded view of a cylinder head**   *Courtesy of Cummins Engine Co*

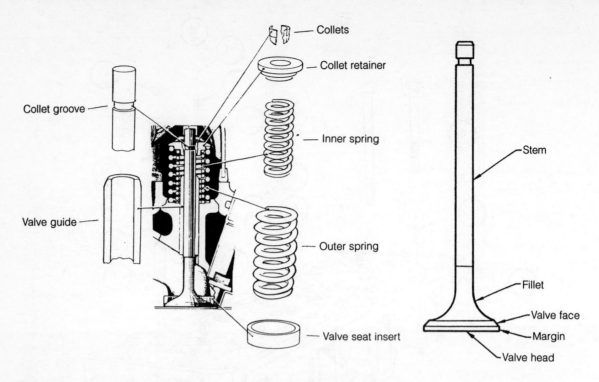

Fig 7.2   Illustration of valve group assembly and valve nomenclature   *Courtesy of Volvo*

The standard diesel engine uses two valves per cylinder; however, on high performance diesel engines, the cylinder head design has changed with an increase in the number of valves being used per cylinder. So as to improve the breathing of the engine, two inlet and exhaust valves are now being used per cylinder as shown in Fig 7.3. Valve actuation is achieved by either cam and/or rocker movement, with one rocker lever being used to operate the two valves. In order to operate two valves from the one rocker lever, a bridge or crosshead is used. The bridge saddles both valve stems and, when pushed down by the rocker lever, transfers equal force to push both valves down evenly. An example of multiple valve operation is the Detroit diesel two-stroke engine which uses four exhaust valves per cylinder so as to improve the efficiency of the exhaust scavenging cycle.

Valve heat dissipation

Both the intake and exhaust valves are subjected to intense heat during engine operation. This heat must be removed from the valves, otherwise they will overheat and be destroyed in a short period of time. Heat dissipation from a valve is approximately 70 per cent through the valve seat and 30 per cent through the valve stem, as shown in Fig 7.4. Because the greater percentage of heat is dissipated through the head of the valve, it is important that the valve face and valve seat mate correctly. Uneven or inadequate valve face-to-seat contact, especially on exhaust valves, will allow hot gases to leak past the valve, creating local hot spots which will eventually burn out the face of the valve.

Valve seat inserts

Valve seat inserts are machined rings made from cast iron or special heat-resistant stellite steel and are fitted to the cylinder head so as to improve and extend valve seat service life. As each insert is made separately to the cylinder head, it is held firmly in the head by means of an interference machine fit. Because

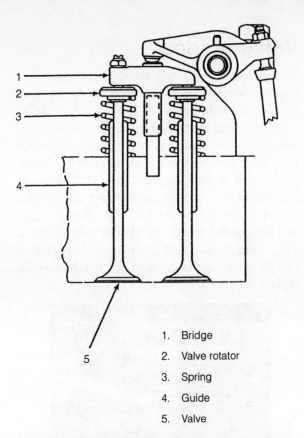

1. Bridge
2. Valve rotator
3. Spring
4. Guide
5. Valve

Fig 7.3 Illustration of a valve bridge being used to operate two valves from the one rocker lever *Courtesy of Caterpillar Inc*

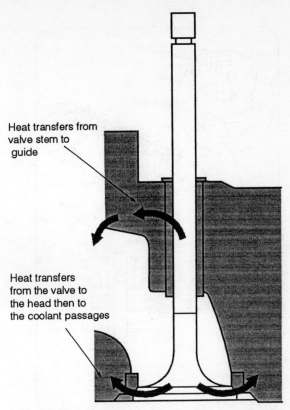

Heat transfers from valve stem to guide

Heat transfers from the valve to the head then to the coolant passages

Fig 7.4 How valves are cooled

of their hardness and resistance to high temperature, inserts maintain an accurate sealing face for a much longer time than do conventional valve seats ground in the cylinder head. Whenever the valve seat inserts have worn beyond serviceable limits, they can be removed from the head and new ones refitted.

Valve springs

The purpose of the valve spring or springs is to return the valve to its seat, keeping it closed until it is opened again by the cam lobe. The most common device used to hold the valve and spring in position is the retainer and collets. The retainer is shaped to fit over the valve stem and sit on top of the valve spring. The hole in the centre of the retainer is tapered to take the two collets. On assembly of the valve and spring, the collets are wedged against the valve stem by the action of the taper in the retainer locking the components in position so they move as one unit.

During high-speed engine operation, coil type valve springs can develop a vibration or surge which can prevent the valve from returning fully to its seat. Valve bounce, as it is known, can cause a loss of engine power and possible breakage of the valve springs. To reduce the tendency of the valves to surge at high speed, double valve springs or a variable pitch spring with a progressive spring rate can be used. Double valve springs sometimes have the coils wound in opposite direction so as to prevent the springs from rotating due to vibration forces. Variable pitch springs are recognised by the close-wound coils at one end and are designed to have a progressive spring rate as they are compressed. In other words, there is only a small force required to compress the spring,

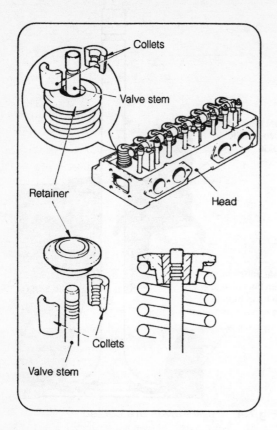

Fig 7.5 Ilustration showing how the spring is secured to the valve stem
Courtesy of AGPS

as the valve initially opens then, as it continues to open, there is a progressive increase in force required to further compress the spring and fully open the valve. Springs of this design are used so as to prevent oscillations which can reduce the spring's effective closing force during high-speed engine operation. Variable-pitch springs must be installed on the cylinder head with the close-wound coils towards the head. If installed upside down, the damping effect of the spring is greatly reduced, contributing to possible spring failure. Also, as there is now extra weight at the top of the valve spring, the increased inertia forces created can cause the valve to bounce off and on its seat during high engine speed operation. Figure 7.6 shows an example of double valve springs being used with close-wound coils at the end of each spring.

Valve guides

The valve guide provides the sliding surface and location for the valve stem as it moves up and down in the cylinder head. The guide is made of cast iron and is precision machined so that when the valve closes, its face makes full contact with the valve seat in the cylinder head. Valve guides can be integral with the cylinder head, but the majority of diesel engines use guides which are made separate to the cylinder head and are pressed into the head after manufacture. Therefore, if the guide is worn or damaged, it can be easily replaced without machining or replacing the cylinder head.

Fig 7.6 Photographs showing the use of double valve springs with close-wound coils at one end. *Note:* The close-wound coils always go towards the head.
Courtesy of Mack Trucks Inc

and valve face fouling due to a buildup of carbon deposits.

Valve rotators as shown in Fig 7.8 and 7.9 are designed to allow the valve to rotate whenever it is off its seat during engine operation. This ensures that there is a continuous wiping action of the valve seat, preventing the buildup of carbon or other deposits and at the same time eliminating the possibility of the valve stem sticking in its guide.

There are two types of valve rotator: the free type rotator and the positive type rotator.

The free type rotator, as shown in Fig 7.8, is positioned on top of the valve spring and forms part of the valve spring retainer. In operation, when the rocker arm moves

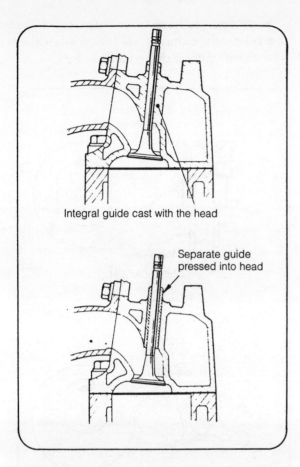

Integral guide cast with the head

Separate guide pressed into head

Fig 7.7   A valve guide machined into the head and a replaceable guide pressed into the head
Courtesy of AGPS

Valve rotators

During normal engine operation, carbon deposits build up on the valve seating surfaces. These deposits, if left on the valve face and seat, prevent the valve from seating properly, resulting in a possible burnt-out valve. Another valve problem is that the valve stem can stick in the valve guide. This can occur when the oil on the valve stem burns and deposits carbon and varnish, which prevent the valve from moving freely in its guide with the possibility of the valve not seating fully and being burnt out. Therefore, if the valve were able to rotate as it moved up and down in its guide, there would be less chance of valve stem sticking

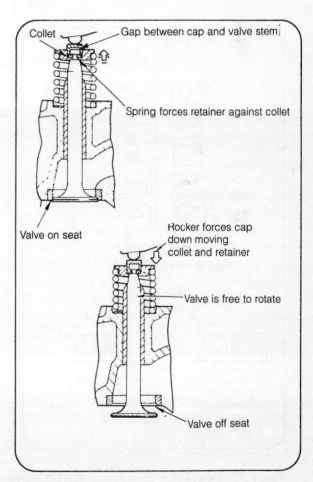

Collet — Gap between cap and valve stem

Spring forces retainer against collet

Valve on seat

Rocker forces cap down moving collet and retainer

Valve is free to rotate

Valve off seat

Fig 7.8   Operation of a free type valve rotator
Courtesy of AGPS

down, the valve clearance is eliminated, as is the clearance which exists under the valve rotator cap. Further downward movement of the rocker arm on to the valve rotator cap pushes the collets away from the shoulder on the valve stem, allowing the valve to rotate freely under the influence of gas swirl and engine vibration.

The positive rotator, which can be either mounted between the valve spring and the head or on top of the valve spring, causes the valve to rotate every time it opens. With reference to Fig 7.9, as the rocker arm pushes the valve down, the garter spring coils are compressed, forcing them to lean sideways, causing the spring seat and the spring/valve assembly to rotate slightly.

Some engines have valve rotators on both the inlet and exhaust valves, while others have them only on the exhaust valves.

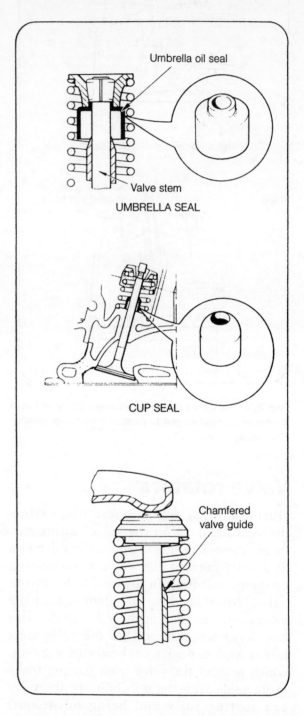

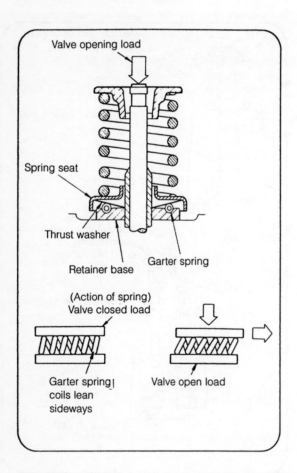

Fig 7.9 Operation of a positive type valve rotator
Courtesy of AGPS

Fig 7.10 Various methods used to seal the valve stem
Courtesy of AGPS

Valve stem seals

Valve stem seals, as shown in Fig 7.10, are designed to prevent excessive amounts of lubricating oil from passing between the valve stem and guide into the combustion chamber. The seal plays a particularly important part during the intake stroke, when the low pressure created within the cylinder tries to draw oil from on top of the cylinder head into the combustion chamber. These seals are either fitted over the valve guide or on the valve stem below the spring retainer. Some manufacturers don't use stem seals at all; instead, they machine a chamfer on the top of the valve guide to scrape oil off the valve stem. This allows a controlled amount of oil leakage for guide and stem lubrication.

Injector sleeve

A number of diesel engines use injector sleeves to house and seal the injector in the cylinder head as shown in Fig 7.11. The sleeve is generally made of copper and is surrounded by coolant; it must therefore be sealed at its top and bottom seating locations. When installed, the injector seats

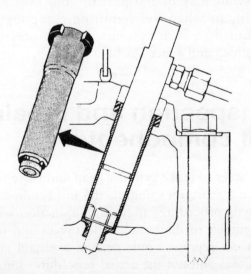

Fig 7.11   Injector sleeve used to seal the injector in the cylinder head
Courtesy of Volvo

on a machined surface in the lower part of the sleeve, preventing combustion gas from leaking out of the combustion chamber. The upper part of the sleeve is sealed by means of swaging the copper tube out into the head.

Cylinder head and valve service

Removal of cylinder head

Before carrying out any dismantling work on the engine, check that it is cold. Removal of a cylinder head which is at or near operating temperature can lead to distortion or possible cracking of the head. Drain the coolant from the radiator and cylinder block. Then begin head removal by taking off the injector lines, manifolds and air cleaner, etc. The injectors can also be removed at this time, taking care to seal both the injector inlet and the ends of the injector pipes with plastic plugs. Remove the rocker cover and the rocker gear from the top of the head. Withdraw the pushrods, making sure that the cam followers are not accidentally pulled out due to the suction of oil on the end of the pushrod ball. With the aid of a drive bar and socket, loosen all the head nuts or bolts evenly, starting from the ends and working to the middle. Remove the nuts or bolts and lift the head off the cylinder block. If the head does not come freely, then tap it on the side with a soft hammer or drive a thin flat wedge between the head and the cylinder block to separate stuck gasket material.

With the cylinder head removed from the cylinder block, mount it on a suitable stand. *Note:* If the injectors are still in the head, do not lay the head face down on a flat surface as the injector tips which protrude past the flat of the head will be damaged. Remove the injectors and seal them as described earlier.

Use a valve spring compressor as shown in Fig 7.12 to compress the valve springs and remove the retaining collets or locks. If the collet retainer does not break away easily from the collets and valve stem then strike the top of the retainer downward with a soft hammer. Take care not to hit the retainer side on, as this could bend the valve stem.

Remove the valve springs and valve stem seals if fitted, then remove the valves. It is important that the valves be stored on a rack so as to keep them in their correct order for reassembly. Use a wire buff to clean the valves so as they can be inspected and wear evaluated.

The head should also be cleaned of all gasket material and decarbonising brushes, as shown in Fig 7.13, should be used to clean carbon from the valve guides, combustion chambers and valve ports.

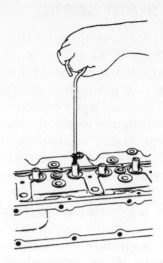

Fig 7.13   Decarbonising brush used to clean valve guides
Courtesy of Fiat Allis

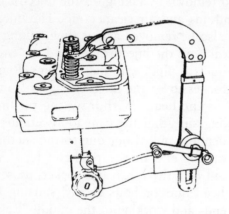

Fig 7.12   Valve spring compressor used to compress valve springs
Courtesy of Fiat Allis

Chemical cleaning

Chemical cleaners can also be used to clean engine components. Amongst the more common chemical cleaning systems are hot and cold tank cleaning. Hot tank cleaning uses a tank containing a caustic solution which is heated to a high temperature. The components to be cleaned are immersed in the solution and, during the cleaning process,

some form of agitation of either the solution or the components is used to maintain the movement of solution over the components. Cold tank cleaning uses a tank containing strong chemical solvents which, by virtue of their chemical composition, strip and clean components back to bare metal.

Warning! Solvents used in cleaning systems may be harmful to your eyes and skin, so whenever handling components cleaned in such systems, wear protective clothing and a face shield.

Inspection and repair of components

In order to make cylinder head and valve servicing more meaningful, the inspection and repair procedures used in conjunction with examples of dimensions, clearances and tolerances represent only general overhaul procedures and not the actual procedures for all engines. Therefore, always refer to the relevant service manual for specifications and correct inspection and repair procedures.

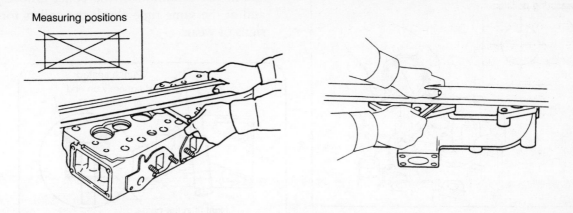

Fig 7.14   Straight edge and feeler gauge used to check the face of the cylinder head and manifolds for warpage   *Courtesy of Mitsubishi*

Cylinder head

Check the face of the cylinder head for flatness. Use a straight edge and feeler gauge to check for warpage across the width of the head and across its diagonal surface as shown in Fig 7.14. Both intake and exhaust manifold faces should also be checked for warpage. If the head or manifolds are warped beyond specifications, they will have to be machined on a surface grinding and/or milling machine.

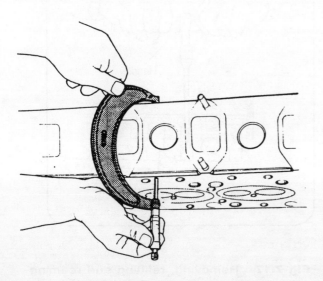

Fig 7.15   Measuring the height of the cylinder head

The head should also be checked for cracks around the injector hole, the combustion chamber, the valve seats, the head face and the coolant passages. If cracks are suspected but not visible to the naked eye, various crack detection methods are available. These are explained in detail later on in this chapter. Measure the height or thickness of the head as shown in Fig 7.15 and refer to the service manual to verify if the head can be machined if required. The head thickness is critical, as it determines the valve protrusion and injector protrusion into the combustion chamber. If the thickness of the head is below specifications, then the head will need to be replaced.

Valve guides

Before inspecting the guides for wear, make sure they have been thoroughly cleaned and decarbonised with a wire brush so as to remove any carbon. With the aid of a dial bore gauge, as shown in Fig 7.16, measure along the full length of the guide, taking particular note of the dimensions at the top and bottom of the guide as these are the areas of greatest wear. Compare these measurements obtained with those listed in the service manual to determine valve guide reuseability

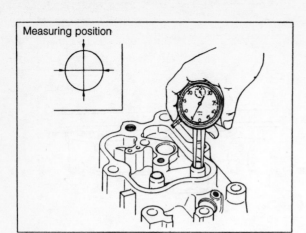

Fig 7.16 **Using a dial bore gauge to measure valve guide wear**
Courtesy of Mitsubishi

If the guides are to be replaced, they should be driven or pressed out of the head with the aid of a stepped punch. The new guides should be pressed into the head until each one protrudes the correct distance above the head surface. Never try to drive valve guides into the head by hitting them directly with a hammer, as this may damage or possibly shatter the guide. If the valves do not move freely within the guides after they have been installed, then the guides will have to be reamed slightly till each valve stem has the correct clearance along the full length of the guide. Figure 7.17 shows the procedure for removing and replacing valve guides in a cylinder head.

Valves

Thoroughly clean all traces of carbon off the valve head and stem with a wire buff as shown in Fig 7.18. Then, with reference to Fig 7.19, inspect and measure the various areas of the valve as follows:

- Using a micrometer, measure the stem for ovality and taper. A general wear limit on the stem is 0.05 millimetres.
- Check the tip of the stem for grooving or damage.

- Check the condition of the collet grooves and at the same time check the collets for signs of wear.

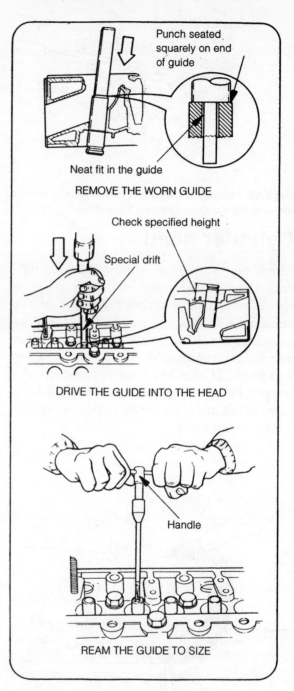

Fig 7.17 **Removing, refitting and reaming valve guides**
Courtesy of AGPS

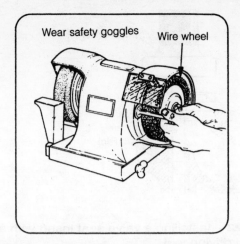

Fig 7.18 **Wire buff machine used to clean carbon off valves**
Courtesy of AGPS

- Check the stem for straightness by placing it between two V blocks. The stem and head should have no noticeable runout when the valve is rotated. Slight valve head runout can be corrected by refacing the valve.
- Inspect the valve face for pitting, grooves and burnt-out areas.
- Measure the thickness of the margin and determine whether there is sufficient metal to allow the valve to be refaced.
- Inspect the stem for possible signs of grooving caused by faulty valve grinding procedures.

If the above inspections find the valves to be faulty in any way, then they should be replaced.

Valve seats (inserts)

Inspect the seat inserts for wear, pitting, looseness or cracks across the seat face. Check also for cracks radiating out from behind the seat insert. Place a pry bar under all the inserts and see if they are loose in their recesses. If any inserts are loose they will have to be removed and the recess checked prior to fitting a new insert. Measure the width of the insert

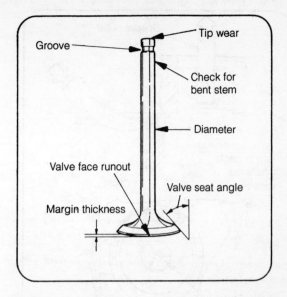

Fig 7.19 **Areas to check and measure when inspecting a valve**
Courtesy of AGPS

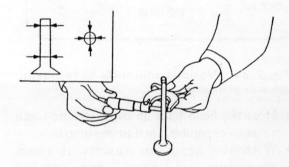

Fig 7.20 **Measure the valve stem for taper and oval wear**
Courtesy of Mitsubishi

seat and if it cannot be brought back to a specified size by grinding, the insert will need to be replaced.

A successful way of removing valve inserts is to run a bead of weld around the inside of insert as shown in Fig 7.21. Allow the weld to cool, which will shrink the insert enough for it be easily pryed out of the head.

Various methods of fitting new inserts to a cylinder head are as follows:

- Freeze the inserts in dry ice so as to shrink them sufficiently so that they can be fitted by hand into the cylinder head.

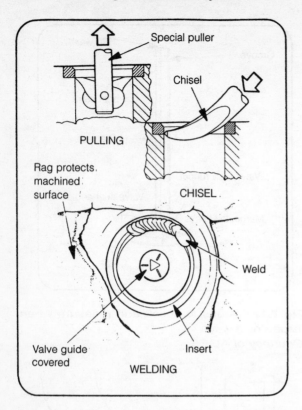

Fig 7.21 Various methods of removing valve seat inserts

- Heat the head with an oxyacetylene torch so as to expand it, then fit the inserts.
- With the head and inserts at room temperature, use a suitable driving tool to drive the inserts into the head as shown in Fig 7.22.

Caution! Handling dry ice can cause frostbite to the skin. To prevent personal injury, wear protective gloves when handling frozen inserts.

After the inserts are fitted to the head, some manufacturers recommend that they should be staked. Staking refers to peening the metal around the outside of the insert with a hammer and punch so as to expand the head metal towards the insert, preventing it from falling out of the head during engine operation. Cast iron inserts expand at the same rate as the cast iron cylinder head, so they don't require staking. Alloy steel inserts have a different rate of expansion

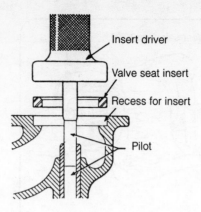

Fig 7.22 Installing a valve seat insert with a special driving tool

and, if not staked, could fall out of the head due to the head expanding at a greater rate than the insert.

As there are a number of different methods for fitting valve inserts, always refer to the service manual for the correct method to use.

Valve springs

Inspect the coils of the springs for rust, corrosion and signs of rubbing wear. Test the springs for squareness and distortion by placing the spring against a square as shown in Fig 7.23 and rotating the spring a full turn to check it for runout. A general allowable tolerance for a spring out of square is 1.5 mm. The springs should also be tested for free and compressed length. If there is no free length specification, check the height of the springs against a new spring. All springs in a set should have free length within 1.5 mm of the specifications. Springs are tested for compressed length by measuring the force required to compress the spring to a set length. A special test stand, as shown in Fig 7.23, is used to compress the spring and at the same time measure its length. Remember, the above specifications are only general, so always refer the manufacturer for the correct specifications.

If any springs fail to come up to specifications, then the whole set of valve springs should be replaced as a simple precaution.

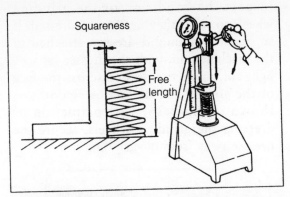

Fig 7.23 Checking a valve spring for squareness, free length and compressed length
Courtesy of Mitsubishi

Injector seat

Check the injector seats in the cylinder head to make sure all the seating washers are removed. Inspect the seat surface for corrosion and pitting. If the injector seat is damaged and has to be machined, be aware that the injector seat location has a direct bearing on the projection of the injector spray tip into the combustion chamber. Injector spray tips which are not positioned correctly in the combustion chamber will have a detrimental effect on the cylinder combustion process. When refitting injectors, always replace the copper sealing washers. If this is not possible, anneal the old washers so as to soften them up for efficient sealing.

To anneal a copper washer, heat it with an oxyacetylene torch until it is cherry red in colour, then cool it down in cold water. Don't heat the washer beyond the cherry red phase as the copper will melt.

Valve rotators

There are no specific measurements or checks for rotators except to ensure that they appear intact and are not externally damaged in any way. There is, however, a simple test that can be carried out on positive rotators to see if the valve will rotate.

Assemble the valves, springs and rotators to the head, then with the aid of a felt pen place a reference line across the valve head and the cylinder head. With the head on its side, strike the top of the valve stem with a hammer so as to lift the valve off its seat. Repeat this a number of times; if the rotators are working, the valves should have rotated in the head.

Whenever the engine is undergoing a major overhaul, it is good practice to renew all rotators. Even though the rotators appear to look in good condition externally, the internal ramps and springs will undoubtedly be worn.

Combustion chamber removal

Some automotive diesel engine cylinder heads are fitted with swirl type combustion chambers which must be removed during cylinder head overhaul or resurfacing of the head.

The combustion chamber design is such that its lower half can be removed from the cylinder head by placing a punch down through the injector hole in the head and driving out the chamber as shown in Fig 7.24.

After all the combustion chambers have been removed, they should be cleaned and inspected for wear and cracking around the throat of the chamber. If cracks are found, then the chamber must be replaced.

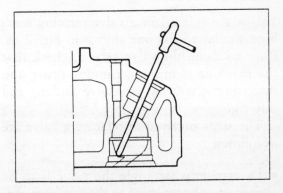

Fig 7.24 Removing a combustion chamber from an indirect injected diesel engine

If the cylinder head has been resurfaced, either the combustion chamber recesses in the head will need to be machined, or the chambers machined to obtain the correct protrusion. Refitting of the chambers to the head requires that they be aligned correctly with the aid of a dowel then pressed into the head. Most engines have chamber protrusion ranging from 0–0.15 mm. Unless specified by the manufacturer, chambers must not lie below the cylinder head face.

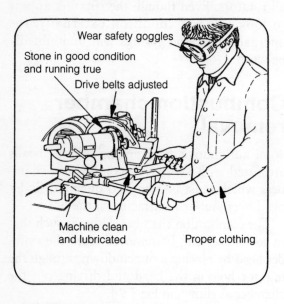

Fig 7.25 Correct procedure for operating and maintaining a valve refacing machine
Courtesy of AGPS

Valve refacing

Valves are refaced in a valve refacing machine similar to the one shown in Fig 7.25. Prior to using the valve refacer, check that the machine is in good running order and that you are wearing protective clothing and safety goggles.

The steps involved in refacing a valve are as follows:

- Determine what angle the valve is to be ground at by referring to the service manual. Then adjust the chuck head of the valve facing machine to suit the required angle.

- Inspect the condition of the grinding wheels to see if they need to be dressed. If so, use the diamond dresser attached to the machine and, with the dresser set to a light cut, move the dresser across the face of the stone until its face is smooth, as shown in Fig 7.26. On completion of dressing the grinding wheels, secure the dresser away from the grinding stone.

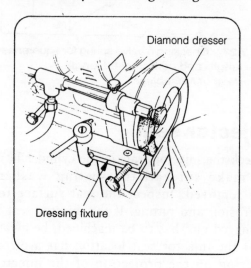

Fig 7.26 Diamond dresser used to dress the grinding wheel on a valve refacing machine
Courtesy of AGPS

- Fit the valve stem into the chuck head so that the valve is neither too far in or out of the chuck, as shown in Fig 7.27.

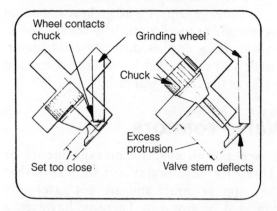

Fig 7.27 Illustration showing incorrect methods of fitting the valve to the valve refacer chuck
Courtesy of AGPS

• Check the travel of the chuck head slide so that the valve can travel across the full face of the stone and not allow the stone to cut the valve stem, as shown in Fig 7.28

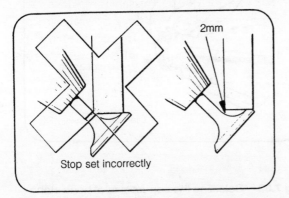

2mm

Stop set incorrectly

Fig 7.28 Adjusting the chuck slide to prevent the valve stem contacting the grinding wheel
Courtesy of AGPS

• Start the machine and check the valve head to see if it has run out, as shown in Fig 7.29. If there is run out in the valve head, remove the valve and reposition it in the chuck. If the run out is still present and cannot be removed by grinding, then the valve will have to be replaced.

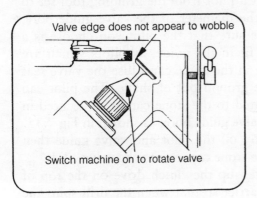

Valve edge does not appear to wobble

Switch machine on to rotate valve

Fig 7.29 Checking the valve for run out
Courtesy of AGPS

• With the valve running true in the chuck head, turn on the coolant, as shown in Fig 7.30, and move the grinding stone until it touches the valve. Move the valve back and forth across the face of the stone. Readjust the grinding stone and repeat the above procedure until the valve face is smooth around its circumference, as shown in Fig 7.31. Avoid removing the valve from the machine to inspect its face, for if the valve requires more grinding, refitting of the valve to the chuck head can slightly alter the relationship of the grind stone to the valve face.

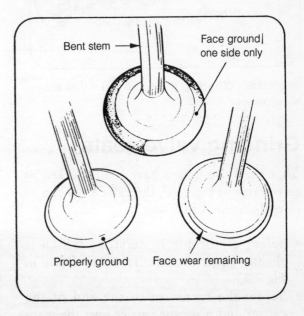

Coolant flow

Lubricates and cools head

Fig 7.30 Coolant used to keep the valve cool when grinding
Courtesy of AGPS

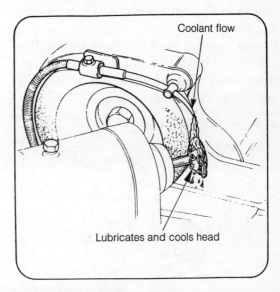

Bent stem

Face ground one side only

Properly ground

Face wear remaining

Fig 7.31 Check the valve face to ensure the valve has been ground properly
Courtesy of AGPS

- Remove the valve from the machine.
- Recheck the valve margin dimension to determine if the valve is still within specifications. If so, proceed to face the end of the valve stem.
- Fit the valve stem into the holding clamp of the machine as shown in Fig 7.32 and grind the tip of the stem until it is smooth and flat.
- Finally, remove the valve from the holding clamp and hold it at an angle to the grindstone so as to grind a chamfer around the end of the valve stem.

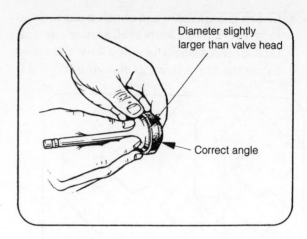

Fig 7.33 Selecting the correct size of hone stone
Courtesy of AGPS

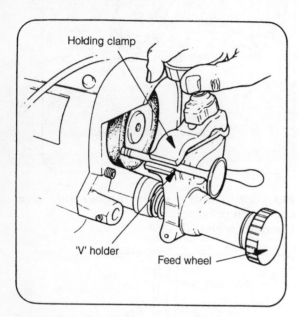

Fig 7.32 Grinding the tip of the valve stem
Courtesy of AGPS

Grinding valve seats

After the valve guides have been checked as serviceable or replaced, the valve seats can be reconditioned as follows:

- Select a suitable hone stone which is slightly larger than the valve, as shown in Fig 7.33.
- Screw the stone on to the end of the carrier and place the carrier over the mandrel of the hone stone dressing tool, as shown in Fig 7. 34. Adjust the angle of the

dressing tool to that required in the service manual. Use an electric drill to drive the carrier at approximately 2000 rpm. Then, with the carrier rotating, set the diamond cutting tool for a light cut and dress the face of the hone to the required angle. The finish on the hone stone will be of a coarse nature which is advantageous for initially rough cutting the valve seats.

- Select a pilot from the grinding tool set to suit the diameter of the valve guide bore. Make sure that the pilot you choose is a neat fit in the guide, as pilots which are loose in the guide can cause the valve seat to be ground out of shape. The pilot can be fitted to the stone carrier or secured in the valve guide bore, as shown in Fig 7.35.
- Lightly oil the pilot and valve guide then fit the stone carrier into the valve guide.
- Tighten up the clutch drive on the top of the carrier so that when the drill spins the carrier at high speed, it will not slip as it rough cuts the seat as shown in Fig 7.36.
- Grind the seat until all the old seat marks are removed.
- For a light, smooth cut of the valve seat, the clutch drive can be slackened off so as to allow the clutch to slip if undue downward force is applied to the clutch drive and hone stone.

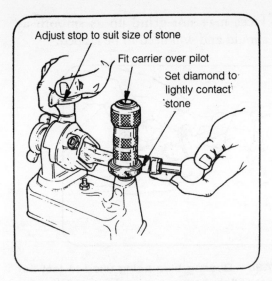

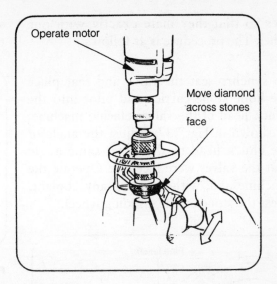

Fig 7.34   Dressing the hone stone   *Courtesy of AGPS*

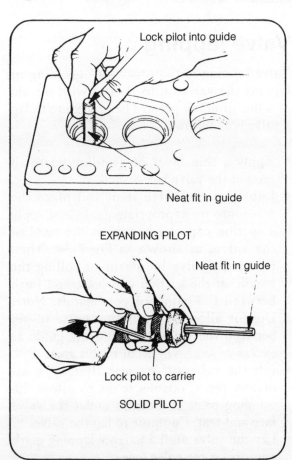

Fig 7.35   Selecting and fitting the pilot to either the hone stone carrier or the cylinder head
Courtesy of AGPS

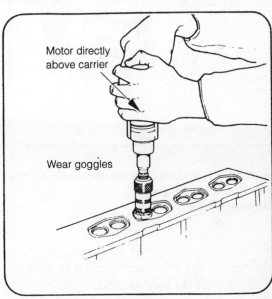

Fig 7.36   Honing the valve seat
Courtesy of AGPS

Synchro-seating of valves and seats

So as to match the valve seat angle with the valve face angle, the seat can now be synchro-seated. Reconditioning of valves and seats by synchro-seating involves grinding both the valve and the valve seat to the exact same angle — that is, synchronising the angles so that they mate exactly with one another. The procedure is as follows.

- To synchro-seat the valve and seat place the hone stone carrier and pilot into the chuck head of the valve refacing machine, as shown in Fig 7.37. Adjust the angle of the chuck head to the exact same angle that the valves were faced at. Operate the machine and, without using any coolant, dress the stone on the grinding wheel.

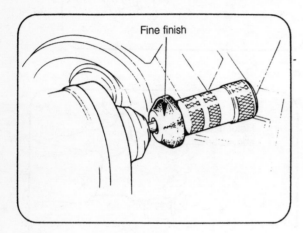

Fine finish

Fig 7.37 Dressing the hone stone to the same angle as the valve
Courtesy of AGPS

- Refit the stone carrier to the valve guide and grind the valve seat until it is smooth and even all the way around.
- To check both seat angles to see that they mate with one another, apply bearing blue to the valve face, as shown in Fig 7.38, and push the valve firmly down on to its seat. Without rotating the valve, push it up off its seat and check the contact pattern on the valve seat. It should be identical to that of the valve face. The valve face and valve seat are now synchro-seated.

Generally, if valves and seats have been synchro-seated, they can be reassembled into the head without lapping the valve to its seat. However, from time to time the valve and seat faces may not grind up as smooth as they should and will need to be lapped.

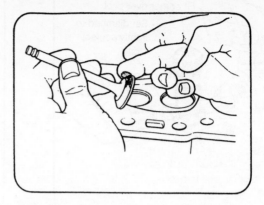

Fig 7.38 Bearing blue being used to test the contact pattern between the valve and its seat
Courtesy of AGPS

Valve lapping

Valve lapping is the process of grinding or lapping the valve on to its seat with the aid of a fine grinding paste. The procedure to lap a valve is as follows.

- Apply a thin layer of grinding paste all around the valve face.
- Lubricate the valve stem and place the valve into its appropriate guide and apply a suction cap and handle to the head of the valve, as shown in Fig 7.39. Then rotate the valve by means of rolling the handle of the suction cup back and forth between the palms of your hands. *Note:* Do not allow any grinding paste to get between the valve stem and the guide as excessive wear will occur in this area.
- Lift the valve off its seat after approximately ten rotations so as to allow the grinding paste to re-form under the valve face and seat. Continue to lap the valve.
- Lap the valve until a narrow lapping mark appears on the valve face.
- Clean off all the grinding paste from the valve and seat with a cloth.
- Lubricate the valve seating face and valve stem then fit the valve back into the head.

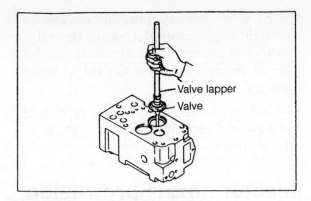

Fig 7.39   Hand lapping a valve on to its seat
Courtesy of Mitsubishi

Valve seat width

The width of the valve seat plays an important part in the valve's sealing ability and its transfer of heat from the valve to the cylinder head. Narrow seats are desirable in that they have a narrow line of contact with the valve face, which helps to form a good seal. Wide seats, on the other hand, are necessary so as to transfer heat away from the valve. A compromise has to be reached between both so as to maintain adequate valve cooling and sealing.

As a general guide to valve seat width, the exhaust valve has a slightly wider seat at 3 mm than the intake valve at 2 mm width.

During valve seat reconditioning, it may be necessary to grind the seat at different angles so as to achieve the specified seat width. Removing metal from the top of the seat is called **crowning** and is achieved by grinding the seat at a 20° angle. Removing metal from the bottom of the seat is called **throating**, as shown in Fig 7.40, and is achieved by grinding the seat at a 60° angle.

These same cutting angles can also be used to raise or lower the contact point on the valve face. Crown cutting the seat will move the contact line towards the stem, and throating will move the contact line away from the stem. The most desirable point of seat contact on the valve face is in the centre.

Interference valve and seat angles

An interference angle is when the valve and the seat are ground at two different angles. The angles vary with different manufacturers, but generally the difference is between half and one degree, as shown in Fig 7.41. The purpose of the interference seat angles is to allow for quick sealing and bedding in of the valve to seat on new engines. As the valve wears on its seat, the interference angle disappears and full face contact is maintained.

Checking valve head height

Valve head height is the distance that the valve protrudes above or below the surface of the cylinder head. Incorrect valve head height can affect the engine compression ratio, or alternatively allow the piston to strike the valve during engine operation. Valve head height can be checked as follows:

* For a valve fitted below the head surface, place a straight edge across the top of the valve and measure the distance between the straight edge and the valve, as shown in Fig 7.42.

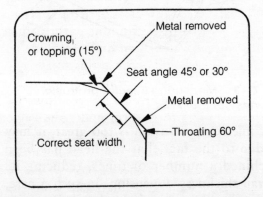

Fig 7.40   Crowning and throating the valve seat to achieve the proper seat position and width
Courtesy of AGPS

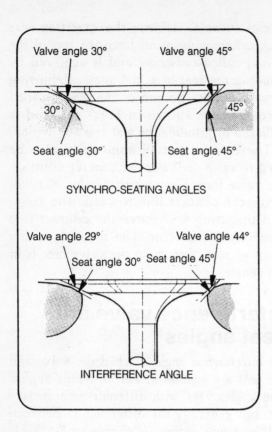

Fig 7.41   Comparing synchro-seated and interference valve and seat angles
Courtesy of AGPS

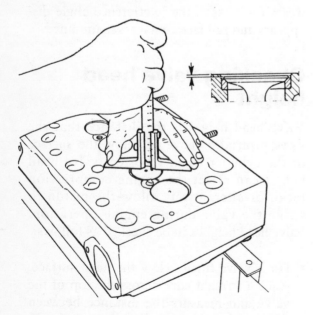

Fig 7.42   Measuring valve depth below the face of the head   Courtesy of Fiat Allis

• For a valve above the head surface, place a straight edge across the top of the valve head and measure from the straight edge down to the head with the aid of feeler gauges.

Grinding of the valve seat or valve face will have a direct effect on the amount of valve protrusion.

Injector nozzle protrusion

Injector nozzle protrusion is the amount that the injector nozzle tip protrudes above the flat surface of the cylinder head. To check for nozzle protrusion, fit a new sealing washer to each injector and, with the injectors bolted into the cylinder head, measure the distance that each injector protrudes above the surface of the head, as shown in Fig 7.43.

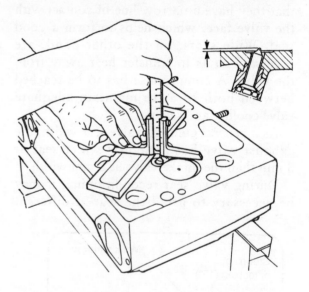

Fig 7.43   Measuring injector protrusion
Courtesy of Fiat Allis

If injector protrusion is too great, it may be due to the fact that the head has been machined a number of times, reducing its overall thickness dimension. In such a case, the head will need to be replaced. Excessive protrusion could also be the result of using sealing washers of incorrect thickness, or could be because the injector seat has been machined beyond its depth specifications. In such cases, selection of the correct size sealing washers could rectify the problem.

If injector protrusion is too small, it may be due to the wrong size of sealing washers being used or an extra sealing washer accidentally being placed in the injector hole.

If injector protrusion is not within specifications, the injector spray will not enter the combustion chamber in the correct position, resulting in inefficient combustion and poor engine performance.

Cylinder head cracking

Cracks in cylinder heads can result from:

- excessive temperature and rapid cooling;
- incorrect cylinder head torque sequence;
- excessive variations between liner protrusion in the cylinder block;
- coolant freezing.

The occurrence of cracking can be greatly reduced by:

- bringing the engine to correct operating temperature before putting it under heavy load. This allows all components of the engine to heat up at the same rate, thus reducing thermal shock stress;
- preventing the engine coolant temperature from rising above normal operating limits. Overheating can cause undue expansion and stress on metal engine components;
- not removing the radiator cap to check coolant level while the engine is at operating temperature. Removing the radiator cap results in a loss of pressure in the cooling system, thereby lowering the boiling point of the coolant. As the coolant boils in and around the head, it causes localised hot spots to occur which can cause cracking;

- fitting block heaters to engines which operate at temperatures at or below freezing point. In this way, when the engine is not operating, the block heater will maintain a satisfactory coolant temperature so as to prevent the coolant from freezing. A characteristic of water is that, when it freezes, it expands and in so doing can cause cracking to occur.

A number of checks can be made to a running engine to verify possible head cracking. With the engine at operating temperature, carefully remove the radiator cap and check the coolant in the radiator for signs of air bubbles. The presence of air bubbles indicates that combustion gas is entering the coolant passages, possibly through a crack in the head, a blown head gasket or reduced cylinder liner protrusion, resulting in poor head gasket sealing. Coolant leaking into the cylinder or cylinders while the engine is not operating can also indicate head cracking or a blown head gasket. Overheating of the engine can also be attributed to a cracked cylinder head as the hot combustion gases enter the coolant, raising its temperature to above normal limits. Alternatively, the presence of coolant in the lubricating oil can indicate the possibility of a crack in the cylinder head which can allow coolant to weep into oil galleries. In such cases the presence of oil in the coolant is also possible.

Cylinder head crack inspection

A visual inspection of the cylinder head will not always reveal cracks, so a more accurate method of detection should be used. Three common methods of crack detection are:
- dye penetrant;
- electro-magnet detection;
- pressure testing.

Note: A detailed explanation about how each of these methods is applied can be found at the end of this chapter.

Cylinder head crack repair

Cylinder heads which are cracked need not always be replaced as some cracks can be repaired by welding or screw plugging.

Welding of the cylinder head requires that the head be pre-heated to avoid distortion and then machined to restore the surface to its original condition. Welding of cast iron cylinder heads is a specialist job, requiring the head to be pre-heated and welded with special welding rods.

Screw plugging — or metal stitching, as it is often referred to — is an alternative repair method to welding and does not involve the heating of the head. The crack is repaired by drilling a hole at the start of the crack then screwing a tapered screw into it. Another hole is drilled next to the original plug in such a way that the screw which is inserted interlocks with the first, as shown in Fig 7.44. This process continues the full length of the crack with all the screws being interlocked together. The heads of the screws are broken off after each one is screwed in and all screw ends are peened over at the completion of the repair to ensure they are all held firmly in place.

Essentially, metal stitching wedges and stresses the localised area on either side of the crack, forming a leak- and movement-free repair.

Welsh plugs

Whenever the cylinder head has been removed for inspection and repair, the welsh plugs which seal off the coolant passages in the head should be renewed. Welsh plugs come in a variety of shapes and sizes and can be constructed from various metals, such as steel, brass and stainless steel.

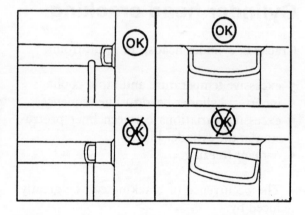

Fig 7.45   Correct installation of welsh plugs
Courtesy of Cummins Engine Co

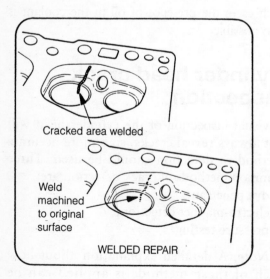

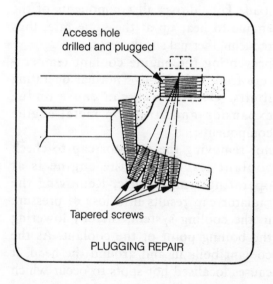

Fig 7.44   Two methods of repairing a crack in the cylinder head   *Courtesy of AGPS*

After all the welsh plugs have been removed from the head, clean the welsh plug mounting area, then refit the new plugs with suitable sealing compound around their circumference. With reference to Fig 7.45, the welsh plugs should be driven squarely into place with the aid of a punch slightly smaller than the size of the plug itself.

Installing cylinder head to block

Cylinder head installation will vary from one manufacturer to another, so whenever refitting a head refer to the service manual for the recommended procedure. In the absence of a service manual, the following general procedure can be used as a guide to refitting the cylinder head:

- Clean the top of the block and the face of the cylinder head with a scraper, emery cloth and a solvent cleaner until both are clean and dry. *Caution!* do not allow the grit from the emery tape to fall into the cylinders, as severe cylinder damage will occur during engine running.
- If the cylinder head is retained by bolts, make sure the bolt holes and threads are clean and that the holes have no oil or water in them. Screwing bolts down into holes which have water or oil in them will cause a hydraulic lock to occur in the bottom of the hole which can crack the cylinder block.
- Fit the head gasket to the block, making sure it is on the correct way, with F to the front or T to the top. If no location markings are present, check water and oil galleries for alignment. Do not apply any sealants or lubricants to the gasket unless specified in the service manual.
- Place the cylinder head gently on the block.
- Clean all retaining bolts and lubricate the threads and up under the head of each bolt

so as to reduce friction during tightening thereby obtaining accurate clamp loads. *Caution!* use only the lubricant specified by the manufacturer (generally engine oil), as the use of EP oils will cause the bolts or nuts to overtighten.

- Use an accurate tension wrench and tension the bolts or nuts down in multiple stages starting from the centre and working out in a circle as shown in Fig 7.46. The amount of torque which should be applied during each stage of tensioning should be around a third of the maximum torque setting. Check the final torque twice.

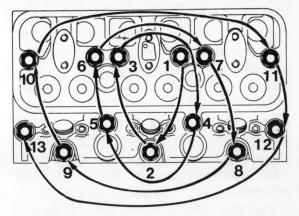

Fig 7.46 Tightening sequence for cylinder head bolts

Another method of tensioning head bolts is **torque turn tightening**. This tensioning procedure requires the bolts to be tightened to an initial torque followed by a further turning of the bolt head to a specified angle as shown in Fig 7.47. This method of tightening eliminates the possibility of the bolt tension being absorbed by friction under the head of the bolt or by an abnormally high turning resistance due to dirty or faulty bolt threads.

- Refit the valve pushrods and rocker shaft assembly.
- Finally, attach the manifolds and refit the injectors.

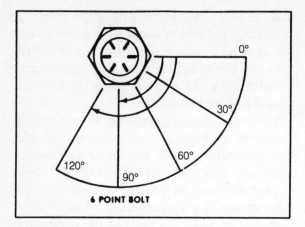

Fig 7.47 Degrees of bolt turn for torque turn tightening
Courtesy of Detroit Diesel

After approximately 20 hours of operation, the cylinder head should be retensioned to ensure that all the bolts or nuts maintain their correct clamping force.

Crack detection

This is a general explanation of the different crack-detecting procedures that can be used to locate cracks in any engine component.

The three most common methods used to detect cracks are as follows:
- dye penetrant;
- electro-magnetic detection;
- pressure testing.

Dye penetrant crack detection

This method of crack detection involves the use of a coloured dye to penetrate a crack and then highlight the crack as a coloured line.

There are four aerosol spray cans used in dye penetrant crack detection. They are:
- the cleaner;
- the dye penetrant;
- the remover;
- the developer.

Fig 7.48 Crack detection by using the dye penetrant test
Courtesy of AGPS

The procedure to detect a crack using the aerosol packs is as follows:

Step 1: Thoroughly clean the area to be tested with the solution from the aerosol 'cleaner' can.

Step 2: With the component clean and dry, spray the coloured 'penetrant' over the area to be tested, as shown in Fig 7.48, and let it sit for approximately five minutes. This will give the coloured dye time to seep into any cracks.

Step 3: With the aid of the spray 'remover' solution and a rag, thoroughly clean all traces of the coloured dye from the test area.

Step 4: With the component perfectly dry and clean, apply the 'developer' evenly over the test area. This will draw out the dye penetrant concealed within any cracks, making them visible as a coloured line against a white background. Apply the developer sparingly, as too great an application may blot out the signs of any fine cracks. An alternative method of detecting a crack with dye penetrant is to use a dye which has fluorescent properties that can be seen under an ultraviolet light.

Electro-magnetic crack detection

This method of crack detection involves the use of magnetic lines of force in conjunction with a metallic powder or liquid solution to locate cracks in engine components.

The suspect component is magnetised by either a portable electro- magnet or a crack-detecting machine. The portable electro-magnet is suitable for crack testing components in workshops where more sophisticated testing equipment is not available. Fine metal powder is sprinkled over the component and the suspected area is magnetised with the electro-magnet. A magnetic field will be formed in the immediate area between the two magnetic poles of the electro-magnet. If a crack is present within the magnetic field, the magnetic lines of force will be broken, resulting in the formation of a north and south pole on respective sides of the crack. The formation of the two poles will attract the metal powder along the crack, identifying its outline as shown in Fig 7.49.

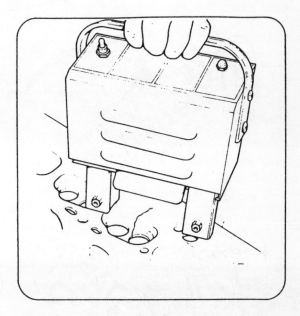

Fig 7.49 Using an electro-magnet to test a cylinder head for cracks
Courtesy of AGPS

An alternative method of crack detection is to magnetise the complete component, such as a crankshaft or cylinder head, then pour a solution of oil, fluorescent dye and magnetic particles over the area to be tested. The test component is held in a special crack-detecting machine, as shown in Fig 7.50, whereby end contacts pass electrical current in a longitudinal pattern through the component.

Once the component is magnetised, the magnetic particles in the solution are attracted to any surface discontinuities, such as cracks. Magnetising the component along its axis is suitable for detecting cracks parallel to the component centre line. A magnetising coil, as shown in Fig 7.50, can also be used

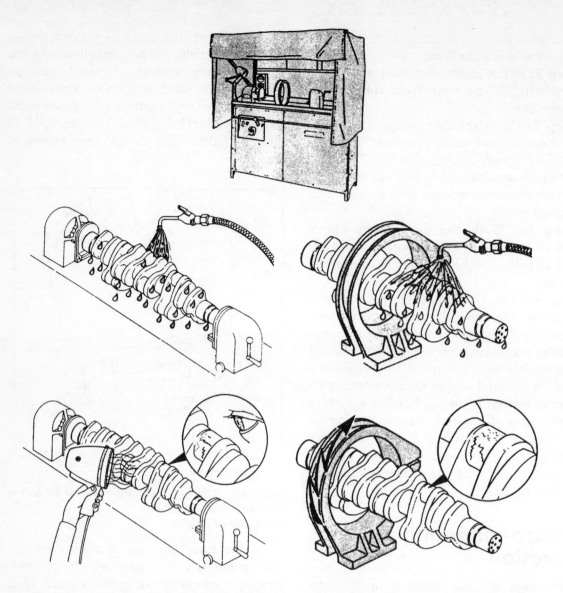

Fig 7.50 Inspecting a crankshaft for cracks using the magnetic particle test procedure
Courtesy of Cummins Engine Co

to pass electrical current across the component which will detect circumferential cracks. Cracks detected using the inspecting solution can be seen with the aid of an ultraviolet light, as shown in Fig 7.50.

Pressure testing

This method of crack detection involves the pressurisation of water passages in the cylinder head and block to see if they leak. Blanking plates are used to seal off the water passages, which are then pressurised with low-pressure air by way of an air fitting attached to one of the blanking-off plates. The component is then submerged in a container of water, as shown in Fig 7.51. The appearance of a continuous stream of bubbles will indicate a crack. To further increase the effectiveness of pressure testing, the water in which the component is submerged should be heated to approximately 70°C. This will heat up and expand the component, thereby opening up fine hairline

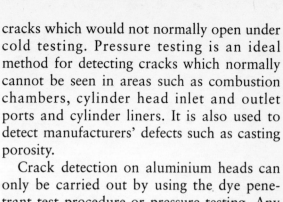

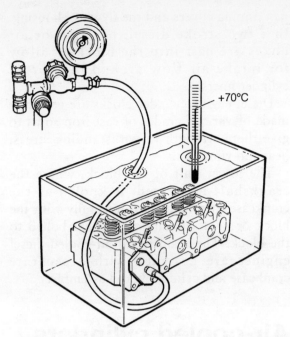

Fig 7.51 Pressure testing a cylinder head for crack detection
Courtesy of Volvo

cracks which would not normally open under cold testing. Pressure testing is an ideal method for detecting cracks which normally cannot be seen in areas such as combustion chambers, cylinder head inlet and outlet ports and cylinder liners. It is also used to detect manufacturers' defects such as casting porosity.

Crack detection on aluminium heads can only be carried out by using the dye penetrant test procedure or pressure testing. Any form of magnetic crack detection is not compatible with aluminium, and therefore cannot be used.

8
Cylinder Block

The cylinder block makes up the basic frame of the engine. Transverse rails cast integral with the block provide rigidity and strength, assuring precise alignment of crankshaft bearings and cylinder bores. The block also contains various passages and galleries, through which coolant and oil circulate to cool and lubricate the engine.

During manufacture, the cast block undergoes a number of machining operations. The cylinders are bored, the crank-shaft main bearing supports are tunnel bored and the camshaft bores are machined. There are also a number of flat surfaces machined on the block to provide for attachment of external components like the cylinder head, water pump, oil filter housing, oil pan, timing covers and the flywheel housing. In a two-stroke diesel, passages or air boxes are cast into the block to allow for intake air flow around the ported cylinder liners.

Diesel engine cylinder blocks are generally made of various grades of cast iron so as to give them strength in withstanding stress, heat and vibration.

The lower half of the block, where the crankshaft is located, is known as the crankcase. It may be cast integrally with the block or be a separate component bolted to the block. The majority of air-cooled diesel engines are designed with a separate crankcase and cylinder barrel assembly.

Air-cooled cylinders

The cylinder barrels on air-cooled diesel engines are designed to be separate from each other and are bolted to a common crankcase. The construction of each cylinder barrel is such that cooling fins completely surround the cylinder. To construct a conventional one-piece cylinder block with cooling fins part way around the cylinders would be inefficient from a cooling point of view, as air must circulate around the total surface area of the cylinder so as to give even and adequate engine cooling. The large volumes of air flow necessary for engine cooling are provided by a combined flywheel/fan which forces air via ducting in and around the finned cylinder barrels.

Cylinder bores and liners

Diesel engine blocks are expensive and have a long service life requirement; consequently many diesel engines use cylinder liners or sleeves of either the 'dry' or 'wet' type which can be replaced when the cylinders become damaged or worn beyond serviceable limits.

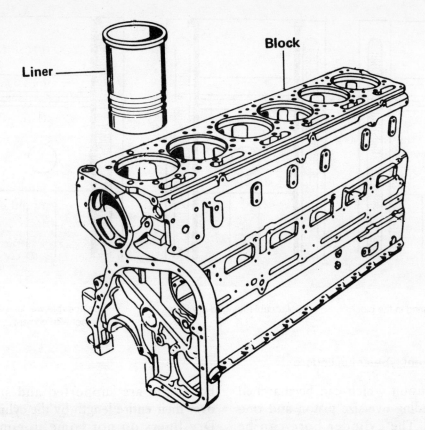

Liner ─

Block

Fig 8.1   Cylinder block for a six-cylinder engine

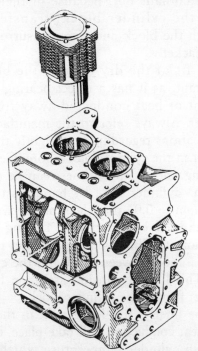

Fig 8.2   Crankcase and cylinder barrel for a
two-cylinder air-cooled engine
Courtesy of Lister Petter

There are a number of cylinder bore/liner designs used in current diesel engines. They are:

- cast cylinder bore (integral with the block);
- the flanged dry liner;
- the wet liner.

Cast cylinder bore

A number of smaller less expensive diesel engines have cylinder bores which are cast integrally with the block. The bores are later machined to a precise measurement to accommodate the piston and rings. During an engine overhaul, worn or damaged cylinder bores can be bored out to an

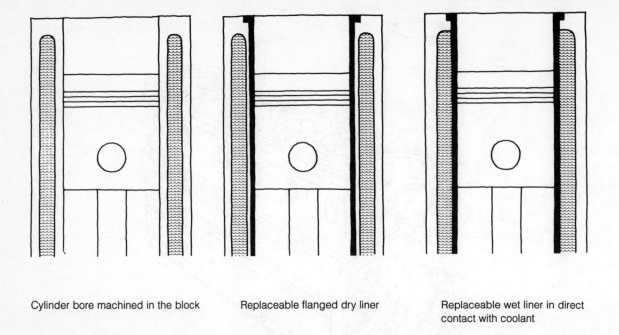

Cylinder bore machined in the block   Replaceable flanged dry liner   Replaceable wet liner in direct contact with coolant

Fig 8.3   Different types of cylinders

oversize dimension which can be matched to a corresponding oversize piston and ring combination. The cylinder bore can be re-bored a number of times, depending on the manufacturer's specifications and availability of parts. However, if the bore is enlarged beyond certain limits, the reduced thickness of the cylinder walls will be such that the cylinder may distort, causing the piston to bind in the cylinder. In many cases, the cylinder bore can be brought back to a standard size by the fitting of a straight liner or cylindrical sleeve into the existing cylinder bore. The liner, which is cylindrical in shape with no flanges attached, is pressed into the oversize cylinder bore with its top flush with the surface of the cylinder block.

Flanged dry liners

Cylinder liners are manufactured as a separate item to the cylinder block and are fitted to it during assembly of the engine. Dry liners are thin metal sleeves approximately 2 mm thick which are fitted into the cylinder

bores and are supported and surrounded over their entire length by the cylinder block. Dry liners do not come in contact with engine coolant but, because of their close fit in the cylinder block, transfer heat through the block and into the surrounding water jacket.

The fit of the dry liner to the block is important, as it has a direct bearing on the amount of heat conducted away from the cylinder. Always refer to the manufacturer's specifications regarding how tightly the liner is to fit in the cylinder block bore. Generally speaking, most flanged liners can be pressed into the cylinder bore by hand, as there is 0.025 mm to 0.04 mm clearance between the liner and the cylinder wall. During engine operation, the liner will expand and take up the clearance between itself and the cylinder wall. This liner expansion assists in holding the liner firm in the cylinder block.

If the liner is too loose a fit in the bore, poor heat conduction will take place, causing a rise in cylinder temperature which could cause the rings and piston to scuff the cylinder

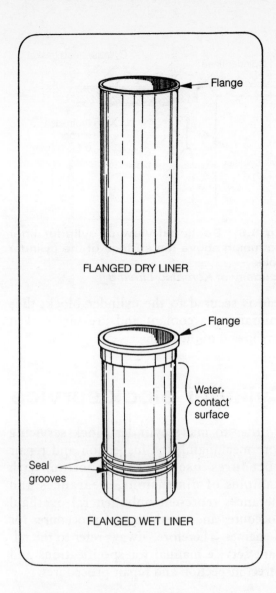

Fig 8.4 Dry and wet type cylinder liners
Courtesy of AGPS

wall. A liner which is too tight a fit may break on assembly or, if assembled, could compress and distort the surface of the cylinder wall, resulting in loss of clearance between the liner and piston with possible scuffing and eventual piston seizure.

Flanged liners are positioned within the cylinder block by way of a flange on top of the liner which fits into a machined recess or counterbore in the top of the block. On assembly, the liner is fitted into the block where its flange sits on the counterbore and

protrudes slightly above the flat surface of the block. Protrusion of the liner above the surface of the block allows the cylinder head to clamp and hold the liner firmly in place on reassembly of the engine.

Dry cylinder liners do not require the same amount of sealing as do wet liners, with sealing being achieved by liner protrusion and the cylinder head gasket.

Wet liners

Wet liners are completely surrounded by coolant which extends the full length of the cylinder wall. Unlike the dry liner, which did not have to seal coolant, the wet liner is required to be sealed at the top flange and at its lower skirt so as to prevent the escape of coolant from the cylinder block water jacket. The liner is sealed at the top by way of a metal-to-metal seal or copper gasket between the liner flange and the counterbore seat. To seal the lower end of the liner, o-rings and sometimes a clevis seal are used to prevent coolant leakage into the crankcase. The clevis seal, which is located at the top of the o-ring sealing group, as shown in Fig 8.5, is designed to protect the o-rings and prevent corrosion occurring adjacent to the o-ring sealing area.

The wall thickness of the wet liner is much greater than that of a dry liner, as the liner does not have the support of the block and must support itself totally during engine operation.

Some engine manufacturers are now constructing tell-tale weep holes in the side of the cylinder block so as to provide an easy means of identifying cylinder liner seal leakage. The weep holes, as shown in Fig 8.5, will allow any coolant which leaks past the liner seals to drain to the outside of the cylinder block instead of down into the crankcase. In this way, a liner seal problem is easily identified before damage can occur to the engine.

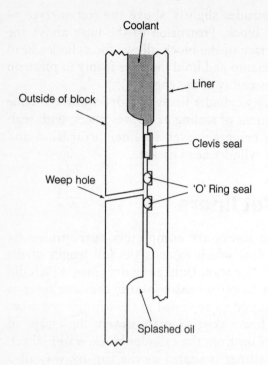

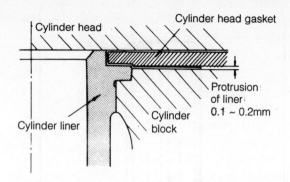

Fig 8.5 Sectional view of a liner and cylinder block showing the location of liner seal weep holes in the side of the cylinder block

Not all wet cylinder liners are exposed to engine coolant over their full length. In fact, some engines use liners which are partly wet and partly dry. The top half of the liner is surrounded by coolant and the bottom half mounted dry in the block. By reducing the coolant contact area around the liner, the volume and consequently the weight of the coolant in the block are reduced, thereby reducing overall engine weight.

Liner protrusion

Both wet and dry liners are designed to be installed with a slight amount of protrusion above the surface of the cylinder block. The liner sits slightly above the flat surface of the cylinder block, as shown in Fig 8.6. This protrusion, which varies from 0.1 mm to 0.17 mm, is designed to ensure that the liner is held firmly on its seat when the cylinder

Fig 8.6 Sectional view of cylinder liner protrusion above the surface of the cylinder block
Courtesy of Komatsu Limited

head is secured to the cylinder block, thus maintaining a coolant and pressure seal at the top end of the liner.

Cylinder block service

In order to make cylinder block servicing more meaningful, the inspection and repair procedures used in conjunction with examples of dimensions, clearances and tolerances represent only general overhaul procedures and not the actual procedures for all engines. Therefore, always refer to the relevant service manual for specifications and correct inspection and repair procedures.

Cleaning the cylinder block

Prior to inspecting and wear evaluating the cylinder block, it should be thoroughly cleaned. A very effective method of cleaning a cylinder block is to leave it to soak in a chemical cleaning solution in a cleaning tank, as shown in Fig 8.7. There are various types of chemical cleaning systems, the most common being hot or cold tank cleaning. Hot tank cleaning uses a tank containing a caustic solution which is heated to a high temperature. The components to be cleaned are immersed in the solution and during the cleaning process some form of agitation of either the solution or the components is used to maintain the movement of solution over the components. Cold tank cleaning uses a tank containing strong chemical solvents which, by virtue of their chemical composition, strip and clean components back to bare metal.

Warning! Solvents used in cleaning systems may be harmful to your eyes and skin, so whenever handling components cleaned in such systems wear protective clothing and a face shield.

Fig 8.7   Cleaning the cylinder block
Courtesy of Cummins Engine Co

After the block is cleaned, it should be inspected all over for cracks, particularly in areas such as around the cylinder counterbore, the top of the block and around the main bearing supports. Areas which are suspected as being cracked and which are not visible to the naked eye can be tested by using dye penetrant. A full explanation on crack testing engine components using dye penetrant can be found in Chapter 7.

Cylinder liner measurement

During disassembly of the engine and before the liners are removed from the block, they can be inspected and measured so as to

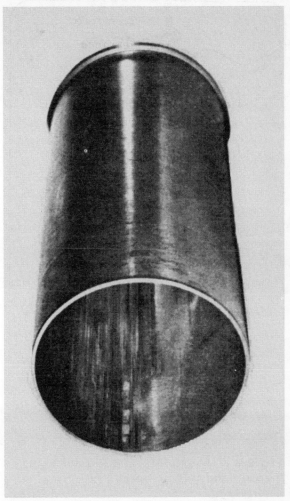

Fig 8.8   Example of a scored cylinder liner
Courtesy of Mack Trucks Inc.

determine their reuseability. The cylinder bore should first be inspected for any signs of scoring or damage, as shown in Fig 8.8. The bore is then to be measured to determine its nominal size, ovality and taper by using either a dial bore gauge, a telescopic gauge or an inside micrometer, as shown in Fig 8.9. The dial bore gauge would be one of the most accurate and easy to use in determining the difference within the bore dimensions as the gauge is moved up and down the bore. The telescopic gauge and the inside micrometer may also be used to determine variations in cylinder bore size, as well as measuring the actual bore diameter.

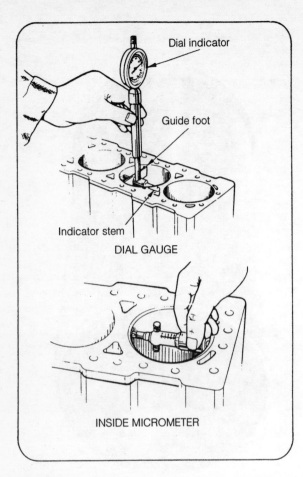

Fig 8.9 Measuring instruments used to measure the cylinder bore
Courtesy of AGPS

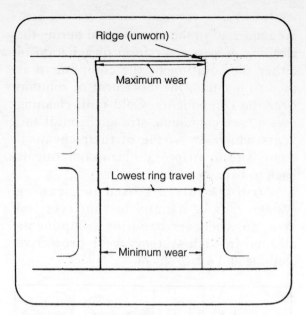

Fig 8.10 Illustration showing cylinder bore wear
Courtesy of AGPS

Nominal bore size

To measure the bore for nominal or actual size, use an inside micrometer and measure the bore at its lower end in an unworn area where the piston skirt does not contact. Alternatively, the bore can be measured at the very top where there is no ring contact provided all the carbon is removed from the area to be measured. Figure 8.10 indicates the general cylinder wear areas.

Cylinder bore ovality

When measuring the bore for ovality or out-of-roundness, first measure in a position parallel to the crankshaft and then at right angles to it, as shown in Fig 8.11. The difference in the two measurements (if any) will determine how oval the bore has worn. These measurements should be taken at several locations, starting at the top of the ring travel and then moving down the bore in increments of 30 mm. A general specification for maximum allowable ovality is 0.075 mm.

Cylinder bore taper

To determine if the bore is worn in a taper, measure at the highest point of ring travel on the piston thrust side, then at a point approximately 25 mm from the bottom of the bore in the same vertical line. The difference between the two measurements will determine the amount of cylinder bore taper. As the allowable taper is dependent on bore length and width, always refer to the service manual for the correct specifications.

Maximum cylinder bore wear

The maximum cylinder bore wear can be determined by measuring the cylinder at its greatest point of wear and then by

Fig 8.11 Measuring the cylinder bore for ovality and taper with the aid of a dial bore gauge
Courtesy of Volvo

subtracting from it the nominal bore size dimension. The point of greatest cylinder wear is at the top of the ring travel just below the ridge at right angles to the crankshaft. Refer to the service manual for the allowable bore wear figures.

Cylinder liner servicing

The type of cylinder liner used will determine the course of action to be taken to repair the worn cylinders. For blocks with pressed sleeves, the sleeve cannot generally be bored oversize, therefore worn sleeves will have to be bored out and new sleeves fitted. For replaceable wet and dry liners, the worn liners are removed and new standard size liners refitted.

Removing cylinder liners

It is important that the proper method be followed when removing a cylinder liner, so as not to damage the liner or the cylinder block. One such method of removing a liner is to fit a puller plate to the bottom of the liner, then, with the aid of a slide hammer or puller, pull the liner up out of the block as shown in Fig 8.12.

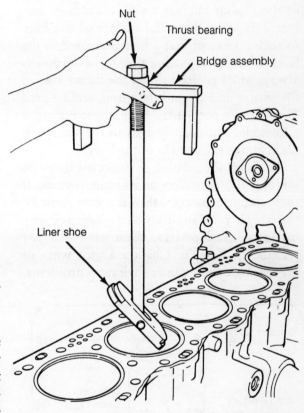

Fig 8.12 Puller used to remove cylinder liners from the cylinder block
Courtesy of Detroit Diesel Corp

Inspection of liners

If the liners are to be reused, they should be numbered on their outside surface so that they go back into their original position. After all the liners have been removed from the block, they should be cleaned and then checked for cracks, flange thickness and pitting of the outside liner walls, as shown in Fig 8.13. Dye penetrant can be used if cracks are suspected and are not visible to the naked eye. The outside surface of wet type liners should be inspected for any signs of pitting due to cavitation. Cavitation occurs only on the outside of wet liners and is due to the liner vibrating within the cylinder block, which causes vapour bubbles to form and implode on its outer surface. This collapsing or imploding of the vapour bubbles on the outer liner surface eats away the metal surface of the liner to such an extent that a hole is created in the liner wall. Liner pitting due to cavitation is always at its greatest down the thrust side of the piston and around the o-ring sealing area of the lower part of the liner. Slight pitting is allowable, but deep gouges in the liner will necessitate replacement of the liner.

The liner should also be inspected for scale buildup and corrosion on its outer surface. If such conditions occur, then the liner must be thoroughly cleaned so as to remove any buildup of deposits, then assessed for reusability. Refer to Chapter 17 for ways of preventing cylinder liner cavitation problems.

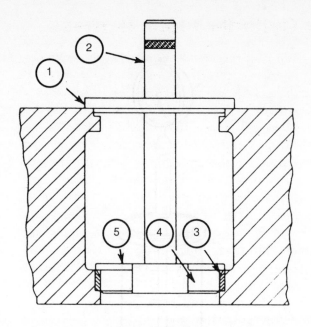

1. Centering plate
2. Handle
3. Insert
4. Pilot
5. Driver

Fig 8.14 Illustration showing how to install a metal insert into the lower part of the cylinder block so as to restore the cylinder liner o-ring sealing surface

The liner sealing area in the lower part of the block should also be thoroughly cleaned and checked for any signs of wear or pitting.

Measure the diameter of this same area and check the service manual to see if it is within specifications. If the bore diameter has increased where the o-rings seal due to o-ring fretting, then poor o-ring tension and possible coolant leakage past the liner seals may result. Deterioration of the o-ring sealing area can be rectified by filling the affected area with epoxy then machining the area or boring the block housing and fitting a metal sleeve, as shown in Fig 8.14.

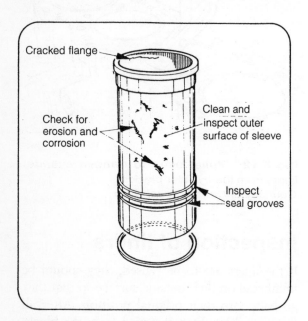

Fig 8.13 Inspecting a wet type liner to determine its reuseability
Courtesy of AGPS

Cylinder block flatness

With all the liners out of the cylinder block, check the top of the block for flatness with the aid of a straight edge and feeler gauge as shown in Fig 8.15. The top surface of the block will have a tolerance as to how much it can be out of level; varying length blocks will have differing amounts of block surface distortion, so always refer the service manual for allowable limits. If the top surface of the block is out of specification, the chances are that water, oil and compression leaks may develop from under the cylinder head during engine operation. If the block requires machining, take care not to remove too much metal, which will reduce its overall height below allowable specifications. It is important that cylinder block flatness always be checked before the cylinder counterbores are measured. For if the block requires machining, the existing counterbore dimensions will no longer be valid once the block is machined. In such cases, the counterbores will require machining also so as to reinstate correct liner protrusion above the surface of the cylinder block.

Fig 8.16   Machining the top surface of the cylinder block
Courtesy of Cummins Engine Co

Checking cylinder counterbores

Counterbore wear can be caused by incorrect cylinder head torque, insufficient liner protrusion or erosion from a long service life.

The counterbore surface should be thoroughly cleaned and checked for distortion, cracking and erosion. To check for counterbore distortion, measure the depth of the counterbore at four places around the block as shown in Fig 8.17. A general specification for allowable variation in counterbore distortion is 0.03 mm. Inspect the counterbore for any signs of cracking in the internal corner area around the circumference of the counterbore. As this is a high stress area, it should be checked carefully and, if need be, dye penetrant used to verify that no cracking exists. Finally, check the counterbore area to see that it is flat and smooth and that the cylinder liner flange fully contacts the counterbore. Figure 8.18 shows a comparison between a good counterbore seat and how a bad seat can lead to stress loading and cracking of the liner flange.

If the counterbore has deteriorated, it will need to be refaced by using a counterbore reseating tool as shown in Fig 8.19. The reseating tool is secured in the block opening

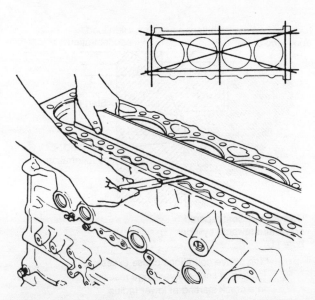

Fig 8.15   Checking the top of the cylinder block for flatness
Courtesy of Detroit Diesel Corp

and consists of a rotating anvil with a cutting tool attached to it. The tool can be adjusted for fine or coarse cuts, depending on the seat condition and surface finish required.

Regardless of how good the counterbore seat may appear to be, a light cut with the reseating tool is beneficial during all engine overhauls so as to ensure full seat contact around the complete counterbore sealing area.

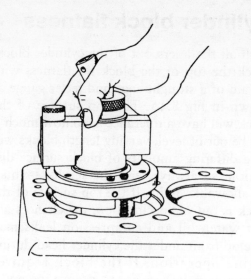

Fig 8.19 A counterbore reseating tool
Courtesy of Fiat Allis

Measuring cylinder liner protrusion

There are various methods of measuring cylinder liner protrusion. Two common methods are as follows:

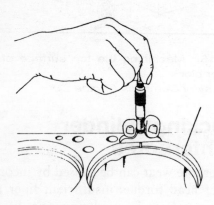

Fig 8.17 Measuring depth of cylinder block counterbore
Courtesy of Fiat Allis

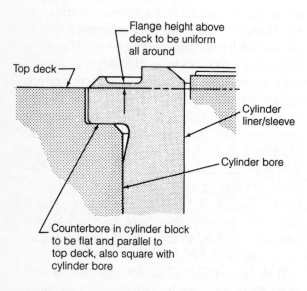

Flange height above deck to be uniform all around

Top deck

Cylinder liner/sleeve

Cylinder bore

Counterbore in cylinder block to be flat and parallel to top deck, also square with cylinder bore

Correct liner to block counterbore relationship

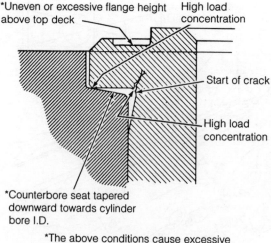

*Uneven or excessive flange height above top deck

High load concentration

Start of crack

High load concentration

*Counterbore seat tapered downward towards cylinder bore I.D.

*The above conditions cause excessive loading of liner/sleeve flange resulting in a crack starting at lower radius

Incorrect cylinder block counterbore

Fig 8.18 A correctly machined cylinder block counterbore and a worn counterbore
Courtesy of Mack Trucks Inc

The **first method** is to measure the width of the cylinder flange at four locations, as shown in Fig 8.20, then the depth of the counterbore at four locations around the bore, as shown previously in Fig 8.17. Subtract one measurement from the other and the result is the amount of liner protrusion.

Fig 8.21   Measuring the cylinder liner protrusion with the liner clamped in position
Courtesy of Cummins Engine Co

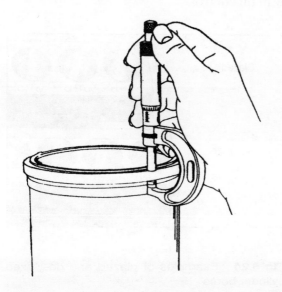

Fig 8.20   Measuring the width of the cylinder liner flange
Courtesy of Fiat Allis

The **second method** of measuring liner protrusion is to place the liner into the cylinder block without any shims or sealing o-rings and clamp it in place. Using a specially designed dial tool, as shown in Fig 8.21, zero the tool on to the top of the cylinder liner flange then move the dial tool on to the flat of the cylinder block and record the dial reading. Measure the protrusion at four equidistant places around the liner and determine the overall average measurement.

A general specification for liner protrusion is between 0.1 mm and 0.2 mm. Failure to retain the specified liner protrusion will cause premature head gasket failure and faulty sealing between the liner flange and the cylinder counterbore. If protrusion is below the specifications, shims can be added under the liner flange to raise the liner to the specified protrusion above the cylinder block surface. (see Fig 8.2)

Variations between adjacent liners under a common cylinder head should not be greater than 0.025 mm within the specified protrusion limit.

After liner protrusion has been established for each cylinder, mark the liner so that on reassembly it goes to its correct position in the block.

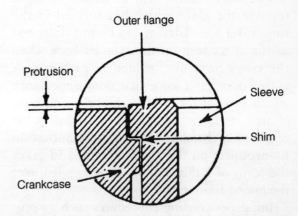

Fig 8.22   Locations where shims can be fitted so as to correct liner or sleeve protrusion

Cylinder ridge removal and deglazing

If the cylinder bore is to be reused, it is important that any ridge above the ring travel area must be removed with the aid of a ridge removing tool similar to the one shown in Fig 8.23. Failure to remove the ridge will result in the new compression ring striking the ridge and being damaged. Removal of the cylinder ridge may sometimes be necessary during the dismantling of the engine so as to allow the pistons to be pushed up unrestricted through the top of the block.

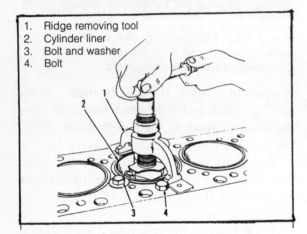

1. Ridge removing tool
2. Cylinder liner
3. Bolt and washer
4. Bolt

Fig 8.23 Ridge removing tool being used to remove a ridge in the top of the cylinder bore
Courtesy of Fiat Allis

The bore should also be honed so as to remove the glaze which has formed in the ring travel area. Glazing can best be described as the effect seen on the cylinder bore when the rings have not bedded in properly. A glazed bore has a somewhat shiny appearance which extends the full length of the ring travel area, as shown in Fig 8.24. Glazing is the result of a chemical build up of combustion by-products on the cylinder bore and takes the form of a thin skin or layer applied over the honed finish of the bore.

Improper running procedures such as prolonged idling or insufficient engine loading are contributing factors to bore glazing. Also

the use of oils containing high levels of anti-friction additives during running-in periods can result in cylinder glazing.

Therefore, during an engine overhaul, the glaze should be removed from the cylinder bore with a honing tool, which will restore the original cylinder bore cross-hatched pattern and thus provide good ring-to-cylinder wall oil control.

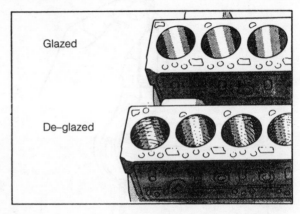

Glazed

De–glazed

Fig 8.24 Examples of glazed and de-glazed cylinder bores
Courtesy of Cummins Engine Co

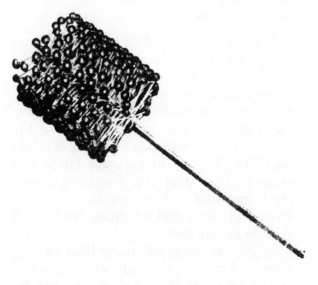

Fig 8.25 Flex hone used to de-glaze cylinder bores

Two types of hone can be used to deglaze cylinder walls: the **flex hone** and the **rigid hone**. The flex hone is a flexible nylon brush with abrasive stones on the tips of the bristles, as shown in Fig 8.25. It can only be used for deglazing and cannot be used to correct any cylinder wear abnormalities. The rigid hone, as shown in Fig 8.26, has four rigid hone stones which can be used for deglazing as well as removing minor grooves or correcting minor cylinder taper wear.

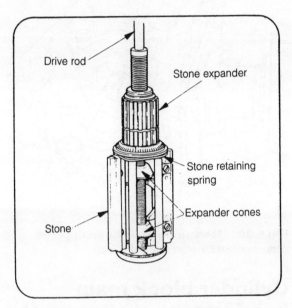

Fig 8.26   Adjustable rigid hone with four hone stones
Courtesy of AGPS

Deglazing the cylinder bore

To deglaze the cylinder bore, first select a 280 grit flex hone which is slightly bigger than the cylinder to be honed. Then, with a suitable variable-speed drill and a mixture of equal parts engine oil and diesel fuel as a lubricant, the cylinder bores can be deglazed. Prior to actually honing the cylinder, place the liner in a suitable holding fixture or clamp it back down into the block. Under no circumstances should a vice be used to hold the liner, as the liner should only be held by

its flange to prevent it from being distorted. *Warning!* Whenever the cylinders are honed while the crankshaft is still installed in the block, the bottom of the bore should be blocked off with cloth so as to prevent abrasive particles falling on to the crankshaft and into the crankcase. Failure to do this will result in abrasives entering the crankshaft bearings, causing major bearing and journal failures.

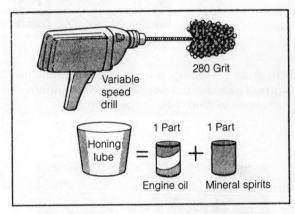

Fig 8.27   Equipment and cutting compound required to deglaze cylinder bores
Courtesy of Cummins Engine Co

With the flex hone spinning at between 300 and 400 rpm, move it up and down the full length of the cylinder in smooth continuous passes at a rate of one stroke per second for 10 to 20 strokes, as shown in Fig 8.28.

A correctly deglazed surface will have a cross-hatched appearance with lines at angles of 15 to 25 degrees with the top of the cylinder block. *Note:* Only hone until the glazing is removed and the cross-hatched pattern is evident throughout the liner, as over-honing will increase the cylinder bore diameter. Figure 8.29 shows the cross-hatched pattern from a properly honed cylinder bore.

It is extremely important to thoroughly clean cylinder bores after honing. If cylinders are not properly cleaned, a considerable quantity of hard abrasives will remain in the engine. These abrasives rapidly wear rings, cylinder walls and bearing surfaces as soon as the engine is assembled and run.

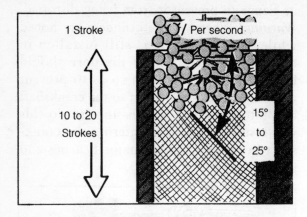

Fig 8.28 Honing procedure to obtain the correct cylinder bore cross-hatched pattern
Courtesy of Cummins Engine Co

Fig 8.29 Cross-hatched pattern from a properly honed cylinder
Courtesy of Mack Trucks Inc

Therefore, clean cylinders thoroughly with the aid of detergent and a scrubbing brush until all honing abrasives are removed. Do not use solvent or petroleum products to clean cylinder walls, as they will not remove abrasives left after honing. As a final check of bore cleanliness, wipe the bore with a white cloth: the cloth should still be clean, without any traces of abrasive material.

Main bearing bores

The main bearing bores should always be checked for size during an engine overhaul. Prior to checking the bore size, install the main bearing caps in their original positions and tension the bolts to the correct torque settings. Use a suitable measuring instrument, as shown in Fig 8.30, and measure each bore for size and out of roundness.

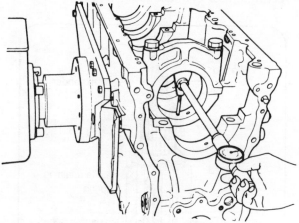

Fig 8.30 Measuring main bearing bores
Courtesy of Detroit Diesel Corp

Cylinder block main bearing tunnel alignment

The main bearing bores should always be checked for alignment whenever the cylinder block is dismantled. Misalignment of the main bearing support webs may be caused by a broken crankshaft, excessive heat or other damage. To check the bearing bores for alignment, place a straight edge along the bores, as shown in Fig 8.31, and with the aid of feeler gauges check to see if any of the main bearing webs are out of alignment. If the main bearing bore alignment is outside the allowable tolerance, then the block must be line bored or replaced.

An alternative check for accurate bearing bore alignment would be to check that the crankshaft rotates and has no tight spots after it has been installed with new bearings and bearing caps torqued down.

To line bore the block, the main bearing caps are to be tightened in place and a boring bar passed through the bearing tunnel, skimming the bearing bores to ensure they are longitudinally aligned. With line boring, it is possible to return the bearing tunnels to their original size and location. This is achieved by machining metal off the mounting faces of the bearing caps, thereby reducing the overall size of the bearing bores, which can then be bored back to a standard size. Line boring is also necessary when a bearing cap must be replaced due to breakage or spun bearing damage.

Line boring can also be used to rectify damaged camshaft housing bearing bores. The repair procedure requires the centring of the boring bar in the camshaft housing whereby a cutting tool attached to the boring bar rotates and at the same time travels through the cylinder block as it machines the bearing housings. Once the cam bearing housings have been bored, oversize outside diameter camshaft bearings must be installed.

Welsh plugs

Whenever the cylinder block has been dismantled for inspection and repair, the welsh plugs which seal off the coolant passages opening on to the outside of the block should be renewed. Welsh plugs come in a variety of shapes and sizes and can be made from various metals such as steel, brass and stainless steel.

After all the welsh plugs have been removed from the side of the block, clean the welsh plug mounting area, then refit the new plugs with a suitable sealing compound around their circumference. The welsh plugs should be installed with the aid of a punch which contacts the outer diameter of the plug and be driven in square until the shoulder on the plug is flush with the outside of the cylinder block, as shown in Fig 8.33.

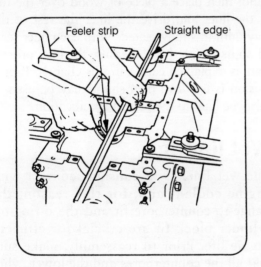

Fig 8.31 Checking the alignment of the main bearing supports
Courtesy of AGPS

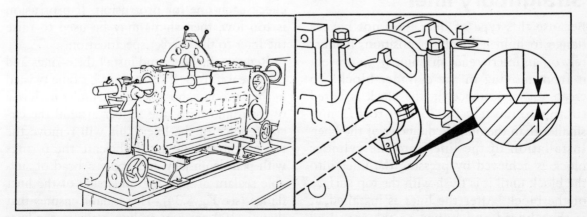

Fig 8.32 Boring bar being used to line bore the main bearing housings
Courtesy of Cummins Engine Co

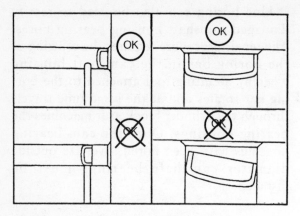

Fig 8.33 Correct installation of welsh plugs
Courtesy of Cummins Engine Co

Installing cylinder liners

As mentioned earlier, various types of liner are used in diesel engines: the straight dry liner, the flanged dry liner and the wet liner. Because of its construction and method of retention, each liner has a different method of installation. Incorrect installation, especially with dry type liners can lead to liner flange breakage on installation, distortion of the liner walls, or local hot spots being formed due to poor heat transfer because of the excessive clearance between the liner and cylinder block.

Straight dry liner

Because this type of liner does not have a flange to hold it firmly in position, it must rely on an interference machine fit to prevent it from moving in the cylinder block. To create an interference fit, the block is bored to approximately 0.025 mm to 0.1 mm smaller than the outside diameter of the liner. Installation of the liner into the cylinder block is achieved by pressing the liner into the block until it is flush with the top surface of the block. After the liner is installed, it is then bored and honed to the specified cylinder diameter.

Flanged dry liners

As the flanged liner is held in place by its flange, it does not require as tight a fit as does the straight dry liner. Prior to installing the liners, inspect the block and make sure that all the counterbores and cylinder walls are clean. Measure the cylinder block bores at several places and, if the liner-to-block clearance is below 0.025 mm to 0.1 mm, lightly hone the block until the correct clearance is obtained. The liners should then be pushed into the cylinder block with the palm of your hand. If the liner does not go fully home when pushed by hand, then place a piece of wood over the top of the liner and drive the liner the rest of the way until it is fully seated. With each liner seated on its counterbore, measure the liner protrusion as explained earlier in this chapter. If protrusion is too low, then shims may be used to raise the liner to the correct specification.

Wet liners

The wet liner is in constant contact with engine coolant and, for this reason, the flange-to-counterbore fit and the o-ring-to-cylinder block fit are crucial for efficient engine life. Prior to reassembly, make sure that all the counterbores and the lower cylinder bores are clean and free of any burrs or corrosion. Before fitting the o-rings to the liners, position the liners in the block and check each one for protrusion. If protrusion is too low, then shims may be used to raise the liner to the correct specification.

Remove the liners and install the o-rings and clevis seal if used. If the o-rings become twisted in their grooves, hook a scriber under each one of them and move the scriber around the circumference of the liner; this will remove the twist from the o-ring. Lubricate the o-rings with petroleum jelly and apply a bead of suitable sealant around the underside of the liner flange (see Fig 8.34). The sealant ensures that there is 100 per cent sealing between the liner and the counterbore seat. Place the liner into the block until it contacts the o-rings then use a liner-driving tool, as shown in Fig 8.35, to drive the liner all the way home into the block counterbore.

As a check for any distortion which may have occurred during liner installation, slide a ring-free piston up and down the cylinder bore and check for any binding between the piston and bore.

With reference to liner protrusion on both dry and wet liners, it is important to ensure that the allowable variation in liner protrusion between individual cylinders is strictly adhered to. Failure to do this will result in some liners not having sufficient clamp force being applied to them, resulting in combustion gas and coolant leakage. Possible head cracking can also occur if liner protrusion is not uniform across all cylinder liners.

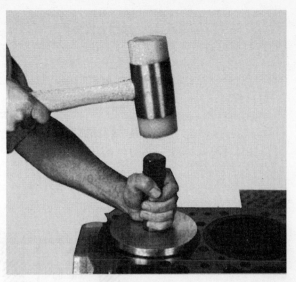

Fig 8.35 Installing a wet type liner with the aid of a liner-driving tool
Courtesy of Cummins Engine Co

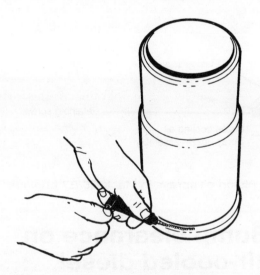

Fig 8.34 Applying a bead of sealant around the underside of the liner flange so as to prevent coolant leakage past the liner
Courtesy of Volvo

After flanged liners have been installed in an engine, be careful the liners don't pop up as the engine is rotated. This is due to a tight piston ring-to-bore fit which is capable of lifting the liner out of its counterbore while the crankshaft is rotated to allow installation of other piston-connecting rod assemblies. To prevent such a problem

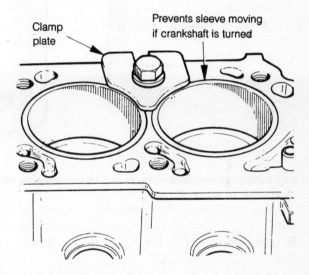

Fig 8.36 Use of clamp plates to retain cylinder liners whenever the crankshaft is rotated
Courtesy of AGPS

occurring, clamp each liner in position, as shown in Fig 8.36.

Piston oil sprays

Oil spray jets which are used to spray oil on the underside of the piston require servicing during an engine overhaul. The oil sprays

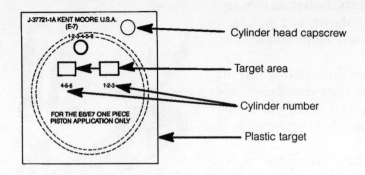

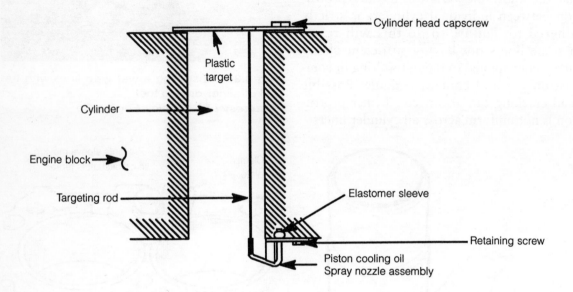

Fig 8.37 Using a targeting rod to accurately align piston oil sprays in Mack E6/E7 engines
Courtesy of Mack Trucks Inc

which are connected to the crankcase should be removed to enable inspection and cleaning of the their nozzle jets.

After the oil sprays are bolted back on to the crankcase, their alignment must be checked to ensure that oil sprays into the correct position on the underside of the piston.

Figure 8.37 shows how an aim indicator rod attached to the oil spray is used in conjunction with a special target placed on top of the cylinder block to check oil spray alignment. Realignment of the oil spray is achieved by bending the oil spray tube to the required position. During the remainder of the engine rebuild, exercise extreme care so as not to bend the oil sprays in any way.

Bump clearance on air-cooled diesel engines

Air cooled diesel engines are built with separate cylinder barrels and crankcase assemblies as shown in Fig 8.38. Due to variations in manufacturing machine tolerances, not all cylinder barrels and pistons are of exactly the same dimensions. This necessitates the use of shims under the barrel so as to be able to set up and maintain a set mechanical clearance between the top of the piston and the cylinder head when the piston is at top dead centre.

This mechanical clearance — or bump

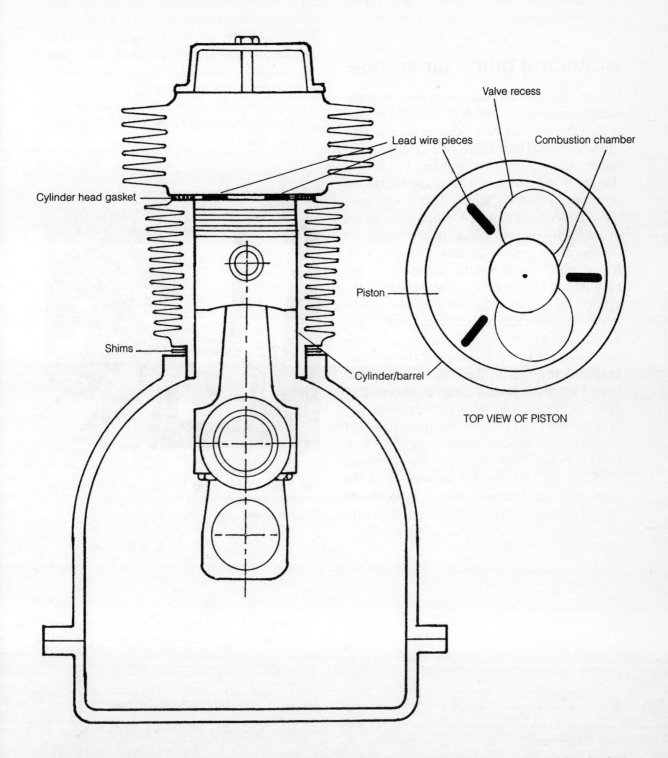

Fig 8.38 Sectional view of an air-cooled diesel engine showing the location of lead wire used to check piston bump clearance

clearance, as it is commonly known — is not only important in that it prevents the piston from hitting the cylinder head; it also predetermines the compression ratio of the engine.

Adjusting bump clearance

During the assembly of the engine, refit the shims which were removed from the underside of the cylinder barrel during disassembly of the engine. These shims will determine the bump clearance for that cylinder. To check if the bump clearance is within specifications, position the piston 10 mm BTDC and, with the cylinder head removed, place three pieces of lead wire or soft solder at 120° intervals on top of the piston, as shown in Fig 8.38. Make sure that when the piston rises up, each piece of wire will contact the flat of the cylinder head and not enter the valve recess or combustion chamber opening, thereby giving a false reading. Fit a new head gasket to the top of the barrel and replace the cylinder head, tightening it to the correct torque setting. Turn the engine over top dead centre so as to compress the wire then remove the cylinder head and measure the three pieces of now-flattened wire, as shown in Fig 8.39. A general bump clearance should be between 0.9 mm and 1.02 mm for an average of the three readings. However, always refer to the manufacturer's specifications for accurate results. If the clearance is outside the limit, it can be altered by changing one or more shims under the cylinder barrel and then rechecking the bump clearance. Every cylinder of a multi-cylinder engine should be individually checked for bump clearance during engine reassembly. To enable accurate bump clearance adjustment to be made, manufacturers have produced a number of shim thicknesses which can be fitted under the cylinder barrel.

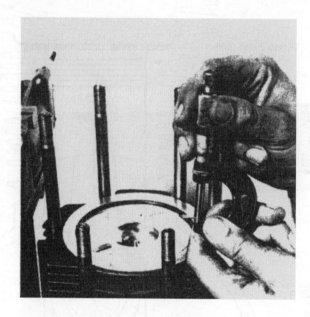

Fig 8.39 Checking the piston bump clearance on an air-cooled diesel engine
Courtesy of Lister Petter

The crankshafts of in-line engines are so designed that each connecting rod is connected to its own individual journal. In 'v' type engine configurations, the big ends of two connecting rods from opposing sides are connected side by side on to the one journal.

Bearings

The main bearings support the revolving crankshaft in precise alignment so that it can rotate freely within the cylinder block. The connecting rod bearings — or big end bearings as they are generally called — allow the crankshaft journal to rotate freely inside the big end of the connecting rod.

Bearing design

A number of factors need to be considered in the selection of bearing materials for modern diesel engines. Some of the more important properties of bearing materials, such as conformability, embeddability, corrosion resistance and fatigue strength, are discussed below.

Conformability

Conformability is the ability of a bearing material to conform or adapt to the shape of the journal. The bearing material must be soft enough so as to change its shape slightly in order to conform to minor variations in the journal shape.

Embeddability

Embeddability is the ability of a bearing material to absorb small particles of contamination. Therefore, the material used in the construction of the bearing must be soft enough to allow small foreign particles to be pressed into it before damaging the journal surface.

9
Crankshaft Assembly

The crankshaft is located in the lower end of the cylinder block and converts the reciprocating motion of the pistons into rotary motion. The crankshaft is forged from heat-treated alloy steel and has precision machined and hardened main and connecting rod journals. The offset throws, or cranks, of the crankshaft are balanced by counterweights to ensure correct weight distribution so as to cancel out any unwanted forces being applied to the rotating shaft.

The rotating crankshaft is supported by main bearings and is constantly being fed by lubricating oil through galleries drilled within the cylinder block. This same oil which feeds the main bearings also feeds the connecting rod journals by way of drilled passages in the throws of the shaft (see Fig 9.3).

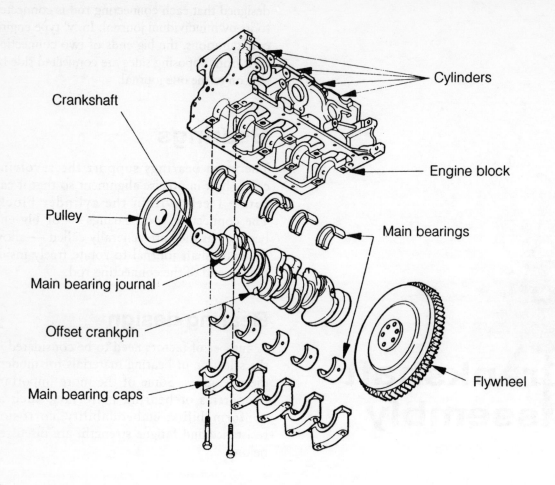

Fig 9.1   Crankshaft assembly   *Courtesy of AGPS*

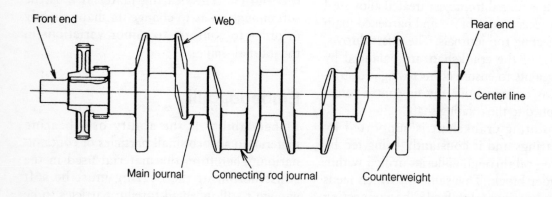

Fig 9.2   Crankshaft nomenclature   *Courtesy of Komatsu Limited*

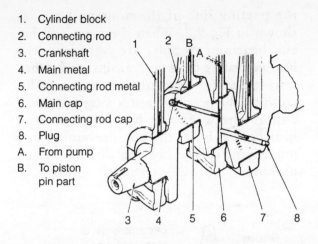

1. Cylinder block
2. Connecting rod
3. Crankshaft
4. Main metal
5. Connecting rod metal
6. Main cap
7. Connecting rod cap
8. Plug
A. From pump
B. To piston pin part

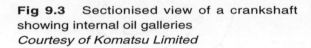

Fig 9.3 Sectionised view of a crankshaft showing internal oil galleries
Courtesy of Komatsu Limited

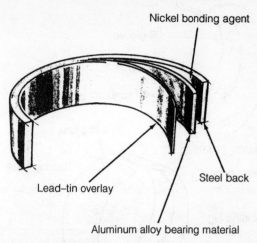

Nickel bonding agent
Lead–tin overlay
Steel back
Aluminum alloy bearing material

Fig 9.4 Bearing construction
Courtesy of Caterpillar Inc

Corrosion resistance

Although today's heavy duty engine lubricating oils contain improved corrosion inhibitors which help to retard the formation of corrosive agents, bearing metals used must still have corrosion resistance to withstand any corrosive agents encountered.

Fatigue strength

This refers to the bearing's construction strength, which must be strong enough to withstand the combustion shock loads during crankshaft rotation.

Bearing construction

Crankshaft bearings are made with layers of different materials, as shown in Fig 9.4. The outer part of the bearing has a steel backing, which gives support to the layers of bearing material. Bonded to this steel backing is an aluminium alloy bearing surface which accounts for the thickest part of the bearing and meets the four requirements mentioned for the selection of bearing material. Next is a lead-tin overlay which protects the aluminium bearing surface when the engine is started and lubrication is at a minimum.

Physical features of crankshaft bearings

With reference to Fig 9.5, crankshaft bearings have a number of distinguishing features. The locating lugs which occur on both bearing halves locate the bearing shells during installation. The upper main bearing shell has an oil hole in it so as to provide oil access from the block to the oil groove in the bearing. This oil groove in the bearing distributes the oil around the journal for continuous lubrication and cooling. Oil holes are also found in the upper big end bearings to allow oil flow from the crank journal to the gudgeon pin bushes.

During engine operation, the crankshaft must rotate with a minimal amount of side movement. To maintain this side movement within close limits, a thrust bearing assembly is fitted beside one of the main bearings. Two types of thrust bearing are used. One is designed so the thrust bearing and main bearing are one unit; the other uses thrust plates which are installed either side of the main bearing, as shown in Fig 9.6. Grooves on the thrust plates face the crankshaft and are used to distribute the oil over the thrust bearing surfaces.

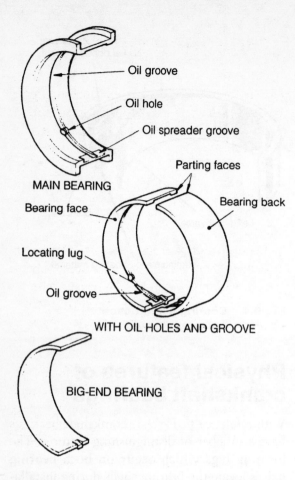

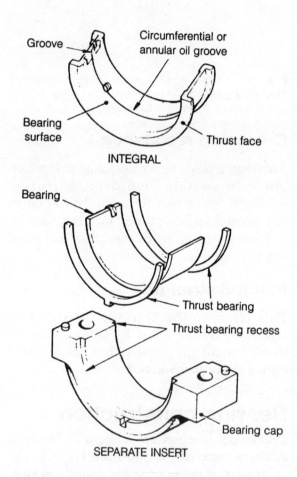

Fig 9.5 Types of crankshaft bearings
Courtesy of AGPS

Bearing spread

Bearings are constructed so that their outside dimension across their parting faces is slightly more than the actual dimension of the bearing housing, as shown in Fig 9.7. Therefore, on assembly, the bearing shell has a slight interference which compresses it slightly when fitted to the cylinder block and connecting rod bearing housings. This compression of the bearing shell retains the bearing firmly in its housing for ease of handling during installation of the crankshaft and the piston/connecting rod assemblies.

Bearing crush

The halves of the bearings are made so the mating faces extend a small amount above

the parting line of the housing bore, as shown in Fig 9.8. When the main and big end bearing cap bolts are tightened, the bearing mating faces push against each other, forcing the bearing tightly into its bore. This crush on the bearing ensures a tight uniform contact between the bearing shell and bearing cap bore, thereby preventing any movement of the bearing during engine operation.

Fig 9.6 Crankshaft thrust bearings
Courtesy of AGPS

Too much crush will cause buckling of the bearing shells and binding on the crankshaft journal, resulting in severe damage to the journal surface. Too little crush can cause the bearing to spin or fret in its housing.

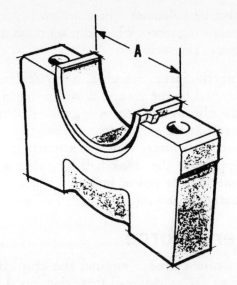

Fig 9.7 Illustration showing bearing spread
Courtesy of Caterpillar Inc

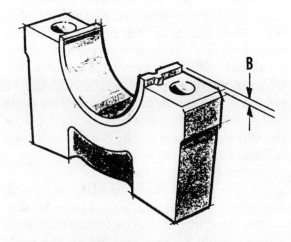

Fig 9.8 Illustration showing protrusion of bearing which is necessary to ensure bearing crush
Courtesy of Caterpillar Inc

Crankshaft oil seals

An oil seal is used at each end of the crankshaft to prevent oil leaking from the engine crankcase. The oil seal is constructed with a single inner sealing lip which is held firmly on to the crankshaft sealing surface by a garter spring.

The general oil seal configuration on most engines is a single-lip type seal at both ends of the crankshaft. However, a dual or double-lip seal (see Fig 9.9)is used in engine applications where oil has to be sealed from both directions — an example would be a transmission with a torque converter mounted to the flywheel. In this type of sealing application, the sealing lips face in opposite directions, thereby preventing the transfer of oil between two compartments.

Oil seals may leak for a number of reasons, such as incorrect installation (seal not in square or seal in back to front), excessive radial movement in the crankshaft due to worn main bearings, a bent crankshaft, a grooved seal running surface on the crankshaft, damaged or worn seal lip, a broken or damaged seal garter spring, or dirt or rust on the shaft.

Crankshaft oil seals are designed to accept a certain amount of runout during normal operation. Such runout is due to the crankshaft moving within its bearing clearance during rotation and can reach as much as 0.2 mm before the seal begins to leak

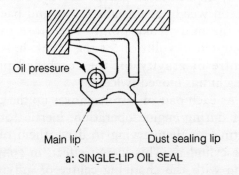

a: SINGLE-LIP OIL SEAL

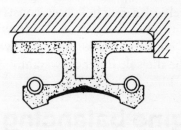

b: DOUBLE-LIP OIL SEAL

Fig 9.9 Two types of rear crankshaft oil seal   *Courtesy of Komatsu Limited*

The flywheel

The flywheel is attached to the rear of the crankshaft and is designed to assist engine operation in a number of ways:

- During engine operation, the flywheel stores up energy for momentum of the crankshaft during the non-productive strokes of the cycle. Remember, out of the four strokes of the engine cycle, the power stroke is the only stroke producing a positive rotational force about the crankshaft. The flywheel helps to rotate the crankshaft through the other three dead strokes.
- The flywheel, with its heavy weight, tends to smooth out the power impulses, resulting in an even crankshaft speed.
- The rear surface of the flywheel serves as a facing for the engine clutch or torque converter, which transmits power to the transmission.
- The flywheel provides a coupling point for the starter motor to rotate the crankshaft via the flywheel ring gear.

The more cylinders there are in an engine, the less need there is for a heavy flywheel, as the power impulses are closer together, resulting in a smoother rotation of the crankshaft. One- and two-cylinder engines require heavier than normal flywheels so as to provide the momentum necessary to rotate the crankshaft through its non-productive cycles of operation. Engines which transmit power through a torque converter generally have flywheels of a much lighter construction as the combined weight of the flywheel and torque converter make up what would normally be the sole flywheel weight.

Engine balancing

Just as the crankshaft is balanced within itself by the location of its cranks and counterbalance weights, so too must the whole engine be balanced. There are two types of unbalancing forces which can act upon diesel engines. They are:

1 **inertia force**, which is a vertical force created by the up and down movement of the pistons and connecting rods that tends to shake the engine up and down;
2 **torsional force**, which is a twisting force applied to the crankshaft by virtue of the intermittent power impulses applied to it during operation.

Inertia force

In a four-cylinder engine, the crankshaft throws are so designed that when no. 1 and no. 4 pistons are at TDC, no. 2 and no. 3 pistons are at BDC. At this point, the centre of gravity for the combined piston weight is at the mid-stroke position, as shown in Fig 9.10. With this as a starting point, observe what happens during one revolution of the crankshaft. When the crankshaft rotates 90°, all four pistons are below the mid-stroke point and the centre of gravity of their combined weight drops to a new location below the mid-stroke point of the pistons as shown in Fig 9.10.

As the crankshaft rotates to 180°, no. 1 and no. 4 pistons move to BDC and no. 2 and no. 3 pistons move to TDC. As this occurs, the centre of gravity for the combined piston weight moves back up to the mid-stroke point. As the crankshaft continues to rotate through the second half of its revolution, the centre of gravity for the combined piston weight again falls below and back up to the mid-stroke point. Therefore in one complete revolution of the crankshaft, the centre of gravity for the combined piston weight has moved twice.

As each pair of pistons moves up the cylinder during engine operation, inertia force is acting on them trying to drive them out of the cylinders. This inertia effect, in conjunction with the changing centre of gravity of the combined piston weight from a lower to

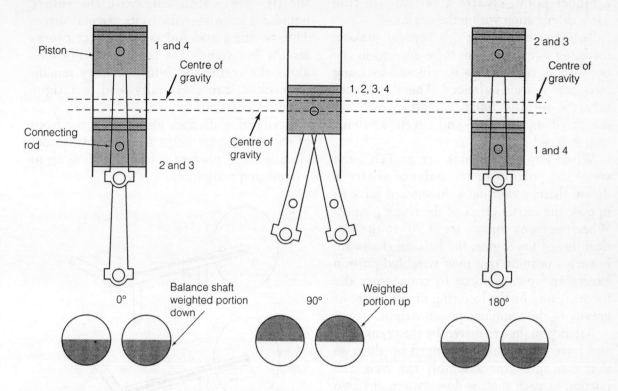

Fig 9.10 Schematic diagram of how balance shafts are used to reduce vertical shaking forces in four-cylinder diesel engines

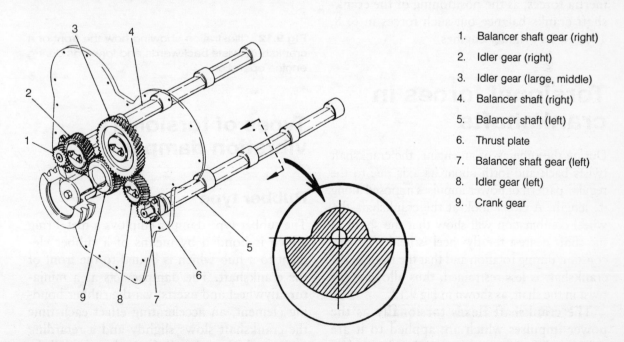

1. Balancer shaft gear (right)
2. Idler gear (right)
3. Idler gear (large, middle)
4. Balancer shaft (right)
5. Balancer shaft (left)
6. Thrust plate
7. Balancer shaft gear (left)
8. Idler gear (left)
9. Crank gear

Fig 9.11 Illustration showing the location of balance shafts in an engine
Courtesy of Komatsu Limited

a higher point, creates a vertical shaking force or vibration within the engine.

To offset or balance this vertical shaking force, an equal force must be applied in the opposite direction. This is achieved by using two gear-driven balances. These balances take the form of balance shafts which are weighted on one side and rotate at twice engine speed.

When any two pistons are at TDC, the weighted portion of the balance shafts is down, thereby exerting a downward force to oppose the inertia effect of the rising pistons. When the crank throws are at 90° to the vertical line of the engine, the balance shafts are in such a position that their weighted portion exerts an upward force to counteract the force created by the lowering of the centre of gravity of the combined piston weight.

Balance shafts are driven by the crankshaft and have timing marks stamped on them so that during engine assembly the weighted portion of each shaft is down when any two pistons are at TDC.

Not all engines are subject to unbalanced inertia forces, as the positioning of the crankshaft cranks balance out such forces in 6, 8, 12, and 16 cylinder engines.

Torsional forces in crankshafts

During the running of an engine, the crankshaft twists back and forth about its axis due to the regular pattern of power impulses imposed along its length. A closer look at the crankshaft–flywheel combination will show that the speed of the shaft nearest the flywheel is held relatively constant during rotation and that the front of the crankshaft is less restrained, thus allowing for twist in the shaft, as shown in Fig 9.12.

The crankshaft flexes torsionally as the power impulses which are applied to it are restrained from speeding up the shaft, thus causing it to twist momentarily, then when the flywheel catches up with the rotary impulse it untwists back to its original shape. This twisting and untwisting effect causes minute but significant torsional vibrations along the crankshaft which, if they remain unchecked, can eventually lead to fatigue fractures and shaft failure.

A vibration damper installed on the front of the crankshaft helps to reduce torsional vibration and prevent it from building up to a damaging magnitude.

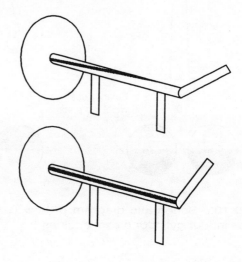

Fig 9.12 Illustration showing how the front of a crankshaft twists backwards and forwards during engine operation

Types of torsional vibration damper

Rubber type

The rubber type damper employs a metal ring which is bonded by means of a rubber element to a hub which is bolted to the front of the crankshaft. The damper acts as a miniature flywheel and exerts, via the rubber bonding element, an accelerating effect each time the crankshaft slows slightly and a retarding effect each time the shaft accelerates slightly. These continual and sudden speed changes

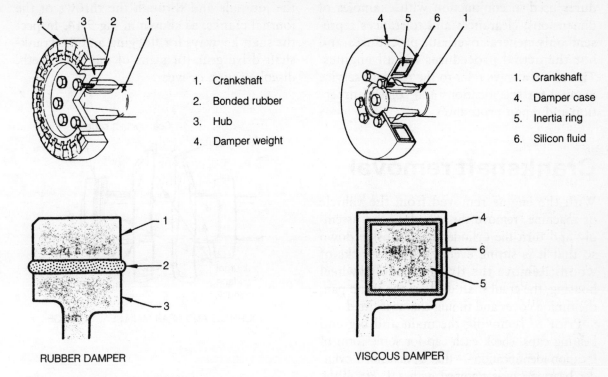

1. Crankshaft
2. Bonded rubber
3. Hub
4. Damper weight

1. Crankshaft
4. Damper case
5. Inertia ring
6. Silicon fluid

RUBBER DAMPER

VISCOUS DAMPER

Fig 9.13   Sectional view of crankshaft vibration dampers   *Courtesy of Komatsu Limited*

which are taking place at the front section of the crankshaft are now being partially absorbed by the combined opposing effect of the metal ring and the flexible rubber element.

Because of its relative inflexibility, the damper's weight and speed range are critical aspects in its design to suit a particular engine application.

Viscous type

The vicous type damper employs a metal ring which is totally enclosed in a rotating housing filled with a highly viscous silicon fluid. During operation, the outer housing which is attached to the crankshaft turns at the same speed as the crankshaft, its motion being transferred to the metal ring through the silicon fluid contained within the housing. Due to the inefficient fluid drive and frequency of speed changes between one end of the crankshaft and the other, there is considerable slippage between the metal ring and the

rotating housing. This slippage is desirable since the acceleration and deceleration of the metal ring in the damper assembly lessen the torsional vibrations through the crankshaft.

Viscous type torsional vibration dampers have a broader engine application as their weight and speed range are less critical than rubber bonded dampers. Viscous dampers can also operate under more adverse temperature conditions and are unaffected by petroleum products and temperature, which can break down the rubber bonding in the rubber type dampers.

Engines of three cylinders or less do not generally require a crankshaft damper due to the minimal amount of twisting associated with such a short crankshaft.

Crankshaft servicing

In order to make crankshaft servicing more meaningful, the inspection and repair procedures used in conjunction with examples of dimensions, clearances and tolerances represent only general overhaul procedures and not the actual procedures for all engines. Therefore, always refer to the relevant service manual for specifications and correct inspection and repair procedures.

Crankshaft removal

With the engine removed from the vehicle or machine, remove the cylinder head assembly and turn the cylinder block upside down so that it is sitting evenly on two blocks of wood. Remove the flywheel, the flywheel housing, the crankshaft damper, the sump pan, the timing cover and timing chains if fitted.

Prior to removing the main and big end bearing caps, check each cap for some form of location identification — that is, that no. 1 cylinder bearing cap is stamped with a 1, etc. If the caps are not appropriately marked then mark them in accordance with the cylinder location, starting from the front of the engine. With all the main and big end caps removed from the crankshaft, lift it from the block with the aid of a sling.

Visual inspection

After the crankshaft has been removed from the block, it should be cleaned and inspected. Remove any plugs which may be installed in the shaft and clean out all the oil passages with a bristle wire brush. Finally, steam clean the shaft.

Check for any signs of discolouration around the bearing journals and thrust faces. If discolouration is excessive due to overheating then the shaft will be fatigued and need replacing. Also, check all journal surfaces for signs of scoring or other forms of damage. Inspect the seal running surfaces at the front and rear of the shaft for oil seal lip wear. Any signs of grooving in these areas can result in oil leakage past the seal.

Carefully inspect the crankshaft for any visible signs of cracking around the radius of

the journals and through the throws of the journal cranks, as shown in Fig 9.14. Inspect the shaft keyways for flogging and the crankshaft drive gear for signs of damaged teeth, discolouration or wear.

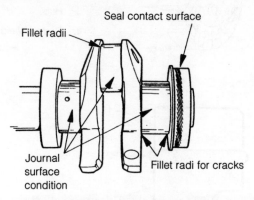

JOURNALS AND REAR MAIN SEAL SURFACE

Fig 9.14 Crankshaft inspection
Courtesy of AGPS

Checking for bent crankshaft

After a long service life or abnormal wear within an engine, the crankshaft may develop a bend. In order to check the crankshaft to see if it is bent, it must be properly supported in one of the following ways:

- Use 'v' blocks to support the front and rear main bearing journals (see Fig 9.15).
- Mount the shaft in a lathe between its centres.
- Turn the block upside down and support the shaft with the front and rear upper bearing shells in place.

With the crankshaft mounted by one of the above methods, use a dial indicator with an extension probe to contact the journal surface through its centre line, as shown in Fig 9.15. Rotate the shaft 360° and measure for any journal out of roundness and repeat the process for the remaining main journals.

The crankshaft should be true, with no runout along its length. However, some runout is possible in worn shafts and, depending on the crankshaft length, can vary from 0.05 mm to 0.13 mm.

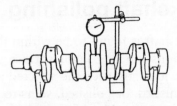

Fig 9.15   Checking crankshaft alignment
Courtesy of Mitsubishi

Crankshafts with slight bending can be repaired by grinding the bearing journal surfaces to an undersize diameter, thereby removing the out of roundness of the journal. Alternatively, the shaft can be straightened by bending it in a press which has been specifically designed for the purpose. However, excessive bending forces placed on the crankshaft during straightening severely stress the metal in the shaft, resulting in possible shaft breakage. After a crankshaft has been straightened by bending, it should be thoroughly tested for any sign of cracking.

Crack inspection

Some of the common areas where cracks may appear in a crankshaft are: the fillet areas of the journal, around the oil holes of journals and in the web area between the main and big end journals, as shown in Fig 9.16.

The crankshaft can be checked for cracks by using either the dye penetrant test or the electro-magnetic metal particle test. A full explanation of each testing method appears at the end of Chapter 7.

All crankshafts are subjected to cyclic loading during engine operation and, regardless of how well the engine is maintained, the crankshaft may incur cracks. Any crankshaft with cracks, as shown in Fig 9.16, is unserviceable

and must be replaced. If a crankshaft does break while in service, it is very important to make a thorough inspection of all engine components so as to determine what the contributing conditions to the failure were. Unless these abnormal conditions are discovered and corrected, there will be a repeat failure of the crankshaft.

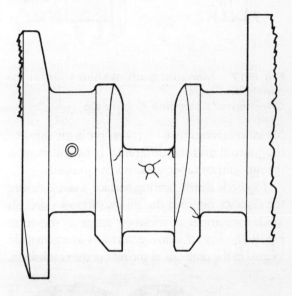

Fig 9.16   Crankshaft fatigue cracks
Courtesy of Detroit Diesel Corp

Crankshaft measurement

To determine crankshaft serviceability, the following wear measurements can be taken:

- journal diameter and ovality;
- journal taper;
- thrust face wear.

To measure the journal for size and ovality, use an outside micrometer and measure each journal in line with the crank throws and at 90° to the crank throws, as shown in Fig 9.17. Subtract the two dimensions to find the journal ovality, if any.

To check for journal taper wear, measure the diameter of the journal by placing the micrometer next to each fillet, but not on the fillet.

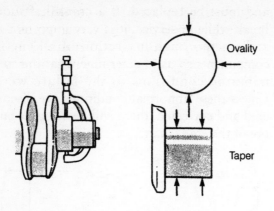

Fig 9.17 Measuring crankshaft journal for ovality and taper
Courtesy of Cummins Engine Co

Measurements must be taken on both sides of the journal and the difference between them is the amount of taper wear on the journal.

To check thrust bearing surface wear, measure the distance between the thrust surfaces using an inside micrometer or telescopic gauge as shown in Fig 9.18. Thrust bearing surfaces are generally located in the centre or at the rear of the crankshaft.

Fig 9.18 Measurement of thrust face wear with an inside micrometer
Courtesy of Caterpillar Inc

After the crankshaft main and big end journals have been accurately measured and recorded, refer to the manufacturer's specifications for correct sizes and allowable tolerances.

Crankshaft polishing

If a crankshaft is found to be within the wear specifications but has slight surface scratching on the journals, then the affected journals may be linished, or polished, so as to remove the scratch marks. Linishing the journal with crocus cloth will remove fine scratch marks and return the journal to a smooth finish.

Do not use emery tape to linish the journal, as this will remove metal from the surface of the journal and reduce its diameter.

Crocus cloth is similar in appearance to emery tape and can be recognised by its smooth rubbing surface, as opposed to emery tape with its abrasive rubbing surface.

Crankshaft grinding

If crankshaft wear evaluation reveals that the journals require grinding then the crankshaft will need to be set up on a crankshaft grinding machine and the journals individually ground, as shown in Fig 9.19. Most engine manufacturers allow their crankshafts to be ground to standard undersize dimensions, which are in increments of 0.25 mm, 0.5 mm and 0.76 mm undersize.

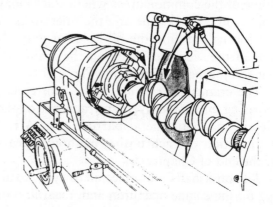

Fig 9.19 Crankshaft grinding machine
Courtesy of Cummins Engine Co

Replacing the crankshaft

If the crankshaft is worn beyond the specified limit or damaged in some way, it will require replacement. In order to provide a better service life for engines, a number of manufacturers have published guidelines for reusing crankshafts and bearings in their engines. The guidelines consist of documentation and pictures of what can and can't be used again, with accompanying information as to what may have caused the failure.

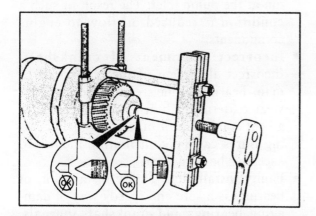

Fig 9.20 Puller used to remove a crank-shaft timing gear

Whenever a crankshaft is to be replaced, the timing gear attached to the front of the shaft will need to be refitted as it is not a standard part of the crankshaft. The timing gear can be removed from the shaft by means of a puller, as shown in Fig 9.20. Prior to refitting the gear to the shaft, heat it using a suitable heating device. Then, with the crankshaft at room temperature, carefully fit the heated gear on to the shaft and, if necessary, drive it home with a hammer and soft metal punch.

Removal of bearing shells

When removing bearing shells, it is important to remove them carefully without damaging them, as they may need to be used again. Some manufacturers recommend the replacement of main bearings while the crankshaft is still in the cylinder block. The upper main bearing shells can be removed by

using the head of a split pin fitted into the journal oil hole to roll the bearing out as the crankshaft is rotated, as shown in Fig 9.21. The same procedure can be used to refit the bearing shells.

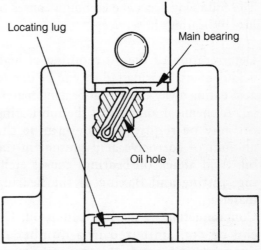

INSERT THE REMOVAL PLUG INTO THE OIL HOLE

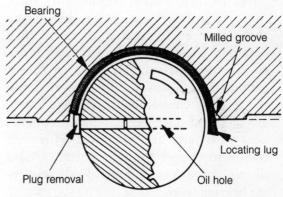

ROTATE THE CRANKSHAFT TO REMOVE THE INSERT

Fig 9.21 Removal of bearing shells with crankshaft still mounted in the block
Courtesy of AGPS

Inspection of bearings

Whenever bearings are removed from an engine, regardless of its condition, always try to evaluate the condition of the bearings and journals to ascertain what might have caused them to wear. Look for irregular wear patterns which characterise certain problems and try to establish whether the worn condition is normal or abnormal. Remember, installing new parts without solving the original problem that caused the damage will eventually lead to a repeat failure.

The following are some common causes of failure of bearings in service:

- **Deterioration of the oil resulting in high acid content.** Bearing failure can be due to acid eating away the actual bearing material. A chemical analysis of the lubricating oil may be required to determine the amount of corrosive acid present in the oil. Acid attack on bearings causes etching, pitting and flaking of the bearing material.

- **Contamination of the lubrication oil.** Oil can be contaminated in a number of ways: the by-products of combustion leave residues in the oil; fine metallic wear particles from engine components enter the oil; and dirt can enter the engine through the air cleaner or crankcase breather. These can all lead to high levels of contamination. All modern diesel engines use full-flow oil filters to minimise the level of contaminants; if these filters are changed on a regular basis, component wear rates are minimised. However, failure to change the lubrication oil and filter/s at the correct interval can accelerate bearing wear.

- **Incorrect oil viscosity.** High oil temperatures resulting from an overheated engine can reduce the viscosity of the oil and reduce the oil film thickness between the crankshaft journals and bearings. The result is that the oil film will not carry the loads imposed by combustion, which in turn causes abnormal bearing wear as the crankshaft journals make contact with the bearings.

- **Wrong grade of oil.** If the oil is too thin it will break down under load conditions, causing metal contact to take place and thereby increased wear to bearings and

journals. On the other hand, if the oil is too thick, it can cause oil pump cavitation, resulting in a lack of lubricating oil during engine running. Cavitation occurs whenever the oil supplied to the oil pump is less than that demanded of the pump. In operation, oil is drawn into the oil pump and then exhausted out the pump outlet; however, due to the oil being too viscous, it cannot enter into the pump quickly enough, therefore creating a void or vacuum at the pump inlet. The result of such a condition is reduced oil flow to engine components.

- **Incorrect alignment of crankshaft.** Incorrect alignment of the crankshaft or main bearing tunnels can cause irregular wear patterns on bearings. Such things as a bent crankshaft or misaligned main bearing bores can be contributing factors to excessive bearing wear.

- **Faulty installation.** Faulty installation of bearings is a sure and speedy way of damaging bearings and crankshaft journals. Common faults are: main bearing caps not tensioned, resulting in limited or no crush on bearing shells, incorrect bearing size fitted, failure to clean out crankshaft oil holes — thus allowing debris to score bearings on initial start up — and installation of bearing shells with dirt behind them, to name just a few.

- **Little or no oil.** Bearing seizure can be due to an inadequate supply of oil to the crankshaft bearings. In such cases, extreme heat is generated around the bearing area, causing metal from the bearings to weld itself to the crankshaft journal, thereby scoring both the bearing and journal surfaces.

- **Oil not changed regularly.** This results in increased oil oxidation, which causes the oil to thicken and thus reduce its flow rate through the engine oil galleries.

- **Clogged suction screen.** A poorly maintained suction screen on the oil pump pick up will cause pump cavitation problems and therefore reduce oil flow through the engine.

For location purposes and the identification of problem areas, bearings should be numbered prior to removing them from their housings. After removal, clean the bearings and inspect the bearing surface for flaking, scoring, pitting, discolouration, loss of metal and irregular wear patterns. The lower bearings, shells of the crankshaft and the upper connecting rod slippers which carry the heavy piston thrust loads during the power stroke will show the greatest wear signs. The general appearance of the bearing may be that of slight pitting and scoring and with some of the initial running in layer of metal worn through. These are the characteristics of normal bearing wear and are not detrimental to the bearing service life. Therefore, such bearings should not be replaced, as these minor surface imperfections will not impair their normal operation.

Inspect the lugs and the backs of the bearings for signs of fretting or rubbing which indicate they have lost their crush and have been moving in their caps or housings. Bearings showing these kinds of symptoms should be replaced and the housings machined if required. If bearing housings are machined, then oversize outside diameter bearing shells will have to be used.

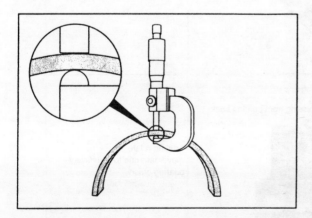

Fig 9.22 Measuring the thickness of a bearing shell
Courtesy of Cummins Engine Co

To further evaluate the condition of the bearings, measure their thickness in the centre of the lower part of the shell semi-circle, as shown in Fig 9.22. The most successful way to measure the curved bearing surface is to put a ball bearing on the inner surface and measure the total thickness of the bearing shell and ball. Subtracting the diameter of the ball from the dimension will then give an accurate bearing thickness.

Bearing clearance

The running clearance between crankshaft bearings and journals on diesel engines is generally within 0.05 mm to 0.11 mm, with a maximum limit up to 0.15 mm. The results of bearing clearances going beyond these limits are as follows: engine oil pressure will be low especially when the oil is hot as there is less resistance for oil to escape from between the bearing and journal; and there will be inadequate oil supply to other engine components and damage to crankshaft journals and bearings due to physical knocking between the bearing and journal.

There are two ways of establishing the running clearance between the bearing and journal: by using 'Flexigauge' or by measuring components individually.

Using Flexigauge to determine bearing clearance

Flexigauge is a soft plastic measuring substance which, when compressed between the journal and the bearing, will spread out, indicating the clearance between them. To use Flexigauge, take a strip of it the width of the bearing and lay it across the bottom of the bearing cap as shown in Fig 9.25. With the crankshaft mounted on its upper bearing shells in the block, fit the bearing cap and tighten it down to the correct tension. Without turning the crankshaft, remove the cap and match the now flattened Flexigauge with the graduations on the Flexigauge

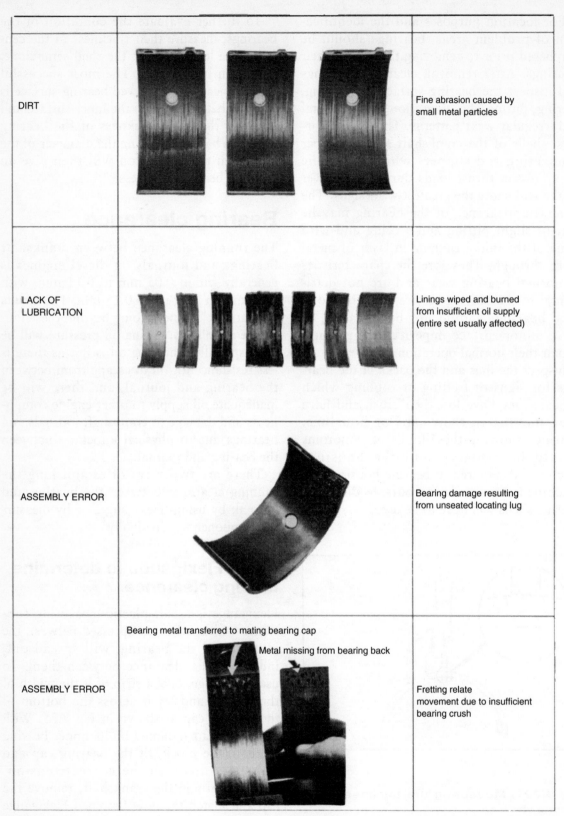

DIRT		Fine abrasion caused by small metal particles
LACK OF LUBRICATION		Linings wiped and burned from insufficient oil supply (entire set usually affected)
ASSEMBLY ERROR		Bearing damage resulting from unseated locating lug
ASSEMBLY ERROR	Bearing metal transferred to mating bearing cap Metal missing from bearing back	Fretting relate movement due to insufficient bearing crush

Fig 9.23

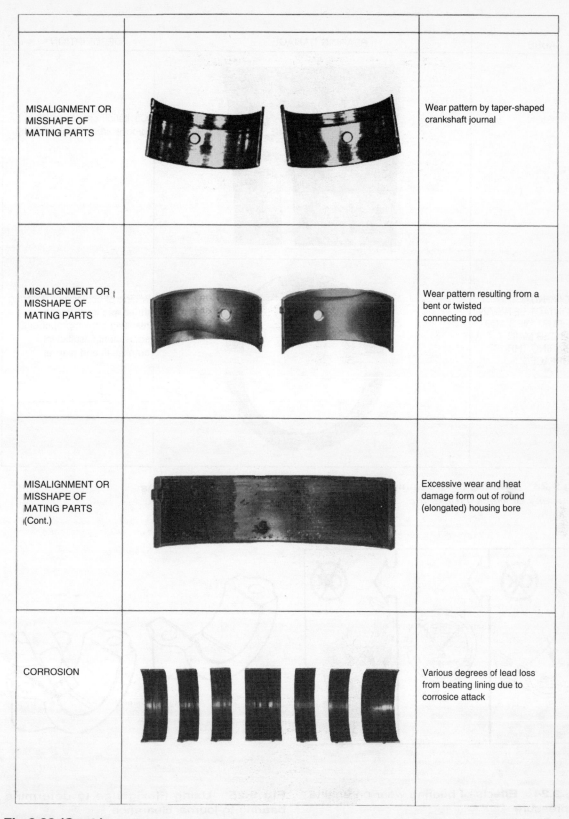

MISALIGNMENT OR MISSHAPE OF MATING PARTS		Wear pattern by taper-shaped crankshaft journal
MISALIGNMENT OR MISSHAPE OF MATING PARTS		Wear pattern resulting from a bent or twisted connecting rod
MISALIGNMENT OR MISSHAPE OF MATING PARTS (Cont.)		Excessive wear and heat damage form out of round (elongated) housing bore
CORROSION		Various degrees of lead loss from beating lining due to corrosice attack

Fig 9.23 (Cont.)

CAUSE	BEARING DAMAGE	DESCRIPTION
EROSION	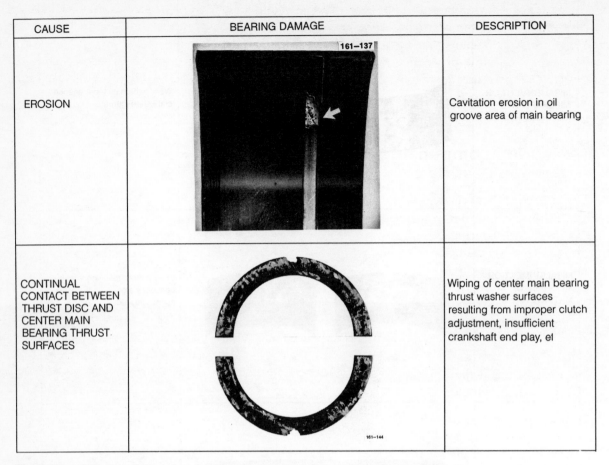	Cavitation erosion in oil groove area of main bearing
CONTINUAL CONTACT BETWEEN THRUST DISC AND CENTER MAIN BEARING THRUST SURFACES		Wiping of center main bearing thrust washer surfaces resulting from improper clutch adjustment, insufficient crankshaft end play, et

Fig 9.23 Bearing failure analysis for main and connecting rod bearings
Courtesy of Mack Trucks Inc

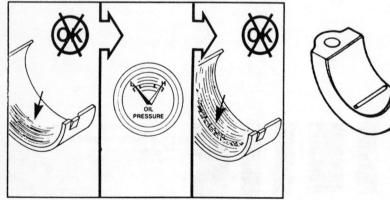

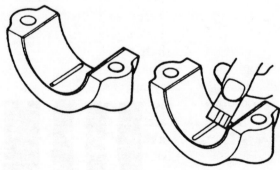

Fig 9.24 Effects of bearing wear on engine oil pressure
Courtesy of Cummins Engine Co

Fig 9.25 Using Flexigauge to determine bearing-to-journal clearance
Courtesy of Mitsubishi

packet. The reading obtained will be the running clearance between the bearing and the journal. Check all the remaining main and big end bearings using the same procedure. Flexigauge is available in three sizes for measuring clearances from 0.025 mm to 0.076 mm; 0.051 mm to 0.152 mm; and 0.10 mm to 0.229 mm.

Measuring components to determine bearing clearance

The difference between the crankshaft journal and the inside diameter of the bearing will give the journal-to-bearing running clearance. To obtain the inside diameter of the main bearing, install the bearing cap with new bearing shells and tighten the cap bolts to the specified torque. Measure the inside diameter of the bearing with the aid of an inside micrometer or cylinder bore gauge. Measure the crankshaft journal diameter and subtract it from the inside diameter of the bearing. The result will be the bearing clearance.

Crankshaft-to-bearing running clearance = main or big end bearing inside diameter minus journal diameter.

Replaceable bearings are obtainable for crankshafts which have been ground in order to rejuvenate journal surfaces. Undersize bearings are available for most crankshafts in increments of 0.25 mm, 0.5 mm and 0.76 mm undersize.

As journal surfaces need grinding from time to time to restore their surface finish, so do the crankshaft thrust surfaces. Upon machining of the thrust surfaces, the crankshaft end float may increase to an unacceptable limit with the standard thrust bearing fitted. In such a case, oversize thrust washers are sometimes available to restore the crankshaft end float to within specifications.

Crankshaft oil seal installation

Before an oil seal is installed, examine the sealing lip and the seal mounting surface for any signs of damage. Crocus cloth can be used to remove any fine scratches on the sealing surface.

If the sealing surface has become grooved, it may be repaired in a number of ways such as:

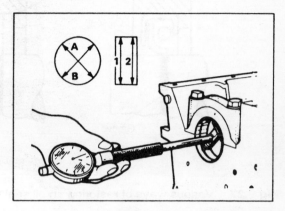

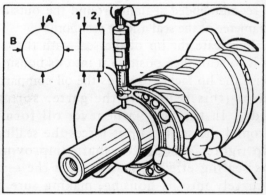

Fig 9.26   Procedure for determining crankshaft running clearance
Courtesy of Mitsubishi

- replacing the steel sleeve on which the seal lip runs;
- fitting a steel sleeve over the worn seal area;
- changing the relative position of the seal by way of a spacer fitted behind it;
- metal spraying the worn area and machining it back to original dimensions. See Fig 9.27 for various ways of restoring oil seal surfaces.

If the seal is rubber encased, do not use sealant around the outside of the case; however, if it is a plain steel case, sparingly apply

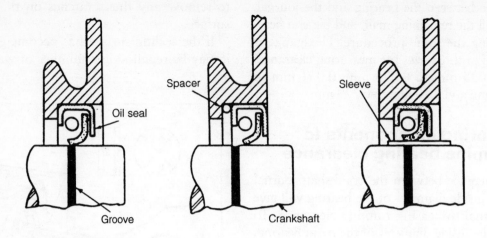

Fig 9.27   Various ways of restoring an oil seal running surface   *Courtesy of Detroit Diesel Corp*

a recommended sealant around the outside diameter of the seal and or seal bore.

Lubricate the lip of the seal with the oil it is to seal, then position it into its housing with the lip facing towards the oil compartment (this is usually the garter spring side). In this way, whenever oil forms around the sealing lip it forces the sealing lip tighter around the shaft, improving its sealing effect. Finally, press the seal squarely into its housing, making sure it goes fully home.

Flywheel service

Wear evaluation

Whenever the engine has been dismantled for repairs, the flywheel should be inspected for:

- damaged ring gear teeth;
- scored or cracked clutch face surface;
- warpage.

If any of the ring gear teeth are damaged or missing, the ring gear will need to be replaced.

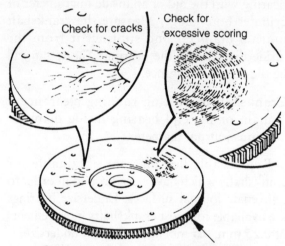

Fig 9.28   Inspecting the flywheel
Courtesy of AGPS

To remove the ring gear from the flywheel, first use a preheating torch to heat the gear then use a hammer and punch to drive the ring gear off the flywheel, as shown in Fig 9.29. Prior to installing a new ring gear, heat it up to a temperature of approximately 180–200°C, then fit it on to the flywheel, as shown in Fig 9.30.

wheel housing and position the dial probe on to the outer face of the flywheel, as shown in Fig 9.31. Rotate the flywheel one whole turn while holding it forwards or backwards to check for the highest reading.

Flywheel runout can generally be rectified by removing it from the engine and machining its face until it is true.

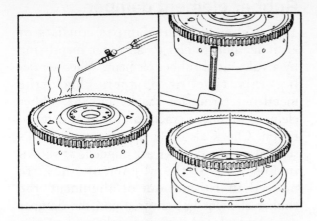

Fig 9.29   Procedure for removing flywheel ring gear
Courtesy of Cummins Engine Co

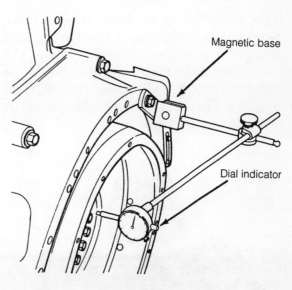

Fig 9.31   Measuring flywheel runout
Courtesy of Detroit Diesel Corp

Balancer and damper servicing

Balance shafts and weights do not require any specific servicing arrangements except bearing and gear replacement if required during engine overhaul. However, on reassembling balance weights or shafts into the block, the balances must be timed to the crankshaft for correct operation. Failure to time both balances correctly will cause severe engine vibration and possible engine damage.

The crankshaft damper on the other hand needs to be inspected thoroughly whenever any of the following occur: the engine is overhauled, there is a failure of the crank-

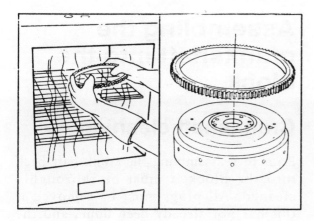

Fig 9.30   Procedure for installing flywheel ring gear
Courtesy of Cummins Engine Co

A flywheel which is scored and or has a lightly cracked clutch face surface can be repaired by machining its face on a lathe or flywheel grinder. Some cracks in the flywheel are too big to be machined out; however, provided the flywheel is not in danger of flying apart, it can be reused in most cases.

With the flywheel installed on the engine, it can be checked for runout. To check for runout, mount a dial indicator on the fly

shaft, the engine timing train gear noise becomes louder than normal, the damper is damaged in any way or the damper is out of alignment and wobbles during operation. Vibration dampers have a limited service life and should be replaced after approximately 500 000 km, or 15 000 hours of service.

Viscous damper

If the damper is dented in any way the inner metal weight and the outer housing may rub against each other. This will restrict the movement of the metal ring and, instead of damping crankshaft vibrations, increase them to such a dangerous level that the crankshaft may fracture and break.

Fig 9.32 Procedure for measuring viscous damper housing thickness
Courtesy of Cummins Engine Co

The damper should be checked for such things as bulges or dents around the damper housing, oil leaking from the housing and damage to the pulley mounting bolt holes. If any of these faults are obvious, the damper should be replaced. To check for a bulged damper housing, remove the paint from four equidistant places on both sides of the damper and measure the thickness of the housing as shown in Fig 9.32. Replace the damper if the difference in the measurements between any two of the four areas is more than 0.25 mm.

Rubber element damper

The rubber element damper consists of an inner hub joined to an outer metal ring by a vulcanised rubber element. When servicing this type of damper, check the metal outer ring for cracks and the rubber element for shear cracks and rubber deterioration. Check also that the alignment marks scribed on the damper are aligned, as shown in Fig 9.33. If the alignment lines are more than 1.6 mm out of alignment, the rubber element has sheared and the damper must be replaced. Use a straight edge to also check the surface alignment of the damper — that is, the outer metal ring and the inner hub should be level with each other.

Assembling the crankshaft into the block

Crankshaft cleaning

Prior to reassembling the crankshaft back into the block it must be thoroughly cleaned. All plugs must be removed if this has not already been done, and the oil passages cleaned with the aid of a nylon brush and suitable cleaning fluid, as shown in Fig 9.34. After the oil passages have been cleaned, install new plugs and circlips if applicable. The block and its oil galleries should also be cleaned prior to assembly.

Assembly

Before fitting the upper main bearings to the block, make sure the bearing bores and the back of all bearing shells are clean and dry. Never put anything between the back of the bearing shell and the bearing housing. After the upper bearing shells are

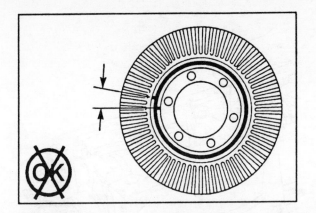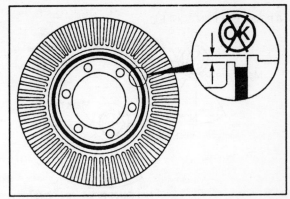

Fig 9.33 Inspecting a rubber type crankshaft damper *Courtesy of Cummins Engine Co*

installed, check for oil hole alignment between the bearing and the block. Lubricate all the bearings, then place the crankshaft gently and squarely on to the main bearings. The main caps with their bearing shells fitted can now be installed in their correct locations. Clean all retaining bolts and lubricate the threads and up under the head of each bolt so as to reduce friction during tightening, thereby obtaining accurate clamp loads. Do not oil internal threads because the hole may partially fill with oil and hydraulic locking will prevent proper tightening of the cap bolts. Tightening of the main bearing cap bolts should be done in stages of one-third torque, two-thirds torque and full torque, or as per the service manual specifications.

An alternative method of tensioning bolts is **torque turn tightening**, which requires the bolts to be tightened to an initial torque followed by a further turning of the bolt head to a specified angle, as shown in Fig 9.35. This procedure eliminates the possibility of the tightening torque applied to the bolt being absorbed by friction under the head of the bolt or by an abnormally high turning resistance due to dirty of faulty bolt threads. Torque turn tightening ensures that correct bolt stretch and clamping loads are applied regardless of the friction incurred during the tightening process.

After all the bearing caps have been tight-

ened in place, use a soft hammer and strike each bearing cap. This will releaseany tension which has built up between the bearing cap and the crankshaft, thereby ensuring that the crankshaft turns freely.

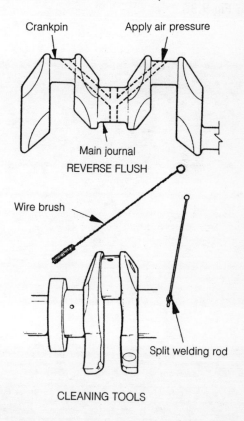

Fig 9.34 Cleaning crankshaft oil passages *Courtesy of AGPS*

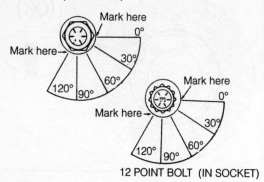

6 POINT BOLT (IN SOCKET)

12 POINT BOLT (IN SOCKET)

Fig 9.35 Degrees of bolt turn for torque turn tightening
Courtesy of Detroit Diesel Corp

Once the crankshaft rotates freely, mount a dial gauge to the cylinder block and measure the end float of the crankshaft, as shown in Fig 9.36.

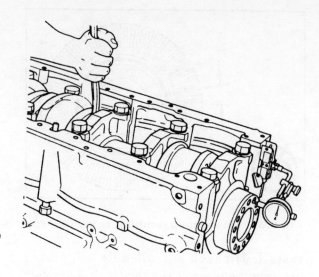

Fig 9.36 Measuring crankshaft end float
Courtesy of Detroit Diesel Corp

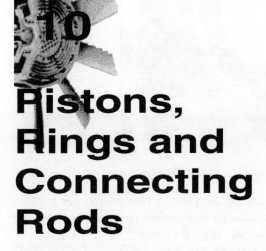

10

Pistons, Rings and Connecting Rods

The piston and piston rings are designed to create a seal within the cylinder and at the same time transmit the forces of combustion via the piston pin and connecting rod to the crankshaft. The movements of the piston and the connecting rod work together to convert the piston's reciprocating motion into rotary motion of the crankshaft. The piston also acts as a pump on the intake and exhaust strokes to draw air into the combustion chamber and push exhaust gas out.

Pistons are usually cast from a high grade aluminium alloy to combine light weight, good strength and high heat conductivity.

Diesel engine pistons are generally of the trunk or two-piece design.

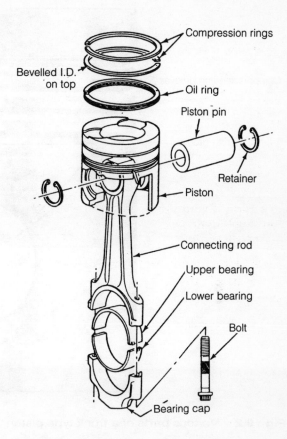

Fig 10.1   Connecting rod and piston assembly
Courtesy of Detroit Diesel Corp

Trunk type piston

The trunk type piston is a one-piece construction, as shown in Fig 10.2, and is made up of piston crown, piston pin bosses, ring grooves, ring lands and piston skirt. The area above the top of the piston rings is called the crown and within it is formed the combustion chamber. There are different combustion chamber shapes, the majority being either a shallow crater or toroidal cavity type. Some pre-combustion chamber engines have an erosion plug inserted into the top of the piston so as to prevent the hot combustion gases leaving the throat of the pre-combustion chamber and burning a hole through the aluminium piston crown.

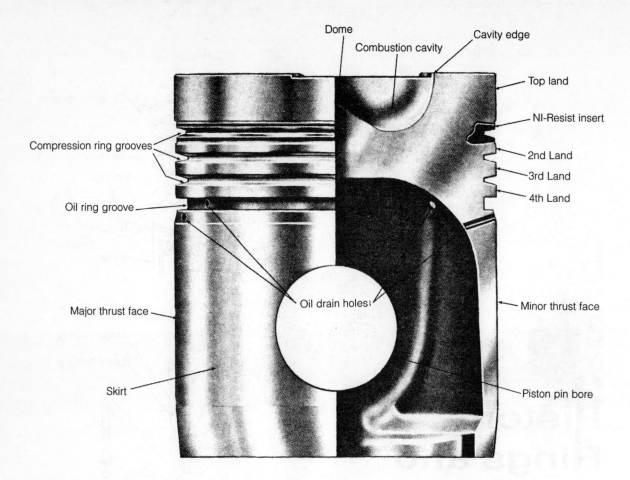

Fig 10.2   Various parts of a trunk type piston   *Courtesy of Mack Trucks Inc*

Below the piston crown are the ring grooves, and separating these grooves are the ring lands. Out of all the ring grooves on the piston, the top groove wears the most, as it is directly subjected to the high cylinder pressures and temperatures.

To overcome this severe wear problem, many pistons are now constructed with an alloy steel insert cast into the piston crown to form the complete ring groove, as shown in Fig 10.2. Such inserts reduce groove and ring side wear, thus increasing the piston and ring service life.

The lower ring groove of the piston contains the oil ring and at the back of the groove, there are multiple oil holes drilled around the circumference of the piston to allow the oil scraped off the cylinder wall to flow to the inside of the piston and into the crankcase. The crown and ring land area of the piston is slightly smaller in diameter than

the skirt of the piston. This allows for greater expansion in this higher temperature area of the piston, thus preventing the crown of the piston from binding on the cylinder wall during engine operation.

Two-piece piston

The two-piece articulated piston design, as shown in Fig 10.3, has been used by Detroit Diesel for many years in their two-stroke design engines. The piston is of a two piece construction, the crown being made of alloy steel and the skirt aluminium or steel. The two components are connected together by the piston pin, which passes through the skirt in the normal way and then through a strut which extends down from the centre of the piston crown. The two-piece piston has a number of advantages over the conventional trunk type piston, which are as follows:

- The construction of the piston in two separate pieces allows for easy access to the crown and top of the skirt area to construct more efficient oil galleries. This results in better piston cooling, which improves piston and ring life.
- The steel crown, being a stronger material than aluminium, allows the piston to withstand much higher cylinder pressures and thermal loads.

Fig 10.3   Two-piece piston design

- The inherent strength of the steel crown allows the top ring to be positioned higher — approximately 5 mm from the top of the crown. This helps in reducing the dead air volume in the cylinder, resulting in improved volumetric efficiency and reduced hydrocarbon exhaust emissions.
- The design of the piston is such that the skirt is now more isolated from the high temperature piston crown, thereby reducing its thermal expansion. This permits a closer skirt-to-cylinder wall clearance, minimising piston slap and engine noise.
- Due to its ability to articulate as two separate

components, the piston is more stable in the bore. The skirt can now absorb the sideways thrust of the connecting rod and at the same time prevent the piston crown and rings from tilting in the bore, as would happen in a trunk type piston. This provides a more stable platform for the rings to work from, resulting in better ring-to-cylinder wall sealing and oil control.

The two-piece piston design has a number of advantages which make it an ideal choice for engine manufacturers who are looking for more thermally efficient engines with reduced exhaust emissions.

Cam-ground piston

Since aluminium pistons are constructed with a greater amount of metal in the piston pin boss area so as to support the piston pin, provision is made for the uneven expansion of metal that results from this design. To ensure that the piston will expand into a round shape from the heat of combustion, the piston skirt is cam ground, or constructed oval in shape. Cam-ground pistons, when cold, have their narrowest diameter across the piston pin bore area, as shown in Fig 10.4 (a). When the piston heats up, the piston pin boss area expands at a greater rate, changing the piston from an oval shape to a round shape. It is important, therefore, that the engine always be run at correct operating temperature so as to obtain normal piston expansion rates and correct piston-to-bore running clearances. Engines run at below-normal operating temperature can have excessive piston-to-bore clearance, resulting in piston slap and accelerated engine wear.

Piston cooling

It is understandable that the piston crown becomes very hot as a result of combustion. This generated heat is dissipated through the piston rings and lubricating oil, maintaining a safe piston operating temperature.

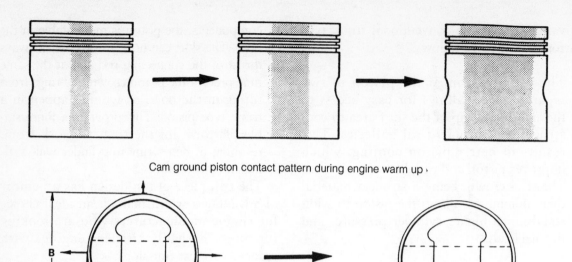

Cam ground piston contact pattern during engine warm up

COLD OPERATION
(a)

HOT OPERATION
(b)

Bottom view of cam ground piston showing the difference in shirt dimensions when the piston is cold.
Distance A is less than B

Fig 10.4   Expansion of a cam-ground piston during engine warmup   *Courtesy of Komatsu Limited*

On turbocharger and some naturally aspirated engines with high performance outputs, the temperature of the piston rises to such a high level that normal methods of heat dissipation are not adequate. Therefore, to increase piston cooling, oil is sprayed up under the piston crown either by piston sprays mounted at the base of the cylinder bore or by oil sprayed out of the top of the connecting rod, as shown in Fig 10.5.

Piston pin

The piston is connected to the connecting rod by means of the piston pin or gudgeon pin. The piston pin is made from hardened alloy steel and is a precision fit within the connecting rod bush and piston pin bosses. The pin is hollow so as to reduce its weight and subsequent inertia force during the reciprocating movements of the piston/connecting rod assembly.

There are different methods of mounting piston pins. Some are fully floating, which means they are free to rotate in both the piston and connecting rod and are retained by circlips in the piston bosses. Other piston pins, known as semi-floating pins, can be bolted to or pressed into the connecting rod, as shown in Fig 10.6. Either way the piston is free to move on the piston pin during engine operation.

Offset piston pin

Some engine manufacturers are offsetting the piston pin so that it is located off the centre line of the piston towards the power thrust side of the piston, as shown in Fig 10.7. By offsetting the piston pin a small amount, the forces of combustion are more evenly distributed over

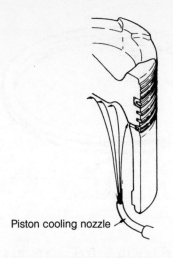

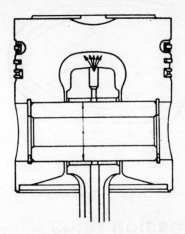

Piston cooling nozzle

Fig 10.5   Two methods of piston cooling   *Courtesy of Komatsu Limited*

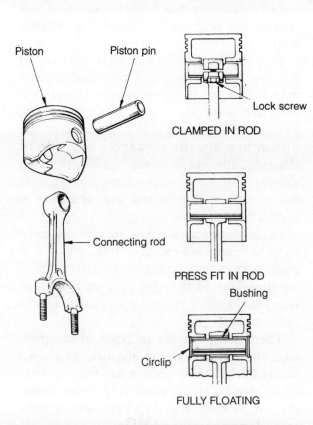

Piston

Piston pin

Lock screw

CLAMPED IN ROD

PRESS FIT IN ROD

Bushing

Circlip

FULLY FLOATING

Connecting rod

Fig 10.6   Three ways of securing the piston pin
Courtesy of AGPS

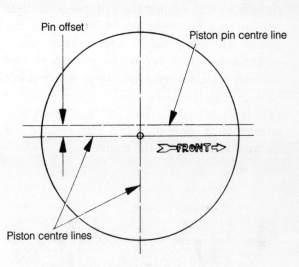

Pin offset

Piston pin centre line

FRONT

Piston centre lines

MARKING ON PISTON INDICATES CORRECT ASSEMBLY

Fig 10.7   Schematic diagram of a piston showing the piston pin offset to the centre line of the piston so as to minimise piston slap and engine noise
Courtesy of AGPS

to a minimum. On reassembly of engines using offset pistons, it is important that the pistons are installed in the cylinder the correct way around.

Piston rings

There are two general categories of piston ring used in diesel engines: the compression ring and the oil control ring, as shown in Fig 10.8.

the top of the piston, with less tilting of the piston during the power stroke. By minimising the tilting or oscillations of the piston in the cylinder, piston slap and engine noise are kept

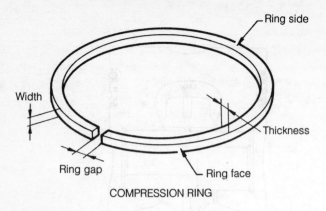

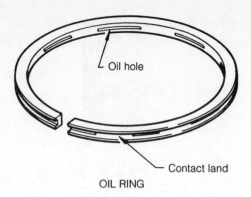

Fig 10.8   Piston rings   *Courtesy of Komatsu Limited*

Compression rings

The primary function of the compression rings is to seal against the cylinder wall, thus providing a gas-tight seal at the top of the piston. The compression ring is also required to transfer heat from the piston to the cylinder wall. Compression rings which don't seal properly cause cold engine starting problems, due to a lack of heat from low compression pressure, and also reduce the thermal efficiency of the engine.

Compression rings in a free state are larger in diameter than the cylinder wall and when installed in the cylinder have a reduced diameter which has the effect of tensioning the ring firmly against the cylinder wall.

In addition to the residual tension of the ring, compression and combustion gases help in forcing the ring to seal against the cylinder wall. During engine operation, gas pressure coming down the side of the piston acts on the top and back side of the ring, forcing it down against the ring groove and at the same time out against the cylinder wall to form a seal, as shown in Fig 10.9.

Many compression rings are chrome faced so as to minimise wear. Such rings are used in conjunction with a cast iron bore and at no time should they be used in a chrome bore, as they will scuff and score the chrome cylinder wall.

There are a number of types of compression ring used in diesel engines, as shown in Fig 10.10. Most pistons use two or three compression rings, each ring being constructed differently so as to perform specific tasks during engine operation.

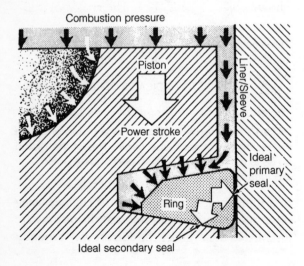

Fig 10.9   Combustion pressure being used to help seal the rings against the cylinder wall and ring groove
Courtesy of Mack Trucks Inc

Rectangular ring

This is the simplest piston ring construction, with full face contact against the cylinder wall as shown in Fig 10.11. It is generally used as either the first or second ring.

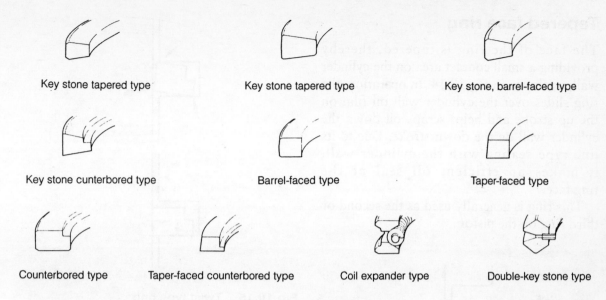

Key stone tapered type

Key stone tapered type

Key stone, barrel-faced type

Key stone cunterbored type

Barrel-faced type

Taper-faced type

Counterbored type

Taper-faced counterbored type

Coil expander type

Double-key stone type

Fig 10.10 Various types of piston rings used in modern diesel engines *Courtesy of Komatsu Limited*

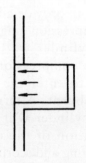

Fig 10.11 Rectangular ring
Courtesy of Komatsu Limited

Barrel faced rings

The face of the ring in contact with the cylinder wall is shaped like a barrel, as shown in

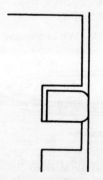

Fig 10.12 Barrel faced ring
Courtesy of Komatsu Limited

Fig 10.12, so that it can operate with a narrow high-pressure contact area, maintaining good sealing capabilities with minimal amount of resistance and wear. It is generally used as a top compression ring.

Keystone ring

This ring has tapered sides and a flat face, as shown in Fig 10.13. When the ring moves out against the cylinder wall, the clearance between the ring and its groove increases. Due to the clearance and movement of the ring in its groove, carbon buildup in the groove is prevented, thereby reducing the possibility of the ring sticking in its groove, as can happen with flat-sided rectangular rings.

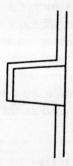

Fig 10.13 Keystone ring
Courtesy of Komatsu Limited

Tapered face ring

The face of the ring is tapered, thereby providing a small contact area on the cylinder wall, as shown in Fig 10.14. In operation, the ring slides over the cylinder wall oil film on the up stroke and helps scrape oil down the cylinder wall on the down stroke. Due to its line type sealing with the cylinder wall, it makes an efficient oil seal at the ring face.

This ring is generally used as the second or third ring on the piston.

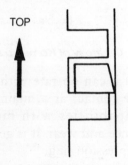

Fig 10.14   Tapered faced ring
Courtesy of Komatsu Limited

Internal step or twist type ring

This type of ring has a step or chamfer cut on the top inside surface of the ring. In operation, as the piston moves down on the intake stroke, internal forces cause the ring to twist slightly, as shown in the top of Fig 10.15. Therefore, as the ring moves down the bore, it provides a scraping action which helps in preventing oil from reaching the top of the piston. During the compression and power strokes, gas pressure acting on the top and back sides of the ring causes it to untwist and be forced to lie flat against the cylinder wall and ring groove, forming an effective gas seal. This ring is often used as the second or third ring on the piston.

Oil control rings

The oil control rings shown in Fig 10.16 are used to control the amount of oil on the

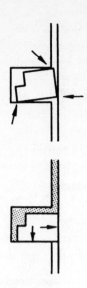

Fig 10.15   Twist type ring
Courtesy of Komatsu Limited

cylinder walls and to provide adequate lubrication to the compression rings. Too much oil left on the cylinder walls cannot be controlled by the compression rings, thus allowing the oil to enter the combustion chamber and be burnt. Alternatively, too little oil on the cylinder will not provide adequate lubrication of the compression rings, causing scuffing and scoring of the ring face and cylinder wall.

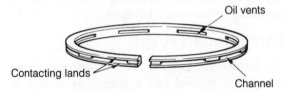

CAST IRON OIL-CONTROL RING

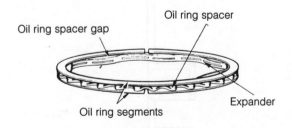

SEGMENTED OIL RING

Fig 10.16   Oil control rings
Courtesy of AGPS

Figure 10.17 shows how the oil control ring functions during the operation of the engine. As the piston moves down the cylinder, the oil ring wipes the excess oil from the walls of the cylinder and allows it to pass through holes in the piston to drain back into the crankcase. On the upstroke of the piston, splashed oil from the crankshaft throws passes through the piston oil holes and through the centre of the oil ring to lubricate the cylinder wall.

Oil control rings rely on the tension of the ring and an expander to help force the ring to seal against the cylinder wall.

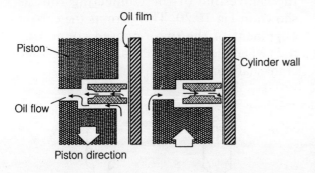

Fig 10.17   Function of an oil control ring

Connecting rod

The connecting rod, as shown in Fig 10.18, is the means by which the piston transmits the force of combustion to the crankshaft. The small or little end of the connecting rod is attached to the piston and the big end to the crankshaft journal.

The big end is constructed with a removable bearing cap which allows the connecting rod to be assembled to the crankshaft. In order to align the bearing cap accurately with the connecting rod, some form of location such as a stepped surface, dowelled bolts or serrated surfaces is provided between the two parting faces of the bearing cap and connecting rod.

With some connecting rods, the parting line of the big end cap may be at a 45° angle to the connecting rod, as shown in Fig 10.19. This facilitates removal and assembly of the connecting rod from the cylinder when the engine is being worked on. It also reduces the inertial forces which normally act on the cap bolts during the exhaust and compression strokes, as these forces are now taken up by the bearing cap-locating device rather than straining the big end bolts.

1.   Connecting rod bushing

2.   Connecting rod

3.   Connecting rod bolt

4.   Connecting rod bearing shell

5.   Connecting rod cap

A: Small end of connecting rod

B: Large end of connecting rod

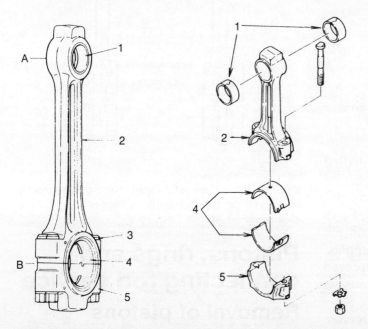

Fig 10.18   Connecting rod assembly   *Courtesy of Komatsu Limited*

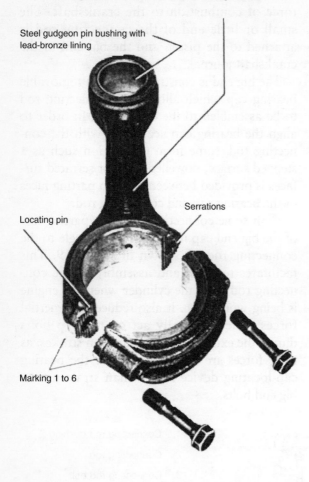

Marking 'FRONT' indicated the direction in which the connecting rod is fitted in the engine and is related to the fact of having the big-end bearing seat at an angle. The connecting rod shouls have the 'FRONT' facing forwards.

Steel gudgeon pin bushing with lead-bronze lining

Serrations

Locating pin

Marking 1 to 6

Fig 10.19 Connecting rod with a 45° serrated parting line between the rod and the cap
Courtesy of Volvo

The connecting rod is normally drilled through the centre from the big end bearing to the piston pin bearing. Lubricating oil, which is supplied to the crank journals, flows up this drilling and lubricates the piston pin and its bearing. In some engines, oil supplied by the connecting rod drilling is also sprayed up under the piston for cooling purposes, as previously shown in Fig 10.5.

Some older engines do not have pressure fed oil to the piston pin; instead they have a funnel-shaped hole in the upper end of each connecting rod which catches oil that is splashed or sprayed within the cylinder block and allows it to flow into the connecting rod bushing for continuous piston pin lubrication.

During engine manufacture, the connecting rod and the big end are etched or stamped with a number, as shown in Figs 10.19 and 10.20, which identifies these two parts as a matched pair and their cylinder location. During an engine overhaul, these matched parts must always be fitted together as a pair and reassembled as such on to the crankshaft.

Some 'V' type engines are fitted with connecting rods in which the big end is offset to the centre line of the connecting rod, as shown in Fig 10.20. This permits the correct alignment of the two opposed connecting rods when they are both attached to the same crankshaft journal.

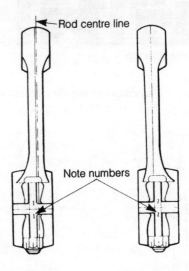

Rod centre line

Note numbers

Fig 10.20 Pair of offset connecting rods used in a 'V' type engine configuration
Courtesy of AGPS

Pistons, rings and connecting rod service
Removal of pistons

Remove the cylinder head and sump from the

For example, the cap number may face the camshaft. If there are no markings visible either side of the parting line of the bearing cap, then stamp appropriate numbers to suit the cylinder location.

If there is a wear ridge at the top of the cylinder wall, it will have to be removed with the aid of a ridge removing tool before the pistons can be withdrawn. Any attempt to remove the pistons while there is a ridge present in the cylinder bore will result in damage to the piston rings and ring grooves.

Remove the big end bolts and detach the bearing cap from the connecting rod. Then, with the aid of a wooden hammer handle, placed on the underside of the piston skirt as shown in Fig 10.21, push the piston and connecting rod out of the cylinder.

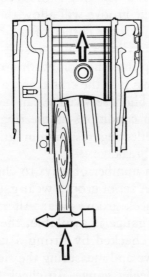

Fig 10.21   A wooden hammer handle being used to push the piston out of the cylinder
Courtesy of Volvo

With all the pistons withdrawn from the cylinders, mount each piston/connecting rod assembly in a vice with soft jaws and proceed to remove the piston rings with the aid of a ring-removing tool, as shown in Fig 10.22. As the rings will not be used again, store them in separate groups for inspection if necessary. With the connecting rod still in the vice, use a pair of internal circlip pliers to remove the circlips or loosen the bolt clamping the little

end of the connecting rod to the piston pin. Before removing the piston from the connecting rod, take note of the piston position on the connecting rod as the piston must go back the same way on reassembly. Depending on what the service manual states, drive or press the piston pin out of the piston. Some manufacturers recommend that the piston be heated prior to removing the piston pin. *Caution!* During piston pin removal, support the piston in a saddle or suitable fixture so that the sides of the piston are not damaged.

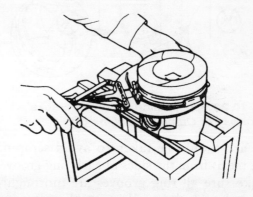

Fig 10.22   Removing piston rings with a piston ring expander
Courtesy of Mitsubishi

Inspection and repair of components

In order to make piston and connecting rod servicing more meaningful, the inspection and repair procedures used in conjunction with examples of dimensions, clearances and tolerances represent only general overhaul procedures and not the actual procedures for all engines. Therefore, always refer to the relevant service manual for specifications and correct inspection and repair procedures.

Piston inspection

If the piston shows obvious signs of damage, scoring or excessive wear then there is no use proceeding with cleaning and inspecting procedures, as the piston will need to be replaced.

Before inspecting the piston for its service-ability, it should be thoroughly cleaned using a suitable cleaning solution. Ring grooves can be cleaned of carbon using a ring groove cleaning tool or, if this is not available, the end of an old ring to scrape the groove clean.

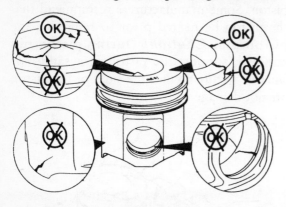

Fig 10.23 Inspecting piston for cracks
Courtesy of Cummins Engine Co

Care should be taken to avoid scraping any metal from the sides of each ring groove. Make sure all ring grooves are thoroughly cleaned of carbon, otherwise the new ring may stick in the groove or be forced to protrude too far out from the groove with high contact pressure and scuffing being caused to the cylinder wall and ring face.

The clean piston can now be examined for cracks, especially in the crown and skirt areas, and for damaged or broken ring lands. Also inspect the piston all over for any signs of scoring. Scored or cracked pistons should

be replaced. However, some manufacturers, in their reuseability guides, do allow for some combustion chamber cracks in the top of the piston, as shown in Fig 10.23.

Ring groove

The top ring groove will be worn the most, as it is exposed to the greatest temperatures and pressures and to all foreign contaminants that may enter the engine. The ideal groove and ring combination is such that the flat surface of the ring fits flat against the piston groove sides around its entire circumference in order to seal and provide both compression and oil control. New rings are smooth and flat, but they cannot form an oil and gas-tight seal against excessively worn and uneven piston groove sides. If a new ring is fitted to a worn ring groove, the groove will allow the ring to tilt, forcing the upper corner of the ring face to contact the cylinder wall, causing the ring to wipe oil up into the combustion chamber instead of down into the crankcase, as shown in Fig 10.24. Short service life can be expected under such conditions as the ring will be continually deflecting, resulting in fatigue and eventual ring breakage.

There are a number of ways to check ring groove wear. A set of groove wear gauges can be used to check groove wear. Alternatively, if no groove gauge is available, the groove wear can be checked by fitting a new ring into the groove and measuring the side clearance with a feeler gauge. To check the side

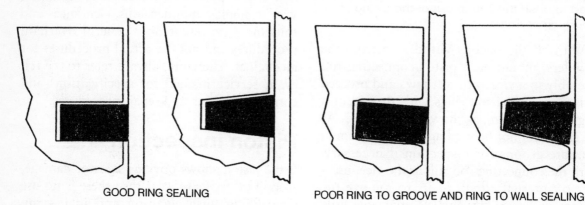

GOOD RING SEALING   POOR RING TO GROOVE AND RING TO WALL SEALING

Fig 10.24   Illustration showing the effects of ring groove wear on piston ring sealing

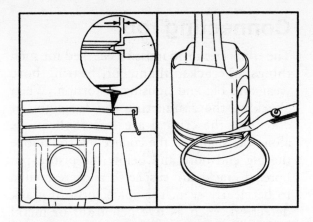

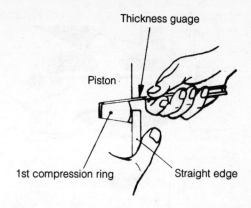

Fig 10.25   Various ways of checking ring groove wear

clearance for keystone rings, use a straight edge to push the ring flush with the skirt of the piston, then measure the ring to groove clearance. Figure 10.25 shows the different ways that ring groove wear can be checked.

As a general rule, the maximum ring-to-groove side clearance is 0.15 mm. Ring grooves should be checked at several places around the piston, as ring grooves can sometimes wear unevenly.

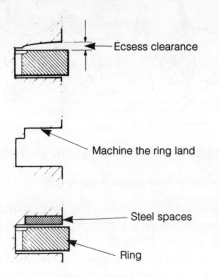

Fig 10.26   Installing steel spacers to repair worn piston ring grooves
Courtesy of AGPS

If ring grooves are worn beyond specification, the piston must be replaced or the ring grooves remachined, depending on the manufacturer's reuseability guide, if available. To rectify a worn piston ring groove, machine the groove to a wider dimension then fit a heat treated spacer above the top of the ring, as shown in Fig 10.26, so as to bring the ring-to-groove clearance back within specifications.

Piston dimension

Because pistons are cam ground, they should be measured at their greatest diameter, which is across the lower part of the skirt at right angles to the piston pin, as shown in Fig 10.27. Do not measure the piston at any other point, as the dimensions obtained will be considerably less than actual piston size specification. The piston crown, ring land and pin bosses areas are all of smaller dimension to allow for heat expansion during engine operation. To obtain the clearance between piston and the cylinder bore, measure the piston across the lower part of the skirt and then measure the cylinder bore and subtract the two dimensions. The difference is the piston to bore clearance.

Finally, measure the piston pin and piston pin bore for actual size. As the piston pin is made of hardened steel, its wear is negligible, but the same cannot be said for the pin bore, which can wear in an oval shape. Therefore, when measuring the piston pin bore, take two measurements at right angles to each other, as shown in Fig 10.28. Subtract the piston pin diameter from the larger pin bore diameter to obtain the clearance.

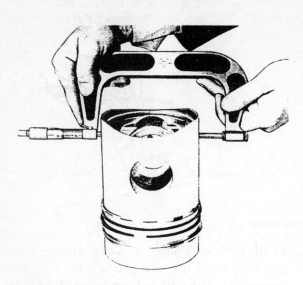

Fig 10.27 Measuring the piston skirt diameter
Courtesy of Volvo

Piston

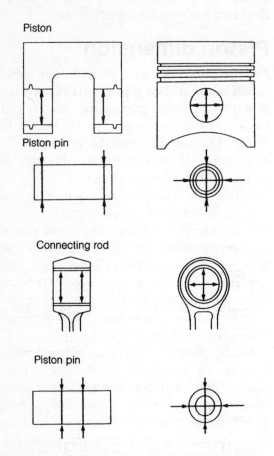

Piston pin

Connecting rod

Piston pin

Fig 10.28 Measuring the piston pin boss, the piston pin and the connecting rod bush
Courtesy of Mitsubishi

Connecting rod

The connecting rod must be checked for such things as cracks, alignment, bearing bore wear and big end housing distortion. When checking the connecting rod for signs of cracking, the critical areas to look at are along the shank of the connecting rod above the big end bore and below the piston pin bore. If cracks are suspected and are unable to be clearly seen, use some form of crack detection, such as dye penetrant or metal particle testing. Crack detection procedures are fully explained in Chapter 7.

If the connecting rod has been damaged or dented in any way, as shown in Fig 10.29, it should be replaced, as the damaged area creates stress lines in the connecting rod which may cause it to break while in service.

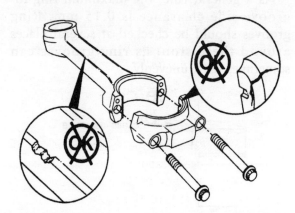

Fig 10.29 Connecting rod showing signs of damage
Courtesy of Cummins Engine Co

Measure the connecting rod piston pin bushing for ovality and taper, as shown in Fig 10.28, and also measure the piston pin if this has not already been done. If the bushing is worn, it should be pressed out and a new bush installed, as shown in Fig 10.30, taking particular note to align the lubricating oil holes on bush installation. After the bush is installed, it may be necessary to ream or machine the bush so that the piston pin will fit correctly. The big end of the connecting rod should also be checked as it can wear out of round.

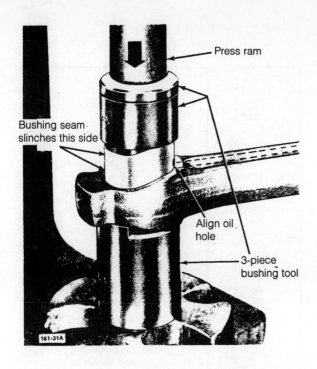

Fig 10.30   Replacing the connecting rod bush
Courtesy of Mack Trucks Inc

Checking the connecting rod big end bore

Over long periods of operation it is possible that the big end bearing bore may become oval in shape. If new bearings are fitted, they will distort slightly to the oval shape of the bore and not provide full bearing surface contact with the crankshaft journal. Therefore, the bearing bore should be checked for signs of rubbing caused by moving bearings shells and also for out of roundness and bore size by measuring the bore as shown in Fig 10.31. If the dimensions obtained are greater than the wear limits, the connecting rod should be replaced or the bearing bore resized. As resizing of connecting rods is a specialist job requiring specialised machining tools, only a general description of the resizing procedure is given below.

To resize the bearing bore, remove the bearing cap and machine metal off the parting faces of the cap and connecting rod so as to

slightly reduce the overall bore size. Refit and tension the bearing cap, then hone the bearing bore back to the standard size.

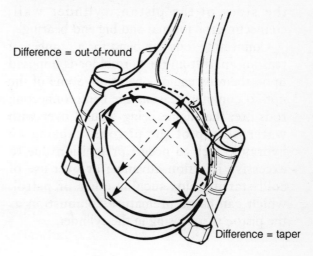

Fig 10.31   Measuring the big end bore for taper and ovality
Courtesy of AGPS

Connecting rod length

The length of the connecting rod, as shown in Fig 10.32, is important in that it determines how far the piston travels up the bore, thus establishing the engine compression ratio and the clearance gap between the piston and the cylinder head.

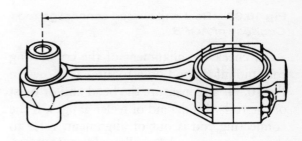

Fig 10.32   Measuring the length of the connecting rod
Courtesy of Caterpillar Inc

Connecting rod alignment

Connecting rod alignment is important in maintaining even wear on the piston, cylinder surfaces and crankshaft journal. A bent or twisted connecting rod, as shown in Fig 10.33, can lead to excessive uneven wear on the sides of the piston, cylinder wall, connecting rod journal and big end bearing.

Connecting rods can bend for a number of reasons apart from the normal loads imposed upon them by engine operation. Some of the not so common reasons for bent connecting rods are: the engine being wound over with water on top of the pistons, causing an hydraulic lock to occur; preignition due to excessive injection advance; or over-use of cold starting aids such as ether or petrol, which can cause premature combustion as the piston is still rising in the cylinder.

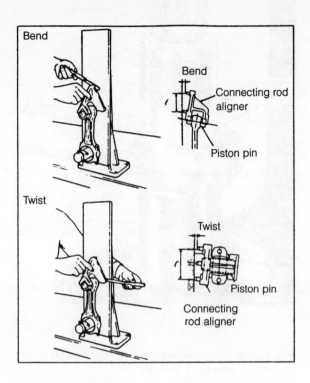

Fig 10.34   Checking a connecting rod for bend and twist
Courtesy of Mitsubishi

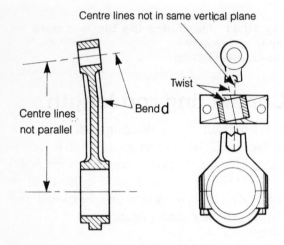

Fig 10.33   Bent and twisted connecting rods
Courtesy of AGPS

To check the alignment of the connecting rod, mount the rod on a fixture, as shown in Fig 10.34, and measure the bend and/or twist of the rod with the aid of feeler gauges. If the connecting rod is out of alignment, refer to the service manual for allowable tolerances. Generally, connecting rods should be replaced if found to be bent; however, refer to the service manual for recommendations on replacement or straightening procedures.

Some diesel engine manufacturers recommend that the connecting rods should be replaced if found to be out of alignment.

Big end bearings

Inspect the big end bearing shells for scoring, chipping, corrosion, cracking or signs of overheating. If any of these conditions are apparent, replace the bearings. Also inspect the backs of the bearing shells to see if they have been fretting in the bearing bore. If so, replace the shells. To measure the big end bearings for wear, assemble the two shells into the connecting rod and correctly tension the bearing cap bolts. Use an inside micrometer or expanding gauge, as shown in Fig 10.35, to measure the diameter of the bearing bore at several places away from the parting line of the cap, then refer to the specifications for the correct size.

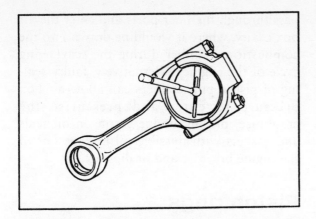

Fig 10.35 Measuring the connecting rod big end bore with a telescopic gauge
Courtesy of Cummins Engine Co

A general recommendation is to replace bearing shells whenever the connecting rods are removed from the engine. The cost of new bearings is minimal compared with the cost of a failure which may occur due to refitting bearings with undetected fatigue or reduced bearing crush.

Assembly of piston to connecting rod

When assembling the connecting rod to the piston, check to see that the piston is positioned relative to the valve recesses and combustion chamber position and that the connecting rod numbers coincide as shown in Fig 10.36. If circlips are used to retain the piston pins, replace them as they would be fatigued and could come out of their grooves if reinstalled.

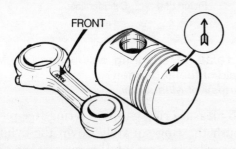

Fig 10.36 Piston and connecting rod assembly marks
Courtesy of Volvo

Refer to the service manual for the correct procedure to install the piston pins, as some pistons have to be heated in hot water before the piston pin is installed so as not to damage the piston pin bores.

With the piston pin installed, secure the connecting rod in a vice with soft jaws and, with one retaining circlip installed in the piston, push the piston pin through the piston and connecting rod until it stops flush against its circlip retainer. Install the other circlip, making sure that both circlips are fitted fully in their grooves and that the eyes or tangs of the circlip are positioned to either

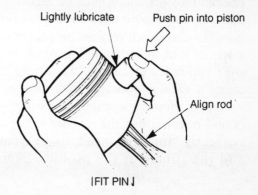

FIT PIN

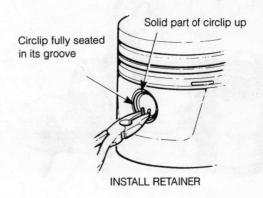

INSTALL RETAINER

Fig 10.37 Installing fully floating piston pin and retainers
Courtesy of AGPS

the top or bottom centre of the hole, as shown in Fig 10.37. If the circlip openings are placed on a horizontal plane rather than a vertical plane as shown, the circlips will be stressed due to the inertia forces of the piston movement which could cause them to fatigue and come out of their grooves during engine operation.

Pistons used in two-stroke engines use piston pin retainers which are similar to that of a welsh plug used in cooling systems. Pin retainers are used for two reasons. The first is to prevent oil leaking past the piston pin and on to the cylinder wall. The second is to prevent the entry of air via the piston pin and bushing into the crankcase whenever the piston pin passes the tangential ports of the cylinder liner. On assembly of the piston and connecting rod, the piston pin retainers are pressed into place and must be checked to see that they form an oil tight seal in the piston pin bore. To check each retainer for proper sealing, a special tool, as shown in Fig 10.38, is placed over the retainer and the tool operated to create a vacuum under the suction cup. If the vacuum cannot be maintained for a specified period of time, then the retainer is not sealing correctly and will need to be removed and the source of the problem rectified.

pass through the liner ports and enter the air box cavity, where it would be drawn into the combustion chamber during the scavenging cycle of the engine. Alternatively, faulty sealing of piston pin retainers can allow air box pressure to enter and pressurise the crankcase, placing undue strain on oil seals and gaskets with possible oil leakage out of the engine breather and or dipstick.

Piston rings

Whenever piston rings are removed from a piston, regardless of how much work they have done, they should be replaced. Before the new rings are fitted to the piston, they should all be checked for ring gap.

Insufficient ring gap can cause the rings to bind on the cylinder wall during engine operation, resulting in damage to both the cylinder bore and the rings. Excessive ring gap, on the other hand, can result in blow-by of combustion gas and oil slippage past the rings and up into the combustion chamber.

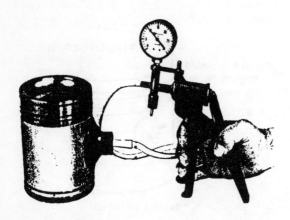

Fig 10.38 Using a suction tool to check that the piston pin retainers on a two-stroke diesel engine are sealing correctly
Courtesy of Detroit Diesel Corp

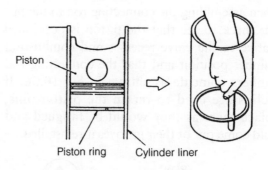

Fig 10.39 Measuring piston ring gap with the aid of feeler gauges
Courtesy of Mitsubishi

If oil were to leak past the piston pin retainers during engine operation, it would form on the cylinder walls and eventually

To measure ring gap, use a ring free piston to push the ring squarely down the cylinder bore until it is in an unworn area of the bore, as shown in Fig 10.39, then use a feeler gauge to check the ring gap opening. If the gap is insufficient, place the end of the ring in a vice with soft jaws and lightly file the end of the ring so as to reduce its circumference. Recheck the gap as before. *Note:* If chrome or molybdenum coated rings are used, file from the outside to the inside of the ring with gentle strokes so as to not chip or peel the chrome or molybdenum coatings off the ring face. In the absence of manufacturer's specifications, piston ring gaps can be set at 0.125 mm per 25 mm of bore size. This figure will provide safe working clearances for satisfactory engine operation.

Installing piston rings

With the piston attached to the connecting rod, clamp the connecting rod in a vice with soft jaws and clean the piston in readiness for ring installation. Examine the sides of each ring near its end for a mark (dot or T), indicating which side of the ring is to go to the top of the piston. Then, using a ring

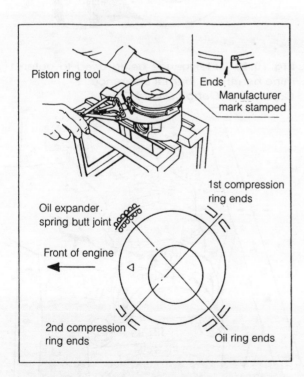

Fig 10.40 Installing and positioning piston rings on a piston
Courtesy of Mitsubishi

expander tool as shown in Fig 10.40, install the rings on to the piston, starting with the oil ring first. After all the rings are installed on the piston, make sure that if the oil ring has an expander spring its ends are placed opposite the oil ring ends. Arrange the compression and oil rings so that their ends are away from the piston thrust face and piston pin and that they alternate 180° apart as shown in Fig 10.40. Finally, lubricate the rings and use a ring compressor to compress them in preparation for the piston installation into the cylinder bore.

Installing piston and connecting rod assembly

The connecting rods are numbered at either side of the big end bearing parting face for identification and must be installed in the corresponding numbered cylinder. Generally, connecting rod numbers face towards the camshaft side of the engine; however, refer to the service manual for the particular engine.

With the bearing cap removed, install the bearing shells, making certain that the backs of the shells are clean and dry and that they align with the locating lug as they are placed in position. With the connecting rod bolts correctly installed, fit plastic tubing over the exposed threaded section of each bolt. This is to prevent the bolts from damaging the journal surface of the crankshaft during connecting rod installation. If piston oil sprays are used in the engine, it may be necessary to turn the connecting rod slightly so that, as it passes down through the cylinder, it will not strike the oil spray and possibly alter its alignment. Also ensure that the crankshaft journal for that cylinder is in its lowest position — that is, at bottom dead centre. Lubricate the top half of the connecting rod bearing with engine oil then install the piston and connecting rod into the cylinder using a wooden hammer handle to press the piston down the cylinder, as shown in Fig 10.41. If undue resistance is felt as the rings are enter-are entering the cylinder, the piston rings may be improperly installed or the ring compressor has allowed a ring to move out and hit on the top of the cylinder block. In such a case, remove the piston assembly and rectify the problem. Before moving the piston further down the cylinder, ensure that the connecting rod is aligned with the journal, then force the piston carefully down the bore until the bearing mates with the journal.

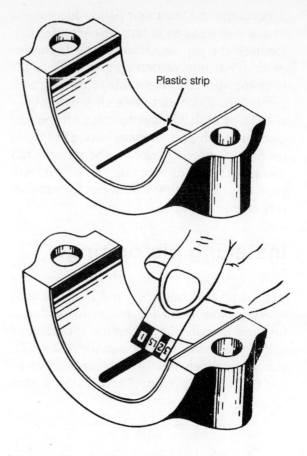

Plastic strip

Fig 10.42 Flexigauge being used to determine bearing to journal clearance
Courtesy of Detroit Diesel Corp

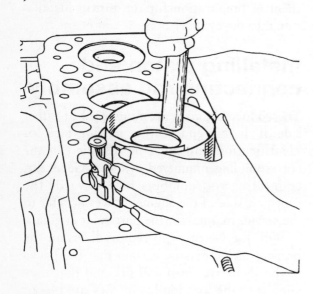

Fig 10.41 Fitting a piston into the cylinder with the aid of a ring compressor to compress the rings

To check the running clearance of the big end bearing, place a piece of suitable size Flexigauge across the big end cap bearing, as shown in Fig 10.42, and install the cap on to the connecting rod. Correctly tension the cap bolts and, without moving the crankshaft, remove the cap and check the width of the compressed Flexigauge with the check scale on the Flexigauge packet. If the clearance is correct, wipe all traces of the Flexigauge from the bearing surface then lubricate the bearing. Reinstall the cap and correctly tension its bolts.

A general running clearance for a medium-sized diesel engine would be 0.05 mm to 0.1 mm.

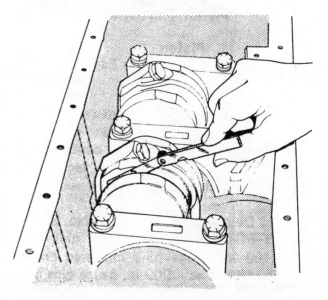

Fig 10.43 Checking connecting rod side clearance

After each connecting rod bearing cap is installed and its bolts tensioned, check the connecting rod side clearance using feeler gauges. A general permissible side clearance between the connecting rod and the side of the crankshaft journal is 0.05 mm. In order to check the clearance accurately, the feeler gauge must be inserted beside the parting line of the bearing cap and connecting rod, as shown in Fig 10.43. Excessive clearance may indicate that the side of the connecting rod is worn or the crank journal flange is worn. Too small a clearance could indicate a bent connecting rod or a bearing cap incorrectly installed.

Piston height

After all the connecting rods are installed, rotate the engine until no. 1 piston is at TDC. (Remember to use clamps to prevent cylinder liners popping up during the rotation of the engine.) Mount a magnetic base dial indicator on to the block and zero the dial needle with the top surface of the block. Then, without altering the height of the dial indicator assembly, rotate the dial gauge arm

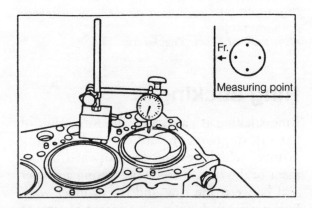

Fig 10.44   Measuring piston height relative to the top of the cylinder block
Courtesy of Mitsubishi

until the dial gauge is above the piston, as shown in Fig 10.44. Measure the piston height at four locations so as to get an average reading and determine the piston height relevant to the block. If the measurement obtained is out of specifications, the piston pin, piston pin bush and big end bearing should be rechecked for wear and the connecting rod rechecked for correct length. Check the remaining piston heights as described above.

Piston height must be within specifications as it affects the engine compression ratio as well as the mechanical clearance between the piston and the cylinder head.

Analysing piston and cylinder problems

Piston, ring and cylinder bore failure can be due to a number of factors relating to inefficient system component operation, faulty assembly or lack of engine maintenance. Engine sub-systems that can have a direct bearing on piston and ring failure are the cooling system, the lubricating system and the air intake system. The human factor can also be responsible, through incorrect assembly of the engine and its running maintenance.

For example, a faulty cooling system which is not controlling engine temperature or insufficient oil being splashed up under the piston crown can cause the cylinder temperature to rise to dangerous levels, resulting in possible scuffing and scoring of the piston and cylinder wall.

Scuffing and scoring

Scuffed surfaces can be identified by a burned or streaked appearance on the face of the piston rings, the piston skirt and the cylinder wall. Scuffing occurs when metal-to-metal contact takes place between components, resulting in temperatures which are higher than the melting point of the metals involved. This causes small areas of localised welding between components, which has the effect of creating a metal buildup on one surface and a cavity on the other. Continued engine running under such conditions enlarges the welded areas until a greater quantity of metal is transferred between parts, resulting in scoring of the piston and/or cylinder wall, as shown in Fig 10.45.

Scuffing and scoring are usually caused by the following:

- engine overheating;
- insufficient lubrication;
- insufficient clearance between moving parts;
- improper cylinder finish.

Fig 10.45 Piston scuffing and scoring
Courtesy of Mack Trucks Inc

Abrasive wear

Dirt-laden air entering a combustion chamber due to a faulty air cleaner or intake plumbing can cause abrasive wear to pistons, rings and cylinder bores. This type of abrasion is not as deep as with metal pickup, but more like fine score marks leaving a matt finish on the cylinder wall and piston surface. Ring gap and ring groove clearance will also show signs of increased wear and may exceed wear specifications. Figure 10.46 shows the effect of abrasive wear on the side of the piston skirt.

Fig 10.46 Piston wear caused by abrasive contaminants
Courtesy of Mack Trucks Inc

Ring sticking

Ring sticking is caused by the formation of carbon deposits in and around the ring groove, which restrict the outward movement of the ring, thereby preventing a proper seal between the ring and the cylinder wall. Piston ring sticking can be caused by any of the following:

- improper grade and quality of oil used;
- incorrect oil and filter change intervals;

- using inferior quality oil filters;
- low engine operating temperature.

Ring breakage

Ring breakage is detrimental to efficient cylinder sealing and can be caused by the following:

- excessively worn ring grooves and rings;
- overstressing of the ring during installation on the piston;
- the ring striking a wear ridge at the top of the cylinder during engine operation;
- excessive cylinder combustion pressure.

Human factor

Faulty work can also be responsible for piston and ring failure. Such things as incorrectly installed piston rings, oil sprays knocked out of alignment during piston installation, and piston pin circlips not installed correctly can lead to ring and piston failure. Alternatively, the engine may have failed due to lack of maintenance. Such things as neglecting to ensure correct oil and coolant levels in the engine are contributing factors to premature engine failure.

Engine diagnosis

An effective way of checking an engine for power related problems such as excessive oil consumption, blow-by and poor performance is to perform a blow-by test and a compression test.

Blow-by test

Blow-by is the term used to describe the leakage of combustion gas past the rings and into the crankcase. Such leakage can occur whenever the rings are not sealing correctly against the cylinder wall, the ring grooves are

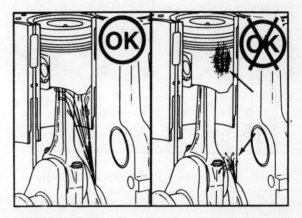

Fig 10.47   The effects of poorly maintained cooling, lubricating and air intake systems
Courtesy of Cummins Engine Co

worn allowing poor ring control or the ring gaps are too wide. Undue combustion gas leakage into the engine crankcase can over-pressurise the crankcase compartment, resulting in oil being blown out the crankcase breather or dip stick tube.

To perform a blow-by test, connect a U-tube water manometer to the engine breather, as shown in Fig 10.48, and run the engine throughout its speed and load range. Record the difference between the highest and lowest points on the manometer and refer to the service manual for the recommended crankcase pressure limits.

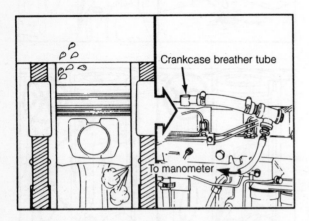

Fig 10.48 Checking for cylinder blow-by
Courtesy of Cummins Engine Co

Compression test

The compression test measures the pressure of the air in the cylinder during the compression stroke. If the pressure is below specifications then it could be due to air leaking past the rings or air leaking past the valves or even a blown cylinder head gasket. With the engine at operating temperature, remove all the injectors, then fit a compression gauge and adaptor as shown in Fig 10.49 into the injector hole. Turn the engine over with the starter motor and record the highest reading. This test is often referred to as a 'dry' test. Repeat the procedure for all the other cylinders. To determine if compression gas is leaking past the valves or the rings, pour a small amount of engine oil into the cylinder to be tested and repeat the compression test, as shown in Fig 10.50. This test is often referred to as a 'wet' test. If the reading remains the same, then the valves in the cylinder head are not sealing correctly, allowing compression gas to escape. If the compression pressure rises dramatically due to the oil improving the seal between the piston and cylinder, then the rings are not sealing in their ring grooves or against the cylinder wall. If two adjacent cylinders have similar low compression, then the problem is most likely a blown cylinder head gasket.

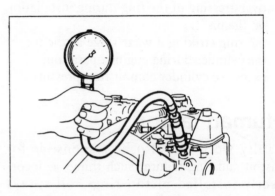

Fig 10.49 Test gauge used to check cylinder compression.

Compression tests can also be performed on running engines. To perform such a test, remove one injector and replace it with a test injector and pressure gauge. Run the engine at idle speed and record the compression pressure. Repeat the process to check the compression on all the other cylinders.

The compression pressures on a diesel engine can range between 2450 kPa and 3500 kPa. Compression pressure readings should be within 10 per cent of each other on multi-cylinder engines so as to avoid engine roughness and maintain even load carrying between cylinders.

Diagnosing the cause of engine problems and failures requires a thorough inspection of all the engine components, along with inspection and testing of the cooling, lubricating and air intake systems for correct operation.

If the cause of the problem is not found and rectified, then there is a strong possibility the same fault will occur again.

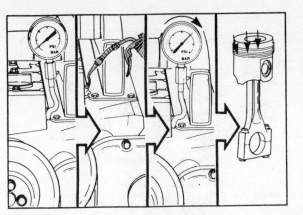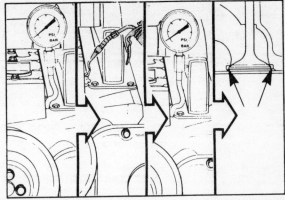

Fig 10.50   Compression testing to determine piston ring and valve sealing   *Courtesy of Cummins Engine Co*

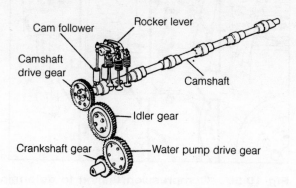

Fig 11.1 Valve train system components
Courtesy of Volvo

Timing Gears, Camshaft and Rocker Gear Assembly

Valve train components

The valve train in an engine is made up of timing gears, a camshaft, cam followers, push rods and rocker levers, as shown in Fig 11.1.

Valve train operation begins at the crankshaft, where the crankshaft timing gear turns the camshaft gear. As the camshaft is rotated, its cam lobes lift the cam followers and push rods which in turn operate the rocker levers. The rocker levers pivot on the rocker shaft and transfer the upward motion of the push rod to a downward motion of the valves.

Timing gears

Figure 11.2 shows the layout and size of the timing gears used on a conventional inline diesel engine. On four-stroke cycle engines, the crankshaft timing gear is small, as opposed to the camshaft gear which is double its size. In operation, the crankshaft gear rotates two revolutions for every one revolution of the camshaft gear. That is, the camshaft rotates at half the speed of the engine. The fuel injection pump, like the camshaft, also rotates at half engine speed. In the case of a two-stroke engine, the camshaft rotates at the same speed as the crankshaft.

Because of the size of some engines and the location of the camshaft, idler or intermediate gears are used to transfer the drive between the crankshaft and camshaft gears. Idler gears can also be used to drive the injection pump, water pump, oil pump and air compressor. Even though idler gears transfer drive to various areas in the front of the engine, they do not alter the ratio between the driving and driven gears. Idler gears can also be used to alter the direction of rotation of the driven gear.

Balance shafts are sometimes fitted to four-cylinder diesel engines above 2.5 litre

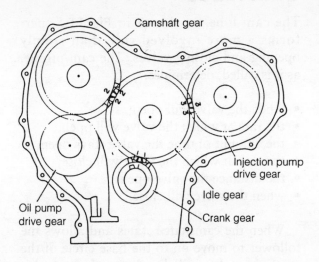

Fig 11.2   Timing gears on the front of a diesel engine

capacity and are driven by the timing gears at the front of the engine. These balance shaft drive gears are half the size of the crankshaft drive gear, making each balance shaft rotate at twice the speed of the crankshaft. In this way, the balance shaft weight is always in opposition to the upward movement of each pair of pistons during engine operation. A more in-depth explanation of why engine balancers are used and how they operate is provided in Chapter 9.

The timing gears on the front of the engine are provided with timing marks so that, during engine assembly, the camshaft, fuel injection pump and balance shafts (if fitted) are all timed correctly to the crankshaft and to each other.

Toothed drive belt

Some small automotive diesel engines use a toothed rubber belt to drive the camshaft and injection pump, as shown in Fig 11.3. As the camshaft on these engines is of the overhead design — that is, on top of or beside the valves — it would be expensive and bulky to use idler gears to transfer the drive from the crankshaft to the top of the engine. The toothed belt is an ideal drive arrangement, as it does not require lubrication and is quiet in operation. To prevent the timing belt from whipping and jumping the toothed pulleys during engine operation, a flat-faced pulley is used to tension the belt on its slack or non-drive side.

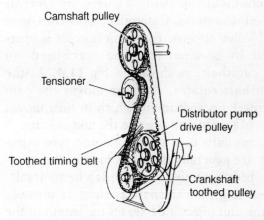

Fig 11.3   Toothed timing belt
Courtesy of AGPS

Camshaft

Camshafts can be cast from cast iron or alloy steel, consisting of nickel chromium and molybdenum. The camshaft runs the full length of the block and is usually mounted in plain bearings which are pressed into the engine crankcase. Camshafts can also be mounted in the cylinder head, whereby they run in the head material or in conventional bearing shells. Cams or lobes are positioned along the shaft which, when rotated, open and close the valves. As the cam lobes are exposed to heavy loading during operation, they are case hardened to ensure adequate service life for both the cam lobe and the follower. Case hardening of cam lobes can be achieved by various processes, one being **induction hardening**.

This type of hardening process uses electric current to pass through the cam lobe, heating it up to a high temperature. Then, by quenching the lobe in either water or oil, the outer surface of the cam is case hardened. Some camshafts have extra cams which are used to operate such components as the fuel feed pump and or individual fuel injection pumps mounted on the side of the cylinder block on an air-cooled diesel engine.

Another fuel injection system which utilises the engine camshaft is unit or mechanical injection, as used by Detroit Diesel, Cummins, Caterpillar, Dorman Diesel and Volvo engines. Each unit injector is operated by a separate lobe machined on the camshaft, as shown in Fig 11.4. As the camshaft rotates, the lobe moves the cam follower up and down, which in turn moves the rocker lever to operate the unit injector.

Camshafts used to operate unit type injectors are generally mounted high in the cylinder block or in the cylinder head itself. Mounting the camshaft as close as possible to the unit injector decreases the length of the pushrod, thereby reducing its deflection which is necessary if high injection pressures of 140 000 kPa are to be sustained during engine operation.

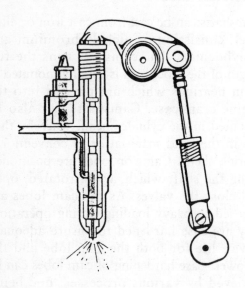

Fig 11.4   Camshaft used to operate a unit injector

Cam lobes

The cam lobe, as shown in Fig 11.5, performs a more involved role than simply opening and closing valves. The cam profile, as it is called, determines:

- when the valve will open;
- the rate at which the valve will open;
- the amount of time the valve stays open;
- the rate at which the valve will close;
- the distance the valve opens;
- when the valve will close.

When the camshaft rotates and allows the follower to move on to the base circle of the cam, the valve will be closed. It is at this point, when the follower is on the base circle of the cam, that the valve or tappet clearances are checked and adjusted if necessary. This corresponds to the end of the compression stroke and the beginning of the power stroke of the engine.

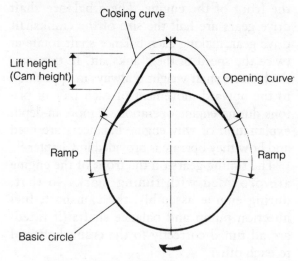

Fig 11.5   Cam lobe profile
Courtesy of Volvo

Cam followers

The three basic types of cam follower commonly used in diesel engines are the mushroom follower, the roller follower and

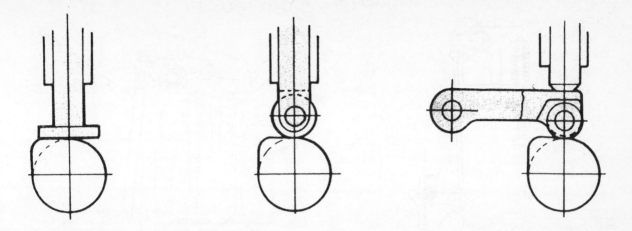

Fig 11.6 Various types of cam follower used in diesel engines

the hinged roller follower, as shown in Fig 11.6. These are all solid type cam followers as opposed to hydraulic type followers which are used extensively in modern petrol engines.

Mushroom followers

The mushroom follower is shaped in the form of an inverted T and has a large surface area on which to contact the cam lobe. This bottom face of the follower is generally machined with a slight convex radius: this, in conjunction with the follower being offset with the centre line of the cam lobe cause the follower

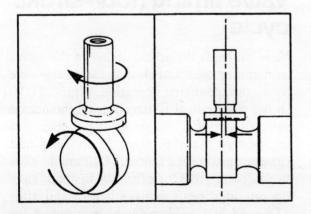

Fig 11.7 Cam follower offset to promote rotation
Courtesy of Cummins Engine Co

to rotate slowly during its up and down operation, as shown in Fig 11.7. As the follower is allowed to rotate, wear is evenly distributed across the face of the follower instead of in just one area, as would be the case if the follower did not rotate.

Roller followers

The roller follower, like the mushroom and flat followers, is housed in the cylinder block. The only difference is that a steel roller, instead of a flat pad, contacts the cam lobe surface.

The roller provides a rolling action instead of a rubbing action, which has the advantage of reducing friction as well as being able to open and close the valves faster and at the same time endure more severe running conditions, such as higher spring pressures, intermittent lubrication and high operating speeds.

Another type of roller follower design is the hinged roller that pivots off the side of the block and rests on top of the camshaft, as shown in Fig 11.8. In operation, the action of the cam lobe lifts the roller and pushrod as the follower lever pivots around its mounting shaft, which is attached to the side of the block.

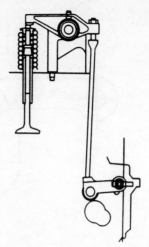

Fig 11.8   Hinged roller cam follower
Courtesy of Caterpillar Inc

Bridge or crosshead

Engines which have a four-valve cylinder head configuration that has two inlet and two exhaust valves use a bridge or crosshead to enable the rocker levers to push two valves open at the one time.

The bridge is constructed in a T shape and moves on a guide located in the cylinder head. The two ends of the bridge sit on top of the valves, as shown in Fig 11.9, and when the rocker pushes down on the centre of the bridge, two valves are moved down at once. The bridge is provided with an adjusting screw located against one of the valve stems. This screw enables the bridge to be adjusted central with its guide and the valves ensuring that valve travel will be equalised during downward movement of the valve bridge. The bridge is prevented from rotating on its guide by means of a recess machined into the bridge valve stem contact face which locates over one of the valve stems

The Cummins Engine Company has released a valve bridge which does not require the use of an adjusting screw or centre guide to locate it between the two valves. The guideless type bridge sits on top of the valvestems and has recesses on its underside so as to locate it above each valve stem.

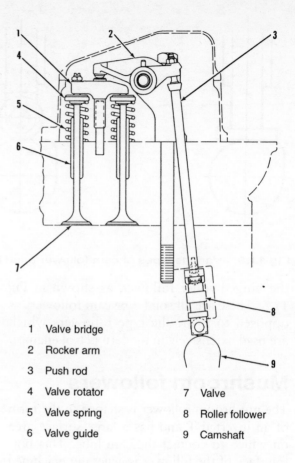

1 Valve bridge	
2 Rocker arm	
3 Push rod	
4 Valve rotator	7 Valve
5 Valve spring	8 Roller follower
6 Valve guide	9 Camshaft

Fig 11.9   Valve bridge and rocker gear assembly
Courtesy of Caterpillar Inc

Valve timing (four-stroke cycle)

Valve timing is the actual timing of the valves so that they open and close at the precise time for optimum engine operation. Figure 11.10 shows a graphical illustration of the actual valve timing of a four-stroke diesel engine. It can be seen that the valves do not open and close at the top dead centre (TDC) and bottom dead centre (BDC) positions. Instead, they operate at various degrees before and after TDC and BDC. This helps to compensate for the inherent shortcomings of the piston engine design, such as decreasing volumetric efficiency as engine speed increases, inefficient cylinder scavenging and exhaust pollution.

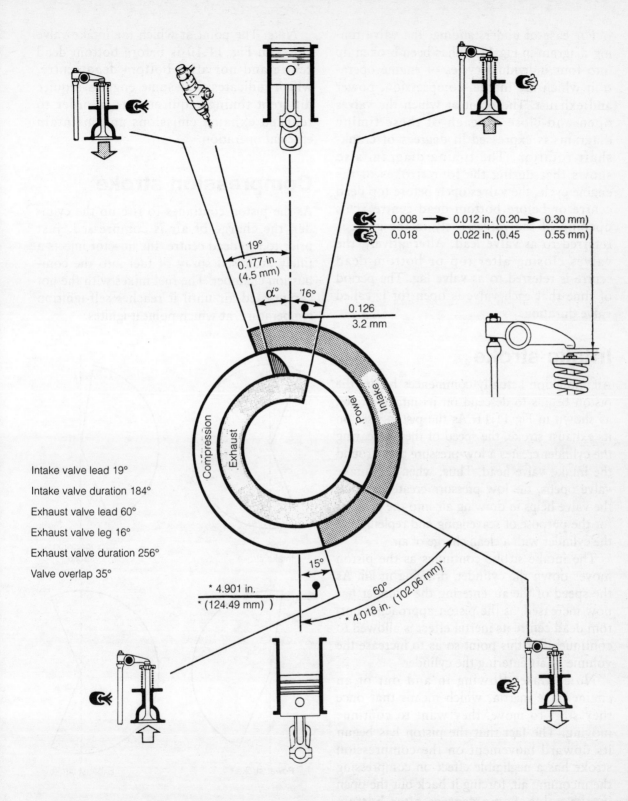

Intake valve lead 19°

Intake valve duration 184°

Exhaust valve lead 60°

Exhaust valve leg 16°

Exhaust valve duration 256°

Valve overlap 35°

Fig 11.10   Valve timing diagram for a right-hand rotation four-stroke cycle diesel engine
Courtesy of Mack Trucks Inc

For ease of understanding, the valve timing diagram in Fig 11.10 has been broken up into four individual cycles of engine operation which are intake, compression, power and exhaust. The point at which the valves open and close on each of these timing diagrams is expressed in degrees of crankshaft rotation. The timing diagram also shows that during the four strokes of the engine cycle, the valves open before top dead centre or before bottom dead centre. This opening of the valves early in the cycle is referred to·as **valve lead**. Alternatively, the valves closing after top or bottom dead centre is referred to as **valve lag**. The period of time that each valve is open for is called **valve duration**.

Intake stroke

Air induction actually commences before the piston begins to descend on its intake stroke, as shown in Fig 11.11. As the piston rises on its exhaust stroke, the speed of the gas leaving the cylinder creates a low-pressure area around the intake valve head. Thus, when the intake valve opens, the low pressure created around the valve helps in drawing air into the cylinder for the purpose of scavenging and replenishing the cylinder with a clean charge of air.

The intake stroke continues as the piston moves down the cylinder, drawing in air. As the speed of the air entering the cylinder has now increased, as the piston approaches bottom dead centre its inertia effect is allowed to continue after this point so as to increase the volume of air entering the cylinder.

Note: Gases flowing in and out of an engine have inertia, which means that once they start to move, they want to continue moving. The fact that the piston has begun its upward movement on the compression stroke has a negligible effect on compressing the incoming air, forcing it back out the open intake valve. Some degrees after bottom dead centre, the intake valve closes and compression begins.

Note: The point at which the intake valve closes in Fig 11.10 is before bottom dead centre and not after bottom dead centre, which indicates that some engines require different timing requirements in order to reduced exhaust emissions and maintain efficient operation.

Compression stroke

As the piston continues to rise up the cylinder, the charge of air is compressed. Just prior to top dead centre, the injector injects a finely atomised spray of fuel into the combustion chamber. The fuel mixes with the hot compressed air until it reaches self-ignition temperature, at which point it ignites.

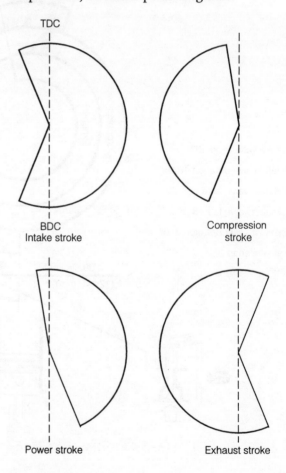

Fig 11.11 Individual strokes of a four-stroke cycle valve timing diagram for a right-hand rotation engine

Power stroke

As the fuel and air begin to combust, the piston is forced down the cylinder on its power stroke. As the piston moves approximately three-quarters of the way down the stroke, combustion pressure acting on top of the piston decreases. At this point the exhaust valve opens. As there is still combustion pressure in the cylinder, the opening of the exhaust valve allows the combusted gas to escape from the cylinder and into the exhaust manifold.

Note: Although there is still combustion pressure in the cylinder as the exhaust valve opens, this pressure is now somewhat reduced and is no longer useful in forcing the piston down the cylinder.

This otherwise wasted gas pressure is now beneficial in ensuring a quick exit of the spent combustion gas from the cylinder.

Exhaust stroke

As the expulsion of the exhaust gas from the cylinder has already begun during the final stages of the power stroke, the piston then moves up the cylinder, forcing out the remainder of the spent gas charge. The exhaust valve remains open after top dead centre so as to increase the time available to expel all the exhaust gas. During the latter part of the exhaust stroke and the early stages of the intake stroke, both the exhaust and intake valves are open together for a short period of time. This is called **valve overlap** and is beneficial in scavenging of the cylinder prior to the start of the next intake stroke. Figure 11.10 shows that the inlet and exhaust valves are both open together for a period of 19° before top dead centre (BTDC) and 16° after top dead centre (ATDC), making a total valve overlap of 35°.

Valve timing (two-stroke cycle)

The two-stroke diesel engine manufactured by the Detroit Diesel Corporation employs a set of intake or tangential ports located around the centre of the cylinder liner, with conventional pushrod-operated poppet type exhaust valves in the cylinder head.

With reference to Fig 11.12, the operation of the two-stroke cycle diesel engine is as follows. Injection of the fuel takes place before top dead centre, which is immediately followed by combustion which forces the piston down on its power stroke. As the piston travels approximately halfway down the cylinder, the exhaust valves (4 off) open, expelling the pressurised gas charge from the cylinder. As the piston continues to move down the cylinder, the top of the piston uncovers the tangential intake ports in the cylinder liner. This allows the entry of low pressure air to flow in a swirling motion from the air box into the cylinder so as to scavenge it. Scavenging continues as both the intake ports and the exhaust valves remain open while the piston travels to the bottom of its stroke and begins to rise up the cylinder again. At 48° after bottom dead centre, the rising piston closes off the intake ports. With the exhaust valves still open for another 7° of crankshaft rotation, the inertia effect of the gas is allowed to continue in order to try to remove the last traces of exhaust gas. The piston continues up the cylinder and begins compressing the new air charge. At

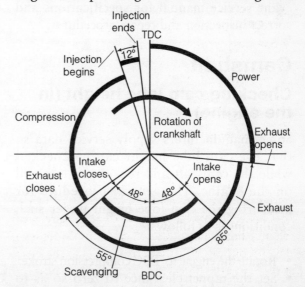

Fig 11.12   Valve timing diagram for a two-stroke cycle diesel engine

ing the new air charge. At approximately 20° before top dead centre, injection takes place and the cycle repeats itself. Two strokes of the piston have taken place to complete the cycle in one revolution of the crankshaft.

It is interesting to note that the two-stroke engine operating on the two-stroke cycle discussed above is considered to be a naturally aspirated engine. Even though the engine has a blower which forces air into the cylinders, this air is primarily used for scavenging. This statement is backed up by the fact that the valve timing diagram shows the intake ports are closed before the exhaust valves, thereby ensuring the cylinder is only charged with air at approximately atmospheric pressure or slightly above it. Hence the name blower and not supercharger is given to the engine driven scavenge pump.

Valve train service

In order to make valve train servicing more meaningful, the inspection and repair procedures used in conjunction with examples of dimensions, clearances and tolerances represent only general overhaul procedures and not the actual procedures for all engines. Therefore, always refer to the relevant service manual for specifications and correct inspection and repair procedures.

Camshaft

Checking cam lobe height (in the engine)

Some manufacturers supply service data so that the cam lobe height can be checked while the camshaft and rocker gear are still on the engine. The general procedure for measuring the cam lobe height under such conditions is as follows:

- Rotate the engine to TDC compression stroke.
- Set the tappet clearance to zero so as to eliminate any possible tappet wear.
- Mount a dial gauge on top of either the

inlet or exhaust valve spring collet retainer, as shown in Fig 11.13. Zero the dial gauge then rotate the engine in the direction of rotation until the dial reaches a maximum reading, then starts turning in reverse. Measure the distance that the valve travels then refer to the service manual for the correct specifications.

- Repeat the above procedure for checking all the other cam lobes.
- Re-set the valve clearances.

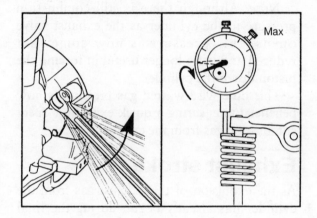

Fig 11.13 Checking cam lobe height
Courtesy of Cummins Engine Co

An alternative method of checking individual cam lobe height is to mount a dial gauge directly above the cam follower, as shown in Fig 11.14. With the dial gauge positioned on top of the pushrod the camshaft is rotated until the cam follower is on the base circle of the cam lobe. At this point the dial gauge is set to zero. The camshaft is then rotated until the lobe lifts the pushrod and the highest dial gauge reading is recorded. This reading is then checked against specification to determine cam lobe wear.

Before the camshaft is removed from the cylinder block, mount a dial gauge on to the timing gear housing and measure the camshaft gear backlash as shown in Fig 11.15. If the backlash is beyond the allowable limits, then the camshaft gear and/or crankshaft gear may have to be replaced.

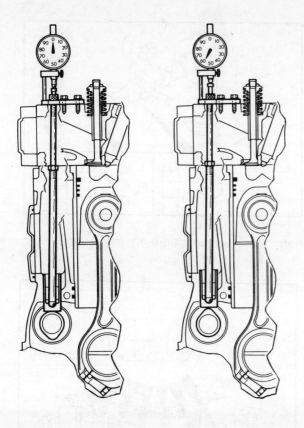

Fig 11.14 Checking cam lobe height with the camshaft installed in the engine
Courtesy of Volvo

Camshaft removal and inspection

To remove the camshaft from the engine, first take out the cam followers then unbolt and withdraw the timing cover from the front of the engine. If mushroom-type cam followers are used, then they will have to be held up off the cam lobe during camshaft removal. Unbolt the camshaft thrust retainer plate and remove the camshaft, being careful not to damage the camshaft bearings as the camshaft is being removed. In engines using mushroom cam followers, the camshaft has to be removed from the block in order to allow access to the cam followers.

Inspect and measure the camshaft and drive gear as follows:

- Check the camshaft for run-out as shown in Fig 11.16.
- Examine the drive gear for damaged or worn teeth.
- Check the cam bearing journals for scoring or wear and measure the journal diameters for ovality and taper as shown in Fig 11.17.
- Check the cam lobe surfaces for pitting, scoring or wear and measure the cam lobe height as shown in Fig 11.17.
- Measure the camshaft thrust plate, drive gear and spigot for wear as shown in Fig 11.18.
- Visually inspect the camshaft drive gear and camshaft for any signs of discolouration.

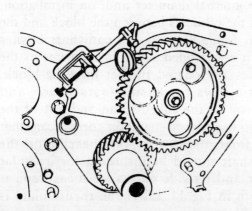

Fig 11.15 Measuring camshaft gear backlash

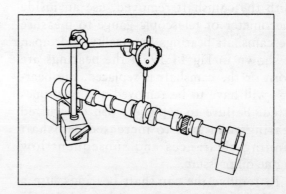

Fig 11.16 Checking camshaft for runout
Courtesy of Mitsubishi

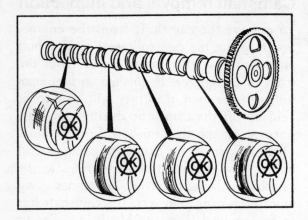

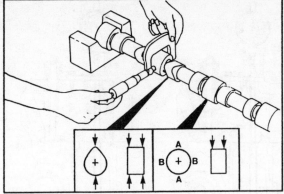

Fig 11.17 Inspecting and measuring the camshaft *Courtesy of Cummins Engine Co*

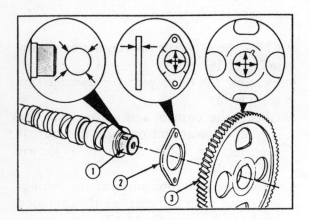

Fig 11.18 Measuring camshaft thrust plate and drive spigot assembly
Courtesy of Cummins Engine Co

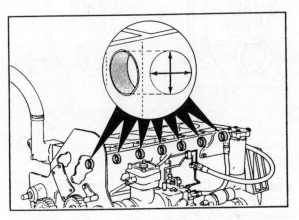

Fig 11.19 How to measure camshaft bearings for wear
Courtesy of Cummins Engine Co

Camshaft bearings

With the camshaft removed, use an inside micrometer or telescopic gauge to measure the camshaft bearings for ovality and taper, as shown in Fig 11.19. If the bearings are worn or the camshaft is replaced, the bearings will have to be removed and new ones fitted. Failure to replace worn or scuffed bearings can lead to increased camshaft running clearances and subsequent low engine oil pressure.

To remove the camshaft bearings, use a camshaft bush removing tool, as shown in Fig 11.21, to press out the old bushes and install the new ones. Prior to installing the new bushes, check that all the bushes are the same internal diameter and, on installation, align the oil holes between the block and the bush. Some engines use camshaft bushes which are stepped down in diameter as the bushes are located further into the block. This allows for easier installation and removal of the camshaft in and out of the block. In order to maintain correct camshaft end float, the thrust plate bearing on the camshaft should be inspected for irregular wear and its side clearance measured, as shown in Fig 11.22. If the thrust plate is worn beyond specifications, the cam gear will have to be pressed off the camshaft and a new thrust plate installed.

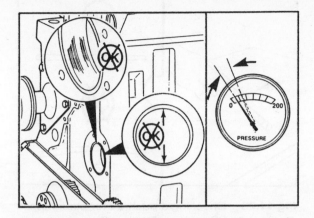

Fig 11.20 Low engine oil pressure due to worn camshaft bearings
Courtesy of Cummins Engine Co

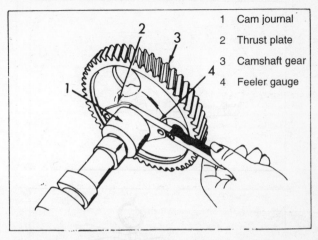

1 Cam journal
2 Thrust plate
3 Camshaft gear
4 Feeler gauge

Fig 11.22 Measuring camshaft thrust plate wear

Cam followers

Cam followers must be checked for wear on their face and stem. The face of the cam follower is slightly convex in shape and if any followers have worn this surface flat or hollow then they should be replaced. Measure the follower stem and its corresponding bore for wear as shown in Fig 11.24.

Roller cam followers should be dismantled and checked for roller and bushing wear. If

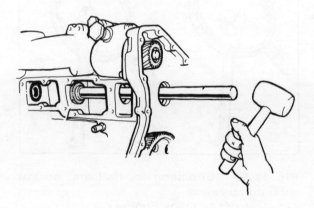

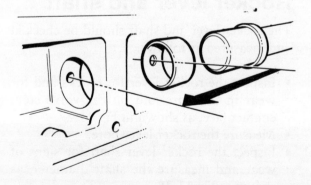

Fig 11.21 Removing and installing camshaft bearings
Courtesy of Volvo

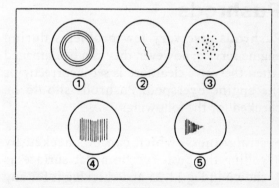

1 Normal contact
2 Cracking
3 Pitting
4 Irregular contact
5 Irregular contact

Fig 11.23 Cam follower wear evaluation

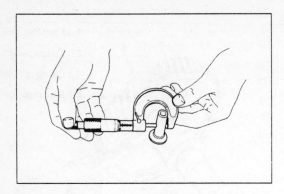

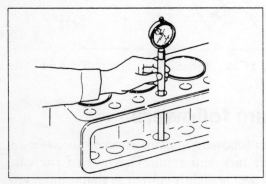

Fig 11.24   Measuring cam follower and its bore
Courtesy of Mitsubishi

the bushing or roller shows signs of wear or pitting, then the follower should be replaced.

Pushrods

Pushrods give very few problems during engine service; however, they can be damaged when the valve clearance is set incorrectly or the engine oversped. Pushrods should be checked for the following:

- straightness, which can be checked by rolling the push rod on a flat surface as shown in Fig 11.25 and checking it for any sign of bending. If the pushrod is bent it should be straightened or replaced, depending on the manufacturer's recommendations;
- cracking around the ball socket and ball end. Pushrods with cracks similar to that in Fig 11.26 must be replaced.

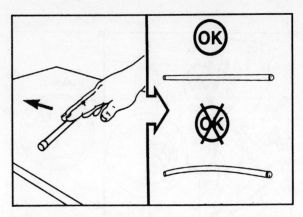

Fig 11.25   Checking a pushrod for straightness
Courtesy of Cummins Engine Co

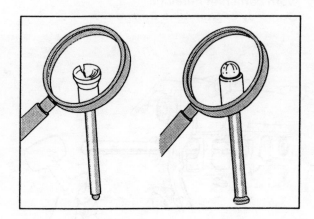

Fig 11.26   Checking for ball and socket wear on pushrods
Courtesy of Cummins Engine Co

Rocker lever and shaft

The rocker lever and shaft should be checked and measured as follows:

- Inspect the rocker lever for cracks and for wear in the bore and on the valve stem contact face, as shown in Fig 11.27.
- Measure the rocker lever bore.
- Inspect the rocker lever shaft for signs of wear and measure the shaft diameter, as shown in Fig 11.28.

If the rocker to valve stem face is worn, it can be ground on a valve refacing machine so as to restore its smooth curved surface.

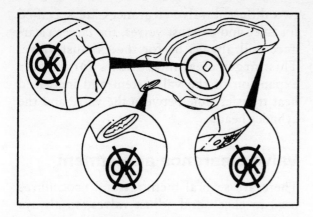

Fig 11.27 Inspecting the rocker lever for cracks and wear
Courtesy of Cummins Engine Co

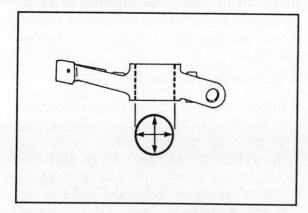

Fig 11.28 Measuring the rocker lever and shaft
Courtesy of Cummins Engine Co

Bridge or crosshead

Inspect and measure the bridge or crosshead for the following:

- cracks;
- the inside diameter of the bridge guide bore;
- the rocker lever contact face;
- the valve stem contact face.
- the adjusting screw and threads in the bridge for wear or damage;
- the bridge guide post in the cylinder head for wear and damage.

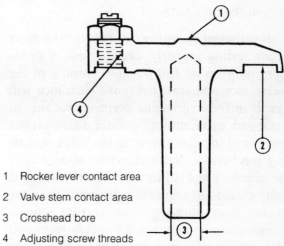

1 Rocker lever contact area
2 Valve stem contact area
3 Crosshead bore
4 Adjusting screw threads

Fig 11.29 Checking a crosshead or bridge for wear
Courtesy of Cummins Engine Co

Camshaft installation

After the camshaft and its bearings have been inspected, the camshaft can be fitted to the engine. Prior to installing the camshaft, turn the crankshaft and camshaft timing gears until the timing marks on both gear teeth align. At this point, install the camshaft into the block and mesh the two gears together, taking note that the timing marks are correctly aligned. Secure the camshaft thrust plate in position then check the camshaft gear backlash as shown previously. Depending on the type of cam followers used, they may have to be installed before or after the camshaft is installed.

Valve clearance

Valve clearance adjustment refers to the adjustment or setting of the clearance between the valve rocker lever and its corresponding valve stem. It can also be referred to as valve tappet or valve lash adjustment.

Valve clearance is necessary for a number of reasons:

- It allows for expansion of the valve stem and rocker assembly.
- It ensures that the valve is fully seated for efficient heat transfer between the valve and the cylinder head.

Insufficient clearance can prevent the valve from seating properly, causing loss of cylinder compression and possible burning of the valve face and seat. Excessive clearance will result in reduced engine performance due to retarded valve timing, greater valve tappet noise and increased wear to the valve operating mechanism. Valve clearance should only be checked and adjusted when the valve is fully closed. To adjust the clearance, turn the rocker lever adjusting screw so that a feeler gauge can pass between the rocker lever and the corresponding valve stem with a slight drag as shown in Fig 11.30.

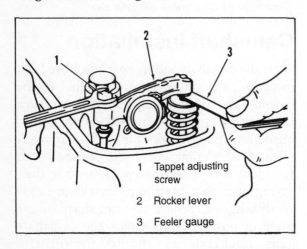

1	Tappet adjusting screw
2	Rocker lever
3	Feeler gauge

Fig 11.30 Checking and adjusting tappet clearance

Some manufacturers specify that the valve clearance should be checked when the engine is at operating temperature, while others recommend that the valve clearances be checked when the engine is cold. Whenever

two different valve clearances are specified for inlet and exhaust valves, the larger clearance will always be for the exhaust valve. This larger clearance allows for greater expansion of the valve stem and increased heat transfer time between the valve and the cylinder head.

Valve clearance adjustment

There are several methods and procedures used to check and adjust valves, so always refer to the service manual for the recommended procedure. In the absence of a valve adjustment procedure, the following general description as to how to adjust valve clearances can be used. The sequence of valve adjustment for an in-line six-cylinder engine with a firing order of 1–5–3–6–2–4 is as follows:

To check the valves on no. 1 cylinder:

- Rotate the engine in the correct direction of rotation (DOR) until the rocker levers on no. 6 cylinder are 'rocking' — that is, the valves are in the overlap position (exhaust just closing, inlet just opening).
- The valves on no. 1 cylinder will now be closed as the piston is on TDC compression stroke. To verify that the valves are closed, the rocker levers will be free to move up and down slightly. Check the valve clearance with a feeler gauge and adjust if necessary.

To check the valves on no. 5 cylinder:

- Continue to rotate the engine until the rocker levers on no. 2 cylinder are 'rocking'.
- Check the valve clearance on no. 5 cylinder and adjust if necessary.

To check the valves on no. 3 cylinder:

- Rotate the engine until the rocker levers on no. 4 cylinder are 'rocking'.
- Check the valve clearance on no. 3 cylinder and adjust if necessary.

To check the valves on no. 6 cylinder:

- Rotate the engine until the rocker levers on no. 1 cylinder are 'rocking'.
- Check the valve clearance on no. 6 cylinder and adjust if necessary.

To check the valves on no. 2 cylinder:

- Rotate the engine until the rocker levers on no. 5 cylinder are 'rocking'.
- Check the valve clearance on no. 2 cylinder and adjust if necessary.

To check the valves on no. 4 cylinder:

- Rotate the engine until the rocker levers on no. 3 cylinder are 'rocking'.
- Check the valve clearance on no. 4 cylinder and adjust if necessary.

The above description may be abbreviated as follows:

TDC compression	TDC valves 'rocking'	Adjust valves
Cylinder 1	Cylinder 6	Cylinder 1
Cylinder 5	Cylinder 2	Cylinder 5
Cylinder 3	Cylinder 4	Cylinder 3
Cylinder 6	Cylinder 1	Cylinder 6
Cylinder 2	Cylinder 5	Cylinder 2
Cylinder 4	Cylinder 3	Cylinder 4

Valve adjustment for a single-cylinder four-stroke engine

To adjust the valves on a single-cylinder engine, rotate the engine in the correct direction of rotation until both the intake and exhaust rocker levers are 'rocking' (valve overlap). With the piston now at TDC, locate the top dead centre timing position on the flywheel. Rotate the engine one complete revolution and realign the top centre timing marks. The piston in now on TDC compression stroke. Check and, if necessary, adjust both the valves.

This same procedure can also be used to adjust the valves on each individual cylinder for any multi-cylinder engine.

Valve adjustment on overhead camshaft engines

Valve clearance adjustment on engines with an overhead camshaft can be adjusted by either rocker lever adjusting screws or by adjusting shims or spacers on top of the valve stem.

Valve adjustment on 'V' type engines

To adjust the valves on 'V' type engines, first establish on which side of the engine no. 1 cylinder is located. Then, with the aid of a suitable turning device, rotate the engine crankshaft until the valves rock on no. 1 cylinder and establish a top centre position. At this point, timing marks on the crankshaft pulley or flywheel will be aligned. Further rotate the engine one complete revolution and again align the timing marks. This will now place no. 1 piston on TDC compression.

Check and adjust the valves if necessary. Continue to rotate the engine until the next piston in the cylinder firing order is on TDC compression. This can be verified by the fact that both rocker levers are loose and the crankshaft timing marks align. Continue the sequence in order of cylinder firing until all the valves are checked and, if necessary, adjusted.

Valve bridge or crosshead adjustment

The valve bridge or crosshead is designed to push two valves down simultaneously via the action of a single rocker lever. The bridge is provided with an adjusting screw which permits it to sit evenly on the valve stem and at the same time sit central with its guide post.

Depending on the manufacturer, the bridge can be adjusted with or without the rocker

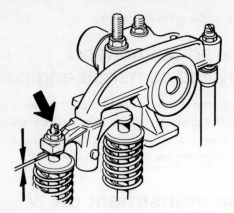

Bridge adjusting screw locked off prior to adjusting the bridge

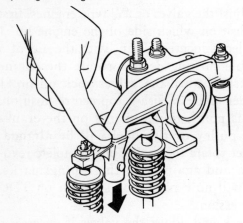

Push the bridge down till it hits on the valve stem

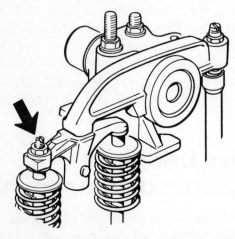

With the bridge still held down, turn the adjusting screw till it just touches the valve stem then turn it down a further eighth to one quarter turn so as to take up the end slack when the lock nut is tightened

Fig 11.31 Valve bridge or crosshead adjustment
Courtesy of Volvo

levers in place. Detroit Diesel require that the bridge must be removed from the head so that it can be held in a vice so as to loosen and retighten the adjusting screw locknut before and after adjustment. This eliminates the possibility of the bridge post being broken or bent as the bridge adjusting screw locknut is loosened while the bridge is installed on the guide post in the head. Other companies usually do the adjustment with the bridge in place.

With the bridge adjusting screw backed off and the bridge sitting in place on top of the valves, push down centrally on the bridge, as shown in Fig 11.31. Screw the adjusting screw down until it just touches the valve stem, turn the screw an additional one-eighth to one-quarter of a turn so as to take up the slack in the screw thread. Tighten the adjusting screw locknut.

An alternative method of checking bridge adjustment is to insert feeler gauges of equal dimension between each valve stem and the bridge. By applying moderate force to the centre of the bridge, equal 'drag' should be felt on both feeler gauges. If the drag is unequal, adjust the bridge adjusting screw until such time as it is equal on both feeler gauges. Once the valve bridges are adjusted, the valve clearances can be adjusted with the aid of a feeler gauge, as shown in Fig 11.32.

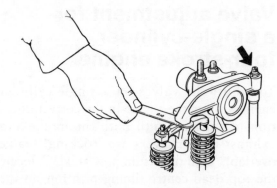

Fig 11.32 Checking and adjusting valve clearance on engines using valve bridges
Courtesy of Volvo

Note: Valve bridge adjustment should always be carried out prior to checking valve rocker clearance.

Timing belt

A number of small automotive diesel engines are using a timing belt to drive the overhead camshaft, the fuel injection pump and other engine accessories. The belt is made of a composite rubber material with a toothed pattern on its inside running surface.

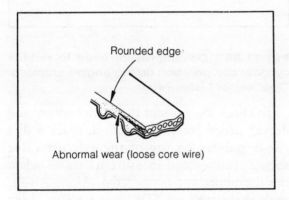

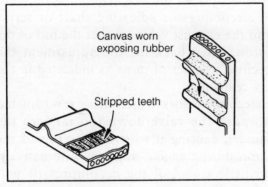

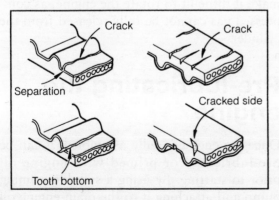

Fig 11.33   Inspecting diesel engine timing belt

During engine operation, the belt wears, and at specified service internals it must be replaced. The majority of timing belts require changing at 100 000 km. However, if the belt shows signs of abnormal wear or deterioration, as shown in Fig 11.33, then it should be replaced earlier than the recommended change interval. Failure to change the timing belt at the correct service interval may result in the belt breaking, which will allow the piston to strike the valves, causing major internal engine damage.

A general procedure for changing a timing belt is as follows:

- Remove all the covers from around the timing belt area.
- Rotate the engine crankshaft and align the timing marks for the crankshaft, the camshaft and the injection pump.
- Release the belt tensioner mounting bolts and pull the tensioner away from the belt.
- Remove the belt.
- Fit the new belt to the pulleys, making sure the timing marks are still aligned (see Fig 11.34). If the old belt is not due for replacement and is to be reinstalled, make sure it runs in the same direction as before.
- Allow the tensioner to tension the belt by means of its tensioning spring. *Note:* The tensioner spring is designed to place the correct amount of tension on the belt, so do not overtension the belt by forcing the tensioner with a lever. An overtensioned timing belt can place undue stress on the fuel injection pump drive shaft bearing, possibly causing it to seize during engine operation.
- With spring tension being applied to the tensioner pulley, rotate the engine two revolutions so as to remove all the slack out of the belt.
- Recheck the timing mark alignment then secure the tensioner in place. If incorrect, repeat the above procedure.
- Refit the timing belt cover/s.

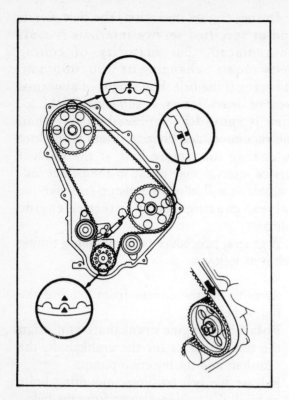

Fig 11.34 Timing belt installed with timing marks correctly aligned
Courtesy of Toyota Motor Corp

Engine decompressor adjustment

Most manual-start air-cooled diesel engines of one to three cylinders configuration use a valve decompressor to unseat the exhaust valves for ease of engine rotation during starting.

Lifting the exhaust valve off its seat releases the compressed air from the cylinder during the compression stroke, thereby allowing the engine to be easily rotated by hand cranking. The decompressor lever is mounted on the rocker cover housing, with a separate lever usually being used for each cylinder.

An easy way of starting a multi-cylinder engine is to release the decompressor levers one at a time during the cranking process. In this way, as the first cylinder starts to fire, it will assist in rotating the engine to attain the necessary speed for ignition of the remaining cylinder/s.

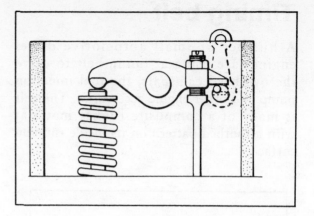

Fig 11.35 Decompressor used to reduce cylinder compression during engine cranking
Courtesy of Lister Petter

To check the amount the valve is depressed during decompressor operation, place a dial gauge pointer on top of the exhaust valve spring retainer and measure its travel when the decompressor is operated. Alternatively, with the piston on TDC compression, turn the decompressor adjusting shaft or screw until the exhaust valve touches the top of the piston. Then back off the adjustment the specified number of turns as indicated in the service manual.

Decompressors which are over-adjusted can push the valve down too far into the cylinder, causing it to strike the top of the piston during engine rotation. Alternatively, too little travel of the decompressor will make it difficult to rotate the engine, as compressed gas cannot be fully released from the cylinder.

Pre-lubricating the engine

Once the engine is fully assembled, it can be pre-lubricated or primed with engine oil prior to starting. By using a suitable priming pump and attaching it to the main engine oil gallery, as shown in Fig 11.36, lubricating oil can be pumped through all the oil passages

Fig 11.36   Pressurised oil reservoir being used to pre-lubricate an overhauled engine prior to running the engine
Courtesy of Caterpillar Inc

and oil filters in the engine. Pre-lubricating the engine in this way ensures that on initial start up there is an immediate supply of oil to all essential moving components. Failure to pressure lubricate an overhauled engine can result in engine damage on initial start up. When an overhauled engine is started without pressure lubrication, there is a short delay before the oil reaches the parts. This delay can be enough to cause damage to the crankshaft bearings.

Engine 'run-in'

After an engine has been overhauled, it should then be 'run-in'. This procedure is necessary to allow the new parts in the engine to bed-in or wear together. This procedure also makes it possible to check for leaks and correct pressures and temperatures, and if necessary make adjustments.

A detailed description of engine run-in procedures and engine testing can be found in Chapter 21.

- reduce friction to an absoulte minimum, with the aid of a suitable lubricant;
- keep parts in alignment;
- reduce maintenance costs. It is less expensive to replace the bearing rather than replace a whole shaft or housing.

Principal classes of bearing

There are two principal classes of bearing in common use. They are:

- plain bearings; and
- ball and rolling contact bearings.

Within these two principal classes of bearing, there are many different types of construction used. The type of bearing selected for a particular application depends upon a number of things, one of which is the type of load which will be applied to it.

Types of load applied to bearings

The load on a bearing comes from internal and external forces acting on a shaft. This load can act on, or be applied to, a shaft as:

- a radial load;
- a thrust load;
- a radial–thrust load, which is a combination of the first two types.

12
Bearings

Purpose of a bearing

A bearing is a part of a mechanism which supports and guides a moving part. By far the commonest type of bearing is that used to support a rotating shaft.

The functions of a bearing are to:

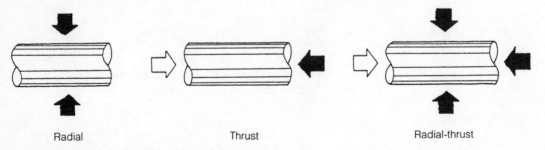

Radial　　　　　　Thrust　　　　　　Radial-thrust

Fig 12.1 Types of load applied to shafts and bearings

Plain bearings

In plain bearings the fundamental action is one of sliding friction between the two mating surfaces. The bearing is constructed so that it has a considerably softer surface than the shaft or journal it is to support, therefore making it the first and least expensive component to wear out.

The plain bearing has an advantages over other types of bearings in that it has a large surface area, which provides rigid shaft support and at the same time is capable of carrying heavy loads.

The main disadvantage of a plain bearing is that, owing to its large contact area, it has greater frictional resistance than ball or roller bearings. However, this unwanted resistance can be reduced considerably by providing constant lubrication to the bearing surface.

There are two types of plain bearing used in engines:

- bushes; and
- split bearings.

Bushes

The simplest type of bearing consists of a plain hole in which a shaft rotates. The bush serves the purpose of providing a suitable combination of materials to minimise friction and wear and also provides a simple and inexpensive way of repairing a worn or damaged bearing.

Types of bush

- **Plain bush.** Used to support a shaft where radial loads only are carried — that is, loads acting at right angles to the shaft centreline.
- **Flanged bush.** Used to support a shaft where both radial and axial loads are encountered. The flange, in conjunction with a collar or shoulder on the shaft, will resist axial load in one direction.

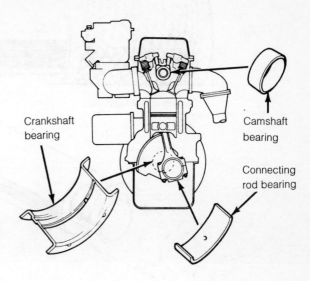

Fig 12.2 Various types of plain bearings used in diesel engines

Split bearings

These are more commonly referred to as bearing shells. Split bearings are made in two halves, and bolted together for convenience of installation. They are commonly used to

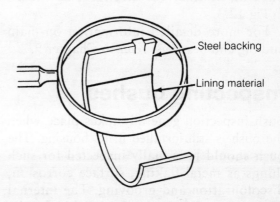

Fig 12.3 Crankshaft bearing construction

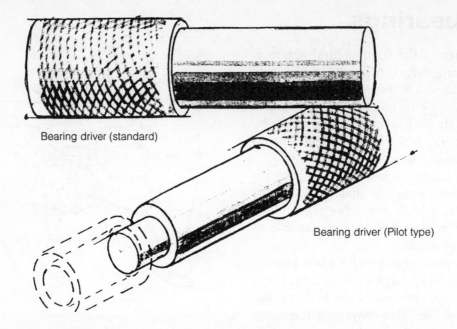

Bearing driver (standard)

Bearing driver (Pilot type)

Fig 12.4   Bearing driver tools used to remove and install bearing bushes

support engine crankshafts and the big ends of the piston connecting rods. Bearing shells are sold in pairs for easy replacement and are precision finished to exact size ready to fit into place in the bearing housing. Big end and main bearing shells have to combine softness with strength. For this reason, a bearing shell consists of a layer of relatively soft anti-friction material bonded on to the surface of a semi-circular shaped backing or liner for strength, as shown in Fig 12.3.

For more detailed information on main and big end bearings, refer to Chapter 9.

Inspecting bushes

Bush inspection generally takes place when the bush is still installed in its housing. The bush should be visually inspected for such things as metal flaking, surface corrosion, discolouration and grooving. The internal dimensions of the bush should also be checked so as to determine whether or not the bush is worn. Finally, check the bush to see that it is still a firm fit in its housing and that it has not spun in the housing during engine operation.

Removal and refitting of bushes

The way the bush is installed into the housing will determine the type of removal procedure used. A bush which is fitted into a bore which is blanked off or blind at one end will need to be reduced in diameter so as to eliminate the tight fit between the bush and the housing. This can be achieved by cutting through the wall of the bush with a chisel or hacksaw blade along its axis line until such time as the bush is relieved in its bore and can be pulled out. *Caution!* Exercise extreme care when cutting the wall of the bush so as not to cut through the bush and damage the housing bore. Removal of a bush from a bore which is open at both ends is somewhat easier in that the bush can be driven from the housing by means of a bush driving tool, as shown in Fig 12.4. This same tool can be used as a guide and press anvil to refit the new bush.

Ball and roller contact bearings

Ball and roller bearings are a very diversified product made in a great variety of types, each with many variations of design. The three basic types, from which all other variations will be found to originate, are the single row ball bearing, the single row roller bearing and the taper roller bearing, as shown in Fig 12.5.

Deep groove ball bearing

The basic ball bearing is known as the deep groove type. Deep groove raceways are provided in each ring so as to give the balls a contact in line with the bearing axis (line drawn through points of contact of ball and races). This type of bearing is the most widely used because of its versatility. Designed primarily to handle radial loads, it can accept an almost equal amount of thrust load in either direction, in combination with the radial load.

Cylindrical roller bearings

Roller bearings have greater load-carrying capacity than ball bearings of the same external dimensions and are suitable for carrying radial loads only. The type shown in Fig 12.5 is a floating bearing in which the cylindrical rollers run between a ribbed inner ring and plain outer ring.

Taper roller bearings

In this type of bearing the contact surfaces of the rolling elements are conical or cone shaped. When used in pairs, these bearings will carry both radial and axial loads and can be set up with a slight amount of preload or shaft end play, depending on the application. A single tapered roller bearing can only deal with thrust in one direction, hence they are usually used in pairs.

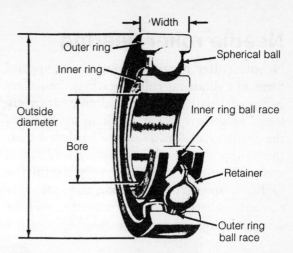

BALL BEARING

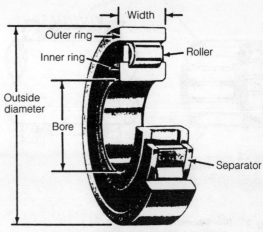

CYLINDRICAL ROLLER BEARING

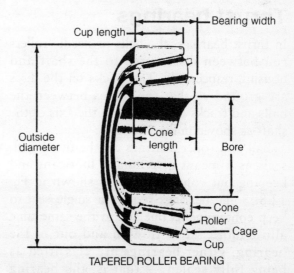

TAPERED ROLLER BEARING

Fig 12.5   Ball and roller contact bearings
Courtesy of Federal-Mogul

Needle roller bearing

Needle roller bearings comprise a special form of cylindrical roller bearing, the rollers being of small diameter and comparatively long, as shown in Fig 12.6. In many cases the needles run directly on the hardened shaft they support, thereby requiring less radial space. These bearings are very useful for high/low speeds or oscillating motions, particularly where the load fluctuates, such as on connecting rod bearings.

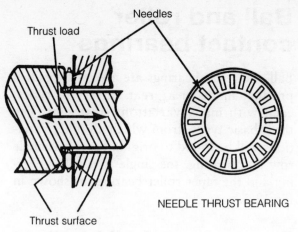

NEEDLE THRUST BEARING

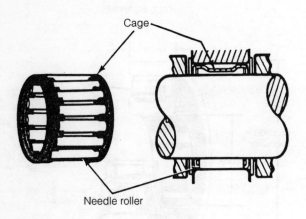

Fig 12.6   Needle roller bearing
Courtesy of Federal-Mogul

Fig 12.7   Needle roller thrust bearing
Courtesy of Federal-Mogul

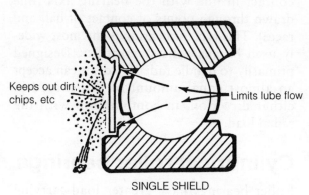

SINGLE SHIELD

Thrust bearings

In thrust bearings, the balls or needle rollers run between discs fitted to the shaft and housing respectively. The tracks on the discs are ground so that the forces between the balls and tracks are parallel to the axis of the shaft as shown in Fig 12.7.

Ball and roller bearings can be fitted with seals as a means of retaining lubricant and keeping out contaminants, as shown in Fig 12.8. Some bearings require a single seal to keep contaminants out and at the same time allow lubricant to flow in and out of the bearing. Other bearings are classified as being fully sealed — that is, the bearing has seals on both sides so as to retain clean

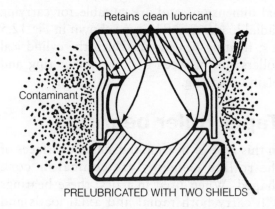

PRELUBRICATED WITH TWO SHIELDS

Fig 12.8   Semi-sealed and sealed bearings
Courtesy of Federal-Mogul

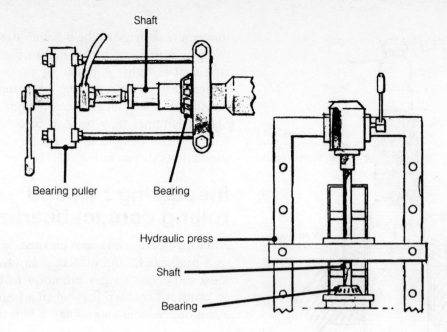

Fig 12.9 Illustration showing how a bearing puller and hydraulic press can be used to remove bearings

lubricant (generally grease) within the bearing and at the same time prevent the entry of contaminants. This type of bearing is pre-lubricated and does not require any other form of lubrication.

Removal of anti-friction bearings

Bearings are generally used to support a shaft in a housing. Of the two races of a bearing, one is a tight fit either on the shaft or in the housing and generally it is when removing or fitting this tight race that damage to the bearing may occur.

When a shaft with a bearing on it has been removed from a housing, the fact that the bearing is on the shaft shows that the inner bearing race is a tight fit on the shaft. To remove the bearing from the shaft, the pushing or pulling effort must be applied only to the race that is tight, in this case the inner one. Figure 12.9 shows various methods of removing a bearing from a shaft.

Figure 12.10 shows a close-up view of how to position and remove a bearing with

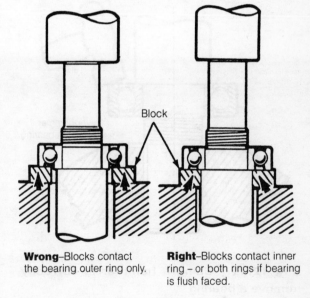

Wrong–Blocks contact the bearing outer ring only.

Right–Blocks contact inner ring – or both rings if bearing is flush faced.

Fig 12.10 The right and wrong way to remove a bearing
Courtesy of Federal-Mogul

the aid of a press. The two illustrations in the figure show the right and wrong way to support the bearing as the shaft is pressed out. By supporting the bearing by its outer ring,

immediate damage to the bearing. Remember, pressure must only be applied to the bearing ring that is tight. A puller or press are the preferred tools for removing a bearing from a housing or shaft. However, if neither is available, a hammer may be used in conjunction with a metal drift to drive the bearing from the shaft as shown in Fig 12.11.

Inspecting ball and rolling contact bearings

After the bearing has been cleaned, hold it up to a bright light and inspect it carefully. It is most important to pay attention to the area of 'constant contact' (e.g. when a bearing has a stationary inner ring — say, a ball bearing).

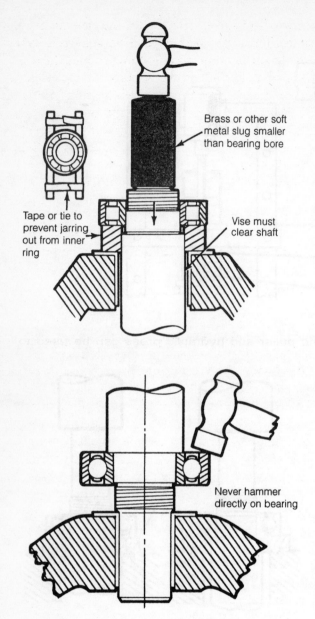

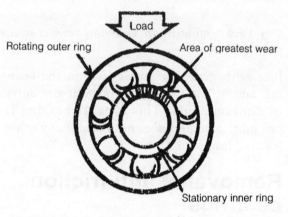

Fig 12.12 Where to examine a bearing for its greatest wear

If a load is applied then the wear is distributed evenly around the inside of the outer ball race, but the load is really concentrated in the area of maximum load on the inner race and that is usually where the bearing starts to fail first, as shown in Fig 12.12. The same thing applies the other way around where it is the outer race that is stationary and the inner race rotates. During the disassembly of the bearing and shaft from the housing, it is a good idea to mark the side of the race where the 'constant contact' occurs with a felt pen and closely examine it first after removal.

Fig 12.11   Using a hammer to correctly remove a bearing
Courtesy of Federal-Mogul

pressure from the press ram will be constantly applied to the bearing balls and raceways. This constant pressure can bruise both the bearing balls and raceways, resulting in rapid failure of the bearing if it is used again.

Never, under any circumstances, try to remove a bearing from a shaft by hitting its outer ring with a hammer. To do so will cause

If the bearing shows signs of discoloration, pitted inner and outer races, pitted balls or rollers, damaged mounting surfaces, or damaged shields and/or seals, then it will need to be replaced. If the bearing is a non-separable type, hold it in your hand and rotate the outer race, taking note of any roughness or tendency to stick. If roughness or sticking does occur, the bearing should be replaced. Bearings that pass inspection but can't be installed the same day should be dipped in oil and wrapped in plastic then stored in a clean environment until they are ready to be used.

Refitting bearings

Prior to refitting bearings, the shafts and housings must be clean and free of any burrs. Bearings must be pressed straight and square on to shafts or into housings with pressure only being applied to the ring that is the tight fit. If a press is not available, the shaft can be held in a vice and the bearing fitted with the aid of a length of clean tube, the diameter of which must fit the inner ring of the bearing, as shown in Fig 12.13.

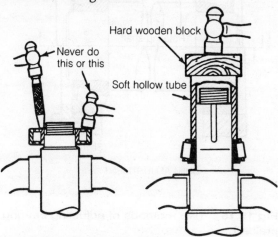

Fig 12.13 Correct procedure for installing ball and roller bearings
Courtesy of Federal-Mogul

An alternative method of fitting bearings on to a shaft is to heat the bearing to expand it then slide it on to the shaft. After the bearing is positioned on the shaft, it will cool down and shrink to form an interference fit. Heating of the bearing can be achieved by boiling it in oil or placing it in a suitable heating oven. If the bearing is heated in oil, care should be taken to ensure even heating of the bearing by suspending it in the oil and not laying it on the bottom of the oil container where it will come in direct contact with the heat source. The oil should be heated to about 100°C–120°C and the bearing left in the oil no longer than five–ten minutes. Do not allow the temperature to exceed the above limits or permanent damage may occur, and the bearing will turn dark blue in colour.

Preloading

When a shaft and bearings are placed under load, deflection can take place between the rolling members and the races with which they are in contact. This deflection results in some degree of movement or end play of the shaft supported by the bearings. (End play refers to the measurable axial looseness of a bearing and shaft.) To reduce this deflection, the shaft and support bearings are preloaded. Preloading is used to remove shaft end play and lightly load the bearings. Applying preload to bearings is important, and must be done with the utmost care. If bearings are preloaded too much they will heat up and destroy themselves. If they are set too loose, the supporting parts will deflect too much, causing them to wear rapidly.

Preload is measured by the resisting torque in Newton metres (Nm) and is the product of a force in Newtons, multiplied by the length or radius of the torque arm in metres.

Bearing preload can be measured with the aid of a spring scale and length of string, as shown in Fig 12.14. The spring scale may read in Newtons or kilograms; if the scale is in kilograms then it will have to be converted to Newtons, for example (1 kg = approx 10 N). Prior to wrapping the string around the hub, measure its diameter at point A in Fig 12.14, then halve the diameter so as to find the radius. For example, if the hub diameter is 0.1 m, then the radius will be 0.05 m. With reference to the same figure, wind the string around the hub on the shaft and, by pulling the string with the spring scale, measure the rolling resistance of the shaft and bearings.

For example, the shaft turns when the scale reads 5 kg. Therefore the preload on the bearings is the radius of the hub in metres or part thereof multiplied by the force in Newtons required to turn the shaft.

The calculation to determine the bearing preload is as follows:

force (N) X distance (m) = torque (Nm)
50N (5kg) X 0.05m = 2.5Nm rolling torque

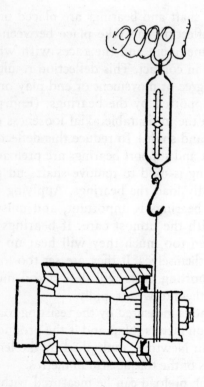

Fig 12.14 Measuring the preload applied to two tapered roller bearings

Another method of checking bearing preload is with the aid of a tension wrench. With the tension wrench attached to the end of the shaft, rotate the wrench and check the resisting strain on the tension wrench torque scale.

In order to obtain the correct amount of bearing preload, the loading on the bearings can be adjusted by either an adjusting nut or the addition or subtraction of shims from behind the bearing retainer, as shown in Fig 12.15.

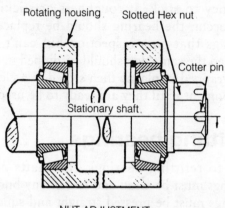

NUT ADJUSTMENT

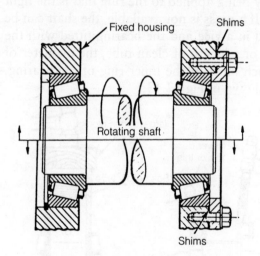

SHIM ADJUSTMENT

Fig 12.15 Two methods of adjusting bearing preload
Courtesy of Federal-Mogul

The majority of bearings do not require preloading on installation; however, when two tapered roller bearings are used to support a shaft or hub, they need to be preloaded.

13

Seals and Gaskets

Seals and gaskets of various types are used in diesel engines to seal the surfaces between two adjoining parts where they are bolted together. Seals are also used on rotating shafts to prevent the passage of fluids along the shaft. Regardless of the type of sealing used, the main aim is to prevent fluid leaking within and out of the engine.

Seals

As the name suggests, seals stop fluids from leaking out of and foreign matter from entering into engine compartments. They are also used to keep fluids separated from one another — for example, engine oil away from diesel fuel. Their construction, operation and application vary widely. While seals are often neglected and considered unimportant, they guard the life of the whole system.

Seals are classified under two general categories:

- static (stationary); and
- dynamic (in motion).

Static seals are used between two stationary components. Dynamic seals are capable of sealing two components which move in relation to one another, as shown in Fig 13.2.

Any one seal cannot be used in all applications. Therefore, the application of the seal will depend on its type, construction and the material it is made of. Consideration must also be given to the type of fluid to be sealed, surrounding conditions, temperature, pressure and speed of operation of the component to be sealed.

The main types of seals which are used in diesel engines are as follows:

- o-ring seals;
- lip type seals;
- exclusion type seals;
- clearance type seals;
- face type seals.

O-ring seals

These seals may be used in either a static or dynamic application. They do not like dirty or abrasive conditions, sparse lubrication, high temperatures or incompatible fluids. They are used extensively in engines, transmissions and hydraulics for sealing coolant, lubricants, fuels and gases, under a wide range of operating conditions. The rubber o-ring comes in a variety of sizes, thicknesses and temperature applications.

The o-ring sits in a square-sided machine groove and may be used alone or with a back-up ring so as to prevent it from squeezing out of its groove under high

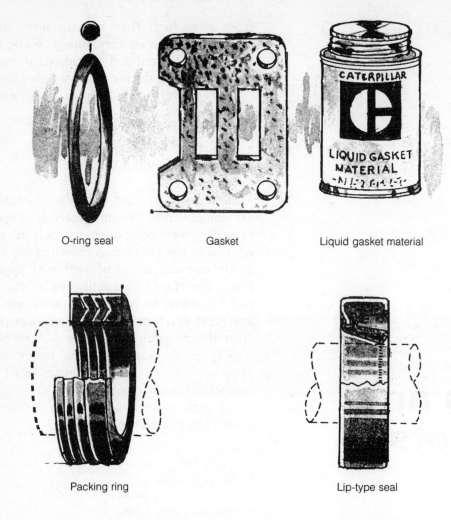

O-ring seal   Gasket   Liquid gasket material

Packing ring   Lip-type seal

Fig 13.1 Various type of seals and gaskets   *Courtesy of Caterpillar Inc*

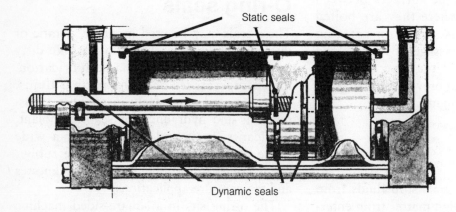

Static seals

Dynamic seals

Fig 13.2 Illustration showing the application of static and dynamic seals
Courtesy of Caterpillar Inc

Fig 13.3   Different coloured o-rings   *Courtesy of Caterpillar Inc*

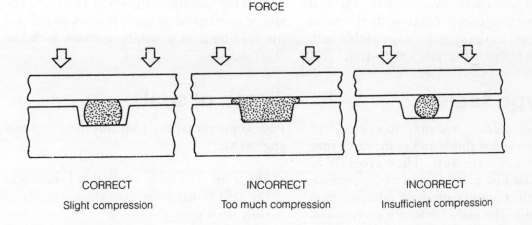

Fig 13.4   O-ring installation

pressure applications. The majority of o-rings are black in colour; however, there are some o-rings which are distinguishable by their yellow or brown colours. These coloured o-rings are used in special applications where extremes of temperature and pressure are encountered.

Operation

An o-ring seals due to initial compression when installed followed by the pressure of the fluid which produces the final deformation and increased sealing efficiency. The correct amount of squeeze for static o-rings is shown in Fig 13.4. An o-ring which is too thick can be pinched when assembling and could leak. An o-ring which is too small will not seal and could also leak.

Installation

Prior to installing an o-ring into its groove or

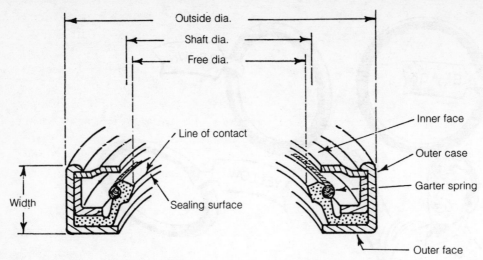

Fig 13.5   Parts of a lip type seal

recess, always check it for correct size and thickness. Also check that the o-ring contact areas and grooves are clean and free of rust, nicks and burrs. Do not stretch or twist the ring on installation, as this can effect its ability to seal correctly. Lubricate the seal and its mating components with the same fluid as used in the system and assemble with care so as not to cut or pinch the o-ring.

Lip type seals

These are purely a dynamic seal. They are used to retain fluids and at the same time keep out contaminants. They are able to seal against low pressure and can accommodate small amounts of shaft misalignment and runout. The main parts of a lip type seal are shown in Fig 13.5.

Some seals use a garter spring to help in maintaining seal lip contact around the shaft. The garter spring is simply a coil spring formed into the shape of a hoop and is fitted behind the seal lip as shown in Fig 13.5. The spring is designed to apply tension to the seal lip holding it in constant contact with the shaft surface.

Types of seal

Four common types of lip seal used in diesel engines are:

- **Single lip**. The lip is not spring loaded and the seal is used for containing fluids at slow shaft speeds.

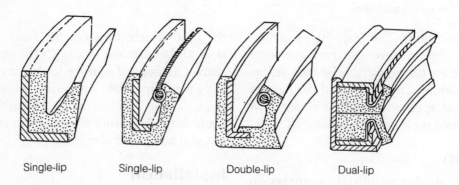

Single-lip   Single-lip   Double-lip   Dual-lip

Fig 13.6   Types of lip seal in common use

- **Single lip spring loaded.** Used for retaining lower viscosity lubricants at higher shaft speeds in a clean working environment.
- **Double lip.** Has two lips facing in opposite directions, with only one lip being spring loaded. Used for retaining lubricant on the spring loaded side, while keeping out dirt on the other side.
- **Dual lip.** Has two lips, both of which are spring loaded. Used in applications where two different fluid compartments are back to back and need to be sealed from one another.

Operation

The outer case of the seal is a press fit in its housing, while the lip seals on the shaft. The seal lip rides on a film of oil and grips the shaft with just enough force to prevent leakage. During shaft rotation, the seal lip compensates for a certain amount of shaft runout by moving with the shaft and at all times maintaining contact with the sealing surface, as shown in Fig 13.7.

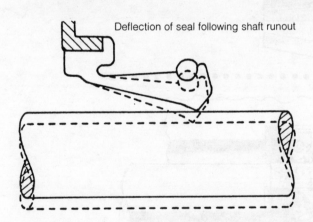

Fig 13.7 Schematic diagram of a lip type seal accounting for shaft runout

Installation

Prior to installing the seal, check that the housing and shaft are clean and free from burrs, nicks, rust or corrosion. The sealing surface may be cleaned by rubbing it with fine wet and dry emery paper.

Note: When cleaning seal contact surfaces, always clean around the shaft and not across it. Finally, lubricate the sealing surfaces with the same lubricant that is to be sealed. Do not use grease, as it breaks down when heated and creates a varnish on the sealing area.

At no time should the garter spring of the seal be shortened to improve its sealing ability. Applying increased pressure to the seal lip will increase the seal wear rate and shorten its service life.

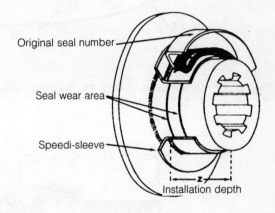

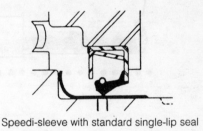

Speedi-sleeve with standard single-lip seal

Fig 13.8 Installation of a sleeve to renew seal running surface

If the shaft has a groove around its circumference, it may be necessary to fit a sleeve to it, as shown in Fig 13.8. Such sleeves are available with accompanying installation tools which make for easy and cost efficient shaft repair. An alternative repair method is to reposition the seal so the seal lip will run on an unworn surface of the shaft. This will require the seal to be moved further into or out of its mounting,

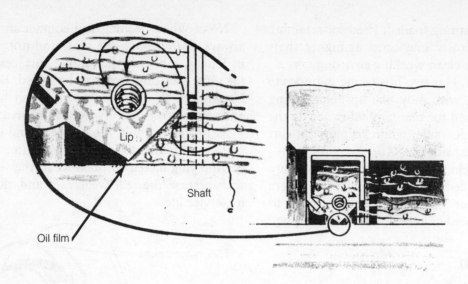

Fig 13.9 Illustration of how oil pressure assists in forcing the seal lip tighter around the shaft
Courtesy of Caterpillar Inc

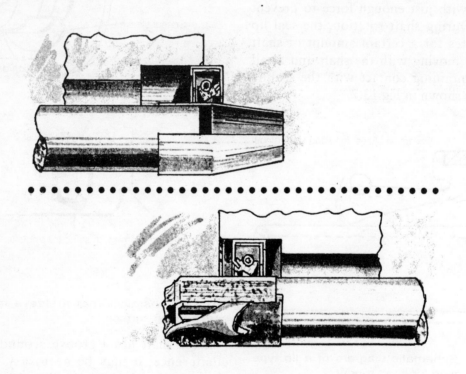

Fig 13.10 A sleeve or tape used to prevent seal damage during shaft installation

depending on how much room is available. If the seal has to be moved, then the use of a spacer washer behind the seal is beneficial to accurate repositioning as well as maintaining seal alignment in the housing. A more

expensive method of repairing a grooved shaft is to metal spray the worn area of the shaft, then use a lathe to turn the shaft down to its original diameter.

When installing seals with a single lip, the

lip should normally face in towards the lubricant. In this way the lubricant and the garter spring form a combined tightening force around the seal lip, as shown in Fig 13.9. If the seal has to be moved over sharp edges during installation, special protective covers are available to protect the lip from being damaged. If a protective cover is not available to protect the seal lip from damage, a piece of plastic tape can be wrapped around the shaft, as shown in Fig 13.10.

Use a seal driving tool, as shown in Fig 13.11, to drive the seal home. If this is not available, use a circular ring such as an old bearing race, making sure that any driving tool always contacts the seal near its outer diameter. Avoid using punches to install seals, as their small contact area bruises the seal housing. Install the seal evenly into the housing and make sure it goes all the way home.

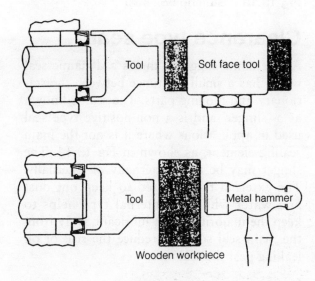

Fig 13.11 Correct installation of an oil seal

Causes of seal leakage

Leakage between the seal mounting recess and the seal outer case may occur if:

- the seal is misaligned in its housing;
- the housing recess is out of round or oversize.

Leakage through the sealing element itself may occur if:

- there is a hole or tear through it from careless installation;
- the rubber has come away from the case.

Leakage from under the seal lip is the most common seal fault and can be caused by the following problems relating to the shaft or the seal lip:

- seal contact surface damaged due to rust or corrosion;
- nicks or burrs on the shaft;
- deep seal grooves in the shaft;
- dirt or foreign material under the sealing lip;
- garter spring broken or fallen off;
- folded seal lip;
- excessive shaft run out due to worn support bearings;
- excessive shaft misalignment;
- a worn, cracked or cut sealing lip.

Exclusion type seals

These are dynamic seals which grip the shaft firm enough to stop fluid leaks and, because of this, create a fair amount of friction. They are capable of sealing oils, greases and diesel fuel. Some exclusion seals can seal against pressure and will operate at low or high speeds, depending on which type is used.

The two basic types are:

- asbestos;
- stuffing box.

Caution should be used to avoid breathing dust that may be generated when handling components containing asbestos fibres. Normal handling is not hazardous as long as airborne dust which contains asbestos is not inhaled.

The asbestos seal has been used in some older engines as a rear crankshaft oil seal, as shown in Fig 13.12. It is made of woven asbestos which is moulded to fit the application — in this case, a groove inside the rear main bearing housing. Such seals are usually coated with a graphite lubricant to assist in 'bedding in' and to reduce friction. Sealing is accomplished by preloading the seal on to the crankshaft and is aided by the lubricant it is to seal.

Prior to installing the new seal, soak it in engine oil until the asbestos is fully saturated. It must then be installed by first fitting the middle part of the seal into its groove then working out to the ends of the seal. A small amount of the seal material should protrude above the bearing cap and engine block surfaces. This seal protrusion will aid in preloading the seal into its grooves when the bearing cap is tightened down.

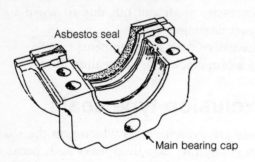

Fig 13.12 Woven asbestos rear crankshaft oil seal as used on older diesel engines

Stuffing box

The stuffing box seal generally uses an asbestos packing which is forced on to the shaft by tightening a gland nut, as shown in Fig 13.13. This type of seal is used on some engine water pumps as well as fuel transfer pumps. It is a cheap and reliable seal, but creates high friction on the shaft. Removal of stuffing box seals is easy and only requires the shaft and gland nut to be removed and the seal lifted out. After cleaning the surfaces inside the housing and on the shaft, lubricate and install the new seal. Finally, adjust up the

gland nut or seal retainer until no fluids pass the sealing surface. Some of these seals are spring loaded and require no adjustment.

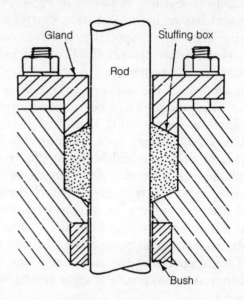

Fig 13.13 Stuffing box seal

Clearance type seal

As the name suggests, this is a dynamic seal which has a small clearance between the stationary and moving parts. The seal is known as a 'slinger' and is a non-positive type seal used in applications where it is not the main sealing element, as shown in Fig 13.14. The slinger may be used externally or internally. The external type is used to keep out dust and water while the internal type helps to keep the majority of the lubricant away from the main seal so as to reduce the risk of oil leaking past the seal face.

Bellows seal

The bellows seal is a face type seal which seals on face contact. It is capable of withstanding high operating temperatures and cooling system pressure and is used as a water pump seal to prevent coolant leaking along the water pump drive shaft.

The seal consists of a brass case which has a rubber bellows bonded to it. Attached to

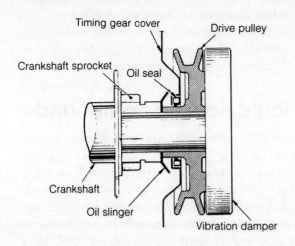

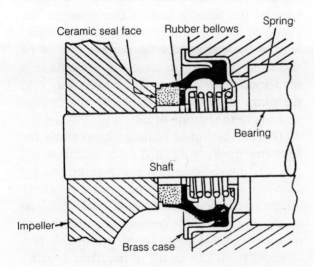

Fig 13.14 Oil slinger used in combination with a crankshaft oil seal

Fig 13.15 Bellows seal used in a water pump

the bellows is a seal face which is usually made of a ceramic compound. When the seal is fitted to the water pump housing, the seal face contacts and seals against a mating ceramic ring bonded to or pressed into the water pump impeller.

In operation, the outer case of the seal, being a press fit into the water pump housing, serves as an efficient seal of the outer diameter of the seal case. The ceramic seal face is held against the ceramic sealing surface on the impeller by a spring which preloads the two sealing surfaces, forming a positive coolant seal.

Gaskets

Gaskets are made of materials which prevent the passage of gas or liquid between two stationary surfaces. When the two components which are separated by the gasket are tightened, the compression of the gasket material causes the gasket to form a seal between the two surfaces. Apart from preventing fluids leaking between two parts, gaskets have several other jobs they must perform in order to seal correctly. They must:

- have resistance against corrosion;
- be able to seal constantly when the temperature and pressure changes;
- be able to flow into surface defects and make a tight seal.

In order for gaskets to suit a variety of applications, they must be made from a number of different materials:

- **Rubberised cork**. Consists of granulated cork mixed with synthetic rubber. Where possible, install dry as gasket cement and grease act as a lubricant promoting extrusion of the gasket.
- **Paper**. A heavy paper-like material used where a thin gasket is required to seal two machined surfaces. If sealing surfaces are not ideal, a gasket cement or sealer can be used to improve sealing.
- **Metal**. This is a shim type gasket made of corrugated steel or copper. It has the ability to withstand high contact pressure applications such as a cylinder head gasket, injector sealing washers and exhaust manifold gaskets. All metal gaskets are

installed dry unless advised otherwise by the engine manufacturer.

- **Asbestos.** An excellent heat-resistant gasket material seldom used by itself, but when combined with copper or steel resists high shearing pressures and temperatures generated by combustion in an internal combustion engine. Asbestos forms the centre core of many head gaskets and exhaust manifold gaskets.

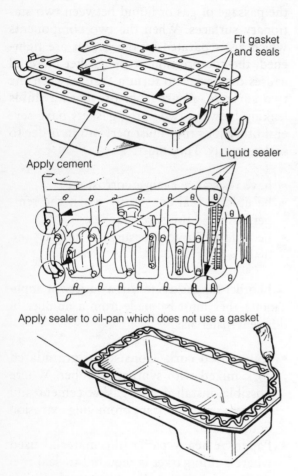

Fit gasket and seals

Apply cement

Liquid sealer

Apply sealer to oil-pan which does not use a gasket

Fig 13.16 Diagram illustrating the use of a gasket or synthetic sealing compound *Courtesy of AGPS*

- **Cellulose compounds.** These are liquid sealing compounds which are being used to replace the conventional paper gasket. They are a more efficient sealing material

than paper and have excellent stability when clamped between two surfaces.

- **Synthetic rubber.** As it is pliable and adapts easily to changing surface conditions, it is widely used under tappet covers.

Liquid sealing compounds

Engine manufacturers are now starting to use liquid sealing compounds to replace the use of gaskets in certain engine applications. After the two adjoining parts have been sealed and clamped together, the sealing compound cures in the presence of air, forming an oil-, water- and heat-resistant seal. It is important, when using a liquid sealing compound, to use only a small continuous bead and apply it to the middle of the sealing surface or as specified by the manufacturer, as shown in Fig 13.17. Applying too heavy a bead or positioning it too close to the inside edge of the sealing surface can result in the excess sealant falling into the internal workings of the engine. As the sealant cannot be dissolved into the engine oil, it remains in a semi-solid state where it can find its way into the sump and block up the oil strainer gauze and starve the engine of oil.

The use of liquid sealing compounds for forming gaskets should only occur when specified by the engine manufacturer. Sealing compound is not recommended in areas where a specified gasket thickness is required to ensure the correct bearing preload or running clearance. Failure to adhere to this recommendation can result in incorrect bearing preloads and reduced running clearance between components, thereby causing possible engine damage.

In operation, gaskets have a number of demands placed on them other than sealing. The necessary characteristics required of a gasket material to enable it to meet these demands are as follows:

- **Compressibility.** Enables the gasket to conform readily to rough and uneven surfaces.

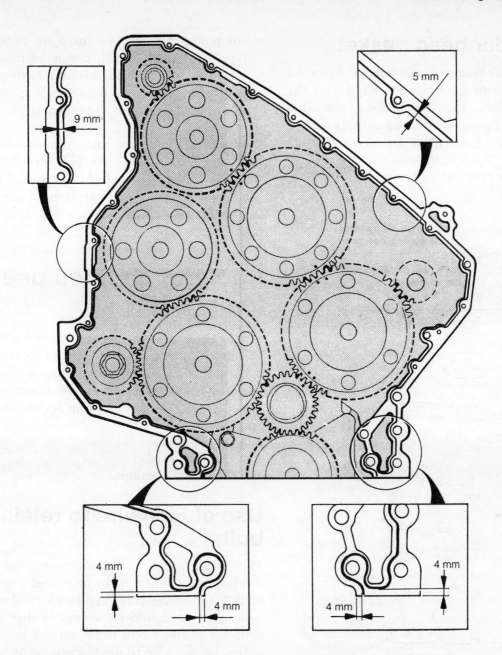

Fig 13.17   An example of how to apply a bead of sealant to a timing cover
Courtesy of Volvo

- **Recoverability from compression.** Expansion and contraction of metal components due to temperature variations continually changes gasket thickness. If the gasket cannot sustain continual expansion and contraction over thousands of cycles, loss of bolt torque will occur and leakage can result.
- **Resistance to wicking.** Some materials, such as cork, pass liquids internally in the same way that kerosene is passed along a lamp's wick. Therefore it is the gasket's job to stop the passage of liquids and make an oil-tight seal.
- **Resistance to flow and extrusion.** This is the gasket's ability to carry the required contact pressure without 'climbing out from under' the two surfaces.

Cylinder head gasket

The cylinder head gasket is designed to form a seal between the cylinder head and the cylinder block. The construction of the cylinder head gasket varies considerably due to differences in basic engine design, compression ratio and cylinder head structure.

Various types of common cylinder head gasket are:

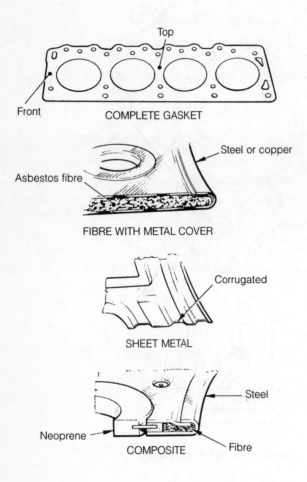

Fig 13.18   Various types of cylinder head gaskets

- asbestos enveloped with copper or tin plate;
- corrugated metal — a single thickness of tin plate especially hardened and preformed to assure concentration of loading at the areas to be sealed;

- composite materials — there are various types used and generally consist of treated asbestos layers vulcanised onto a crimped steel plate core. Neoprene sealing rings assist in sealing water and oil passages.

When installing head gaskets, always look for the 'TOP' and 'FRONT' markings stamped on the gasket. Failure to install the head gasket correctly can result in oil starvation to the rocker shaft or coolant leaks from under the head.

Locking devices used in engines

There are many applications where locking devices are being used in engines to retain nuts, bolts, studs or bearings from working loose or moving during engine operation. Three common types of locking device are:

- lockwire;
- tab locking washers;
- lock-type compounds.

Use of lockwire to retain bolts

There are a number of applications, such as flywheel bolts, where lockwire is used to stop bolts from unscrewing. Figure 13.19 shows how lockwire should be wound so that any tendency of either bolt to loosen will be prevented by the wire trying to tighten the bolt beside it.

Tab locking washers

These are widely used and come in many types, some of which are shown in Fig 13.20. Lock tabs are mainly used to lock nuts or bolts. Note that some types have two tabs which allow the second tab to be used on reassembly. It is important to remember that each tab can only be used once. The correct method of bending the tab, where the tab must sit up against the flat on the bolt hexagon, is shown in Fig 13.20.

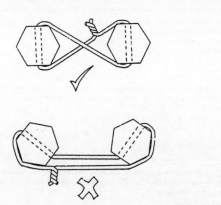

Fig 13.19 Correct use of lock wire to retain bolts

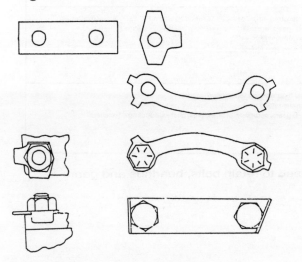

Fig 13.20 Lock tab washers

Lock type compounds

These are liquid resin adhesives which, when applied to nut and bolt threads during component assembly, harden into a solid, thereby preventing the fastener from coming loose.

A complete range of these lock type compounds is available to give a wide range of strengths and types of adhesive properties for various purposes such as:

- retaining gears on shafts;
- locking threads on studs, bolts and screws;
- mounting bearings on shaft and in housings.

These highly specialised adhesives are quite different to ordinary everyday adhesives. The chemical hardening action of ordinary adhesives depends upon the evaporation of a solvent, or the reaction of a catalyst, and must be exposed to air for hardening to take place. Anaerobic resins, as they are sometimes called, only react and cure when air is excluded from around them. Anaerobic means 'without air'. In their stored form, anaerobic resins contain air which is dissolved in the liquid preventing the resin from hardening. When the resin is confined between closely fitting parts, the air is expelled, allowing a chemical reaction to take place, causing the resin to cure and harden.

Disassembly of components

Selection of the correct grade of lock type compound during assembly will allow disassembly with normal tools or pulling equipment. Initially, a larger than normal force or torque will be required to move parts locked with a lock type compound, but once movement occurs, the compound breaks up into granules and will not cause any damage to mating surfaces.

PRODUCT	PROPERTIES	FUNCTIONS AND BENEFITS
222 Screwlock	• Best strength for screws • Will undo with normal tools • Maintains torque/tension within specifications • Does not wick into adjoining parts • Fast cure	• Low strength locking of screws having long thread engagements • Low strength locking of adjustment screws allows adjustment anytime without loss of locking benefit • Stops loosening due to vibration or shock loading • Seals threads against leakage of fluids and gases
242 Nutlock	• Medium strength • Will undo with normal tools • Maintains torque/tension within specifications • Does not wick into adjoining parts • Excellent chemical resistance • Fast cure	• Best strength for nuts under all operating conditions • Stops loosening due to vibration and shock loading • Seal threads against leakage of fluids and gases • Prevents thread corrosion and seizure • Best product to overcome or prevent backlash in splines and keyways
262 Studlock	• High strength • Will need extra effort to undo • Maintains torque/tension within specifications • Does not wick into adjoining parts • Excellent chemical resistance • Fast cure	• Heavy duty product for studs and for threadlocking in severe operating conditions • Stops loosening due to vibration and shock loading • Seals threads against leakage of fluids and gases • Prevents thread corrosion and seizure
241 Bearing Mount	• Medium strength • Allows removal with press or standard pullers • Excellent chemical resistance • Fast cure • Cured strength 7000 - 14000 kPa (1000 - 2000 psi) • Fills gaps to .13mm (.005 inch)	• General purpose strength product for mounting bearings, bushes, sleeves, oil seals • Can be used in pressfit or slipfit situations to prevent unwanted movement • Prevents fretting corrosion • Improves heat transfer • Seals outside diameter of oil seals • Retains oil seals in high pressure applications • Reduces downtime and maintenance costs
601 Retaining Compound	• High strength • Allows removal with press and pullers • Excellent chemical resistance • Fast cure • Cured strength 14000 - 21000 kPa (2000 - 3000 psi) • Fills gaps to .13mm (.005 inch)• High strength	• Load transmitting grade for parts needing removal for maintenance or repair • Pulleys, gears, sprockets, sleeves, pins, bushes, couplings • Stops fretting corrosion • Stops corrosion lock-up
602 Retaining Compound	• Allows removal with press and pullers • Working temperatures up to 230°C (450F) continuous • Cure speeds 8 - 10 hours at 23°C 1/2 hour at 121C • Cured strength 21000 - 25000 kPa (3000 - 35000 psi) • Fixtures in 30 min. In 5 min. with Primer T	• Special high working temperature grade • Load transmitting • Pulleys, gears, sprockets, sleeves, pins, bushes, couplings, fasteners

Fig 13.21   Various types of Loctite compound used to retain bolts, bearings and gears
Courtesy of Loctite

14

Cold Starting Aids

Because of its compact form, the open combustion chamber system presents only a small surface area to the compressed air, and the amount of heat lost by conduction to the combustion chamber is relatively small. As a result, the temperature of the compressed air at the moment of injection is always considerably higher than the fuel's self-ignition temperature, and the fuel ignites readily.

Unfortunately, the other combustion chamber systems present a large surface area to the compressed air, resulting in a large loss of heat. When the engine (and combustion chamber) is cold, the large difference in temperature between the compressed air and the combustion chamber causes a rapid transfer of heat from the air to the chamber. This heat loss, coupled with the fact that compression only raises the air temperature a certain amount above its initial temperature, makes starting from cold a problem.

Many systems have been developed to overcome this, the most common being:

- glow plugs;
- thermostart devices; and
- the use of volatile fuel.

Glow plugs

Glow plugs screw into the combustion chamber and supply additional heat to the air during the compression stroke. A heater element on the plug lies flush with the combustion chamber wall. When, prior to starting, a current of 20 to 35 amperes is supplied from the battery for between five and fifteen seconds, this element glows bright red. If the engine is then cranked, some of the heat from the element is transferred to the compressed air, giving a final air temperature high enough to ensure efficient ignition and combustion.

Although other types have been used, almost all glow plugs used today are of the single-pole type, which provides one insulated terminal post for electrical connection with the circuit being completed to earth through the body of the glow plug (see Fig 14.1).

Single-pole glow plugs are said to be connected **in parallel**. This means that the current is supplied from the battery to the single terminal of each plug, and the circuit is completed through the cylinder head to earth. In this system, full battery voltage is applied to each plug, and one plug can fail without affecting the others. Thus, for a vehicle using a 12-volt electrical system, 12-volt single-pole glow plugs can be employed.

Many automotive diesel engines are equipped with a glow plug control system, usually known as a 'quick start' system. The

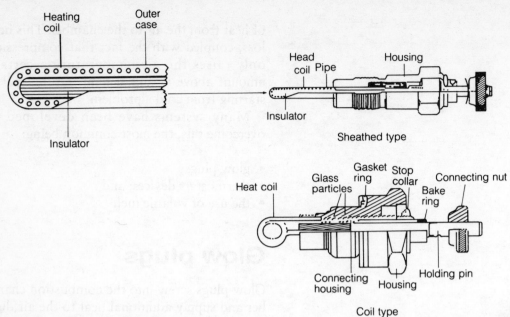

Fig 14.1 Typical glow plugs

basic quick start system is designed to control the preheating time of the glow plugs by the use of an automatic timer; the more sophisticated models modify that timer operation to take into account the engine water temperature.

When starting a cold engine fitted with a typical system, immediately the starting switch is turned to the 'on' position, the glow plug warning lamp is illuminated and the main glow plug relay becomes operative. This allows a high current flow

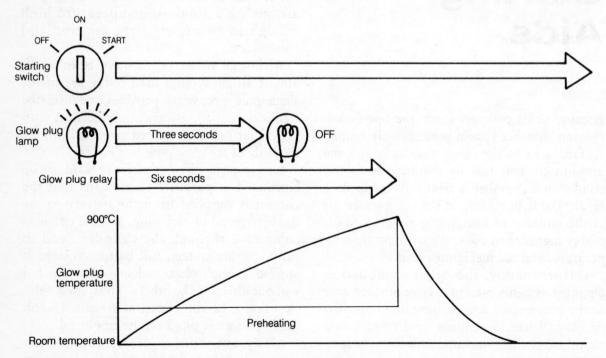

Fig 14.2 Operation of the quick-start system with the starting switch turned to the 'on' position
Courtesy of Mazda

through the glow plugs to earth, causing rapid heating of the glow plugs.

After a set time, the automatic timer switches off the glow plug warning lamp, indicating that the engine is ready to be started, but leaves the glow plugs on. The engine is started by turning the key to the 'start' position (see Fig 14.2). Once the engine has

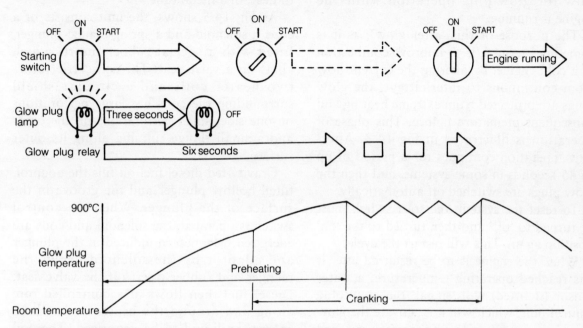

Fig 14.3 Glow plug operation during engine cranking and intial running periods
Courtesy of Mazda

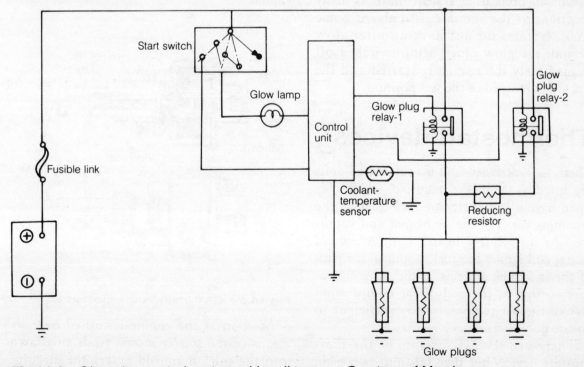

Fig 14.4 Glow plug control system wiring diagram *Courtesy of Mazda*

started and the start switch returned to the 'on' position, the main glow plug relay will turn 'off', but a second relay will become operative, supplying intermittent current flow for glow plug operation while the engine is running.

The purpose of this 'after glow', as it is sometimes termed, is to improve combustion in a cold engine. By altering the current flow from continuous to intermittent, the glow plugs are protected from extreme heating and subsequent premature failure. This phase of operation is illustrated in Fig 14.3. After-glow operation continues for a period of up to 45 seconds in some systems, and then the glow plugs are switched off automatically.

To reset the system, the start switch must be turned to 'off' and then turned to the 'on' position again. This will restart the cycle.

When the engine is to be restarted after it has reached operating temperature, a water sensor (if fitted) will 'signal' the glow plug control unit, which will not activate the glow plugs, thus preventing unnecessary use and overheating.

Not all preheating systems have as many functions as the one discussed above. Some basic systems do not have an after-glow period, the glow plugs being switched off immediately the engine is started and the start key returned to the run position.

Thermostart devices

These CAV-designed and manufactured units are fitted to the intake manifold, where they burn a small quantity of fuel to heat the incoming air. The fuel is heated and vapor-ised by an electric heater coil. A second heater coil ignites the fuel vapour in the path of the incoming air, raising the air tempera-ture so that at the end of the compression stroke the air temperature is sufficient to ensure good starting.

There are several variants of the ther-mostart device, but they fall into two main types: an early type, which controls the entry of fuel to the heater element by means of a solenoid; and a later type, which controls the entry of fuel by means of the expansion, due to heat, of a metal tube.

As Fig 14.5 shows, the unit consists of a core, a solenoid and a spring-loaded plunger, fitted with a special rubber insert, which abuts on a valve seat. The coil carrier bears two heater coils and a circular shield surrounding the coils has large perforations on one side, small perforations on the other and a small flange running along its outer surface.

Gravity-fed diesel fuel oil fills the adaptor, filter, hollow plunger and the groove in the surface of the plunger. When the control switch is operated, the solenoid and coils are energised. Magnetism induced in the plunger and adaptor by the solenoid draws the plunger and rubber insert off the valve seat. Diesel fuel then flows at a controlled rate along and around the heater coil, which causes the liquid to be vaporised. The coil reaches the ignition temperature of the fuel vapour.

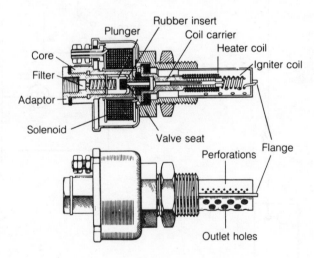

Fig 14.5 CAV 'mark' 1 thermostart

As soon as the engine is turned over by means of the starter motor, fresh air drawn into the inlet manifold enters the circular shield through the small perforations and mixes with the vaporised fuel within. The resultant mixture is ignited by the igniter coil heating the air to facilitate combustion by promoting easier ignition of the fuel injected into the engine cylinders.

The flange running along the outer surface of the shield provides a sheltered zone around the outlet holes and protects the flame from the incoming air stream.

Fig 14.6 shows the second type of thermostart device. The holder screws into the inlet manifold, and contains the tubular valve body, which is surrounded by the heater coil, an extension of which forms an igniter coil. The valve body houses a needle, the stem of which holds a ball valve in position against its seating. The assembly is surrounded by an open perforated shield. Diesel fuel from the reservoir enters through an adaptor on the end of the valve body.

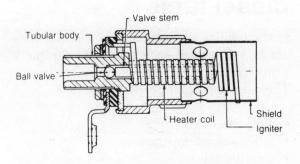

Fig 14.6 CAV 'mark' 3 thermostart

When the unit is cold, the ball valve is held closed. When the coil is switched on, the valve body is heated and expands, carrying the valve stem away from the ball. This opens the ball valve and permits entry of fuel. The fuel is vaporised by the heat of the valve body and, when the engine is cranked and air is drawn into the manifold, the vapour is ignited by the coil extension and continues to burn, thus heating the inlet air.

When the coil is switched off, the flow of air in the manifold cools the valve body rapidly, causing it to contract. The valve closes.

The cold-start aid is a sealed unit and cannot be dismantled. If the unit ceases to function, it must be replaced.

Volatile fuel

Instead of using some means of providing extra heat for the air before or during the compression stroke in order to achieve a sufficiently high temperature at the completion of the compression stroke, thus giving efficient starting, a volatile fuel, which has a much lower self-ignition temperature than diesel fuel, is sometimes used. The fuel used is usually some form of ether, and an ether–air mixture will ignite at a much lower temperature than diesel fuel.

The ether fuel may be packed in pressurised cans so that it can be sprayed into the air intake as the starter is operated. Or it may be supplied in a capsule, which fits into the base chamber of a special carburettor in the inlet manifold. The base chamber is removed for fitting the capsule, which is automatically punctured when the base chamber is refitted. Puncturing the capsule releases the ether compound, and air, being drawn through the inlet manifold into the combustion chamber, carries a quantity of ether with it. This ether–air mixture ignites readily on the compression stroke.

The manifold is fitted with a butterfly valve, which is nearly closed for starting to give a very high air speed past the fuel chamber. The high speed of the air causes a depression, which draws the ether from the chamber to mix with the air. As soon as the engine runs evenly, the butterfly is opened fully, so removing its restricting effect from the air intake.

15
Diesel Engine Fuels

A number of grades of fuel are available for compression ignition engines, and the use of the correct fuel is extremely important. The fuels available in Australia are listed below.

Automotive distillate

Automotive distillate is a highly refined fuel for use in high-speed diesel engines as fitted to tractors, trucks and motor cars. The distillate is also known as automotive diesel fuel, automotive diesel oil, distillate, diesolene and diesoleum. It is clear to light-straw coloured.

Winter fuels

Because wax solidifies in diesel fuel under very cold conditions and blocks the fuel flow, winter-grade diesel fuel has been introduced. This contains special additives to prevent the wax from solidifying at low ambient temperatures.

Industrial diesel fuel

This is the name given to a less refined fuel suitable for use in slow- to medium-speed diesels and commercial heating installations. It is a heavier grade of fuel, but is free flowing and does not require preheating. Its colour is light straw to black.

Specifications of diesel fuels

In the refining of fuels, certain specifications are laid down for each type, and the fuel's properties must lie within these set limits. The most important properties include:

- ignition quality;
- self-ignition temperature;
- calorific value;
- flashpoint;
- pour point;
- cloud point;
- viscosity;
- specific gravity;
- carbon residue;
- sulphur content;
- ash content;
- water and sediment content.

Ignition quality

The ignition quality of a fuel may be described as its degree of readiness to burn when injected into the combustion chamber. Fuels with low ignition quality will take longer to ignite than fuels with high ignition quality. Fuels with a low ignition quality therefore cause a longer delay period or ignition lag, with resultant greater diesel knock.

The **cetane number** of a diesel fuel is the most common method of measuring the fuel's ignition quality. Cetane is a chemical fuel that has the highest known ignition quality, and is given the rating of 100. Alpha-methyl-naphthalene is another chemical fuel which has a very low ignition quality; it is given the number 0.

When testing a fuel to find its ignition quality, a test engine is first run on a sample of the fuel. The knocking tendency and the delay period of the engine are noted.

Then the same engine is run on a mixture of cetane and alpha-methyl-naphthalene. The amount of cetane in this mixture is slowly increased or decreased, until the engine gives the same test results as were obtained when it was run on the fuel sample. For example, if the mixture of cetane and alpha-methyl-naphthalene giving the same test results contained 40 per cent cetane and 60 per cent alpha-methyl-naphthalene, the cetane number of the fuel would be 40.

As an alternative to testing a fuel in an engine laboratory to ascertain its cetane number, an approximate equivalent can be calculated after some simple testing of the fuel. This is known as the **calculated cetane number** of the fuel.

It is worthwhile noting at this stage that the average high-speed diesel engine requires a fuel with a minimum calculated cetane number of 47.

The effects of the quality of the fuel on the engine may be summarised as follows:

- **Diesel knock.** The use of a fuel of too low an ignition quality results in severe diesel knock, rough running and severe shock loading on pistons and bearings.
- **Engine deposits.** When a low ignition-quality fuel is used, deposits in combustion chambers, on rings and on piston skirts become excessive. The use of a suitable fuel keeps these deposits to a minimum.
- **Starting.** The higher the ignition quality of the fuel used, the lower the efficient starting temperature. The use of a fuel of lower ignition quality than is recommended results in harder starting and longer warm-up periods, during which the engine produces white exhaust smoke.
- **Odour and fumes.** If the engine is in good condition, a fuel with a high ignition quality keeps fumes, odour and smoke to a minimum, while a lower grade fuel will aggravate the situation.

Self-ignition temperature

This is the temperature at which the fuel will ignite without the aid of a spark. The lower this temperature, the easier the engine will be to start and the less diesel knock will occur; the lower the self-ignition temperature, the higher the ignition quality of the fuel will be.

Calorific value

This is the quantity of heat released when the fuel is completely burnt. It is measured in joules per kilogram of fuel. Distillate has an approximate calorific value of 44 joules per kilogram (44 MJ/kg), while lower grade fuels have a slightly higher value. Since IC engines are dependent on heat to produce power, the calorific value of the fuel has a direct bearing on the power output.

Flashpoint (open or closed)

This is the temperature at which the fuel will give off a flammable vapour. To ascertain the flashpoint, a quantity of fuel is heated in a container (open or closed) and a flame is passed through the hot oily vapour. The temperature at which the vapour burns momentarily and then goes out is the flashpoint.

Flashpoint has no bearing on the engine's

performance, but is important with regard to safety precautions during storage and handling of the fuel.

Pour point

This is the lowest temperature, under test conditions, at which the fuel will flow under its own weight. It is necessary for a fuel to flow freely at the lowest temperature likely to be encountered, hence pour point is an important factor. However, low pour point is often obtained at the expense of ignition quality, and the use of low pour point fuels, where they are not necessary, should be avoided.

Cloud point

This is the temperature at which the wax in the diesel fuel will begin to crystallise and form a solid and, in so doing, will give the fuel a cloudy appearance. The winter-grade cloud point in southern and eastern Australia is around –1°C to –2°C, while that for summer is around 5°C. The cloud point variation now allows users the benefits of summer and winter grades of diesel fuel.

Viscosity

Viscosity may be defined as the reluctance of a fluid to flow; the more viscous a fluid, the greater its resistance to flowing. From a practical point of view, the viscosity of a fuel is a measure of thickness or thinness.

Viscosity is measured by means of a viscometer, which measures the time taken for a specific quantity of a fluid to pass through a set orifice.

Note: There are three viscosity scales in common use, and each gives a different reading. To compare, one reading may be converted to the other from the formula:

Redwood = 29 × Englar = 0.85 × Saybolt.
(The Redwood value is numerically equal to 29 times the Englar value and to 0.85 times the Saybolt value.)

The viscosity of a diesel fuel is very important. If the fuel is not viscous enough, then the lubricating film between the moving parts in the injectors and fuel pump may break down, causing rapid failure of this very expensive equipment. On the other hand, an excessively viscous fuel may not fully charge the pumping element at high speeds, resulting in loss of power. Again, the more viscous a fuel, the less the atomisation, but the greater the fuel spray penetration, so that the combustion process may be severely altered if a fuel of the incorrect viscosity is used.

Specific gravity

The specific gravity of a substance is the ratio of the mass of a certain volume of the substance to the mass of an equal volume of water. This specification is not only significant from a combustion or performance point of view, but is used for converting weight of fuel to volume of fuel and vice versa.

Carbon residue

The carbon residue value is found by burning a fuel sample, weighing the residue and expressing this mass as a percentage of the mass of the fuel sample. The conditions under which the test is made are not the same as those existing in the combustion chamber, so the result is not directly related to engine deposits. However, it is an indication of the quantity of slow-burning constituents likely to cause engine deposits.

Sulphur content

Although sulphur is undesirable in fuels, operating conditions have a very considerable bearing on the maximum allowable sulphur content.

When sulphur burns, a very small proportion of it forms sulphur trioxide, and if this combines with any water vapour formed during the combustion process, sulphuric acid results. If this sulphuric acid vapour is condensed by any cool surfaces, such as cylinder liners, it will settle on and attack these surfaces.

Ash content

The ash content of a fuel is a measure of the incombustible material in the fuel. The incombustible material exists in two forms:

- hard abrasive solids;
- soluble metallic soaps.

Both forms contribute to engine deposits, particularly in high-speed engines, while the solids, which consist of silica, iron oxide and other impurities, are extremely abrasive and contribute to injector and fuel pump wear, as well as piston ring wear.

Water and sediment content

Water in the fuel can wreck the fuel injection equipment very rapidly, and every attempt must be made to keep the water content to a minimum. Unfortunately, water collects in fuel tanks due to condensation, so the only way to draw off clean fuel is to have the fuel pick-up some distance above the bottom of the storage tank, and to regularly drain the water and sludge from the tank.

The same holds for sediment. A certain amount of rust (for example) builds up during storage; this should be allowed to settle and should be drained regularly with the water.

Fuel storage

When it is realised that the clearances in the injection equipment are in the order of 0.0025 mm or a quarter of a hundredth of a millimetre, it is obvious that even small particles of abrasive material are capable of

doing severe damage to this equipment. Furthermore, since diesel fuel is a heavy fuel, solids take a considerable time to settle out. For these reasons, diesel fuel containers should not be moved for a few days prior to drawing off fuel.

Storage drums and tanks

Storage tanks should be of as large a capacity as practical, and preferably cylindrical. Ideally, they should be set up almost horizontal, with a slope of 40 mm per metre of length away from the outlet connection. The outlet connection should be not less than 75 mm above the bottom of the tank, and a sludge drain cock should be fitted to the bottom of the tank at the low end. Regular draining of sludge and water accumulations is essential if clean fuel is to remain so.

Key factors in the proper storage of fuel are as follows:

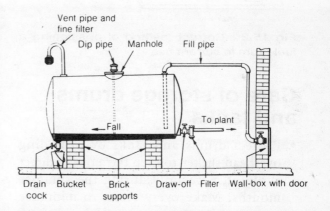

Fig 15.1   Ideal fuel storage tank

- Store fuel in steel drums and tanks. Never use galvanised lined drums or tanks; the zinc reacts with the diesel oil and forms a sludge.
- Diesel fuel has a shelf life of twelve months, when correctly stored under cool, dry conditions. Always empty drums or tanks before refilling with new fuel.
- Drain sediment and condensed water from tanks before refilling.

- Avoid carrying over summer fuel for winter use.
- After moving or refilling storage drums, allow them to stand for a number of hours before drawing off fuel.
- Install a filter in the drum or tank outlet hose.

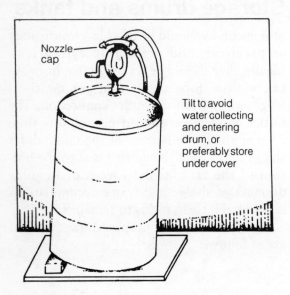

Fig 15.2 Correct method of positioning a fuel drum in current use

Nozzle cap

Tilt to avoid water collecting and entering drum, or preferably store under cover

Care of storage drums and tanks

- Protect drums and tanks by providing overhead shelter to keep them out of direct sunlight, especially during the summer months. Make every effort to minimise variations in temperature, which can cause moisture-laden air to enter the container.
- Store drums off the ground and on their sides with the bungs at the '3 o'clock' and '9 o'clock' positions, as shown in Fig 15.3.

Biological contamination

This fuel contamination problem generally occurs in storage tanks and marine diesel fuel tanks. The contamination begins when micro-organisms multiply at the interface between water on the bottom of the tank and the fuel. The micro-organisms, present in the air at all times, enter the tanks through the breathers or fillers and form a layer of algae.

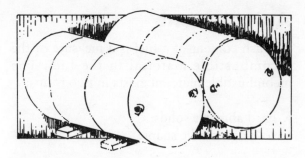

Fig 15.3 Correct positioning of drums in storage

As a result of vehicle motion or the disturbance caused by refilling of the tank, the algae become broken and dispersed throughout the fuel. Carried in the fuel, the algae then block the engine fuel filters to the extent that the engine may stop because of fuel 'starvation'.

Two approaches can be taken to overcome the problem. The first is to remove the inspection cover and manually clean the inside of the tank; the second is to treat the fuel chemically to kill the micro-organisms.

Biological contamination of diesel fuel is more prevalent in areas where a lot of moisture is present in the surrounding air — for example, wet tropical areas, coastal areas and in marine applications.

Care of fuel systems

Machine maintenance

- Refill the fuel tank after use or at the end of the day's operation; this will exclude the moisture-laden air in the tank.
- Drain the sediment and water from the fuel tank and filter once a week.
- Change the fuel filters at recommended service intervals.

- Have enough fuel-filtering equipment on the engine to thoroughly filter the fuel.

Cold weather operation

- Change to the correct fuel and oil for winter operation.
- Store the machine under cover overnight.
- Insulate the fuel-tank and fuel-system components with a suitable cover to protect them from the elements.
- If the engine will not start due to fuel starvation:
  - renew the filter(s);
  - warm the fuel system with hot water or a steam cleaner.

This will dissolve the wax crystals in the fuel lines. Never light a fire under the machine, as disastrous results may occur.

- Use 20–25 per cent heating oil mixed into the diesel fuel to reduce waxing. Heating oil has a lower cloud point than diesel fuel.

16
Engine Lubrication

During the initial stages of development of internal combustion engines, simple — even crude — lubrication systems were used and were satisfactory. However, internal combustion engines have developed from the low-powered, unreliable engines of the late 1800s to the highly sophisticated high-speed machines they are today. As the speed, power, reliability and performance of these machines have rapidly advanced, so the lubrication systems have advanced to keep pace with changing engine designs, for no engine can perform reliably unless it is efficiently lubricated.

Engine lubricating systems

The first lubrication systems to be used were known as 'splash' systems. This was an apt name, for the engine components were lubricated by oil splashed on to them by the engine connecting rod big end and the crankshaft web ends. In the more sophisticated designs, a dipper on the big-end bearing cap picked up oil from the sump, and a drilling led this oil into the big-end bearing surfaces. The main bearings were lubricated by oil splashed into troughs on the inside of the crankcase by the big ends and crankshaft, and led to the bearings through drillings in the housing. However, those early systems have long since been superseded by the pressure system in which oil is pumped by an engine-driven oil pump to the various engine components.

In a typical system, oil from the sump passes through a strainer into a positive displacement oil pump. Leaving the pump (under pressure), the oil flows past a relief valve, which opens whenever the oil pressure exceeds a set maximum to dump sufficient oil to the sump to limit the pressure. Typically, the oil then flows via galleries to the oil cooler, where it is cooled by the engine radiator water or ambient air, although not all engines are fitted with a cooler. Some engines incorporate an oil bypass valve, which allows the flow of oil to bypass the oil cooler when the oil is below a certain temperature — for example, on engine startup.

On leaving the oil cooler, the oil flows through a full-flow oil filter; on some lubrication systems a percentage of this oil flow is directed to a bypass filter, where it is filtered and returned to the sump. From the full-flow filter, the main volume of filtered oil flows to the main oil gallery, which runs the length of the engine block.

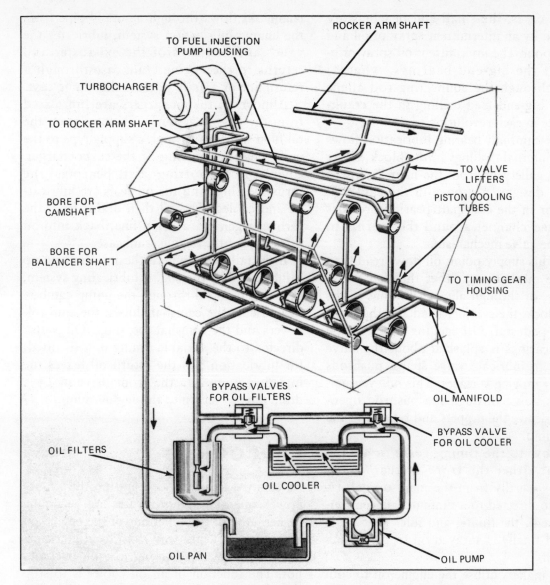

Fig 16.1   Oil flow diagram for a diesel engine   *Courtesy of Caterpillar Inc*

The oil flow from this gallery is directed to the following engine components:

- crankshaft;
- camshaft and valve mechanism;
- timing gears;
- underside of the piston;
- exhauster or vacuum pump (if fitted);
- turbocharger (if fitted);
- fuel injection pump.

Oil for lubricating the crankshaft bearings flows directly to the main bearings through drillings in the engine block. An oil channel cut in the surface of the main bearings carries oil completely around the journal. From this channel, oil passes through drillings in the crankshaft webs to the big-end bearings.

In most designs, the connecting rod small-end bearings (or gudgeon bushes) receive oil from the big-end bearings via axial drillings in the connecting rods.

In other cases, the small-end bearings are lubricated by an intermittent spray of oil and by oil vapour. The intermittent oil spray originates at the big-end bearings, where a drilling through the connecting rod aligns with the big-end feed drilling in the crankshaft once in each revolution.

Oil for camshaft bearing lubrication flows through internal drillings in the block, either from the gallery or from the main bearings. In many designs, a groove in the camshaft journal or in the camshaft bearing provides an oil-feed channel around the journal to supply the valve mechanism.

From this supply point, oil flows readily to the valve mechanism, either through an oil feed pipe, or through aligned drillings in the engine block, the cylinder head and the rocker shaft pedestal. Oil seeping through the rocker bearings is splashed about the valve chamber to lubricate valve stems, pushrods and other moving surfaces. This oil eventually drains down through the pushrod openings, lubricates the tappets and returns to the engine sump.

Oil flow to the timing gears or timing chain (at either the front or rear of the engine) is usually from the main oil gallery. Oil is also directed to a timing chain tensioner (if fitted), the timing and idler gear bearings, and finally is sprayed on to the timing gear teeth.

Many makers utilise the engine oil to cool the pistons, either by actually passing oil through channels in the piston crown, or by directing an oil spray on to the underside of the piston crown.

In a typical system, oil is sprayed upwards under the piston through spray nozzles located at the bottom of the cylinder bore. The oil enters special passages in the underside of the piston, circulates under the crown of the piston and drains out through another passage on the other side of the piston.

Where an engine is fitted with an exhauster (or vacuum pump), it is usually lubricated from the engine lubrication system. The engine oil flows through a supply pipe from the engine lubrication system, lubricates the vanes and bearings of the exhauster and returns to the engine crankcase through a return line or a drain port via the timing case.

Almost all turbochargers are lubricated from the engine system. Oil flows from the oil filter housing through a supply pipe to the main bearing housing of the turbocharger. There the supporting shaft bearings, the thrust bearings and the oil seals are lubricated and cooled. The oil then drains from the turbocharger, via a drain line, back into an open part of the engine crankcase.

In installations where the injection pump is lubricated by the engine lubricating system, the oil is pumped through the pump cambox to lubricate the camshaft lobes, the cam followers and the camshaft bearings. Oil is also directed to the variable timing unit (if fitted) for lubrication. All the return oil leaves the injection pump via the front drive or by a drain pipe to return to the engine sump.

Oil coolers

As engines are developed and produce more power, operating temperatures are becoming higher. One of the functions of the engine oil is to conduct heat away from local hot spots in the engine; in so doing, the oil becomes hot. The function of an oil cooler is to stop the engine oil from becoming excessively hot under heavy load conditions. The hotter the oil becomes, the greater the danger of lubrication failure and oil oxidation.

The operation of an oil cooler is similar to that of an engine radiator, particularly an air-cooled unit, where the oil is passed through the core, which is cooled by ambient air flow.

In a typical water-cooled system (see Fig. 16.2), the hot oil is circulated through a chamber containing a large number of tubes carrying engine-cooling water. Heat passes from the hotter oil to the cooler water, lowering the oil temperature.

Oil filters

During service, engine oil becomes contaminated by oxidation, the products of combustion, abraded metal particles and foreign matter that has entered the engine through the oil filler, engine breather and so on. Oil filters are included in the lubrication circuit to remove any solid contaminants that may cause abrasion or destroy the oil's lubricating quality.

If the oil is passed through a porous material, any solids in the oil larger than the pores will not pass through and will be filtered from the oil. However, the material will eventually become choked, preventing the oil from passing through. The time taken for the filter material to become choked depends on three factors:

1 the size of the pores in the material;
2 the area of filtering material used;
3 the operating conditions, which directly influence how rapidly the oil is contaminated.

Clearly, the size of the pores in the material must determine the filtering efficiency, but a filter material that is too efficient may remove necessary oil additives from the oil and may become choked far too rapidly to be practical. Many different filter materials have

been and are still being used. By far the most common, however, are felt and resin impregnated paper. Many manufacturers of engines using felt filters recommend that dirty elements be washed in petrol a couple of times before being renewed, thus extending the working life of the filter. This is not recommended with paper filters, but their high efficiency has made them the most popular.

The larger the area of filtering material available, the longer it will take to become choked. Hence it is desirable to make oil filters with the largest possible filtering area, but available space limits the overall size, and therefore manufacturers must design their products to present the greatest possible filter area in the most compact form. Most filters are manufactured from sheet material folded or plated to satisfy both requirements.

If an engine is operating under severe conditions of dust and load, the oil will become contaminated sooner than under normal conditions. Consequently, the oil filter will choke more rapidly and will require servicing more frequently.

Full-flow oil filters

By far the most extensively used, full-flow oil filters are fitted between the oil pump and the gallery where they filter all the oil

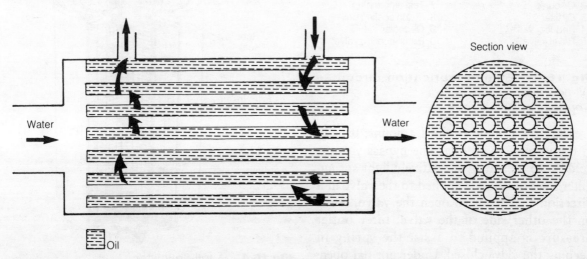

Fig 16.2   Typical engine oil cooler showing oil and water flow paths

delivered to the engine components. Since all the oil flowing to the engine gallery must pass through a filter of this type, the element must not be so fine as to restrict the flow of oil while the filter remains clean and the oil is not abnormally viscous. To prevent oil starvation should a full-flow oil filter become blocked or choked, a bypass is incorporated in the filter housing to provide an alternative oil circuit to the gallery. This bypass is controlled by a valve that opens when the pressure at the filter outlet is less than the inlet

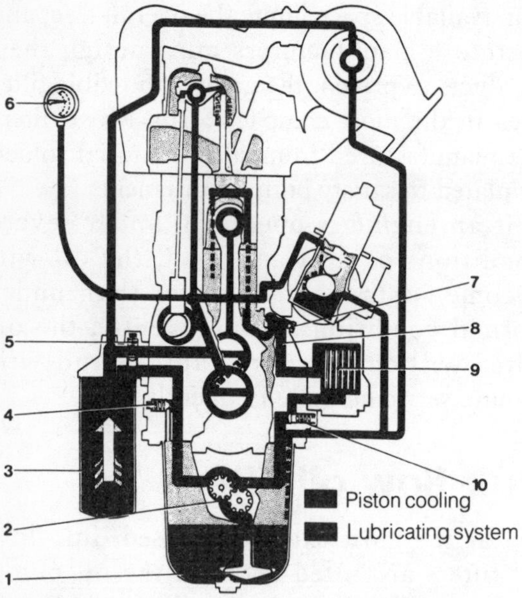

are very nearly equal and the spring holds the valve on its seat, but when the filter element becomes blocked, the outlet pressure drops. If the pressure drops approximately 70 kPa, the total force applied by the spring and outlet pressure will be overcome by the force resulting from the inlet pressure, and the valve will be forced from its seat, allowing the oil to bypass the filter. While this allows unfiltered oil to pass to the engine components, it is preferable to an insufficient flow of oil.

Bypass oil filters

A bypass filter makes use of a finer element than a full-flow filter, but filters only a proportion of the oil delivered by the oil pump. As its name suggests, the filter is incorporated in a bypass circuit, the filtered oil being returned to the sump. However, because a proportion of the oil is constantly being filtered, all the oil is eventually filtered and kept reasonably clean.

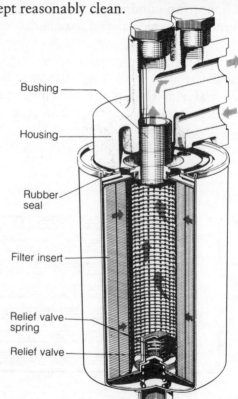

1 Strainer **6** Oil pressure gauge
2 Oil pump **7** Test nipple plug
3 Oil filter **8** Piston cooling drilling
4 Reducer valve **9** Oil cooler
5 Relief valve **10** Piston cooling valve

Fig 16.3   **Engine lubrication circuit —** **full-flow filter system** *Courtesy of Volvo*

pressure by a predetermined amount, usually in the vicinity of 70 kPa. The bypass valve is held on to its seat by a relatively light spring. Filter inlet pressure is applied to the valve in a direction that tends to open the valve, while on the other side of the valve, filter outlet pressure is applied to assist the spring in keeping the valve closed. Under normal operating conditions, the inlet and outlet pressures

Fig 16.4   **A full-flow filter** *Courtesy of Volvo*

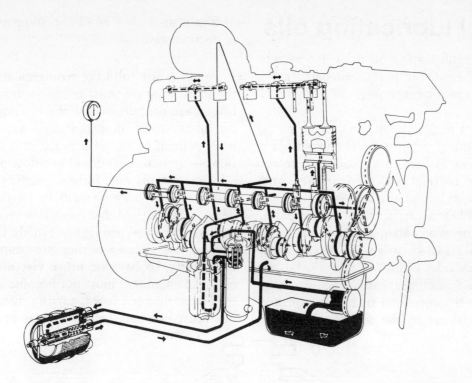

Fig 16.5   Engine lubrication circuit — bypass filter system   *Courtesy of Volvo*

Because of its position in the circuit, a bypass filter must offer sufficient restriction to oil flow to maintain pressure in the lubricating system. If it offered no restriction, almost all the oil would escape back to the sump through the filter and the oil pressure would not build up sufficiently to lubricate the engine components. For this reason, a restricting orifice is usually incorporated in the filter housing outlet.

In many cases, a bypass filter may appear to be similar to a full-flow filter, but it will have a finer element and no bypass valve, since a blockage of the filter cannot restrict the flow of oil to the engine components but must increase it.

Centrifugal oil filters

Filters that have no element, but separate heavy solids from the oil by centrifugal force, are becoming increasingly popular with many engine manufacturers. Filters of this type are known as centrifugal filters,

and may be driven either by the oil that is being filtered or directly by the engine.

The operation of a typical centrifugal filter may be readily followed by reference to Fig 16.6. Oil from the oil pump enters the filter unit through the oil inlet, passes up the spindle and flows into the rotating canister. When the rotor fills, oil enters the outlet tubes through the gauze strainers and escapes through a nozzle at the lower end of each tube. The oil sprays squirting out of the nozzles spin the rotor (turbine action), the rotor being supported in plain bearings in the top and bottom housings.

The speed at which the rotor spins is governed by the oil pressure, and generally lies between 2000 and 6000 rpm. Any solids in the oil are flung by centrifugal force against the sides of the rotor, where they remain until the unit is dismantled and cleaned during service. Centrifugal filters of this type may be employed as either full-flow or bypass units, the outlet being restricted in bypass applications.

Diesel lubricating oils

The engine lubricating oil does not merely lubricate the moving parts, but performs a number of specific functions:

1 It forms a film between the moving parts, so preventing metal-to-metal contact. As a result, wear is kept to a minimum, power loss due to friction is minimised and engine noise is kept at a low level.
2 It carries heat away from hot engine parts, thus acting as a cooling agent.
3 It forms a seal between the piston rings and the cylinder walls.
4 It acts as a cleaning agent.
5 It resists the corrosion of highly polished engine surfaces by the acidic products of combustion that enter the sump past the piston rings.

To efficiently fulfil the requirements listed, the lubricating oil must possess a number of important properties. Of these, viscosity is one of the most important, and has already been defined as the reluctance of a fluid to flow — a viscous fluid will not flow as freely as a less viscous one. In less specific terms, a viscous fluid may be said to be thick or heavy, while a fluid that has a low viscosity is said to be thin, or light. Fluids tend to become less viscous as they are heated and, conversely, to become more viscous when cold. An engine oil must not become so thick in winter that it causes starting difficulties, but must not become so thin at operating

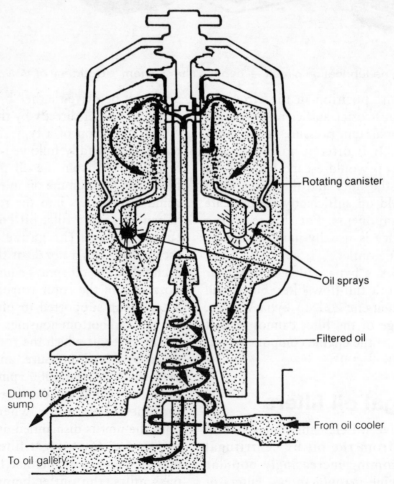

Rotating canister

Oil sprays

Filtered oil

Dump to sump

From oil cooler

To oil gallery

Fig 16.6 Schematic diagram of a bypass centrifugal oil filter *Courtesy of Scania*

temperatures as to fail in its requirements as a lubricant. The oil should resist any tendency to become oxidised at high temperatures, since the oxidation of the oil creates deposits and acid products. However, deposits and acids are also formed through the combustion of the fuel, and the oil should have the ability to wash the deposits from engine components and to neutralise the acids. Further, the oil should not foam when agitated in the sump and should be able to withstand the extreme pressures encountered between certain engine components.

Mineral oil, by itself, cannot fulfil all the requirements of an engine lubricating oil, and certain chemicals are added to the basic mineral oil.

Lubricating oil additives

All lubricating oils suitable for use in medium- and high-speed diesel engines contain most, if not all of the following additives. Indeed, many contain more than the major ones listed below:

- detergent/dispersants;
- oxidation inhibitors (anti-oxidants)
- corrosion inhibitors (alkaline additives)
- viscosity index improvers;
- pour point depressants;
- anti-scuff (extreme pressure) additives;
- foam inhibitors (anti-foam additives)

Detergent/dispersant additives

The detergent component of these additives is included to wash deposits from the engine components, while the dispersant component is provided to ensure that the solids washed from the engine components by the detergent do not clot and form sludge.

The intense heat in the engine cylinder causes the oil film on the piston rings and cylinder walls to be broken down, producing tarry deposits, which may cause the rings to stick in the ring grooves. In addition, small quantities of unburnt fuel may be broken down into similar substances in the same area, aggravating the situation. It is to prevent these deposits from building up that the detergent additives are included in the lubricating oil. However, if the deposits were simply washed from the pistons and rings, they would accumulate as sludge elsewhere and would eventually restrict the oil passages. Dispersant additives prevent any particles from clotting and forming sludge by maintaining the particles in suspension in the oil. Any such particles are then filtered out of the oil by the oil filter, or drained from the engine when the oil is changed.

Oxidation inhibitors

When mineral oil is heated and agitated in the presence of air, the oil oxidises. The oxidation of oil causes three products to be formed — **gum**, which causes components to stick and/or become coated with varnish and oil-ways to become blocked; **acids**, which attach bearing surfaces; and **sludges**, which cause thickening of the oil. The ideal conditions for the promotion of oil oxidation exist in the crankcase of a running engine, and to reduce this tendency, additives known as **oxidation inhibitors**, or **anti-oxidants**, are included in the oil.

Corrosion inhibitors

Alkaline additives, known as **corrosion inhibitors**, are included in the engine oil to neutralise any acids created by oil oxidation or combustion. During combustion, sulphur in the fuel combines with oxygen to form oxides of sulphur. The sulphur trioxide so formed then combines with water vapour created during combustion to form sulphuric acid, while other sulphur compounds combine with water vapour to form less corrosive acids. These acids naturally attack highly polished metal surfaces, particularly if they pass the piston rings and condense on the cooler metal surfaces in the crankcase. Once these acids have entered the sump, they will corrode the running surfaces of the engine, whether it is operating or not.

Viscosity index improvers

The rate of change of viscosity with temperature is known as the **viscosity index** of the oil; the higher the viscosity index, the lower the oil's viscosity change per degree of temperature change. Thus an oil with a high viscosity index maintains a fairly stable viscosity over a wide temperature range. To improve this very desirable characteristic of lubricating oils, viscosity index improvers are added.

If a lubricating oil is too thick (too viscous), the amount of power necessary to overcome friction will be extremely high, while if the oil is too thin, the oil film will be easily fractured and lubrication will fail. But the viscosity of oil changes with temperature — the hotter the oil, the less viscous it becomes. If the oil's viscosity changes very much over the engine's operating temperature range, it is likely that difficult starting (owing to the high friction value) will occur when the engine is cold, and subsequently the quality of the lubrication at operating temperature will be poor.

Pour point depressants

At very low temperatures, oil may become so thick that it will no longer flow. When this occurs, it is impossible to start the engine without first heating the oil in the sump until it becomes fluid enough to permit the engine to be turned over and to ensure adequate lubrication. To lower the temperature at which the oil will remain fluid, pour point depressants are added.

Anti-scuff additives

Certain engine components are subjected to extreme pressure of contact during normal conditions. This high-contact pressure is usually combined with a wiping action and this combination readily breaks through the oil film, allowing metal-to-metal contact. To prevent damage, anti-scuff additives are usually incorporated in engine oil. These additives react chemically with the metal surfaces to form very thin films that are slippery and extremely strong. These films prevent metal-to-metal contact during moments when the oil film is broken.

Anti-foam additives

The churning action in the engine crankcase, coupled with a secondary action of some additives, may cause the engine oil to froth and foam. If this occurs, inefficient lubrication and loss of oil from the engine breather, filler and/or dipstick hole result. The foaming tendency is prevented by the addition of anti-foam additives or foam inhibitors.

Diesel engine oil classification

There are two important aspects to consider in the selection of a lubrication oil. The first is viscosity, which may be considered as the 'body' or thickness of the oil; the second is its additive concentration and content, which determine whether the oil is suitable for use under particular operating conditions.

SAE oil viscosity gradings

Note: This system originated in the United States, where °F are used to designate temperature and test specifications are not given in °C. The following information is given using the original temperature system, but can be converted as follows: 212°F = 100°C; 0°F = –17.80°C.

The viscosity of an oil is indicated by the manufacturer in terms of SAE grade numbers. The higher the number, the more viscous the oil. This number indicates the oil's viscosity at a specific test temperature, namely 210°F. This is a good guide to the viscosity of the oil at operating temperature, but gives no indication of its viscosity at low temperatures; thus there is nothing to indicate that the oil will not become too heavy (too viscous) at low temperatures. However, if an SAE number is following by a 'W', it indicates that the viscosity is based on a 0°F test temperature, and this gives a good indication of the oil's viscosity under winter starting conditions.

Multigrade oils have been developed to give suitable viscosity under winter cold-starting conditions and yet remain viscous enough to ensure efficient lubrication at normal operating temperatures. For example, an oil rated 101W–30 will meet the viscosity requirements of an SAE 30 oil (at 210°F), but will not become any more viscous at 0°F than is specified for an SAE 10W oil.

Note: The viscosity specifications for an SAE 10W oil (at 0°F) are not the same as those for an SAE 10 oil (at 210°F). An SAE 10W oil is much more viscous at test temperature than an SAE 10 oil at its test temperature. Further, at 0°F, an oil rated SAE 10W is much more viscous than an SAE 30 oil at 210°F.

Engine service classifications

Diesel engine lubricants are subjected to greater oxidising influences within the engine cylinder than are the oils used in petrol engines. This is due to greater compression pressures and a much more adequate air supply during combustion.

When a lubricating oil is oxidised on the cylinder walls, pistons and rings, and this combines with the products of the partial combustion of any of this oil that has combined with fuel, gums and lacquers are formed that cause sticking rings and which build up on the piston skirt. Extreme cases of such buildup may ultimately cause engine seizure and must be prevented. Detergent additives will dissolve such deposits, preventing the above problems. The need to use the correct grade of oil cannot be over-emphasised.

If an engine is called on to deliver a high continuous power output, then the oxidising tendencies are very high. Operating an engine to deliver fairly high power at a low temperature promotes, in high addition to deposits, the formation of acids. The use of fuels with a high sulphur content also causes acid formation, while inefficient combustion, regardless of the cause, leads to engine deposits and dilution of the engine oil.

On the other hand, intermittent operation at the rated load and at normal operating temperature, together with the use of high-grade, low sulphur content fuel and efficient combustion, can minimise or prevent the formation of excessive deposits, large quantities of corrosive compounds and oil dilution.

Without some standard, manufacturers would each tend to give an oil a classification that may well have no basis for comparison with another oil, or give any indication of its applications. The standard system of classification in Australia is the API (America Petroleum Institute) Engine Service Classification System.

This system provides the standards for the performance characteristics of engine crankcase oils, and for the operating conditions for which they are intended.

There are two classifications within the system: the Commercial 'C' classification (primarily for diesel engines) and the Services 'S' classification (primarily for petrol engines).

Other classifications have also been widely used: the United States military systems, as in MIL-L-2104B, or the Caterpillar Tractor specifications such as Series 3.

C — 'commercial' classification (primarily for diesel engines)

CE, for very severe-duty turbocharged engines. this classification meets the service typical of turbocharged or supercharged heavy-duty diesel engines manufactured since 1983 and operated under both low-speed, high-load and high-speed, high-load conditions. Oil designed for this service may also be used when previous API engine service categories for diesel engines are recommended.

CF4. This category was adopted in 1990 and describes oils for use in high-speed, four-stroke cycle diesel engines. API CF-4 oils exceed the requirements of the CE category providing improved control of oil consumption and piston deposits. These oils should be used in place of CE oils. They are particularly suited for on-highway, heavy-duty truck applications. When combined with the appropriate 'S' category — for example, SG — they can also be used in petrol- and diesel-powered personal vehicles such as automobiles, light trucks and vans when recommended by the vehicle or engine manufacturer.

Selection procedure

Oil companies are responsible for producing oil that meet the performance requirements of various API classifications.

Engine manufacturers are responsible for deciding which API classification oil meets the requirements of a particular engine under the conditions of intended use. This API classification will normally be listed in the engine or equipment users' handbook (or on the filler cap), as a guide to indicate the most suitable oil to be used.

The equipment owner or user should then purchase an oil which meets this API classification.

Contamination and degradation of engine oil

Contamination

Contamination refers to the presence of unwanted material or contaminants in the engine oil. There are seven contaminants commonly found in contaminated oil.

1 **Wear elements.** Wear elements are regarded as those elements whose presence indicates a part or component which is wearing. Wear elements include copper, iron, chromium, aluminium, lead-tin, molybdenum, nickel and magnesium.
2 **Dirt and soot.** Dirt can enter the crankcase of the engine by way of dirty air entering the cylinders, where it sticks to the oil film and is scraped down from the cylinder walls. Dirt can also enter through a faulty or poorly serviced crankcase breather. Soot is partly burnt fuel. A dirty air cleaner element and subsequent black smoke from the exhaust indicate its presence. When soot by-passes the rings and enters the sump it turns the engine oil black.
3 **Fuel.** Wear in the fuel injection pump plungers and or a faulty injector spray pattern can allow fuel to enter into the engine crankcase and dilute the engine oil.
4 **Water.** Water is a by-product of combustion and is usually removed from the engine via the exhaust pipe or as a vapour out the crankcase breather. However, lower than normal operating temperatures, reduced work loads or long periods of idling can increase the percentage of water in the engine oil.
5 **Ethylene glycol/antifreeze.** Internal leaks within the cooling system allow the entry of coolant into the engine oil.
6 **Sulphur by-products.** Sulphur is present in the fuel after it is refined and, when burnt

in the combustion process, forms sulphur trioxide. Water, which is also a by-product of combustion, enters the crankcase, where it mixes with the sulphur trioxide-forming sulphuric acid.

7 **Oxidation by-products.** Oxidation of the oil is accelerated by high engine operating temperatures, which cause the oil to thicken and produce varnish and lacquer deposits.

Degradation

Apart from contaminants, there are other factors at work which decrease the oil's overall effectiveness. These factors do not directly 'contaminate' the oil, like soot or dirt, but they do contribute to the degradation or breakdown of the oil. They are low coolant temperature, high humidity, engine load and quality of fuel. These factors are explained in more detail below.

• **Low engine coolant temperature.** Low coolant temperature influences the formation of corrosive acids in the engine crankcase. Low engine operating temperature reduces the amount of water vapour leaving the crankcase, thereby increasing the available amount of water to produce sulphuric acid in the engine oil. When using fuel with a sulphur content of 0.5 per cent or less, operating the engine below 80°C will cause acid vapour to form and corrosive attack to occur.

• **High humidity.** When operating under conditions of high humidity, there is additional water content in the air which can increase acid formation in the engine oil.

• **Engine load.** The loads placed on the engine play a critical role in oil degradation. Engines running at rated speed and high load will be operating at maximum efficiency for both lubrication and cooling systems. If, however, the load is reduced with the engine still running at rated speed, the lubrication and cooling systems

will continue to operate efficiently, but the engine can become overcooled. This can affect the wear rates of pistons, rings and liners and cause increased cylinder blowby.

• **Lower grade fuels.** Fuels which have not been refined to a high degree can cause engine damage because the heavier distillate materials cannot be totally burned in the high-speed diesel engine cycle. The engine is subjected to higher concentrations of soot and other unburned or partially burned fuel products which accelerate deposit formation and oil contamination.

Diagnostic tests

A number of oil companies and engine manufacturers offer oil condition monitoring programs consisting of a series of diagnostic tests designed to identify and measure contamination and degradation in a sample of oil.

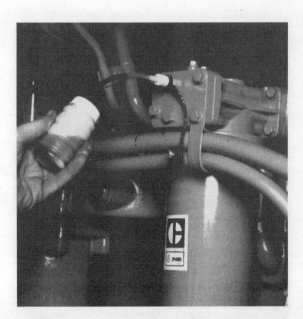

Fig 16.7 Taking an oil sample
Courtesy of Caterpillar Inc

One such condition-monitoring program is composed of three basic tests:

1 wear particle analysis;
2 chemical and physical tests;
3 oil condition analysis.

A brief explanation of what each of these tests involves is given below.

Wear particle analysis

Wear analysis is performed with an atomic absorption spectrophotometer. Essentially, the test monitors a given component's wear rate by identifying and measuring concentrations of wear elements such as copper, iron, chromium, aluminium, lead-tin, molybdenum, nickel, and magnesium in the oil. Based on known normal concentration levels, maximum limits of wear elements are established. After a number of oil samples are taken, trend lines for the various wear elements can be established for the particular engine, and impending failures can be identified when trend lines deviate from the established norm.

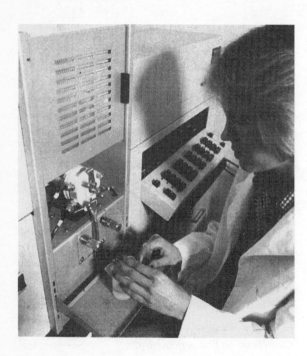

Fig 16.8 Analysing an oil sample using an atomic absorption spectrophotometer
Courtesy of Caterpillar Inc

Chemical and physical tests

Chemical and physical tests detect water, fuel and antifreeze in the oil and determine whether or not their concentrations exceed established maximum limits.

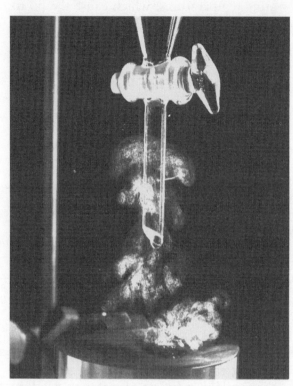

Fig 16.9 The presence of water in the oil is verified and measured by the Sputter Test
Courtesy of Caterpillar Inc

Oil condition analysis

Oil condition analysis is performed via infrared analysis. This test determines and measures the amount of contaminants such as soot, sulphur and oxidation products, as well as checking the viscosity of the oil. Although it can also detect water and antifreeze in the oil, infrared analysis is always accompanied by wear analysis and chemical and physical tests to ensure accurate diagnosis.

Fig 16.10   The presence of fuel in the oil is verified and measured by the Setaflash Tester
Courtesy of Caterpillar Inc

Fig 16.11   Infrared analysis is used to determine the condition of used engine oil
Courtesy of Caterpillar Inc

Oil samples

Cleanliness is of the utmost importance when taking an oil sample — so much so that companies who conduct the oil monitoring service provide a special vacuum pump and sample containers so as to extract the oil sample under conditions which are as clean as possible.

To take an oil sample, run the engine until it is at the correct operating temperature then shut it down. With the vacuum pump assembled and the suction tube cut to the length of the dipstick, place the suction tube down the dipstick tube. Draw up enough oil to fill the sample bottle. Remove the sample bottle from the pump and place the cap on it. It is important that the sample of oil taken is from an open section of the oil compartment, as samples taken at the bottom or side of the sump can contain a high percentage of sludge and therefore give false contamination readings.

One engine manufacturer now provides a sample valve which is built into the oil filter housing for the purpose of extracting oil samples for testing. To obtain an oil sample, fit the tube from the oil sample bottle into the sample valve as shown in Fig 16.7; this will open the valve, allowing oil to flow out with the engine running at idle.

Lubricating system service

Oil pump overhaul

After the oil pump is removed from the engine, it can be dismantled and inspected for wear. To dismantle the oil pump, first remove the drive gear with the aid of a puller, then unbolt the top cover from the pump. Remove the pump gears from the housing. Check the sides of the housing for scoring and wear and also check the ends of the housing and the housing cover for circular wear patterns. If any component shows signs of wear or damage, it will need to be replaced. It is possible on some oil pumps to lightly machine the top cover so as to remove wear marks or scoring. Alternatively, fine scratch marks can be removed from the cover by rubbing it on wet and dry emery paper while on a surface plate.

Also check the pump gears and shafts for wear in areas such as the side of each gear

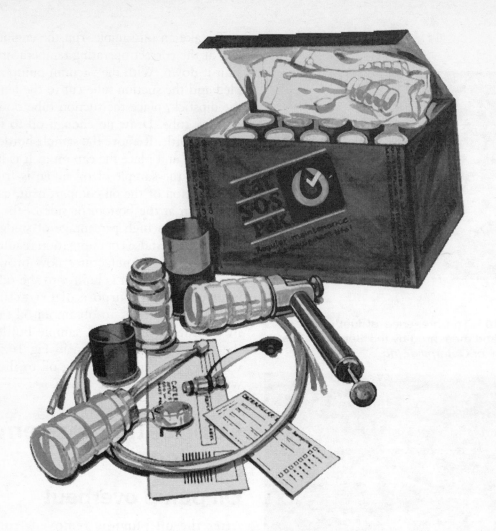

Fig 16.12 Oil sample test kit *Courtesy of Caterpillar Inc*

tooth, the outer diameter and the end faces and the shaft-to-bearing running surfaces.

Once again if the gears or shafts are worn or damaged they must be replaced.

During an oil pump overhaul, all the shaft bushings should be replaced by pressing the bushings out of the housings with a suitable bush driving tool, as shown in Fig 16.14. Refit the new bushings by using the same tool. Upon fitting the new bushes, check that the gears can be installed into the housing and that they turn freely. If this cannot be done, then the bushes will need to be reamed so as to enlarge their diameter. In order to ream the bushes parallel to each other, the pump housing and its end cover must be bolted together.

Then, with the aid of a parallel reamer, as shown in Fig 16.15, ream the bushings until the gears turn freely in the housing.

Carefully clean the pump housings and remove all swarf left after the reaming process. Lubricate the pump gears and bushings with engine oil and fit the gears into the housing.

Oil pump assembly checks

End clearance

With the gears installed in the pump housing, place either the end cover or a straight edge

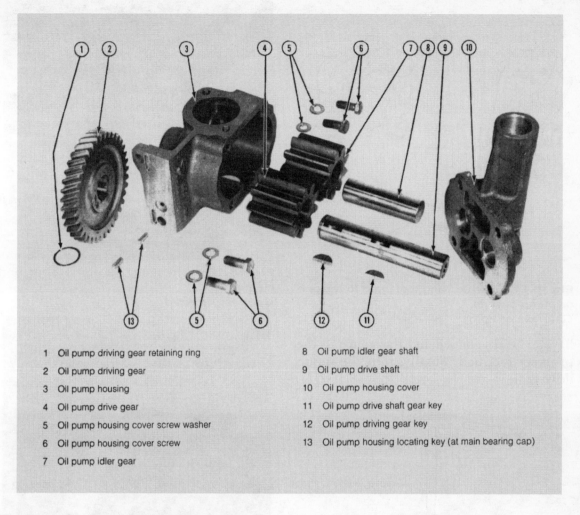

Fig 16.13 Exploded view of a lubricating oil pump   *Courtesy of Mack Trucks Inc*

1   Oil pump driving gear retaining ring

2   Oil pump driving gear

3   Oil pump housing

4   Oil pump drive gear

5   Oil pump housing cover screw washer

6   Oil pump housing cover screw

7   Oil pump idler gear

8   Oil pump idler gear shaft

9   Oil pump drive shaft

10   Oil pump housing cover

11   Oil pump drive shaft gear key

12   Oil pump driving gear key

13   Oil pump housing locating key (at main bearing cap)

across the top of the pump housing and check the gear end float with a feeler gauge, as shown in Fig 16.16. An approximate end clearance should by 0.07 mm–0.15 mm. If the end clearance is greater than specified with the pump housings in good condition, then the gears will need to be replaced.

Side clearance

With both gears installed in the pump housing, check the clearance between the side of the gears and the housing with the aid of a feeler gauge, as shown in Fig 16.17. An approximate side clearance should be 0.050 mm–0.1 mm. If the clearance is greater than

this, either the gears or housing are faulty and need to be replaced.

Backlash

With the gears meshed together, check their backlash using a feeler gauge as shown in Fig 16.18. An approximate backlash figure should be 0.15 mm–0.30 mm.

After checking all the above clearances, the pump end cover should be installed and tightened down. Before installing the pump drive gear, rotate the pump drive shaft and check for any signs of roughness or binding of the gears in the housing. If there are signs of roughness or binding, then the pump will

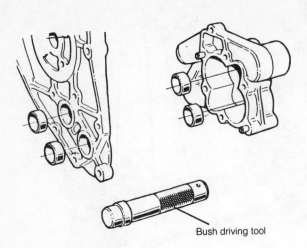

Bush driving tool

Fig 16.14   Bush driving tool used to replace oil pump bushes
Courtesy of Volvo

have to be dismantled and the source of the problem rectified. Finally, refit the pump drive gear.

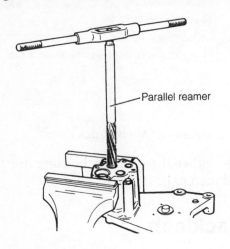

Parallel reamer

Fig 16.15   Reaming new oil pump bushes
Courtesy of Volvo

Oil pressure relief valve

The oil pressure relief valve is generally mounted in the oil pump housing or in the cylinder block next to the oil pump. During an oil pump overhaul, the relief valve should

Fig 16.16   Checking oil pump gear end clearance
Courtesy of Volvo

Fig 16.17   Checking oil pump gear side clearance
Courtesy of Mack Trucks

be dismantled and inspected for wear and/or damage. Upon disassembly of the valve its spring tension should be checked for free length and, if the specifications are available, for compressed length. Also check the valve plunger and housing for wear and/or scoring. Replace any parts which show signs of wear or damage. When reassembling the valve, make sure that the plunger moves freely in its housing. Restricted movement of the relief

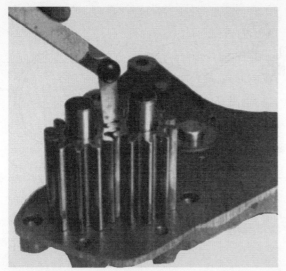

Fig 16.18 Checking oil pump gears for backlash
Courtesy of Volvo

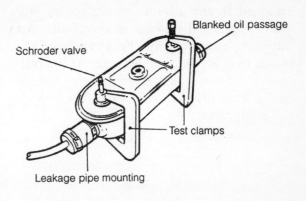

Fig 16.20 Leakage test equipment attached to an oil cooler
Courtesy of Volvo

valve plunger can result in over-pressure and possible damage to engine components such as the oil filter and oil cooler.

Oil cooler leakage test

If the oil cooler shows signs of malfunctioning, then it should be tested for leakage. Prior to testing the cooler, clean out the coolant side and the oil side of the cooler with a suitable cleaning agent. In order to discover any small leakages, the cooler must be tested under temperature conditions similar to those which occur during engine operation.

Prepare the cooler for testing by attaching

leak-detection equipment to the oil cooler as shown in Fig 16.20. The oil side of the cooler is blanked off at one end and a hose is attached to the other end. A schroder valve is attached to one of the sealing clamps on the coolant side of the cooler so as to retain air in the cooler during testing.

With reference to Fig 16.21, lower the oil cooler into a bath containing water heated to approximately 70°C. During the leakage test, do not allow water to enter the test hose attached to the cooler oil passages. Air pressure should then be applied to the cooler so that leakage testing can be carried out at three different pressures: 15 kpa, 100 kpa and 250 kpa. Each testing pressure should

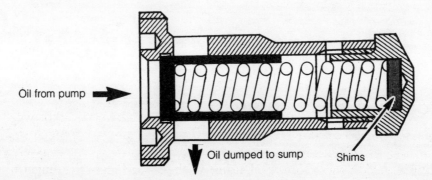

Fig 16.19 Oil pump pressure relief valve   *Courtesy of Scania*

be checked for a minimum of one minute. Air bubbles emerging from the hose attached to the oil side of the cooler will indicate internal leakage in the cooler. Air bubbles from around the outside of the cooler indicate external leakage. At the conclusion of the leakage test remove the oil cooler from the bath and detach the leakage test equipment.

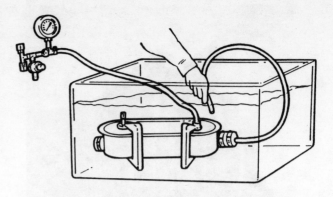

Fig 16.21   Oil cooler being tested for leaks
Courtesy of Volvo

associated with engine operation. These components, which transfer heat to the engine cooling system, are:

- transmission and torque converter oil cooler;
- hydraulic oil cooler;
- retarder oil cooler;
- aftercooler;
- water-cooled exhaust manifolds; and
- marine gear oil cooler.

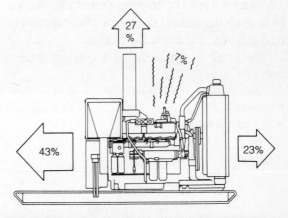

Fig 17.1 Percentages of heat dissipation from a diesel engine

The operation and service life of a diesel engine are directly affected by the cooling system. If the cooling system is of an inadequate size, is poorly maintained or does not function correctly, the result can be overheating or overcooling. Because overheating or over-cooling can cause excessive and unnecessary internal engine wear, with a resultant decreased in engine performance, it is very important that the cause of any problem in the cooling system be rectified as soon as possible.

Types of cooling system

There are two types of cooling system used in modern engines:

1 **Liquid-cooled systems.** These use a liquid to remove the heat from the engine and air or another fluid to cool the liquid.

17

Cooling Systems

In the course of the work cycle of the internal combustion engine, a lot of heat is created. During the combustion phase of the engine operation, the temperature of the burning fuel may reach 1900°C. With modern engine design, a greater percentage of this heat generated during combustion is converted into useful work at the engine's flywheel. Out of the total heat produced by a modern engine, up to 43 per cent is converted into usable power, 27 per cent is lost out the exhaust, 7 per cent is lost in radiation and the remaining 23 per cent is dissipated out into the atmosphere via the cooling system.

The cooling systems of many diesel engines are not only called upon to remove heat generated by combustion, but to remove heat from a number of other components

2 **Air-cooled systems.** These use air flowing around the engine surfaces to remove heat.

Liquid-cooled system components and operation

There are a number of different types of cooling system. The conventional system uses a liquid coolant, a radiator and a fan to remove the heat from the engine.

Different engine applications demand alternative types of cooling system, such as a heat exchanger, keel cooler or cooling towers to dissipate heat from the engine.

The basic components of a cooling system are:

- coolant;
- water pump;
- radiator and pressure cap;
- engine-oil cooler;
- fan;
- thermostat.

Operation

See Fig 17.2. On starting a cold engine, the water pump impeller forces coolant through the engine-oil cooler and then into the cylinder block. The coolant then flows around the cylinders in the block and into the cylinder head. The coolant leaves the head and enters the thermostat housing. As the engine is cold, the thermostat, being closed, prevents the flow of coolant to the radiator and allows it to circulate back to the water pump via a by-pass pipe. In the thermostat-controlled cooling system, the coolant is circulated

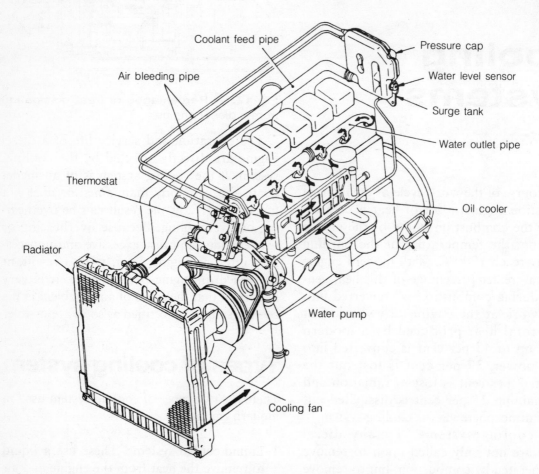

Fig 17.2 Schematic diagram of a typical engine cooling system   *Courtesy of Volvo*

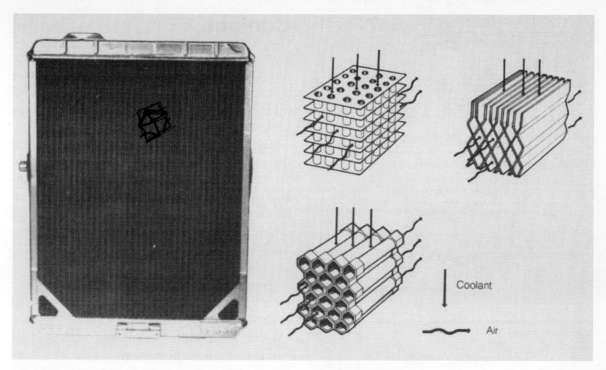

Coolant

Air

Fig 17.3   Radiator and various core patterns   *Courtesy of Volvo*

around the block and head until it reaches the correct engine operating temperature of between 85°C and 99°C. At this point, the thermostat opens and blocks off the by-pass pipe, thus allowing the coolant to circulate down through the radiator and back through the block to repeat its cycle. If at any time the engine coolant temperature were to drop below the normal operating temperature, the thermostat would close slightly, restricting the coolant flow to the radiator, thereby once again raising the temperature of the coolant to the correct operating level. The engine load and the outside ambient air temperature determine how far the thermostat opens, thus allowing coolant flow to the radiator. At the same time as the coolant circulates through the system, the fan pushes or pulls air through the radiator fins and around the tubes that extend from top to bottom of the radiator. Heat then moves quickly from the radiator tubes to the air moving around them. In this way, excess engine heat is dissipated to the surrounding air, keeping the engine at a safe operating temperature.

Cooling system components

Radiator

The radiator is made up of a top and a bottom tank with a tube and fin-type core mounted in between them. Coolant from the engine enters the radiator at the top tank, then passes down through a series of small tubes surrounded by fins and air passages. Radiators are either mounted horizontally or vertically, depending on the allowable space requirements. As far as the actual cooling is concerned, it does not matter whether the coolant flows vertically or horizontally through the radiator core.

Often used in conjunction with a radiator is a surge or expansion tank, which is mounted beside or above the radiator. The main functions of the surge tank are to absorb any increase in coolant volume when the coolant temperature rises, and also to allow for checking and topping up the coolant level.

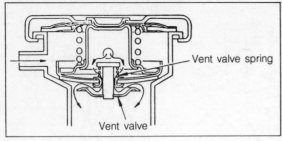

Vacuum valve open

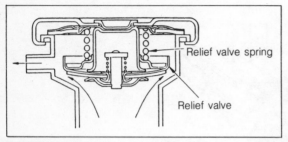

Relief valve open

Fig 17.4   Radiator cap operation

Radiator cap

A pressurised cooling system allows the engine to operate at a higher temperature without boiling the coolant or losing it through evaporation. A radiator cap is used to seal the cooling system and raise its pressure to the required limit. For every 7 kPa of pressure exerted on the coolant, the boiling point is increased by 2°C.

The cap contains two valves, a relief valve and a vacuum valve, as seen in Fig 17.4. The relief valve in the cap allows coolant to escape whenever the system pressure reaches a certain point. An average radiator cap will release pressure from the radiator when system pressure reaches approximately 90 kPa. The vacuum valve in the cap allows air and sometimes water to re-enter the radiator when the coolant cools and contracts. This is to prevent the collapse of some hoses which may not be internally supported.

Coolant

Coolant generally consists of water combined with corrosion inhibitor or water combined with anti-freeze and corrosion inhibitor. It is important to the efficiency and service life of the engine and cooling system that the correct coolant be used. It is the job of the coolant to transfer heat from around the hot engine components to a radiator or heat exchanger where the heat can be dissipated. The coolant has a number of other functions other than to transfer heat. They are:

- to provide corrosion resistance;
- to prevent the buildup of scale and deposits;
- to be compatible with hoses, seals and all metals used in the system.

If an engine is to be used in an area where extremes of cold temperature are not going to be encountered, the water need only have a corrosion inhibitor added to it. However, some engine manufacturers recommend that corrosion inhibitor as well as anti-freeze be used all year around.

Corrosion inhibitor is designed to reduce the effects of corrosion on the metallic components of the system. It is especially important in wet sleeve engines, where it provides a protective layer on the cylinder liner so as to help reduce the damage caused by cavitation on the surface of the metal.

If an engine is to operate under very cold conditions, the water will have to be mixed with an anti-freeze (ethylene glycol) in an approximate ratio of 50–50. This will prevent the coolant in the engine from freezing. If, however, the coolant does not have an anti-freeze added to it, when the coolant temperature drops to freezing point, the coolant will freeze and expand in size. This in turn puts extreme pressure on the cooling system components, and could result in the block or head cracking. By using a 30–50 per cent concentration of ethylene glycol, the boiling point of the coolant is elevated from 100°C to approximately 108°C. However, the degree of heat transfer out of the system using a concentrated mixture of ethylene glycol is less than if straight water were used in the cooling system. Therefore, some of the loss in coolant heat dissipation is recovered by obtaining a higher temperature in the top tank of the radiator without the loss of coolant because of boiling. For this reason, the concentration of ethylene glycol to water should not exceed a 50–50 ratio. If it does, coolant heat transfer and dissipation will be proportionally reduced. Recent research has found that, by using anti-freeze in the cooling system, water pump cavitation can be reduced. One manufacturer recommends that a 30 per cent minimum concentration of anti-freeze should be used at all times to reduce cavitation of the engine water pump.

is made up of a filter element containing corrosion inhibitor. The filter serves to remove any impurities, such as dirt and rust particles, suspended in the coolant, and the corrosion inhibitor imbedded in the filter element dissolves into the coolant, forming a protective film on all the metal surfaces of the cooling system. The filter conditioner performs the function of cleaning and maintaining the cooling passages, while the corrosion inhibitor protects them from corroding.

Thermostat

The thermostat is designed to bring the engine to correct operating temperature as soon as possible and to maintain that temperature.

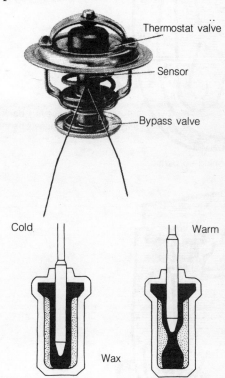

Fig 17.6 Illustration of a thermostat
Courtesy of Volvo

Fig 17.5 Cooling system filter conditioner
Courtesy of Caterpillar Inc

As an alternative to using liquid coolant additives, a coolant filter and conditioner can be fitted to the engine. The filter/conditioner

Types of thermostat

The two most common types of thermostat are the by-pass type and the full-flow type.

The bypass thermostat is designed to divert coolant flow through a bypass circuit, allowing recirculation in the cylinder block during engine warm-up. When the coolant reaches a certain temperature, the valve in the thermostat opens, allowing coolant to flow from the cylinder head to the top tank of the radiator. The coolant also continues to flow through the bypass line in the cylinder block, as it is unaffected by the opening of the thermostat.

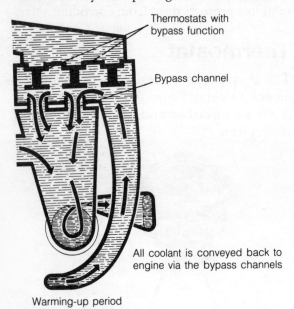

Thermostats with bypass function

Bypass channel

All coolant is conveyed back to engine via the bypass channels

Warming-up period

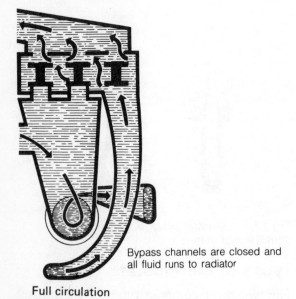

Bypass channels are closed and all fluid runs to radiator

Full circulation

Fig 17.7   Operation of a full-flow thermostat
Courtesy of Volvo

The full-flow thermostat performs the same job as the bypass thermostat during the warm-up period. However, as the coolant reaches the correct operating temperature, the thermostat opens and at the same time closes the bypass line, allowing full flow of coolant from the engine to the radiator.

Thermostats are opened and closed by the expansion and contraction of a special type of wax (see Fig 17.6). At a predetermined coolant temperature (e.g. 80°C), the wax starts to melt; it is fully melted at approximately 90°C, the point at which the thermostat is fully open. When the wax melts, it expands and actuates a piston either directly or by compressing a rubber diaphragm surrounding the piston. The piston in turn regulates the thermostat valve, which gradually opens the water passage to the radiator.

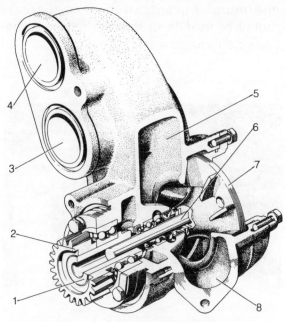

1 Bearing journal	5 Pump body
2 Drive gear	6 Pump shaft
3 Pump outlet	7 Impeller
4 Pump inlet, warming-up period	8 Pump inlet at full circulation

Fig 17.8   Cross-section of a gear-driven water pump
Courtesy of Volvo

The thermostat is also called upon to act as a restrictor for the coolant flowing from the head to the top tank of the radiator. Due to the fact that the coolant temperature in the head is higher than that of the radiator, there is a natural surge of coolant from the head to the radiator. However, if this coolant surge were not restricted in some way, the top tank of the radiator would be subjected to over-pressurising. Thus the relief valve in the radiator cap would relieve and coolant would be lost from the system, which could result in overheating problems.

Water pump

The water pump is of the centrifugal type, consisting of a spiral-shaped body in which an impeller is fitted. The impeller is a press fit on to the driving shaft, which is either gear or belt driven. When the pump is operating, coolant is drawn via the pump inlet into the rotating impeller. Rotation of the impeller forces the coolant against the pump body wall and into the pump outlet passage.

Centrifugal pumps are particularly suitable for cooling systems because they pump large capacities of coolant at relatively low pressures.

The fan

There are three types of fan which can be used in a cooling system: blower, suction and reversible. All three do the same thing: force air through the radiator core. Suction fans are more effective than blower fans because the cooling air doesn't pass around the engine before entering the radiator core. However, the use of a suction fan on a tractor may not be desirable in high ambient temperatures because hot air from the radiator is blown towards the operator. The blower fan is used in applications where there is a high risk of radiator core plugging due to a suction fan pulling thrash into the radiator core (e.g. land clearing).

The reversible fan quickly adapts to various conditions, but it is not as efficient as the other fans. It is important that all the fan blades are positioned the same for either blower or suction operation. In an effort to reduce fan noise, some fans are constructed with their blades unevenly spaced around the fan hub.

Fig 17.9   Reversible fan and fan shroud
Courtesy of Caterpillar Inc

All cooling systems are today designed with a fan shroud, which is located around the fan and attached to the radiator. The fan shroud increases fan efficiency by controlling and directing air flow through the radiator housing. Fan shrouds are designed to fit close to the fan blades so as to prevent recirculation of air at the blade tips.

Because the fan requires a substantial amount of power to drive it, manufacturers have designed temperature-controlled fans which operate at varying speeds relative to the coolant temperature of the engine. Therefore engine power is not wasted unnecessarily in driving the fan at its full speed when it is not required.

A temperature-controlled fan regulates fan speed and thus fan cooling by means of a bimetallic washer mounted in the middle of the fan hub. The fan hub is connected to a drive shaft and is driven via a fluid coupling.

When the cooling air flowing through the radiator reaches a certain temperature, the bi-metallic washer starts to bend and continues bending as the cooling air becomes hotter. The movement of the bi-metallic washer is transmitted via a control pin to a spring-loaded valve in the fan coupling.

At low engine temperatures, the coupling control valve is closed and oil flows from the coupling housing through the return channel to the storage chamber in the cover (see Fig 17.10). Because of the lack of oil which is the driving medium, fan speed is thereby reduced to about a quarter the speed of the drive hub, which is the slowest speed at which the fan will rotate.

At higher coolant temperatures, the coupling control valve opens, allowing oil to flow through the valve and around the drive plate in the coupling housing. The more the valve opens, the greater the amount of oil that flows into the coupling housing; thus the

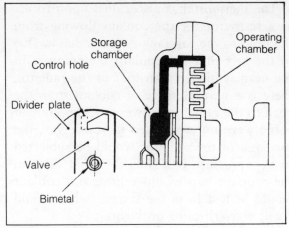

(a) Slow fan speed engine heating up

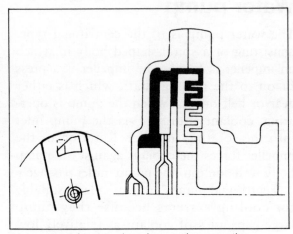

(b) Increased fan speed engine nearing operating temperature

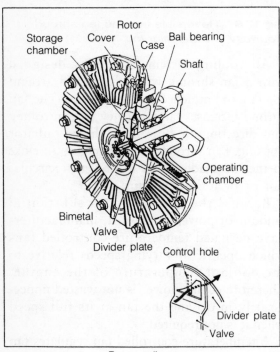

Fan coupling

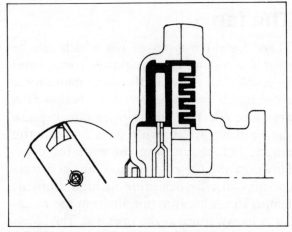

(c) Full fan speed engine at operating temperature

Fig 17.10   Operation of a temperature-controlled cooling fan coupling: (a) Slow fan speed engine heating up; (b) Increased fan speed engine approach operating temperature; (c) Full fan speed engine at operating temperature   *Courtesy of Mitsubishi*

higher will be the speed at which the fan rotates. The fluid used in the fan coupling is a silicon oil of high viscosity, which can be neither topped up nor changed during the life of the coupling.

Marine engine cooling systems

The marine engine cooling system operates in a slightly different way from the conventional system, but still uses the same basic cooling system principles.

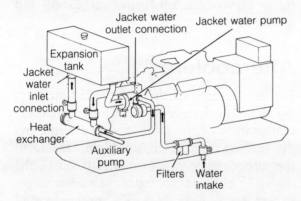

Fig 17.11 Schematic diagram of a typical heat exchanger cooling system

An expansion tank and heat exchanger are used to perform the same task as a radiator (see Fig 17.11). However, instead of transferring heat into the air, a heat exchanger system transfers coolant heat to an external water supply.

On a boat, for instance, the external water supply is sea water, which is pumped from the sea through the heat exchanger then back into the sea. Another variation of the heat exchanger cooling system is keel cooling, as shown in Fig 17.12. The keel cooler is attached to the hull of the boat and the surrounding sea water absorbs heat from the keel cooler.

A simpler type of cooling system used on small marine diesel engines is raw water cooling. This system uses an impeller-type

pump to draw water from the sea and pump it directly through the engine. A thermostat is used to regulate the flow of water through the system, thereby maintaining the engine at its correct operating temperature. The coolant water generally leaves the engine through the exhaust pipe.

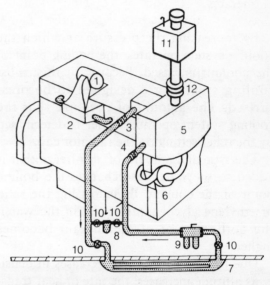

1 Turbocharger
2 Aftercooler, jacket water cooled
3 Jacket water outlet connection
4 Jacket water inlet connection
5 Expansion tank
6 Jacket water pump
7 Keel cooler
8 Bypass filter
9 Duplex full-flow strainer
10 Shut-off valve
11 Auxiliary expansion tank
12 Flexible connection

Fig 17.12 Schematic of a typical keel cooling system

Cooling system temperature

The design of the cooling system is such that it allows an engine to operate within a desired temperature range. During engine operation, the temperature of the coolant must remain high so as to maintain engine operating efficiency, but not too high as to cause the coolant to boil.

There are three factors that can change the temperature at which coolant will boil:

1 the pressure at which the cooling system operates;
2 the amount and type of anti-freeze in the coolant;
3 the altitude at which the cooling system operates.

By increasing the pressure at which the cooling system operates, the boiling point of the coolant is raised. Because of this, most cooling systems are designed to be pressurised. The amount of pressure that the cooling system operates under is determined by the relief setting on the radiator cap.

The type and amount of anti-freeze that is added to the water also changes the boiling point of the coolant. By increasing the ratio of ethylene glycol (anti-freeze) in the water, the boiling point of the coolant becomes higher.

Due to the fact that air decreases in density as altitude increases, the rate of heat transfer to the air will decrease accordingly as the altitude increases. Thus the higher the altitude in which an engine operates, the lower the boiling point of the coolant will be. Therefore higher altitudes cause higher coolant temperatures. In compensation for this, an increase in altitude results in a decrease in ambient air temperature, so the effects can often counterbalance one another.

Heat from other sources

The cooling system is designed primarily to control and regulate the coolant temperature of the engine and remove unwanted heat generated during the combustion process. With the introduction of power shift transmissions, hydraulic systems and turbochargers has come the problem of the production of

unwanted heat from these systems. Therefore it has been left to the cooling system to help remove heat from the engine oil, intake air, transmission oil and hydraulic oil via coolers attached to the engine.

Engine-oil coolers

Because of the higher internal temperatures of turbocharged engines, oil sprays are being fitted to spray oil up under the piston crown so as to help remove some of the heat generated in this area. The oil is then channelled through an oil cooler where the engine coolant must remove enough heat from the oil to prevent the oil from overheating and oxidising.

Aftercoolers

The temperature of the compressed air leaving the turbocharger is much higher than the temperature of the atmospheric air entering the turbocharger. If air inlet temperature to the turbocharger is approximately 30°C, the outlet air temperature from the turbocharger can reach as high as 115°C under loaded engine conditions. Therefore, in an effort to lower the temperature of the air in the engine intake manifold and increase its density, some engines are fitted with an aftercooler or intercooler, which relies on engine coolant to help remove unwanted heat from the intake air.

Transmission oil cooler

During the operation of a power shift transmission, there is a lot of friction between the oil as it flows through the torque converter and transmission system. The bulk of the heat produced in the transmission system comes from the shearing of the oil between the rotating parts in the torque converter. The greatest amount of heat generated in the system occurs when the torque converter operates at or near stall speed.

Hydraulic oil coolers

Some machines have hydraulic oil coolers which are of a radiator-type construction and are mounted between the fan and the radiator. As the air must pass through the cooler before it goes through the radiator, any overheating of the hydraulic oil can cause the cooling system to overheat also.

Troubleshooting the cooling system

The two main problem areas associated with the cooling system are:

1 overheating;
2 overcooling.

Engine overheating

When overheating is suspected, first determine whether it is actual or only indicated. Overheating is usually accompanied by coolant loss. Make a visual inspection of the simple things first: gauges, coolant level, blocked radiator core or slipping fan. Also fit a known accurate temperature gauge into the system to verify actual overheating of the system. Overheating usually results from reduced cooling system efficiency and/or increased demands being placed on the cooling system.

Engine overheating may not necessarily be caused by engine-related malfunctions. Heat from other sources is introduced into the cooling system via engine-mounted oil coolers. If the transmission is operated at or near stall for lengthy periods of time, the temperature of the oil in the torque converter rises sharply, resulting in extra heat being dissipated into the cooling system. At the same time, fan and water pump speeds are reduced due to the low lugging speed of the engine, thereby reducing the heat dissipation capacity of the cooling system. Another factor affecting cooling system efficiency is that the rate of heat dissipation from the radiator to the air is directly related to the difference between the coolant and ambient air temperatures. High ambient air temperature will cause the cooling system to operate at a higher temperature. If a simple visual inspection does not locate the cause of the overheating problem, more in-depth checks of the system will be necessary.

The most common cause of engine overheating is a lack of sufficient coolant. After making sure the radiator is cool, check the level of the coolant. A low coolant level can sometimes cause overheating, but it can also be the result of overheating. If the coolant boils, the pressure buildup will cause the relief valve under the radiator cap to open, thereby relieving system pressure and allowing coolant to be lost from the system. If the coolant level is found to be low, top up the system to the required level; if the engine overheats again, it will be evident that the low coolant level is not the cause of overheating.

When filling the top tank of the radiator, always allow some free space for coolant expansion. If the top tank is filled completely, excess coolant will be forced out the overflow via the relief valve.

Radiator cap

A faulty radiator cap allows loss of pressure and coolant from the system. Use a radiator cap pressure tester to check the pressure at which the relief valve relieves. This relief valve setting can generally be found stamped on top of the radiator cap. A general radiator cap relief valve setting is 90 kPa. If the relief valve relieves at a lower pressure than that specified on the radiator cap, replace it. Using the same tester, attach it to the radiator filler opening and pressurise the system. However, do not pressurise the system any more than 14 kPa above the specified system pressure. Leave the system under pressure and carefully inspect the radiator core, hoses, head gasket and water pump for water leaks.

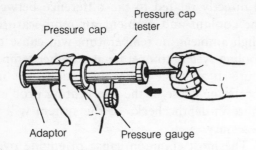

Fig 17.13 Radiator cap pressure tester

Thermostat

As mentioned earlier, the thermostat prevents coolant from flowing between the engine and the radiator until it reaches the correct operating temperature. However, if the thermostat fails to open, the coolant in the block cannot dissipate combustion heat quickly enough, therefore causing the engine to overheat.

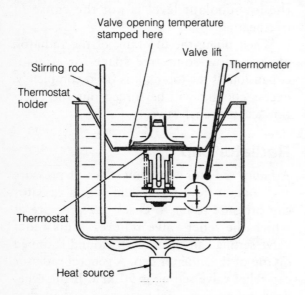

Fig 17.14 Testing a thermostat

A thermostat can be checked by placing it with a thermometer in water and heating the water slowly until the thermostat valve opens. Check the thermometer to see at exactly what temperature the thermostat starts to open and compare this with the opening temperature stamped on the thermostat itself. If the thermostat does not operate correctly, replace it. Never operate an engine without a thermostat, as overheating can occur.

Coolant condition

The condition of the coolant in the system also has a bearing on overheating. If the coolant in the system has not been changed on a regular basis and new corrosion inhibitor added, scale deposits can form in the radiator and engine. Scale deposits can cause serious engine damage by retarding the transfer of heat to the coolant. A deposit of lime 2 mm thick insulates the same as 50 mm of steel. Consequently, heat transfer out of the cooling system is substantially reduced.

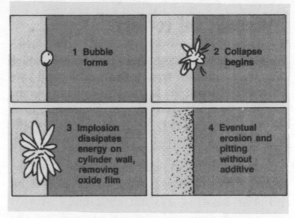

Fig 17.15 Progression of cavitation and pitting on a cylinder wall

Cylinder liner cavitation erosion

Cylinder liner cavitation is a special type of corrosion caused by the collapse of vapour bubbles at the surface of a vibrating liner. As the piston descends down the cylinder during the power stroke, a certain amount of piston slap takes place. This causes the liner to vibrate and create vapour bubbles in the coolant. The outside wall of the liner first moves away from the coolant, causing an area of low pressure near the liner surface. The low pressure allows the coolant to vaporise and form bubbles. When the liner vibrates or moves towards the coolant, the pressure at the liner surface increases greatly, causing the bubbles to collapse. The collapsing vapour bubbles implode inward and physically attack the cylinder wall's protective oxide film, causing corrosion and pitting of the liner walls to take place at a fast rate. The most severe pitting is on the side of the liner where the piston thrusts during the power stroke. The use of a corrosion inhib-itor in the coolant is the most effective way of preventing cavitation damage. The chemicals in the inhibitor create a tough, thin oxide protective layer on the metal surface which can withstand the shockwave generated by the collapsing bubbles. Cylinder liner cavitation erosion generally occurs on wet-sleeve engines, as opposed to dry-sleeve engines.

Fig 17.16   Cylinder liner showing the results of cavitation

Water pump

If the water pump does not circulate coolant

through the cylinder block, the head, the aftercooler (if equipped) and the oil cooler at a certain rate, the engine will overheat. Poor coolant circulation generally indicates a badly corroded or worn water pump impeller or slipping fan/water pump drive belt.

Aftercooler

The aftercooler fitted to a turbocharged engine cools the inlet air so as to make it more dense. If, for any reason, there are restrictions to either the coolant or air flow through the aftercooler, reduced aftercooler efficiency will result. If the aftercooler does not cool the intake air to an acceptable point, then a rise in inlet air temperature will result in a threefold rise in exhaust temperature, which would be a cause for engine overheating. For example, a 1°C rise in inlet air temperature will result in a 3°C or more rise in exhaust temperature.

Fan operation

Reduced fan speed will result in inadequate heat transfer from the coolant to the atmosphere, thereby causing overheating of the system. Lower-than-normal fan speed can be caused by loose or worn drive belts, or worn pulley grooves.

Air flow obstruction

Reduced air flow through the radiator core due to blocked fins can result in an engine overheating. Check for any blockages in the radiator core by lowering a light down one side of the radiator and visually inspecting the opposite side.

Temperature gauge

If the temperature gauge indicates overheating and there has been no coolant loss or extremes of engine temperature, replace the gauge and recheck the coolant temperature.

Engine overcooling

Overcooling can be as harmful to the engine as overheating and occurs when normal operating temperatures are not reached.

When an engine operates at or below the normal operating temperature, the heat of compression and subsequent heat of combustion are reduced. This results in incomplete burning of the fuel, which settles out on the sides of the cylinder walls, washing away the lubricating oil film and thus increasing component wear rate. Therefore the engine will use more fuel in an effort to make up for the resultant loss of power. At the same time, the piston has not expanded to its normal dimensions resulting in increased piston-to-bore clearance. This increased clearance allows excessive movement between the piston and cylinder, once again increasing cylinder and bore wear rates.

The usual cause of overcooling is coolant flowing through a defective fully open thermostat back into the radiator. Another cause of overcooling is when the engine is operated under low ambient temperatures and for prolonged idle periods, even though coolant is not flowing through the radiator. To verify whether an overcooling problem exists, install an accurate temperature gauge into the cooling system and run the engine for a period of time under normal operating conditions.

Air cooling

Air cooled engines rely on air to contact the metal fins on the surfaces of the engine, thereby transferring heat from the engine to the cooler surrounding air.

Good heat dissipation in an air cooled engine depends on three things:

1 the cooling fin design;
2 the velocity of the air passing over the fins;
3 the temperature difference between the air and the fin surface.

Methods of air cooling

In small single- and multi-cylinder engines, flywheel fans are used to force air through special ducting surrounding the head and cylinder assembly.

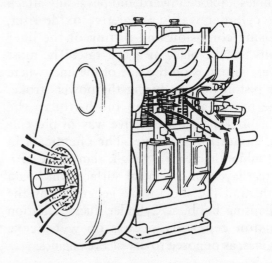

Fig 17.17   Cooling air flow through an air-cooled engine

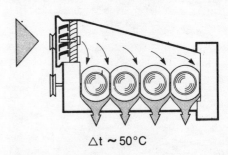

$\Delta t \sim 50°C$

Fig 17.18   Cooling air flow through a multi-cylinder Deutz engine

In larger engines (four through to eight cylinders), engine cooling is via high-speed axial-flow fans through carefully designed ducting which concentrates the air flow on the critical heat areas of the engine.

The operating temperature of some Deutz engines is regulated by the use of a variable-speed cooling fan. With this type of design, the amount of air cooling through the engine is directly related to engine temperature. The

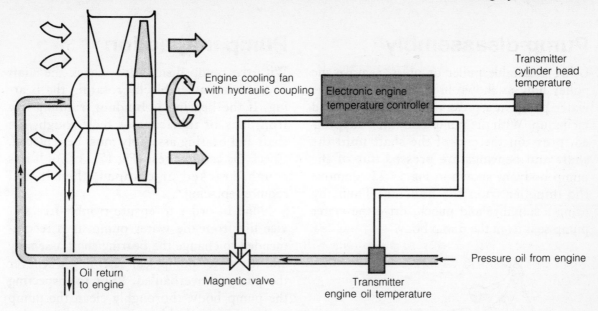

Engine cooling fan
with hydraulic coupling

Electronic engine
temperature controller

Transmitter
cylinder head
temperature

Pressure oil from engine

Oil return
to engine

Magnetic valve

Transmitter
engine oil temperature

Fig 17.19   Schematic of an electronic engine temperature control as used on a Deutz air-cooled diesel engine   *Courtesy of Deutz*

cooling fan is driven by the engine timing gears through an hydraulic coupling whose speed is automatically controlled (see Fig 17.19). The electronic engine temperature controller senses engine temperature and, if necessary, varies the amount of engine oil flowing to the hydraulic coupling to alter its speed. Thus the cooling-fan speed is controlled by the temperature of the engine, which relates directly to how hard the engine works. During engine warm-up, cylinder-head temperature and engine-oil temperature are monitored by the electronic controller which reduces oil flowing to the fan hydraulic coupling. This results in a low fan speed which helps bring the engine to correct operating temperature quickly. After the correct operating temperature is reached, the amount of cooling air required is directly related to the temperature of the engine. Thus the engine is not unnecessarily deprived of energy in driving the cooling fan.

Water pump service

The explanation and diagrams below represent the overhaul procedure for one

particular design of water pump. As water pump design varies from one engine manufacturer to the next, the relevant workshop manual should always be used so as to ensure correct dismantle and reassemble procedures.

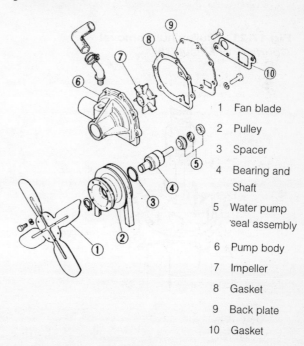

1 Fan blade

2 Pulley

3 Spacer

4 Bearing and
   Shaft

5 Water pump
   seal assembly

6 Pump body

7 Impeller

8 Gasket

9 Back plate

10 Gasket

Fig 17.20   Water pump

Pump disassembly

Using a suitable puller or press, remove the pulley hub, as shown in Fig 17.21. Place the water pump in a press with the impeller end facing up. With the pump body well supported, press on the end of the shaft until the shaft and bearings are pressed out of the pump body, as shown in Fig 17.22. Remove the impeller from the housing. Then, by using a hammer and punch, drive the water pump seal from the pump body.

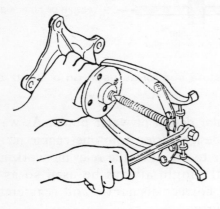

Fig 17.21   Pulley hub removal
Courtesy of Mitsubishi

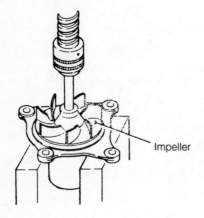

Impeller

Fig 17.22   Using a press to remove the shaft and bearing from a water pump housing
Courtesy of Mitsubishi

Pump inspection

With the pump dismantled, check the shaft and bearing assembly by rotating the bearing. If the bearing is binding, running dry from lack of lubricant or feels rough, the shaft and bearing assembly must be replaced. Check the ceramic seat (Fig 17.23 (2)). If it is rough, cracked or chipped, then it will require replacing.

Note: In order to ensure trouble-free service life from the water pump, it is recommended to change the bearing/shaft assembly and the water pump seal assembly whenever the pump is overhauled. Prior to inspecting the pump body, thoroughly clean the pump body with a suitable solvent, then examine the bearing bore for signs of bearing spinning. If measurements are available, measure the bearing bore for correct size. Also examine the pump body for signs of cracking and/or impeller vane rubbing. If any of these conditions exist, then the pump body must be replaced.

Pump assembly

Prior to fitting the new water pump seal, apply a thin coating of sealant around the outer metal case of the seal. Then, with the impeller side of the pump facing up, use a suitable adaptor or sleeve that contacts the outside diameter of the seal body and carefully press the seal into the pump body.

Note: Do not press on the spring loaded face of the seal, otherwise it will be damaged. With the seal installed, reposition the pump so that the bearing bore is facing up. Place the shaft and bearing assembly into the bore, taking note that the impeller end of the shaft goes in first. Using a suitable adapter or sleeve that contacts the outer ring of the bearing, press the shaft and bearing assembly into the pump body until it is seated in the housing bore.

If a new ceramic seat is to be fitted to the impeller, pry out the old seat and clean the seat location area. Install the new seat into the impeller, ceramic side facing out, and press it fully home using hand pressure. If greater pressure is required, then protect the ceramic face and, using a press, carefully press the seat into the recess in the impeller.

Note: Before installing the impeller, the ceramic face of the impeller seat and the seal face in the pump body must be free of oil, grease and fingerprints. Support the water pump in a press so that the pulley hub end of the shaft sits on a solid base. Using a suitable adaptor, press the impeller onto the opposite end of the shaft. The impeller is pressed on to the shaft until either a set distance between the impeller and the cover mounting face is achieved or the impeller vanes are a specific distance from the pump body, as shown in Fig 17.23.

Turn the water pump over and support the impeller end of the shaft. Using a suitable adaptor, press the pulley hub on to the shaft. The hub will need to be pressed on a certain distance to correctly locate the fan and drive belt pulley, as shown in Fig 17.23.

On completion of pump assembly, rotate the pulley hub and check for proper pump operation. A slight drag caused by the mating surfaces of the water pump seal is normal.

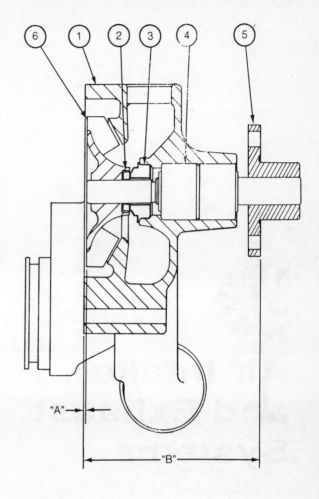

1	Water pump body	5	Pulley hub
2	Ceramic seat	6	Impeller
3	Water pump seal	Dim. "A" Refer specification
4	Shaft and bearing	Dim. "B" Refer specification

Fig 17.23 Cross-section of a water pump assembly showing fan hub and impeller positioning *Courtesy of Fiat Allis*

18
Air Intake and Exhaust Systems

Air intake system

The air intake system supplies clean air for engine combustion while the exhaust system takes away the by-products of combustion in the form of exhaust gases. The components that make up the air intake and exhaust system are as follows.

- **Pre-cleaner**. The pre-cleaner removes large particles of dirt and debris.
- **Air cleaner**. Usually there are two air cleaning elements, a primary and a safety element. The elements filter dust and dirt from the air passing through them en route to the engine cylinders.
- **Air cleaner service indicator**. The indicator monitors air inlet restriction through the air cleaner element and determines when the element should be serviced.
- **Turbocharger** (if used). Heat expansion from the exhaust gases drives the turbocharger, which pumps additional air into the engine, allowing more fuel to be burned, and thereby increasing the power output of the engine.
- **Aftercooler** (if used). The aftercooler cools the air after it leaves the turbocharger prior to entering the engine. This increases the air density, so more air can be packed into the cylinders, thereby increasing engine power output.
- **Intake manifold**. The air intake manifold connects directly to the cylinder head(s). The intake manifold distributes clean air from the air cleaner or turbocharger into each cylinder.
- **Exhaust manifold**. The exhaust manifold connects directly to the cylinder head(s) and collects exhaust gases from each cylinder, then directs them to the turbocharger and/or to the muffler.
- **Muffler**. The muffler reduces the sound level of the exhausting gas.

Pre-cleaners

Although several types of air cleaning device are used as preliminary pre-cleaners, probably those used most extensively are centrifugal in action. The Donaldson PB series (Fig 18.2) is an excellent example of this type of device. It is probably simplest to consider the unit as consisting of three concentric components enclosed under a cover, although the two inner components are in fact manufactured as one piece: the base. In the centre lies the air outlet through which the air, with up to 80 per cent of the dust removed, passes to the main air cleaner element. Surrounding this outlet, but integral with it, lies a set of angled air inlet vanes which cause rotation of the air as it enters the assembly. Around this again lies the transparent dust receptacle.

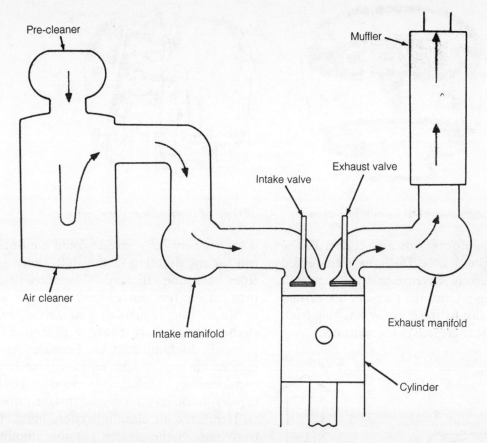

Fig 18.1 Air intake and exhaust system *Courtesy of John Deere*

Contaminated air, entering through the vaned inlet, is caused to move upwards and to rotate around inside the inner face of the dust receptacle. Heavy dust particles are carried outwards by centrifugal force and pass over the top lip of the dust receptacle inner face to fall into the collection area, while clean air is taken from the centre of the vortex down through the outlet. When the dust level reaches an indicator line on the transparent receptacle, it should be emptied by unscrewing the knurled nut on the top, removing the cover, lifting the receptacle from the base and emptying it.

When an engine is being used under conditions where light, coarse materials such as chaff and leaves may be carried into the air cleaner, a gauze screen may be used as well as or instead of a pre-cleaner to prevent such materials from entering the air cleaner, where they could seriously impair the efficiency of any cyclone-type separator. Such screens are also readily available and are called 'pre-screeners'.

The Donaspin pre-cleaner

The Donaspin pre-cleaner is designed to remove heavy contaminants from the incoming air and automatically eject them from the system via the exhaust pipe. The advantages of this system over the conventional pre-cleaner include higher engine volumetric efficiency as a result of the less restricted air flow and, most of all, lower maintenance.

Air flows into the Donaspin pre-cleaner via angled slots on the pre-cleaner housing; these slots direct the air in a swirling motion around the inside of the pre-cleaner. Due to centrifugal force, the heavy particles in the

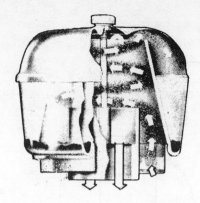

Fig 18.2   Donaldson PB series pre-cleaner   *Courtesy of Donaldson Air Cleaners*

air are thrown outwards and collect in the base of the pre-cleaner. This area is connected via a low-pressure scavenge line to a venturi in the exhaust pipe, and the particles are carried into the exhaust by the air flow resulting from the low pressure created in the venturi.

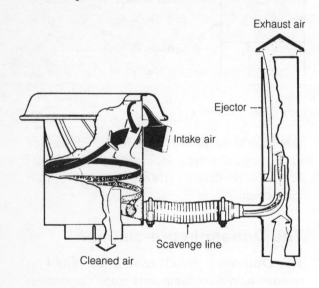

Fig 18.3   Schematic diagram of a Donaspin pre-cleaner
Courtesy of Donaldson Air Cleaners

Air cleaners

In earthmoving applications, air cleaners have been known to remove over 3.5 kg of dust in an eight-hour shift. Should dust enter the engine at this rate, it is extremely doubtful if even a very large engine could continue to run for the duration of the shift, quite apart from operating efficiently. The entry of dust into an engine causes fast abrasive wear of rings, liners, pistons and valves, while turbochargers are rapidly destroyed by pumping contaminated air. Because the volume of air required by an IC engine is very considerable, a small abrasive dust content rapidly amounts to a very damaging quantity. Hence the air cleaning system must effectively remove the greatest possible amount of foreign particles from the air.

A naturally aspirated engine must have an unrestricted air supply if it is to develop anything like its maximum possible power, and even a turbocharged engine will suffer from considerable loss of power if its air supply is restricted. This power loss is caused by insufficient air being available to allow full combustion of the quantity of fuel being injected, and is evidenced by black exhaust smoke. Thus the air cleaning system should offer no restriction to airflow.

While the achievement of maximum cleaning efficiency is the most important factor in air cleaner design, closely followed by unrestricted airflow, factors such as durability, service accessibility, service life and cost are also important considerations.

The type of air cleaner fitted to a high-speed diesel engine depends largely on the size of the engine and the environment in which it has to operate. Of the many types available to suit various operating conditions, most manufacturers of modern high-speed diesel engines use a dry element type air cleaner. If the engine has to operate under extremely dusty conditions, a preliminary air cleaner (pre-cleaner), usually of the centrifugal type, is generally fitted in addition to the dry type cleaner.

When selecting an air cleaner to suit a particular engine, whether setting up a new installation or improving an existing one, it is of the utmost importance that the air cleaner is suitable for the application. Air cleaner manufacturers have full data available for their various models, including dimensions and airflow capacity. The capacity must be suitable for the engine, so the engine requirements must be known. Although the engine manufacturer can best supply this information, it is possible to calculate the requirements in most instances from the following formula, bearing in mind that it applies to naturally aspirated engines. For others, refer to the manufacturer's figures.

For naturally aspirated four-stroke engines:

$$\text{airflow} = \frac{\text{displacement} \times \text{rpm} \times \text{VE}}{2000}$$

where airflow is in m^3/min
displacement is in litres and
VE is volumetric efficiency

For naturally aspirated two-stroke engines, double the requirements by halving the denominator.

Note: The volumetric efficiency of IC engines varies as follows:

4-stroke side valve petrol engine	70%
4-stroke OHV petrol engine	75%
4-stroke OHV diesel engine	85%
4-stroke OHV turbocharged diesel engine	130% (av)

Dry element type air cleaners

Although oil bath air cleaners have been extensively used, they are rapidly being replaced by dry element type (paper element) air cleaners throughout their entire range of applications. There are a number of reasons for their fall from favour:

- Although the oil bath air cleaners are quoted at 95–98 per cent efficient, dry element air cleaners are rated at 99.5 per cent efficient for the same size dust particles. Hence the oil bath air cleaner may pass from four to ten times as much dust as the dry element type.
- Because the oil bath air cleaner depends on high air velocity to cause dust particles to impinge on the oil surface, its efficiency is affected by engine speed and may fall to 90 per cent at reduced engine speeds. Should it fall to this low figure, the oil bath air cleaner would pass twenty times as much dust as a dry element air cleaner, the efficiency of which does not fall with engine speed.
- The oil bath air cleaner is less efficient at low temperatures due to increased oil viscosity.
- A well designed air cleaning system of the dry element type is less likely to cause restriction to airflow over the entire speed range.
- There is danger of the airflow picking up air cleaner oil as a result of an overfilled oil container or an extremely steep operating angle. Should oil be carried into a diesel engine from the air cleaner, the engine will run uncontrolledly as it burns this oil and will stop only when the oil is used or when the air intake is closed. Such runaway conditions usually cause extremely high speed and engine damage may well occur.
- An oil bath air cleaner gives no warning when it is in need of service and its efficiency has fallen. A dry element air cleaner, on the other hand, causes air restriction when in need of service, causing loss of power and black exhaust smoke, but suffers no fall off in cleaning efficiency. If a service indicator is fitted to the system — a service indicator is a warning device operated by the pressure differential across

the element (although it may be dash mounted), and gives a visible indication when the element is so restricted by dust as to require service — the engine may be operated without risk until the indicator warns that service is required, so extending service periods to the maximum for the prevailing operating conditions, with complete safety.

- In general, the dry element type air cleaner is simpler to service.
- The dry element type air cleaner can be mounted in any position, while the oil bath air cleaner must be vertical.

Although the air cleaning elements range from small, simple automotive types, perhaps 150 mm in diameter and 50 mm thick, to large industrial types, 300 mm in diameter and 450 mm long (and larger), the filtering material used in their manufacture is resin-impregnated paper. The element may consist simply of a ring of pleated paper carrying a moulded rubber gasket on its sealing face, or may well carry a series of fins or vanes on its outer surface, which acts as a pre-cleaner by imparting a swirl to the incoming air, so that large dirt particles are separated by centrifugal force and are deposited in the bottom of the

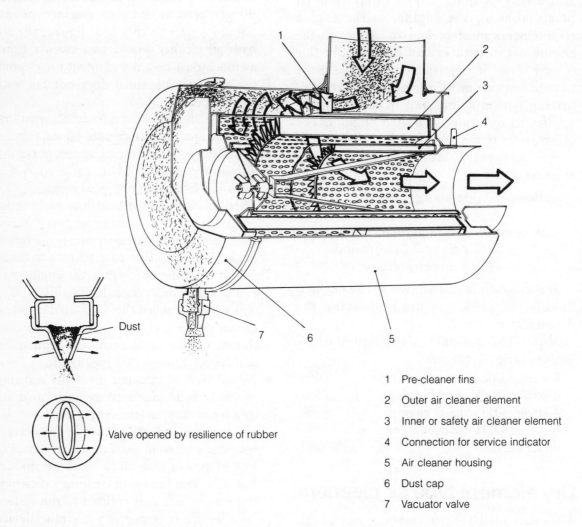

Dust

Valve opened by resilience of rubber

1   Pre-cleaner fins

2   Outer air cleaner element

3   Inner or safety air cleaner element

4   Connection for service indicator

5   Air cleaner housing

6   Dust cap

7   Vacuator valve

Fig 18.4   Donaldson FH Cyclopac air cleaner   *Courtesy of Donaldson Air Cleaners*

unit in the dust cup. Many industrial air cleaners feature a safety element — a second dry element inside the main or primary one — to protect the engine should the main element be damaged and to prevent any dust disturbed during removal of the primary element from entering the engine.

Instead of manufacturing their own air cleaners, most engine and equipment manufacturers buy them from or have them manufactured by specialists in this field. Probably the most extensively used dry element air cleaners would be those manufactured by the Donaldson Company Inc of the United States, which are fitted to an extremely large variety of IC-engined machines. We will examine the Donaldson 'Cyclopac' series and the 'Donaclone' series and, in doing so, we should cover the operation and service requirements of those types of air cleaner used extensively on heavy equipment.

There are two types of Cyclopac currently available — the FW series and the FH series — and both use the same system of air movement to centrifugally remove heavy contaminants. The FW series is a single-element air cleaner and the FH, as shown in Fig 18.4, is a duel-element two-stage air cleaner. Both air cleaners can be mounted in either a horizontal or vertical position.

In operation, incoming air enters the inlet of the air cleaner housing and flows around the outside of the element, where it passes through the pre-cleaner fins. The fins cause the air to rotate rapidly around the outside of the element so that large dust particles are separated from the air and carried to the bottom of the air cleaner where they are collected in the dust cup. Those finer dust particles that remain are separated from the air when they pass through the filter paper of the outer or primary element. Finally, the air flows through the safety element and on into the engine.

Vacuator valve

The installation of a vacuator valve on the dust cup will eliminate the need for regular dust cup service, as this valve will automatically eject dust and water. The vacuator valve is made of rubber and fits on to the bottom of the dust cup, as shown in Fig 18.4. Even though the dust cup is normally under a slight vacuum when the engine is running, pulsing of the vacuum opens and closes the valve, expelling dust and water. The vacuator valve will also unload and expel dust when the engine is stopped.

Within the Donaclone series of air cleaners, there are three basic types: the SBG series for medium- to heavy-duty service, the STG series for medium-duty service and the SRG series for heavy-duty service. All types utilise a number of Donaclone tubes for primary dust separation with a dry element for final filtration.

The Donaclone tube (Fig 18.6) consists of a nylon outer tube with an aluminium inner. Vanes at the top impart a cyclonic twist to the air as it enters the unit, causing heavy particles of dust to be thrown to the outside, from where they fall to the bottom of the tube and into the dust cup. Relatively cleaner air is taken up through the centre tube to pass to the paper element. This air leaving the tubes is claimed to be as clean as that obtained from some oil bath air cleaners.

The SBG series Donaclone (Fig 18.5) features the dry element mounted vertically above the lower section containing the Donaclone tubes. Contaminated air enters the unit from one side, passes down into the tubes and moves up into the section carrying the dry element, from whence it leaves via a side air outlet. Access to the element is from above in the standard type, but specific models are available for horizontal mounting with end access to the element.

The STG series Donaclone air cleaner is made in a 'T' configuration with the Donaclone tubes in the lower section and the dry element mounted horizontally in the upper, where a safety element can be fitted as required. Air entry is through holes in the side of the lower section; from here, it passes

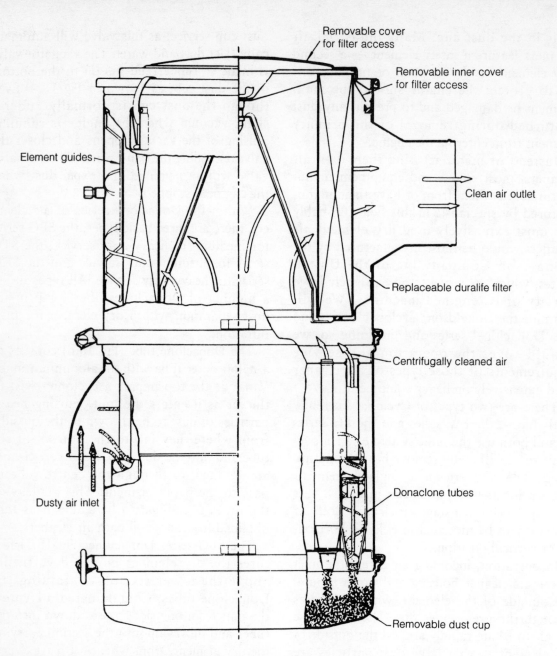

Removable cover
for filter access

Removable inner cover
for filter access

Clean air outlet

Element guides

Replaceable duralife filter

Centrifugally cleaned air

Donaclone tubes

Dusty air inlet

Removable dust cup

Fig 18.5 Donaldson Donaclone SBG dry type air cleaner
Courtesy of Donaldson Air Cleaners

down through the outer portion of the tubes, up the centres and into the chamber housing the dry element. By situating the element horizontally above the tubes, ready access is gained when servicing.

SRG series Donaclone air cleaners are designed for the higher airflow requirements of today's high-output engines. They are available in three basic models. The smallest utilises single elements (primary and safety), a single dust cup and a single outlet, while the larger models both feature dual elements (in parallel), dual outlet and three dust cups. In standard form, these air cleaners cover the airflow requirement of 56 m³/min (2000 cu ft per min) to 112m³/min (4000 cu ft per min) and are designed to operate under heavy dust conditions for periods of 1000 to

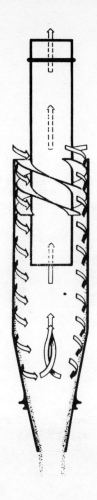

Fig 18.6   Layout of a Donaclone tube
Courtesy of Donaldson Air Cleaners

2000 hours without need of for periods of service. Special models are available for power levels and airflows below these.

Air cleaner service (paper element)

Common sense is one of the most important tools required for efficient element service, and while the following recommendations apply to Donaldson air cleaners, servicing of other types will be made possible by applying the same procedures discussed here. However, it should be borne in mind that all elements cannot be treated alike. Some are specially treated and must not be wet, while the manufacturers of others do not approve the use of compressed air for cleaning. Reference to the manufacturer's manual is always the best guide to service.

Dust cups should be regularly emptied when they are about two-thirds full, unless a vacuator valve is fitted, in which case a quick check to see that the valve is not choked, inverted or damaged is all that is necessary.

Service indicator

Many air cleaner systems now incorporate a service indicator, as shown in Fig 18.7, which is factory set to show when the air cleaner element is due to be serviced. Dust collected by the air cleaner element increases the restriction within the air cleaner, activating the indicator signal. When the red signal locks in full view, air cleaner service is required. After cleaning or replacement of the air cleaner element(s), depress the reset button to release the red signal from view. Some engine manufacturers specify that air cleaner servicing should only be carried out when the service indicator is in the red. The reason for this is that servicing an air cleaner too often can actually do more harm than good, because the more times the element is removed, the greater the chance of dirt entry into the engine.

Fig 18.7   Air cleaner service indicator
Courtesy of Donaldson Air Cleaners

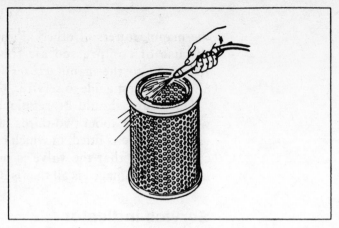

Air flow through the element should always be from the inside to the outside of the element

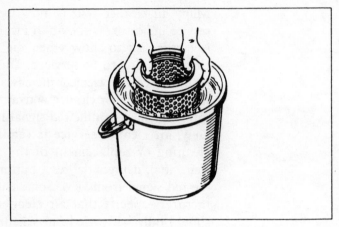

Element being cleaned in special cleaning solution

With a bright light placed inside the element examine the outside of the element for visible signs of light rays passing through holes in the filter paper

Fig 18.8 Various ways of cleaning and inspecting a paper type air cleaner element
Courtesy of Mitsubishi

On Cyclopac models, the pre-cleaner fins should be checked for fouling, while the Donaclone tubes should be checked on Donaclone models. If these tubes are fouled, light dust may be removed with a stiff fibre brush, but if severe plugging with fibrous

material is evident, the lower body section must be removed so that the tubes can be cleaned with compressed air or water at a temperature not exceeding 70°C.

Warning! Never clean Donaclone tubes with compressed air unless both primary and

and safety elements are installed in the air cleaner. Do not steam clean Donaclone tubes.

When the fins or tubes are clean, the replacement element may be fitted, care being taken to ensure that all gaskets are in first-class condition and are correctly located. The safety element should be **renewed** every third primary element service, and should not be cleaned and reused.

The primary element can readily be cleaned in one of two ways: by the use of compressed air or by washing in **special** detergent (see Fig 18.8). Compressed air must be employed when the element is to be immediately reinstalled, but this method is not as efficient as washing the element. When using compressed air, there are three points to remember: direct the air through the element in the direction opposite to normal airflow, moving the nozzle up and down while rotating the element; keep the nozzle at least 25 mm from the paper; and limit the air pressure to a maximum of 700 kPa.

Element washing instructions should be included with the detergent, but basically the process consists of soaking the element for fifteen minutes or more in the solution recommended by the element manufacturer, rinsing the element until the water is clear and drying with warm flowing air (maximum temperature 70°C), or simply air-drying. To check the element for damage after either method of cleaning, place a bright light inside the element and rotate the element slowly. Any holes in the element will readily be seen by looking in the direction of the light through the element. If any holes, ruptures or damaged gaskets are discovered during inspection, discard the element immediately so that there is no danger of it being subsequently refitted. After an element has been cleaned and is ready for further service, it should be stored under extremely clean conditions in a safe place where it will not be subjected to physical damage.

Oil bath air cleaners

Although oil bath air cleaners may vary in design to suit particular applications, the principle on which they operate remains unchanged.

The type of oil bath air cleaner illustrated in Fig 18.9 is fitted mainly to tractor engines, but may in some instances be fitted to transport vehicle engines that are required to operate under extremely dusty conditions. A pre-cleaner is usually fitted to the air inlet connection of this type of air cleaner to remove the larger particles of dirt from the air before it enters the main cleaner, thus increasing the interval between successive air cleaner services.

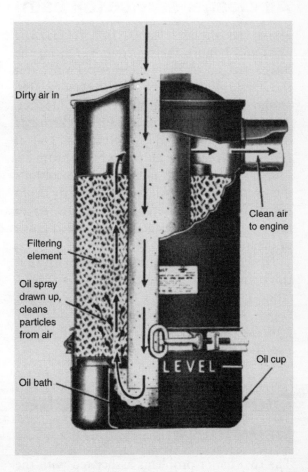

Fig 18.9   Oil bath air cleaner
Courtesy of John Deere

As Fig 18.9 shows, air enters the cleaner through the inlet pipe and moves down through the centre to the oil bowl. Here the air impinges on the surface of the oil, and the majority of the dust particles contained in the air are carried into the oil and trapped. The air then turns outwards, travels upwards through the oil-wetted wire element where the remaining dust particles are removed, and passes out through the connection at the top of the air cleaner.

The tractor-type oil bath air cleaner is usually serviced daily, or after ten hours of engine operation. However, if the engine is operating under extremely dusty conditions, it may be necessary to service the air cleaner twice daily.

Air cleaner service (oil bath)

To service the air cleaner, first release the clips and remove the oil container from the lower section of the air cleaner. Empty out the dirty oil and scrape all the accumulated sludge from the bottom of the container. Thoroughly wash the oil container in kerosene or distillate. Inspect the wire element and, if necessary, remove the filter body from its installation and wash in either of the solvents mentioned above. Allow the unit to drain before reassembly. Refill the oil container to the correct level with the recommended grade of oil and reassemble to the filter.

Note: Care must be taken to ensure that the container is not overfilled, as an overfilled cleaner restricts the airflow to the engine as well as allowing possible oil entry into the engine cylinders, resulting in engine overspeeding.

Diagnosing air intake problems

The two major problems associated with the air intake system that can affect engine performance and life expectancy are:

- dirty air;
- insufficient air.

Dirty air

Indicators of unfiltered air entry into an engine are:

- high oil consumption;
- worn rings, liners, bearings, turbocharger components.

In order to prevent unfiltered air entering the engine, the following air intake components should be regularly inspected and if necessary special tests performed to determine faults in the system.

Air cleaner

During air cleaner servicing, take care not to damage seals and gaskets when removing the air cleaner element. Before refitting the air cleaner element, inspect seals for cuts or deterioration and replace if necessary. Also inspect the surfaces where the seal is to seat, as a warped or dented sealing surface will prevent an air-tight seal. Remember, faulty seals, gaskets and sealing surfaces can allow the entry of unfiltered air into the engine, regardless of how efficient the rest of the system is.

The location of the air cleaner inlet stack on farm tractors is also important in ensuring efficient air filtering. An air cleaner inlet which is located too close to the exhaust stack can draw in exhaust soot, which can foul the air cleaner element.

A way of checking to see if unfiltered air is getting past the air cleaner element seals is to smear a film of grease around where the element seals in its housing. With the air cleaner reassembled, run the engine and sprinkle chalk dust down the air cleaner intake pipe. Stop the engine, remove the air cleaner element and inspect the sealing area for signs of chalk dust tracking across the sealed area. If the chalk dust has tracked across the sealing area, either the seal is at fault or the mating sealing surface is warped or damaged.

Ducting

Examine all the ducting and rubber hosing for signs of damage or deterioration. Loose retaining clamps or damaged ducting can also allow unfiltered air into the engine; alternatively, faulty ducting between the turbocharger and the engine will allow boost air to escape, thereby reducing the available air intake into the engine.

A way of checking for unfiltered air entry on the suction side of the intake system is to run the engine and spray 'ether start' around all the sealing joints. If the engine suddenly increases speed, then there is a hole in the system, allowing the entry of ether, which burns in the engine causing it to momentarily increase in speed.

Air leaks on the pressure side of the air intake system (turbocharged engines) can be detected by applying soap suds around all the sealed joints and, with the engine running, examining each joint for signs of air bubbles.

Dirt in an engine causes wear. As little as one teaspoon of dirt can cause severe damage to the engine's internal parts. Whenever dirt enters the engine, it collects on the oil film on the cylinder walls, forming an abrasive wear compound. As the piston rings move up and down the cylinder walls, the dirt causes increased wear similar to that produced by rubbing sandpaper on the piston rings, their grooves and the cylinder walls. Continual dirt entry into the engine will cause wear, resulting in cylinder blowby and increased oil consumption. A very successful method of determining if dirt has entered the engine is to have a sample of the lubrication oil laboratory tested to determine the level of silicon in the oil.

Insufficient air

Indicators of not enough air entering the engine are:

- black smoke;
- reduced power;
- hard starting.

When the air cleaner becomes blocked with dirt or there is a restriction in the air intake system, the engine will be starved for air. With reduced air intake, the engine cannot efficiently or completely burn the fuel, resulting in excessive amounts of black smoke from the exhaust and a loss of engine power. The most common causes of air restriction include the following.

- **Blocked air cleaner element.** A dirty, blocked air cleaner is the most overlooked and yet the primary cause of air restriction in diesel engines. The first item that should be checked if the engine is blowing black smoke or lacks power is the air cleaner element.
- **Faulty turbocharger.** If the bearings supporting the turbine and compressor wheel rotating assembly within the turbocharger are worn, then the blades of the rotating assembly may contact housings which will reduce turbocharger speed. Reduced turbocharger speed will result in insufficient air going to the cylinders for complete combustion.
- **Blocked aftercooler.** Any restriction in the core of the aftercooler will decrease the amount of air entering the cylinders.

For further information and diagrams on how to test the air inlet restriction and intake manifold boost pressure on diesel engines refer to Chapter 21.

Exhaust system

The function of the exhaust system is to remove the spent combustion gases from the engine and discharge them into the atmos-

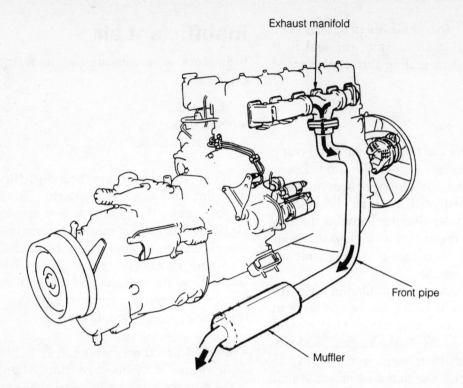

Fig 18.10 Exhaust system for an automotive truck

phere. The system is also designed so that it will create the minimum amount of exhaust back-pressure or restriction and at the same time reduce the noise level of the exhausting gas to an acceptable level.

Excessive exhaust back-pressure has a detrimental effect on engine performance in that more work has to be expended on pushing the exhaust out of the engine so less is available for useful work. This becomes apparent as a loss of power and an increase in specific fuel consumption. Another indicator of increased back-pressure is higher than normal coolant temperature because of increased cooling required due to higher pressure and temperature of the exhaust gas.

Mufflers

Mufflers or silencers are used in the exhaust system to reduce the level of exhaust gas noise by the use of internal baffling.

Whenever gas flows through a muffler, its velocity decreases and pressure increases. The more effective the silencing, the greater the back-pressure in the system. Therefore, muffler selection by the engine manufacturer is a compromise between noise reduction and back-pressure increase.

The two most commonly used exhaust mufflers are the straight-through and reverse-flow types.

Straight-through muffler

This muffler design, as shown in Fig 18.11, carries the exhaust gas straight through the muffler via a perforated tube which is surrounded by a sound-absorbing material. The vibrating exhaust gas passes through the holes in the perforated tube and penetrates into the sound-absorbent material — generally metal shavings or glass wool. This process lowers the frequency of the gas vibrations, which lowers the pitch of the exhaust sound. There

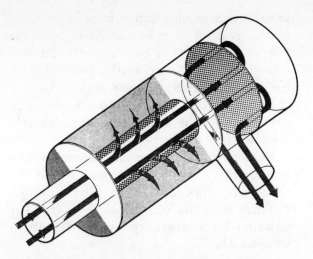

Fig 18.11   Exhaust gas flow through a straight-through muffler

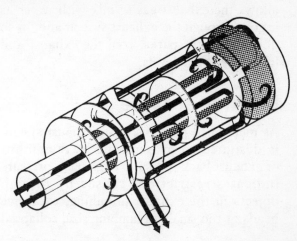

Fig 18.12   Exhaust gas flow through a reverse-flow muffler

is very little back-pressure with this design of muffler, which makes it suitable for use on two-stroke diesel engines that operate on the Kadency principle of exhaust scavenging.

Reverse-flow muffler

This design, as shown in Fig 18.12, helps to reduce sound levels by channelling the exhaust gas back and forth through expansion chambers within the muffler. The effect of this is to reduce the pressure and temperature of the gas as it passes through baffles and tubes where its turbulence dies out and noise levels are reduced. The degree of noise reduction in reverse-flow mufflers can be varied by the size of the expansion chambers within the muffler. When comparing the two muffler designs, the reverse-flow type can achieve the lowest noise levels.

Spark arrester muffler

The reverse-flow muffler can be varied in its design so as to act as a spark arrester for engines operating near combustible material. This type of muffler is therefore dual purpose in that it acts as a sound-suppressing unit as well as extinguishing any burning pieces of carbon which may be present in the exhaust

gas. With reference to Fig 18.13, the spark arrester muffler contains two spark extinguisher inserts, so-called 'lip screens'. When the exhaust gases flow through these screens, they cause the screens to rotate, thereby forcing any sparks towards the muffler outer jacket, where they are extinguished.

On some underground minimg equipment, special provision is made to eliminate sparks in high fire-hazard areas. The design of muffler

Lip screens

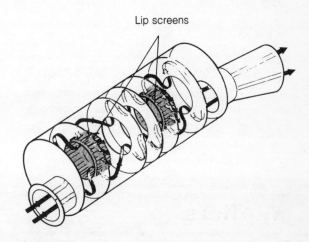

Fig 18.13   Exhaust gas flow through a spark extinguisher muffler

used on such equipment is a wet type which allows the exhaust gas to mix with water as it goes through the exhaust system and, in so doing, quench sparks, cool the exhaust and lower the sound levels.

Muffler service

As mentioned previously, the exhaust system is designed to provide the least amount of exhaust back-pressure. High back-pressure indicates restrictions caused by foreign objects in the exhaust plumbing, excessive bends or too small a plumbing size, collapsed exhaust pipe or obstruction from loose baffle plates. This, in turn, can cause high engine temperatures, loss of power and higherfuel consumption. As an indication of how back-pressure effects engine performance, it is estimated that for each 14 kpa of back-pressure there is a loss of approximately 3 kilowatts of engine power.

Exhaust back-pressure can be measured by connecting a u-tube manometer into the exhaust pipe just after the exhaust manifold. Further information on how to test for exhaust back-pressure can be found in Chapter 21.

burned efficiently. In this way, the torque and power output of an engine can be increased by up to 35 per cent by the addition of a turbocharger.

Turbocharger construction

The turbocharger is made up of three sections, the centre bearing housing assembly, the turbine housing and the compressor housing, as shown in Fig 19.2. The bearing housing contains two plain bearings, piston ring-type seals, retainers and a thrust bearing. There are also passages for the supply and dumping of oil to and from the housing.

The turbine wheel turns in the turbine housing, and is usually integral with the turbine shaft, which is carried in the plain bearings in the bearing housing. The compressor wheel, which is fitted to the opposite end of the turbine shaft, forming a combined rotating assembly, turns in the compressor housing. Turbocharger rotational speeds can reach 120 000 rpm on some small high-performance units.

Turbocharger operation

In general terms, there are two types of turbocharger — the pulse type and the constant pressure type — each with its own operating characteristics. However, both operate in the same basic way.

Exhaust gas from the engine passes through the exhaust manifold and into the turbocharger turbine housing, where it impinges on the turbine blades, causing the turbine, shaft and compressor wheel assembly to rotate.

It is important to understand that the speed of the turbine is directly related to the temperature of the exhaust gas and its rate of expansion as it passes through the turbine housing. The amount of heat produced by an engine running under light load conditions or at maximum no-load speed is considerably less than that produced under heavy

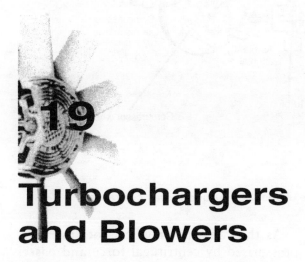

19 Turbochargers and Blowers

Turbocharging

The turbocharger was invented by a Swiss named Buchi in 1906, and has been seen from time to time in various versions ever since. However, it is only in the past two decades that it has been developed to such a degree of reliability and performance that it is now being fitted to a continually increasing percentage of new IC engines.

The turbocharger is essentially an exhaust-driven supercharger, its primary purpose being to pressurise the intake air, so increasing the quantity entering the engine cylinders on the inlet stroke, and allowing more fuel to be

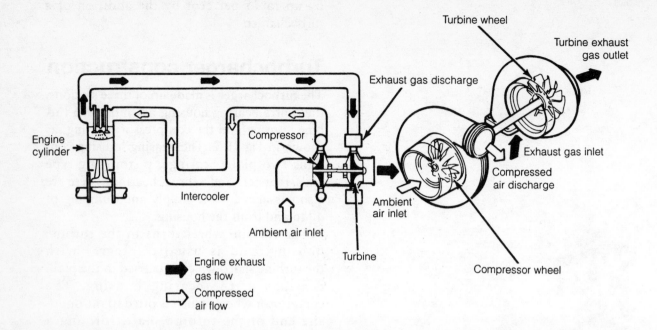

Fig 19.1 Schematic diagram showing how an exhaust gas turbocharger operates *Courtesy of Detroit Diesel Corp*

load conditions such as at maximum torque speed. Therefore, as there is less heat produced under light load conditions, the intensity of exhaust gas expansion in the turbine housing will be less, resulting in a slower turbine and compressor wheel speed. Under heavy load conditions, such as at maximum torque, there will be a greater amount of heat produced, resulting in a significant increase in exhaust gas expansion and turbine and compressor wheel speed.

As the compressor wheel rotates, air is pressurised by centrifugal force and passes from the compressor housing to the engine inlet manifold, the quantity and/or pressure of the air being proportional to the speed of rotation of the compressor wheel.

Pulse-type turbocharger

The pulse-type turbocharger requires a specially designed exhaust manifold to deliver high-

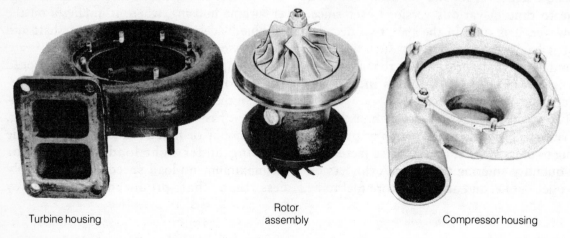

Fig 19.2 Turbocharger sub-assemblies *Courtesy of Volvo*

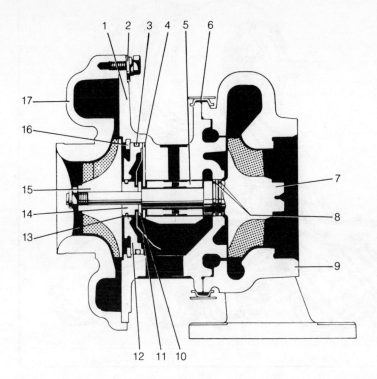

1 Bearing housing
2 Washers
3 'O'-ring
4 Thrust bearing
5 Bearing bushing
6 Tensioning band
7 Turbine wheel
8 Piston rings
9 Turbine housing
10 Thrust washer
11 Oil distributor plate
12 Cover
13 Piston ring
14 Piston ring holder
15 Compressor wheel
16 Circlip
17 Compressor housing

Fig 19.3   Sectional view of a typical turbocharger   *Courtesy of Volvo*

energy exhaust pulses to the turbocharger turbine. This design, with its individual branches, as shown in Fig 19.4, prevents interference between the exhaust gas discharges from the separate cylinders, thus promoting a high-speed pulsing flow not achieved with other designs.

In some applications, a split-pulse turbine housing can be used to further aid in the excitation of the rotating assembly. This design has two volute chambers instead of one. The term 'volute chamber' is used in reference to the spiral-shaped turbine housing, which decreases in volume towards its centre in the manner of a snail shell.

Each chamber receives half of the engine exhaust flow; for example, in a four-cylinder engine, the front two cylinders are fed into the first chamber, while the back two are fed into the second chamber, as shown in Fig 19.5.

Constant pressure-type turbocharger

With the constant-pressure type of turbocharger, the exhaust gas from all cylinders flows into a common manifold, where the pulses are smoothed out, resulting in exhaust gas entering the turbine housing at an even pressure.

With both types of turbocharger, the exhaust gas then enters a volute-shaped annular ring in the turbine housing, which accelerates it radially inwards at reduced pressure and increased velocity on to the turbine blades. The blades are so designed that the force of the high-velocity gas drives the turbine and its shaft assembly.

The compressor assembly is of similar design and construction in both pulse and constant-pressure turbochargers (see

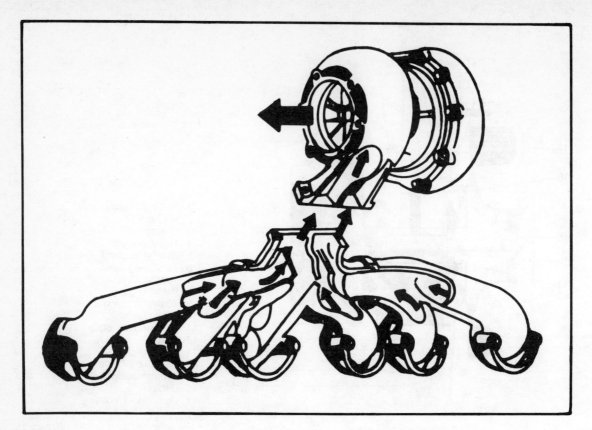

Fig 19.4   Pulse-type exhaust manifold   *Courtesy of Cummins Engine Co*

Fig 19.6). The compressor consists of a wheel and a housing incorporating a single volute or diffuser. Air in the compressor chamber mainly lies between the blades of the compressor wheel, and is thrown out radially by centrifugal force into the volute during rotation of the wheel. Here the air velocity decreases and a corresponding increase in air pressure results. As the air progresses around the volute, its velocity decreases further and the pressure increases as the cross-sectional diameter of the chamber increases.

In summary, the pulse-type turbocharger offers a quick excitation of the rotating assembly due to the rapid succession of the exhaust gas pulses on the turbine assembly. It is predominantly used in automotive applications, where acceleration response is important.

Constant-pressure turbochargers are used mainly on large diesel engines in earth-moving equipment and in marine applications. In these applications, acceleration response is not so critical.

Turbocharger lubrication

In most applications, turbochargers are lubricated by the lubrication system of the engine to which they are fitted. Oil under pressure from the engine oil pump enters the top of the bearing housing and flows around the shaft and to the thrust bearings and oil seals. The oil flows both inside and around the outside of the shaft bearings, which fully float in oil during operation. The oil also flows to the piston ring-type oil seals at either end of the rotating shaft to aid in sealing and lubrication. The thrust bearing located at the compressor end of the rotating assembly is lubricated by the same oil before it leaves the bearing housing and flows back to the engine sump.

On large diesel engines such as those used in marine and power-generation applications,

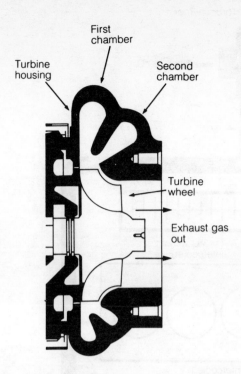

Fig 19.5 Split-pulse turbine housing
Courtesy of Volvo

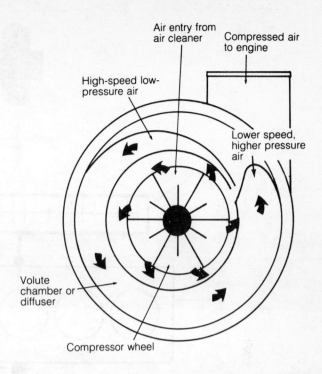

Fig 19.6 Turbocharger compressor housing

the turbocharger has its own oil reservoir in the main bearing housing and does not rely on engine oil for lubrication.

Advantages of turbocharging

Because the turbocharger is driven by exhaust gas energy that would otherwise have been lost, a turbocharged engine offers several advantages over a naturally aspirated version:

- **Increased power-to-weight ratio.** A turbocharger can generally increase the power and torque output of a diesel engine by as much as 35 per cent above that of a naturally aspirated version. Thus many turbocharged smaller four and six-cylinder diesel engines are able to do the work of naturally aspirated larger capacity V8 engines.
- **Reduced engine noise.** The turbine housing acts as a noise absorption unit for the

pulsating engine exhaust gases. The compressor section also helps to reduce pulsating intake noises in the intake manifold. As a result of these factors, a turbocharged engine is generally quieter than a naturally aspirated unit, although a characteristic whine is usually audible when the engine is under load or accelerating.
- **Better fuel economy.** A turbocharged engine has a higher volumetric efficiency than a naturally aspirated engine, giving more complete combustion of the fuel and resulting in lower specific fuel consumption.
- **Reduced smoke output.** Turbochargers supply a surplus amount of air during medium- to high-speed operation, resulting in a much cleaner and efficient combustion phase, which reduces smoke output considerably.

Intercooling

Intercoolers are used to reduce the high temperature of the air leaving the turbocharger,

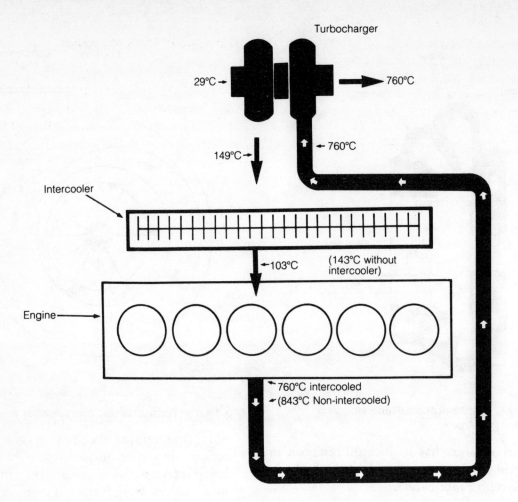

Fig 19.7 Intake/exhaust temperature comparisons — intercooled and non-intercooled engine
Courtesy of Cummins Engine Co

so increasing the density of the intake air. The denser the air, the greater the quantity of fuel that can be burned efficiently, and the greater the subsequent power and torque output of the engine.

When air is compressed, it becomes hot. When the air charge leaves the compressor section of the turbocharger, it is at a much higher temperature than the ambient air temperature. When it is heated, the air expands and becomes less dense, so that less oxygen is available in the engine cylinder for combustion. Further, the addition of heated air to the engine can increase engine operating temperature.

These effects become noticeable when the charge-air pressure exceeds 140 kPa, and the high temperature of the air starts to have an adverse effect on the engine performance and operating temperature. Charge-air temperature on non-intercooled turbocharged engines can reach temperatures of 100°C and above.

Intercooling or charge-air cooling is the process of cooling the heated compressed air before it enters the engine cylinders. In so doing, the air charge becomes more dense, allowing additional fuel to be efficiently burned, resulting in increased engine power and torque above that possible with a non-intercooled turbocharged engine. Fig 19.7 shows typical air and exhaust gas temperatures for intercooled and non-intercooled engines.

There are two types of intercooler in current use, namely the air-to-water and the air-to-air intercooler. Both are heat exchangers, devices that bring a hot medium (in this case, the charge air) into close contact with a cooler medium (either water or air), allowing heat to be conducted from the hot to the cold.

Air-to-water intercooler

This type of intercooler operates by passing the charge air through a water-cooled heat exchanger mounted in the intake manifold beside the cylinder head, as shown in Fig 19.8. Because the charge air is hotter than the engine cooling water, which runs through the intercooler, some heat transfer will take place. This transfer of heat reduces the charge-air temperature to a (possible) 85°C (engine operating temperature), if the cooling system is operating efficiently.

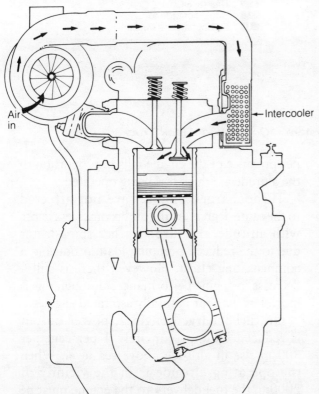

Fig 19.8 Air-to-water intercooler — inlet manifold installation
Courtesy of Caterpillar Inc

Air-to-air intercooler

With air-to-air intercooling, the charge air is passed through a finned heat exchanger (like water in an engine radiator), and the vehicle's forward movement causes air to flow across the fins of the heat exchanger, thus cooling the charge air. A typical system is shown in Fig 19.9.

This type of intercooler can reduce charge-air temperature to as low as 15°C above ambient air temperature. With charge-air temperatures as low as this and under pressure between 175 and 189 kPa, it is possible to provide three times as much air for combustion as is possible in a naturally aspirated engine. Air-to-air intercoolers are used on mobile machines and are mounted in front of the engine radiator.

Engine design changes when turbocharging

Because turbocharged engines operate under higher stress and temperature than naturally aspirated engines, original equipment manufacturers design such engines to tolerate these conditions. Engine oil coolers are practically a standard fitting on turbocharged diesels; so too are oil sprays (as shown in Fig 19.10), which spray engine oil on the underside of the piston crown for efficient cooling. To cater for the extra oil-flow requirements of these additional features, larger capacity oil pumps are fitted. Further, stronger pistons are fitted to handle the increased loads.

Effects of altitude on turbocharged diesel engines

When an internal combustion engine is operated at a high altitude where the air is less dense than at sea level, the quantity of air (and oxygen) entering the engine cylinder on the induction stroke is insufficient for combustion of the normal fuel charge. As a result, the

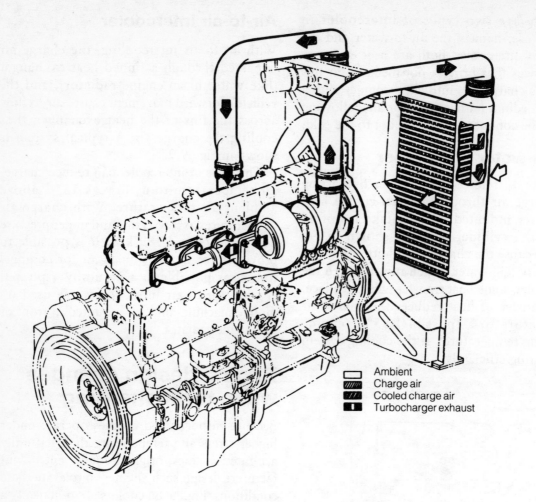

Fig 19.9   Layout of an air-to-air intercooler system   *Courtesy of Mack Trucks*

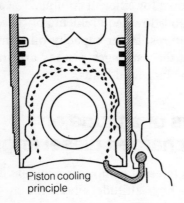

Piston cooling
principle

Fig 19.10   Oil-spray piston cooling
Courtesy of Volvo

performance of the engine falls in proportion to the altitude at which it is being operated.

Turbocharged engines are not affected to the same degree. As the air becomes less dense with altitude, the turbocharger spins faster due to the reduced pumping load, producing a compensating effect. However, there is still a decrease in engine performance, although this is much less than for naturally aspirated engines.

On turbocharged engines, power output is reduced by approximately 1 per cent per 300 m rise in altitude above sea level. When the operating altitude is in the vicinity of 2000m, the fuel delivery to the engine must be decreased according to engine specifications to prevent damage to the turbocharger due to overspeeding.

Turbocharger controls

In certain applications where fast acceleration is needed, engines are fitted with large-capacity turbochargers that require a speed-control device. This device, commonly referred to as a **wastegate** (as shown in Fig 19.11), prevents the turbocharger from over-speeding and subsequently over-boosting and damaging the engine.

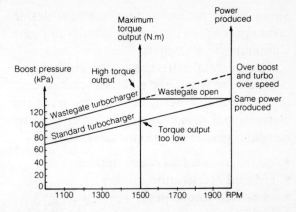

Fig 19.12 Wastegate turbocharger/standard turbocharger performance comparison

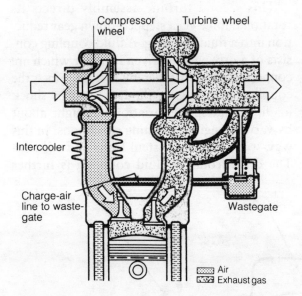

Fig 19.11 Turbocharger with wastegate and intercooler
Courtesy of Robert Bosch GmbH

On the other hand, the smaller turbochargers fitted to stationary engines or slow moving diesel-powered equipment are self-regulating in their maximum speed and charge pressure by the design of the turbine and compressor housings. Because these engines operate in a narrow speed band with constant high-charge pressures, there is no need for controls that regulate charge pressures relative to changing engine speeds.

Therefore it is essential that the turbocharger which is installed be matched to the engine and performance requirements. Fig 19.12 shows a typical performance comparison between a standard turbocharger and a turbocharger fitted with a wastegate.

The standard turbocharger, with its smaller output capacity, supplies sufficient charge air for combustion of a full fuel charge only when the engine is operating in the high torque and speed ranges. But down in the medium speed range, the charge-air pressure is considerably lower, generally resulting in incomplete combustion, black exhaust smoke, poor acceleration and lack of power.

The wastegate turbocharger, however, is of a higher output capacity and capable of delivering sufficient charge air for complete combustion of the fuel during acceleration as well as in high-torque situations. As the engine speed and exhaust-gas energy increase, so the turbocharger speed increases and the charge-air pressure rises. Without the wastegate charge, pressure would continue to rise with considerable risk to both the engine and the turbocharger.

However, the increasing air pressure acts on the diaphragm in the wastegate until, at a predetermined pressure, the resulting force is sufficient to compress the spring and open the exhaust bypass passage. This allows sufficient exhaust gas to bypass the turbine to prevent any further rise in turbocharger speed and subsequent charge-air pressure.

Wastegate turbochargers are generally fitted to faster moving earthmoving equipment — for example, dump trucks and road scrapers — as well as high-performance automotive vehicles.

Series turbocharging

Series boost turbocharging is a new design concept currently being used on some Cummins diesel engines.

The system utilises two turbochargers connected in series, and is shown schematically in Fig 19.13. Several advantages over the conventional design using one larger capacity turbocharger are claimed for this concept:

- better specific fuel consumption;
- reduced acceleration smoke;
- improved torque peak;
- higher overall pumping efficiency.

Turbocompounding

In an effort to increase engine efficiency and performance, some engine manufacturers are turbocompounding their engines. In a conventional turbocharged engine, the exhaust gas is directed to the turbine wheel and then exits into the atmosphere via the exhaust pipe.

With turbocompounding, the exhaust gas leaves the turbocharger and is redirected through a second turbine assembly which harnesses some of the remaining exhaust energy to help drive the engine's flywheel, as shown in Fig 19.14.

This second turbine assembly directs its rotational force via a stepped-down gear reduction into a fluid coupling. A fluid coupling consists of a driving and driven member which are connected to each other by a fluid. Since the coupling is through a fluid, it absorbs shock loadings and speed variations brought about by varying engine operating conditions. In this way, it protects the system from undue stress. The drive from the fluid coupling is further

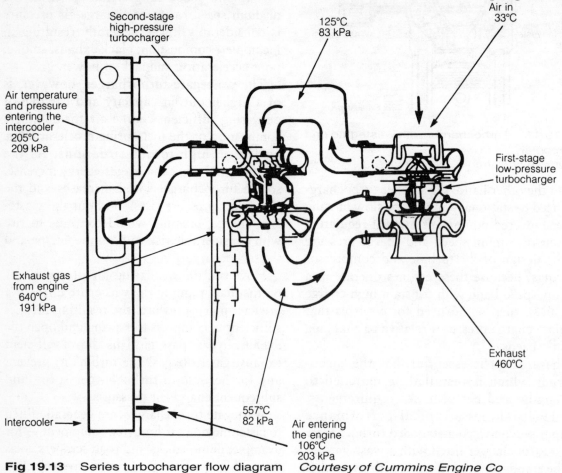

Fig 19.13 Series turbocharger flow diagram *Courtesy of Cummins Engine Co*

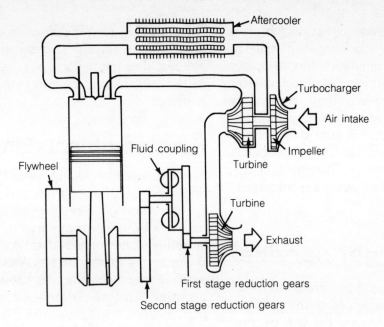

Fig 19.14   Schematic diagram of a turbocompounded diesel engine

reduced in speed as it is geared down and coupled directly to the flywheel.

Overall, the drive through the fluid coupling and gear reductions combine to link a turbine spinning at a maximum of 55 000 RPM to a crankshaft which runs at a speed of up to 2200 RPM.

Some of the advantages of using turbocompounding are lower specific fuel consumption, reduced exhaust emission, better power-to-weight ratio and increased thermal efficiency. Claims have been made by some manufacturers that, by using turbocompounding, the thermal efficiency of their engines has risen from 44 per cent to 46 per cent.

Precautions when operating turbocharged engines

Engine starting procedure

A turbocharged engine should always be allowed to idle when it is started until the engine oil pressure has built up to normal operating pressure.

Starting an engine with the throttle wide open will result in the turbocharger operating at high speed with very little oil being circulated through its bearings, with resultant accelerated wear on the rotating assembly and bearings of the turbocharger.

Engine shutdown

Before a turbocharged diesel engine is shut down, the engine should be run at idle speed for three to four minutes. This will allow the high-speed rotating assembly to slow down, allow the engine operating temperature to normalise, and allow excessive heat to be dissipated from the turbocharger.

If a turbocharged engine is shut down while operating at high speeds or under load, the turbocharger rotating assembly will continue to rotate for some time without oil for essential lubrication and cooling. Because the exhaust turbine shaft operates at high temperature during engine operation, once the oil flow to the bearing housing stops, the heat in the shaft and housing is sufficient to decompose the oil to form gums and varnish, leaving no lubricating residue and causing premature wear to the rotating shaft, its support bearings and the bearing housing.

There are now ways of protecting the turbocharger against sudden engine shutdown. An automatic timer unit can be fitted to the to the engine shutdown system, which overrides the stop control and allows the engine to idle for a number of minutes before stopping.

Another method utilises an oil accumulator mounted on the engine, which is charged by the engine lubrication system during operation. When the engine is shut down, oil is forced from the accumulator, via a check valve, to the turbocharger bearing housing, and lubricates the bearings for approximately 30 seconds.

Turbocharger service

Being unlike any other component of the engine, turbochargers have the need for specific service procedures. Further, because of the high operating temperatures and high operating speeds, turbochargers are susceptible to heat cracking and unbalance to a degree seldom seen in engine equipment.

Although not specifically a turbocharger service item, it is of the utmost importance to carry out regular oil and filter changes on turbocharged engines. It is just as important to monitor engine oil pressure and the quality of engine oil used. Turbocharged diesel engines should only operate on the lubricating oil recommended by the engine manufacturer, which is usually of a different classification from that required for naturally aspirated engines.

Inspection and cleaning

Many engine manufacturers and/or turbocharger manufacturers recommend periodic disassembly, inspection and cleaning of the compressor housing and turbine. A small deposit on the turbine wheel can seriously affect turbocharger performance and should be removed. The usually recommended cleaning procedure is to use a solvent and soft (not wire) brush, taking care to ensure that solvent does not enter the turbocharger bearing housing.

In addition to inspecting for deposits, the components should also be inspected for physical damage, with special attention paid to the turbine and compressor wheels and housings.

Foreign-object damage

The high-speed rotating assembly of a turbocharger is balanced to exacting standards. For this reason, a turbocharger should not be put back in service if any part of the rotating assembly or housings is damaged in any way. If damage by foreign objects does occur to the rotating members, the unit should be disassembled and the damaged component replaced, in consultation with the appropriate workshop manual.

Turbocharger installation

When a turbocharger is installed on an engine, and before the engine is started, engine oil should be poured into the oil intake hole in the bearing housing. This prelubricates all the bearings and sealing rings. The oil intake pipe can then be refitted and the engine started.

Turbochargers that have not operated for long periods will lose their residual lubrication. Therefore the engine should be cranked over in the 'no-fuel' position (stop lever actuated) until oil pressure registers on the gauge — this will prelubricate the turbocharger prior to start-up.

Operating checks

With experience, it is possible to gain a good indication of turbocharger operation from the sounds it produces in operation. The engine should be operated through all speed and load ranges while paying particular attention to unusual noises coming from the turbocharger. Generally the only noise that should be heard is a high-pitched whine that occurs when the engine is placed under load or accelerated.

Turbocharger overhaul

Overhauling a turbocharger should not be attempted without reference to the appropriate workshop manual. However, the following provides a general overall description of the disassembly, inspection and reassembly of a typical turbocharger.

Disassembly

Clean the exterior of the turbocharger with a non-caustic cleaning solvent. Mount the unit on to a special fixture or in a vice, as shown in Fig 19.15.

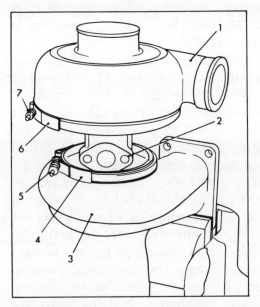

1	Compressor cover	5	Locknut – 'V' clamp
2	Bearing housing		
3	Turbine housing	6	'V' clamp
4	'V' clamp	7	Locknut – 'V' clamp

Fig 19.15 Turbocharger correctly held in a vice

Before removing the housings, use a scribing tool to mark the relative location of compressor and turbine housings to the bearing housing.

Remove the clamp or bolts securing the compressor housing and lift off the housing. Next remove the turbine housing clamp or bolts and lift the bearing housing clear of the turbine housing.

Mount the bearing housing in an upright position in a special fixture or soft-jawed vice, as seen in Fig 19.16, making sure that the vice jaws grip the turbine wheel extension nut only, and not the turbine fins.

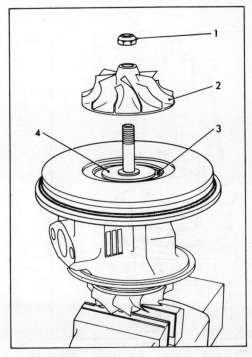

1 Locknut
2 Compressor wheel
3 Circlip
4 Bearing housing

Fig 19.16 Bearing housing correctly held in a vice

Unscrew the locknut retaining the compressor wheel and lift the wheel off the turbine shaft. On some turbochargers the compressor wheel is shrunk on to the shaft and will have to be pressed off, as shown in Fig 19.17.

With the compressor wheel removed, the turbine shaft can be removed from the turbine end of the bearing housing.

Next remove the circlip or capscrews from the thrust assembly located at the compressor end of the bearing housing and, with a piece of wood dowling inserted into the centre hole of the thrust assembly, lever the assembly out of the bearing housing. Remove the remainder of the thrust assembly and the two plain turbine shaft support bearings and circlips. Finally, remove all piston ring seals from the turbine shaft and thrust assembly spacer sleeves. The disassembled turbocharger is now ready for cleaning and inspection.

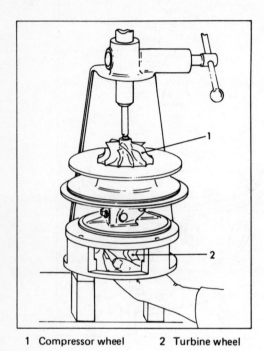

1 Compressor wheel   2 Turbine wheel

Fig 19.17 Pressing the turbine shaft from the compressor wheel

Inspection

Clean all components for inspection, using an approved cleaner; caustic solutions will damage aluminium components and must not be used. All parts should be soaked in cleaning fluid until all foreign deposits have been removed. The turbine wheel and turbine housing can be bead blasted to remove carbon deposits, provided that the smooth surface of the turbine shaft is protected. After soaking the components, blow out all passages and compartments with compressed air.

Generally, no parts should show signs of wear, corrosion or damage. A wear evaluation in accordance with the manufacturer's specifications will determine whether parts are replaced or reused. Refer to Fig 19.18 for an exploded view of the layout of the turbocharger parts described below.

- **Bearing housing.** The bearing housing must not show wear marks due to contact with rotating parts. Inspect the bores in which the bearings run for scores, and measure their diameter with a telescopic gauge. The bore diameter is critical, with permissible wear approximately 0.025 mm. If the bores are scored or are worn oversize or oval, a new housing should be fitted or the old housing sleeved.
- **Turbine shaft bearings.** Whenever the turbocharger is overhauled, the shaft bearings (21, 14) must be renewed, regardless of their condition.
- **Thrust bearing assembly.** The thrust bearing (10) and thrust rings (12, 9) should be renewed, regardless of their condition. Measure the thrust spacer (11) and spacer sleeve (7) and inspect their surfaces for scoring or heat discolouration. Discard if worn, scored or discoloured.
- **Rotating assembly.** Examine the turbine wheel (16) and shaft (18) for any signs of wear. Inspect the fins of the wheel for cracks, carbon deposits, distortion of shape, erosion wear on the tips and foreign-object damage. The shaft must show no signs of wear, scoring or discolouration. Measure the shaft journals for exact size and ovalness and check against the manufacturer's figures. Check the width of the seal ring groove in front of the turbine wheel to ensure that the groove has not worn oversize. Inspect the compressor wheel blades for tip damage due to foreign objects or rubbing on the compressor housing. The wheel should also be checked for signs of rubbing between the underside of the wheel and the bearing housing. Any foreign object damage or wear marks on either the turbine or compressor wheels will cause them to run out of balance, creating undue vibration and wear within

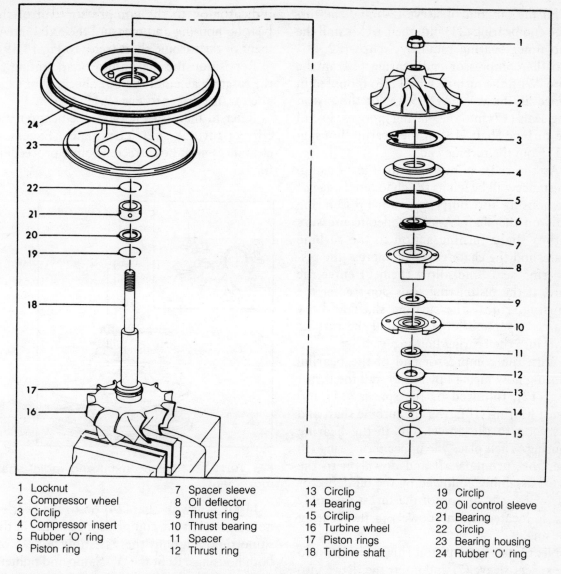

1 Locknut	7 Spacer sleeve
2 Compressor wheel	8 Oil deflector
3 Circlip	9 Thrust ring
4 Compressor insert	10 Thrust bearing
5 Rubber 'O' ring	11 Spacer
6 Piston ring	12 Thrust ring

13 Circlip	19 Circlip
14 Bearing	20 Oil control sleeve
15 Circlip	21 Bearing
16 Turbine wheel	22 Circlip
17 Piston rings	23 Bearing housing
18 Turbine shaft	24 Rubber 'O' ring

Fig 19.18   Exploded view of bearing housing assembly

the turbocharger. Check that the bore of the compressor wheel is of the correct size — it may be either an interference fit or a slide fit on to the turbine shaft, depending on the type of turbocharger.

- **Turbine and compressor housing.** Inspect the turbine housing for erosion, cracking and rub marks in the vicinity of the turbine wheel. Also, the turbine housing to the exhaust manifold mounting flange is to be checked for surface trueness. The compressor housing should also be checked for wheel rub marks and cracking.

Reassembly

When reassembling a turbocharger, cleanliness is vital to a long service life. All piston ring-type seals, o-rings, lock tabs, circlips and the compressor wheel retaining nut should be automatically renewed, together with all other parts that require replacement during the inspection period. Throughout assembly, lubricate all rotating parts with clean engine oil. Install the bearing retaining circlip (19) into the turbine end of the housing, taking care not to scratch the bearing bore.

Fit the oil control sleeve (20) and the turbine end bearing (21) into the bore. Install the two inner bearing retainer circlips (22, 15) and the compressor end bearing (14) in the bore. With the turbine wheel (16) mounted in a vice as shown in Fig 19.18, fit the piston ring seals (17) into the oil ring grooves. Install the turbine shaft (18) in the bearing housing (23) from the turbine end.

As the shaft is pushed into the housing, resistance will be felt as the chamfered edge of the housing bore butts against the piston ring seals on the shaft. Apply moderate pressure with a slight turning action to the turbine shaft, and the chamfer will compress the piston ring seals and allow them to enter the bore. If the piston ring seals don't enter the housing, rotate the turbine shaft and try again. Never use force to install the turbine shaft into the bearing housing.

With the compressor end of the bearing housing now facing upward, install the thrust ring (12), followed by the spacer (11) and thrust bearing (10), over the turbine shaft and down on to the dowel pins in the bearing housing. Then place the upper thrust ring (9) over the turbine shaft and down on to the thrust assembly, followed by the oil deflector (8), which sits on top of the thrust assembly and is located by the dowels in the bearing housing.

Next, install the piston ring seal (6) on to the spacer sleeve (7) and insert the sleeve into the compressor insert (4), using light finger pressure. Fit a new o-ring (5) to the compressor insert, and place the insert over the turbine shaft and down into the bearing housing. Secure the insert with the retaining circlip (3).

Install the compressor wheel (2) on the turbine shaft. If it is an interference fit, it will have to be heated in hot clean engine oil to expand it before sliding it on to the turbine shaft. (Refer to the manual for correct oil temperature.) Secure the wheel with the self-locking nut, tensioned to the required torque.

In order to check for correct running clearances of the rotating assembly, mount a dial indicator on to the compressor end of the bearing housing and measure the axial movement of the turbine shaft (refer to Fig 19.19).

Reposition the dial indicator mounting so the rotating assembly can be checked for radial clearance (refer to Fig 19.19).

Refer to the turbocharger specifications for correct turbine shaft clearances. Excessive clearances must be corrected before proceeding further.

Fig 19.19 Checking axial and radial shaft movement

Install a new o-ring (24) on to the bearing housing and fit the compressor housing, at the same time aligning the assembly marks on both housings. Refit the 'V' clamp and tighten.

Turn the turbocharger over and install the turbine housing, once again aligning the assembly marks. Secure the housing with the 'V' clamp or the bolts and lock tabs (as the case may be).

Finally, cover all openings until the turbocharger is to be installed on the engine.

Testing the intercooler core for leakage

As mentioned previously, there are two types of intercooler used on diesel engines: the air-to-air and the air-to-water intercoolers.

From time to time these units may malfunction and will require removal from the engine or vehicle for inspection and testing. The following inspection and testing procedure relates directly to the air-to-air intercooler; however, a similar procedure can be adapted to testing air-to-water intercoolers.

With the intercooler removed from the vehicle, inspect the cooler core for core damage and also for dirt and debris buildup in the core fins. If the core is damaged, it will require repair or replacement. If the core is blocked with debris, it will need to be cleaned.

Intercooler problems generally fall into two categories: low charge air pressure, or too high a charge air temperature. Low charge air pressure can generally be attributed to faulty pipe connections, holes in the intake plumbing or air leaks in the intercooler core. High charge air temperature can be the result of restricted air flow past the intercooler core due to a partly blocked core. As the intercooler is placed before the radiator in the front of the vehicle, it is not affected by the transfer of heat from the engine coolant.

To test the cooler for leakage, proceed as follows. With reference to Fig 19.20, plug off one cooler outlet and install an air pressure adapter in the other, making sure both fittings are air tight. Connect a pressure regulator similar to the one shown in Fig 19.21 "to the intercooler air pressure adapter. Turn on the air pressure and adjust the pressure regulator valve until the pressure in the intercooler stabilises at 100 kPa. Turn off the air supply so as to prevent the air leaking back out the regulator and the air supply line. During a one-minute test period, the intercooler should maintain approximately 100 kPa air pressure; however, the pressure can fall to a minimum of 75 kPa (refer specifications) and the intercooler still be in satisfactory condition. If the pressure falls below 75 kPa, recharge the intercooler and pour soapy water over the core so as to find any air leaks.

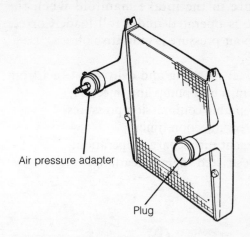

Air pressure adapter

Plug

Fig 19.20 Preparing an air-to-air intercooler core for pressure testing
Courtesy of Volvo

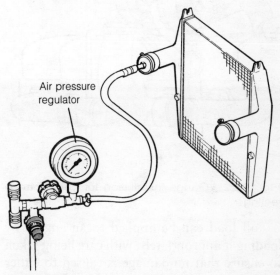

Air pressure regulator

Fig 19.21 Pressurising an air-to-air intercooler core for leakage testing
Courtesy of Volvo

Performance testing

An accurate method of gauging an engine's performance output is by using test gauges to measure certain aspects of engine operation (see Fig 19.22). A quick and accurate way of checking that the turbocharged engine's output is in accordance with the manufacturer's specifications is to measure the charge-air pressure in the intake manifold when the engine is operated under full load. Correct charge-air pressure is indicative of:

- correct metering and delivery of fuel from the injection pump and injectors;
- acceptable compression pressures;
- correct injection timing;
- efficient turbocharger operation;
- unrestricted engine breathing.

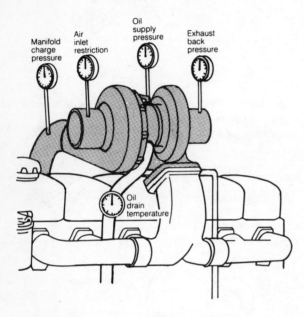

Fig 19.22 Gauge installation for performance testing

Full load can be applied to an engine by loading it appropriately, with care being taken to ensure that no damage is caused to either the engine or the equipment being driven.

If the engine is installed in a piece of mobile equipment fitted with a torque converter, full load can be applied by applying the brakes and stalling out the torque converter with the transmission engaged in top gear. The engine should be running at full throttle and rated engine speed during any stall test.

Note: Do not run the engine under stall conditions for more than 30 seconds at one time, as serious overheating of the engine and torque converter will occur.

Blowers

The term 'blower' is used to refer to the air supply pump that supplies the air under pressure to two-stroke engines, the primary purpose being to scavenge burnt gas from the engine cylinder. As a secondary function, blowers usually ensure that the cylinder is completely filled with fresh air by raising the cylinder pressure to above atmospheric pressure. The primary function is achieved by having both the inlet and exhaust ports open together, allowing the fresh air to sweep through the entire cylinder, while the secondary function is performed by closing the exhaust port (or valve) before the inlet port (or valve), thus allowing the pressure to build up in the engine cylinder before the air supply is shut off. Almost all engine manufacturers use Roots blowers for this purpose.

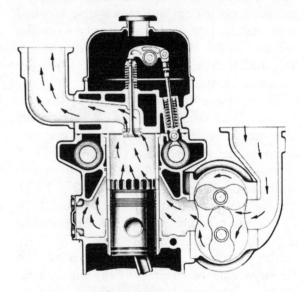

Fig 19.23 Scavenge air flow through two-stroke diesel engine
Courtesy of Detroit Diesel Corp

Construction

The basic Roots blower consists of three sub-assemblies: an oval housing, a pair of rotors and associated bearings, gears and seals, and two end covers.

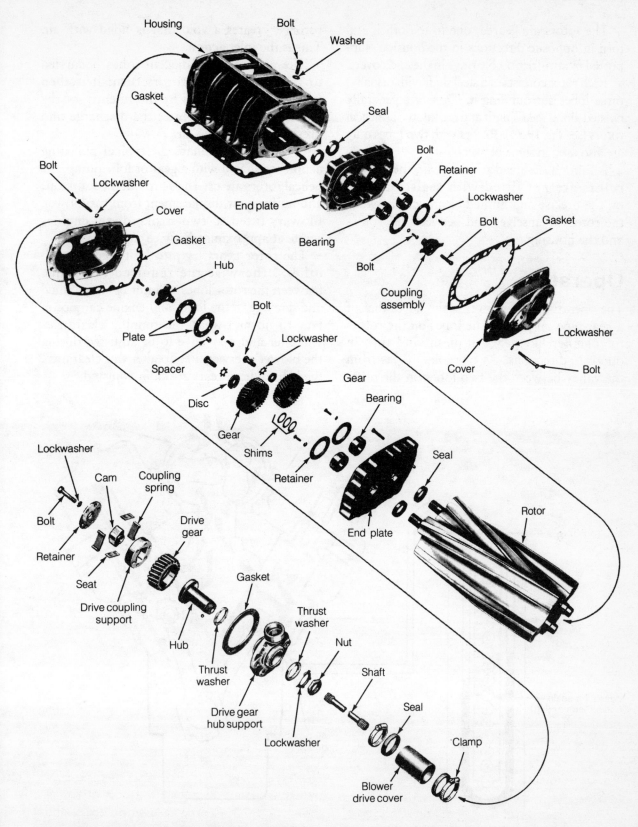

Fig 19.24 Exploded view of blower assembly and drive *Courtesy of Detroit Diesel Corp*

The rotors are geared, one to the other, and turn in opposite directions in the housing, supported in anti-friction bearings in the end covers.

Each rotor consists of a steel shaft with (usually) three lobes surrounding it. These are generally twisted along their length and are known as **helical rotors** (see Fig 19.24). Rotors with two lobes only are also used in some blowers.

Although designed to pump air, the blower rotors are not fitted with seals, but rely on the precise and limited clearances between the rotors themselves and between the rotors and the housing.

Operation

The operation of a blower is similar to that of a gear-type oil pump. The lobes on the rotors fit together like gears in mesh, and turn in opposite directions. As one lobe moves from the valley between the two lobes on the other rotor, it creates a void that is filled with air. This is the inlet action.

The air between adjacent lobes is carried to the outlet as the rotors turn; it is then forced from the valley by the re-entry of the meshing lobe. This creates the discharge and pressurisation of the air.

In order to eliminate the typical pulsating action associated with a gear or lobe pump, the helical rotors are used and provide a continuous and uniform air displacement from the blower. Blowers fitted to two-stroke diesel engines rotate at approximately twice engine speed.

The rotor gears have to be timed to each other, otherwise the required clearance between the rotor lobes will not be maintained and damage to the lobes and engine can occur. Due to normal wear, the running clearances will alter and may have to be adjusted during the blower's service life. To alter this clearance, the helical drive gears are shim adjusted.

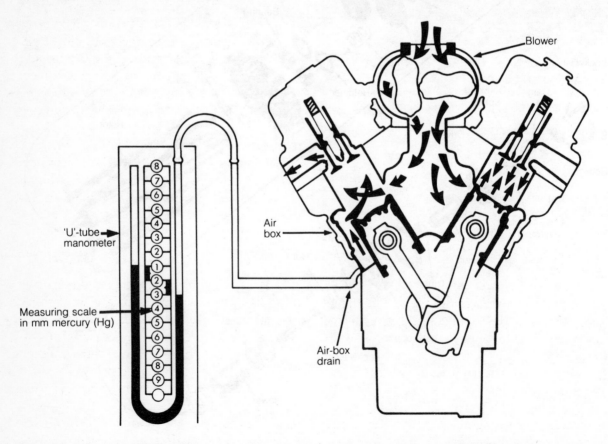

Fig 19.25   Measuring blower pressure with 'U'-tube manometer — schematic view

Because the rotor lobes turn within close tolerances and never contact one another, no form of lubrication is necessary within the blower housing. However, the support bearings and timing gears at the end of the rotors need constant lubrication from the engine lubrication system. To prevent engine oil from entering the rotor compartment, lip or piston ring-type oil seals are fitted within the blower end plates to separate the two sections of the blower and prevent the entry of oil into the air chamber (Fig 19.24).

The drive coupling used between the engine and the blower is a flexible or dampening type, which reduces the torsional twisting loads placed on the blower drive shaft during normal engine operation (Fig 19.24).

When in service, the efficiency of the blower is checked by measuring the discharge pressure by means of a mercury-filled manometer — a 'U'-tube device that indicates pressure by means of the difference between fluid levels in the arms of the tube (Fig 19.25). To check blower output (or airbox pressure), connect the manometer to an air-box drain, usually located on the lower side of the cylinder block, just below inlet-port level. (The air box is the compartment that surrounds the tangential ports area of the cylinder liners.)

To carry out a static inspection of the blower, the air inlet housing and safety screen leading into the blower inlet must be removed. The safety screen is a wire gauze screen located at the blower inlet to prevent the entry of foreign objects.

To detect a worn flexible drive coupling, hold the driving rotor and try to rotate it. The rotor should move, against the flexing of the coupling, from 10–16 mm as measured at the lobe crown. On release, the rotor should spring back at least 6 mm. If the rotors cannot be moved as described above, the drive coupling should be inspected and replaced if necessary. A faulty blower drive coupling can be detected by a rattling noise within the vicinity of the coupling during engine operation.

The rotors should be examined for evidence of contact by visually checking the edges of the rotor lobe crowns and mating rotor roots for signs of scoring or contact wear marks. At the same time, the drive gear backlash should be checked by mounting a dial indicator on the blower housing with the indicator probe perpendicular to, and in contact with, the side of the lobe. The backlash is measured by moving the rotor in one direction and then the other within the limits of the gear teeth clearance (the second rotor must not move). The allowable backlash is generally 0.1 mm; if this is exceeded, the blower drive gears will have to be renewed.

During an inspection, oil on the blower rotors indicates leaking rotor shaft oil seals, which may be the result of worn rotor bearings, worn seals or lip-type seals that have been turned inside out due to the closure of the emergency shutdown flaps during high-speed engine operation. The emergency shutdown flap is a shutter mounted on the inlet to the blower which, when operated, closes off the air supply to the blower (and engine), thereby stopping the engine. The emergency shutdown flap is to be used only in an emergency when the normal method of engine shutdown is inoperative.

Finally, the safety screen should be checked for signs of damage and, after the emergency shutdown flap has been refitted, the latch checked to ensure that the flap remains open during engine operation.

Disassembly of the blower

When disassembling, inspecting and reassembling a blower, the appropriate workshop manual should always be used. However, as a guide to procedures, a general description of overhauling a blower fitted to a Detroit Diesel 'V' series 71 engine is detailed below.

After the governor assembly and fuel feed pump have been removed from the blower, the drive gears are ready to be pulled off the rotor shafts. By placing rag between the two rotor lobes to prevent the rotors from turning, unscrew and remove the allen-headed bolts retaining the drive gears. Mount a suitable puller and remove both drive gears together — because they are helical gears, pulling one alone will cause partial rotation of one rotor against the other. Also remove the spacer shims from behind the gears and mark the gears and shims to ensure correct positioning of parts on reassembly.

Remove the bearing retainer bolts and retainers for all four bearings and, with the aid of a puller, remove the rear end plate and bearing assembly. Repeat the procedure for the front end plate. Next, remove the two rotors from the blower housing. With the aid of a press, remove the bearings and oil seals from both end plates.

Inspection of components

Prior to inspection, all the blower components should be washed in a suitable cleaning solution and dried off with compressed air. All the parts of the blower should be examined and measured to determine whether they should be reused.

The rotor lobes should be examined for burrs and scoring, especially on the sealing edges. Witness marks along the full length of the lobe usually indicate worn bearings or excessive backlash in the timing gears. Small imperfections on the lobe or rotor roots can be removed with fine emery tape.

The internal surface area of the blower housing and the blower end housings should be checked for scoring. Any fine score marks can be removed with fine emery tape. Deep score marks will necessitate replacement of the housing. The blower end housings should also be checked for surface flatness and for evidence of bearing rotation in the housing.

Oil seal ring carriers and running surfaces (if fitted) should be examined for wear and scoring. All oil seals, bearings and lock tabs should automatically be renewed during a complete overhaul.

Assembly

The assembly procedure as described below is that for a typical blower with lip-type oil seals sealing the rotor shafts (some blowers use other types of seal).

Install the lip-type oil seals in both of the end plates so that they sit approximately 0.125 mm below the finished surface of each end plate.

Fit the front end plate to the blower housing with the three oil holes on the side of the end plate facing the cylinder block. Because no gaskets are used between the end plates and housing, ensure that the mating surfaces are smooth and clean.

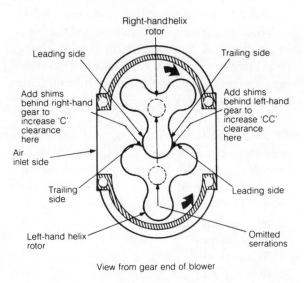

Fig 19.26 Blower lobe clearance adjustment guide
Courtesy of Detroit Diesel Corp

Before installing the rotors, establish where the driving rotor is to be placed in the blower housing relative to the drive shaft coming from the engine. The driving rotor lobe and its associated drive gear are identified by the way they both form a right-hand helix. The driven rotor lobe and drive gear form a left-hand helix.

Match the rotors together so that the master splines (omitted serrations) lie in a horizontal position (as shown in Fig 19.26), and face the left when looking at the rear of the blower

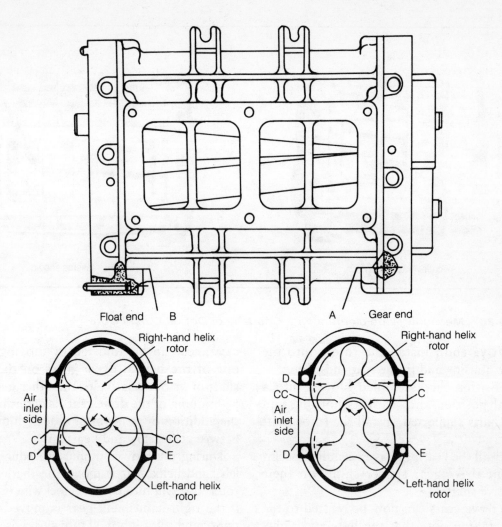

Views from gear end of blower

ENGINE	BLOWER	IDENT*	A	B	C	CC	D	E
6 & 12 CYL.	STD.		.007″	.012″	.008″	.006″ TO .010″	.015″	.004″
6 & 12 CYL.	TURBO		.007″	.012″	.008″	.006″ TO .010″	.015″	.004″
8 & 16 CYL.	STD.		.007″	.014″	.010″	.004″ TO .008″	.015″	.004″
8 & 16 CYL.	TURBO		.007″	.014″	.010″	.004″ TO .008″	.015″	.004″
8 & 16 CYL.	TURBO	LT	.007″	.024″	.010″	.004″ TO .008″	.030″	.004″

Chart indicating the areas where rotor lobe clearances are to be checked and the allowable clearances in these areas.

*Identification stamped on blower
†Dimensions are in inches as supplied by manufacturer.
Note: Time rotors to dimensions on chart for clearance between trailing side of right-hand helix rotor and leading side of left-hand helix rotor (CC) from both inlet and outlet side of blower.

Fig 19.27 Rotor clearance data *Courtesy of Detroit Diesel Corp*

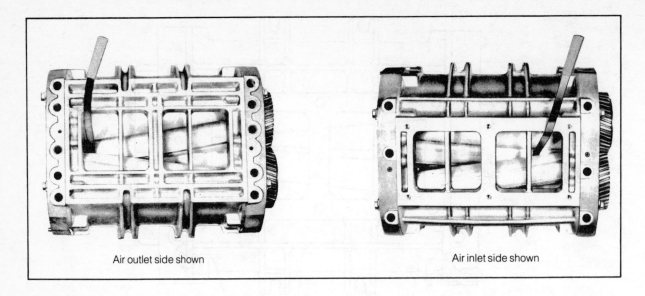

Air outlet side shown

Air inlet side shown

Fig 19.28 Measuring lobe clearances *Courtesy of Detroit Diesel Corp*

(non-drive end). Install the rotors into the blower housing and fit the rear end plate.

Reposition the assembled blower into a vertical position and, with its housing and rotor shafts supported, install the rotor shaft bearings.

After all the bearings have been fitted, reinstall the drive gear spacer shims on their respective shafts.

The drive gears can now be refitted to the shafts, taking note that the left- and right-hand helical gears are matched to their corresponding rotor lobes, and that the master splines on the rotor shafts and drive gears are in alignment with one another prior to the gears being pressed on.

With rag placed between the rotor lobes to prevent them from turning, the drive gears can be pressed on to the shafts by means of a puller bolt screwed into the end of the blower shaft. As with removal, the gears must be installed together, to prevent rotation of one in relation to the other.

With the end plates bolted up and the drive gears installed, the rotors can be timed to each other. During operation, the rotor lobes run with a slight clearance between them. This clearance can be adjusted by moving either one of the helical drive gears on the rotor shaft in or out relative to the other gear. The positioning of the drive gears is determined by the addition or removal of spacer shims from between the gears and bearings.

During the blower timing procedure, if the left-hand helix gear is moved in, the left-hand rotor lobe will turn counter-clockwise (CC) and if the right-hand helix gear is moved in, the right-hand rotor lobe will turn clockwise (C).

The running clearance between the rotor lobes should be checked with the aid of a feeler strip, as shown in Fig 19.28. The trailing and leading edges, as shown in Fig 19.26, must be measured from the inlet and outlet side of the blower.

The measured running clearances can be compared with the specifications (Fig 19.27) and the necessary repositioning of the timing gears carried out. As a reference, the adding or subtracting of 0.075 mm shim material will revolve the rotor approximately 0.025 mm.

When timing of the blower rotors is completed, any accessories mounted on the blower can be refitted and the blower installed on to the engine.

Bypass blowers

Detroit Diesel are now installing a modified form of Roots blower to turbocharged Detroit Diesel two-stroke engines. This 'bypass' blower, as it is known, directs excess and unnecessary boost air back into the intake of the blower, thus helping to drive it. This in turn reduces the internal power loss of the engine and ultimately increases engine power and torque output.

The modification is the addition of a bypass valve in a passage between the inlet and discharge sides of the blower, as shown in Fig 19.29. The valve is a simple spring-loaded relief valve, held closed by its load spring to keep the bypass passage blocked while the engine is stopped or running at low speed or under light load conditions.

When engine speed or load increases, the turbocharger output alone can provide adequate air flow for scavenging and charging the engine cylinders, making the use of the blower unnecessary. As air-box pressure increases to 34 kPa, the bypass valve begins to open, and is fully open at 44 kPa, allowing the excess air to flow back into the inlet port of the blower, thus helping to drive it. The blower does less work and so requires less power input, increasing the engine's fuel economy.

To keep the blower bypass valve clean and to maintain its proper function, a small amount of air is allowed to bleed past the valve and through a vent hose into the engine crankcase

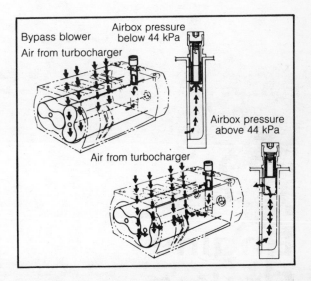

Fig 19.29 Bypass blower airflow
Courtesy of Detroit Diesel Corp

20
Engine
Brakes

When used in vehicle applications, the diesel engine is often called on to drive or provide a range of ancillary systems or equipment, necessary for the operation of the vehicle. Such equipment is predominantly associated with the vehicle braking system.

In heavy trucks, an engine brake is often used to assist the conventional (wheel) braking system in retarding the vehicle. In simple terms, the engine brake is designed to effectively turn the engine into an air compressor that absorbs power while compressing the air charge within the cylinders. In so doing, the engine is converted into a retarder coupled to the vehicle's drive train, which helps slow the vehicle, giving greater safety with added brake and tyre savings.

Another style of engine braking system is the exhaust brake, which moves a shutter across the exhaust pipe to restrict the exit of exhaust gas; this in turn slows the engine and vehicle.

Jacobs engine brake

In a conventional four-stroke engine, air is compressed during the engine's compression stroke. As each piston passes TDC, this air will act on the piston (like a compressed spring) to drive it back towards BDC. The energy used in compressing the air is thus stored as potential energy, which then drives the piston down again. Because of inefficiencies — heating, leakage, friction — this positive driving effect is somewhat less than the power input.

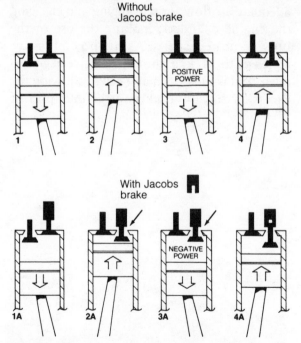

Fig 20.1 Operating principle of the Jacobs engine brake
Courtesy of Jacobs Brake Division

However, with an engine brake, the exhaust valves are opened just prior to TDC on the compression stroke, thus releasing the compressed air (and, effectively, its potential

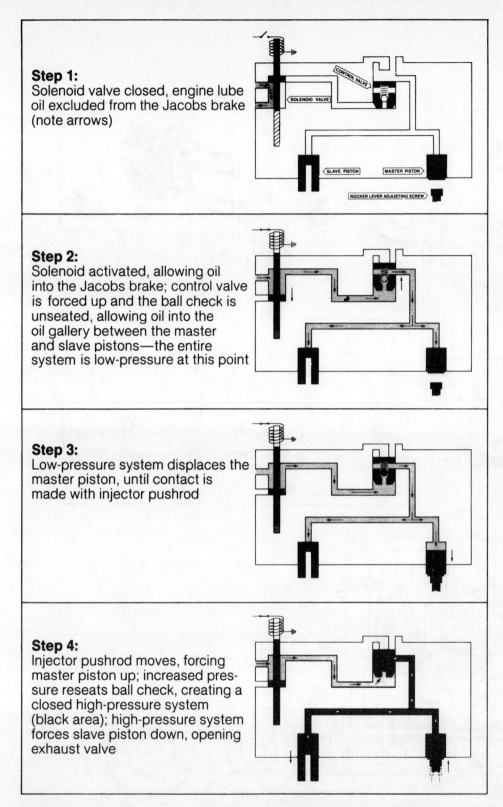

Step 1:
Solenoid valve closed, engine lube oil excluded from the Jacobs brake (note arrows)

Step 2:
Solenoid activated, allowing oil into the Jacobs brake; control valve is forced up and the ball check is unseated, allowing oil into the oil gallery between the master and slave pistons—the entire system is low-pressure at this point

Step 3:
Low-pressure system displaces the master piston, until contact is made with injector pushrod

Step 4:
Injector pushrod moves, forcing master piston up; increased pressure reseats ball check, creating a closed high-pressure system (black area); high-pressure system forces slave piston down, opening exhaust valve

Fig 20.2   Operation of a Jacobs engine brake hydraulic system   *Courtesy of Jacobs Brake Division*

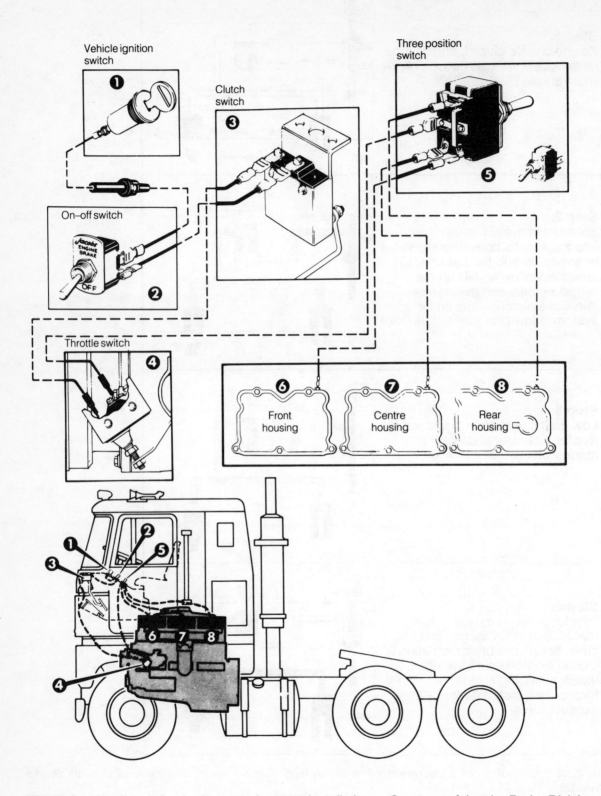

Fig 20.3 Jacobs engine brake control system installation *Courtesy of Jacobs Brake Division*

energy) into the exhaust system. The energy required to return each piston to the bottom of its stroke as well as compressing the air on the compression stroke is gained from the momentum of the vehicle. It is this two-step process of releasing the compressed air from the cylinders and using the vehicle's momentum to move the pistons that develops the engine brake retarding force.

Operation of the Jacobs engine brake

Under all 'run' conditions in an engine without a Jacobs engine brake, air is compressed in the engine cylinders during the compression stroke to a high pressure (3100–3800 kPa) and temperature (550°C). Fuel is then injected and combustion occurs, raising the cylinder pressure and temperature to even greater levels than before. As combustion continues, the pressure of the expanding gas in the cylinder forces the piston down, to turn the crankshaft. In other words, the engine produces power.

In an engine equipped with a Jacobs engine brake, whether it be a two-stroke or four-stroke, something very different happens in each engine cylinder during braking, as shown in Fig 20.1. The key component is a slave piston mounted in a housing over the exhaust crosshead or the exhaust valve which is hydraulically connected to a master piston in another section of the housing. As shown in Fig 20.2, the oil gallery between the master and slave pistons is charged with oil. At the precise engine timing position, the master piston is driven up, displacing the trapped oil to force the slave piston down, opening the exhaust valve.

The compressed air, with its potential energy, is released into the exhaust system. By venting the compressed air at this point, no positive driving effort is exerted on the piston, thereby dramatically increasing the retarding effect of the engine and subsequent vehicle movement.

In conclusion, the Jacobs engine brake is a hydraulically operated device, which converts a power-producing diesel engine into a power-absorbing retarding mechanism.

Jacobs engine brake controls

Activation of the Jacobs engine brake is controlled by three main switches, as shown in Fig 20.3:

1 An **on–off dash switch** designed to initially activate the engine brake unit, which is left in the 'on' position during vehicle operation. Also, a three-position selector switch mounted on the dash is used to engage the engine brake on selected cylinders only, so altering the intensity of the engine braking, dependent on driving conditions.

2 A **clutch switch** mounted beside the clutch pedal with a probe in contact with the pedal itself. The engine brake will only operate when the drive line from the engine to the transmission is coupled. Therefore, when the clutch pedal is depressed to change gears, the clutch switch will operate, preventing the engine brake from operating. However, if there were a malfunction in a switch and the brake did not cease to operate, the engine would stall.

3 A **rack travel** or **throttle switch** mounted on the governor housing of the fuel injection pump, which has a probe in contact with the fuel rack. When the vehicle is being operated with the driveline fully engaged and the throttle backed off, the rack travel or throttle switch is activated, due to governor action moving the rack to the 'no fuel' position, thereby setting the engine brake into operation.

In summary, to operate a Jacobs engine brake, the dash on–off switch has to be in the 'on' position, the clutch pedal has to be fully released and the throttle must be closed.

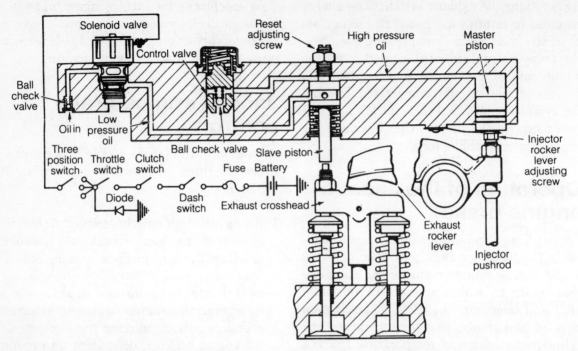

Fig 20.4   Schematic diagram of engine brake operation on a Cummins engine
Courtesy of Jacobs Brake Division

Operation of the Jacobs engine brake hydraulic system (Cummins engine installation)

Whenever the Jacobs brake fitted to a Cummins engine is operated (with reference to one cylinder only), the solenoid valve is activated, which allows engine oil to enter the brake housing mounted on top of the valve rocker gear, as shown in Fig 20.4. The oil then flows to the control valve, where it simultaneously moves the control valve up, against the force of a spring, and the ball valve off its seat, allowing oil to charge the slave and master piston housings. The oil pressure creates sufficient force to move the piston down to contact the injector rocker adjusting screw. Once the oil gallery between the pistons has filled with low-pressure oil, the spring closes the check ball valve, trapping the oil.

As the engine piston continues to move towards TDC on the compression stroke, the injector pushrod rises and begins to lift the master piston. This movement displaces oil from the master piston housing into the slave piston housing through the oil gallery, forcing the slave piston down on to the exhaust crosshead, opening the exhaust valves and allowing the compressed air to escape into the exhaust system.

For continued engine braking, the solenoid valve remains activated with the control valve maintaining a charge of oil between the slave and master pistons.

Once the operator opens one of the four control switches, the solenoid valve will be deactivated, closing off the engine oil flow to the control valve. Therefore, the control valve under spring force will move down and allow the trapped oil in the slave and master pistons to bleed off into the rocker gear housing. At this point, the engine brake will cease to operate.

Note: Cummins have now developed their own engine brake called the 'C' brake; its operation and construction are similar to those of the Jacobs brake previously used on Cummins engines.

Jacobs brake used on engines with in-line injection pumps

A number of diesel engines, such as Caterpillar and Volvo, which use in-line fuel injection pumps also use Jacobs engine brakes. The basic operation of the brake unit is the same as that described earlier on the Cummins engines; however, the means of signalling when each cylinder is to be exhausted is different. On the unit injected engines (Cummins and Detroit), the upward movement of the unit injector pushrod signals when the exhaust valves on the same cylinder are to open.

On engines with conventional fuel injection systems, the master piston within the engine brake assembly is operated by the upward movement of an exhaust valve pushrod. Master piston operation transfers oil to a slave piston, which moves downward to open an exhaust valve/s on a different cylinder within the engine. For example, when the number 1 piston is beginning the exhaust stroke, the exhaust pushrod is moved upwards, which causes the master piston to transfer oil to the slave piston, thereby opening the exhaust valve/s on cylinder number 3 (which is on the compression stroke). Table 20.1 shows the relationship between the master and slave pistons on a six-cylinder engine with a firing order of 1–5–3–6–2–4.

Table 20.1 Relationship between the master and slave pistons on a six-cylinder engine fitted with a Jacobs engine brake

Master piston exhaust valve	Slave piston exhaust valve
Cylinder 1	Cylinder 3
Cylinder 5	Cylinder 6
Cylinder 3	Cylinder 2
Cylinder 6	Cylinder 4
Cylinder 2	Cylinder 1
Cylinder 4	Cylinder 5

The Dynatard engine brake used on Mack trucks

The Dynatard engine brake works on the same principle as the Jacobs brake. However, the mode of operation and construction is very different. Again, engine braking is achieved by opening the exhaust valve just prior to TDC on the compression stroke, thereby preventing the compressed air from helping to drive the piston down the cylinder.

Dynatard engine brake controls

The Dynatard engine brake system is activated by three controls:

1 the cab switch;
2 the injection pump switch;
3 the solenoids.

For engine brake operation, both the cab switch and the injection pump switch must be activated. The cab switch is operated by selecting 'on', and the injection pump switch operates automatically when the throttle is fully released as in deceleration, which allows the fuel rack to move to the 'no fuel' position. With both of these switches activated, the electric solenoids on the rocker shafts will operate. However, when the engine speed falls to idle speed, the governor will move the rack from the 'no fuel' position to slight fuel delivery, thus opening the injection pump switch and cutting off the engine brake, as shown in Fig 20.5.

Dynatard engine brake operation

With the dash switch on, and the injection pump switch activated by the accelerator pedal being fully released, the engine brake

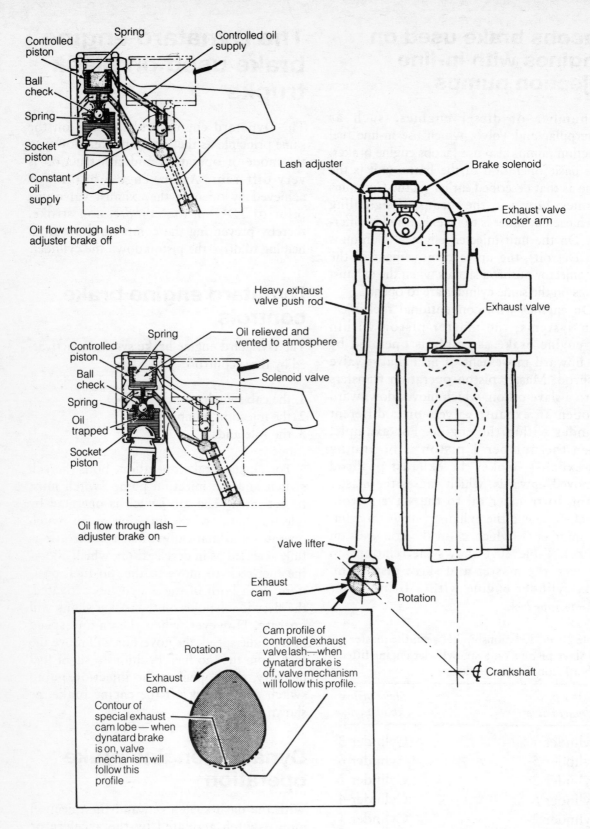

Controlled piston
Spring
Controlled oil supply
Ball check
Spring
Socket piston
Constant oil supply

Oil flow through lash — adjuster brake off

Lash adjuster
Brake solenoid
Exhaust valve rocker arm
Heavy exhaust valve push rod
Exhaust valve

Spring
Controlled piston
Oil relieved and vented to atmosphere
Ball check
Solenoid valve
Spring
Oil trapped
Socket piston

Oil flow through lash — adjuster brake on

Valve lifter
Exhaust cam
Rotation
Crankshaft

Rotation
Cam profile of controlled exhaust valve lash—when dynatard brake is off, valve mechanism will follow this profile.
Exhaust cam
Contour of special exhaust cam lobe — when dynatard brake is on, valve mechanism will follow this profile

Fig 20.5   Operating components of a Dynatard engine brake   *Courtesy of Mack Trucks Inc*

will start to operate, with a number of functions occurring simultaneously, as shown in Fig 20.5.

Considering the actions relative to one engine cylinder only, as the Dynatard system is activated, oil pressure acting on top of the controlled piston is allowed to dump to the atmosphere through the upper section of the solenoid valve. At the same time, oil pressure acting on the underside of the controlled piston pushes it up against the controlled piston spring. This allows the ball check valve in the socket piston to seat. Just before the ball valve seats, the socket spring pushes the socket piston down and oil fills the socket piston chamber. With the ball check valve now seated, oil is trapped in the piston chamber, forming an hydraulic lock which keeps the lash adjuster fully extended for engine brake operation.

With the exhaust valve lash reduced to zero, the valve mechanism will follow a special contour on the cam lobe, causing the cam follower to ride up on the lobe contour, pushing the exhaust valve open as the piston approaches TDC. Consequently, the compressed air charge will escape into the exhaust manifold. Thus the engine goes through a power-absorbing cycle without a corresponding power-producing one, resulting in a braking effect by the engine.

When the engine brake is deactivated due to either the clutch pedal or the engine throttle being depressed, the solenoid valve opens, allowing oil to flow into and act on top of the controlled piston. As there is now equal pressure on both sides of the piston, the controlled piston spring pushes the controlled piston down, unseating the ball check valve. The oil which was previously trapped in the socket piston is now released, allowing the lash - adjuster to operate in a collapsed position, thereby maintaining normal exhaust valve clearance.

The exhaust brake

Another design of engine brake generally known as an exhaust brake features a shutter which, when operated, closes the exhaust system outlet and restricts the exit of exhaust gas. This type of exhaust brake serves the same purpose as the previously discussed engine brake in that it causes the engine to operate as a power-absorbing compressor. Although it is not the most efficient type, the exhaust brake is widely used in engines of smaller vehicles. In this application, it provides adequate engine braking, is a lot quieter during operation, places a uniform load on the engine during braking and is probably the least expensive type of engine brake.

A typical exhaust brake system (Fig 20.6) shows the exhaust brake unit fitted into the engine exhaust pipe. It is simply a shutter or a butterfly which, when operated, closes during engine operation, restricting the exit of the exhaust gas. The result is the production of a large back pressure in the engine cylinders, which opposes the piston travel, hence slowing the engine and vehicle. The exhaust brake is only effective above 1500 engine rpm.

Exhaust brake operation

When the exhaust brake is to be used, the operator activates a switch in the cabin, which causes a compressed air- (or vacuum-) operated cylinder to close the exhaust brake butterfly. Engine braking begins immediately this happens.

Brake service

All engine brake and exhaust brake systems need to be serviced at various times. However, because adjustment procedures vary from one brake to the next, it is recommended that the appropriate workshop manual be consulted prior to servicing any engine braking system.

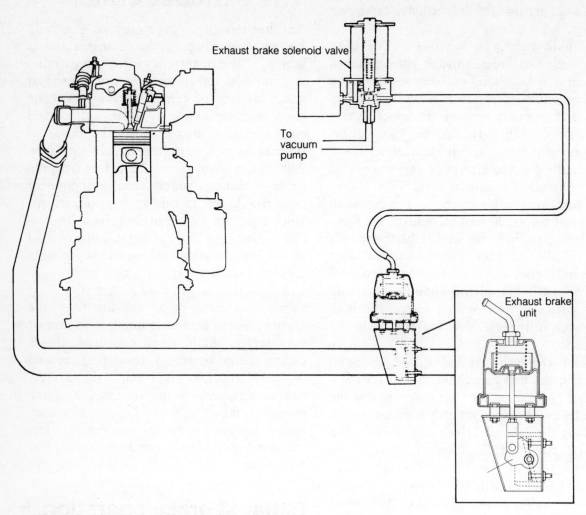

Fig 20.6   Typical exhaust brake unit   *Courtesy of Mazda*

21
Engine Faultfinding and Testing

Fault diagnosis is a skill in which the diesel serviceperson must become extremely proficient in order to determine the cause of an engine malfunction and effect repairs quickly and efficiently. The serviceperson must be able to recognise from the various symptoms shown that certain adjustments are necessary, or that a particular engine component is worn, is about to fail or has failed.

The following basic faultfinding steps have been laid down as a guide to finding out what the engine problem is and how to solve it.

- Gather as much information as possible from the owner/operator about the complaint as to when and how it occurred.

- Operate the engine so as to confirm for yourself that the problem exists.
- Inspect the engine and always look for the simplest and smallest things that may be causing the problem.
- Check the service records to see if any recent work has been carried out on the engine.
- Know the operation of the system and relate the problem symptoms to basic operating and safety principles.
- Examine the service manual faultfinding guide for information concerning the type of problem and what could cause it.
- Where possible, use diagnostic test equipment to check pressures and temperatures so as to pinpoint the problem area. If possible, dynamometer test the engine to check for correct performance.
- Examine the gathered information relating to the complaint and determine what the problem is and what might be causing it.
- List the possible causes of the problem and carry out the necessary repairs.
- After the problem has been repaired, run and test the engine to confirm that the problem has been rectified.

Faultfinding

Table 21.1, by courtesy of Perkins Engines Ltd, lists some of the possible causes of an engine failing to operate satisfactorily. As in the original Perkins table, the term 'atomisers' has been retained instead of the alternative 'injectors'.

Compression testing

A compression test is given to each cylinder of an engine in order to ascertain its compression pressure. Because a diesel engine relies on compression ignition, it is essential that the compression pressure in each cylinder remains as close as possible to that at which the engine is designed to operate. If

Table 21.1 Engine faultfinding

Fault and possible cause	Remedy
Engine will not start	
1 No fuel at atomisers	
• Stop control in 'no fuel' position.	Turn control to 'run' position.
• Insufficient fuel in tank, air has drawn into the system.	Replenish fuel tank, then 'bleed' system.
• Fuel lift pump inoperative.	Remove lift pump and rectify or fit replacement pump.
• Fuel filters choked or fuel feed pipe blocked.	Check fuel feed to fuel pump and filters, rectify as necessary.
• Fuel pump not delivering fuel to the atomisers.	Remove pump for attention of specialised work shop and fit replacement.
Fuel at atomisers	
• Atomisers require servicing.	Service or fit replacement set.
• Wrong type of thermostart unit fitted.	Check that correct type is fitted.
• Thermostart unit inoperative.	Visually check unit, fit new unit if unserviceable.
• Valve and/or pump timing incorrect.	Check and reset if necessary.
2 Cranking speed too low	
• Battery not in well-charged condition	Fit fully charged replacement.
• Incorrect grade of lubricating oil.	Check oil viscosity against approved lists in manual for temperature range.
• Poor electrical connections between battery and starter motor.	Check and tighten or remake connections if necessary.
• Starter motor faulty.	Examine and rectify if necessary.
3 Poor compression. With poor compression, starting may just be difficult in normal weather, but in cold weather the engine may refuse to start altogether, depending on how much compression there is and the cranking speed. The causes are numerous, and include worn liners, piston rings and leaking valves.	There is no quick remedy for this condition; generally, the engine will have been in service for some time. At least a top overhaul or probably a complete overhaul would be indicated to restore the lost compression, which is so vital for the efficient running of a diesel engine.
Engine starts, runs for a few moments, then stops	
• Partially choked fuel feed pipe or filter.	Trace and rectify.
• Fuel lift pump not giving adequate delivery.	Check output of lift pump and rectify or replace as necessary.
• Fuel tank vent hole blocked.	Check and clear if necessary.
• Restriction in induction or exhaust systems.	Check and rectify if necessary.
• Air leaking into supply or return fuel pipes.	Check and trace.
Engine misfiring or running erratically	
• Atomiser(s) require attention.	Isolate offender(s), remove and test; if faulty, service or fit replacement(s).
• Air in fuel system.	Check for air in fuel pump; if present, prime the the fuel system.
• Water in fuel pump.	Thoroughly check fuel system for signs of water; remove if present, then prime with clean fuel

Table 21.1 Engine faultfinding (cont.)

Fault and possible cause	*Remedy*
• Valve and/or pump timing incorrect.	Check and reset if necessary.
• Valve clearances incorrect.	Check and reset if necessary.
• Fuel leaking from high-pressure pipe.	Observe with engine running and replace pipe if necessary.

Engine runs evenly but suffers from loss of power

• Atomisers require servicing.	Remove and service or fit a replacement set.
• Loss of compression.	Refer to previous remarks on poor compression.
• Pump not delivering sufficient quantity of fuel to meet engine requirements.	Observe throttle linkage for unrestricted travel; if satisfactory, pump should be checked for correct output in specialist workshop.
• Air cleaner causing restriction to the flow of air.	Check that the correct type is fitted and that it has been serviced in accordance with the instructions given in manual.
• Fuel pump timing incorrect.	Check and reset if necessary.
• Brakes binding, causing excessive load on engine and apparent loss of power.	Stop vehicle and check if any brake drum(s) appear over-heated; if drum(s) over-heated, take immediate remedial action.

Engine runs but with a smoky exhaust

• Incorrect air–fuel ratio.	Check diaphragm and adjustment of air–fuel ratio control. Check for any restriction to the airflow; if satisfactory, have the fuel pump maximum fuel output checked.
• Cold starting aid (thermostart) valve leaking.	Replace with a serviceable unit.
• Valve and/or fuel pump timing incorrect.	Check and reset if necessary.
• Atomiser(s) require servicing.	Remove and service or fit a replacement set
• Excessive oil consumption.	Generally consistent with poor compression and long engine life; workshop examination required to give precise details.
• Vehicle overloaded.	Check that the loading is consistent with the manufacturer's load classification.

Engine knocking

• Faulty atomiser (nozzle needle sticking).	Fit replacement atomiser.
• Fuel pump timing too far advanced.	Check timing and reset if necessary.
• Piston striking a valve.	Check valve timing, piston topping and valve head depth relative to cylinder head face.
• Incorrect fuel.	Check that the tank has been filled with diesel fuel and not petrol by mistake.
• Worn or damaged bearings, etc.	Engine overhaul required.

Engine overheating

• Coolant level in system too low.	Replenish and check if leakage is taking place; if so, rectify at once.
• Radiator or system partially blocked.	Flush system through thoroughly in accordance with the manufacturer's instructions.
• Blockage or restriction due to ice formation.	Locate trouble spot and take any action necessary to prevent recurrence.

Table 21.1   Engine faultfinding (cont.)

Fault and possible cause	Remedy
• Fan belt slipping or incorrect type of fan fitted.	Check fan belt tension and fan type.
• Valve and/or fuel pump timing(s) incorrect.	Check and reset if necessary.
• Thermostart stuck in the closed position	Check and replace with a new one if found to be unserviceable.
Low oil pressure	
• Oil level in sump too low.	Replenish to correct level.
• Incorrect grade or inferior oil being used.	Change to approved grade.
• Oil leaking externally from engine.	Rectify immediately.
• Pressure gauge or oil warning light switch inaccurate.	Check either against a master unit.
• Oil pump worn or pressure relief valve sticking open.	Remove and examine.
• Suction pipe to oil pump allowing air to be drawn in.	Rectify leak or renew pipe as necessary.
• Worn main or big end bearings.	Engine overhaul required.
High oil pressure	
• Incorrect grade of oil being used.	Change to approved grade.
• Pressure gauge inaccurate.	Check against a master unit.
• Pressure relief valve sticking closed.	Remove and examine.
Excessive crankcase pressure	
• Partially choked breather pipe.	Check pipe for any obstruction.
• Worn or sticking piston rings.	Engine examination required.
• Pipework or tank on vacuum side of exhauster allowing entry of air into the system (only where exhauster is fitted).	Check system for leaks and rectify if necessary.

the compression pressure in one or more cylinders is reduced by any marked degree, the engine will not operate smoothly and effciently, or may not even start at all. Symptoms such as difficult starting, uneven running, misfiring, excessive fuel consumption or loss of pulling power are usually indicative of low or uneven compression, and when they are present the engine should be given a compression test.

The information gained from a compression test is most helpful in determining the mechanical condition of an engine. For example, low but relatively even compression pressure in all cylinders usually indicates faulty or worn piston rings, or worn pistons and/or cylinder liners. Low but uneven compression pressure readings usually indicate leaking cylinder valves, but may indicate faulty or worn piston rings or worn pistons and/or cylinder liners. Leaking cylinder valves, which result from insufficient tappet clearance, faulty valve operation or incorrectly seated valves, are usually responsible for low compression pressure in a particular cylinder. This, however, is not always the case, as broken compression rings or a damaged piston will also cause low compression in a particular cylinder.

Procedure

While the procedure adopted for taking compression tests on both petrol and diesel engines is somewhat similar, care must be taken to ensure that the pressure gauge chosen for a diesel engine is capable of registering pressures up to 5000 kPa. This is necessary as the compression pressure of most high-speed diesel engines is in the vicinity of 3000 kPa — more than twice that of a petrol engine of comparable size. Owing to this high compression pressure, it is not advisable, when taking a compression test, to try to hold the gauge in the injector pocket or hole by hand. If a suitable adaptor is not supplied with the gauge to enable it to be clamped in the injector pocket, one should be made before starting the compression test.

Once a suitable pressure gauge and adaptor have been selected, the compression test should be carried out as follows:

1 Remove no. 1 injector from its pocket in the cylinder head and then cover both the fuel inlet connection of the injector and the disconnected end of the delivery line with clean rag to prevent the entry of dirt or dust.
2 Clean the injector pocket and fit the compression gauge, making sure that it is firmly clamped in position to prevent leakage.
3 Either start the engine and increase its speed to a fast idle (e.g. 600 rpm) or crank the engine over continuously by means of the starter motor. (See the workshop manual for the recommended method.) If the latter method is adopted, the remaining injectors must either be removed from the cylinder head or the appropriate decompression levers set so that compression is not possible in any cylinder other than the one being tested. This allows the engine to be cranked over at a sufficiently high speed for satisfactory testing, while keeping battery drain to a minimum. Should the engine be fitted with a pneumatic governor, it is essential that the venturi butterfly remains in the full open position during the cranking operation, since a restriction in the inlet will cause a low reading.
4 Note the pressure gauge reading and compare it with the recommended compression pressure specified by the engine manufacturer in the workshop manual. In the absence of a workshop manual, an approximate compression of 3100 kPa may be assumed for most high-speed diesel engines tested at idling speed. If the test is taken while the engine is being cranked over by the starter motor, the compression pressure will be decreased by approximately 700 kPa because of reduced volumetric efficiency at lower speeds. The figures quoted above are valid at sea level only and will decrease with altitude. For each 800 m increase in altitude (up to 3000 m), the compression pressure will be reduced by approximately 240 kPa.
5 Test each remaining cylinder in turn, making sure that the pressure gauge readings are accurately noted for further reference.
6 Compare the readings from the different engine cylinders. If they differ from each other by more than 175 kPa, or if any reading is more than 350 kPa below the recommended compression pressure, it is evident that the engine is in need of attention. While a top overhaul (i.e. a valve grind) is necessary in most cases, this should not be started before all other possibilities such as loose cylinder head studs, incorrect valve clearances, weak or broken valve springs or incorrect decompressor settings have been eliminated.

Note: Once the engine cylinder head has been removed and a burnt valve discovered, the possibility of worn piston rings and/or cylinder liner is not positively eliminated. Therefore the engine should be examined carefully for evidence of other faults.

Diesel exhaust smoke

One good aid to faultfinding is the correct interpretation of the exhaust smoke colour. Table 21.2, provided courtesy of CAV, gives a comprehensive guide to the causes of exhaust smoke colours, suggests cures and lists some pertinent comments.

Table 21.2   The use of exhaust-smoke colour in engine faultfinding

Colour of smoke	Symptom	Probable diagnosis
Black or dark grey	Smoke at full load at any engine speed, but particularly at highest and lowest speeds, and power at least normal.	Maximum fuel setting of injection pump too high. Excess fuel device not tripping automatically to normal after starting.
	Smoke at full load, particularly at high and medium speeds, engine quieter than normal	Pump timing retarded (or advanced device not correct if fitted).
	Smoke at full load, particularly at low and medium speeds, engine noisier than normal	Pump timing too advanced.
	Smoke at full load, particularly at high and medium speeds, probably with loss of power.	Injector nozzle holes (or some of them) wholly or partially blocked.
	Smoke at full load at higher speeds only.	Air cleaner restricted due to blockage with dirt, or damage.
	Intermittent or puffy exhaust smoke, sometimes with white or blue tinge, usually coupled with knocking.	Injector nozzle valve stuck open intermittently
	Smoke at full loads at high speed, engine running faster than normal when on governor.	Governor speed setting considerably above engine maker's maximum.
	Smoke at full loads at high speed, engine running slower than normal on governor (vacuum type).	Governor venturi throat partially choked with carbon.
	Smoke at most speeds and loads, tending to blue or white when cold and when starting.	Nozzle sprays impinging on cylinder head, due to incorrect fitting of injector into cylinder head.
	Smoke at higher loads and speeds, not necessarily at maximum.	Injector nozzle valve lift excessive, due to repeated valve or seat refacing, without lift correction.
	Smoke at all speeds at high loads, mostly low and medium speeds and probably coupled with poor starting.	Loss of cylinder compression due to stuck rings, bore wear, valve wear or burning, sticking valves, incorrect valve setting.
	Smoke at full load, either at lower or higher speeds only, but in some cases at all speeds.	Incorrect nozzle type fitted, or mixe types, or out-of-date type, or type for different duty.

Table 21.2 The use of exhaust-smoke colour in engine faultfinding (cont.)

Cure	Remarks
Remove pump, have reset to engine maker's maximum flow figure (or less) by authorised service agent if own equipment not available.	Some operators may be tempted to reset by trial and error; this may be very misleading as smoke may be caused by another fault.
Have repaired by authorised agent — removal of pump may be necessary.	The fault is rare except when caused by deliberate tampering (now illegal).
Correct timing according to engine maker's instructions, taking up pump drive backlash (or rectify advance device if fitted).	Often becomes retarded owing to chain stretch, or backlash not taken up when set;may be critical to two crankshaft degrees.
	More likely to apply to indirect injection engines.
Replace injectors by reconditioned set on maker's service exchange scheme or clean and recondition with proper equipment.	Loss of power will lead to even more smoke if there is an attempt to restore by increasing pump setting.
Clean or replace air cleaner element according to type.	See note about vacuum governors below.
Have injectors examined for sticking valve, broken spring or grossly low opening pressure, or sign of cross-binding in cylinder head; replace as necessary.	May be due to neglect of filter maintenance, or water in fuel or bad fitting of injector in head; injector should fit freely in head and should be tightened down evenly and not too tightly.
With mechanical or hydraulic governors, reduce governor speed adjustment and seal stops, or preferably remove pump for attention; with vacuum governors, reset stops on venturi butterfly valve.	
Clean carbon from venturi throat.	Applies to vacuum governors where engine breather is upstream of venturi.
Examine for number of washers between injector and cylinder head — only one required at most. (Some engines none required — refer instruction book.)	Washer often left behind when removing injector and new one fitted on top of old; some injectors fitted with heat shield, which might be incorrectly assembled — refer to instruction book.
Can be rectified by proper equipment during reconditioning.	Many improperly trained fuel injection equipment mechanics will not rectify lift.
Engine requires top overhaul at least; re-ringing or sleeving, piston renewal if wear indications shown.	May be due to unsuitable lubricant or incorrect valve tappet clearance; may cause blue smoke too (if lubricating oil consumption is excessive).
Will be automatically corrected if injectors are reconditioned by an authorised agent, but it is essential to quote exact details of engine type and application.	Engine makers sometimes change the nozzle type with new engine marks or for different duties; power may or may not seem satisfactory if the wrong nozzle is fitted.

Table 21.2 The use of exhaust-smoke colour in engine faultfinding (cont.)

Colour of smoke	Symptom	Probable diagnosis
Black or dark grey	Smoke at full load, mostly at medium and high speeds, probably coupled with low power	Injection high-pressure pipes of incorrect length or bore, or having badly closed-in bore at ends, or due to sharp bends.
Blue, bluish-grey or greyish-white	Blue or whitish smoke particularly when cold, and at high speeds and light load, but reducing or changing to black when hot and at full load, and with loss of power at least at.	Pump timing retarded (or advance device not correct if fitted).
	Blue or whitish smoke when cold, particularly at light loads, but persisting probably with knocking.	Injector nozzle valve stuck open, or tip broken off nozzle.
	Blue smoke at all speeds and loads, hot or cold.	Engine oil being passed by piston rings due to sticking or worn bores.
	Blue smoke particularly when accelerating from period of idling, tending to clear with running.	Engine oil being passed by inlet valve guides due to wear, or valve guide oil shields misplaced.
	Blue smoke when running at maximum speed, full or light load.	Oil bath air cleaner overfilled.
	Light blue smoke at high-speed light loads, or running downhill, usually with acrid odour.	Engine running too cold, thermostat stuck or not fitted.

Diesel engine testing

The most satisfactory method of testing an engine for performance, as well as providing an ideal environment for faultfinding, is to operate the engine on a dynamometer in an engine testing installation. It is also a very convenient way of gaining open access to the engine under varying loads for tuning.

Before proceeding to further discussion on dynamometers and testing procedures, the terminology of testing should be defined to avoid any possible misinterpretations.

Power measurement terminology

Power is the rate at which an engine will do work. Reference to Chapter 1 will provide further basic explanation. Figure 1.2 in Chapter 1 shows that the maximum power a typical engine can produce is in the upper end of the engine's speed range, as might be expected, since power, by definition, is a 'rate'.

Power is measured in kW (kilowatts) or HP (horsepower). For conversion, 1 kW = 1.341 HP or 1 HP = 0.746 kW.

Torque is an indication of an engine's ability to produce a rotational force about its crankshaft. This is also explained more fully in Chapter 1. In addition, the torque curve of a typical engine can be seen in Fig 21.1. It shows that the optimum engine speed to obtain the greatest torque output is less than for maximum power.

The torque output of an engine is rated in newton metres (Nm) or lbs ft. For conversion, 1 N.m = 0.737 lbs ft or 1 lb ft = 1.36 Nm.

Brake power is the usable power available at the flywheel of an engine when the engine is placed under load. The brake power of an engine is found by applying a load to the engine output shaft by means of a dynamome-

Table 21.2   The use of exhaust-smoke colour in engine faultfinding (cont.)

Cure	Remarks
Fit only the engine maker's listed pipe; check ends for closing-in.	Pipe bores for vehicle engines are never less than 11/2 mm—a 3/64" or no. 56 drill should enter freely.
Reset timing (or rectify advance device if fitted).	Some engines, particularly indirect injection, show this symptom for less retard than gives rise to black smoke, but usually a gross retard is required to give blue smoke when running hot and under load.
Examine for sticking valve or broken spring, but suspect handling of injectors out of engine if tip is found broken.	Injector nozzle valve sticking or blocked spray holes can lead to this condition if not dealt with quickly.
Engine recondition indicated.	May be due to unsuitable lubricant; will be associated with high oil consumption.
Recondition cylinder head, and make certain that guide oil shields (if any) are in place.	May be aggravated with vacuum governors due to depression in inlet manifold when idling; oil consumption may not be moticeably affected.
Fill only to the mark or recommended level.	May cause an engine uncontrolled run away in severe cases.
Replace thermostat.	Low jacket temperatures also increase bore wear.

ter and measuring, throughout the engine speed range, the maximum torque (in Nm) the engine can sustain without loss of rpm. The brake power of the engine is found by calculation from the torque reading and the engine rpm at which the reading was taken.

Below is an example of calculating the kWbp (kilowatt brake power) of an engine when loaded by a dynamometer. The torque produced under load is 400 Nm at 1800 engine rpm. The calculation formula for the particular dynamometer is:

$$kWbp = \frac{rpm \times Nm}{9549}$$

Therefore,

$$kWbp = \frac{1800 \times 400}{9549}$$

$$= 75.4 \text{ kWbp}$$

The 9549 is an internal correction factor, or constant, for the particular dynamometer being used. It is specific to a particular dynamometer based on its performance under test and is supplied by the manufacturer with the machine.

Note: A dynamometer provides a means of applying a variable load to the engine and measuring its torque output and speed. Generally, it is only by using a dynamometer that the kWbp can be obtained.

Purpose of engine testing

There are many reasons for performing an engine test on a dynamometer, particularly after an engine overhaul. In particular, the tests enable the serviceperson to:

- make sure the engine will start and does not run out of control;
- check for oil and water leaks;
- check for correct oil and water temperature and pressure, both under load and without load;

- adjust the idle and maximum no-load speed of the engine;
- detect unusual noises;
- run the engine in, under varying loads;
- establish that the engine will produce its rated power and torque as per the manufacturer's specifications;
- check the operation of the turbocharger and record the manifold boost pressure;
- check for air cleaner inlet restriction;
- check for crankcase blowby;
- check air-box pressure on two-stroke engines;
- check exhaust back-pressure.

If before, during or after testing an engine, it is found that the engine does not perform correctly, some form of fault diagnosis will be necessary to locate the cause before it can be rectified. Guidance can be obtained from the engine manufacturer's manual, or from the faultfinding schedule listed in Table 21.1.

Engine-testing standards

To have any significance, the power and torque output of an engine must be in accordance with set of standard codes. The most common codes in use throughout the world are the:

- SAE Standard (Society Automotive Engineers);
- DIN Standard (Deutsche lndustrie Normen);
- ISO Standard (International Standards Organisation).

The above standards can be expressed either as gross kWbp or net kWbp.

Gross kWbp is the power developed by a bare engine. A bare engine is defined as an engine fitted only with the accessories essential for its operation, such as flywheel, oil pump and fuel pump.

Net kWbp is the power output of a fully equipped engine fitted with all accessories necessary to perform its intended function. It is the usable power from the engine after all accessories are installed — unlike gross power, which, in practical terms, is over-rated and can never be achieved from a fully equipped engine in service.

Intermittent power is the maximum power the engine is capable of producing at a stated speed. The engine should be capable of producing this power for a maximum period of up to one hour, after which it should be operated at a reduced power output.

Continuous power is less than intermittent power and is the amount of power an engine can produce continuously for a minimum of twelve hours.

Variations in power output

Engine power output may vary considerably under certain circumstances or conditions of operation. The effect can be quite considerable, and some engine manufacturers give a 5 per cent tolerance in power output rating to cover variations in engine operating conditions.

The major conditions affecting engine performance include variations in:

- ambient air temperature;
- barometric pressure;
- altitude;
- fuel temperature.

Variations in ambient air temperature

As the temperature of the air increases, the air becomes less dense, with a corresponding decrease in combustion efficiency and engine power output, due to the reduction in the amount of oxygen entering the engine cylinder. Conversely, as the temperature of the air decreases, the air increases in density, which improves combustion and increases engine power output.

Variations in barometric pressure

The increase in barometric air pressure has the effect of forcing more air into the cylinders, promoting greater combustion efficiency, with the capacity to burn more fuel, thus slightly increasing the power developed. The opposite effect is caused by a decrease in barometric pressure, producing a corresponding decrease in power.

Variations in altitude

All engines will operate successfully at sea level and to approximately 2500 m above without the fuel setting needing to be changed. Naturally aspirated engines operating above the 100 m level will experience a loss of power, because the reduced air density (and subsequent reduced air charge) will lead to less fuel being burned, resulting in a decrease in engine performance. Therefore, adjustments to the fuel system are required to prevent over fueling and excessive exhaust smoke. However, turbocharged engines automatically compensate for the decreasing air density as the turbocharger rotates faster, forcing more (less dense) air into the engine cylinders.

Variations in fuel temperature

As diesel fuel becomes heated, it becomes less dense and the mass of fuel injected decreases. This causes a corresponding decrease in the power output of the engine. On the other hand, as the fuel becomes cooler and its density increases, a greater mass of fuel is injected to give an increase in power output.

The density of the fuel is measured by its specific gravity (see Chapter 15). One engine manufacturer states that a power loss of 2 per cent per 1°C rise in fuel temperature above 32°C can be expected. Therefore, in a diesel engine, the operational temperature of the diesel fuel is proportional to its available heat energy and subsequent power output.

Dynamometers

A dynamometer is used to simulate engine operational loadings and, from this measure, the engine's torque reaction to the varying loads. Remember, a dynamometer does not measure the direct power output of an engine, but only provides a means of measuring the torque that an engine is capable of producing at the flywheel. After recording the torque output and the speed at which this output was measured, the kWbp of the engine can be calculated using a simple formula supplied with the dynamometer.

A number of different types of dynamometer are used to test engine performance:

1 the **engine dynamometer**, which attaches directly to the engine flywheel during testing, as shown in Fig 21.1;
2 the **chassis-type dynamometer**, which applies a braking load to the rear wheels of the vehicle, as shown in Fig 21.2;
3 the **power-take-off dynamometer** (PTO), which is connected to the PTO shaft of tractors for engine testing (Fig 21.3).

Engine dynamometers can be further classified according to the method by which the

Fig 21.1 Go Power DT 1000 engine dynamometer
Courtesy of Go Power Dynamometers

Fig 21.2   A heavy-duty chassis dynamometer   *Courtesy of Go Power Dynamometers*

load is applied to the engine under test. The load may be applied:

- hydraulically; or
- electrically.

Fig 21.3   A PTO dynamometer attached to the tractor power take off
Courtesy of Go Power Dynamometers

Hydraulic dynamometers

There are two types in common use: the water brake type and the gear pump type. Dynamometers operating on the water brake design have testing capacities as high as 2700 Nm or 600 kW. However, dynamometers of the gear pump type are designed for use with smaller engines, with a maximum output of approximately 50 Nm or 15 kW.

With the water brake dynamometer, illustrated in Fig 21.4, the braking action or loading is developed by an impeller (driven by the engine), which directs water against a turbine housing fitted to, or part of, the main dynamometer housing. This turns the dynamometer housing, within limits, in its mountings, so that the turning effort, or torque, of the engine can be measured.

The finned turbine housing is designed to divert the water back against the impeller, so opposing its rotation. It is this turbulence and back-flow that causes the braking action on the engine. Engine braking only occurs when water is fed into the dynamometer and the

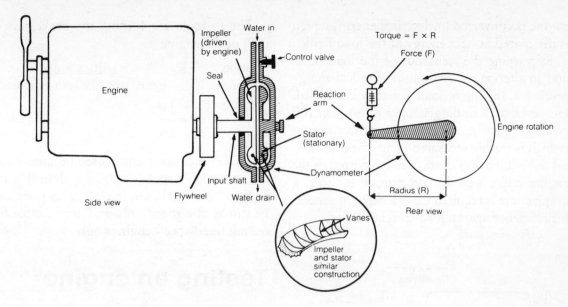

Fig 21.4   Schematic diagram of a water brake engine dynamometer

braking action on the engine can be increased by simply increasing the flow of water through the dynamometer.

The second method of providing hydraulic braking action is by means of a gear pump, suspended in mounting bearings to allow partial rotation, and directly driven from the engine crankshaft. Loading of the engine by progressively restricting the outflow of fluid from the pump causes the pump to turn in its mountings, so that the torque produced can be measured (see Fig 21.5).

Electrical dynamometers

There are several types of electrical dynamometer being used today to test engines. One such type is the direct-reading dynamometer, so named because the brake power of the engine is found directly from the generator's output.

With this type, the engine to be tested is close coupled to a generator, the output of which is connected to a resistance load bank as shown in Fig 21.6. The output of the

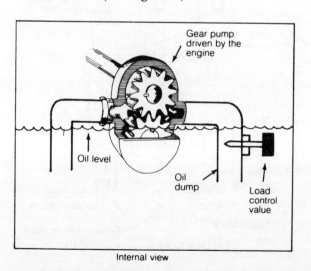

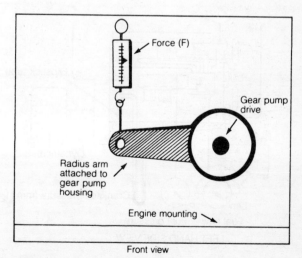

Fig 21.5   Principle of the gear-pump type dynamometer

engine is converted to electrical energy, which is dissipated as heat energy at the load bank.

By varying the resistance of the load bank and so altering the amount of electrical energy produced, the engine load is readily controlled. However, because the generator is less than 100 per cent efficient, the generator power output (which is readily measured by means of electrical test equipment) is less than the output of the engine under test. To compensate for this, a graph curve is required for determining generator efficiency against load current output.

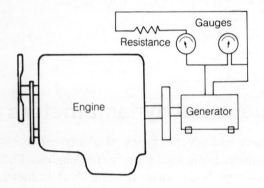

Fig 21.6   Schematic diagram of an electric engine dynamometer

The formula for finding the brake power (BP) of the engine is:

$$\frac{\text{brake}}{\text{power}} = \frac{\text{volts x amps}}{\text{generator per cent efficiency}}$$

$$BP = \frac{IV}{\eta g}$$

A DC generator is often used because it can run at variable speeds, which is desirable for engine testing. However, AC generators can be run at one speed only and are suitable for testing fixed-speed engines only.

Testing an engine

Engine testing is not simply testing an engine to determine its power and torque outputs, but rather a systematic approach to testing and problem-solving the whole operational condition of the engine.

In order to accurately check the performance of the engine, test instruments will need to be connected to the engine as shown in Fig 21.7 so as to monitor individual operational conditions such as:

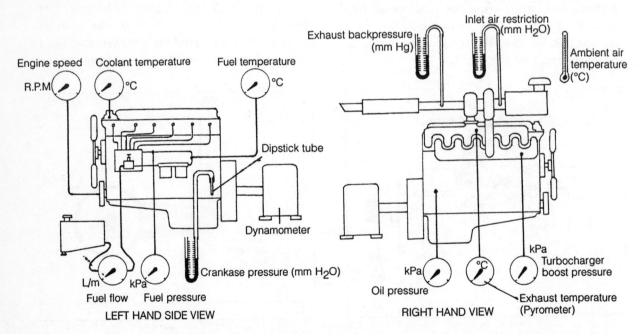

Fig 21.7   Schematic diagram showing where various test instruments can be connected to a turbocharged engine in order to monitor its operating condition

The height of a column of mercury is read differently than that of a column of water. Mercury does not wet the inside surface; therefore, the top of the column has a convex meniscus (shape). Water wets the surface and therefore has a concave meniscus. A mercury column is read by sighting horizontally between the top of the convex mercury surface and the scale

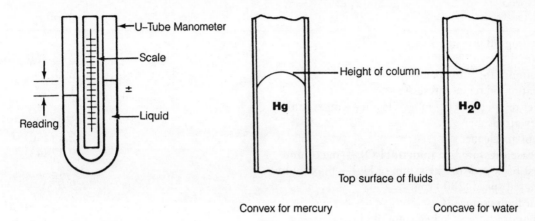

Fig 21.8   Reading a U-tube manometer   *Courtesy of Detroit Diesel Corp*

- fuel consumption;
- inlet manifold pressure;
- fuel pressure;
- fuel temperature;
- ambient air temperature;
- engine speed;
- crankcase pressure;
- exhaust back pressure;
- air inlet restriction;
- exhaust temperature;
- coolant temperature;
- oil pressure.

Fuel consumption

The fuel consumption of an engine is determined by measuring the flow of fuel to the engine with a flow meter while the engine is operating under various load and speed conditions. Fuel consumption can be rated in a number of ways. Two of the more commom methods are to use litres per minute (L/m) or grams per kilowatt hour (g/kW/hr).

Inlet manifold pressure

Inlet manifold pressure refers to the boost or charge air pressure in the inlet manifold on a turbocharged engine. Alternatively, on two stroke engines such as the Detroit Diesel, the air box pressure refers to the pressure of air surrounding the intake ports in the cylinders.

To measure inlet manifold pressure, connect a low-pressure gauge or a U-tube manometer to a test point on the inlet manifold. Air box pressure on Detroit Diesel engines is determined by measuring the pressure of the air coming out of the engine's air box drain. This can be achieved by connecting a manometer to the end of one of the two air box drains located on the lower side of the cylinder block.

U-tube manometer

The U-tube manometer is a measuring device used to indicate positive or negative pressure by the difference in the height of two columns of fluid (see Fig 21.8). Manometers can be filled with either mercury (Hg) or water (H_2O). The mercury manometer can be identified by its silver-coloured fluid, whereas the water manometer has a dye in the water to enable its high and low levels to be easily seen. The mercury manometer is used to measure higher level pressures, while the water

Table 21.3   Complete set of operating conditions for an engine undergoing performance testing

Engine operating conditions

Maximum no-load speed	3000 rpm
Rated speed	2800 rpm

	3000 rpm
Lubricating oil pressure kPa:	
Normal	240–350
Minimum for safe operation	200
Lubricating oil temperature °C	110–127
Air inlet restriction kPa (mm of H_2O) — maximum:	
Dirty air cleaner	5.0 (500)
Clean air cleaner	2.5 (250)
Crankcase pressure kPa (mm of H_2O) — maximum	0.42 (43)
Exhaust back pressure kPa (mm of Hg)— maximum:	
@ Rated speed (2800 rpm)	9 (63)
Inlet air temperature °C	36
Inlet manifold pressure kPa (mm of Hg):	
@ Maximum torque (1800 rpm)	121 (900)
Fuel pressure kPa	175–350
Coolant temperature °C	85–90
Exhaust temperature °C — maximum	590
Fuel consumption g/kW/hr:	
low limit	200
high limit	230
Fuel temperature °C	30

manometer is used to measure lower level and negative pressures.

As inlet manifold pressure on turbocharger engines is a higher level pressure, so a mercury filled manometer must be used in this case. In order to find the pressure recorded by the manometer, subtract the lowest fluid level reading from the highest reading. *Note*: When mercury is used in the manometer, read the top of the meniscus; when water is used, read the bottom of the meniscus, as shown in Fig 21.8.

Inlet manifold pressure is one of the simplest and quickest ways of determining engine performance on turbocharged engines and is indicative of the heat produced during the combustion cycle of the engine. That is, if the heat produced during combustion is at a high level, the turbocharger, which is driven by the expansion of hot gases, will rotate at sufficient speed to ensure

correct charge pressure in the intake manifold. Conversely, if the heat produced is lower than normal, the speed of the turbocharger turbine assembly will be slower, with a resultant lower intake manifold pressure. *Note*: Faulty turbocharger operation can also cause inlet manifold pressure to be low. Operating an engine at its maximum torque or stall speed will produce the highest possible charge air pressure in the intake manifold. Stall speed refers to the speed at which the engine will operate when the output shaft of a power shift transmission is stalled or prevented from turning due to the application of the vehicle brakes.

Fuel pressure

Fuel pressure in conventional in-line and rotary fuel systems refers to the pressure of the fuel flowing through the fuel filter and injector pump fuel gallery. It is generally of a low pressure, ranging between 50 and 350 kPa with the engine running at maximum speed. To measure fuel pressure, connect a suitable pressure gauge into a fuel filter housing or the injection pump fuel gallery. Low fuel pressure can generally be attributed to blocked fuel filters, worn fuel feed pump or restrictions in the fuel line.

Fuel temperature

This is the temperature of the fuel as it enters the fuel injection pump. Fuel temperature which is above the limits set by the manufacturer will result in reduced engine performance, as mentioned earlier in this chapter.

Ambient air temperature

This is the temperature of the air surrounding the engine before it goes into the air cleaner. It can be measured by a thermometer placed witin the engine test cell area adjacent to the air cleaner inlet.
Note: High ambient air temperature can result in reduced engine performance, as opposed to low ambient air temperature, which helps to improve engine performance.

Engine speed

This is a measurement of the revolutions per minute of the engine throughout the complete engine test. Engine speed can be measured in a number of ways, the most common being a mechanical tachometer attached to th camshaft or the use of a photo tachometer gauge which senses the rotational speed of the flywheel or front crankshaft pulley.

The maximum speed of the engine should always be set in accordance with the manufacturer's specifications.
Note: Increasing engine speed beyond the specified limits can have a detrimental effect

on the service life of the engine — and also void engine warranty.

Crankcase pressure

Crankcase pressure is the pressure of the gas within the engine crankcase during engine operation. The engine will normally have a slight amount of crankcase pressure due to a combination of piston movement within the cylinders and a small amount of blowby past the piston rings. However, as the rings and piston wear against the cylinder wall, the amount of gas leakage past them increases. This increased gas leakage, or blowby as it is commonly known, can cause the pressure in the crankcase to rise above acceptable limits, resulting in heavy engine fuming and/or engine oil being pumped out the engine dipstick or breather openings.

Crankcase pressure can be measured by removing the crankcase dipstick and fitting a tube from a manometer down the dipstick hole. To obtain accurate readings, the manometer tube must be sealed in the dipstick opening. The greatest amount of blowby will occur when the engine is operating under heavy load conditions.

As crankcase pressure is generally low, a water-filled manometer should be used in order to get an accurate pressure measurement.

Exhaust back pressure

Exhaust back pressure is the pressure created in the exhaust manifold due to the restriction to the flow of the exhaust gases as they flow through the muffler and exhaust pipe on their way out into the atmosphere.

Increased back pressure in the exhaust system can be caused by a partly blocked muffler, incorrect exhaust pipe size, too long an exhaust pipe, too many bends in the pipe or a restriction in the pipe.

To measure exhaust back pressure, use a mercury-filled manometer and connect the manometer to the exhaust pipe just as it leaves the exhaust manifold.

Air inlet restriction

All engines operate with some degree of air inlet restriction as air passes through the air cleaner. This negative pressure, or vacuum, which is created in the intake system is due to the restriction of the air flow as it passes through the small holes in the air cleaner element. A clean filter element will cause minimal restriction to intake air flow; however, as the air cleaner element becomes blocked with impurities, the air flow restriction becomes greater. Increased restriction to the air flow will decrease the volumetric efficiency and subsequent performance output of the engine. To check for air inlet restriction, connect a water-filled manometer into the intake pipe between the air cleaner and the engine.

Note: So as to obtain an accurate reading always connect to mamometer well away from any bends in the pipe

Exhaust temperature

This is the temperature of the exhaust gas as it leaves the cylinder head. Exhaust temperature can be used to determine the engine's ability to produce heat. The greater the amount of heat produced, the greater the thermal efficiency of the engine. The measurement of exhaust gas temperature from individual exhaust branches can be used to determine the operating efficiency of each individual cylinder assembly.

Exhaust temperature can be measured with a pyrometer mounted in the exhaust manifold where all the branch pipes come together, or by rubbing thermal crayons on the exhaust manifold. When the crayons are rubbed on the exhaust manifold, the colour of the crayon on the hot surface will change to another colour, which then can be cross-referenced to a particular heat range.

Coolant temperature

Measuring the coolant temperature will determine the operating temperature of the engine. Alternatively, some engine manufacturers prefer to monitor the temperature of the engine oil as a more accurate means of establishing engine operating conditions. Coolant temperature is generally taken at a point on the cylinder head, whereas oil temperature is taken at the main oil gallery on the side of the cylinder block. Correct engine operating temperature is important, as too low an engine temperature can result in increased piston slap as well as increased fuel consumption due to the low thermal efficiency of the engine. Too high an operating temperature can cause oxidation of the engine oil and scuffing of the cylinder liner and piston due to a breakdown of the lubricating oil film.

Table 21.3 shows a set of manufacturer's engine operating conditions which can be used as an aid for correct engine operation and fault finding. Any variation from the conditions listed may indicate an abnormal operating condition which must be corrected.

Note: Before attempting to make corrections to the engine, verify that the readings obtained represent true values and that the test instruments are accurate.

Running in an engine

After an engine has been rebuilt, and before it is put back into service, it must be 'run in' and tested for performance. To do this, the engine must be secured to a test bed and a suitable dynamometer attached to the engine flywheel. The engine should initially be run at low speed to check for oil, fuel and coolant leaks, as well as for oil pressure and coolant temperature, then run up to maximum speed to verify that the engine is in an operable condition for further testing.

With the engine set at half-speed position, open the dynamometer control valve to allow fluid flow into the dynamometer. This will cause the engine to lug down relative to the

ENGINE TEST REPORT

Date: _____   Unit number: _____

Repair Order Number: _____   Model Number: _____

Engine make: _____   Engine Size: _____

Rated F/L RPM: _____   Max. N/L RPM: _____

Idle RPM: _____   Max. Torque RPM:

A. PRESTART		
1. PRIME LUBE OIL SYSTEM	2. PRIME FUEL OIL SYSTEM	3. FILL COOLING SYSTEM

B. START UP AND IDLE FOR 30 SECONDS.

START _____ STOP _____ OIL PRESSURE _____ WATER TEMPERATURE _____

C. WARM UP—5 MINUTES   START _____ STOP _____

RPM MAX. SPEED	LOAD 50%	OIL PRESSURE	WATER TEMPERATURE
1. LUBE OIL LEAKS	2. FUEL OIL LEAKS	3. COOLANT LEAKS	4. LOOSE BOLTS

D. RUN IN—5 MINUTES   START _____ STOP _____

RPM MAX. SPEED	LOAD 75%	OIL PRESSURE	WATER TEMPERATURE

E. FINAL RUN IN—20 MINUTES   START _____ STOP _____

RPM MAX. SPEED	LOAD 100%	CRANKCASE PRESSURE AT F/L	EXHAUST BACK PRESSURE AT F/L
LUBE OIL PRESSURE AT F/L	LUBE OIL TEMPERATURE AT F/L	FUEL OIL TEMPERATURE AT F/L	FUEL OIL PRESSURE AT F/L
WATER TEMPERATURE AT F/L	TURBO BOOST PRESSURE AT F/L	LUBE OIL PRESSURE AT IDLE	IDLE RPM

REMARKS: _____

_____

OK _____ Reject _____ Dynamometer Operator _____ Date _____

Fig 21.9   Engine test report   *Courtesy of Detroit Deisel*

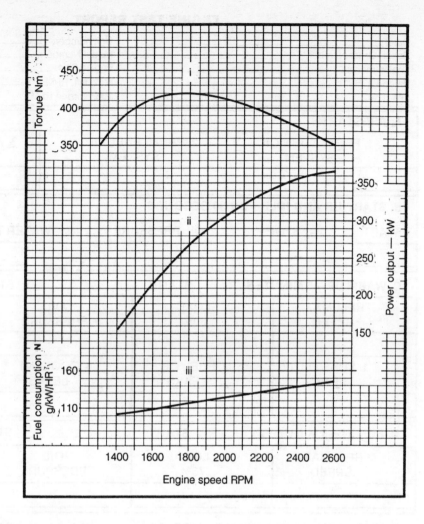

Fig 21.10   Dynamometer test results being used to plot a graph to show power, torque and fuel consumption curves for a diesel engine

i   Torque curve
ii   Power curve
iii   Fuel consumption

flow of fluid through the dynamometer unit. Lug the engine down until it is running at 50 per cent of its normal load. Maintain this speed and load condition for five minutes so as to allow the coolant temperature to reach the correct operating range. At the end of the test, record the time the test took, the engine speed, the torque output, coolant temperature and oil pressure on an engine test report sheet similar to the one shown in Fig 21.9.

Following the five-minute warmup period, increase the engine speed to maximum and the load on the engine to 75 per cent for another five-minute period. During this time,

engine performance will improve as new parts, namely the rings, 'bed-in'. Once again, record on the test report sheet the length of time the test lasted, the torque produced, the oil pressure and the coolant temperature. During the final part of the running-in period, the engine should be loaded to 100 per cent and run for 20 minutes or more, at which time all operating conditions should be monitored and checked against specifications as per the engine test report.

After the running-in period, the engine is ready for final performance testing to ensure that it has been rebuilt correctly and can produce its required power and torque output. With the throttle in the maximum position, increase the load on the engine with the dynamometer so that it will lug down to its rated or full load speed. Maintain this speed for a few minutes, during which time you record the engine speed and torque reading from the dynamometer torque gauge. The engine should develop its maximum rated power at this speed.

Continue to lug the engine down below its rated speed in increments of 100 rpm by increasing the fluid flow through the dynamometer. At each 100 rpm speed drop, record the torque produced by the engine until the engine has been lugged down to at least 200 rpm below maximum torque speed. Upon completion of the performance test, decrease the water flow through the dynamometer and reduce the engine speed gradually to idle then stop the engine. *Note:* Allow turbocharged engines to idle at least three minutes prior to shutdown so that the turbocharger can cool down and reduce speed.

With all the speed and torque readings recorded, use the appropriate formula relative to the dynamometer and calculate the engine power produced throughout the speed ranges.

An example of a formula for determining the power of the engine is as follows:

$$kW = \frac{Nm \times rpm}{9549}$$

Where:
kW = Kilowatts
Nm = Newton metres
rpm = revolutions per minute
9549 = dynamometer constant

Some dynamometers indicate direct brake kilowatt power readings. Therefore, the use of the above formula is not required when using this type of unit.

Note: Some manufacturers allow up to 5 per cent tolerance in engine power output to cover variations in engine operating conditions as compared with the conditions under which the engine was originally tested and certified. Such varying test conditions would be ambient air temperature, barometric pressure and altitude. Consequently, the specified engine power output may not be achievable due to unfavourable operating conditions beyond our control.

With all the torque and power readings recorded, a graph can be plotted showing torque, power and fuel consumption curves for the engine, as shown in Fig 21.10.

Fuel Supply Systems

Two systems are commonly employed to feed fuel from the fuel tank, through the fuel filters, and on to the injection pump of a diesel engine: the **gravity feed system** and the **pressure feed system**.

The gravity feed system can only be used when the fuel tank is mounted at a height above the fuel injection pump sufficient to provide a plentiful supply of fuel at all times. With modern fuel filters, using very fine filtering media, the tank must be well above the injection pump to ensure that an adequate fuel supply is maintained even when fuel flow through the filters is restricted by foreign matter that has been filtered from the fuel and chokes the filter element.

Almost all high-speed diesel engines utilise pressure feed systems, even though in stationary applications the fuel tank is mounted above the injection pump. The use of a pressure feed system, with its mechanical feed pump, ensures a constant fuel pressure and guarantees an adequate supply of fuel to the injection pump.

In addition to carrying fuel from the fuel tank through the filters to the injection pump and on to the injectors, the fuel system must include a means of carrying leak-off fuel (see Chapter 25) from the injectors, fuel (and air) from the self-bleeding filters and, in many cases, fuel from the injection pump cambox where it accumulates after leaking past the injection pump plungers.

One, two or three filters are commonly used between the fuel tank and the fuel injection pump. The fuel tank itself is usually treated to prevent rust, and mounted so that the bottom slopes away from the pick-up pipe towards a drain cock. The pick-up pipe is generally situated above the bottom of the tank, and is usually fitted with a gauze strainer.

The fuel system often used for large marine and stationary engines is worthy of note. The fuel is pumped up from storage tanks below the engine, through a fuel purifier, to the service tank — a fuel tank of sufficient capacity to carry enough fuel for approximately half a day's continuous running. From the service tank, the fuel is gravity fed, via the filters, to the injection pump.

Gravity feed fuel systems

The CAV gravity feed fuel system shown in Fig 22.1 features a hand primer pump, one fuel filter and a distributor-type fuel injection pump. In this system, the fuel tank must be located so that the bottom lies at least 300 mm above the injection pump.

The hand primer pump is fitted between the fuel tank and filter in order to facilitate

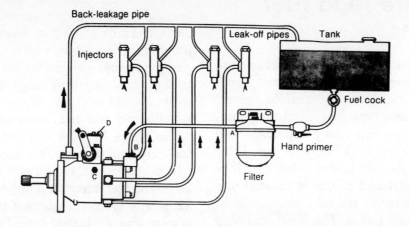

Fig 22.1   Schematic diagram of a CAV gravity fuel feed system for a DPA fuel injection pump
Courtesy of CAV

bleeding of the system; because of their design, CAV DPA fuel injection pumps require a pressure of about 20 kPa to force fuel through the pump during bleeding. When an in-line injection pump is used in conjunction with a gravity feed system, the primer pump is not necessary, because the pressure due to gravity is enough to bleed the system.

Because the system relies on gravity alone and has the fuel tank above the fuel filter, a self-bleeding type of filter cannot be used, since the fuel cannot flow from the filter back to the tank. However, any fuel that leaks past the pumping elements and injector components flows back to the fuel tank, since pressure soon builds up in the back leakage pipe.

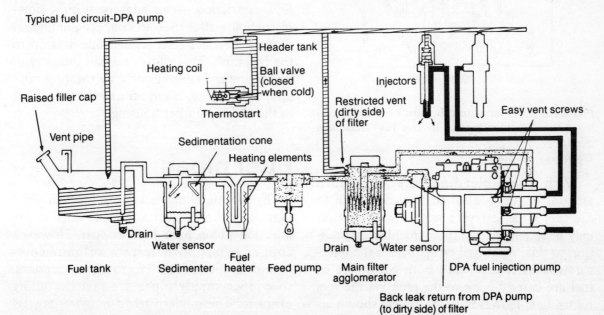

Fig 22.2   Schematic diagram of a CAV pressure feed fuel system for a DPA fuel injection pump
Courtesy of CAV

Pressure feed fuel systems

Fig 22.2 shows a pressure feed fuel system, featuring a sedimenter, fuel heater, self-bleeding filter, thermostart (or manifold heater) and a distributor-type fuel injection pump. The engine-driven fuel feed pump draws fuel from the tank through the sediment filter then through the fuel heater (when fitted, as in this example) and pumps it through the self-bleeding filter to the inlet connection of the fuel injection pump. The injection pump raises the pressure of the fuel, which is passed via the injection pipes to the injectors, which spray the fuel into the engine cylinders.

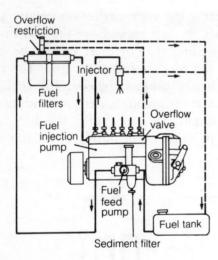

Fig 22.3 Schematic diagram of a pressure feed fuel system for an in-line fuel injection pump
Courtesy of Volvo

With a self-bleeding filter, a certain amount of fuel is allowed to escape back to the fuel tank, carrying with it any air that may have entered the filter chamber. In addition to this, some fuel escapes from the injectors (back-leakage) and both quantities of fuel are carried back to the tank via the fuel return line. However, in the system shown, as the fuel returns to the tank, some of it fills a header tank for the manifold heater. (Refer to Chapter 14 for manifold heater operation.) During injection pump operation, there is a certain amount of fuel leakage past the pumping components, which builds up in the pump housing. This excess fuel from the distributor-type injection pump is carried back to the second inlet on the fuel filter, where it is refiltered and circulated to the injection pump again. In some systems, however, this fuel may be returned to the fuel tank.

A pressure feed system of a type used with an in-line fuel injection pump is shown in Fig 22.3. The system features a two-stage filter system and a plunger-type fuel feed pump which is mounted on and driven by the fuel injection pump.

The fuel circuit follows a fairly conventional layout for an in-line injection pump, with continuous fuel circulation through an overflow valve located in the injection pump fuel gallery. The overflow valve determines fuel feed pressure and allows fuel which is excess to engine requirements to circulate back to the fuel tank to purge the gallery of any gas or air, and to cool the injection pump.

The main fuel filter is fitted with an overflow restriction — an adaptor with a flow-restricting orifice used to connect the highest part of the filter to a return pipe and on to the fuel tank. This allows a small quantity of fuel to return continuously to the fuel tank and, in so doing, bleed off any entrapped air in the main fuel filter housing.

Fuel pipes

In the past, in almost all cases, the fuel pipes that carry the fuel from the fuel tank to the injection pump have been copper. However, copper reacts with certain sulphur compounds in diesel fuel to form greasy deposits, so copper supply pipes are fast becoming obsolete. The modern trend is towards steel pipes and synthetic rubber flexible hoses, or flexible plastic fuel lines.

To ensure an adequate supply of fuel at the injection pump, supply lines of suitable size must be provided. An 8 mm bore supply line is generally adequate for use on a multicylinder engine with injection pump plungers that do not exceed 11 mm, while a 10 mm bore fuel line is necessary when the plunger diameters are between 12 and 15 mm. If the pump plunger diameters are between 15 and 17 mm, either 13 or 14 mm bore pipes are used.

Although all injector leak-off fuel passes through one pipe, the rate of leakage is very slight, and 4.5 mm bore tubing is adequate.

Note: When fuel feed pipes are being shaped, sharp bends should be avoided — the bending radius should never be less than 50 mm.

The injector lines — the pipes connecting the injection pump to the injectors — have to withstand fuel pressures that may reach 70 MPa. Because of the pressures involved, cold drawn, annealed, seamless steel tubing must be used.

Both the length and the bore diameter of the injector lines affect the injection characteristics, so the lines are kept to minimum length with the minimum bore diameter that will give efficient fuel delivery to the injectors at high speed. To ensure correct timing at each cylinder and uniform injection characteristics, all lines on multicylinder engines should be as near equal length as practicable since a change in the pipe length can alter the injection timing by up to 1° per 100 mm of pipe. The manufacturer's manual should be checked to ascertain the recommended bore diameter when making replacement injector lines, but in the absence of specific information the following chart should provide a satisfactory guide:

Pump plunger diameter (mm)	Injector line bore diameter (mm)
Up to 7.0	1.5 or 2.0
8.0 to 10.0	2.0 or 3.0
11.0 to 18.0	3.0

Three systems are used to provide a suitable end on injection lines to facilitate attachment to the injection pump and injectors. The oldest method consists of silver brazing conical sleeves or collars to the line, and tightening the collar against the face of the union with the nut.

The second, and most extensively used, system entails cold-forming a conical end or nipple on the end of the line by forcing special dies against the end of the line by hydraulic pressure. This is done in a nipple-forming tool, which utilises a small hydraulic ram completely enclosed in the tool. The nipple-forming tools are supplied with a set of collets to hold each size of pipe likely to be encountered — 6, 8 and 10 mm outside diameter — and a separate die or former for each size.

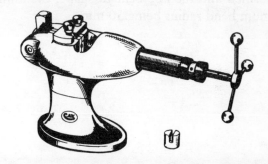

Fig 22.4 Hydraulic nipple-forming tool

Note: Some manufacturers of fuel injection equipment recommend that the fuel line be annealed after the nipple has been formed by heating to cherry red and cooling slowly.

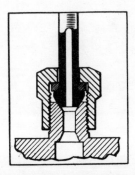

Fig 22.5 Typical pressure-formed nipple and pipe connection

The third system makes use of a compression-type sleeve, which is clamped on to the pipe when the union nut is tightened, forcing the sleeve into a taper that compresses it. This provides a readily replaceable fitting and is ideal for rapid, on-the-spot repairs.

While actual conditions may make this difficult to achieve, new injection lines should be thoroughly cleaned before being fitted to ensure that no dirt enters the injectors. Ideally, the pipe should be cut to length, the burrs removed, and the pipe then left for 24 hours in kerosene. After soaking, the pipe should be blown out with compressed air and pulled 20 to 30 times over a steel wire about 0.5 mm smaller in diameter than the inside of the pipe. The nipples may then be formed and the line bent to shape, the minimum bend radius being 50 mm.

Once the line has been shaped, it should be flushed for ten minutes with test oil or kerosene at a pressure of from 140 to 250 atmospheres. This can be accomplished best by fitting the line to an injector tester, and fitting an injector with a pintle nozzle (see Chapter 25) and an edge-type filter (see Chapter 24) to the other end. The injector should be set to open at the required pressure (i.e. 140–25 atmospheres). After flushing in this way, the line is ready for attachment to the engine. If not fitted immediately, the ends of the line should be covered with some suitable device (such as small plastic sleeves) to prevent the entry of foreign matter.

23

Fuel Supply Pumps

In all pressure feed systems, a fuel supply pump is required to pump the fuel from the fuel tank, carry it through the fuel system, including the filters, and supply it to the injection pump at constant pressure, and in sufficient quantity for the engine's requirements. Many types of fuel supply or feed pumps are in extensive use today, but most of them fall into one of the following categories:

- plunger-type feed pumps;
- diaphragm-type feed pumps.

The plunger-type feed pump

This type of pump is manufactured by a number of makers of fuel injection equip-

ment, including American Bosch, CAV, Zexel (formerly Diesel Kiki) and Nippon Denso. The pump is mounted on the fuel injection pump and is driven by the pump camshaft. It is self-regulating and will build up to, and maintain, a predetermined pressure.

Construction

The pump consists of:

- an alloy housing;
- a spring-loaded, roller-type cam follower, which reciprocates in the housing under the action of a cam;

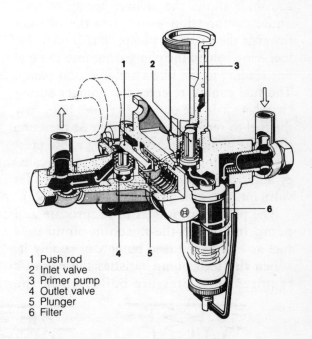

1 Push rod
2 Inlet valve
3 Primer pump
4 Outlet valve
5 Plunger
6 Filter

Fig 23.1 Plunger-type fuel feed pump
Courtesy of Robert Bosch GmbH

- a spring-loaded plunger, which is a neat fit in the bore of the housing and which is forced away from the injection pump by the cam follower;
- two spring-loaded fibre valves, which control the passage of fuel to and from the pump cylinder or plunger spring chamber.

Operation

When the injection pump camshaft is in such a position that the feed pump cam follower lies against the back of its cam lobe, the pump plunger is forced by the spring towards the camshaft, creating a low-pressure area in the plunger spring chamber. The fuel on the inlet side of the pump, being under atmospheric pressure, opens the inlet valve and fuel enters the chamber (see Fig 23.2a). Then, as the cam lobe drives the plunger against its spring, the fuel is forced by the plunger through the outlet valve and passes around to fill the chamber behind the plunger, which has been left vacant by its movement (see Fig 23.2b).

Further rotation of the injection pump camshaft allows the plunger spring — now under compression — to press the plunger towards the injection pump, thus forcing the fuel lying behind the plunger out into the fuel line leading to the filters and injection pump. The fuel cannot re-enter the plunger spring chamber since the outlet valve does not allow the fuel to return (see Fig 23.2c). At the same time, the plunger is again creating a low-pressure area in the spring chamber and this causes additional fuel to flow through the inlet valve into the spring chamber (see Fig 23.2a).

The plunger continues to reciprocate and pump fuel while the injection pump uses fuel as fast as the feed pump can supply it. When the feed pump satisfies the engine's requirements, pressure builds up in the supply line to the injection pump and under the plunger until it is high enough to prevent the plunger from returning with the follower. The supply pressure to the injection pump is controlled by the force exerted by the plunger spring.

As fuel is used, the plunger is forced towards the cam by the spring, causing an intake of fuel into the plunger spring chamber, and the operating cycle starts again. Thus the pump maintains an adequate supply of fuel at a constant pressure, the pressure being controlled by the spring force.

A hand-operated primer pump is usually fitted to this type of feed pump, so that bleeding of the fuel system can be carried out. This consists of a plunger and barrel assembly, which is screwed into the pump housing directly above the inlet valve.

When the plunger is lifted, a low-pressure area is created beneath it, causing the supply pump inlet valve to be forced from its seat, and allowing fuel to flow into the hand-priming pump barrel. When the priming pump plunger is pressed downwards, the fuel is forced into the supply pump spring chamber. This causes the outlet valve to open and the fuel to be forced into the supply line leading to the injection pump.

After use, the hand knob must be firmly screwed on to the top of the plunger barrel. This action seals the top of the plunger barrel to prevent fuel, which can pass the plunger during engine operation, from escaping.

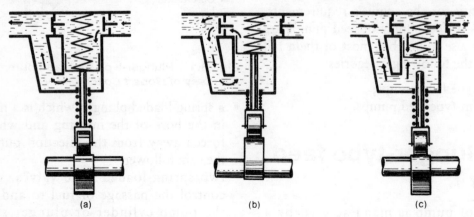

(a) (b) (c)

Fig 23.2 Plunger pump operation

Diaphragm-type feed pumps

There are many variants of the mechanically operated diaphragm-type feed pump, but they are all driven in one of two ways — either by an eccentric on the engine camshaft or by a special cam, or an eccentric on the injection pump camshaft.

The AC-type diaphragm feed pump

This type of pump is identical with the fuel pumps fitted on many petrol engines, and is driven in the same way by an eccentric on the engine camshaft.

Construction

This type of pump consists of an upper and a lower alloy body with a diaphragm (made of fabric impregnated with synthetic rubber) sandwiched between them. The upper body carries the inlet and outlet valves, usually spring-loaded fibre discs.

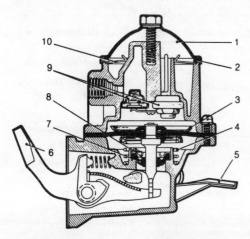

1	Domed cover	6	Rocker arm
2	Gasket	7	Seal
3	Diaphragm assembly	8	Seal retainer
4	Diaphragm return spring	9	Valve assemblies
5	Priming lever	10	Filter gauze

Fig 23.3   AC-type fuel feed pump

The centre of the diaphragm is clamped between dished circular plates attached to one end of a diaphragm pull rod. A diaphragm return spring is located between the lower circular plate and the lower diaphragm body. A two-piece lever, pivoted on a pin through the lower body, connects at one end to the diaphragm pull rod, while the other end bears against an eccentric on the engine camshaft.

A light spring maintains the lever in contact with the eccentric.

Operation

When the engine is turned over with the starter or is running, the eccentric causes the lever to rock on its pivot pin. This draws the pull rod and diaphragm down, compressing the diaphragm return spring and creating a low-pressure area above the diaphragm. The pressure difference — atmospheric at the fuel tank, less in the fuel chamber — causes the fuel to force open the inlet valve and flow into the fuel chamber (Fig 23.4a).

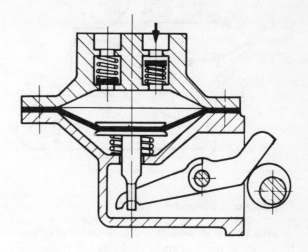

Fig 23.4a   Intake

When the lever rocks back, the spring forces the diaphragm upwards, forcing the fuel through the outlet valve (Fig 23.4b).

This cycle continues until the pressure builds up above the diaphragm on the outlet side — when more fuel is pumped than the engine can use — to the extent that the

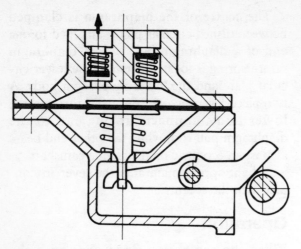

Fig 23.4b   Delivery

spring is not strong enough to force the diaphragm up. When this occurs, the diaphragm and one lever will remain stationary, while the other lever will continue to move due to its contact with the eccentric (Fig 23.4c).

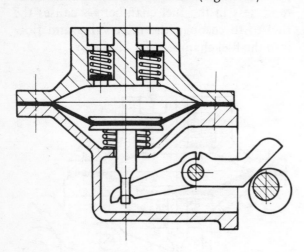

Fig 23.4c   'Freewheeling'

This two-lever action is due to both lever sections being pivoted independently on the same pin, the only connection occurring when a shoulder on the cam section strikes the corresponding shoulder on the other section. This only occurs when the diaphragm is able to move under spring action — when the engine requires fuel. When the diaphragm is held down by the fuel trapped above it, the second lever section is also held down and the shoulders do not meet, producing the necessary 'free linkage' action.

In practice, the diaphragm does not perform a full stroke nor does it remain stationary, but is continually moving in very short strokes to replenish the fuel supply as soon as even a minute quantity is used.

Faults in fuel feed pumps

In Table 23.1, we have attempted to indicate the cause of some of the more common faults that occur in fuel feed pumps. Correct fuel pressure is very important, for low fuel pressure will not allow the engine to develop full power at large throttle openings, since the pumping element (see Chapter 26) will not be fully charged. Fuel pressure is usually measured at a specified rate of flow — neither pressure nor pumping capacity alone indicates clearly the pump condition. However, the manufacturer's recommended procedure and specifications should always be followed when testing a feed pump.

Table 23.1   Some common faults in fuel feed pumps

Symptom	Cause
Low fuel pressure.	Weak diaphragm or plunger spring. Worn actuating link age or eccentric. Leaking fuel pump valves. Choked, fractured or loose inlet pipes. Fractured or torn diaphragm.
Fuel output low or nil.	Worn actuating linkage or eccentric. Fractured or torn diaphragm. Leaking valves. Choked, fractured or loose inlet pipes.
Fuel running from injection pump cambox overflow pipe.	Fractured or torn diaphragm.

24

Fuel Filters

Due to the high pressures and accurate metering necessary when injecting fuel, the pumping components of the injection system are extremely accurately made and finely finished. Research has shown that, while particles of foreign matter of all sizes cause wear to this equipment, most wear is caused by particles from 6 to 12 microns in size (1 micron = 0.001 mm).

Water, even in small quantities, causes corrosion of the highly polished surfaces and contributes to the ultimate failure of both injection pumps and injectors. Therefore, in order to obtain the longest possible working life from this expensive equipment, efficient fuel filters are indispensable.

The best fuel filtering system is generally considered to be a progressive one, the first or primary filter removing the large particles of foreign matter, the second or secondary filter removing the finer particles. A third or final stage filter is sometimes fitted in a progressive system, the secondary filter being responsible for the removal of the intermediate particles.

However, there are many systems used widely throughout the world in which two identical elements in series are used, the second providing a safety element should the first become damaged.

Fuel filters range from simple sediment bowls, capable of removing water and heavy particles only, to replaceable element filters capable of removing particles down to 2–4 microns.

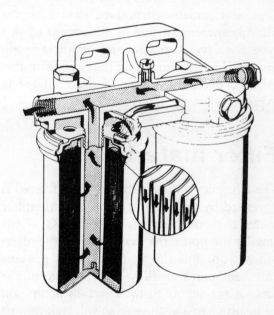

Fig 24.1 Dual filter paper element type
Courtesy of Robert Bosch GmbH

A sediment bowl is simply a bowl or chamber in the fuel system, and has no filtering element. However, because of its relatively large volume, the fuel passes very slowly through it and heavy particles of foreign matter and water settle to the bottom of the sediment bowl, from where they are periodically drained. Many sediment bowls are made of glass, so that accumulations of foreign matter can be easily seen by the operator, who can then drain or clean the bowl.

Element-type filters are made in a wide variety of types and designs. The self-bleeding filters referred to in the previous chapter are element filters, with a small restricting orifice or spring-loaded pressure relief ball valve in the top of the housing. A pipe leading from this hole carries a small quantity of fuel continuously back to the tank. Any air entering the fuel filter assembly in the fuel rises to the top and passes back to the fuel tank as a bubble in the return line.

Modern filter elements are generally made to one of two designs. The first design consists of a replaceable cartridge or element fitted inside a filter bowl. The second — and fast becoming the most popular — type consists of a canister of pressed steel with the filtering material inside. Replacement of this type consists of unscrewing or unclamping the old element and fitting the new. With this latter type, the outside of the canister is exposed when the element is in service.

Filter materials

The efficiency with which the fuel is filtered is governed by the size of the pores in the filter material through which it must pass — the smaller the pores, the more efficient the filtering action. But the material must present sufficient pores to allow free passage of the fuel, or the supply to the injection pump will be insufficient and the engine will lack power; this problem will worsen with use, since the filter will become more and more restricted.

The ideal filtering material must therefore efficiently filter the fuel, but must also have sufficient area to allow free and adequate fuel flow for a reasonable period — a filter that requires renewal after only a short period of running is not satisfactory.

During the development of fuel injection equipment to its present level of efficiency, many different filtering materials have been tried.

Fuel filter elements made from resin-impregnated paper are by far the most common and are generally considered to be the most efficient. The paper filtering material is invariably folded or pleated to present a very large surface area to the fuel, thus giving maximum life between changes.

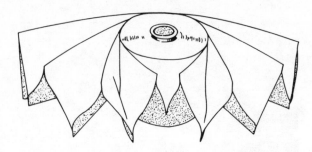

Fig 24.2   V-form resin-impregnated fuel filter paper

Fuel filter service

The need for absolute cleanliness when servicing fuel filters cannot be stressed too greatly.

Where filter bowls and sediment bowls are fitted with a drain plug, this should be removed periodically to allow accumulated sediment and water to drain away.

Before changing a filter element or servicing a filter, it is good practice to thoroughly wash the filter bowl and surrounding engine area with petrol to remove impurities that could fall into the filter components. The filter unit may then be dismantled and the element removed. If the element is a type that can be washed, this must be done in the recommended solvent in a clean container. If the element is to be discarded, ensure that there are no sealing plates adhering to it.

Any parts removed from the filter unit to allow the element to be removed should be washed in clean solvent but should not be wiped with rag. All rubber o-rings and seals should be renewed. The new element may then be fitted and the unit reassembled.

After servicing the filter, the air bleed screw should be opened and any trapped air bled from the system.

Fuel filter types

Although there are a large number of manufacturers of fuel filtration systems, the majority follow a limited number of basic designs. For this reason, coverage will be restricted to the typical filters manufactured by Robert Bosch and CAV.

Bosch fuel filters

Robert Bosch manufacture a range of fuel filters, the most common of which is a box-type spin-on paper element filter.

The type of filter element used by Bosch is of the 'V'-form spiral design, as shown in Fig 24.3. In this type of element, the filter paper is wound around a tube and adjacent layers are glued together, alternately at the top and the bottom. This forms pockets with their openings at the top.

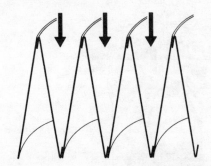

Fig 24.3   Sectioned and expanded 'V'-form spiral element

The fuel flows through the 'V'-form spiral element axially from the top to the bottom; the dirt particles that are held back accumulate in the filter pockets. The filtered fuel then flows upwards through the tube in the middle of the filter.

Bosch paper filter elements perform with a high degree of efficiency in separating water from the fuel. In addition to a certain amount of molecularly bound water, diesel fuel often contains free water. This free water may enter the fuel through carelessness when the tank is being filled, by unsuitable storage in drums or through condensation in the fuel tank.

The molecularly bound water does not cause any adverse effects during operation. However, it is absolutely essential to separate the free water from the fuel for trouble-free operation of the injection system; this is particularly true for distributor-type injection pumps.

The filter paper used by Bosch not only has an exceptionally high filtering efficiency, but it is also a good water separator due to a special impregnation technique, in which a surface-active precipitation agent is deposited on the paper. This chemical treatment enables the water to be retained on the filter paper, but allows the diesel fuel to flow through.

In a spiral element, the diesel fuel passes through the filter while the water accumulates on the dirty side of the paper pockets. Therefore the filter surface area available for the passage of fuel is reduced, and the pressure differential across the element increases and finally forces the water through to the clean side. Here it forms larger drops that collect in the lower part of the filter. The spiral filter ceases to function when the water level in the bowl rises above the lower edge of the element.

Bosch fuel filter box

The filter box consists of a metal housing in which a 'V'-form spiral paper element is fitted. At the top of the housing there is a leakproof cover with its edges rolled over. This cover is provided with an M16 x 1.5 mm threaded hole in the centre, four outlet holes and a gasket. The threaded hole is used for attachment to the filter head and as the fuel outlet.

The unfiltered fuel enters through the head, flows through the four holes into the

Fig 24.4   Fuel filter box

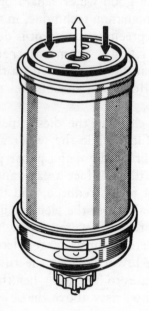

Fig 24.5   Filter box with transparent water trap
Courtesy of Robert Bosch GmbH

filter box, through the filter element and finally exits through the inner tube and the threaded hole.

When the unit no longer allows the passage of sufficient fuel, the filter box must be unscrewed and replaced by a new one. The new filter box should be screwed on by hand until the gasket makes contact with the filter head. It is then tightened a quarter turn. The fuel system should then be bled to remove any air.

Two forms of water trap are used with box-type fuel filters: transparent and non-transparent. In the first case there is an end cover on the bottom of the filter box, which serves for screwing the glass bowl on to the filter with a bolt. In both cases, there is a drain screw with a drain hole in the middle so that the water can be drained out without dirtying the hands. The water level should be checked daily and excess water drained off by turning the drain screw to the left. Replacement of a filter box with a water trap and bleeding of the system is done in the same basic manner as with plain box-type filters.

The Bosch water separator

If the water or dirt content of the diesel fuel is particularly high, it is recommended that a water separator be fitted to increase the service life of the fuel filter. It will not only retain the larger water drops in the fuel, but also the larger rust, metal and dirt particles.

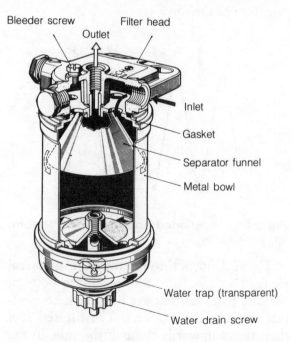

Fig 24.6   Water separator (sectional view) with a filter head for horizontal mounting
Courtesy of Robert Bosch GmbH

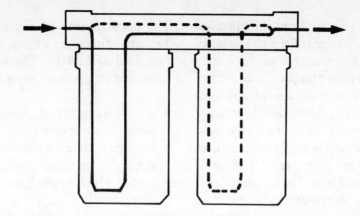

Fig 24.7   Flow principle for fuel filters connected in parallel   *Courtesy of Robert Bosch GmbH*

At low ambient temperatures, the water separator can also hold back paraffinic precipitation without causing the filter to clog.

The water separator is similar in appearance to a box filter with a transparent water trap, but the construction is somewhat different. Instead of the filter element, there is a separator funnel.

The fuel, containing droplets of water, flows over the separator funnel and is accelerated between the edge of the inverted funnel and the wall of the bowl. Because of the higher density, the water droplets absorb more energy and continue in the direction of movement for a longer time. In a relatively large bowl, the fuel slows down and the water droplets sink to the bottom. Inlet and outlet are kept far apart by the separator funnel. Because the flow speed is low, water droplets in suspension are not entrained. The fuel flows out through the funnel hole and the threaded connection.

The water level can be checked through the transparent water bowl, and the water drained, when required, by the drain screw. To obtain good water separation, the water separator must be installed upstream of the fuel feed pump because fuel and water would be homogeneously mixed by the pump due to the pulsating action.

Box filter types

Bosch filter boxes without water traps are available in sizes of 0.4 litres and 0.6 litres;

those with water traps are available in the 0.6 litre size only. They are screwed to the filter head, and the assembly is called a box filter. The threads for fuel inlet and outlet connections are in the filter head and the installation holes are in the mounting flange. Filter heads are supplied for vertical or horizontal mounting.

The range of box filters includes single-box filters (as previously discussed), parallel box filters and two-stage box filters.

The required fuel flow rate determines the size of the filter and the filter configuration. Where there is a large fuel flow requirement, one filter would be insufficient, either because of inadequate flow capacity or limited service life, so a set of filters in parallel are used (Fig 24.7).

It is interesting to note that two filters in parallel will more than double the service interval of a single unit; apart from halving the quantity of fuel to be filtered, each element can become more restricted by contaminants, while together they can continue to pass sufficient fuel for the engine.

With a two-stage filter configuration, the fuel flows first through a primary (coarse) filter, which removes the larger particles, and then through a secondary finer filter and on to the fuel injection pump as shown in Fig 24.8.

Various possibilities in selecting a filter also present themselves in regard to quality. The aim in the development of fuel filters is to obtain, besides a sufficient filter life, the longest possible service life from the injection equipment. Bosch has matched the quality of its filters to the requirements of the widely known Bosch injection pumps. Thus a filter paper with an average pore size of approximately 9 microns has been developed for standard requirements. It is generally used with in-line injection pumps. A micro filter paper with an average pore size of 4 microns is available for more exacting requirements — for example, for distributor-type injection pumps.

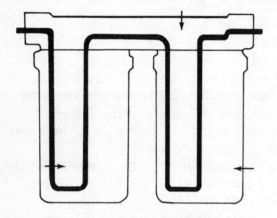

Fig 24.8 Two-stage series filter
Courtesy of Robert Bosch GmbH

CAV fuel filters

CAV Ltd manufacture a large range of fuel filters that feature 'V'-form impregnated paper elements. These may be configured in one of several ways — as single units, as a parallel assembly, or as a series arrangement, depending on the requirements of the engine manufacturer, the rate of fuel flow needed and the desired service life.

FS filter

The FS filter is of the crossflow type. The element is contained within a strengthened steel canister, which forms an integral part of the filter assembly.

With this type of filter, the fuel may be passed through in either of two directions.

The construction of the filter and the two available directions of fuel flow are shown in Figs 24.9 and 24.10. The unit consists of the following component parts (refer to Fig 24.9):

- a cast aluminium head with inlet and outlet connections and a mounting flange;
- a paper filter element enclosed in a strengthened metal canister; and
- a cast aluminium base, together with a centre stud.

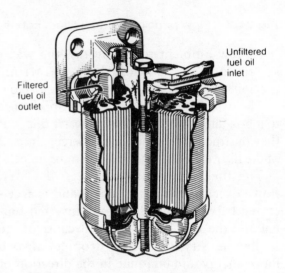

Fig 24.9 FS bowl-less filter, showing filter-flow element
Courtesy of CAV

The three units are held together by the centre bolt, which passes through the head casting and screws into the centre stud.

Synthetic rubber sealing rings located at the top and bottom of the filter element canister prevent external fuel leakage. The clean outgoing filtered fuel is sealed off from the incoming unfiltered fuel by a synthetic o-ring held in a groove on the filter head centre boss.

The filter head is supplied with galleries drilled to provide for either filter flow or agglomerator flow. Filter flow is illustrated in Fig 24.9, which shows the incoming unfiltered fuel passing through the centre bolt housing and into the base. It then passes upwards through the filter element and out through the filtered fuel outlet port.

Agglomerator flow takes advantage of the fact that when fuel containing fine water droplets is passed through a porous medium such as the filter element, the water droplets will join together (or agglomerate) into larger droplets, which may then be removed from the fuel by sedimentation. Fig 24.10 shows the FS filter arranged for agglomerator flow. Incoming fuel entering through the inlet passes downwards through the filter element into the base, and then upwards through the centre tube and out via the filtered fuel outlet. Abrasive particles are retained by the filter element and the water particles are deposited in the base to be drained off at convenient intervals. Certain models of this filter have a nylon drain plug incorporated in the base for this purpose.

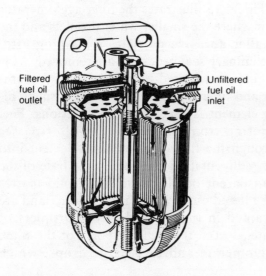

Fig 24.10 FS bowl-less filter showing agglomerator-flow element
Courtesy of CAV

The standard filter head for an FS-type filter has two inlet and two outlet connections to provide alternative piping connections for different types of engine installation. It is suitable for both distributor and in-line fuel injection pumps, but when used with a distributor pump the fuel return from the pump will be to the unfiltered side of the filter. Closing plugs are fitted to the connection ports not used for pump connections.

2FS twin bowl-less filter

This filter is a twin version of the FS-type filter and has a common head casting and mounting flange, with two separate elements. It provides alternative arrangements for fuel flow:

- series flow, for engines working in exceptionally dirty conditions;
- parallel flow, for engines requiring double the fuel flow rate of that provided by the single FS filter.

The Filtrap system

The Filtrap system of fuel filtration is designed to give the best possible protection against abrasive matter and water carried in the fuel. The system consists of two parts: a simple sedimenter and a filter-agglomerator.

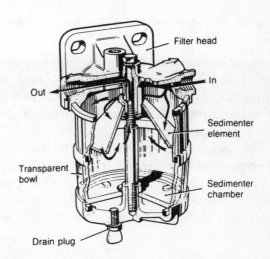

Fig 24.11 Simple sedimenter — Filtrap system
Courtesy of CAV

A cutaway view of the simple sedimenter is shown in Fig 24.11. Incoming fuel is fed into the unit above the sedimenter element and passes through a clearance between the sedimenter cone and the sedimenter wall. Sedimentation takes place in the lower transparent bowl, and the fuel, relieved of the large droplets of water and the larger particles of abrasive matter, passes out of the

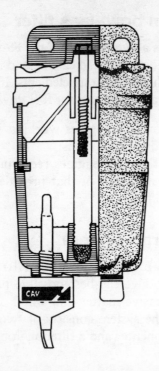

Fig 24.12 Waterscan sedimenter fuel filter
Courtesy of CAV

unit via ports in the central portion and galleries in the head. Accumulated water and solid matter are visible in the transparent bowl and may be drained off through the drain plug provided in the base.

This same sedimenter is also available with a water-level detector. Known as a waterscan sedimenter, it operates in exactly the same way as a simple sedimenter, but has the addition of a water-level detector at the base of the filter housing. This detector senses the water level, and at a certain point activates a warning light in the instrument panel.

Another type of sedimenter, the waterstop pre-filter (Fig 24.14), operates on the normal sediment filter principles, but has, in addition, a piston and needle valve which float on the water in the bottom of the bowl. When the water level in the bowl of the filter rises, the piston and needle valve also rise and block off the exit of fuel from the filter to the injection pump at a predetermined point, so stopping the engine. On draining the water from the filter, the piston and needle valve drop, opening the passage and allowing fuel to flow again. No bleeding of the fuel system is required after draining water from the waterstop filter.

Fig 24.15 illustrates the filter-agglomerator unit where the smaller water droplets and the smaller abrasive particles remaining after preliminary sedimentation are removed.

Since the desired properties of agglomerator and filter elements are similar, a single filter element is used for both functions. Fuel entering from the top of the filter passes through the filter-agglomerator element into the sedimentation chamber in the base of the transparent bowl. Particles of solid matter are filtered out in the normal manner and are retained in the filter element. Droplets of water, forced through the pores of the filter, agglomerate and form large drops, which

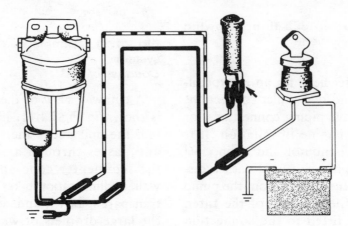

Fig 24.13 Waterscan system wiring diagram   *Courtesy of CAV*

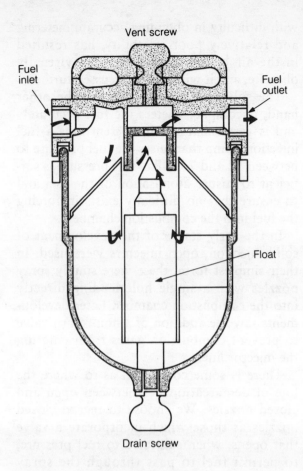

Fig 24.14 Water fuel filter
Courtesy of CAV

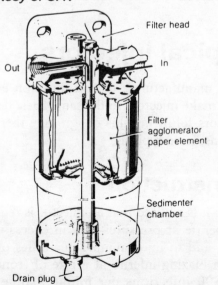

Fig 24.15 Filter-agglomerator sedimenter, type FAS
Courtesy of CAV

separate from the fuel by sedimentation and accumulate in the base of the housing. The fuel, free from solid matter and water droplets, then passes upwards through the element centre tube to the outlet connection in the unit cover. The accumulated water, visible within the transparent bowl, may be drained off by unscrewing the drain plug provided.

Injector filters

Some injector manufacturers incorporate a filter in the injector inlet connection. In some cases, this filter takes the form of a very fine brass gauze held between the injector inlet adaptor and the housing. Alternatively, an **edge-type** filter may be used.

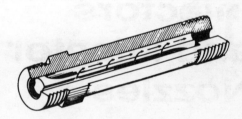

Fig 24.16 Edge-type filter

The edge-type filter consists of a hardened steel rod fitted inside a rather long inlet adaptor. Four grooves are ground along the rod, two from each end, but these do not run the full length of the rod and do not connect. Fuel can run along the two grooves from the inlet end, but to get to the other grooves and on to the injector it must pass around the outside of the rod. The clearance between the edge and the inlet adaptor is very small, so that no particles of dirt can pass.

Filters of this type are, of course, serviced during injector maintenance. The edges should be inspected for any damage that could allow dirt particles to pass.

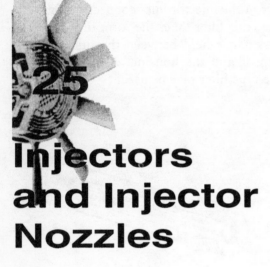

25
Injectors and Injector Nozzles

Over the years, two systems of injecting fuel into the combustion chamber have emerged: the air blast fuel injection system and the solid fuel injection system.

The air blast system, the first to be developed, was used on Dr Diesel's first operative engine and was developed and used on marine and large stationary engines until the 1930s, when it fell into disfavour. This system relied on compressed air to blast the fuel into the combustion chamber. When the pressure existing in the cylinder before and during combustion is considered, it becomes obvious that a very efficient compressor is required. Furthermore, not only a compressor but also an air receiver or reservoir is necessary, making it a relatively bulky system. This, coupled

with difficulty in obtaining accurate metering and relatively poor reliability, has resulted in the air blast system becoming virtually obsolete, and it will not be discussed further.

The solid injection system, on the other hand, is compact, meters the fuel accurately and is very reliable. The system uses a fuel injection pump that raises the fuel pressure to between 12 and 70 MPa. This pressure is sufficient to ensure atomisation of the fuel and to ensure that no difficulty exists in forcing the fuel into the combustion chambers.

In the early stages of the development of solid injection, open injectors were used. In their simplest form, these were simply spray nozzles with a single hole leading directly into the combustion chamber. Later developments saw the addition of a non-return valve to prevent combustion gases from entering the injector line.

There is some contention as to where the line of demarcation lies between open and closed nozzles. We choose to regard closed nozzles as those which incorporate a valve that opens, when subjected to fuel pressure, to permit fuel to pass through the spray holes; those that do not include such a valve are considered to be open nozzles.

Typical injectors

Most manufacturers of fuel injection equipment make injectors to the same basic design; injectors following this design may therefore be considered typical.

Construction

When it is realised that an injector is required to operate at pressures well in excess of 20 MPa, and to inject minute quantities of fuel into a blazing inferno at a rate of from 150 to 1500 injections per minute, some idea must be gained of the quality of materials and manufacture going into the ordinary fuel injector. With the exception of copper sealing washers, all parts are manufactured from heat-treated alloy steel.

A basic fuel injector consists of seven essential parts:

1 A nozzle assembly consisting of two parts, a nozzle body and a needle valve or nozzle valve. The two components are lapped together to form an assembly, the needle valve being free to slide, but with minimum clearance, in the bore of the nozzle body. The upper surface of the nozzle body is accurately ground and lapped to form a precision sealing surface where it contacts the body of the injector.

One or more drillings in the nozzle body lead from the upper lapped surface, which may carry an annular groove, to a pressure chamber (or fuel gallery) above the needle valve seat. The needle valve is stepped or shouldered where it passes through the pressure chamber.

At the lower end of the nozzle body, below the needle valve seat, lies the passage (or passages) through which the fuel passes to the engine combustion chamber.

2 A steel nozzle holder, complete with mounting flanges for securing the unit in the cylinder head, and with drilled passages for conducting fuel from the inlet connection to the nozzle. The lower end of the holder is provided with an accurately ground and lapped surface, which makes a leak-proof seal with the corresponding lapped surface on the upper end of the nozzle body. A leak-off connection is also provided in the nozzle holder in some cases.
3 A steel nozzle nut or nozzle cap nut, which screws on to the lower end of the nozzle holder, securing the nozzle assembly in place.
4 A heavy-duty compression spring, which holds the needle valve on its seat.
5 A steel spindle located inside the nozzle holder between the spring and the needle valve, transmitting the spring force to the needle valve.
6 A spring adjusting mechanism, which is needed for the spring force to be varied. This usually takes the form of a screw and lock nut.

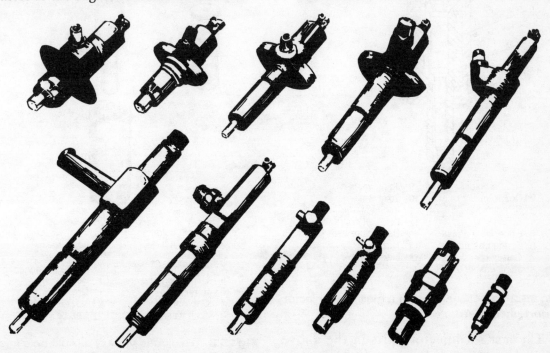

Fig 25.1   A range of typical injectors   *Courtesy of CAV*

7 A cap nut, which is screwed on to the top of the nozzle holder to keep out dirt, etc. This nut may be drilled and tapped to accommodate a leak-off connection.

collectively as the **injector body assembly**, while the first one, the **nozzle assembly**, is usually termed the injector nozzle.

Operation

When the metered quantity of fuel enters the nozzle holder through the inlet connection, it passes through the drilled passage(s) to the pressure chamber above the needle valve seat.

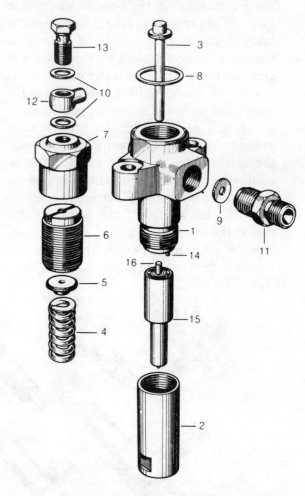

1	Nozzle holder	9	Joint washer
2	Nozzle nut	10	Joint washer
3	Spindle	11	Inlet adaptor
4	Spring	12	Leak-off connection
5	Upper spring plate	13	Banjo screw
6	Spring cap nut	14	Nozzle
7	Cap nut	15	Needle valve
8	Joint washer		

Fig 25.2 Sectional view of a multi-hole injector
Courtesy of CAV

The last six injector parts in the above list, when assembled, are often referred to

1	Nozzle holder	9	Joint washer
2	Nozzle nut	10	Joint washer
3	Spindle	11	Inlet adaptor
4	Spring	12	Leak-off connection
5	Upper spring plate	13	Banjo screw
6	Spring cap nut	14	Dowel
7	Cap nut	15	Nozzle
8	Joint washer	16	Needle valve

Fig 25.3 Exploded view of a multi-hole injector
Courtesy of CAV

In some cases, the injector nozzle body drillings may not align with the nozzle holder drilling but, where this can occur, the nozzle body has an annular groove machined in the lapped surface to which the nozzle drillings join. Thus fuel can flow from the holder, around the top of the nozzle and down the nozzle drillings. When the pressure of the fuel in the pressure chamber applies sufficient force to the needle valve shoulder to overcome the spring force, it lifts the valve from its seat, allowing fuel to flow from the nozzle until delivery from the pump ceases, at which point a positive instantaneous cut-off of fuel occurs because the valve is snapped to its seat by the spring force, eliminating the possibility of after-dripping or dribbling.

A certain amount of seepage of fuel between the lapped guide surfaces of the needle valve and nozzle body is necessary for lubrication. This leakage of fuel accumulates around the spindle and in the spring compartment, and the excess is carried away through the leak-off connection provided for that purpose.

Injector nozzles

Injector nozzles may be divided into two major classes: hole-type nozzles and pintle-type nozzles.

Each nozzle, regardless of the class into which it falls, is designed for a particular application, and will not function satisfactorily in any other. It cannot be too highly stressed that the correct nozzle must be used, and that any nozzle that fits will not do.

Hole-type nozzles

Hole-type nozzles give a fairly hard spray, open at a high pressure (from 150–200 atmospheres) and take one of four forms: single hole, conical-end single-hole, multi-hole and long-stem multi-hole.

The most common form of single-hole nozzle has one spray hole drilled axially, the hole diameter ranging upwards from 0.2 mm. A variation, known as a conical-end nozzle, features a spray hole drilled at an angle to the nozzle axis. This latter type must be located in relation to the injector body by dowels in the nozzle holder lower face, so that the fuel sprays in the required direction.

Multi-hole nozzles are widely used and are fitted in direct injection engines. These nozzles utilise a number of spray holes, two or four being the most common. The holes are drilled in such a way as to give the best possible distribution of fuel, and may consist of one axial hole with a number of holes, at an angle to the nozzle axis, surrounding it.

In many applications, the injector is not located vertically above the piston cavity, but lies at an angle to the cylinder axis. The holes on one side of the nozzle must be drilled at a different angle from those on the other side to ensure that the spray does not strike the piston crown on one side and the cylinder head on the other. In applications of this type, the nozzle is again dowelled to the nozzle holder.

In many direct-injection engines, long-stem nozzles are used. As can be seen from Fig 25.6, the extra length of the long-stem nozzle lies in the greater distance between the fuel gallery and the nozzle tip. The extended small-diameter section of the nozzle makes it suitable for use in direct injection engines, where the space between the valves is limited, and the machining necessary for fitting the thicker, standard type may weaken the head to the extent that it will crack in service. In certain applications there is a tendency for the needle in standard nozzles to seize due to distortion caused by the heat of combustion. This problem is eliminated when long-stem nozzles are employed, since the close-fitting guide section lies a relatively great distance from the combustion chamber, there being considerable clearance between the needle (below the gallery) and the nozzle body.

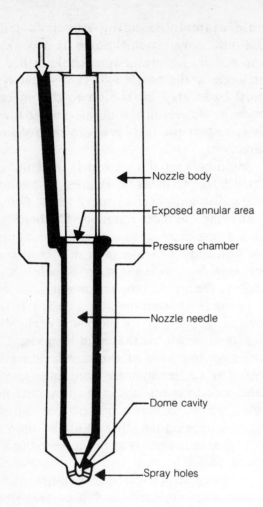

Fig 25.4 A typical multi-hole injector nozzle
Courtesy of Robert Bosch GmbH

- Nozzle body
- Exposed annular area
- Pressure chamber
- Nozzle needle
- Dome cavity
- Spray holes

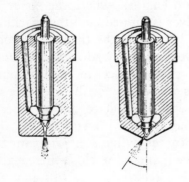

Fig 25.5 Single-hole nozzle (left) and conical end single-hole nozzle
Courtesy of CAV

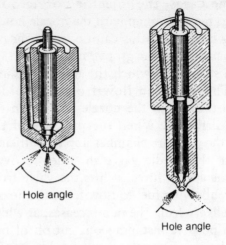

Hole angle

Hole angle

Fig 25.6 Short-term multi-hole nozzle (left) and long-stem multi-hole nozzle
Courtesy of CAV

Pintle nozzles

Pintle nozzles have a pin that protrudes through a single spray hole and are, to a large extent, self-cleaning. They are not as inclined to become blocked with carbon deposits as hole-type nozzles. The diameter of the pin or pintle is slightly less than the diameter of the hole through which it passes, and the fuel is sprayed from between the pintle and the nozzle body. Because the pintle lies in the centre of the fuel spray, the characteristics of the fuel spray are controlled by the shape of this pintle. Pintle nozzles generally give a soft spray, open at low pressure — usually between 85 and 145 atmospheres — and are suitable for use in indirect injection engines.

Plain pintle nozzles are the standard version. The shape of the pintle controls the spray form, and various nozzles are available to provide sprays from a hollow, parallel-sided pencil form to a hollow cone with an angle of 60° or more.

To reduce diesel knock in certain precombustion chamber engines, a special type of pintle nozzle was developed. This delay (or throttling) nozzle allows only a limited quantity of fuel to be injected at first by providing only a narrow gap between the pintle and the nozzle body. As injection continues, the nozzle opens fully, allowing a normal injection rate, but by the time this stage is reached the initially injected fuel has ignited. The limited quantity of fuel injected during the delay period ensures minimum diesel knock.

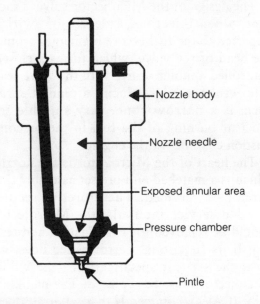

Fig 25.7   A pintle nozzle
Courtesy of Robert Bosch GmbH

Pintaux nozzles

The Pintaux nozzle was developed by Sir Harry Ricardo and the CAV organisation for use in Ricardo Comet combustion chambers. Basically, it is a plain pintle nozzle with a fine spray hole leading from below the needle valve seat at an angle to the nozzle axis. The pintle itself has a fairly long parallel section, which passes through the main nozzle orifice.

It must be realised that a quantity of fluid can be forced slowly through a small orifice without raising the pressure beyond a certain point. If an attempt is made to force it through at a faster rate the pressure will rise rapidly, but the fuel flow will not increase in proportion.

Now the Pintaux nozzle is designed to spray the fuel through the small hole at cranking speeds, and to spray most of the fuel through the main hole when the engine starts. At low injection speeds the fuel can escape through the small hole so fast that the fuel pressure does not lift the needle valve far off its seat.

This allows the parallel part of the pintle to stay in the main fuel orifice, stopping the passage of fuel. As soon as the engine starts and the speed of injection is increased, the fuel cannot escape from the small hole rapidly enough and the fuel pressure increases. This lifts the needle valve well clear of its seat, the parallel section of the pintle lifts clear of the main hole, and normal injection occurs.

It has been definitely established that the area of greatest heat in a Comet combustion chamber on compression stroke lies in the

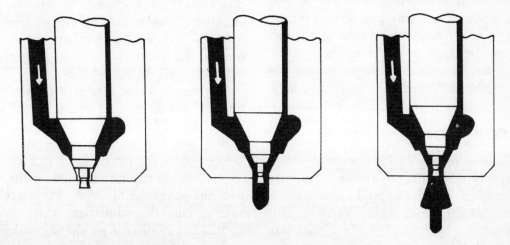

Fig 25.8   Spray characteristics of a delay (or throttling) nozzle
Courtesy of Robert Bosch GmbH

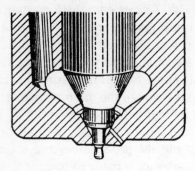

Fig 25.9 Pintaux nozzle
Courtesy of CAV

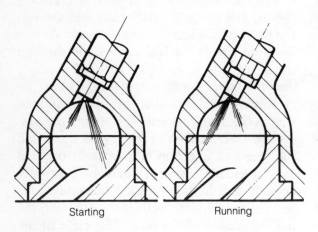

Starting   Running

Fig 25.10 Action of the Pintaux nozzle

auxiliary chamber at the mouth of the tangential passage. It is towards this point that the fine hole directs the fuel at cranking speed, giving easy starting. However, to ensure good combustion and mixing, the fuel must be directed at right angles to the swirling air. As soon as the engine starts, this is accomplished through the main pintle hole.

Microjector

The Microjector (Fig 25.11) is more compact than the typical injector and has recently been fitted to some high-speed indirect injection automotive diesel engines. The injector screws into the cylinder head in a similar way to the spark plug in a petrol engine.

The nozzle design is of the outward opening type as opposed to the conventional inward opening type. In an outward opening type of injector nozzle, the nozzle valve — similar to a poppet valve as opposed to the conventional needle valve — opens outwards towards the combustion chamber.

The design of the Microjector valve is such that, when injecting, a degree of swirl is imparted to the fuel before it emerges around the head of the valve, which forms a closely controlled annular orifice with the valve seat. The resultant high-velocity atomised spray form is a narrow cone, very suitable for efficient burning of the fuel in the precombustion chamber of the engine.

The heart of the Microjector is the nozzle, which is a matched and pre-set assembly that cannot be serviced. Therefore, at recommended service intervals, the Microjector should be removed for examination and testing. If its functional performance does not meet the set test specifications, the whole Microjector must be replaced. The manufacturer (CAV) recommends that, after an operating period of 80 000 km, the Microjector be replaced anyway.

Operation of the Microjector is straightforward. With reference to Fig 25.11, once the unit is filled with fuel, injection occurs as extra fuel is supplied from the injection pump.

Fuel enters the unit at the top, and flows down via the edge-type filter into the spring chamber. It then flows through feed ports into the nozzle body and continues down around the nozzle valve until it reaches the valve head via the swirl helices.

The nozzle valve lifts at a predetermined opening pressure (approximately 70 atmospheres or 7175 kPa), set by the pre-loaded spring, and continues to move until the lift stop contacts the nozzle body just above the feed ports. As the nozzle valve opens, atomised fuel leaves the tip of the Microjector in a swirling cone-shaped pattern, which continues as fuel is supplied from the injection pump and the nozzle remains open. When the supply of fuel stops and injection ceases, the nozzle valve is returned to its seat by the spring action and engine combustion pressure.

Some of the advantages claimed for Microjectors are:

- lower nozzle opening pressure;
- reduced injection dribble;
- no injector back-leakage.

The combination of low opening pressure and reduced nozzle dribble is due to the fact that combustion pressure helps the relatively low spring force to close the needle firmly on to its seat.

The absence of back-leakage is because all the fuel flows in one direction — down along the needle and out into the combustion chamber.

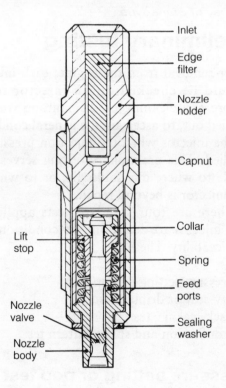

Fig 25.11 Section view of a Microjector
Courtesy of CAV

Roosa Master pencil nozzles

While injectors of the Roosa Master pencil nozzle type operate on the same general prin-

ciple as almost all injectors, they have a number of features that make their construction unique. These features are probably best shown as follows:

- The small body diameter of 9.5 mm allows more room for cylinder valves and large water jackets.
- The thin, light needle valve is claimed by the manufacturer to increase seat life due to its light impact and to allow high engine speed due to low reciprocating weight.
- The precision fit of the needle valve is in the main injector body, well away from the heat of combustion.
- Both injector opening pressure and needle lift are adjustable by means of adjusting screws.
- The inlet connection pipe and body length are available in a number of variations to suit different applications.
- The nozzle body, or tip as it is called, cannot be detached from the main body.
- Because of its small size, there is less likelihood of leakage between the injector and cylinder head and a simple clamping device is sufficient.

The operation of the injector follows the standard pattern: fuel flows through the inlet connection and fills the space between the precision needle valve-to-body fit and the seat. As the fuel pressure builds up, it acts against the shoulder of the needle valve, lifting it from its seat. Injection then occurs. Back-leakage fuel escapes by passing upwards through the spring chamber and adjustments to the leak-off connection.

Injector service

Injectors will give long periods of service without trouble, provided the fuel filters receive regular attention to ensure a clean fuel supply.

Some of the symptoms that indicate inefficient operation are as follows:

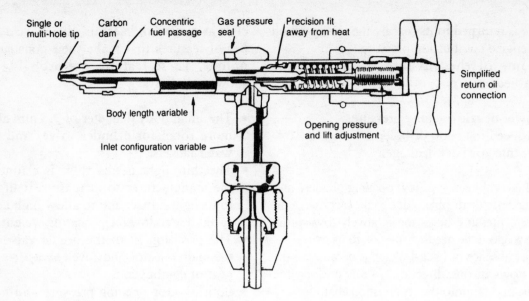

Single or multi-hole tip — Carbon dam — Concentric fuel passage — Gas pressure seal — Precision fit away from heat — Simplified return oil connection — Body length variable — Inlet configuration variable — Opening pressure and lift adjustment

Fig 25.12 The Roosa Master pencil nozzle *Courtesy of Stanadyne*

- intermittent misfiring on one or more cylinders;
- smoky exhaust-black smoke indicating an injector discharging unatomised fuel;
- pronounced knock in one or more cylinders;
- increased fuel consumption and engine overheating.

The injectors should be removed periodically from the engine (in accordance with the engine manufacturer's instructions) about every 16 000 km for routine testing and examination. Dismantling, cleaning and reconditioning are carried out according to the condition of the injectors.

The injectors are generally tested by means of a lever-operated pump, fitted with a pressure gauge graduated in 'atmospheres'. Clean fuel (or test oil) is pumped through the injector, the pressure, spray pattern, etc. indicating the injector condition.

Note: If a test pump is not available, a rough test can be carried out on the engine by removing the injectors, then reconnecting them to the fuel supply pipes so that the nozzles are positioned away from the engine. After bleeding the air from the supply pipes, the sprays from the injectors can be examined while the engine is turned by the starter motor or by hand, cranking.

Preliminary testing

After removal from the engine, each injector should be checked on an injector tester before any cleaning or dismantling work is carried out, to ascertain the general condition of the injector when the injection pressure is applied. This preliminary testing serves as a guide to where any faults lie, or to whether the injector is beyond repair.

There are four standard tests applied to any injector to determine its condition and serviceability. These are:

1 pressure setting or pop test;
2 dry-seat or dribble test;
3 back-leakage test;
4 atomisation and spray pattern test.

Pressure setting or pop test

To pressure test an injector, expel the air from the injector tester, fit the injector to the adaptor provided for the purpose, depress the lever very slowly and observe the highest pressure reading obtained before the pressure gauge needle flicks. This is the pressure at which injection begins (although the injection pressure **may** rise to many times this figure when the engine is running), and must correspond with the manufacturer's recommendations.

The injector opening pressure is almost invariably expressed in atmospheres. The term 'atmosphere' means the pressure of the atmosphere, and as this is very nearly 101.3 kPa, a pressure of 100 atmospheres is 10 130 kPa or 10.13 MPa.

If the injector opening pressure is lower than it should be, poor fuel atomisation will result. This will lead to black smoke, difficulty in starting and loss of power.

The effects of high injector opening pressure will vary from combustion chamber to combustion chamber. In some cases, the finer atomisation from the high pressure will result in lack of penetration by the fuel spray, while in other combustion chambers a slightly higher pressure may cause the spray to touch some part of the engine, and overheating of this part may follow.

Fig 25.13   Hartridge Testmaster
Courtesy of Hartridge

If the injector opening pressure is incorrect, it should be able to be adjusted by means of the spring tension adjustment — either screw and lock nut or shim. If it cannot be adjusted in this way, this indicates a major fault and the injector will have to be dismantled for further checking.

Note: When a new injector spring has been fitted, the injector opening pressure must be set slightly higher than normal to allow for bedding-in (e.g. CAV injector opening pressure should be increased by 5 atmospheres).

Dry-seat or dribble test

Injector manufacturers' recommendations regarding dry-seat testing vary, but the basic test may be performed as follows. Fit the injector to the injector tester, wipe the nozzle dry, and raise the pressure to approximately 10 atmospheres below the injector opening pressure. After a specified time, during which the pressure is maintained, the nozzle tip should remain dry.

CAV injectors are checked by holding a piece of blotting paper against the dry nozzle, raising the pressure to 10 atmospheres below injection pressure, and noting the stain produced on the blotting paper. It should be not more than 12 mm in diameter after 60 seconds, the pressure being maintained constant during the test.

However, there is an exception to the above pressure and that is with pencil injectors which are allowed to dribble during a dry seat or dribble test. Depending on the type of injector, the dribble rate ranges from three to twenty drops within a maximum time frame of fifteen seconds.

The dry-seat test shows whether fuel is leaking past the needle valve seat or not when the needle is held on its seat by the spring. An injector that dribbles may cause one or more of the following faults:

• **engine overheating and/or piston seizure.**
The fuel entering the combustion chamber will be both excessive and poorly atomised in part. The possible consequences include extra fuel being burnt after combustion should have finished, incomplete combustion leaving unburnt fuel to destroy cylinder lubrication, and oxidation of unburnt fuel in and above the ring area causing gum and lacquer formation;

- **severe engine wear**, due to dilution of the lubricating oil by unburnt fuel escaping past the rings;
- **carbon deposits** on the nozzle tip.

If the nozzle does not remain dry, the injector will have to be dismantled and cleaned, but it is most unlikely that this will rectify the fault and the nozzle will probably have to be reconditioned. It should be noted at this stage, however, that a loose nozzle nut or distorted faces where the nozzle body and nozzle holder mate will allow the leakage of fuel, which will collect on the nozzle tip. This condition is often confused with a leaking needle valve seat.

Back-leakage test

The generally accepted procedure when testing an injector for back-leakage is to pump the injector tester to near opening pressure, then isolate the pump if possible. The pressure shown on the gauge will slowly fall, due to fuel leakage past the needle valve. The rate at which the pressure falls indicates the clearance between the needle valve and the nozzle body.

Most manufacturers give maximum and minimum amounts of time for the pressure drop through a specified range (e.g. for some CAV injectors, the time for the pressure to fall from 150 to 100 atmospheres should be not less than fifteen seconds and not more than 35 seconds).

Note: Some manufacturers recommend that the back-leakage test be done at pressures in excess of normal opening pressures. In these cases, the injector pressure setting must be altered before the tests are made.

There are a number of faults that may produce the symptoms of excessive back-leakage. These include:

- dirt between the nozzle body and the nozzle holder, which allows fuel to escape;
- a loose nozzle cap nut, again allowing leakage;
- loose fuel pipe connections;

- high temperatures, causing thinning of the test oil.

The back-leakage test indicates the amount of fuel leaking between the needle valve stem and the nozzle body. Some leakage at this point is necessary for lubrication purposes, but when an excessive amount of fuel is lost at this point, the quantity of fuel injected is less than it should be. If the time taken for the specified pressure drop is too long, then the clearance between the needle valve and the nozzle body is not sufficient and the nozzle will probably seize.

This test is very important at the preliminary stage, since it indicates whether or not the nozzle is worth reconditioning. Once the needle-to-body clearance is excessive, the nozzle cannot be repaired.

Atomisation and spray pattern test

The atomisation and spray pattern test is simply a visual check in most instances. The usual procedure is to fit the injector to the injector tester, isolate the pressure gauge and pump the handle at about 60 strokes per minute. The spray should be without distortion and without visible streaks of unvaporised fuel. A multi-hole nozzle should produce sprays of equal length.

It is good practice to check the angle of the sprays when a new multi-hole nozzle has been fitted by allowing the spray to strike a piece of paper and checking this against the manufacturer's recommendations. There have been cases where all the holes have not been drilled right through the nozzle body and cases where one of the holes has been drilled at the wrong angle.

Note: Usually, an audible 'grunt' is made when the fuel issues from the nozzle. This is the result of the needle being lifted from its seat, snapping down again and being lifted once more. Thus the needle 'chatters' on its seat. Although this chatter is often considered to be an indication of a good nozzle, this is not always so. A delay pintle nozzle in top condition may operate without the noise. Again, nozzles with leaking seats may quite often chatter very well, as will nozzles with excessive back-leakage. Thus chattering may only indicate that the needle is free in the body.

If the injector does not atomise the fuel completely, incomplete combustion, causing black smoke, a loss in engine power and poor fuel economy, will result. Increased diesel knock, due to the longer delay period that follows poor atomisation, will also become evident.

Poor atomisation and/or distorted spray pattern usually result from semi-blocked nozzle holes, provided the opening pressure is correct. In such a case the injector should be dismantled, the nozzle cleaned and the unit reassembled and tested again.

If the injector operates satisfactorily on preliminary testing, it may not have to be dismantled. The nozzle should be cleaned with a brass wire brush to remove any carbon deposit. The exterior of the injector should then be cleaned with a suitable cleaning fluid and dried off with compressed air. After cleaning the exterior, the injector should be checked again for operation on the test pump.

Dismantling a typical injector

If the injector is faulty on preliminary testing or is due for injector service, it must be dismantled for cleaning the interior, examination and further testing.

For dismantling and reassembling, the injector should be held in a jig fixture instead of a bench vice to avoid damaging the components.

For any type of injector, the usual practice is to begin dismantling at the top to release the spring force before removing the nozzle. To dismantle the injector shown in Fig 25.14:

1 Remove the cap nut (9) and joint washer (10).
2 Slacken the lock nut (8) and adjusting screw (7) to release the spring force.

3 Remove the nozzle nut (2) and nozzle (16), complete with needle (17).
4 Remove the spring cap nut (6), upper spring plate (5), spring (4) and spindle assembly (3).
5 If a filter is fitted in the inlet adaptor (13), remove the inlet adaptor, filter (14) and nipple (15).

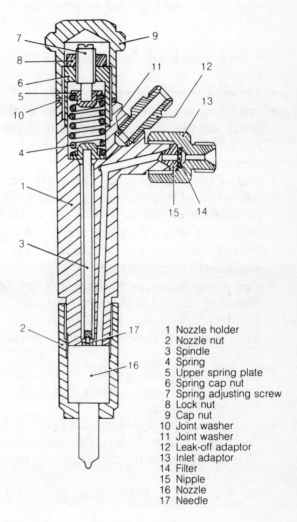

1 Nozzle holder
2 Nozzle nut
3 Spindle
4 Spring
5 Upper spring plate
6 Spring cap nut
7 Spring adjusting screw
8 Lock nut
9 Cap nut
10 Joint washer
11 Joint washer
12 Leak-off adaptor
13 Inlet adaptor
14 Filter
15 Nipple
16 Nozzle
17 Needle

Fig 25.14 Injector with spring-adjusting screw
Courtesy of CAV

6 Place the nozzle holder (1) and the dismantled parts in a container. When several injectors need to be dismantled at the same time, it is important that there is a container for each injector to avoid any interchanging of parts.

Cleaning the dismantled injector

Clean all the parts with a suitable cleaning fluid and dry off with compressed air. Do not use rags or fluffy cloths. Special tools to facilitate cleaning are available.

A nozzle-cleaning kit consisting of the following tools should be used for removing the carbon deposits:

- a brass wire brush for the exterior of the nozzle;
- a brass scraper for the gallery;
- one or more scrapers for the cavity in the nozzle tip (the scraper stems are of different diameters, to suit the nozzles in which they are used);
- one or more scrapers for the nozzle seat (the stems of these scrapers are also made in different diameters to suit the various nozzles in which they are used, and the cutting end of the tool is made to the same angle as the nozzle seat);
- steel pricker wires for the spray holes (these wires are supplied in different diameters to suit the nozzles in which they are used);
- a pin vice or pin chuck to carry the pricker wires;
- one or more brass needle scrapers (these are designed to accommodate needles of different diameters);
- a number of brass cleaners for pintle nozzles (these fit into holders, with stems of different diameters to suit various nozzles).

To clean a multi-hole nozzle, proceed as follows:

1 Remove all traces of carbon from the exterior of the nozzle with the brass wire brush (Fig 25.15).
2 Clean carbon from the feed hole (between the annular groove and gallery) with a piece of wire or a drill of the correct size (Fig 25.16).
3 Clean the gallery with the correct scraper (Fig 25.17).

4 Remove any carbon from the dome in the end of the nozzle with the correct scraper. Select a scraper with a stem that fits neatly in the nozzle body (Fig 25.18).
Note: Pintle nozzles do not have a dome end. Special pintle hole cleaners are supplied for cleaning nozzles of this type.
5 Clean all carbon from the nozzle seat with the brass scraper. Again ensure that the stem fits neatly in the body, and check that the scraper tip angle coincides with the angle of the seat (Fig 25.19).
6 Check the size of the spray holes in the manufacturer's manual, and select the appropriate pricker wire. The wire should be fitted in the pin vice so that just sufficient protrudes to clean the full depth of the hole. Avoid having an excessive length of wire protruding, as it is very easy to break part off in the hole. Grinding a chamfer (about 45°) on the end of the pricker wire to form a cutting edge facilitates the cleaning operation.
7 Hold the nozzle body firmly, and move the pricker wire carefully in and out of the spray holes, while rotating the pin vice slightly between the thumb and forefinger (Fig 25.20).

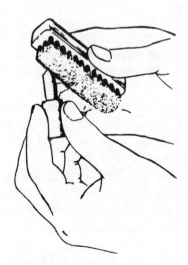

Fig 25.15 Cleaning the exterior of the nozzle

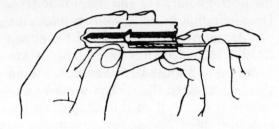

Fig 25.16   Cleaning the fuel feed hole

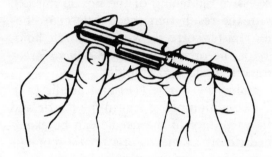

Fig 25.17   Cleaning the fuel feed gallery

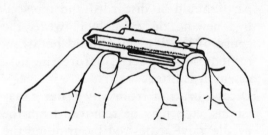

Fig 25.18   Cleaning the dome

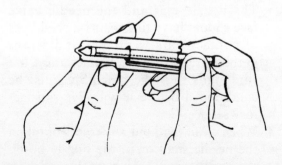

Fig 25.19   Cleaning the nozzle seat

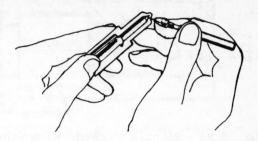

Fig 25.20   Cleaning the spray hole

A hard carbon deposit in the spray holes may be softened by the following method:

- Dissolve 50 grams of caustic soda in 0.5 litres of water, and add 12.5 grams of detergent.
- Place the nozzle in the liquid and boil for a minimum period of one hour and not more than one and a half hours.
- The concentration of caustic soda must not exceed 15 per cent and water should be added to replace that lost by evaporation. Should the concentration of caustic soda exceed 15 per cent, the bore and the joint face on the nozzle may be corroded and thus render the nozzle unserviceable.
- Remove the nozzle and wash it in running water. Remove surplus by draining or by using compressed air.

8 Flush all carbon particles from the nozzle body by fitting it in a reverse flushing adaptor and fitting the adaptor to the injector test pump. When the pump is operated, the fuel is forced through the spray holes and nozzle body in the reverse direction to normal fuel flow, thus washing foreign particles out through the top of the nozzle body (Fig 25.21).

9 Clean any carbon from the needle with the brush and finish with the brass needle scraper (Figs 25.22 and 25.23). Instead of a scraper, CAV recommend the use of a piece of soft wood for polishing the needle.

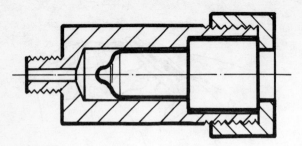

Fig 25.21 Nozzle in reverse flushing adaptor

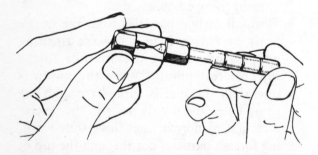

Fig 25.22 Cleaning the needle with a brass wire brush

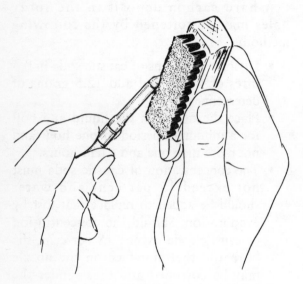

Fig 25.23 Cleaning the needle with a brass scraper

Inspection of the injector components

Referring to Fig 25.14:

1 Examine the condition of the joint faces of the nozzle holder (1) and the nozzle (16). Discolouration or dark stains between the annular groove and the edge of the nozzle holder indicate that the surfaces are distorted and must be 'trued-up'. Should this be necessary, the correct procedure to follow is outlined in this chapter in the section entitled 'Nozzle reconditioning'.

2 Examine for distortion of the dowels (if fitted) in the nozzle holder. The dowels may be distorted (partially sheared) by excessive tightening of the nozzle nut (2), with the result that the nozzle (16) does not register correctly with the nozzle holder for the offset spray. The dowels are a press fit in the nozzle holder.

3 Examine the nozzle (16) and needle (17). The condition of the seat in the nozzle and the valve face of the needle can be examined closely by means of a nozzle-scope — a simple form of microscope incorporating a beam of light:

- If the nozzle seat and the valve face are 'blued', indicating overheating, the two parts should be discarded and replaced by a new nozzle assembly. However, the cause of the blueing should be ascertained and corrected before the new assembly is fitted.

- Discolouration from any other cause (stains, etc.) may be removed from the needle valve if desired by gripping the needle in a lapping chuck and rotating it, while firmly gripping the discoloured area of the needle between two pieces of pine.

- The nozzle seat and the needle valve face should have fine matt finished lines of contact. Pits, scratches and scores in these areas, or wide contact areas, are sure signs that the assembly must be conditioned before it will give satisfactory service.

- When clean (without any traces of oil on the needle stem or in the nozzle bore), the needle should drop freely under its own weight on to the nozzle seat.

- As another check for binding, the needle should be pressed by hand against the nozzle seat (nozzle in normal vertical position). The needle should fall freely when the nozzle is inverted and the hand is removed.

4 Examine the spindle (3). If the recessed end of the spindle is flattened, a new spindle complete with spring cup must be fitted.

5 Examine the inlet adaptor filter (14). Renew the filter if damaged.

6 Examine the spring (4). It may be corroded due to condensation of moisture on the spring as a result of temperature changes in service. It should be cleaned.

7 Examine the nozzle nut (2). Carbon deposits can lodge inside the nut, particularly in the hole for the nozzle. Remove the carbon with a suitable tool.

Reassembly of the injector

All the injector's parts should be reassembled wet with clean fuel.

Cleanliness in handling the parts is of paramount importance because of the fine clearances of the operating parts. A minute particle of dirt can upset the performance of any injector. It is essential that the tools and work bench are clean.

If the injector is being reassembled in anything but dust-free conditions, it should be done under the surface of clean fuel.

Note: An adjustable torque wrench should be used to ensure correct tightening of several of the injector parts.

To reassemble the components, as shown in Fig 25.14:

1 Reassemble the nipple (15), filter (14) and inlet adaptor (13).

2 Fit the spindle (3), spring (4), upper spring plate (5) and spring cap nut (6).

3 Fit the nozzle (16) complete with needle (17) to the nozzle holder (1) and ensure that the dowels (if fitted) locate the nozzle. Tighten the nozzle nut (2).

4 Screw down the adjusting screw (7) temporarily until pressure is felt on the spring (4). Adjustment of the injection pressure setting is carried out as described earlier in this section under the heading 'Preliminary testing'. After adjustment, tighten the lock nut (8).

5 Reassemble the cap nut (9) with a new joint washer (10).

After reassembly, the four basic injector tests should again be applied to the injector. The pressure setting or pop pressure, however, must be correct, since it is set during reassembly.

If the injector dry-seat test does not come up to specifications, and all other possible points of leakage have been eliminated, the nozzle will have to be reconditioned.

If the original nozzle is being tested, the rate of back-leakage should be the same as in the preliminary test. If excessive back-leakage during preliminary testing indicated the need for a new nozzle, then the rate of back-leakage of the new nozzle should be correct. In either case, then, the rate of back-leakage will probably be correct but should be checked.

Nozzle reconditioning

Should inspection of the injector components indicate the need for reconditioning the nozzle, the following procedures should be followed.

To true nozzle body and nozzle holder joint faces

Lapping the joint face of the nozzle or nozzle holder is usually done on a power-driven machine or by hand on a cast-iron surface plate.

In the latter method, the lapping compound should be smeared sparingly on the surface plate. The nozzle or nozzle holder (with dowels removed) should be held evenly and firmly between finger and thumb of both hands, and moved lightly in a figure-8 motion on the plate.

Note: The operation of lapping a nozzle joint face should be carried out before lapping the nozzle seat. The impact of the needle shoulder on the joint face of a nozzle holder is usually indicated by a mark around the centre hole. Removal of this mark by lapping is not necessary.

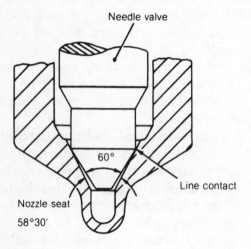

Fig 25.24 Typical needle and seat details

To recondition valve face and seat

The two parts of an injector most affected by the stress of operation are the nozzle and the needle valve. The continual hammering effect caused by the opening and closing of the needle valve ultimately affects the needle seat and the nozzle seat.

The reconditioning of an injector nozzle involves the restoration of the nozzle seat surface and the face of the needle valve. The needle face is almost invariably refaced by a grinding process; the nozzle seat may be ground using specialised equipment, or resurfaced by a lapping process.

It is important to realise that the angle of the nozzle seat is different from the angle of the needle face and, when reconditioning is carried out, it is necessary to maintain these angles. The purpose of having this interference angle or differential angle is to maintain a line contact between the two. Line contact ensures three desirable factors:

1 a sharp cut-off of fuel, since there can be no fuel trapped between the valve faces as the needle snaps closed;
2 extremely high pressure of contact, because the seat is narrow and therefore has a very small area. Thus, in terms of the force applied and the area of contact, a small seat area ensures a higher contact pressure than a large seat area;
3 little likelihood of any minute particles being trapped between the needle and its seat because of the very narrow contact.

After long service, leakage occurs when the needle seat and the nozzle seat become pitted and scored. The line contact may become wider or the seat may become grooved where the needle seats against it. If the wear and pitting are excessive, reconditioning should not be attempted.

The nozzle seat and the needle face are reconditioned separately. The nozzle seat and the needle face must never be lapped together to rectify seat leakage because such an operation would create the very conditions (wide contact and seating impression) that have to be corrected.

The needle is made of a harder steel than that of the nozzle, while the nozzle is case-hardened to a depth of about 0.4 mm. The hardened surface of the nozzle seat can be removed if reconditioning is carried out several times. It may be assumed, broadly, that about 0.05–0.075 mm of metal is removed each time a nozzle seat is rectified. Under normal conditions of wear, therefore, the nozzle should be reconditioned only five times at the most, after which it should be scrapped.

Lapping nozzle seats

To recondition nozzle seats by the lapping process, two items of equipment are required: a lapping machine and the 'lap'. A lap may be likened to a long nozzle needle with a hardened body where it fits into the nozzle body. The tip of the lap (equivalent to the face of the needle) may be made of one of a number of materials, cast iron being the most popular. When a small quantity of lapping compound — an extremely fine grinding paste — is applied to the tip, it is retained in the pores of the cast iron. The lap becomes, in effect, a fine grinding tool. Usually, two grades of lapping compound are used, a coarse one for 'roughing' and a fine one for 'finishing'.

Laps are made to suit the different types of nozzle with different bore diameters, and for each type of nozzle, laps are made with stem diameter increases of 0.01 mm. The correct lap should be selected to recondition each nozzle seat, and should be a very fine clearance fit in the nozzle bore. Once the lap has been selected, it should be fitted into a nozzle grinding and lapping machine and the tip ground carefully to the correct angle for the nozzle body seat. If there is any doubt as to the trueness of the grinding wheel, this should first be dressed.

In machines of this type, the lap is turned, while it is being ground, by a rubber belt or wheel (depending on the make of machine). The lap body fits against a 'V'-block and is held and turned in this 'V' by the drive mechanism. Thus a centreless grinding process is used, and this ensures concentricity.

Very fine cuts should be taken when grinding the lap, which should be moved back and forth across the full face of the wheel.

As soon as a true, fine finish on the lap end is obtained, the nozzle seat may be lapped. A very good lapping procedure (by courtesy of CAV) is outlined below:

1 Mount the lap in the collet of the machine lapping head. Smear the stem of the lap with tallow.
2 Place a small bead of lapping compound such as chromic oxide (about 1 or 2 mm

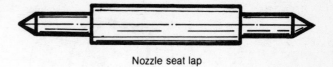

Nozzle seat lap

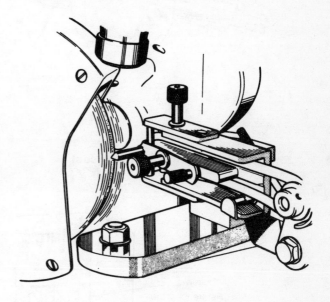

Fig 25.25   Grinding the nozzle seat lap

diameter) on the lap face. Too much lapping compound should not be applied.
3 Hold the nozzle between finger and thumb and slide it on the revolving lap. Care must be exercised that the nozzle bore is not damaged by contact with the lapping compound.
4 Move the nozzle quickly to and fro, at the some time partially rotating the nozzle back and forth, so that the lap comes into contact with the nozzle seat. The nozzle seat should not be in contact with the lap for more than five seconds at a time.
5 After about 30 seconds, remove the nozzle and wipe the lap. Apply lapping compound and repeat the procedure.
6 After one or two lappings, depending on the condition of the nozzle seat, wash out the nozzle with cleaning fluid by reverse flushing. Then examine the seat in a nozzlescope. The correct finish should appear as a clean unbroken surface.

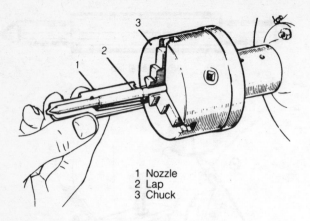

1 Nozzle
2 Lap
3 Chuck

Fig 25.26 Lapping the nozzle seat

Machine grinding nozzle seats

For faster and more precise reconditioning of nozzle seats than can be obtained by hand lapping, automatic nozzle reseating machines are now being used. One such machine is the Hartridge Injectomatic shown in Fig 25.27.

A grinding tool similar to a nozzle needle but with a grinding stone attached to the tip is used to grind the nozzle seat. After a correctly fitting grinding tool has been selected, it is placed in a needle grinding machine and faced to the correct seat angle. The grinding tip of the tool is then dipped in cutting oil and the tool placed inside the nozzle.

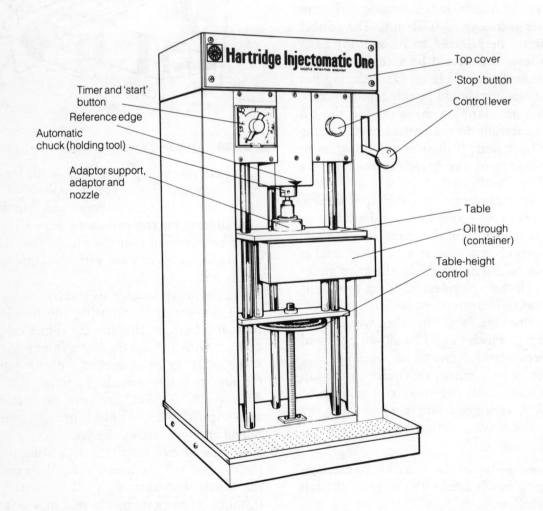

Timer and 'start' button
Reference edge
Automatic chuck (holding tool)
Adaptor support, adaptor and nozzle

Top cover
'Stop' button
Control lever

Table
Oil trough (container)
Table-height control

Fig 25.27 'Hartridge Injectomatic One' nozzle reseating machine   *Courtesy of Hartridge*

The nozzle is mounted on the adaption plate of the reseating machine and the machine is set into operation for a period of from 30 seconds to two minutes, depending on the seat condition and the type of grinding stone used. Experience is the best guide to selection of the grinding time.

Valve reconditioning

The needle valve face itself may be reconditioned in one of two ways. The first entails fitting the needle into the lapping and grinding machine and carefully grinding just enough metal from the face to eliminate pits and marks. Of course, since the needle face

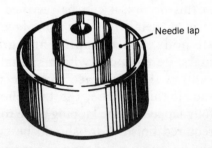

Fig 25.28 Needle lap

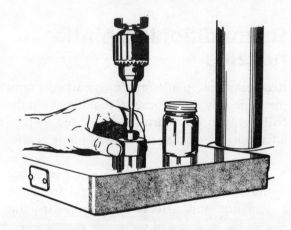

Fig 25.29 Lapping the needle

angle is invariably different from the nozzle body seat angle, the machine will have to be reset to grind the needle correctly. Once the face has been ground, it should be examined

through a microscope to ensure that any pitting has been completely removed.

An alternative method of reconditioning the needle valve is by the lapping sequence, which is clearly outlined below:

1 Mount the needle in the chuck of a vertical spindle machine, as shown in Fig 25.29. *Note:* The need for the needle to run true cannot be too greatly stressed.
2 Apply a small bead of lapping compound to the lapping face of the needle lap. Run the machine at about 460 rpm.
3 While holding the lap, move the revolving needle quickly up and down so that the needle face comes lightly in contact with the lap; contact should be not more than five seconds at a time.
4 After about 30 seconds, remove and clean the needle. Examine the needle face in a nozzlescope. Repeat the lapping procedure if necessary.

Needle lift

Once the needle valve face and the nozzle body seat have been reconditioned, no further work should be necessary — if the job is carefully done, a perfect seal will result. The two components should be thoroughly cleaned and assembled while wet with fuel or test oil. However, the removal of metal from the seat area lets the needle move deeper into the body, while the removal of metal from the joint face of the nozzle body results in the needle sitting relatively higher in the body. Thus both these reconditioning procedures affect the **needle lift**, which is described below.

The amount the needle can lift off its seat during injection is limited by the amount the needle can move before the shoulder on its upper end strikes the joint face of the main injector body. Thus needle lift may be defined as the maximum distance that the needle may lift off its seat to allow the passage of fuel during injection.

Needle lift must lie within certain limits if efficient injection and/or reasonable nozzle life are to be obtained. If the needle lift is below specifications, the clearance between the needle valve face and the nozzle body seat will be insufficient to allow the full charge of fuel to pass, unrestricted, to the injector hole or holes. Restriction of fuel at the valve area will cause a considerable drop in fuel pressure, so that the pressure applied to force the fuel through the hole(s) will be less than that required for atomisation and penetration. Thus insufficient needle lift considerably affects the fuel spray characteristics.

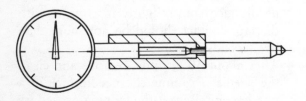

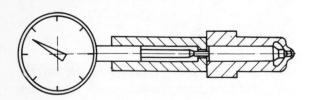

Fig 25.30 Checking needle lift

If, on the other hand, the needle lift is greater than is required for efficient injection (the area through the open valve seat should be approximately twice the orifice area), the needle valve will travel through a greater distance than is necessary. When the valve closes under the influence of the injector spring, any extra distance of travel results in an increase in the impact of the needle on the seat. Thus excessive needle lift greatly reduces the life of a nozzle assembly, due to the hammering of the needle on the seat.

The needle lift may be found very easily by using a dial gauge and adaptor.

First, take the needle and place the spigot in the adaptor hole. Hold the needle so that the shoulder is firmly and squarely against the face of the adaptor. Note the dial gauge reading. Then refit the needle to the nozzle body, making sure it seats properly. Hold the nozzle assembly to the adaptor, so that the joint face of the nozzle body is firmly and squarely against the adaptor face. Note the dial gauge reading.

Now the difference between the two readings is the amount of needle lift from when it is on its seat to when its shoulder is against the join face of the main injector body. Thus it is a measurement of the amount the needle can lift from its seat — the needle lift.

During service, no problems will occur with insufficient needle lift, but on many occasions excessive needle lift will develop after a nozzle has been reconditioned a number of times. When this occurs, it can be rectified by the removal of metal from the joint face of the nozzle body. Some lapping and grinding machines are equipped with a special chuck that allows the joint face to be accurately ground. If this is done, the face should be carefully lapped on the lapping plate to obtain the required finish. Care should be taken to remove no more metal than is required, and the needle lift should be carefully rechecked after the face has been lapped.

Reconditioning pintle nozzles

Reconditioning pintle nozzles is carried out in the same way as for other types. However, the following points should be noted before attempting to reclaim any type of pintle nozzle:

- The seat is lapped in the normal way, but the removal of excessive metal from the seat not only affects the needle lift, but also the position of the pintle during injection, relative to the pintle hole. This can result in an entirely different spray pattern.
- The removal of excessive metal from the needle face also affects the position of the pintle relative to the pintle hole, and again the spray can be affected.

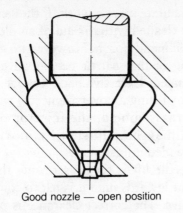

Good nozzle — open position

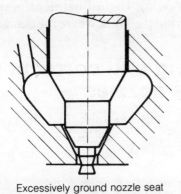

Excessively ground nozzle seat

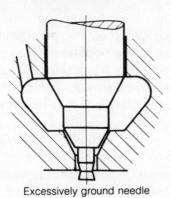

Excessively ground needle

Fig 25.31   Faults when reconditioning pintle nozzles

- The clearance between the pintle and the nozzle hole is extremely critical, and care must be taken not to damage the hole in any way during reconditioning.
- Care must be taken not to damage the pintle during needle valve face repairs. If the face is reground, the wheel will probably

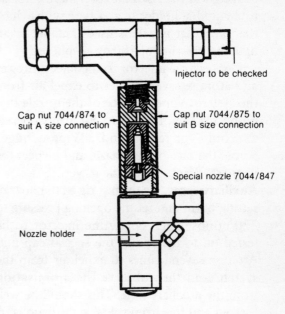

Fig 25.32   Test rig for checking Pintaux nozzles

have to be specially faced to accommodate the pintle. If the face is lapped, the correct laps — with a hole to accommodate the pintle — must be employed.

Testing Pintaux nozzles

In order to check the required injection rate and delivery of this type of nozzle, it is necessary to fit the injector to a special test rig, which is, in turn, connected to the injector tester. The rig consists of an additional nozzle holder fitted with a special nozzle. A cap nut to suit A size (12 mm) or B size (14 mm) connections is available.

The cap nut enables the injector, complete with the Pintaux nozzle under test, to be screwed on to the end as shown in Fig 25.32. By setting the opening pressure of the special nozzle to a value where its closing pressure is higher than the opening pressure of the Pintaux nozzle, a sufficiently high rate of injection can be obtained on hand test to determine the quality and form of atomisation of both auxiliary and main sprays.

To test a Pintaux nozzle, the following procedure (by courtesy of CAV) should be followed:

1 **Seat tightness.** Assemble the Pintaux nozzle to a suitable holder (e.g. a type with which the particular nozzle is used) and set to an opening pressure of 100 atmospheres.

Connect the injector to the injector tester and atomise several times to expel air from the system. Wipe the face of the nozzle dry, pump up the pressure to 90 atmospheres, and hold for ten seconds. Wipe a finger across the face of the nozzle and inspect for wetness. Reject the nozzle if wet.

2 **Auxiliary spray.** Fit the test rig to the nozzle-setting outfit and set the opening pressure to 220 atmospheres. Screw the injector to be tested on to the end of the special cap nut. Atomise several times to expel air from the system and then observe the atomisation from the auxiliary hole. This should be well formed and free from splits or distortions. A slight centre core may be disregarded.

The hand lever of the nozzle setting outfit should be operated at a minimum frequency of 60 strokes per minute during this test.

3 **Main spray.** Operate the hand lever at 140 strokes per minute and observe the main spray. This should be well atomised and free from large splits or distortions. A slight centre core may be disregarded.

Servicing pencil nozzles

Because of their compact construction, pencil nozzles are not able to stand rough treatment and two spanners must always be used when disconnecting and adjusting these injectors. To undo the inlet pipe, for example, the two spanners should be used in one hand — one spanner on the union nut, the other on the hexagon provided on the inlet connection. This will ensure that the injector is not distorted.

These injectors should be subjected to the four standard tests during service.

The injector opening pressure may be adjusted without dismantling the injector, but a leaking seat or excessive back-leakage indicates that the injector requires dismantling.

Dismantling is obviously done from the top, and a special injector service kit is available to facilitate service work. If the seat leaks, it may be cleaned with the aid of an old needle and a little metal polish. However, no grinding or lapping of the seat or needle valve face is recommended. Excessive back-leakage may be rectified by fitting an oversize needle valve.

Once reassembled, the injector opening pressure may be adjusted by moving the outer threaded adjustment.

The needle lift is set by screwing the inner adjustment inwards until it is felt to contact the needle valve. The correct clearance is obtained by unscrewing the adjustment a specified amount from the point where the contact is felt.

Testing and correcting faulty nozzles

The chart shown in Table 25.1, by courtesy of CAV, lists the common nozzle faults and gives an indication of the necessary service procedure.

Unit injectors

As an alternative to the conventional injector and separate fuel injection pump, unit injectors have grown in popularity in recent times due to their compact design and improved injection characteristics. The unit injector combines an individual fuel injection pump and fuel injector in a single compact unit that is fitted directly into the engine cylinder head, where it is operated from a lobe on the engine camshaft in a similar way to the engine valves. Apart from the widely used Detroit Diesel system, unit injectors are now being fitted to some Caterpillar engines, while Lucas Bryce manufacture unit injectors for several engine manufacturers.

The operation of a basic unit injector is described in Chapter 30 under Detroit Diesel fuel systems. Because the operating principles are the same with all unit injectors, only the manufacturers' design and installation variations will be discussed.

Unit injectors are currently fitted to a number of Caterpillar industrial and automotive truck engines. GEC diesel have also fitted unit injectors to their six- and eight-cylinder Dorman engines.

The unit injector used by Caterpillar is comparable in design and operation to the unit injector used in the Detroit Diesel series engines. The Dorman diesel uses a injector developed by Lucas Bryce and, although different in construction, its basic design and operation are the same as for the Detroit Diesel unit.

Unit injection offers a number of advantages over the conventional separate pump and injector system. The injector itself contains a much smaller volume of fuel trapped under high pressure than conventional systems, thereby allowing higher mean effective injection pressures to be employed. This increases the injection rate

and atomisation of the fuel, and is claimed to give improved performance and reduce fuel consumption.

Another advantage of the unit injector is the elimination of the high pressure flow losses through the injector lines and the problems associated with fuel compressibility that occur in separate pump and injector systems (Chapter 26).

Servicing of unit injectors

Due to installation variations between various unit injectors, the timing, calibration and maximum fuel adjustments vary from one engine installation to another. Therefore, prior to carrying out unit injector adjustments, the workshop manual should be consulted.

Table 25.1 Service procedure for common nozzle faults

Fault	Possible cause	Remedy
Nozzle does not buzz when injecting.	1. Needle valve too tight, binding, or valve seating leaky.	CleanNozzle. Examine cap nut; if necessary replace nozzle and needle valve.
	2. Nozzle cap nut distorted.	(*Note:* Delay -type nozzles and poppet nozzles do not usually buzz at slow plunger velocities given by testing outfit.)
Excessive leak-off	1. Needle valve slack,	Replace nozzle and needle valve.
	2. Foreign matter present bvetween pressure faces of nozzle and nozzle holder.	clean.
	3. Nozzle cap nut not tight.	Tighten cap nut after inspecting joint faces.
Nozzle blueing.	Faulty installing, tightening or cooling.	Replace nozzle and needle valve. Check cooling system.
Nozzle opening pressure.	1. Compression screw shifted.	Adjust for prescribed pressure.
	2 Needle valve seized up, corroded.	Replace nozzle and needle valve.
	3 Needle valve seized up, dirty, sticky.	Clean nozzle.
	4 Nozzle openings clogged with dirt or carbon.	Clean nozzle.
Nozzle pressure too low.	Nozzle spring broken.	Replace spring and readjest pressure.
Nozzle drip.	Nozzle leak due to carbon deposit; sticking needle valve.	Clean nozzle. If this does not clear fault, replace nozzle and needle valve.
Form of spray distorted.	1. Excessive carbon deposit on tip of needle valve.	Clean nozzle.
	2. Injection holes partially blocked.	Clean nozzle.
	3. Nozzle needle valve damaged (pintle type only.)	Replace nozzle and pintle valve.

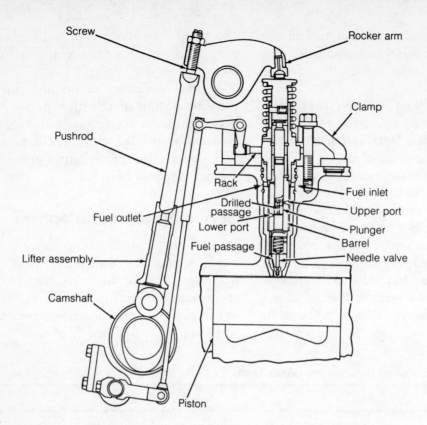

Fig 25.33   Unit injector installation in a Caterpillar diesel engine
Courtesy of Caterpillar Inc

26

Single and Multi-element In-line Injection Systems

The solid fuel injection system, as mentioned in Chapter 25, consists of two (usually separate) components: the fuel injector and the fuel injection pump. While these two units are united to form a single camshaft-operated component in some specific cases, the common practice is to use a separate fuel injection pump, which is connected to the injectors by steel injector pipes.

The function of the injector in such a system was clearly shown in Chapter 25: the fuel injection pump must perform three separate functions, which involve very high pressures and accurate control. These functions are as follows:

1 **To raise the pressure of the fuel high enough to be injected into the engine combustion chamber before and during combustion.** Fuel is supplied, either by gravity or by feed pump, to the fuel injection pump at a pressure that usually lies between 20 and 105 kPa. The fuel injection pump must raise the fuel pressure to between 12 and 70 MPa, depending on the injector type, engine speed, etc. This very high pressure is required for two reasons: to force the fuel into the combustion chamber of the engine against the gas pressure and to thoroughly atomise the fuel as it leaves the injector nozzle and passes into the combustion chamber.

2 **To accurately meter the quantity of fuel passing to the injector over the entire fuel requirement range.** The quantity of fuel required per cylinder for each firing is very small — a droplet of fuel about the size of a matchhead is sufficient for an average-sized engine operating under normal load conditions. The fuel pump must measure out the **exact** quantity of fuel for each engine cylinder and pass it on to the cylinder via the injector pipe and injector to be burnt. It is vital that the each cylinder receives the same amount of fuel per injection if the engine is to run smoothly.

3 **To accurately time the fuel injection for each cylinder.** For efficient combustion of the fuel charge, injection must begin at a specific point in the engine cycle before the piston reaches TDC on its compression stroke, continue for a certain time, and then cut off sharply. The fuel injection pump must start to supply fuel to each engine cylinder at a specific point in the engine cycle. The point of commencement of injection is determined by the engine manufacturer and usually lies between 15° and 30° before TDC for high-speed diesel engines.

It may be seen, then, that the fuel injection pump must force fuel into the combustion

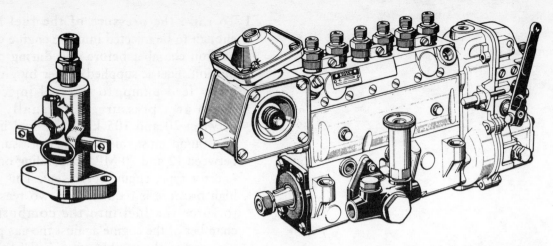

Fig 26.1   Single- and multi-element fuel injection pumps   *Courtesy of Robert Bosch GmbH*

chamber via the injector(s) at a pressure high enough to enable it to be atomised, measure out the fuel charge to be distributed to each cylinder and send this fuel charge to its respective cylinder at exactly the right moment. Since these operations may occur more than a hundred times per second when the engine is operating, the fuel injection pump must be capable of accurately and reliably fulfilling its functions at a very high rate and of resisting wear under high-speed, high-pressure conditions. While being able to satisfy all the demanding requirements outlined above, the pump must remain light and compact enough to be fitted to the engine without any inconvenience.

One of the most extensively used and entirely satisfactory fuel pump systems is the in-line injection pump, which was designed by Robert Bosch, and is now manufactured by almost every manufacturer of fuel injection equipment. Pumps of this type are made in a variety of forms — from single pumping element units operated by a special engine camshaft provided for the purpose to multi-element units with a camshaft enclosed within the pump housing. Single-element pumps are usually located along one side of the engine block to which they are flange mounted, where they are readily operated by the camshaft provided by the engine manufacturer for the purpose, while the multi-element,

enclosed camshaft units are generally mounted on the side of the block where their camshaft is driven (at half engine crankshaft speed in four-stroke engines) from the engine crankshaft via the timing gears.

Flange-mounted injection pumps

Flange-mounted injection pumps may be described as cam-operated, single-acting, constant-stroke plunger-type pumps, attached by a flange mounting plate to the engine. Usually mounted vertically, pumps of this type are generally operated by a special engine camshaft driven from the engine crankshaft by chain or gears, or by a special lobe(s) on the engine camshaft.

Fuel injection pumps of this type may be used for either single- or multi-cylinder engines that operate at low, medium or high speeds.

The majority of engine manufacturers who use flange-mounted pumps have them made by such companies as American Bosch (Ambac Industries Incorporated), CAV, Robert Bosch, Nippon Denso and Zexel (formerly Diesel Kiki), which specialise in the manufacture of fuel injection equipment.

The majority of flange-mounted fuel injection pumps are single-element units, able only to serve one engine cylinder. Multi-element units are also manufactured, but for reasons of simplicity and because of their greater use by engine manufacturers, we will restrict all basic discussion to single-element units.

Construction of a typical single-element, flange-mounted pump

By reference to Fig 26.2, it can be seen that the typical pump consists of the following major parts:

- the pump housing;
- the pumping element, consisting of two parts — a plunger and a barrel;
- the plunger return mechanism, consisting of a compression spring and two spring plates;

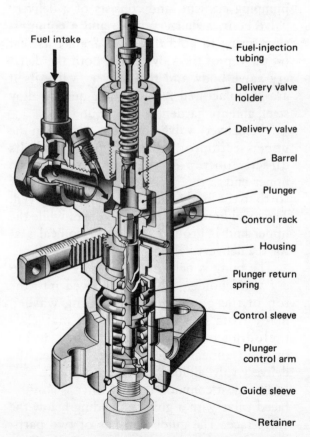

Fig 26.2   Typical single-element flange-mounted fuel injection pump
Courtesy of Robert Bosch GmbH

- the plunger rotating mechanism, made up in two parts — a control rack and a control sleeve;
- the delivery valve assembly;
- the plunger guide cup.

The pump housing

The pump housing is usually manufactured from high-quality cast iron and provides the 'body' of the pump in which all components are housed, as well as a flange for attaching the pump to the engine. A fuel gallery is cast in the top portion of the housing to carry the fuel supply for the pumping element. An air-bleed drilling, sealed with a threaded plug, leads upwards from the gallery to facilitate the removal of entrapped air. The lower portion of the housing is accurately machined internally to accommodate the pumping element and associated components. For ease of timing, a sight window is provided in the side of the housing through which a line on the plunger guide cup can be seen and aligned with a line inscribed on the housing.

The pumping element

The pumping element consists of two parts, a barrel and a plunger, each of which is manufactured from high-quality alloy steel, hardened, ground and lapped to the finest limits. The components are mated in manufacture and are lapped to such a degree of accuracy that they provide an efficient seal at extremely high pressures and very low speeds without the use of packing or seals of any type. Consequently, the barrel and plunger must be kept together as a mated pair during service, and never interchanged or replaced separately.

The barrel, which is a firm fit in the pump housing, is located in position by a screw and locked in place by the delivery valve holder, which screws down on top of both the delivery valve body and the flanged end of the barrel. The barrel carries two diametrically opposed holes — an inlet port and a control or spill port, through which the fuel from the fuel gallery can enter the barrel to be pressurised by the plunger. Although it is common practice to use a pump barrel that is equipped with both inlet and control ports, some pumps are fitted with a barrel with only the control port.

The pump plunger reciprocates inside the barrel, and both pressurises and meters the fuel charge that is sent to the engine cylinder. To make it possible for the pump to vary the quantity of fuel delivered per stroke, the upper part of the plunger is provided with a vertical channel extending from its top face to an annular groove, the top edge of which is milled in the form of a helix and is called the **control edge**. In some pumps the plunger has an additional helix on the top, and this allows the point at which injection begins to be changed.

The lower end of the plunger, which protrudes from the bottom of the barrel, is supported by the plunger guide cup and is equipped with two lugs or vanes to facilitate plunger rotation.

The plunger return mechanism

This mechanism consists of a compression spring (called the plunger return spring) and two spring plates, the lower portion of the spring and the bottom spring plate being situated inside the plunger guide cup. The lower spring plate and the end of the plunger are held against the bottom of the plunger guide cup by the action of the plunger return spring. During the delivery stroke, the plunger guide cup and plunger are raised by the action of the cam and returned to bottom dead centre by the plunger return spring

The plunger rotating mechanism

The object of this mechanism is to rotate the pump plunger and so control the amount of fuel it delivers to the engine cylinder. It consists essentially of a control rack and a control sleeve, the top of which is provided with an integral gear ring or pinion. The control sleeve, which is fitted over the pump barrel, has two longitudinal slots in its lower end. The vanes on the bottom end of the plunger are engaged in these two slots, and the gear ring at the top of the control sleeve is in mesh with the teeth of the control rack. By this arrangement, the movement of the control rack, either manually or by the governor, will rotate the plunger even while the engine is running. It is this controlled rotation of the plunger within the barrel that gives control over the quantity of fuel delivered to the engine cylinder.

The delivery valve

The delivery valve assembly is situated in the upper part of the pump body above the pumping element, and consists of a delivery valve body, a delivery valve and a compression spring to hold the valve against its seat on the top of the valve body. Both the delivery valve body and the delivery valve itself are manufactured from highest quality alloy steel, and are hardened and ground.

The delivery valve body is a close fit in the upper section of the pump body, and sits directly on top of the pump barrel. The upper end is threaded for attaching a puller so that the body may be readily removed. The axial bore is accurately lapped, while the upper end is ground to form a conical seat for the delivery valve.

The body is held in position by the delivery valve holder, which is screwed into the top of the pump body. A sealing washer, made from one of a variety of materials including phenolic-bonded fibre, nylon or solid annealed copper, lies between the delivery valve holder and the valve body.

The most common type of valve is a mitre-faced valve with a guide extending below the valve face. The guide consists of two parts: an upper section that forms a small piston or plunger, and a lower section that carries four axial grooves on its surface to form a cross-section in the form of a cross. The guide is a very close fit in the axial bore of the valve body, and an annular groove divides the two sections. Above the mitre valve face, the top of the delivery valve is reduced in diameter to fit inside the lower end of the delivery valve spring.

Note: Some delivery valve assemblies incorporate a stop to prevent the valve lifting further from its seat than is desirable. This is also known as a **volume reducer**, since it reduces the total volume of fuel between the delivery valve and injector and so prevents any misfiring tendency that may result at idling speed when the addition of a minute quantity of fuel does not always raise the fuel pressure sufficiently to open the injector.

The plunger guide cup

The plunger guide cup is retained in the pump housing by a circlip, and reciprocates under the action of the cam provided for the purpose, either directly or via a tappet assembly. The plunger guide cup in turn imparts the necessary reciprocating motion to the pump plunger.

The guide cup usually has a line inscribed around its circumference, and this is used in conjunction with a line inscribed on the edge of the window in the pump housing to facilitate timing the pump to the engine.

Operation of a typical single-element, flange-mounted pump

The pumping principle

Fuel from the supply system enters the pump body through the inlet connection and fills the gallery that surrounds the top of the barrel. With the plunger at the bottom of its stroke (Fig 26.3a), fuel from the gallery flows through the barrel ports, filling the space above the plunger, the vertical slot in the plunger and the cut-away area below the

plunger helix (or scroll). As the plunger moves upwards, the barrel ports are closed by the plunger (Fig 26.3b), and fuel is trapped above the plunger. Further movement of the plunger forces the fuel from the barrel through the delivery valve into the delivery line and on to the injector (Fig 26.3c).

Delivery of fuel ceases when the plunger helix passes the barrel spill port (or control port), as shown in Fig 26.3d, and the delivery valve returns to its seat. During the remainder of the stroke, the fuel displaced by the plunger simply returns to the gallery via the vertical slot, cut-away area and spill port. Thus fuel ceases to be injected when the helix passes the spill port.

Metering the fuel charge

Since the plunger is driven by a cam, its stroke is constant and cannot be varied to control the quantity of fuel injected per stroke. However, the effective part of the pumping stroke can be varied to control the quantity of fuel injected per stroke simply by rotating the plunger in the barrel.

Fuel delivery begins at the instant the upper end of the plunger covers the barrel ports and continues until the helix edge uncovers the spill port, at which point fuel trapped above the plunger is allowed to return to the fuel gallery. Thus the effective pumping stroke ceases when the spill port is uncovered, and is directly controlled by the distance through which the plunger must travel before the edge of the helix passes the bottom of the spill port.

Because the edge of the helix lies at an angle to the top of the plunger, the distance through which the plunger must travel before the spill port is uncovered is dependent on the angular position of the plunger in relation to the barrel spill port. Thus turning the plunger in the barrel by means of the plunger rotating mechanism varies the effective plunger stroke, and hence the quantity of fuel injected may be controlled.

The position of the plunger for maximum fuel delivery is shown in Fig 26.4a, while

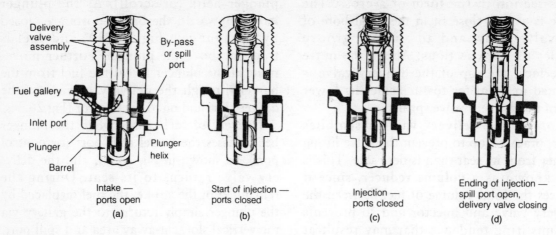

Fig 26.3 The pumping principle

Labels for (a): Delivery valve assembly, By-pass or spill port, Fuel gallery, Inlet port, Plunger, Barrel, Plunger helix

(a) Intake — ports open

(b) Start of injection — ports closed

(c) Injection — ports closed

(d) Ending of injection — spill port open, delivery valve closing

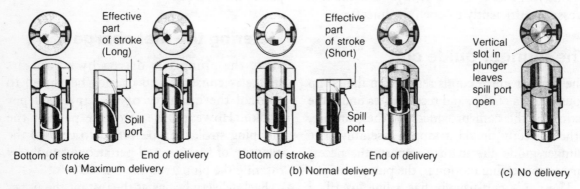

Fig 26.4 The metering principle

(a) Maximum delivery — Effective part of stroke (Long), Bottom of stroke, Spill port, End of delivery

(b) Normal delivery — Effective part of stroke (Short), Bottom of stroke, Spill port, End of delivery

(c) No delivery — Vertical slot in plunger leaves spill port open

Fig 26.4b illustrates the plunger position for normal delivery.

In Fig 26.4c, the plunger is shown rotated to the point where the vertical slot aligns with the spill port. Since in this position the spill port must remain open regardless of the vertical movement of the plunger, the entire stroke is ineffective and no fuel can be delivered. This, then, is the 'engine stop' position.

Function and operation of the delivery valve

The delivery valve, often referred to as an 'anti-dribble' device, performs two essential functions:

1 It acts as a non-return valve, so maintaining some pressure in the injector line.

2 It reduces the pressure in the injector line to a level well below the injector opening pressure, so preventing dribble from the injector nozzle.

During the effective stroke of the plunger, the delivery valve is lifted from its seat in the body by the fuel acting against the underside of the delivery valve piston (or relief plunger) and against the end of the delivery valve. The relief plunger is lifted clear of the delivery valve body bore, and fuel from on top of the pump plunger is delivered into the injector pipe, which conveys it to the injector and so into the combustion chamber. When the helical edge of the pump plunger uncovers the spill port in the barrel, the effective pumping stroke is terminated and the pressure of the fuel in the barrel immediately drops to feed pump pressure. The delivery valve instantly resumes its seat, due to the force exerted by the spring and the high fuel pressure above the valve in the injector pipe. Thus the delivery valve cuts communication between the pumping element and the injector until the next delivery stroke takes place, and retains some pressure in the line so that the element does not have to 'pump up' the pressure in the line to any extent before the next injection can take place.

In moving down on to its seat to act as a non-return valve, the delivery valve performs its other important function of reducing, by a predetermined amount, the pressure of the fuel in the injector line. As the delivery valve resumes its seat, the small piston on the guide sweeps down the bore of the valve with a plunger-like action, thereby increasing the volume enclosed in the injector pipe between the top of the delivery valve piston and the injector. Thus the volume enclosed in the delivery line is increased by an amount equal to the cross-sectional area of the delivery valve bore multiplied by the distance the piston section moves on its return down the bore. This **increase** in volume is directly associated with a **decrease** in pressure. The pressure is reduced to a level well below the opening pressure of the injector, thus allowing the injector needle valve to snap to its seat, instantly terminating the spray of fuel entirely without dribble.

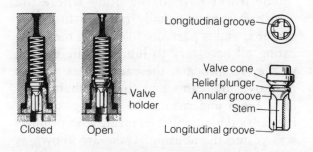

Fig 26.5 A typical delivery valve

Injection pump lubrication

The method of lubrication of the tappet and roller assembly is arranged by the engine manufacturer, since these parts are incorporated in the engine. The only lubrication required by the injection pump is a few drops of engine oil applied periodically to the plunger guide cup, through the inspection window in the lower part of the pump housing. The pump element is lubricated by fuel that escapes, in minute quantities, between the plunger and barrel.

Enclosed-camshaft injection pumps

Before the development of satisfactory rotary or distributor-type fuel injection pumps, most high-speed, multi-cylinder diesel engines were equipped with multi-element, enclosed-camshaft, fuel injection pumps of one make or another. Now, however, owing to the development of the distributor-type fuel injection pump, the multi-element pump is not used as extensively in this field as it once was.

Single-element, enclosed-camshaft pumps are still made, but these are rarely seen. In general, these pumps are simply one element of a multi-element type, and may be treated in the same way. However, because balancing of fuel deliveries is not required, the control pinion is an integral part of the control sleeve and the rack and pinion have only to be correctly timed one to the other to ensure correct fuel delivery, as is the case with a single-element flange-mounted pump.

Enclosed camshaft injection pumps operate in the same way as flange-mounted jerk pumps and so may also be described as cam-operated, single-acting, constant-stroke plunger pumps, the effective working stroke of which can be varied. Unlike flange-mounted pumps, which are operated by a camshaft running in the engine block, these pumps feature a camshaft running in bearings in the pump housing.

Like most items of injection equipment, there are many makes and models of the enclosed-camshaft fuel injection pump, although the basic construction and operating principles are the same. Therefore we will first consider a typical example before examining some of the various makes and models.

Construction of a typical enclosed-camshaft pump

Figure 26.6 shows a typical pump, which consists of the following major parts or assemblies:

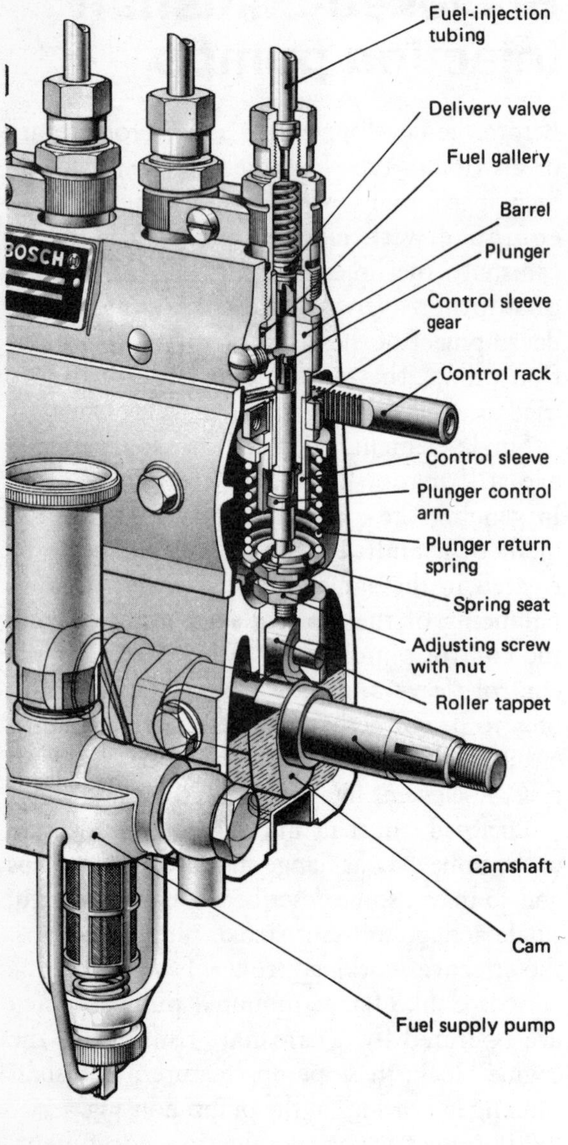
Fuel-injection tubing
Delivery valve
Fuel gallery
Barrel
Plunger
Control sleeve gear
Control rack
Control sleeve
Plunger control arm
Plunger return spring
Spring seat
Adjusting screw with nut
Roller tappet
Camshaft
Cam
Fuel supply pump
BOSCH

Fig 26.6 A typical multi-element enclosed camshaft pump
Courtesy of Robert Bosch GmbH

- the pump body or housing;
- the pumping elements, each consisting of two parts — a plunger and a barrel;
- the plunger return mechanisms, each consisting of a compression spring and two spring plates;
- the plunger rotating mechanism, made up of a control rack or control rod and a set of control sleeves;
- the delivery valve assemblies;
- the tappet assemblies;
- the camshaft;
- the control rod stop.

The pump body or housing

The body is cast from aluminium alloy and is accurately machined, where necessary, to house the other pump components. As is the case with all in-line injection pumps, a gallery is cast in the upper half of the housing, and fuel is held here prior to being taken into the pumping element to be pressurised and pumped to the injectors. A bleed screw is provided to allow the removal of air from the gallery.

The pumping elements are located in the upper half of the housing, where the barrels are a firm fit. They are located in their correct position by spigot-ended locating screws, which engage an elongated depression provided for the purpose in each barrel.

The lower half of the body where the camshaft runs is usually referred to as the **cambox**, and is partially filled with the lubricating oil necessary to lubricate the tappets as they reciprocate, the cam rollers as they pass over the cams and the camshaft bearings. From underneath the housing, directly beneath each pumping element, a set of plugs screws into the housing. These are known as **closing plugs**, and must be removed to allow the tappet, plunger, spring and spring plate to be removed.

At either end of the cambox, and bolted to the housing, lie the two end plates, which are machined to accommodate the bearings that carry the camshaft.

The pumping elements

A multi-element pump must, of course, have the same number of elements as the engine it is to serve has cylinders. The elements used in pumps of this type are identical in design and operation to those used in flange-mounted pumps.

- **The plunger return mechanism.** Each pumping element is provided with its own plunger return mechanism. This consists of a plunger return spring, an upper spring plate and a lower spring plate. Its action is straightforward and its purpose twofold:
  1 to return the plunger to the bottom of its stroke when its upward stroke is completed;
  2 to keep tension on the tappet assembly to ensure that the roller remains in contact with the cam lobe.
- **The plunger rotating mechanism.** As is the case in flange-mounted pumps, the effective pumping stroke of an enclosed-camshaft pump is controlled by rotating the plungers in their barrels. The mechanism employed to achieve this is identical with that used in multi-element flange-mounted pumps, and consists of a number of control sleeves (one for each element) and a control rack. Since individual adjustment of the fuel delivery from each element is necessary if balanced deliveries are to be obtained, the brass control pinions are clamped to the sleeves.

In almost every case, movement of the control rack is controlled by the governor, which is usually mounted on one end of the pump housing and is connected to the end of the rack that protrudes from the pump housing. The other end of the rack also protrudes from the pump housing into a 'rack stop' housing. The rack stop is an adjustable stop, the purpose of which is to limit the movement of the control rack in the maximum fuel direction and thus control the maximum amount of fuel delivered by the pump.

The delivery valve assemblies

Each element of an in-line pump has its own delivery valve assembly. These valves are identical in design and operation to those used in flange-mounted pumps.

The tappet assemblies

Each pumping element is operated by its own tappet assembly, which consists of a body, a hardened adjusting screw and lock nut and a shaft supporting a hardened roller. The shafts protrude slightly from the sides of the body and engage in two slots in the side of the bores in which the tappets reciprocate, thus preventing the tappets from turning in the housing. The top of each adjusting screw head makes direct contact with the bottom of its plunger, while the tappet rollers are held in contact with the camshaft lobes by the plunger return springs. As the camshaft rotates, the rollers follow the contour of the cams and so the necessary reciprocating motion is given to the plungers. Adjustment of the plungers' strokes is made possible by the set screws that are used to raise or lower the plungers in their barrels.

The camshaft

The camshaft is usually made of high-grade nicked alloy steel, the lobes being heat treated and precision ground. There are the same number of cam lobes on the shaft as there are pumping elements, the lobes being set to operate the pump elements in the same sequence as the firing order of the engine to which the pump is fitted. If the injection pump has a fuel lift pump mounted to it, this pump is driven from the injection pump camshaft, either by one of the cams used to operate the plungers or by a separate cam or eccentric specially provided for the purpose.

Two basic cam profiles are employed (see Fig 26.7), although there are many variations of each to give specific injection characteristics. Because of its shape, the early type of camshaft would cause injection to occur on compression stroke in either direction of the engine rotation — a very undesirable characteristic if the engine were to kick back, since it could fire and turn backwards. Consequently, a design to prevent this from happening was introduced.

The camshaft is carried in two bearings — usually single row ball races, although tapered roller bearings are used in some pumps — and generally has a thread, taper and Woodruff keyway machined on the drive end to allow the drive coupling to be fitted.

The end of the camshaft remote from the drive coupling is usually provided with either a thread, taper and Woodruff keyway or a spline to allow a governor to be driven.

Most injection pump camshafts are provided with a dot or some other means of identification on one end. In cases such as this, the camshaft can be fitted in either of two ways, and the mark provides a means of identification to ensure that it is fitted correctly.

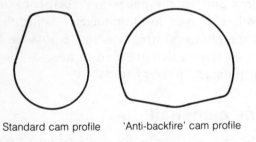

Standard cam profile   'Anti-backfire' cam profile

Fig 26.7   Basic cam profiles

The control rod stop

The control rod stop, also known as the rack stop and the smoke stop, is fitted to the main housing of a multi-element pump to prevent the control rod (or rack) from moving too far in the direction of maximum fuel delivery, and so limits the amount of fuel able to be delivered to the correct maximum. If the control rod setting is not correct and more fuel is delivered to the engine cylinders than can be burnt completely, fuel is wasted and black exhaust smoke results. On the other hand, if the stop is incorrectly adjusted and the rack

cannot move far enough, the engine will lack power due to insufficient fuel being supplied to the cylinders.

A large variety of rack stops is employed over the complete range of enclosed camshaft pumps. However, those shown in Fig 26.8 are representative of the more commonly used types.

The fixed stop shown in Fig 26.8 is adjusted with a screw secured in its correct position by means of a split pin. However, in many applications, engines require injection to continue for a longer period under cold conditions than is required under full load conditions, and a fixed stop is not suitable. For these applications, a rack stop that can be temporarily disengaged or over-ridden when starting, but that will correctly limit the rack travel under normal operating conditions, is required.

The lever-actuated stop in Fig 26.8 incorporates a manual over-ride to allow extra fuel for cold starts. It is adjusted by turning the guide in its threaded socket and securing it in position by means of its lock nut. In its normal position, this stop will limit the control rack travel for full load delivery. When the lever is moved forwards or backwards axially (for the purpose of starting), the spring-loaded stop will move away from the control rod so that the rod can move beyond the full-load position.

The automatic control rod stop in Fig 26.8 can be used in conjunction with idling and maximum-speed governors (see Chapter 31). The stop is adjusted by turning the guide bushing in its threaded sleeve. The guide bushing, which is secured in its adjusted position by a lock nut, sets the limit to the full load fuel delivery at pump speeds above 400 to 500 rpm. When the driver fully depresses the accelerator pedal with the engine stopped, the spring in the stop sleeve will yield to pedal pressure so that the rack will travel beyond the full load position and thus the rack will travel the greater distance required for starting. However, when the engine is running, the automatic stop will no

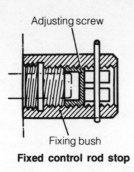

Fixing bush

Fixed control rod stop

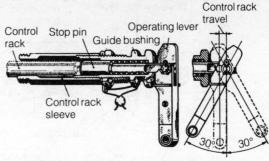

Lever-actuated control rack stop for supplementary fuel delivery for starting

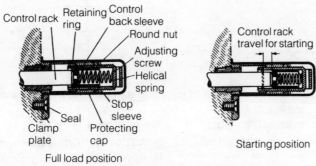

Automatic control rack stop

Fig 26.8   Typical control rack stops

longer yield to the pedal pressure since the governor, assisted by the spring of the stop device, will return the control rod to the driving (full load) position before the engine has reached medium idling speed.

Operation of a typical multi-element enclosed-camshaft pump

Since pumps of this type use the same pumping components as flange-mounted jerk pumps, it is obvious that the operation of these components will be identical with that of the typical single-element, flange-mounted pump.

Electric fuel pump control device

A number of automotive diesel engines fitted with in-line injection pumps are fitted with an electric fuel pump control device to facilitate the starting, running and stopping of the engine.

A typical fuel pump control device, as shown in Fig 26.9, is controlled by the engine control (stop/start) switch located in the cabin of the vehicle.

Operational modes

- **Engine starting** (refer to Fig 26.10a). When the engine control switch is turned to the start position, the fuel pump control device operates and moves the governor stop lever away from the engine stop (no fuel) position and into the maximum fuel position. This in turn allows the governor mechanism to move the rack into the maximum fuel delivery position, thereby creating optimum starting conditions.
- **Run** (refer to Fig 26.10b). When the engine starts and the control switch is returned to the run position, the control system moves independently of the governor stop lever,

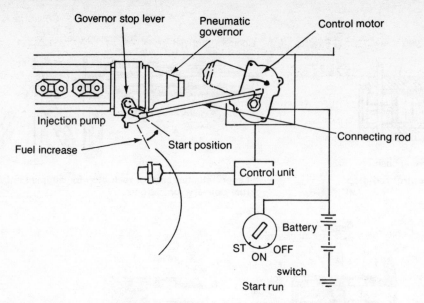

Fig 26.9 Schematic layout and circuit diagram of a typical electric fuel pump control device

and positions itself in a non-active position, about midway between the stop and start positions.

- **Stopping the engine** (Fig 26.10c). Turning the control switch to the stop position activates the control device, which moves

the governor stop lever to over-ride normal governor action. The injection pump rack is moved to the 'no fuel' position, thus stopping the engine.

- **Anti-reverse operation** (Fig 26.10d). Some fuel pump control devices monitor the

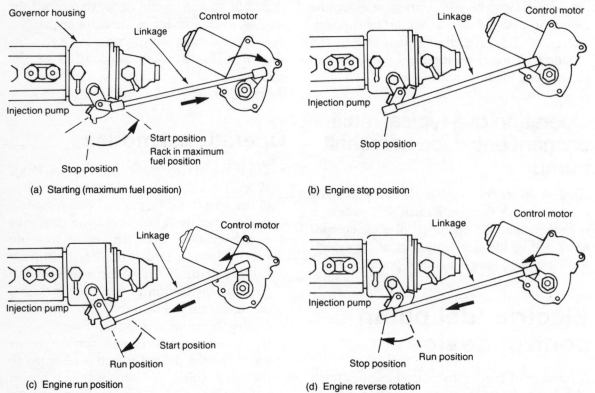

(a) Starting (maximum fuel position)

(b) Engine stop position

(c) Engine run position

(d) Engine reverse rotation

Fig 26.10 Operational positions for a typical electric fuel pump control device

engine oil pressure at all times. If the engine were to start in reverse rotation (which can happen in diesel engines), the oil pressure would fail to build up. Unless the control unit receives a signal indicating that engine oil pressure has reached a pre-set minimum level, it will move the governor stop lever to shut down the engine, so preventing engine damage.

- **Oil pressure switch.** There are two oil pressure sender switches mounted on a diesel engine fitted with a fuel pump control device. One is the sender for the normal oil pressure gauge in the cabin and the other is the oil pressure signal for the fuel pump control device.

Should the engine oil pressure fall below the pre-set minimum (approximately 28 kPa) during operation, the control device will move the injection pump operating lever to the 'no fuel' position within thirteen seconds, again stopping the engine. Under these conditions, the engine can be restarted, but will stop after another thirteen seconds' delay.

Manual over-ride

Should the fuel pump control device fail to function correctly in any or all of its different modes, the unit may be manually over-riden to start or stop the engine. This is carried out by removing the linkage between the control device and the injection pump, and manually moving the governor stop lever to the required operating position.

Servicing a typical single-element flange-mounted pump

The need for the utmost cleanliness in any service operation performed on fuel injection equipment cannot be over-emphasised. The ideal conditions as regards cleanliness can only be created in an air-conditioned, dust-proofed room, and injection pumps should only be dismantled in such a room. In addition to a suitable room, special tools, specialised equipment and pump data sheets are necessary before any pump service can be carried out, so trained personnel with the necessary equipment and information are the only persons who should attempt pump service.

Once it has been removed from the engine, and all dirt washed from the exterior, the service procedure for a typical single-element, flange-mounted fuel injection pump may be divided into six separate operations:

1 preliminary testing;
2 disassembly;
3 cleaning components;
4 inspection of components;
5 reassembly;
6 final testing.

Preliminary testing

The main object of a preliminary test is to determine the condition of the pumping element. However, a defective delivery valve, or a faulty delivery valve body joint, may also be detected by means of this test.

The required test rig consists of a reservoir or tank to carry fuel or test oil, from which fuel flows through a flexible fuel line to the inlet connection of the fuel injection pump, mounted on a pump test bracket. This pump test bracket consists of a means of mounting the pump, and an operating lever to operate the pump plunger via the plunger guide cup and so on in the normal way. A high-pressure line carries fuel from the pump outlet (when the operating lever is operated) to a pressure gauge. A release valve is provided in the high-pressure line to faciliate bleeding air from the system.

To perform the test, the rig must be set up as described above. The fuel supply to the pump should be switched on, and the release valve opened. All air should be expelled from

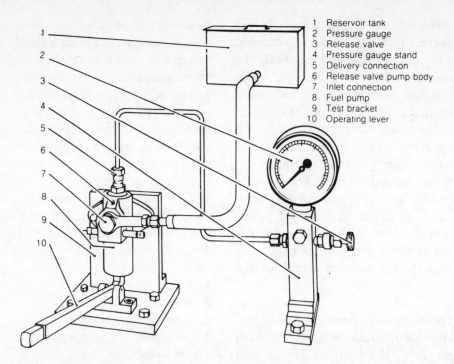

1 Reservoir tank
2 Pressure gauge
3 Release valve
4 Pressure gauge stand
5 Delivery connection
6 Release valve pump body
7 Inlet connection
8 Fuel pump
9 Test bracket
10 Operating lever

Fig 26.11 The test-rig layout

the system by pumping the operating lever, and the release valve is then tightened.

Before starting the actual testing, it is essential to ensure that there are no leaks in the test system, or on the pump or pump connections.

Note: The pump will not operate if the fuel control rack is in the 'engine stopped' position. During bleeding and throughout the test, the rack should be set in the normal running position.

The test is performed in three phases:

1 Operate the pump by working the hand lever of the test rig. No actual test is made for 'suction' on this type of pump, as no inlet valve is fitted, but the intake side is checked by the feel of the pump when operating the lever. Any defect on the intake side of the pump will allow the admission of air and will be readily apparent because of the loose or elastic feeling of the lever. The reason for this can be either lack of fuel in the supply tank or a leak on the intake side of the test system.

Any defect must be rectified before proceeding further with the test.

2 The delivery of the pump is proved and tested by the regular increase of pressure with each pumping stroke, indicated on the pressure gauge.

During the delivery test, pumping should be stopped at any pressure reading and the indicated pressure noted. This pressure should remain steady. Any falling back of pressure indicates either a leak on the delivery side of the test system or a defect at either the delivery valve or the delivery valve seat joint.

3 Defective parts should be corrected or removed. The final phase of this test is to check that the pump can readily provide fuel at a pressure high enough to overcome the injector opening pressure.

Note the injector opening pressure. (This should be found in the manufacturer's manual.) Operate the pump until the indicated pressure is equal to the injector opening pressure. Further operation of the lever through one pumping stroke only must ensure that the pressure reading is well in excess of the injector opening pressure. This test indicates that the clearances between the pump plunger and the barrel are satisfactory; if the pump fails to meet the requirements of the test, the pumping assembly will require further checking.

Note: This preliminary testing on the equipment described does not give accurate, detailed information such as is obtained with a power test bench or similar test equipment, but the results obtained are satisfactory for most purposes.

Disassembly

When the injection pump is being dismantled, the manufacturer's recommended dismantling sequence should be followed. The following sequence (by courtesy of CAV) outlines a good, easy-to-follow procedure that can be readily applied to a typical single-element flange-mounted fuel injection pump.

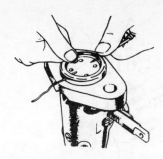

Fig 26.13   Removing the circlip

Insert a tool into the hole breaking into the circlip groove and lift the circlip. Remove the circlip by inserting a screwdriver under it. Remove the pin holding the plunger guide cup depressed and allow it to rise gently under the action of the plunger return spring, clear of the pump body.

Remove the plunger guide cup and the lower spring plate.

Fig 26.14   Removing the lower spring plate

Remove the plunger return spring and carefully withdraw the plunger and place it in a container of clean test oil where no possibility of scratching, burring or damaging of the lapped surfaces can occur.

With the aid of pliers, pull out the control sleeve and pinion, together with the upper spring plate and retaining circlips (if fitted). Before removing the control sleeve and pinion, however, note the position of the plunger vane in the control sleeve slot and also the assembly marks on the pinion and control rod teeth.

Fig 26.12   Holding the pump

Grip the pump by the discharge union in a vice with plain jaws. Depress the plunger guide cup against its spring until it is clear of the cross-hole drilled in the pump body spigot. Insert a pin or suitable piece of wire into this hole to retain the plunger guide cup in the depressed condition.

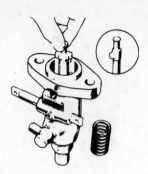

Fig 26.15   Withdrawing the plunger

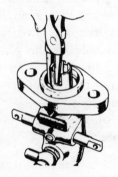

Fig 26.16   Removing the control sleeve

Withdraw the control rod after removing the control rod-locating screw (where fitted).

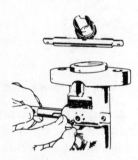

Fig 26.17   Withdrawing the control rod

Reverse the pump body in the vice and unscrew the delivery valve holder. Remove the delivery valve spring or springs, the delivery valve and the valve stop (if used), care being taken not to damage the lapped surfaces. Remove the air vent screw and washer.

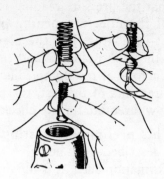

Fig 26.18   Removing the delivery valve and spring

With the delivery valve extractor, remove the valve body and the discharge union washer. Remove the barrel locating screw and washer. On removal of the pump from the vice, the barrel can be easily pushed out.

Fig 26.19   Withdrawing the delivery valve body

The plunger and barrel should immediately be mated to avoid damage and to prevent confusion when servicing a number of pumps.

Cleaning components

Wash and thoroughly clean the body, discharge union, rack, pinion, spring plates, circlip, etc. Rinse all the components with lapped surfaces in a suitable cleaning liquid. Gently rotate and reciprocate the plunger in its barrel, rinsing frequently. After cleaning, place all parts on clean, lintless paper.

Inspection of components

Once the pump has been dismantled and cleaned, the various components must be inspected thoroughly to determine whether they should be renewed.

The body

Check the passage in the housing through which the control rod passes. If the pump is used on an engine that is subjected to varying loads, this passage may be excessively worn. The body must also be checked externally and internally for cracks or chips and all threads should be closely examined.

The plunger

The end of the plunger that comes in contact with the guide cup will eventually wear. As this wear develops, it will gradually affect the pump timing. The manufacturer's recommendations should be followed when checking the extent of this wear, although the general rule would seem to be as follows:

- Hang the plunger vertically from the lower spring plate and place a straight edge across the spring plate and plunger. With a feeler gauge, measure the distance the plunger end protrudes above the spring plate face or lies below the face.
- Check the measurement against the manufacturer's figures.
- Excessive wear indicates that a new plunger and barrel assembly is required.

Pitting or erosion of the plunger is caused by cavitation in the vicinity of the barrel ports of pumps fitted to high-performing engines where the plunger speeds (and, consequently, the fuel velocities) are high. This abnormal condition is permissible if the eroded area is not too close to the leading edge of the plunger helix. The most usual position for erosion on a plunger is along a line parallel to and approximately one port diameter distant from the helix. It is rare for cavitation to affect the actual helix edge.

When helix edge deterioration occurs in service, it is probably due to solid particles in the fuel abrading the edge.

If the leading edge of the plunger helix does become damaged by erosion, it will seriously affect the pump timing and fuel delivery. Any plunger showing erosion approaching that on the helix, as illustrated on plunger A in Fig 26.20, should be renewed with a new plunger and barrel assembly, of course, being fitted. On any plunger, 0.8 mm is the absolute minimum distance allowable between the edge of the helix and the eroded area. The number of engine running hours between overhauls will determine whether a minimum of more than 0.8 mm should be established. The erosion on plunger B is acceptable, and the plunger is fit for further service.

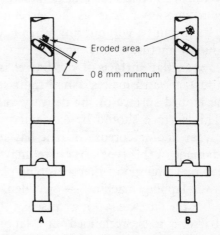

Eroded area

0 8 mm minimum

A   B

Fig. 26.20   Eroded plungers

The plunger should also be inspected for signs of wear or scoring caused by dirt in the fuel. The wear is usually confined largely to the region that passes over the barrel ports, and consists of deep straight scratches uniformly spread over most of the length of the effective stroke. The presence of fine score marks does not indicate a faulty plunger; these fine marks appear after a short period of service and do not impair the efficiency of the plunger. It is interesting to note that, while all abrasive particles cause wear, the most damaging particles lie in the size range from 5–15 microns.

Water in the fuel will also cause plunger damage in the form of corrosion, and the plunger should be examined for signs of this during the inspection.

The barrel

Like the plunger, the barrel may also be scored by particles of dirt in the fuel. Consequently, the barrel should be inspected carefully to ascertain the extent of the damage, which usually occurs in the vicinity of the barrel ports. The barrel should also be inspected for erosion, which results from cavitation — if erosion damage does occur, it usually takes the form of pits in the barrel ports.

When inspecting the barrel, particular care must be taken to check for cracks. However, it is rare to find any cracks, as the barrel usually bursts instantly, without any warning, if it fails due to fracture of any type.

The upper, flat surface of the barrel is a lapped surface, and makes a fuel-tight seal with the lapped surface of the delivery valve body. This surface should be examined for scores, wear and/or corrosion. If it has sustained damage of this type, the barrel may be reclaimed by lapping on either a lapping plate or a power lapping machine — provided, of course, that the damage is not excessive.

If a barrel is to be reclaimed on a lapping plate, the following procedure is recommended:

1 Spread a small quantity of coarse lapping paste across the surface of the plate.
2 Hold the barrel so that the surface to be lapped can be pressed evenly and squarely against the surface of the lapping plate. It is probably best to use both hands. This will prevent the formation of uneven, non-parallel surfaces. Move the barrel in a smooth, figure-8 motion, occasionally rotating it between strokes, to provide a smooth flat finish.
3 When a smooth surface is obtained, wipe the plate with a clean cloth and repeat the lapping procedure using a fine lapping paste to polish the surface.
4 Thoroughly wash and flush the barrel with clean test oil, distillate or kerosene, and blow dry with clean compressed air. Coat the lapped surface of the barrel with some rust-inhibiting preparation and place it on clean lintless paper until final assembly.
5 If it is desired that the lapped surface be tested for flatness, this may be done using mono-chromatic light and optical flats.

The delivery valve

Both the conical face and the unloading collar of the delivery valve, together with the valve seat and bore in the delivery valve body, must be carefully inspected for signs of wear or damage, and the complete assembly renewed if the damage is too great.

If dirty fuel is being passed through the injection pump, the unloading collar (or relief plunger) will become severely scored. Should this scoring be evident when the pump is dismantled, the delivery valve assembly must be renewed. This is such an important indication of dirty fuel that it is probably the first pump component at which the experienced serviceperson looks when faulty filtration is suspected.

When the delivery valve unloading collar becomes worn, it is possible that the amount of fuel withdrawn from the delivery line will be insufficient to adequately lower the line pressure. As a result of this, injector dribble may develop. Alternatively, if the valve seating also becomes worn, the pressure may be reduced too much, due to the fuel leaking back past the seat and collar. The fuel delivery will then be insufficient due to the line pressure having to be built up by the pump before the injector opens.

If excessive wear develops between the valve guide and the bore of the delivery valve body, it is possible for the unloading collar to stick on the valve seat, thus preventing the valve from functioning correctly.

The sealing face of the delivery valve housing, which makes a metal-to-metal contact with the lapped upper face of the pump barrel, should be inspected for evidence of leakage. This will take the form of fine, irregular radial tracks on the surface.

If the tracks are not very deep, they may be removed by lapping on a lapping plate as described previously. If, however, the marks are too deep to allow reclaiming by this method, the complete delivery valve assembly should be renewed.

The upper surface of the delivery valve that is in contact with the delivery valve sealing washer should also be checked for any signs of damage. If there is severe damage, the delivery valve assembly must be renewed, but minor damage at this point can be rectified in the following way:

1 Cover the precision lapped surface of the delivery valve with masking tape or some similar protective covering that can be easily removed.
2 Carefully secure the delivery valve body in a lathe fitted with a three-jaw chuck, placing small pieces of soft metal such as copper between the jaws of the chuck and the delivery valve threads. Wrap a piece of fine emery cloth (320 grit) around a piece of flat metal. As the body is rotated in the lathe, bring the emery cloth into contact with the washer mating surface, at the same angle as that to which the surface was originally ground. This angle is important, and must not be changed.
3 When a perfectly smooth, clean surface is obtained, polish it with a piece of crocus cloth using the above procedure.
4 Remove the delivery valve body from the lathe and remove the protective covering. Thoroughly wash the body in clean fuel or kerosene, blow off with clean compressed air, and place it on clean lintless paper.

The delivery valve holder should also be inspected, with particular attention being paid to the threads and the lower surface of the holder that comes in contact with the delivery valve sealing washer. If this surface needs attention, it may be gripped in a three-jaw lathe chunk and dressed in a similar manner to that previously outlined for dressing the upper surface of the delivery valve body. If a delivery valve stop is fitted as in the CAV CC size pump, for example, it should be checked for tightness of fit.

The delivery valve sealing washer should always be discarded and replaced with a new one when the injection pump is being reconditioned. If this is not done, fuel leakage could result from 'channelling' between the delivery valve sealing washing and its mating surfaces.

The delivery valve spring and stop (if fitted) should be carefully tested and examined for any possible defects. A broken or weak spring has a marked effect on the fuel delivery to the engine, and thus has a serious influence on the engine's performance.

The plunger guide cup

The base of the plunger guide cup should be checked for wear at the point where it makes contact with the engine tappet. In time, a depression will develop in the guide cup surface, and as this progresses it will gradually affect the pump timing. The manufacturer's specifications should be checked to ascertain the maximum allowable wear, but a figure of 0.38 mm would seem to be generally acceptable. Once the plunger guide cup becomes worn to excess, it must be renewed.

The plunger return spring

The plunger return spring should be carefully inspected for cracks, fractures or any other damage, and tested on a spring tester to determine whether its tension is sufficient for efficient operation.

The control sleeve

If the teeth on the control sleeve pinion show signs of excessive wear, the control sleeve must be renewed. It must also be renewed if the vertical slots in its lower end are excessively worn.

The control rack

The teeth on the control rack should be checked for wear, and the rack renewed if necessary. The amount of movement between the rack and pinion has a direct bearing on fuel metering efficiency, and so must directly affect engine performance. For this reason, it is desirable to keep the amount of movement between the rack and pinion to a minimum. The body of the rack must also be inspected for wear to ensure that it is not a sloppy fit in the pump housing.

As linkage wear will have a detrimental effect on engine performance, the clevis pin holes in either end of the control rack must be examined for signs of excessive wear, the presence of which will also indicate the necessity for renewal of the control rack.

Erosion plugs (or pressure screws)

Erosion plugs, or pressure screws, are used in some fuel injection pumps to prevent erosion damage to the pump body. Body erosion, which seems most likely to occur in large-capacity pumps working at high pressures and speeds, takes place on the plunger upstroke when the metering edge of the helix reaches the lower edge of the spill port. At this point, a high-velocity jet of fuel is released from the barrel into the fuel gallery in the pump body. The force with which this jet of fuel strikes the gallery wall is so great that in time it will erode the hardest metal. To prevent erosion damage to the pump body, a hard, erosion-resistant, replaceable metal plug — known either as an erosion plug or a pressure screw is fitted to the pump housing at a position where it will bear the attack of the eroding fuel.

After the fuel has struck the plug, its force is lost, and the high-pressure fuel disperses throughout the rest of the fuel in the gallery.

If inspection of the plug reveals signs of erosion, the depth of the affected area should be measured. The maximum allowable depth of erosion varies, but 0.5 mm would seem to be a fairly acceptable figure. Continued erosion of the erosion plug beyond service limits may result in irreparable damage to the pump body.

Reassembly

Before reassembly, all pump components must be thoroughly cleaned and oiled. The plunger and barrel should be reassembled while completely coated with clean test oil. The parts of the lower section of the pump should be oiled with test oil or clean lubricating oil. The injection pump should be reassembled by working in the reverse order to the dismantling sequence, particular attention being paid to the following points:

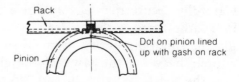

Fig 26.21   Rack-pinion timing

- The barrel must be placed in the pump body so that its locating groove aligns with the locating screw hole. When the barrel locating screw is fitted it should not bottom on the barrel, which should be left free to move slightly up and down. If this slight movement cannot be felt, it indicates that the locating screw spigot is not correctly engaged in the barrel locating groove, and the barrel must be repositioned.
- When the control sleeve is fitted, take care to ensure that timing marks on the control sleeve pinion and the control rack are carefully aligned.

- Start the plunger squarely when entering it in the barrel, so that it will move down the barrel under its own weight. When the plunger is inserted in the barrel, turn it so that the marked end of the plunger vane fits into the marked control sleeve slot (see Fig 26.22). The mark on the plunger vane must coincide with the mark on the control sleeve to properly locate the plunger helix in relation to the barrel spill port.
- Position the plunger guide cup retaining circlip so that the ends are not less than 20 mm from the removal slot.
- When the injection pump is fully reassembled, hold it horizontally with the control rack vertical. The rack should settle to its lower extreme due to its own weight.

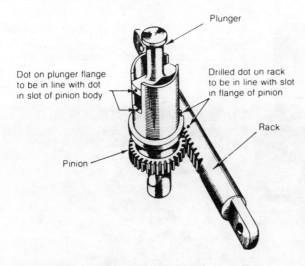

Fig 26.22 Internal pump timing

Dot on plunger flange to be in line with dot in slot of pinion body

Plunger

Drilled dot on rack to be in line with slot in flange of pinion

Rack

Pinion

Final testing

When the injection pump has been reassembled, it must be subjected to several tests before it may be declared ready for use. For the sake of clarity, the testing may be divided into two phases — static testing and dynamic testing.

Static testing

Static testing usually involves three operations: testing for leaks; checking the spill cut-off point; and checking the 'dead rack' setting.

1 **Testing for leaks.** This is sometimes referred to as a 'gallery air test'. It may be performed either with the pump completely assembled, or (provided that a suitable bridge piece is bolted to the underside of the flange to support the plunger foot) without the guide cup, spring, pinion and associated components. This test is carried out as follows:

- Ensure that the air vent is fitted to the pump body, and connect a compressed air line to the fuel inlet connection of the pump.
- Apply air at a pressure of 350 kPa and immerse the complete pump in test oil. This pressure should not be sufficient to open the delivery valve, and no air should escape from the delivery valve holder.
- Watch closely for bubbles, which indicate that air is escaping from the pump. Bubbles issuing from the top of the pump could mean that the delivery valve washer is leaking, and bubbles issuing from the bottom of the pump could indicate a leak at the barrel-to-housing seat. It is possible that some air will escape through the clearance between the plunger and barrel, but this can be disregarded at this stage since excessive clearance will show up during subsequent tests.

Any defects revealed by this test should be corrected before proceeding further.

2 **Checking the spill cut-off point.** Before checking the spill cut-off point or checking the dead rack setting, the injection pump should be fitted to a cambox and the cambox mounted on a calibrating machine.

Note: A cambox is a device designed to operate a flange-mounted fuel injection pump 'on the bench'. It consists of a housing, a camshaft and one or more tappets (or cam followers). The number of cam lobes and cam followers depends on the number of pumps it is designed to operate. When the pump is mounted on the cambox and the camshaft is turned, the pump is operated as it would be on the engine. In this way the pump can be tested on the bench.

A calibrating machine or injection pump test bench is a machine on which injection pumps are fitted to ascertain their performance and to make any adjustments. Basically, a test bench consists of:

- a horizontal mounting table with suitable clamps, adaptors and fittings to carry the large variety of injection pumps;
- a horizontal drive coupling shaft, some distance above the mounting table, driven through a variable speed mechanism by an electric motor;
- a revolution counter connected to the drive coupling to register the pump camshaft rpm;
- a test oil supply tank and fuel supply system — the test oil supply pressure is variable by means of a control, and a pressure gauge is included to indicate the pressure of the supply to the pump;
- a set of special test injectors mounted to discharge into a set of graduated test tubes — an automatic cut-off device allows only a specified number of injections (usually 100) to enter the tubes, after which the spray is deflected away;
- flexible hoses to connect the test oil supply to the pump under test and steel injector lines to run from the pump to the injectors.

Once the cambox is mounted on the calibrating machine, and the calibrating

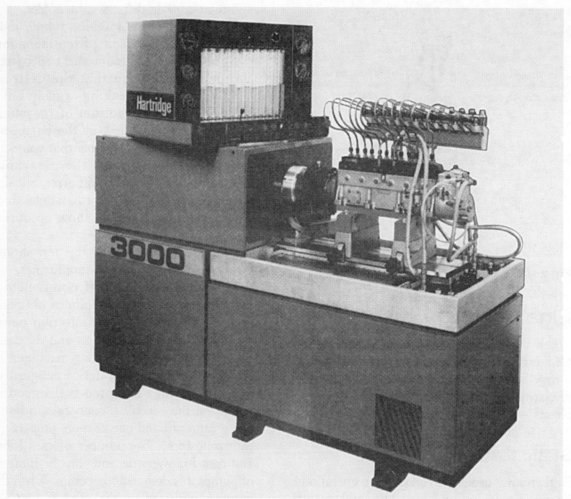

Fig 26.23 Hartridge series 3000 fuel pump test stand

machine drive is connected to the cambox, proceed as follows:

- Connect the fuel supply line from the calibrating machine to the fuel pump inlet connection.
- Remove the delivery valve holder, delivery valve and spring. Do not remove the delivery valve body.
- Refit the delivery valve holder and tighten to the correct tension.
- Fit a spill pipe to the delivery valve holder.
- Move the control rack to the full fuel position and ensure that the plunger is at the bottom of its stroke. Fuel will be seen to issue from the spill pipe.
- Rotate the drive shaft of the calibrating machine slowly by hand until the flow of fuel from the spill pipe just ceases. This is the spill cut-off point — the point at which the plunger just covers the barrel ports and injection begins.

On pumps provided with timing windows, the timing line on the plunger guide cup should coincide with the line inscribed on the pump window at spill cut-off point. If the pump element assembly has been renewed during reconditioning, the lines may not coincide, and the pump body will have to be re-marked.

If the pump is not provided with a sight window, the spill cut-off point should occur when the bottom of the plunger guide cup is a certain distance (specified by the manufacturer) from the base of the pump.

3 **Checking the dead rack setting.** With the pump mounted on the calibrating machine as described previously, proceed as follows:

- Move the control rack to the full fuel position.
- Rotate the calibrating machine drive shaft slowly by hand until the fuel flow from the spill pipe ceases.
- Slowly move the rack towards the stop position until fuel flow begins again. This must occur before the rack reaches the end of its travel.

This final test is important, since it gives an indication of the relative positions of the rack and the control sleeve. If fuel does not begin to flow as the rack is moved towards the stop position, it indicates that the plunger is not being rotated to the stop position. The engine would not stop if the pump were fitted in this condition.

If the fuel begins to flow before the rack has been moved far from the full fuel position, it may be an indication that the rack-to-pinion timing is incorrect.

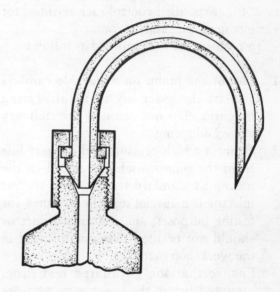

Fig 26.24 A spill pipe

Dynamic testing

The aim of dynamic testing is to determine if, under operating conditions, the pump is delivering the correct quantity of fuel at all rack positions. Since there is no means of adjustment, it is only possible to check the pump delivery at various rack positions; if the pump fails to make the correct fuel delivery, this is an indication of a fault in the pump.

To check the pump delivery, a test sheet, which may be supplied by either the pump manufacturer or the engine manufacturer, is necessary. This sheet specifies the amount of fuel that must be delivered by the pump in a

Engine type	Pump type	Camshaft speed rpm	Rack setting at full load	Second position			Third position		
				Rack setting	Max	Min	Rack setting	Max	Min
ATX	FATC/B 20000A and all future	250	32	28	142	128	24	92	82
ATC	FATC/B	250	35	30	167	151	25	102	93

Note: All distances are in mm; all volumes are in cm³ per 100 strokes

Fig 26.25   Example of test sheet

specified number of injections (usually 100 or 200), at specified control rack settings, for various specified cambox rpm.

To perform the test, proceed as follows:

1 Mount the pump on a suitable cambox and fit the assembly to a calibrating machine. Do not remove the delivery valve and spring.

2 Connect a high-pressure fuel delivery line from the pump discharge union to the machine's standard test injector. (A test injector is a special injector designed for testing purposes, and a standard injector should not be used unless authorised in the workshop manual.)

3 Ensure that the graduated test tube, mounted below the injector to measure the fuel delivery, is empty.

4 Ensure that the calibrating machine tank is filled with an approved test oil (such as Shell Calibrating Fluid 'B'), and the test oil temperature is as specified by the pump manufacturer.

5 Connect the fuel supply line to the pump and bleed all air from the system.

6 Run the pump at maximum rpm for not less than ten minutes to ensure that all pump components are at operating temperature.

7 Adjust the pump control rod to the first specified setting (in mm) given on the test sheet. Although a graduated rack setting device is usually used to set and secure the control rack in the desired position, an accurate result may also be obtained by holding the rack by hand and using a depth gauge to set the rack in the specified position.

8 Start the calibrating machine and adjust its speed to that specified on the test sheet for the particular control rack setting.

9 Allow the pump to operate for the specified number of injections. To facilitate accurate counting of the injection strokes, which would be impossible at speed anyway, calibrating machines are fitted with an automatic timing device which, when engaged, allows only that fuel supplied by the required number of pumping strokes to enter the test tube and be recorded.

10 Note the quantity of fuel in the test tube.

11 Adjust the control rack setting and the calibrating machine rpm to conform with the remaining settings specified on the test sheet, and measure and note the quantity of fuel delivered in each case.

The fuel deliveries at the various rack and rpm settings must correspond with those specified on the test sheet. Failure of the fuel deliveries at all or any setting to conform to specifications is an indication of a fault in the pump, and this must be rectified. Provided there are no leaks or external faults, the trouble will probably be found to lie in the pumping element or the delivery valve. High readings or low readings on all tests may be due to incorrect timing of the control rack to the pinion.

Once the pump has been dismantled, the fault rectified and the pump reassembled, it should be subjected to all final tests before refitting to the engine.

Figure 26.25 shows an example of a test sheet.

Installation of typical single-element, flange-mounted pumps

Mounting and driving arrangements

Figure 26.26 illustrates a typical mounting and driving arrangement for a single-element, flange-mounted fuel injection pump. Clearly, there are two main sections:

1 cam;
2 tappet assembly, consisting of a roller, a tappet shell, an oil deflector and (in this case) a tappet-adjusting screw with a lock nut.

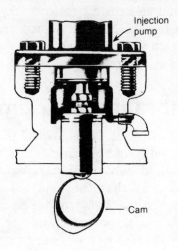

Injection pump

Cam

Fig 26.26   Details of a typical pump mounting

Fig 26.27   Inspection window showing the three critical positions

The tappet assembly is located directly above the cam, the profile of which is designed to give injection characteristics. The tappet-adjusting screw and lock nut are provided so that the piston of the plunger stroke in the barrel may be adjusted as required. Some manufacturers, however, utilise shims placed between the mounting flange of the pump housing and the engine block instead of the adjusting screw to adjust the position of the plunger stroke.

Setting the plunger stroke

When a flange-mounted fuel injection pump is fitted to an engine, it is essential that the plunger rises to the correct height in the barrel. Not only must the plunger cover the ports before the unit can pump, but the helix must rise high enough to allow fuel to spill from the barrel ports at the completion of the stroke, or full fuel delivery will not be achieved. Again, if the plunger guide cup does not rise high enough, it may touch the retaining circlip at the bottom of its stroke.

Should the plunger rise too high in the barrel, however, it will strike the bottom of the delivery valve body and serious damage may result.

For ease of checking the position of the plunger stroke, a reference line is provided around the plunger guide cup, and this should remain visible in the inspection window in the pump body throughout the entire pump stroke (see Fig 26.27). If the guide cup reference line rises out of sight at TDC, or falls out of sight at BDC, the position of the stroke must be corrected by adjusting the tappet-adjusting screw (if one is provided), or by varying the thickness of shims between the pump mounting flange and the engine mounting bracket. When ascertaining the limits of the plunger stroke, the engine must be carefully turned over by hand.

Installing and timing procedure

The following instructions (by courtesy of Ambac Industries Incorporated) for fitting and timing a flange-mounted fuel injection pump to an engine refer specifically to American Bosch single-element, flange-mounted fuel injection pumps, but are given to provide a guide to the general procedure. Detailed instructions for fitting and timing the fuel injection pump to a specific engine are given in the engine workshop manual, and they should be carefully followed and strictly adhered to in all cases.

1 Turn the engine crankshaft until the cam is in its lower position, at which the roller of the tappet assembly rides on the base circle of the cam.
2 Carefully wipe all dirt from the face of the engine mounting block and the pump mounting flange. Dirt will prevent the pump from seating squarely. Use a lint-free wiping cloth for this purpose. Then mount the injection pump on the top of the operating mechanism. Tighten the hold-down nuts or bolts evenly and securely.
3 Turn the engine crankshaft until the piston of the cylinder that is to be served by the injection pump to be timed reaches the position at which fuel injection is to begin. This position is usually marked on the flywheel of the engine by the manufacturer and complete details of the flywheel markings are contained in the engine instruction manual. At this position, the line on the plunger guide cup and those on the inspection window should register. If they do not, then the adjusting screw on the tappet assembly must be raised or lowered accordingly, until exact registration is obtained. Be sure to tighten firmly the lock nut of the tappet adjusting scew.
4 Next, turn the engine crankshaft until the pump plunger reaches the top of its stroke, at which the roller of the tappet assembly rides on the highest part of the cam. The movement of the plunger can be followed by simply observing the reference mark on the plunger guide cup visible through the pump housing window.

Important note: With the plunger in either extreme position, top or bottom, it is of the utmost importance that the reference line mark on the plunger guide cup remains visible below the upper, and above the lower, edge of the inspection window in the pump housing (see Fig 26.27). Otherwise considerable damage to the injection pump may result.

Multiple pump applications

If a multi-cylinder engine is to operate smoothly and efficiently, it is essential that all engine cylinders receive exactly the same amount of fuel for each power stroke. In the case of a multi-cylinder engine that employs an individual injection pump for each cylinder, it is necessary to make sure that all injection pumps deliver the same amout of fuel at any throttle position, when the individual pump control racks are connected together. Ensuring an equal and correct fuel delivery from each pump (when separate pumps are used), or from each element of a multi-element pump, is known as **calibrating** the pump(s).

Calibrating the pumps

During overhaul, the individual pump deliveries should have been checked, so the calibration should only entail marking the racks in such a way that they may be connected together on the engine to give equal deliveries, regardless of throttle position.

To calibrate two or more single-element flange-mounted pumps, proceed as follows:

1 Mount the pumps to a suitable cambox, and mount the cambox in a calibrating machine.
2 Connect a fuel supply to each pump, and connect each pump outlet to one of the machine's test injectors.
3 Move each pump rack to the engine stop position.

4 Attach each pump rack to a common control rod (or balancing shaft) via adjustable linkages. Ensure that the common control rod scale reads zero. (A common control rod is simply a rod, free to move in the horizontal plane, one end of which is graduated in millimetres. The individual pump racks are connected to this rod so that they may be moved together.)

5 Operate the calibrating machine at the rpm specification shown on the test sheet and move the common control rod to the highest rack position shown on the test sheet.

6 Note the fuel delivered by each pump over the specified number of injections.

7 Adjust the control rack of any pump with an incorrect delivery by means of the adjustable linkage. Continue to test and adjust the control racks until the fuel deliveries are equal and correct.

8 Mark each control rack with a scriber or centre punch level with the face of the pump body. This will ensure that each pump rack can be returned to this exact position when required. (Ruston pumps use a pointer and a line engraved on the rack. Once the pumps are balanced, various spacers may be fitted between the housing and the pointer until the pointer and line coincide.)

9 Adjust the common control rod to any of the other positions specified on the test sheet. The deliveries from all pumps should be equal and correct.

Timing the pumps on the engine

Once the pumps have been calibrated, they may be fitted to the engine. Once fitted, it is very important that each pump is timed to the engine so that firing in each cylinder starts at the correct point. To ensure that the timing is correct, proceed as follows:

1 Turn the engine over slowly by hand in the direction of rotation, until the line on the plunger guide cup of no. 1 pump coincides with the line on the housing. This is the spill cut-off point — the point at which injection begins — and the no. 1 cylinder injection marks (usually on the flywheel and housing) should coincide at this point.

2 If necessary, adjust the tappet or fit the necessary shims to ensure correct timing.

3 Turn the engine over until the next pump (in firing order) reaches the spill cut-off point.

4 Check the injection marks, and make any necessary adjustment.

5 Continue the above operation until all pumps are timed.

Note: When pumps without a sight window are used, the spill cut-off point of each pump may be found by connecting the fuel supply, removing the delivery valve and spring, and fitting a spill pipe as was described previously in this chapter (see 'Checking the spill cut-off point').

Balancing the fuel deliveries

As has been mentioned, even distribution of the fuel to the engine cylinders is essential for efficient running. For this reason, the fuel deliveries should be balanced after the pumps have been fitted and timed. The recommended procedure varies from one engine to the next, and the manufacturer's manual should be consulted when balancing the pumps. However, in the absence of the correct manual, the following procedure should ensure satisfactory results:

1 Move each pump rack to the position marked during calibration.

2 Connect the control rod and linkages to the pump racks, adjusting the linkages if necessary to ensure that the racks all lie at the marked position.

3 Operate the linkage system to ensure that full rack travel will be possible with governor and/or throttle movement.

4 Move the linkages back and forth a couple of times, and move one rack to the marked position.
5 Check that all racks lie at the marked position. Make any adjustment necessary.

The above procedure should ensure that all pump deliveries are very close to being equal. A final check may be made in one of the following two ways:

1 Remove the exhaust manifold and start the engine. (The fuel lines, etc. must be fitted and bled first, of course.) Pass your hand through the exhaust gases issuing from each cylinder. The gases should be at the same temperature. If one cylinder is running a low temperature, it is an indication of a low fuel delivery to that cylinder and the pump rack must be adjusted accordingly. Careful, fine adjustments and frequent checking should ensure accurate balancing of the fuel deliveries.
2 Remove the injectors, swing the pipes away from the engine and fit the injectors to the pipes. Bleed the fuel lines and mount a calibrating tube under each injector. Turn the engine over by hand for approximately 100 injections. The quantities of fuel in the tubes should be equal, and the individual racks should be carefully adjusted to give this result.

The individual fuel injection pumps of a large slow-speed diesel engine are checked for balanced fuel delivery by comparing the temperatures of the exhaust gas from each cylinder. As the temperature of the exhaust gas for each cylinder is proportional to the amount of fuel being burnt in that cylinder, it should be obvious that the injection pumps' deliveries are in balance when the exhaust gas temperatures are the same. Since a standard thermometer could not be used due to the high temperatures involved, an instrument known as a **pyrometer** is used to indicate the temperatures of the exhaust gases.

If the pyrometer readings are not the same when the engine is operating under load, adjustment must be made to the control rod settings of the pumps until the readings are equal. If, for example, the exhaust gas temperatures of a six-cylinder engine were 225°C, 250°C, 250°C, 250°C, 250°C and 250°C, it would be necessary to adjust no. 1 pump rack to give more fuel. By slowly increasing the fuel delivery from no. 1 pump, the temperatures could be made all equal at 250°C. This would indicate that each pump was delivering the same amount of fuel.

Note: A leaking exhaust valve can cause high exhaust gas temperature, and care should be taken to avoid confusing this fault with excessive fuel delivery.

Servicing a typical enclosed camshaft pump

Again, it should be stressed that dust-free conditions, special tools and equipment, detailed information and data, and knowledge and experience are necessities before any major service is attempted on a fuel injection pump. If these prerequisites are not available, the pump in question should be forwarded to the nearest manufacturer's service depot or agent.

Once again, the complete service procedure may be divided into six separate operations:

1 preliminary testing;
2 disassembly;
3 cleaning components;
4 inspection of components;
5 reassembly;
6 final testing and setting.

Preliminary testing

When the pump has been removed from the engine and all dirt and grease have been washed from its exterior, it should first be subjected to a preliminary test. Although this test may reveal other pump defects, its primary objective is to determine the extent of wear between the barrel and plunger of each pumping element. The following test procedure, which is recommended by CAV for testing the elements of SPE-A series fuel injection pumps, may be used as a general guide for testing the elements of all multi-element pumps in the absence of specific instructions from the manufacturer.

1 Before dismantling the pump, set it up on the calibrating machine. Make sure that the pump governor is inactive and that the control rod of the pump is locked in the maximum fuel delivery position.
2 Run the pump at 600 rpm and note the amount of fuel delivered by 200 pumping strokes.
3 Run the pump at 100 rpm and note the amount of fuel delivered by 200 pumping strokes.
4 The decrease in the amount of fuel delivered at 100 rpm **should not be more than 40 per cent**. For example, an element delivering 16 cm^3 for 200 strokes at 600 rpm should deliver at least 9.6 cm^3 at 100 rpm.
5 These readings must be taken under standard test conditions with test nozzles set at an opening pressure of 175 atmospheres.

Note 1: The fall in delivery between 600 rpm and 100 rpm is not entirely due to wear, the delivery characteristic of the pump being such that, even with new elements, there is a certain output drop between the two test speeds.

Note 2: The above test should only be carried out if it is certain that no dirt has entered the pump gallery or delivery unions.

In applying this test, it will inevitably be found that a large proportion of elements show a delivery drop very close to the permitted 40 per cent for A size pumps, and the question will arise whether such borderline cases are suitable for further use. The answer is that elements showing 40 per cent drop are still capable of satisfactory service, even for considerable engine hours, but are approaching the end of their useful lives and their future use depends on whether it is desired to rebuild the pump to 'as new' standards, or whether it is merely desired put the pump into running order and to secure the use of the remainder of the useful lives of the elements.

It must be stressed that wear on a pump element and its useful life are dependent almost entirely on the efficiency with which the fuel is filtered. With filtration of reasonable efficiency, the useful life should be approximately 250 000–325 000 km on road vehicles, or about 8000–10 000 hours' running time. These figures can be exceeded with good filtration, while with poor filtration they will be very considerably reduced.

The individual elements of a multi-element pump may also be tested for wear in the same manner as the element of a single-element pump. However, as this procedure takes a considerable amount of time, it is rarely used in modern practice when a power-driven test bench is available.

During preliminary testing, particular attention should be given to the control rod to ascertain whether it moves freely back and forth. If it does not move freely, the reason for its stiffness (a tight element plunger or excessive dust in the control rod bushes) should be determined. Also, other defects, such as a faulty delivery valve (a sticking delivery valve will give erratic calibration deliveries) or a leaking delivery valve seat joint, should be watched for. Any defects revealed during preliminary testing should be noted so that either reconditioning or replacement of parts may be carried out at the appropriate time in the servicing sequence.

Disassembly

When a multi-element fuel injection pump has to be dismantled, the procedure recommended by the manufacturer of the pump concerned should be strictly adhered to. The following disassembly sequence (by courtesy of CAV) is specified for CAV type BPE injection pumps, but may be used (with slight variations) as a general guide for most makes and models of multi-element pump (with the exception of CAV SPE Series pumps) if specific information from the manufacturer is not available.

To dismantle a CAV BPE fuel injection pump, proceed as follows (refer to Fig 26.29):

1 Attach the pump to the mounting plate of a universal pump vice.
2 Disconnect and remove the governor mechanism.
3 Remove the inspection cover plate (5).
4 Rotate the camshaft (8) to bring the tappet (20) to its top dead centre position and insert the tappet holder (19) under the head of the tappet-adjusting screw. This should be repeated for each element.
5 Remove the bearing end plate (9) and withdraw the camshaft (8). The oil seals, which are a push fit in the bearing end plates, should not be removed unless it is intended to renew them, as removal may cause damage. Should renewal be necessary, the outer race of the bearing must first be extracted, followed by the shim washer and then the oil seal. When replacing, the spring loaded lip of the seal should be facing towards the bearing.
6 The pump half coupling need only be removed from the camshaft if it is fitted at the opposite end to the bearing end plate. Should this be done, care should be taken that the shaft position is marked so that, on reassembling the pump, the firing sequence will be correct. The removal of the coupling from the taper of the camshaft should never, at any time, be done with the use of a hammer. A properly fitting extractor should be used for this purpose.
7 Unscrew the closing plugs (1) at the base of the housing and push up the tappet (20) until it is possible to withdraw the

tappet holder, after which the tappet assembly (20), the lower spring plate, the plunger spring (12) and plunger (10) may be withdrawn through the holes in the base of the pump housing.

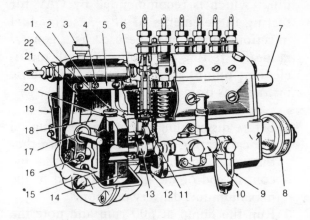

1	Adjusting nut	12	Closing plug
2	Outer link fork	13	Camshaft
3	Oil lubricator	14	Flyweights
4	Screw for link forks	15	Bell crank pin
5	Inner link fork		retaining cage
6	Control rod	16	Coupling cross-head pin
7	Control rod stop	17	Eccentric
8	Drive coupling	18	Bell crank lever
9	Preliminary filter	19	Control lever
10	Plunger-type feed	20	Governor spring
	pump	21	Fuel inlet connection
11	Tappet screw	22	Floating lever

Fig 26.28 CAV fuel injection pump, type BPE

8 The next step is to remove the delivery valve assembly. This is done by unscrewing the delivery valve holder (15), withdrawing the spring peg if fitted (not fitted to BPE pumps), the delivery valve spring (14) and the delivery valve. The delivery valve housing and its joint are now removed by means of the extracting tool (18).
9 To remove the pump barrel, unscrew the locking pin (7) and push the barrel from below by means of a fibre or soft brass drift.
10 It is seldom necessary to remove the control rack. In the event of it having to be removed, this is usually done by removing a screw from the housing since the spigot end of the screw retains the rack by engaging in a groove machined in the rack.

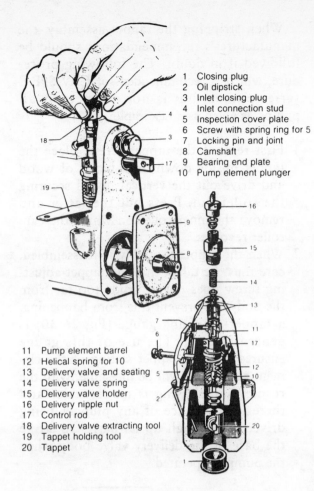

1 Closing plug
2 Oil dipstick
3 Inlet closing plug
4 Inlet connection stud
5 Inspection cover plate
6 Screw with spring ring for 5
7 Locking pin and joint
8 Camshaft
9 Bearing end plate
10 Pump element plunger

11 Pump element barrel
12 Helical spring for 10
13 Delivery valve and seating
14 Delivery valve spring
15 Delivery valve holder
16 Delivery nipple nut
17 Control rod
18 Delivery valve extracting tool
19 Tappet holding tool
20 Tappet

Fig 26.29   Dismantling a CAV BPE fuel injection pump

Cleaning components

All pump components should be thoroughly cleaned with a soft brush (not rag), washed in clean kerosene or other suitable cleaning medium and blown dry with clean compressed air. Special care should be taken when cleaning to make sure that the fuel gallery in the pump body is cleaned with the appropriate brush. To prevent rusting of highly finished surfaces, all steel components should be smeared with light oil.

Inspection of components

Once the pump has been dismantled and cleaned, the various components must be inspected thoroughly to determine whether they are fit for further service or whether they should be reconditioned or renewed.

The body

Check the passage in the body (or bushes if used) through which the control rod passes for excessive wear, and examine the body closely for any signs of cracks. An internal crack in the upper half of the pump body in the vicinity of the fuel gallery could allow fuel to leak from the gallery and cause either an excessive buildup of fuel in the cambox of the pump or crankcase dilution, if the pump cambox components are lubricated by the engine lubricating system. Also check all threads in the pump body for damage or excessive wear, and ascertain the fitness of the barrel seats situated just below the fuel gallery.

The elements

Although the elements have been subjected to a delivery drop test during preliminary testing, they should also be given a visual examination after the pump is dismantled. Elements that have passed the delivery drop test should not be rejected for visual defects unless these are serious. Too much importance should not be attached to fine scratch marks, which are usually visible on the lapped surface of the plunger adjacent to the control edges. These are caused by very fine particles of abrasive matter in the fuel and will appear after a comparatively short period of service, but they have little effect on the pumping efficiency of the element unless they are deep and extensive.

It should be noted that wear is mainly concentrated at the upper end of the element and that the lower or guide portion of the barrel and plunger wears very little, so that after long periods of service there is no serious increase in the leakage of fuel oil from the elements. Normal element wear does not seriously diminish the power output of the engine over its normal speed range, since the loss of fuel delivery can be corrected by adjustment of the maximum fuel delivery stops. It may, however, cause difficulty in starting owing to reduced delivery at cranking speeds and erratic idling arising from the same cause.

Note: A difference in wear between the various elements will make calibration difficult. As each element consists of a barrel and plunger, these components must be examined closely for individual faults.

The plungers of a multi-element pump are inspected in a similar manner to those of single-element pumps, the depth of score marks and the extent of erosion damage (if any) being carefully noted. The foot of the plunger should be examined for chips, cracks or wear.

The barrels should be inspected for deep scoring, erosion damage and cracking. Particular attention should be paid to the upper flat surface of the barrel for signs of **fretting**, a form of corrosion caused by 'breathing', which takes place between the upper flat surface of the barrel and the delivery valve body. Fretting marks may be removed by lapping.

Delivery valve assemblies

Mitre-type, volume unloading delivery valves are used in most makes of multi-element fuel injection pumps. The inspection and servicing procedure is the same as for the delivery valve used in a single-element pump.

Tappet assemblies

Each tappet assembly should be carefully inspected for damage and wear, careful attention being paid to ensure that the roller is free to rotate on its shaft. If the roller is not free, it tends to skid over the cam lobe and so causes wear. The hardened roller should be examined for chips or cracks and the hardened top of the tappet adjusting screw should be inspected for damage and dressed if required.

When stripping the tappet assembly, the manufacturer's recommendations should be followed if in doubt. The following procedure, which is recommended for CAV SPE-B series pumps, but is not correct for all pumps, is given as an example:

1 First remove the tappet screw, place the tappet upside down on a block of wood and drive out the vertical dowel securing the roller pin. Press out the latter and remove the inner roller on which the cam roller revolves.

2 When the tappet assembly is reassembled, care must be taken that the tappet-adjusting screw does not protrude too far from the body. To prevent this from happening, a tappet-adjusting gauge (Fig 26.30) is generally used. The use of this gauge ensures that the tappet setting of the element assemblies will be the same, with the result that phasing is made easier and there is no chance of any plunger being driven far enough up its barrel to strike the base of the delivery valve body when the pump is operated.

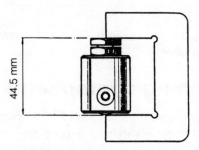

44.5 mm

Fig 26.30   Method of setting tappet adjustment

Plunger return springs

The plunger return springs should be inspected for signs of cracks, fractures, distortion or any other damage, as a plunger spring that breaks in service will cause the engine to misfire in the cylinder concerned. They should be tested on a spring tester or have their free length checked to determine whether they are fit for further use.

Control sleeve and quadrants

If the teeth of a control quadrant (or control pinion) show signs of excessive wear or are damaged, the quadrant should be renewed. In addition, if the plunger vane slots in the lower half of one of the control sleeves are damaged, then that control sleeve should be renewed. If a new control quadrant has to be fitted to either the original or a new control sleeve, care should be taken to ensure that the clamping screw of the new quadrant bears the same relative position to the slots in the control sleeve as did the clamping screw in the previous quadrant. If this is done, time will be saved when the pump is being calibrated.

Control rack or control rod

Examine the teeth of the control rack itself for signs of excessive wear or damage. Make sure that the control rack is not bent and that it moves freely, but has no slop, in the pump housing. Excessive backlash between the teeth of the control rack and the control quadrant, or a sticking control rack, will not allow efficient metering and delivery of fuel and the engine will run erratically. The governor link pin hole in the rack should be checked, and the rack renewed if wear is evident.

Camshaft and bearings

Inspect the threads, tapered ends and Woodruff keyways on both ends (if applicable) of the camshaft for wear or damage, and repair if possible. Although camshafts are robustly constructed, during pump overhaul it is advisable to inspect the camshaft for any signs of cracks developing. The lobes of the camshaft should be checked for signs of wear or chipping on their leading edges and the camshaft either reground or renewed if wear is excessive. The camshaft bearings (either ball or roller) should be checked for signs of excessive wear. The balls or rollers and the races should be inspected for pitting, flaking, rusting or surface cracks, and the bearing cages inspected for damage. If in doubt, replace the bearings.

Reassembly

When the pump is being reassembled, great care should be taken to ensure that all joint faces and other parts are entirely clean. They should be rinsed in clean petrol, kerosene or fuel, allowed to drip, smeared with light lubricating oil, and finally brought together entirely without the use of cotton waste or cloth wipers of any kind. In the absence of the correct manual, the reassembly sequence for a CAV type BPE fuel injection pump, which is given below, will serve as a general guide for most multi-element, enclosed-camshaft fuel injection pumps, with the exception of CAV SPE Series pumps.

1 Refit the first element barrel, making sure that the locating slot in its upper end aligns with the hole for the barrel locating screw. Tighten the barrel-locating screw after ensuring that its sealing washer is in place. When the screw is tight, the barrel should be free to move slightly up and down in the pump body. Repeat for the other barrels.

2 Place the first delivery valve body in position, after ascertaining that the top face of the barrel and the lower face of the delivery valve body are perfectly clean. Fit the sealing washer to the delivery valve body, drop the valve and its spring into position, and tighten down the valve holder after ensuring that the valve spring seats correctly on the valve. Tighten with a tension wrench to the manufacturer's specification. Repeat for the other delivery valve assemblies.

3 Invert the pump and insert the control rack and its retaining screw.

4 Set the control rack in middle position so that the centre punch marks on each end of the rod are the same distance from each side of the pump housing.

5 Refit the control sleeves (with the control pinions fitted) and the upper spring plates. Make sure that when the teeth of each control pinion are in mesh with the teeth of the control rack, the gap in the control pinion is in line with the mark on the plunger vane slot at the lower end of the control sleeve — in other words, the gap in the control pinion is at right angles to the control rack. Check to ensure that the tommy-bar holes in the control sleeve are on the same side as the control pinion clamping screw.

6 Insert, in turn, the plungers, with the springs and lower spring plates in place, into the barrels. Take care to ensure that the marks on the plunger vanes lie opposite the marks on the plunger vane slots in the control sleeves.

7 Insert the first tappet assembly, and press against the plunger return spring until a tappet holder (or tappet bridge) can be located between the head of the tappet-adjusting screw and the pump housing. Repeat for the other tappet assemblies.

8 Refit the correct bearing end plate to the no. 1 end of the pump body. (The no. 1 end of the pump body is the left-hand end when looking directly at the inspection window of the pump.) Install the camshaft and refit the bearing end plate to the no. 2 end of the pump body, taking care not to damage the oil seal.

Note: If the camshaft ball races have been renewed, check that these are pressed hard against their abutments on the shaft and in the bearing housings before installing the camshaft. A trial assembly of the camshaft should also be made to check that the amount of preload is to the manufacturer's specifications. If preload is incorrect, adjust by inserting or removing shims behind the bearing inner races, equalising the shims at each end. Care must be taken when refitting the camshaft to make sure that the correct firing order is maintained. If, for example,

a four-lobe camshaft, correctly fitted, has a firing order of 1–3–4–2, it will have a firing order of 1–2–4–3 if reversed. In order to eliminate any confusion as to how the camshaft should be fitted, a notch or cut is usually made on one of the threaded ends of the camshaft of four-, six- and eight-element pumps. The formula given on the pump body indicates the correct way to fit the camshaft, and it should be fitted with the notch at the specified end. However, if the firing order of the pump is ascertained before dismantling, there should be no chance of the camshaft being incorrectly fitted.

9 Rotate the camshaft and remove the tappet holders from beneath the heads of the adjusting screws as each tappet is at the TDC position.

10 Refit the inlet connection union nut, inlet closing plug and oil dipstick (if fitted).

11 Smear the mitre joint face of the closing plugs with white lead or other sealing compound and tighten up hard. On some types of pump, such as CAV type AA, a new set of closing plugs should be fitted.

12 Fill the cambox to the prescribed level with first quality engine lubrication oil.

13 Replace the inspection cover plate.

14 Refit the governor mechanism.

ISO test conditions

With more stringent guidelines being implemented on power and exhaust emissions from diesel engines, manufacturers of fuel injection equipment have had to devise more accurate testing and measurement procedures for fuel injection equipment.

In an effort to standardise testing conditions and reduce discrepancies between test results of various manufacturers and improve the correlation between test bench results and engine performance, the International Standards Organisation (ISO) has devised a new set of standards for testing fuel injection equipment. The biggest change in the testing of injection pumps is the type of testing fluid used. The fluid used for testing to ISO standards is of a lower viscosity than the previously used calibration 'B' fluid, is nearer in characteristics to normal diesel fuel and conforms to ISO standard 4113.

Other ISO standards relate to the use of high-pressure injection pipes, test injectors, test bench drive and coupling anti-backlash requirements, delivery measurement system and various other conditions.

For an in-depth explanation of the setting up and testing of pumps to ISO standards, refer to the pump manufacturer or service agent.

Final testing and setting

After the pump has been reassembled, it must:

- be tested for leaks or other defects;
- be phased and calibrated;
- have the various stops adjusted.

Testing for leaks

The multi-element, enclosed-camshaft fuel injection pump should be subjected to a gallery air test in a similar manner to the single-element pump. As the main purpose of this test is to reveal leakage from the delivery valve assembly and the barrel-to-body seating, it is best carried out during reassembly, or after the barrels, delivery valve assemblies and plungers have been fitted. The advantage gained by conducting the gallery air test at this stage of reassembly is that a confirmed leak between the barrel and body can be eliminated with less work than would be the case if the pump were fully assembled. However, if the gallery air test is to be carried out before the pump is completely assembled, a device must be made to support the plungers in the barrels so that they will not be forced out by the air pressure.

The control rack should be checked for freedom of movement and if it is found to be sticking or does not move with a free, smooth action, the cause of the trouble must be found and corrective action taken.

Phasing and calibrating

There are, of course, two separate operations included under this heading: phasing, which is setting the pump so that each element will be correctly timed to its engine cylinder; and calibrating, which is setting the fuel deliveries from the elements to give equal and correct injection quantity.

Phasing involves checking — and adjusting, if necessary — the number of degrees of pump camshaft rotation between successive injections. On a pump fitted to a four-cylinder engine with a firing order of 1–3–4–2, fuel delivery from no. 3 element must start exactly 90° of pump camshaft rotation after the beginning of fuel delivery from no. 1. If no. 3 is corrected to give the exact phase angle, no. 4 may be adjusted to start injection 90° after no. 3, but greater accuracy is obtained by using no. 1 as the reference point and timing no. 4 at 180° after no. 1.

Phasing may be carried out by using either a hand- or motor-driven phasing and calibrating machine, commonly referred to as a test bench or test stand. Because of their many advantages, motor-driven test benches, which are made by various companies such as Hartridge and Merlin, are now used in all modern pump rooms. In keeping with modern practice, therefore, the phasing procedure given applies to power-driven test benches.

The actual method employed to phase a pump will depend on the type of test bench used and the equipment available, but should be one of the following three:

1 low-pressure phasing;
2 high-pressure phasing;
3 electronic (stroboscopic) phasing.

Low-pressure phasing

This method (phasing by spill cut-off) may be carried out as follows:

1   Mount the fuel injection pump on the table of a test bench fitted with a degree plate for measuring the angular rotation of the pump camshaft. Connect the pump drive coupling to the test bench drive, making sure that there is a small end clearance. Attach the rack setting gauge (if required) to the end of the control rack, set the rack in its middle position and lock it.
    Note: A rack setting gauge is an accessory to the test bench, and is fitted to the end of the rack where it indicates the distance the rack is moved from the stop (no fuel) position.

2   Fit the fuel supply line from the test bench to the inlet connection of the pump, turn on the fuel supply and bleed all air from the pump. Turn off the fuel supply.

3   Disengage the power drive mechanism so that the pump camshaft may be turned by hand. Rotate the pump camshaft until no. 1 plunger is at TDC. This position may be verified by checking the drive end of the pump-at TDC; a mark on the camshaft or the pump half coupling lines up with a datum line scribed on the end of the pump body. Where there are three lines, the two on the outside are timing marks and are usually marked R and L to indicate the direction of rotation; the middle line is the TDC mark.

4   Check the clearance between the top of the plunger and the base of the delivery valve body — the recommended clearance will be specified by the pump manufacturer and must be strictly adhered to. In this discussion, we will assume that the correct clearance is 0.5 mm since this is not an uncommon figure, and each of the following three methods of checking this clearance will relate to it:

   • With the plunger at TDC, carefully screw up the tappet-adjusting screw until the top of the plunger contacts the base of the delivery valve body. Back off the tappet-adjusting screw half a turn. In cases where this method

is recommended, the pitch of the tappet-adjusting screw is usually twice the recommended clearance (or almost exactly so), and the required clearance can be obtained by backing off the tappet-adjusting screw half a turn.

   • Adjust the tappet-adjusting screw so that a 0.5 mm feeler gauge will just fit between the bottom of the plunger and the top of the tappet screw when the top of the plunger is in contact with the base of the delivery valve housing.

   • Remove the delivery valve assembly and use a depth gauge micrometer to measure the distance between the top of the plunger and the top face of the pump body. Then measure the distance between the top of the barrel and the top face of the pump body — since the delivery valve body seats on the barrel, this measurement should be the same as that from the base of the delivery valve body to the top face of the pump body. Therefore, by subtracting the second distance from the first, the clearance measurement can be obtained.

5   Unscrew the delivery valve holder and remove the delivery valve and its spring from no. 1 element. Refit the delivery valve holder and attach a gooseneck spill pipe to it.

6   Turn the test bench drive shaft by hand using the tommy bar supplied until no. 1 plunger is at the bottom of its stroke.

7   Turn on the fuel supply. Fuel will flow from the fuel gallery, through the barrel ports and out of the spill pipe.

8   Begin rotating the pump camshaft slowly by hand, in the direction of rotation, until spill cut-off point is found.
    Note: There are two spill cut-off points per revolution of the pump camshaft — one as the plunger is moving up the barrel, and one as the plunger is moving down. It is important, therefore, to watch the tappet to make sure that the spill cut-off point is found when the plunger is on the up-stroke.

Check the coupling end of the pump to make sure that the appropriate timing line coincides with the datum line on the drive end of the pump body. If the pump rotates in a clockwise direction when driven by the engine, the timing line R should coincide with the datum line on the pump body. If the pump rotates in an anticlockwise direction, timing line L and the datum line should coincide.

9 The point at which spill cut-off occurs should be checked several times and care taken to ensure that the appropriate timing line coincides with the datum line on the pump body. If the specified timing mark does not coincide exactly with the datum line of the pump body when the spill cut-off point has been accurately found, a new timing mark should be scribed on either the camshaft or the drive coupling so that the pump may be accurately timed when fitted to the engine.

Note: The position and number of reference marks on either the periphery of the pump camshaft or drive coupling and the pump body vary for different makes and models. For example, some pumps have one line only instead of three. Usually, with markings of this nature, the spill cut-off point is reached when the scribed line on either the camshaft or the drive coupling coincides with the datum line on the pump body.

10 Hold the camshaft securely and rotate the graduated phasing dial until the zero mark on the dial coincides with the datum line on the front panel of the test bench. To facilitate this operation, the phasing dial may be either frictionally secured to the test bench drive shaft or held positively by a locking screw. After setting the phasing dial, recheck to make sure that spill cut-off occurs when the zero mark on the phasing dial coincides exactly with the datum line on the front panel of the test bench.

11 Turn off the fuel supply to the pump and remove the gooseneck spill pipe and the delivery valve holder from no. 1 element. Wash and refit the delivery valve, spring and delivery valve holder to no. 1 element.

12 Remove the delivery valve holder, delivery valve and spring from the next element in firing order of the pump (i.e. no. 5 element from a six-element pump, firing 1–5–3–6–2–4). Replace the delivery valve holder and attach the gooseneck spill pipe.

13 Turn on the fuel supply to the pump and rotate the test bench drive shaft in the correct direction by hand until spill cut-off occurs. The appropriate degree marking on the phasing dial — 60° for a six-element pump or 90° for a four-element pump — should now coincide with the datum line on the front of the test bench panel. If this is not the case, the element tappet-adjusting screw must be adjusted so that spill cut-off does occur when the appropriate lines coincide. If spill cut-off occurs too soon, the tappet-adjusting screw must be screwed down into the tappet; if spill cut-off occurs too late, it must be screwed upwards.

Note: If tappet-adjusting screws are used — in some particular pumps they are not — the lock nuts must be securely tightened after each adjustment has been made.

14 Turn off the fuel supply, remove the gooseneck spill pipe and delivery valve holder, wash and refit the delivery valve components, and check the angles between spill cut-off points of the remaining elements (in correct firing order) as previously described, making any necessary adjustments.

Note: The normal tolerance allowed between successive injections is half a degree.

15 After all adjustments have been made, a final check should be carried out, starting at no. 1 element and proceeding in the correct firing order, to make sure that the spill cut-off point of each element occurs at exactly the specified number of degrees of camshaft rotation.

High-pressure phasing

This is similar to low-pressure phasing in that the spill cut-off point of each element is found when the flow of fuel from the top of the delivery valve holder ceases. It differs from the low-pressure phasing, however, in that the pressure of the test oil used is much higher and that it is not necessary to remove the delivery valve and spring in order to find the spill cut-off point.

To enable high-pressure phasing to be performed, the test bench must be fitted with a fuel supply pump capable of delivering fuel to the injection pump at a pressure approaching 2000 kPa. When the high-pressure fuel enters the fuel gallery of the injection pump and the top of the element plunger is below the barrel ports, it flows from the gallery into the barrel via the ports and acts on the underside of the delivery valve. The pressure of the fuel exerts a force on the delivery valve that overcomes the force exerted by the valve spring and lifts the valve off its seat, allowing fuel to flow from the top of the valve holder. When the plunger moves up the barrel and closes the inlet and spill ports, high-pressure fuel can no longer flow from the pump gallery; the delivery valve returns to its seat, the flow of fuel from the valve holder ceases and so the spill cut-off point is determined.

High-pressure phasing techniques vary according to the make and model of the test bench used. The following procedure should serve as a useful guide for most high-pressure phasing operations:

1   Make sure that the storage tank of the test bench is filled with clean test oil and prime the high-pressure lift pump (if necessary).
2   Mount the pump on the test bench and connect the flexible pipe from the pressure connection of the machine to the fuel inlet connection of the injection pump, using an adaptor if necessary.
3   Attach the gooseneck phasing pipe to no. 1 pump element and attach a small drain funnel with an affixed length of suitable tubing to the straight, lower section of the gooseneck phasing pipe. Insert the free end of the tubing into the return connection of the test bench so that test oil flowing from no. 1 element will be returned via the tubing to the storage tank of the test bench.
4   Connect the injector pipes to the remaining elements of the pump.
5   Slacken the phasing dial locking screw so that the phasing dial may be rotated freely on the spindle and set the spindle clutch of the test bench in the off or neutral position for phasing.
6   Use the tommy bar provided to rotate the spindle by hand until no. 1 plunger is at TDC.
7   Check the clearance between the top of the plunger and the base of the delivery valve housing as described previously and adjust this clearance if necessary. Rotate the drive spindle of the test bench by hand in the correct direction of rotation until no. 1 plunger is at BDC.
8   Set the test bench controls for pressure feed according to the instruction book, start up the motor and adjust the pressure regulating valve to give a test oil pressure of approximately 1700 kPa. Fuel will flow from the gooseneck phasing pipe.
9   Rotate the spindle slowly by hand, in the correct direction of rotation, until spill cut-off occurs. Note the position of the mark on either the pump half coupling or camshaft periphery in relation to the datum mark on the end of the pump body, and re-mark if necessary.
10 Set the appropriate mark on the phasing dial to the datum line on the front panel of the test bench, and tighten the phasing dial locking screw. Recheck that the timing mark and the datum line coincide at spill cut-off point.
11 Stop the test bench motor, remove the gooseneck phasing pipe from no. 1 element and fit the injector pipe. Remove

the injector pipe from the next element in firing order, and attach the gooseneck phasing pipe. Start the test bench motor and adjust the test oil pressure to 1700 kPa. Find the spill cut-off point for this element as for no. 1 element, and make any necessary adjustments to give the correct phase angle.

12 Check the spill cut-off points of the remaining elements in correct firing order, and make any necessary adjustments to the phase angles. When all adjustments have been made, a final check should be carried out, starting at no. 1 element and proceeding in firing order, to make sure that all phase angles are correct.

Electronic (or stroboscopic) phasing

This refers to the modern trend in phasing systems. With this system, the pump is run on the test bench and the spray from the injectors triggers an electronic circuit. When the circuit is triggered, a neon light is flashed and this light falls on the phasing dial. Due to the very short duration of the light, the phasing dial appears to be stationary every time the light flashes and the angular rotation between successive firings can be instantly and conveniently seen. Thus the phasing operation is carried out with the pump operating, all phase angles can be very quickly seen, and rapid adjustments can be made and checked.

Calibrating

As explained previously, it is imperative that each cylinder of a multi-cylinder engine be supplied with exactly the same amount of fuel if the engine is to operate smoothly, and that each cylinder receive the correct amount of fuel if the engine is to operate efficiently. In order to achieve this objective, the pumping elements of a multi-element, enclosed-camshaft pump must be adjusted so that the amount of fuel delivered by the elements is equal and correct for any control rack setting.

This operation is called **calibrating** and, before it is attempted, a test sheet for the pump concerned and a power-driven test bench must be available.

To calibrate a multi-element, enclosed camshaft pump proceed as follows:

1 Mount the pump on the table of the test bench, ensuring that there is a minimum clearance of 0.5 mm between the pump coupling and the drive coupling of the machine. Connect the fuel supply line to the pump inlet connection and the delivery lines from the various elements to the pump's test injectors. Fill the cambox with lubricating oil and attach a rack travel indicator to the end of the control rod. Disconnect the governor linkage if a governor is fitted.

2 Turn on the fuel to the pump, move the control rod to its mid-travel position and run the pump at approximately 400 rpm. Either open the bleed screws on the pump body or loosen the delivery lines and bleed all air from the pump. Continue to run for about ten minutes to ensure that the pump is at operating temperature.

3 Stop the test bench. Move the control rod to the no-fuel position first, and then advance it towards the maximum fuel position for the distance first specified (in mm) on the test sheet. Start the test bench and adjust its speed to the lower figure stated on the test sheet. Operate the test bench controls to direct the fuel delivered by the test injectors of the machine into the graduated measuring test tubes and to automatically cut off at the specified number of 'shots'. Stop the test bench and compare the quantity of test oil in the test tubes with the figure given on the test sheet for a pump using the corresponding diameter plungers.

Note: The 'size' of a pump (A size, B size, etc.) refers to the stroke of the pump. Each size pump may be fitted with a variety of plungers to provide a variety of deliveries to suit engines of different sizes.

If the variation in the reading of the test tubes is not within the limits specified by the test sheet, adjustment must be made. To do this, slacken the screw clamping the pinion to the control sleeve, and, by inserting a small pin in the tommy-hole in the regulating sleeve, move it in the required direction as follows:

- For elements with a right-hand helix, rotate the sleeve to the right to increase delivery and to the left to decrease delivery.
- For elements with a left-hand helix, rotate the sleeve to the left to increase delivery and to the right to decrease delivery.

When corrected, the pump should be run again and the variation in delivery of the elements should not exceed ±2.5 per cent.

Camshaft speed (rpm)	Plunger diameter (mm)	Delivery at given control rod openings					
		7 mm		9 mm		12 mm	
		Min	Max	Min	Max	Min	Max
200	6.5	1.4	1.8	2.3	3.2	4.4	5.2
	6.0	0.6	1.0	1.4	2.1	3.1	3.6
	5.0	0.3	0.9	1.1	1.7	2.1	2.7
1000	6.5	1.9	2.5	2.6	3.4	4.9	5.7
	6.0	1.0	1.4	1.5	2.3	3.3	3.9
	5.0	0.9	1.2	1.2	1.9	2.4	3.0

Delivery quantities in cm^3 per 100

Fig 26.31   Test sheet

4 With the control rod settings as specified by the test sheet (e.g. 6, 9 and 12 mm), run the test bench at the specified speeds (e.g. 200 and 600 rpm) for each setting and compare the amount of fuel delivered by each element for the specified number of injections with the amount specified on the test sheet. If the deliveries are within the limits stated by the test sheet, no further adjustment is necessary. If, however, the deliveries are not within the limits specified, compromise adjustments should be made. It may be necessary, for example, to set one element's delivery near to

maximum when the pump is run at high speed to ensure that the delivery at low speed does not fall below minimum.

5 Check the fuel cut-off position by moving the control rod to the no-fuel position and running the test bench. When the control rod is in this position, fuel should not be delivered by any element.

A typical test sheet for an A size fuel injection pump is shown in Fig 26.31

Note: The various stops to be adjusted which are incorporated in or connected with the governor, and the adjustment of these stops, will be covered in Chapter 31.

Installation of typical enclosed-camshaft pumps

Mounting and driving arrangements

Many enclosed-camshaft pumps are mounted by means of bolts or clamping straps that secure them to either a flat bracket or a semi-circular cradle on the side of the engine. Some pumps, however, are secured to the engine by means of a mounting flange. The mounting flange carries a large spigot concentric with the pump shaft to ensure positive location of the pump drive gear when the pump is in position bolted to the engine timing gear case.

When the pump is in position on the engine, the camshaft should lie in a horizontal plane to ensure adequate lubrication of all the camshaft lobes. To this end, the pump is usually mounted with the pumping elements in a vertical plane. Should the pump be required to lie in anything but a position with the elements vertical, a specially adapted pump must be used.

Many pumps are designed so that they can be driven from either end as necessary or can be used to drive some accessory mounted behind them. In pumps of this type, both camshaft ends protrude from the pump housing and both are machined to accommodate a drive coupling.

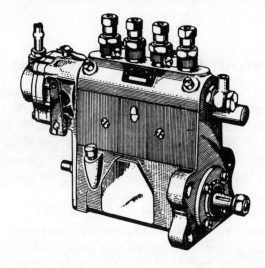

Fig 26.32   Pump with mounting flange

A positive drive is required for fuel injection pumps. So-called 'elastic' couplings, which drive through a rubber composition core, are best avoided, as they fatigue with age and correct timing becomes impossible. However, special couplings designed for the purpose are necessary since they compensate for slight misalignment between the engine drive and the pump. When mounting the pump, a small end clearance (approximately 1.5 mm) should be given to the coupling in order to prevent axial stress on the pump bearings.

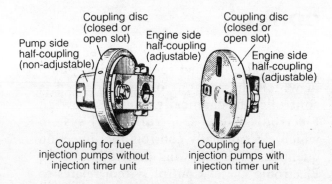

Fig 26.33   Pump couplings

Most multi-element pumps can be driven in either direction, since the cams are symmetrical. However, changing the direction of rotation reverses the injection sequence of the pump and care should be taken to correctly connect the pump elements to their respective engine cylinders.

Timing the pump to the engine

The best procedure for timing a multi-element, enclosed-camshaft pump to a particular engine is given in the engine manufacturer's manual, and this should be carefully followed. If, however, a workshop manual is not available, the following timing procedure will be found to be correct in most cases:

1 Turn the engine over by hand, in the direction of rotation, until no. 1 cylinder is on compression stroke. Continue turning slowly until the no. 1 injection mark is in alignment with the pointer. (The injection timing mark is usually on the flywheel, and quite often a cover plate has to be removed to expose it.)
2 Ensure that the timing mark on the boss of the pump half of the drive coupling is in line with the timing mark or pointer on the pump body.
3 Couple the pump to the engine drive by tightening the coupling bolts and secure the pump firmly to the engine.

The injection pump should be correctly timed to the engine. If, however, a further check is required, or if there were no timing marks on the coupling, spill timing may be carried out. This is done by finding spill cut-off point for no. 1 pumping element, as for a flange-mounted pump. At this point, no. 1 cylinder should be at injection point — or on compression stroke, with the injection mark in alignment with the pointer. If the spill timing check indicates that it is necessary to advance or retard the injection timing slightly, adjustment can usually be made by means of the adjusting slots and set screws provided in the drive coupling. In order that accurate adjustment may be made, the coupling flange is usually graduated so that each division is equal to one degree of pump camshaft rotation.

Advanced and retarded timing

An engine is designed so that the maximum pressure within the cylinder occurs at a point when the piston is just past TDC. This ensures that the maximum cylinder pressure will be exerted on top of the piston for the longest possible time, and the maximum amount of energy will be delivered to the engine crankshaft. Thus the correct timing of the start of fuel injection is necessary if an engine is to deliver maximum power.

Advanced (or early) injection

If fuel injection occurs too early, maximum cylinder pressure will occur before TDC. Momentarily, this will oppose the engine's forward rotary motion, causing the net energy supplied to the crankshaft to do useful work to be reduced, resulting in reduced engine power. In addition, excessive cylinder pressures will result, placing the piston and connecting rod components under excessive load.

Retarded (or late) injection

When injection commences later or closer to TDC, the piston will have started on its downward movement before the pressure due to combustion has reached its maximum level. But, because the enclosed cylinder volume is already expanding when the maximum pressure is reached, it will not reach its designed peak, and the force acting on the piston will fail to reach its potential. Consequently, the force applied to the crankshaft will be reduced, with a resultant decrease in engine performance. In addition, because the conversion of the heat of combustion to pressure has not been fully utilised during the power stroke, the exhaust gas temperature will be higher than normal when injection timing is retarded.

Dynamic timing advance

In theory, it is considered that injection commences when the rising plunger completely covers the spill port in the pump element. In fact, when the engine is running, a 'pre-flow' of fuel occurs before the spill port is covered, advancing the injection timing. This is known as dynamic timing advance.

Because of the speed of the plunger's movement and the amount of fuel that has to be displaced through the spill port, fuel pressure builds up in the pump element as the plunger nears the top of the port and restricts the area through which the fuel must escape. This results in injection pressure being reached before the port is totally covered. The effect increases with engine (and pump) speed, since the time for the fuel to escape through the restricted opening diminishes with engine speed increase.

Dynamic timing advance will cause timing to be advanced approximately one degree for every 100 rpm beyond the normal static timing.

Electronic diesel control

As an alternative to the conventional centrifugal governed fuel injection pump in which the amount of fuel injected is controlled mechanically, there is now an Electronic Diesel Control (EDC) system which electronically controls fuel injection quantities. The following description of the Electronic Diesel Control system relates to that used on in-line injection pumps.

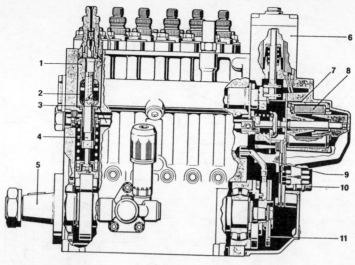

1	Pump cylinder	4	Pump plunger	7	Control sleeve	10	Connector
2	Control sleeve	5	Camshaft	8	Rod-travel actuator solenoid	11	Inductive speed sensor
3	Control rod	6	Part-closing actuator solenoid	9	Inductive rod-travel sensor		

Fig 26.34 Electronically controlled in-line fuel injection pump
Courtesy of Robert Bosch GmbH

Differences between mechanical and electronic governors

An injection pump with a centrifugal governor (see Fig 26.34) mechanically controls the amount of fuel injected into the engine. During pump operation, the centrifugal governor continually senses the position of the accelerator pedal and compares this with the speed of the injection pump. If engine fuelling is not in accordance with that set by the accelerator pedal position, then the governor will move the injection pump control rack accordingly, so as to increase or decrease engine speed to that determined by the position of the accelerator pedal.

In the EDC system, the centrifugal governor attached to the back of the fuel injection pump has been replaced by an electromagnetic actuator. The actuator is controlled by a control unit which receives input signals from various sensors and switches situated on the engine and elsewhere on the vehicle. With the aid of this information, the control unit determines the appropriate amount of fuel to be injected then signals the electromagnetic actuator to move the control rack to attain the desired fuel injection quantity.

System control unit

The EDC system shown in Fig 26.35 receives a number of signals from sensors and contact switches throughout the vehicle and, on the basis of these, determines the operational status of the complete engine/vehicle system. Some of the more important sensors and switches used in the EDC system are as follows:

- accelerator pedal position;
- speedometer;
- engine speed;
- inlet manifold boost pressure;
- boost air temperature;
- coolant temperature.

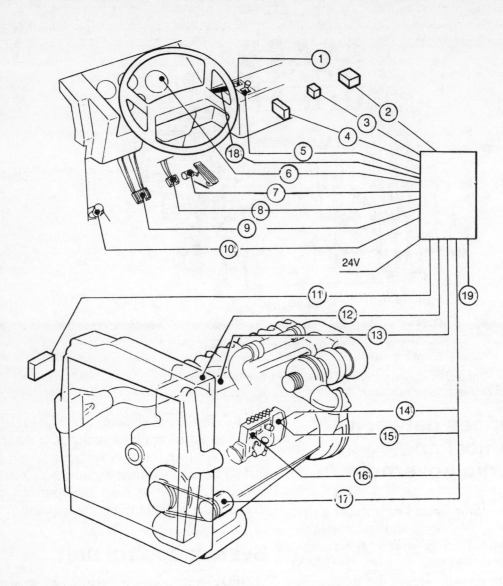

1	Diagnostic lamp	11	Sensor, turbo pressure
2	Relay box	12	Sensor, boost air temperature
3	Fuse holder	13	Sensor, coolant temperature
4	Test socket	14	Fuel quantity
5	EDC control	15	Sensor, revs
6	Speedometer	16	Fuel cut-off
7	Sensor, accelerator pedal	17	Sensor, assist revs
8	Contact, brake pedal	18	Trailer brakes
9	Contact, clutch pedal	19	Control unit
10	Contact, exhaust brake		

Fig 26.35 Electronic diesel control system (EDC)   *Courtesy of Volvo*

In addition to these signals, a number of other components provide signal information such as:

- EDC control;
- brake pedal contact switch;
- clutch pedal contact switch;
- exhaust brake contact switch.

Special functions

The EDC system also offers a number of other functions which are beneficial to the operation of the engine and vehicle. They are:

- **Cruise control.** Cruise control can be used whenever the vehicle is to be kept to a pre-set speed regardless of the load or road conditions.
- **Constant PTO speed.** The speed of the engine can be set to a predetermined level by means of a dash-mounted toggle switch. Constant engine speed is an advantage when operating equipment driven by the power take-off.
- **Vehicle speed limiter.** The maximum speed of the vehicle can be limited to a value programmed into the control unit.
- **Engine stop.** The engine can now be switched off by a key instead of by a separate mechanical stop.
- **Engine protection with cold start.** When starting in cold weather, the maximum speed of the engine can be limited immediately after start-up so that oil pressure can build up.

Monitoring functions

The EDC system also monitors the following engine sub-systems. If any system should move outside the set operating parameters programmed into the EDC system, the operator is alerted by the illumination of a diagnostic light mounted on the vehicle dash. The sub-systems continually monitored by the EDC are:

- coolant temperature;
- coolant level;
- engine oil pressure.

Whenever the diagnostic light is activated on the EDC dash control, the fault within the system can be identified by pressing the 'diagnos' button on the control panel, as shown in Fig 26.37. This will then cause the diagnosis light to flash a numerical fault code, identifying the problem area.

EDC component description

Control unit

The control unit which makes up the central part of the EDC system receives information continuously from sensors and switches on the engine and inside the vehicle cabin. This information is sent by way of a closed-loop circuit to the control unit, which then compares these input values with those pre-set values which are programmed into the system. If the input values are not in accordance with the pre-set values, then the control unit will monitor the abnormal sensor signal for a period of time so as to verify that it is an actual fault and not a voltage surge in the system. If the sensor continues to operate outside safe operating limits, then the control unit will log a fault code in the EDC memory and at the same time alert the vehicle driver.

Injection pump

The injection pump supplies fuel to the engine and the electronic governor controls the amount of fuel injected. Apart from the electronic governor, the rest of the injection pump is unchanged in that it still uses individual mechanical pump units to supply fuel to the injectors.

Governor

The governor, which is attached to the rear of the injection pump as shown in Fig 26.36, is electronic and is controlled by a control unit mounted on the governor housing. The electronic governor incorporates the following components:

- **The actuator and position sensor.** The governor comprises an electromagnetic actuator (6) that controls the movement of the injection pump control rod and a position sensor (5) that determines the position of the control rod. The positioning of the control rod determines the amount of fuel which is to be injected into the engine. The control unit monitors the position of the control rod via the position sensor and signals the control rod actuator to move the control rod whenever the accelerator pedal and or engine speed conditions change. The fuel control rod operates against spring compression and if the rod actuator is de-energised — that is, the ignition switch is turned off — then the control rod spring will release, moving the control rod to the no-fuel position, causing the engine to stop.
- **Speed sensor.** The speed sensor (7) is mounted on the side of the injection pump and records the speed of the injection pump camshaft. This is achieved by registering the time it takes for a master tooth on the camshaft drive gear to pass the stationary speed-sensing probe during pump camshaft rotation.

Accelerator pedal

The accelerator pedal consists of a potentiometer (variable resistor) which is activated by movement of the pedal. Every position of the accelerator pedal corresponds to a specific number of revolutions of the engine. This means that when the driver pushes the accelerator down, an electrical signal is sent to the control unit which signals the control rod actuator to move the control rod to increase engine fuelling.

Brake pedal contact switch

This switch is attached to the brake pedal and is operated whenever the brakes are applied. While the vehicle is in cruise control, application of the service brakes will cancel the cruise control function.

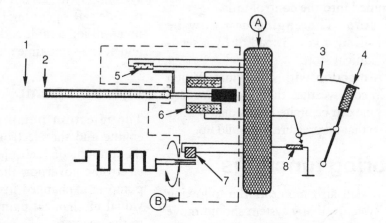

1	Max. fuel quantity	6	Actuator
2	Min. fuel quantity	7	Speed sensor
3	Full acceleration	8	Position sensor for accelerator pedal
4	Idling	A	Control unit
5	Position sensor for control rod	B	Governor

Fig 26.36 Schematic diagram of an electronically governed fuel injection pump
Courtesy of Volvo

Clutch pedal contact switch

This switch is attached to the clutch pedal and operates whenever the clutch is disengaged. Once again, whenever cruise control is activated, the control unit will sense clutch disengagement and therefore deactivate cruise control.

Exhaust brake contact switch

This switch is mounted on the exhaust brake and is used to signal the EDC control unit whenever the brake is used. This input signal is necessary in order to control engine fuelling during exhaust brake application.

Boost pressure sensor

This sensor is attached to the inlet manifold and measures the sum of turbo boost pressure and atmospheric pressure, emitting a proportional voltage representative of this pressure. This signal voltage is sent to the control unit which in turn determines the quantity of fuel injected relevant to the amount of air available to ensure efficient combustion. Smoke emissions during acceleration, which have previously been a problem with mechanically governed engines, are now eliminated under electronic governor control.

Coolant temperature sensor

The system continuously monitors the temperature of the coolant in the engine. If the temperature rises to a level outside the set operating limits, the control unit sends a signal to the governor to reduce engine fuelling and subsequently engine power output. At the same time, the driver is warned of the overheating problem by means of the diagnostic warning light on the vehicle dash.

Charge air temperature sensor

The system constantly monitors the temperature of the air entering the engine. This sensor is mounted on the intake manifold and is able to detect changes in air temperature in order to determine engine fuelling relevant to how cold or hot the air flow is into the engine.

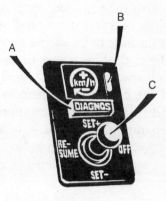

A   Diagnostic button

B   Diagnostic lamp

C   Toggle switch

Fig 26.37 **EDC fault diagnosis monitor and dash control unit**
Courtesy of Volvo

EDC dash control unit

The control unit, as shown in Fig 26.37, is mounted on the vehicle dash and consists of three components, a 'diagnos' button, a diagnostic light and a toggle switch. The 'diagnos' button and the diagnostic light are used in conjunction with each other to detect and report faults in the EDC system. The control unit monitors the sensors in all the sub-systems and generates fault codes should malfunctions occur. If the system develops a problem, a fault code is stored in the control unit memory and at the same time the diagnostic light on the vehicle dash either flashes or remains on, depending on the severity of the fault detected. A flashing light indicates a serious engine problem such as high coolant temperature. On the other hand, minor problems are indicated by the continual illumination of the diagnostic light.

The fault code allows for the fault to be traced by providing information as to where in the system the fault can be found. Fault code information is obtained by depressing the 'diagnos' button on the EDC dash control unit, which will activate the diagnostic light to flash the code sequence. A fault code 23 (i.e. low oil pressure) would be shown as the light flashing twice then a pause followed by the light flashing three times. If two or more fault codes have been stored simultaneously in the control unit memory, the faults will be displayed one after another with a pause separating each code sequence.

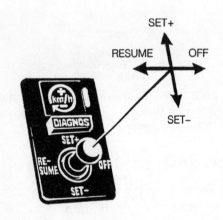

SET+	Increases speed
OFF	Disengage
SET−	Reduces speed
RESUME	Revert to former speed

Fig 26.38 Speed control positions on the EDC control unit
Courtesy of Volvo

The toggle switch on the EDC dash control unit, as shown in Fig 26.38, is used to control three different functions:

1 **Idling speed.** The toggle switch can be used to alter the idling speed of the engine. Movement of the switch to the 'set +' position will cause the engine to increase in speed in increments of 10 rpm; alternatively, moving the toggle switch to 'set −' will decrease engine speed.
2 **Constant engine speed.** Constant engine speed is adjusted in the same way as idling speed, except that the speed range is generally higher so as to operate equipment driven off the power take-off. The engine speed can be returned to that of idle by moving the toggle switch to 'resume'. The resume mode is designed to return the speed to that which was previously programmed into the control unit, in this case idle speed.
3 **Cruise control.** To engage the vehicle cruise control, first attain the required road speed, then push the toggle switch to 'set +' and release it. The vehicle will now maintain this speed constantly. Vehicle speed can be altered at any time by moving the toggle switch to 'set +' to increase or 'set −' to decrease speed.

Cruise control is automatically disengaged whenever any of the following occur:
• the service brake, the exhaust brake or clutch pedal are used;
• the accelerator pedal is depressed for longer than two minutes;
• the cruise control toggle switch is moved to the 'off' position on the EDC dash control unit.

single element, and the fuel charges are distributed in the correct firing order and at the required timing interval to each cylinder in turn by means of a rotary distributor, integral with the pump. In consequence, equality of delivery to each injector is an inherent feature of the pump and deliveries are not subject to maladjustment.

Similarly, since the timing interval between injection strokes is determined by the accurate spacing of distribution ports and high-precision operating cams that are not subject to adjustment, accurate phasing is also an inherent feature.

The pump is a compact, oil-tight unit, lubricated throughout by fuel and requiring no separate lubrication system. It contains no ball or roller bearings, gears or highly stressed springs, and the number of parts and overall size of the pump remain the same irrespective of the number of engine cylinders it is required to serve.

Sensitive speed control is maintained by a governor, either mechanically or hydraulically operated, embodied in the pump.

Variation of injection timing, which is required on some applications, can be obtained on models of the pump fitted with an advance device. Except where a manually operated start retard is incorporated, the advance device is fully automatic and requires no attention from the operator.

Construction and operation

Briefly, the pump operates as follows (refer to Figs 27.1 and 27.2). Fuel is pumped to the inlet connection (1) incorporated in the end plate assembly (2). The fuel passes through an inlet port (4) to the top of the transfer pump (3) where its pressure is raised to an intermediate level. The fuel leaves the transfer pump through two outlets — one leading forwards from the transfer pump along a drilling (5) in the hydraulic head (6), and one (7) leading backwards from the transfer pump to the pressure regulating valve assembly.

27

Distributor-type Injection Systems

The idea of using the same pumping element for all engine cylinders, with a distributor to supply the fuel to the injectors in turn, is very old — in fact, it was patented in 1917. While many manufacturers are supplying injection equipment operating on this principle, two of the most commonly used systems today are the CAV DPA and the Robert Bosch VE type fuel injection pumps.

The CAV DPA fuel injection pump

In the CAV DPA (distributor pump, size A) fuel injection pump, the fuel is pumped by a

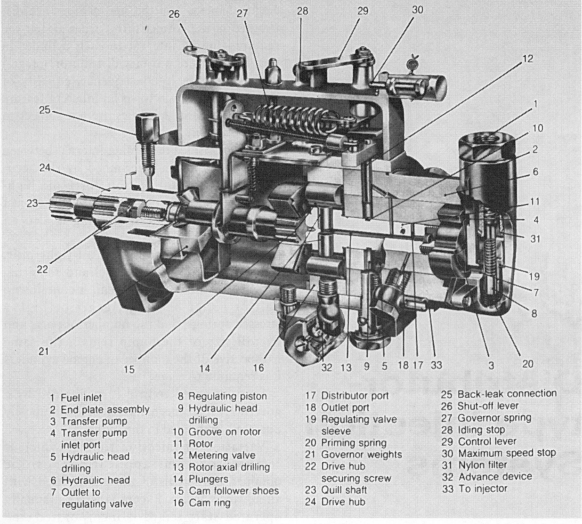

1 Fuel inlet	8 Regulating piston	17 Distributor port	25 Back-leak connection
2 End plate assembly	9 Hydraulic head	18 Outlet port	26 Shut-off lever
3 Transfer pump	drilling	19 Regulating valve	27 Governor spring
4 Transfer pump	10 Groove on rotor	sleeve	28 Idling stop
inlet port	11 Rotor	20 Priming spring	29 Control lever
5 Hydraulic head	12 Metering valve	21 Governor weights	30 Maximum speed stop
drilling	13 Rotor axial drilling	22 Drive hub	31 Nylon filter
6 Hydraulic head	14 Plungers	securing screw	32 Advance device
7 Outlet to	15 Cam follower shoes	23 Quill shaft	33 To injector
regulating valve	16 Cam ring	24 Drive hub	

Fig 27.1 DPA pump with a mechanical governor and automatic advance   *Courtesy of CAV*

The pressure regulating valve controls the pressure of the fuel from the transfer pump by allowing a certain amount of the fuel to bypass back to the inlet side of the pump when a certain pressure is reached.

The fuel from the transfer pump that passes through the hydraulic head passes to a second drilling (9) at right angles to the first. The fuel then passes round a groove (10) on the outside of the rotor (11) to pass up to the metering valve (12). The metering valve is controlled by the governor, and regulates the quantity of fuel that passes to the rotor (11), when the ports are in alignment, as shown in Fig 27.3a.

The fuel passes along the axial drilling (13) in the rotor to fill the space between the plungers (14). The rotor turns, carrying the trapped fuel with it until the cam followers (15) strike lobes on the stationary cam ring (16). The lobes force the cam followers inwards, taking the plungers with them. The fuel between the plungers is forced back through the axial drilling to pass to the injector lines through the distributor port (17) in the rotor, and one of the outlet ports (18) in the hydraulic head.

Detailed construction

The foregoing explanation gives only an outline of the construction and operation of a CAV DPA fuel injection pump. In order to

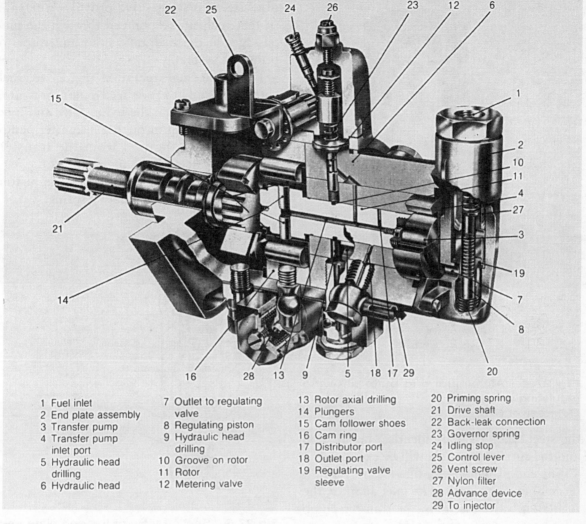

1 Fuel inlet	7 Outlet to regulating valve	13 Rotor axial drilling	20 Priming spring
2 End plate assembly	8 Regulating piston	14 Plungers	21 Drive shaft
3 Transfer pump	9 Hydraulic head drilling	15 Cam follower shoes	22 Back-leak connection
4 Transfer pump inlet port	10 Groove on rotor	16 Cam ring	23 Governor spring
5 Hydraulic head drilling	11 Rotor	17 Distributor port	24 Idling stop
6 Hydraulic head	12 Metering valve	18 Outlet port	25 Control lever
		19 Regulating valve sleeve	26 Vent screw
			27 Nylon filter
			28 Advance device
			29 To injector

Fig 27.2   DPA pump with a hydraulic governor and automatic advance   *Courtesy of CAV*

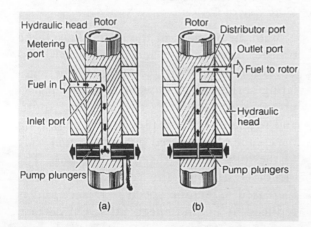

Fig 27.3   Diagram of pumping section, showing (a) charging, and (b) pumping
Courtesy of CAV

fully understand the unit, it will be necessary to examine each of the following major section in detail:

- end plate and regulating valve;
- transfer pump;
- metering valve;
- pumping and distributing section.

End plate and regulating valve

Two designs of end plate assembly have been used: an early steel type and the current aluminium type. Though different in appearance and layout (the regulating valve assembly lies at right angles to the fuel inlet connection in

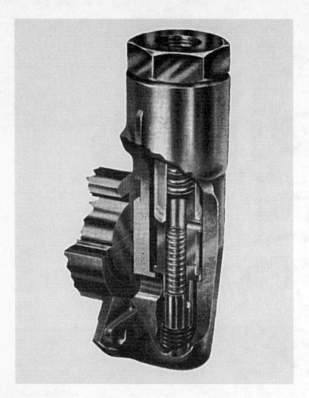

Fig 27.4 Aluminium end plate showing regulating valve
Courtesy of CAV

the steel type), they are identical in function and the current type only will be examined.

The end plate houses a fine-mesh nylon filter held in place by the fuel inlet adaptor, the regulating valve assembly, the transfer pump inlet port and one of the transfer pump outlets. It is secured to the end of the hydraulic head by four studs, thereby enclosing the transfer pump, which is fitted in a recess at the rear of the hydraulic head.

The regulating valve performs two separate functions. First, it controls the level to which the transfer pump raises the fuel pressure, maintaining a predetermined relationship between the pressure and the speed of rotation. Transfer pressure — the pressure of the fuel from the transfer pump — ranges from 80 kPa to a pressure in excess of 825 kPa in some cases, depending on the engine (and pump) speed. Second, because of its design, fuel cannot be made to flow through the transfer pump when it is stationary. The

pressure regulating valve provides a bypass so that fuel can be pumped through the fuel passages in the hydraulic head and rotor to prime the system.

During normal operation (Fig 27.6), fuel enters the end plate at feed pump pressure, then passes through the nylon filter and into the transfer pump through the transfer pump inlet. Some of the fuel from the transfer pump outlet acts on the underside of the regulating valve piston, and forces the piston upwards against the regulating spring.

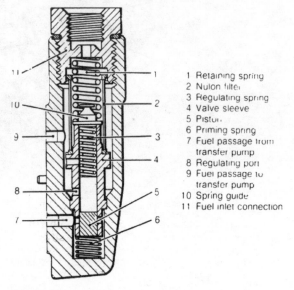

1 Retaining spring
2 Nylon filter
3 Regulating spring
4 Valve sleeve
5 Piston
6 Priming spring
7 Fuel passage from transfer pump
8 Regulating port
9 Fuel passage to transfer pump
10 Spring guide
11 Fuel inlet connection

Fig 27.5 Section view of the end plate and regulating valve at rest
Courtesy of CAV

With an increase in the engine speed, the transfer pressure rises and the regulating piston is forced upwards, compressing the regulating spring. Such movement of the piston progressively uncovers the regulating port, and regulates transfer pressure by permitting the escape of a metered quantity of fuel back to the inlet side of the transfer pump. The effective area of the regulating port is increased as engine speed is raised, and is reduced as engine speed falls. On certain pumps, the maximum movement of the piston is restricted by a screw in order to increase the rate at which transfer pressure

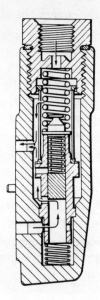

Fig 27.6 Regulating valve, operating position
Courtesy of CAV

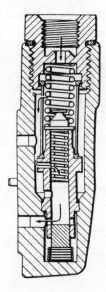

Fig 27.7 Regulating valve, priming position
Courtesy of CAV

rises. The screw, which is referred to as a **transfer pressure adjuster**, is set during manufacture to suit the application concerned.

When priming the pump, fuel entering the end plate cannot pass through the transfer pump and into the fuel passages in the hydraulic head and rotor in the normal way.

Fuel at priming pressure enters the valve sleeve and acts on the upper face of the regulating piston. The piston is forced to the lower end of the valve sleeve, compressing the priming spring and uncovering the priming ports. Fuel then passes through the priming ports, to the transfer pump outlet port, through the lower part of the transfer pump to the second transfer pump outlet, which leads along the drilling in the hydraulic head (Fig 27.7).

As soon as priming is completed and fuel is no longer forced through the regulating valve, the priming spring forces the piston slightly upwards, so that it covers the priming ports. During normal operation, fuel enters the regulating valve through the priming ports, but with these covered, it cannot do so. When the starter is operated, fuel from the transfer pump passes down outside the regulating valve sleeve and up into the sleeve from the vicinity of the priming spring. The regulating piston is thus forced back to its normal operating position.

Transfer pump

The purpose of the transfer pump is to raise the pressure of the fuel to an intermediate level, the pressure being controlled by the pressure regulating valve.

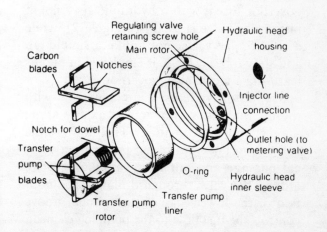

Fig 27.8 Exploded view of the transfer pump
Courtesy of CAV

The transfer pump is a positive displacement, vane-type pump, which functions in the same way as a vane-type lubrication system oil pump or a vane-type blower. The transfer pump rotor, a steel unit screwed on to the rear of the injection pump rotor, carries two slots in which lie two sliding carbon vanes. The outer section of the pump consists of a hardened steel liner with inner and outer surfaces not concentric. This liner is prevented from turning by a locating dowel in the end plate, which engages with a corresponding slot in the liner.

The transfer pump inlet lies in the end plate, while one outlet lies in the end plate and one in the hydraulic head. A fuel-tight seal between the end plate and hydraulic head is provided by an o-ring in a recess around the transfer pump liner.

Metering valve

The purpose of the metering valve is to provide a means of governor control over the quantity of fuel passing to the pumping element.

Fuel from the transfer pump flows through the two connecting drillings in the hydraulic head, around an annular groove on the rotor and into a chamber in the hydraulic head that houses the metering valve.

The type of metering valve used in a particular pump is determined by the type of governor fitted; with a hydraulic governor, a piston-like valve is used (see Fig 27.2), while a semi-rotary valve, not unlike a simple tap and shown in Fig 27.1, is employed in pumps featuring a mechanical governor.

The piston valve used in conjunction with the hydraulic governor moves axially along the metering valve chamber. Fuel flows to the valve from underneath and passes up a vertical passage and out to an annular groove around the valve through drillings. The position of the lower edge of the annular groove controls the fuel flow to the pumping element. As the plunger rises, the edge partially covers the drilling in the hydraulic head to reduce the flow; as the plunger descends and the groove edge progressively uncovers the drilling, the flow increases.

The semi-rotary valve used in pumps fitted with mechanical governors is caused to rotate through a limited arc by the governor. A groove, similar to a very small keyway, runs axially along one side of the round valve body and carries fuel upwards to the drilling in the hydraulic head leading to the pumping element. Rotation of the valve in one direction aligns the groove in the valve body with the hydraulic head drilling, while rotation in the other direction causes the edge of the groove to progressively cover the drilling, reducing the fuel supply to the pumping components.

Pumping and distributing section

The function of this section of the pump is to raise the fuel pressure from transfer pressure to injection pressure, to distribute the fuel charges to the correct engine cylinders in turn, and to reduce fuel pressure in the injector lines after injection to preclude the possibility of the injector nozzle dribbling.

The section is composed of six sub-sections of components:

- hydraulic head;
- rotor and plunger assembly;
- cam followers;
- cam ring;
- maximum fuel adjusting plates;
- drive plate.

Hydraulic head

The hydraulic head provides a housing in which the rotor turns. It combines with the rotor to distribute the fuel charges to the injector pipes. In addition to these primary functions, the hydraulic head carries the metering valve, conveys fuel from the metering valve to the rotor, conveys fuel from the transfer pump to a groove on the rotor from where it passes to the metering valve and provides the injection line connections.

The hydraulic head is constructed of two separate components — an inner sleeve and an outer barrel (Fig 27.9). The sleeve is an interference fit in the barrel, which is heated in manufacture to allow the sleeve to be fitted.

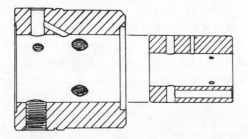

Fig 27.9   Hydraulic head
Courtesy of CAV

Because the sleeve is shorter than the barrel, and because they are flush at the rotor drive end, the necessary recess to accommodate the transfer pump is provided without any special machining.

The inner sleeve carries the horizontal fuel feed drilling from the transfer pump, the large feed drillings at right angles to the horizontal drilling carry the fuel to the metering valve, and inlet and outlet drillings. The barrel is drilled and tapped to provide accommodation for the fuel outlet unions, etc., and carries the metering valve drilling and an angled drilling that conveys fuel from the metering valve to the fuel inlet in the sleeve. The transfer pump end is counter-bored to accommodate the o-ring seal, which prevents leakage at the transfer pump. The outside of the large diameter end that fits into the pump housing is machined to accommodate a second o-ring, which provides a seal between the hydraulic head and the housing.

Rotor and plunger assembly

The rotor and plunger assembly is driven by the drive shaft, which connects to the drive plate bolted to the rotor, and rotates in the axial bore of the hydraulic head. The rotor comprises two sections: a pumping section and a distributing section. The distributing section is a precision, minimum-clearance fit in the hydraulic head, while the pumping section is of larger diameter and has two diametrically opposed slots machined in it. A transverse bore runs between the slots and carries the two opposed pumping plungers.

An axial drilling running the length of the distributing section connects to the transverse bore. Along the distributing section, and connecting to the axial drilling, are a number of radial drillings — a single-outlet port remote from the pumping section and a group of radial inlet or charging ports nearer to the pumping section. (The number of ports is governed by and is equal to the number of engine cylinders the pump is to serve.) The charging ports are so positioned that they align in turn with the inlet port in the hydraulic head sleeve, while the outlet port in the rotor aligns with the outlet ports in the hydraulic head, also in turn.

Between the charging and the pumping section of the rotor lies a groove around the outside of the distributing section of the rotor. This groove provides the channel through which the fuel passes to reach the metering valve from the drilling in the lower side of the hydraulic head. Between this groove and the pumping section, the rotor diameter is slightly reduced.

The transfer pump end of the rotor is counterbored and internally threaded to accommodate the threaded spigot of the transfer pump rotor — thus the rotor provides the means of conveying the drive to the transfer pump. A screwed plug seals the end of the axial drilling in the rotor, and is centrally situated within the counterbore.

Cam followers

The cam followers are made in two parts — a roller and a shoe. The followers are situated in the pumping section of the rotor, and ears or lugs on the ends of the shoes protrude slightly past the surfaces of the rotor pumping section. The cam followers rotate with the rotor and force the pumping plungers together when the rollers strike the lobes of the stationary cam ring situated around the rotor pumping section.

Cam ring

The cam ring (Fig 27.10) is located around the pumping section of the rotor between the end of the hydraulic head and a circlip in the housing. (This circlip carries timing reference marks and is known as a timing ring.) Cylindrical in general terms, the cam ring has one small flat on its outer surface with a tapped hole in the centre, and a number of lobes on its inner surface. Normally the cam ring has as many lobes as the engine for which the pump is designed has cylinders, the lobes being diametrically opposed to operate both pumping plungers together. The exception is the case where the pump has to be fitted to an engine with an uneven number of cylinders, in which case the cam ring will feature twice as many lobes as the engine has cylinders.

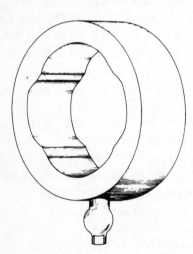

Fig 27.10   Cam ring
Courtesy of CAV

The cam lobes are designed to fulfil two functions — to force the plungers together via the cam followers and raise the fuel pressure to injection pressure, and to reduce the pressure of fuel in the injector line to slightly below injector opening pressure to prevent dribbling at the nozzle. Each cam lobe is so shaped that the plungers move outwards slightly after injection while the outlet ports are still in register. That part of the lobe that allows the plunger movement is known as a **retraction curve** (Fig 27.11). This outward movement increases the volume enclosed between the plungers, thus lowering the pressure slightly, and since the injector line is still connected to this space, the line pressure is allowed to drop.

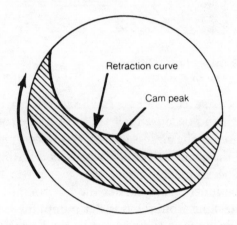

Fig 27.11   Enlarged view of the cam lobe
Courtesy of CAV

Note: As a further means of preventing injector dribble, some DPA fuel pumps are now being fitted with conventional delivery valves, located in the fuel outlet fittings.

The cam ring is either locked in position by means of a stud that screws into the cam ring from the bottom of the pump, or it is provided with a ball coupling that screws into the cam ring and engages with a piston in an automatic advance cylinder housed underneath the pump. The automatic advance system partially turns the cam ring in the housing to advance or retard the injection point.

Maximum fuel adjusting plates

The maximum amount of fuel the pump is capable of delivering is governed by the distance the plungers can move outwards before being forced together. Therefore the maximum fuel delivery must be controlled at this point. To provide a maximum fuel stroke that can be adjusted to suit the requirements of different engines, two adjusting plates are fitted to the rotor pumping section, one on each side (Fig 27.12). These plates are provided with eccentric slots or cut-outs, which engage with the ears or lugs on the cam follower shoes. The ears' protrusion through the slot provides the stop that limits the plunger's outward movement, and since these slots are eccentric, partial rotation of the plates varies the maximum outward movement. The two plates move together because of two lugs on the forward plate, which engage with slots in the rear one. These plates are adjusted in manufacture and should only need readjusting after the pump has been dismantled.

Drive plate

Bolted to the front of the rotor, and clamping the forward maximum fuel adjusting plate in position, is the drive plate. This ground plate carries a number of lines on its outer surface,

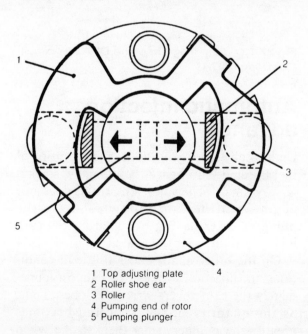

1 Top adjusting plate
2 Roller shoe ear
3 Roller
4 Pumping end of rotor
5 Pumping plunger

Fig 27.12 Maximum fuel control
Courtesy of CAV

each with an associated letter. These lines are used for timing purposes. The centre of the drive plate is splined to carry the drive from the drive shaft to the rotor, a master spline being provided to ensure correct timing.

Detailed pump operation

Fuel is supplied to the inlet connection incorporated in the end plate, from the fuel tank, by the fuel feed pump (usually) via two fuel filters. The fuel passes through a fine (usually) nylon filter to the transfer pump inlet port. The transfer pump, being a positive-displacement unit, increases its fuel delivery with its speed of rotation. Since fuel flow through the system is somewhat restricted, the transfer pump pressure rises as the speed of pump rotation increases. The resulting pressure varies between 80 kPa and an upper maximum, which may be 825 kPa or more in some applications, depending on pump speed, the relationship being controlled by the pressure regulating valve.

From the transfer pump, the fuel passes either to the pressure regulating valve through the fuel outlet in the end plate or along the drilling in the hydraulic head sleeve. The fuel passing into the regulating valve acts against the end of the regulating valve piston, which is moved against the regulating valve spring. When the fuel pressure becomes high enough, the piston compresses the spring sufficiently to allow the fuel to pass through the regulating port to the transfer pump inlet.

The fuel passing along the drilling in the hydraulic head sleeve flows around the rotor groove and into the metering valve drilling. The rate at which the fuel passes through the metering valve is dependent on two factors: the position of the metering valve as determined by the governor, and the fuel pressure as controlled by pump speed per medium of the transfer pump. Hence at high engine speed and large throttle opening, although the inlet ports are in register for only a very short time, the high transfer pressure and large opening at the metering valve allow the required large quantity of fuel to enter the rotor. Conversely, at low speeds with only a small throttle opening, the combination of low fuel pressure and small metering valve opening results in only a small quantity of fuel passing to the rotor.

After passing through the metering valve, the fuel passes through an angled drilling in the hydraulic head barrel, through a radial drilling in the hydraulic head sleeve and through one of the radial inlet ports in the rotor (when they are in alignment) to the axial drilling in the rotor. The fuel enters the space between the plungers, forcing them apart. The distance the plungers are forced apart is dependent on the quantity of fuel passing through the metering valve and is limited, as previously discussed, by side plates on the pumping section of the rotor, to a predetermined maximum. Hence, at low speed, the plungers are forced apart a small distance only and the subsequent injection is of a small fuel quantity, while at large throttle opening the plungers are pushed apart to their limit, giving the maximum injection quantity. That part of the pump's operation during which the fuel flows to the rotor and forces the plungers apart is known as the **charging stroke** and is shown in Fig 27.3a.

Further rotation of the rotor causes the rotor inlet port to move out of alignment with the hydraulic head charging port, and the rotor outlet port moves into alignment with one of the delivery drillings in the hydraulic head, and the cam followers strike the lobes on the cam ring and force the plungers together. This is the **pumping stroke** and is shown in Fig 27.3b.

After passing the peaks of the cam lobes, the cam followers move outwards slightly due to the cam ring retraction curve. This outward movement of the plungers occurs while the rotor outlet is still in register with the hydraulic head outlet drilling, and the pressure in the injector lines is reduced slightly due to the plungers' outward movement.

Once the ports are no longer in register, due to further rotation of the rotor, the cam followers move outwards to the stops due to centrifugal force.

As soon as the next rotor inlet port aligns with the hydraulic head charging port, the flow of fuel into the rotor pushes the plungers apart and the cycle begins again.

A line diagram of the DPA fuel circuit is shown in Fig 27.13.

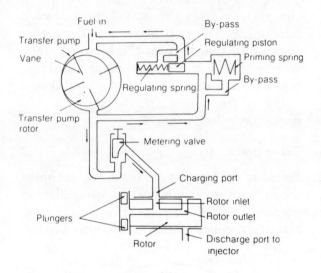

Fig 27.13   Line diagram of the DPA fuel circuit
Courtesy of CAV

Automatic injection advance

Under light load conditions, the quantity of fuel injected (and hence the plungers' stroke) is very small. The injection stroke does not begin until the cam followers strike the plungers, after having travelled up the cam lobe to a point near the peak.

On the other hand, under full load conditions, the injection stroke begins almost immediately the cam rollers strike the lobes. Thus, as the quantity of fuel required becomes greater, the plungers start their stroke when the rollers are at a lower point on the cam lobe — that is, earlier in rotor rotation.

It follows, then, that injection timing becomes progressively advanced as fuelling is increased, since contact between the plungers and followers occurs progressively earlier in the pump's rotation.

In many applications, some form of automatic advance device is also included to increase the amount of advance. This extra automatic advance of the fuel injection timing is accomplished by partially rotating the cam ring in the pump housing. This movement of the cam ring is accomplished by means of an automatic advance unit, a typical example being shown in Fig 27.14. The unit fits on the underside of the pump and consists of a housing containing a cylindrical bore, a piston which operates in the bore, and a spring(s), which biases the piston to one extreme of the piston to one extreme of the cylinder. The piston connects to a ball-headed screw or stud, which screws into the cam ring, and the spring force is in such a direction that the cam ring is held in the direction of pump rotation, namely in the retarded position. The piston is moved against the spring by fuel from the transfer pump. As the pump speed and transfer pump pressure rise, so the piston is moved progressively to compress the spring, thereby advancing the injection timing in proportion to the pump's speed of rotation. The fuel supply to the automatic advance mechanism passes from the hydraulic head horizontal drilling (which leads from the transfer pump), travels down through a hollow locating stud that secures the hydraulic head in the housing, and passes through a radial drilling in the locating stud to flow into the automatic advance cylinder through a drilling in the advance unit housing.

In some instances, a means of cutting off the fuel supply to the automatic advance unit when starting from cold is incorporated in the locating stud; this may be either a cock or a cable-actuated valve. If automatic advance cannot be prevented, starting under cold conditions may become virtually impossible, since transfer pressure may be sufficient at

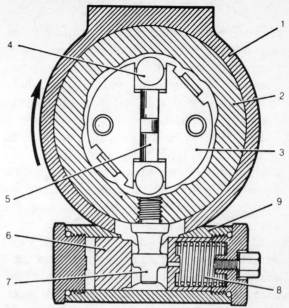

1 Pump housing
2 Cam ring
3 Pumping and distributing rotor
4 Roller
5 Pumping plunger
6 Automatic advance piston
7 Cam advance screw
8 Piston spring
9 Automatic advance housing

Fig 27.14   Automatic advance mechanism
Courtesy of CAV

cranking speed to carry the cam ring (per medium of the piston) towards the advance position, and cylinder air temperature at cranking speed is insufficient before TDC to efficiently ignite the fuel. As soon as the engine starts, the device is opened and the piston (and cam ring) move to the correct (more advanced) position.

Any tendency for the cam ring to be dragged towards the retarded position by the impact of the cam follower rollers on the cam ring lobes is prevented by a ball check valve in the fuel supply stud, which causes fuel to be trapped in the cylinder. When the engine is stopped or its speed is reduced, the advance mechanism is allowed to return to the retarded position under the influence of the spring due to a slight but controlled-rate leakage of fuel between the piston and the cylinder.

Mounting and driving arrangements

Both types of DPA pump — mechanically or hydraulically governed — are equipped with a triangular mounting flange for attachment to the engine's timing case or cylinder block. Because the pump is filled completely with fuel during operation for lubrication purposes, it can be mounted horizontally, vertically or in any intermediate attitude that may be necessary for a particular engine installation.

Both types of pump are driven by a splined shaft provided with a master spline. The master spline is engaged with a corresponding master spline on the engine drive during fitting, and ensures correct location of the pump in relation to the drive.

On mechanically driven pumps, a short detachable splined shaft, known as a quill shaft, engages with splines in the drive hub that protrudes from the mounting flange. Carrying the drive from the drive hub to the rotor drive plate and secured to the drive hub by an axial stud is a second drive shaft. Hence the drive passes from quill shaft to drive hub to drive shaft to drive plate via two clamping studs to the rotor, and to the transfer pump rotor. On some applications, the quill shaft is replaced by a special keyed drive hub that bolts to the engine coupling — some early models of mechanically governed pumps have a quill shaft with a small locking screw at one end. It is important that this screw is engaged in the socket head of the drive hub securing screw before tightening the pump to the engine.

On hydraulically governed pumps, the detachable quill shaft is not employed, and a one-piece drive shaft engages at one end with the engine drive and at the other with the rotor drive plate. On certain hydraulically governed pumps, a torsion bar is fitted to iron out backlash in the drive shaft. The device consists of a flat bar engaged between the end of the rotor and the pump drive coupling on the engine. The bar runs through the centre of the drive shaft and is made to twist during engagement of the pump to the engine.

Lubrication

Reference has already been made to the fact that the pump housing is filled with fuel. Fuel reaches the annular groove on the rotor at transfer pump pressure, and a small quantity leaks from this groove around the rotor shank (which at this point is of slightly reduced diameter) to fill the pump housing. The rest of the rotor and hydraulic head is lubricated by slight fuel leakage from the various ports. Once the housing is full, the fuel is returned to the secondary fuel filter for recirculation to the pump. When an automatic advance unit is fitted, additional fuel enters the body after leaking past the automatic advance piston.

DPA pump governors

The need for an effective governing device on a diesel engine was clearly shown in Chapter 31, and engines equipped with CAV DPA fuel injection pumps are naturally no exception. Because the governors are integral with the pump and directly control the metering valve, they are included in this work with the pumps rather than in the chapter on governors.

As the preceding comments on these pumps have clearly shown, there are two entirely different types of governor fitted — the mechanical governor and the hydraulic governor. While the type of governor has a great deal of bearing on the appearance of the pump, the pumping sections are identical except for the metering valve. The mechanically governed pump is somewhat longer than the other, due to the governor weight assembly, which is situated within the pump housing.

The mechanical governor

The mechanically governed DPA fuel injection pump is shown in Fig 27.1. Reference to this figure will show that the flyweight assembly is carried on the splined drive shaft within the pump housing, and that the governor-controlled linkage is enclosed by a cover fitted to the upper face of the housing.

Governor operation can readily be understood if reference is made to Fig 27.15, which shows the governor weights and control sleeve diagrammatically.

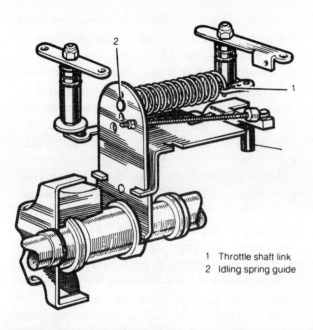

Fig 27.15 Mechanical governor layout
Courtesy of CAV

1 Throttle shaft link
2 Idling spring guide

The governor weights are housed in pockets in the weight carrier, which is rigidly clamped between the end of the drive hub and a step on the drive shaft. Drive hub, governor weight assembly and drive shaft thus rotate as a single unit when the pump is operating. The weights are so shaped that they pivot about one corner under the influence of centrifugal force. Such movement causes a thrust sleeve, with which they are engaged, to slide along the drive shaft.

Movement of the thrust sleeve is transmitted to the metering valve by the pivoted governor arm and the spring-loaded hook lever.

Outward movement of the weights tends to close the metering orifice by rotating the metering valve, thus reducing the quantity of fuel reaching the engine cylinders at each injection.

The governor arm is spring loaded by the governor spring; the tension of this spring acts in opposition to centrifugal force, tending to oppose outward movement of the weights and to hold the metering valve in the maximum fuel position. Spring tension can be varied by moving the control lever to which the spring is connected, tension being increased as the throttle control is moved towards the maximum speed setting.

When the control lever is moved to a position that calls for engine acceleration, increased spring tension is applied to the governor arm. This increased spring tension overcomes centrifugal force acting on the governor weights, and the metering valve is rotated to the maximum fuel position. Engine speed builds up until the centrifugal force acting on the weights is sufficient to overcome the increased spring tension. The weights then move outwards and reduce the fuelling by rotating the metering valve until the two opposed forces acting on the thrust sleeve are in equilibrium.

While running at a selected speed, the spring tension opposing movement of the governor weights remains constant. When speed fluctuations occur, the resulting change of centrifugal force causes movement of the weights and brings about a compensating change of fuelling — increased fuelling when engine speed falls below the selected speed and decreased fuelling when it is exceeded.

It will be noted that the governor spring is connected directly to the governor arm. It is coupled to the idling spring guide, which passes through a hole in the governor arm and is, in most cases, spring loaded by a light idling spring. At speeds outside the idling range, the tension applied to the governor spring is sufficient to compress the idling spring completely, thus rendering it ineffective. At idling speeds, when the tension of the governor spring is reduced to a minimum, the idling spring comes into action. Movement of the control arm by governor action is opposed by the light idling spring only, so that stable idling can be maintained when changes of centrifugal force are small.

Idling and maximum speed adjustment screws are provided on both hydraulically and mechanically governed pumps. Maximum speed and idling stops are adjusted while the pump is on the engine and should be set in accordance with the engine manufacturer's instructions.

Fuel shut-off is achieved by rotating the metering valve to a position where the metering orifice is completely closed. An eccentric on the shut-off shaft engages a bar, which is brought into contact with the arm on the metering valve when the control is operated. The hook lever connecting the metering valve to the governor arm is spring loaded so that the control can be operated at any engine speed without need for over-riding the governor.

The hydraulic governor

A CAV DPA fuel injection pump featuring a hydraulic governor was shown in Fig 27.2.

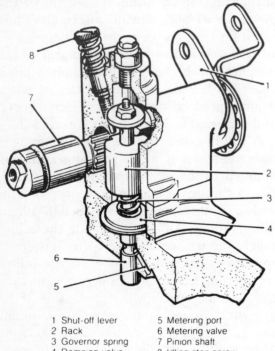

1 Shut-off lever	5 Metering port
2 Rack	6 Metering valve
3 Governor spring	7 Pinion shaft
4 Damping valve	8 Idling stop screw

Fig 27.16 Section through a hydraulic governor
Courtesy of CAV

The components of the hydraulic governor are contained in a small casting secured to the upper face of the injection pump housing, a speed control lever and a shut-off being externally mounted.

Within the governor is a pinion that engages with a rack carried on the stem of the metering valve. The rack is not secured to the valve stem, but is usually located between two springs, a lower governor spring and an upper light idling spring. In some instances the governor spring only is fitted, as is the case with the hydraulic governor shown in Fig 27.16.

Movement of the piston-type metering valve controls the effective area of the metering orifice, thus controlling the metering pressure at the inlet port in the rotor, and regulating the quantity of fuel admitted to the pumping element at each charging stroke.

Two forces act on the metering valve: the force exerted by the governor spring and the force exerted by the fuel at transfer pressure acting on the underside of the valve. The two forces are opposed, spring force tending to hold the valve in the maximum fuel position and transfer pressure tending to hold it in the idling position. During operation the valve assumes a position where the two forces acting on it are in equilibrium.

When the control lever is moved towards the full throttle setting, the metering valve moves to the maximum fuel position and the governor spring is compressed. Engine speed increases in response to increased fuelling, thus causing a rise in transfer pressure. As transfer pressure becomes sufficiently high to overcome spring force, the metering valve moves towards the idling position until the two forces are in equilibrium. The engine will then run at a speed corresponding to the setting of the speed control lever, and the selected speed will be maintained by governor action.

Any change in engine speed resulting from a change of loading is accompanied by a corresponding change of transfer pressure. This will cause movement of the metering valve and bring about a compensating change of fuelling — increased fuelling when engine speed falls below the selected speed and decreased fuelling when the selected speed is exceeded.

Within the idling range, the idling spring is compressed. The force exerted by it on the metering valve is in the same direction as the force exerted by transfer pressure. Thus, at idling speeds, a reduced force exerted by the governor spring is opposed by transfer pressure plus the force exerted by the idling spring. This enables close governing to be maintained at low speeds where transfer pressure changes are relatively small.

The dished damper plate is immersed in fuel oil, and prevents violent metering valve movement by dashpot action.

A cam, controlled by the shut-off lever, contacts the underside of a washer fitted at the upper end of the metering valve stem. When the control is operated, the valve is lifted upwards and the metering orifice completely closed. The control can be operated at any engine speed, thus enabling the operator to shut off the engine in an emergency.

Special application DPA fuel injection pumps

Some DPA fuel injection pumps are used in automotive applications. For driver convenience and improved performance, certain modifications are carried out on many of these pumps. The modification options available include:

- a **manual advance lever** to allow injection timing to be advanced by the driver for easier cold weather starting. This is the reverse of standard DPA pumps because of the considerably modified pump timing and advance systems;

- an **electric solenoid shut-off control valve** to allow the engine to be stopped by means of the operator key;

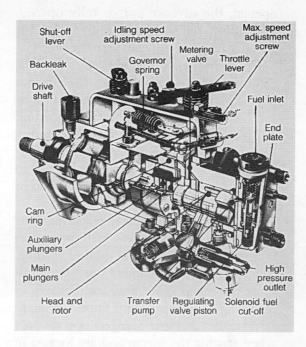

Fig 27.17 Special application DPA fuel injection pump
Courtesy of CAV

- a **light load advance system** to ensure smooth running during light-loaded operation. In this modification, fuel supply to the advance unit passes through a helical groove on the metering valve and a drilling in the hydraulic head, instead of directly from the transfer pump.

As the metering valve moves under governor action, this helix covers and uncovers the port leading to the automatic advance mechanism. Because there is a constant leakage past the automatic advance piston, the restriction in the supply circuit causes a pressure drop, the amount of pressure loss being dependent on the amount of restriction.

Thus the amount of advance is determined by the position of the metering valve helix, which controls the fuel pressure to the automatic advance. Because of the relative positions of the helix and the normal fuel passage in the metering valve, under light load conditions (moderate to high engine speed) with the metering valve partly opened, the advance port is fully opened. This allows full fuel pressure to act on the advance unit and fully advance the timing.

Under heavy load conditions, when the metering valve is fully opened, the advance port is partly closed, reducing the fuel pressure acting on the automatic advance unit and therefore retarding injection timing slightly. Light load advance pumps are distinguished by a circular groove machined in the outside of the hydraulic head adjacent to the transfer pump housing;

- a **modified rotor assembly** featuring four plungers to provide excess fuel above normal maximum delivery for ease of starting. The main pair of plungers operates at all times the pump is running, and behaves as the plungers in the standard rotor. The auxiliary, smaller diameter plungers operate only when starting the engine and are located in tandem beside the existing main plungers in the rotor. At cranking speed, all four plungers operate, but once the engine has started, fuel at transfer pressure acts against a piston valve, which closes off the fuel drillings to the auxiliary plungers, leaving only the larger plungers operational.

DPA pump service

Once again, the need for absolutely clean working conditions, specialised equipment, special service tools, detailed service information and experience must be stressed before any thoughts of injection pump service can be entertained. Provided that these prerequisites are available, the DPA pump does not present any special service difficulties.

To ensure that the correct service information is used, the pump type and model should be identified from the pump typeplate on the housing, and reference should then be made to the appropriate pump test sheet. However, a setting code below the type/model data also provides specific information on assembly and setting details.

For example, in the setting code EX52/600/4/2850, the '52/600' indicates that the pump will deliver 52 millilitres of fuel per 1000 shots when it is running at 600 rpm on an injection pump test bench. The '4' indicates the governor spring location code on mechanically governed pumps; a zero appears in this position for hydraulically governed pumps. The '2850' is the maximum no-load speed of the engine.

Both calibrating and phasing, as they apply to in-line pumps, are eliminated with the DPA pump — calibrating because all fuel deliveries come from the same element and cannot be adjusted individually, and phasing because the firing intervals are set in manufacture when the cam ring lobes are ground at the correct positions.

The condition of the hydraulic head assembly can be ascertained when the pump is assembled by setting it up on the test bench and running it at a specified speed. The fuel escaping from the pump is made up of that escaping from between the plungers and their bore and between the rotor and hydraulic head, as well as a small quantity escaping past the automatic advance piston. Hence the quantity of fuel escaping is a direct indication of the clearances between the pumping and distributing components of the pump. If this fuel is passed into a calibrated glass and measured during a specified number of injections, a good indication of the hydraulic head condition can be gained, since a maximum allowable leakage rate is quoted in the manufacturer's manual.

However, it only takes a very small quantity of dirt entering the inlet connection when the pump is removed from the engine to destroy the pumping components if the pump is run. Again, a speck of dirt in an outlet union will be pumped into the test injectors and will damage them if the pump is run on a test bench. Because of these dangers, many service people prefer to dismantle the pump without performing any preliminary test.

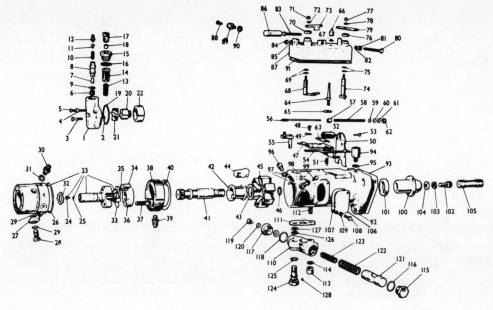

Fig 27.18 Exploded view of CAV DPA mechanically governed fuel injection pump
Courtesy of CAV

Dismantling a mechanically governed DPA pump

A number of special tools are necessary before a DPA pump can be dismantled. All engine manufacturers, as well as service equipment manufacturers, make these tools available. The following dismantling sequence by courtesy of British Leyland Motor Corporation of Australia Limited may well be applied to almost any mechanically governed DPA pump, the special tools necessary being listed under this manufacturer's part numbers.

To dismantle the pump, proceed as follows (part numbers refer to Fig 27.18).

1   Remove the cover-plate (106) from the side of the pump housing, and drain the fuel from the injection pump.

2   Withdraw the quill shaft (105) from the drive hub (100) and check the drive hub end float by inserting a feeler gauge between the drive hub and the pump body (92). The end-float should not exceed 0.254 mm. Excessive end-float can be corrected by renewing the pump body and the governor weight retainer (45).

3   Mount the pump on an assembly base (a mounting plate for service work, part no. 18G633) secured in a vice and remove any high-pressure connections (27) from the hydraulic head.

4   Unscrew the nuts and remove the shut-off lever (79) and throttle arm (73) from their shafts. Withdraw the dust cover from each shaft and remove the two nuts (66) and washers (67) securing the control cover (87).

5   Press the throttle shaft downwards and withdraw the control cover complete with the shut-off shaft (74). Discard the control cover gasket.

6   Detach the governor spring (52) from the governor arm (50) and the shut-off bar (54) from the control bracket (47). Remove the two control cover studs (64) and the small set screw (48) securing the control bracket. Detach the keep plate (63) and lift the control bracket assembly from the pump. This assembly will include the control bracket (47), the governor arm (50), the spring for the governor arm (51), the spring guide (53) and its associated idle spring, governor spring (52), linkage hook (56) (complete with spring retainer

(57), linkage spring (58), linkage washer (59), pivot ball washer (60), backing washer (61) and linkage nut (62), and the metering valve (55).

7 Disconnect the metering valve from the linkage hook and place it in a clean container of test oil to protect its precision-ground surface.

8 Disconnect the governor spring from the idle spring guide, and remove the idle spring and guide from the governor arm.

9 Disconnect the linkage hook from the governor arm. Detach the governor arm spring and separate the governor arm from the control bracket.

10 Slacken both the spring cap (117) and end plug (115) in the automatic advance unit (if fitted). Remove the hydraulic head locating bolt (124) complete with its outer o-ring (125), and take care not to lose the non-return valve ball (128) located in the side of the head locating bolt.

11 Remove the cap-nut (113) and washer (114) and withdraw the advance unit from the pump. Detach the inner o-ring (126) and washer (127) from the head locating bolt hole, and discard the advance unit gasket.

12 Unscrew the spring cap (117) (complete with o-ring) (118) from the advance unit, and withdraw the spring(s) and the piston. Note that there is a shim inside the spring cap.

13 Remove the end plug (115) and o-ring (116) from the advance unit.

14 Unscrew the cam advance screw (39) from the cam ring (38) with the special spanner (part no. 18G646).

15 Slacken the fuel inlet connection (15) and remove the screws and studs (3, 4) securing the end plate to the hydraulic head (23). Lift out the transfer pump vanes (21) and withdraw the transfer pump liner (22).

16 Unscrew the fuel inlet connection (15) and withdraw the regulating valve components in the following order: sleeve retaining spring (13), nylon filter (14),

transfer pressure adjuster (12), regulating spring (10) and peg (11), regulating sleeve (8) with piston (7) and joint washer (9), and lastly the piston retaining spring (priming spring) (6). If necessary, remove the transfer pump liner-locating pin from the inner face of the end plate. The pin can be in one of two positions, marked 'A' and 'C' on the end plate outer face, depending whether the pump's rotation is anti-clockwise or clockwise.

17 Hold the drive hub (100) with the special tool for the purpose (part no. 18G659) and, using the special tool (part no. 18G634), slacken the transfer pump rotor (20) by turning it in the direction of pump rotation as shown on the pump nameplate.

18 Remove the two hydraulic head locking screws (96, 98), one of which incorporates an air vent screw (99), and withdraw the hydraulic head and rotor assembly (23) from the pump. Remove the o-ring (26) from the groove in the periphery of the hydraulic head.

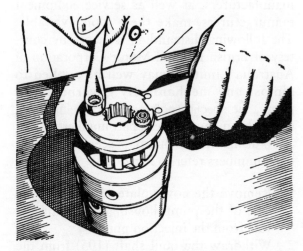

Fig 27.19 Holding the drive plate while removing the drive plate screws
Courtesy of CAV

19 Unscrew the transfer pump rotor (20), but do not allow the pumping and distributing rotor assembly to fall out of the hydraulic head.

20 Stand the hydraulic head on the bench with the drive plate (36) uppermost. Hold the drive plate with the special tool (part no. 18G641) and unscrew the two drive plate screws (37) (see Fig 27.19). Remove the drive plate and top adjusting plate (33) and withdraw the rollers (34) and shoes (35) from the pumping and distributing rotor.

21 Withdraw the rotor from the hydraulic head, remove the bottom adjusting plate (32) and refit the rotor to the hydraulic head. Immerse the assembly in test oil to protect the working surfaces.

22 Withdraw the cam ring from the pump housing, noting the arrow etched on the visible face of the cam ring. This arrow indicates the direction of rotation as shown on the pump's nameplate.

23 Remove the cam ring locating circlip (40) from inside the pump, using suitable circlip pliers.

24 Hold the drive hub with the special tool (part no. 18G659) and, with a suitable Allen key or special tool, unscrew the drive shaft screw (102) from inside the drive hub. Withdraw the drive shaft (41) and governor weight assembly from inside the pump housing as an assembly.

25 Remove the o-ring (46), the weight retainer (45), weights (44), thrust washer (43) and sleeve (42) from the drive shaft.

26 Withdraw the drive hub from the pump and remove the spring washer (103) and support washer (104) from inside the drive hub.

27 Remove the drive hub oil seal (101) from the pump housing using a suitable tool (such as part no. 18G658).

Inspection of components

All components should be washed in clean test oil, after which the following procedure should be followed:

1 Remove the rotor plug (24) and washer (25). Hold the pumping plungers in their bores and blow out the passages in the rotor with compressed air. Coat the threads of the plug with Araldite and refit the plug.

2 Remove the pumping plungers one at a time and examine them and their bore in the rotor for wear and abrasion. The end of each plunger will be polished where it contacts the roller shoe. The plungers should be replaced in their original positions.

3 Examine the hydraulic head bore and its mating surface on the rotor for wear or scoring. If either of these components or one of the pumping plungers is worn, renew the rotor and head as a unit.

4 Check the cam ring lobes for wear, the plunger rollers for flats and the roller shoes for freedom in their guides in the rotor.

5 Refit the drive plate to the drive shaft and ensure that there is no excessive radial movement on the splines.

6 Check that the transfer pump vanes are a sliding fit in their slots when lubricated with fuel.

7 Inspect the bore of the regulating valve sleeve for wear and ensure that the valve piston can move freely through it.

8 Check all springs for fractures and signs of weakness, and the governor weight retainer, thrust washer and sleeve for signs of wear.

9 Inspect the bore in which the drive hub runs. If it is worn or scored, the housing must be renewed.

Note: One method that may be used to gauge the amount of wear sustained by the hydraulic head components is as follows:

1 Machine a cylindrical sleeve of fair wall thickness to fit over the roller and plunger assembly in the position the cam ring normally occupies. The inner diameter of the sleeve should be such that it will just fit over the rollers when the plungers are forced together.

2   Connect the hydraulic head assembly to an injector tester, as shown in Fig 27.22. Operate the injector tester and turn the rotor until the rotor outlet port registers with one of the hydraulic head outlet ports connected to the tester. At this point, the rollers will be forced out against the sleeve by the plungers.

3   Note the quantity of fuel leaking from the assembly. Experience will provide the necessary judgment as to how great this leakage may be.

Reassembly of the mechanically governed DPA pump

All components should be rinsed in clean test oil and assembled wet in the following order (all component numbers again refer to Fig 27.18):

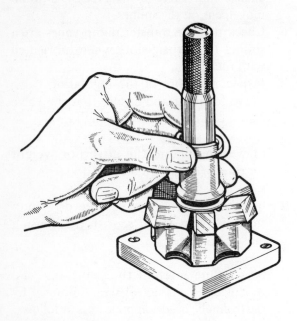

Fig 27.20   Assembling the governor weights
Courtesy of CAV

1   Fit a new hub oil seal (101) to the pump housing (using tool part no. 18G663). Insert the correct inspection plug (part no. 660) into the oil seal; a continuous black line should be visible through the plug.

2   Fit the two washers (104, 103) into the drive hub (100) and insert the hub into the hub oil seal.

3   Using the special tools (part nos 18G661, 18G662) assemble the governor weights (44), thrust washer (43) and sleeve (42) to the weight retainer (45). (See Fig 27.20.) The stepped flange of the sleeve must go away from the thrust washer.

4   Slide the governor weight assembly on to the drive shaft (41) and fit a protection cap (part no. 18G657) over the drive shaft splines and a new o-ring (46) in the groove on the drive shaft.

5   Insert the drive shaft and weight assembly into the pump housing and engage the drive shaft splines with the splines in the drive hub. Fit the drive shaft screw (102) and, using a drive hub holding tool (part no. 18G659), hold the drive hub while tightening the screw with an adaptor (part no. 18G664) and torque wrench to the figure laid down in the specifications. Check the drive hub end float as described in 'Dismantling a mechanically governed DPA pump' (2).

6   Using circlip pliers, fit the cam ring locating circlip (40) against the shoulder in the pump housing. If the circlip is the type that has a timing line scribed on one face, ensure that the timing line faces forward to the inspection cover.

7   Place the cam ring (38) in position against the circlip, and ensure that the direction of the arrow on the visible face of the cam ring conforms with the direction of the arrow on the pump name plate. Fit the cam advance screw (39) finger tight and check the cam ring for freedom of rotation. If the hydraulic head and rotor are being renewed, ensure that the direction of the arrow on the pumping end of the rotor conforms with the direction of the arrow on the pump nameplate.

8   Withdraw the rotor from the hydraulic head and fit the top adjusting plate (33) so that the slot in its periphery is in line with the mark on the rotor (see Fig 27.21).

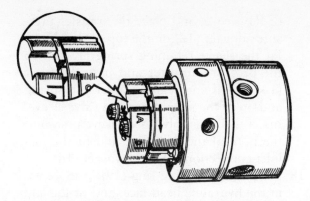

Fig 27.21   Hydraulic head and rotor assembly, showing the top adjusting plate position relative to the rotor
Courtesy of CAV

9   Fit the drive plate (36) to the rotor with its relieved face next to the top adjusting plate, and the slot in the periphery of the drive plate in line with the mark on the rotor (see Fig 27.21). Tighten the drive plate screws (37) lightly and insert the roller (34) and shoe (35) assemblies into their guides in the rotor. Make sure that the contour of the roller shoe ears conforms with the contour of the eccentric slots in the top adjusting plate.

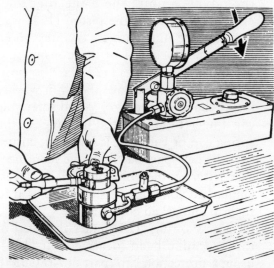

Fig 27.22   Setting the roller-to-roller dimension
Courtesy of CAV

10 Fit the bottom adjusting plate (32), engaging its slot with the lugs on the top adjusting plate, and ensuring that the contour of the eccentric slots matches the contour of the roller shoe ears.

11 Insert the rotor assembly into the hydraulic head, then fit and lightly tighten the transfer pump rotor (20).

12 Stand the hydraulic head and rotor assembly on the bench, drive plate uppermost. Fit the relief valve timing adaptor (part no. 18G653), preset to 15 atmospheres, to two opposite high-pressure outlet on the hydraulic head and connect this assembly to the injector tester (see Fig 27.22).

   Note: The relief valve timing adaptor connects to the injector tester and provides two connections for attachment to the hydraulic head. The unit contains a relief valve, which can be adjusted to any recommended pressure. The hydraulic head outlets are each stamped with a letter for identification and the choice of outlets to which the relief valve timing adaptor is connected is specified by the manufacturer, and varies from one pump application to the next.

13 Operate the pumping lever of the injector tester and turn the rotor in the normal direction of rotation until the pumping plungers are forced outwards as far as the eccentric slots in the adjusting plates will allow; this is the maximum fuel position. Using a maximum fuel adjusting probe (part no. 18G656), rotate the adjusting plates as necessary to set the roller-to-roller dimension at the figure given in the specifications (see Fig 27.22). Hold the drive plate with the correct tool (part no. 18G641) and tighten the drive plate screws to the torque figure given in the specifications. Recheck the roller-to-roller dimension. Disconnect the adaptor from the hydraulic head.

14 Rotate the drive shaft in the pump housing to position the master spline at 12 o'clock. Fit a new o-ring (26) to the groove in the periphery of the hydraulic head and align the master spline in the

drive plate with the metering valve bore in the hydraulic head. Lubricate the periphery of the hydraulic head and the bore of the pump housing liberally with clean test oil, and assemble the hydraulic head to the pump body. Fit the two hydraulic head locking screws (96, 98) finger tight, positioning the screw with the vent valve in the position where it will be readily accessible when the pump is fitted to the engine.

15 Hold the drive hub with the correct tool (18G659) and, using the spanner designed for the purpose (part no. 18G634), tighten the transfer pump rotor to the torque figure given in the specifications (see Fig 27.23). Fit the transfer pump liner (22), and insert the transfer pump vanes (21) in their slots.

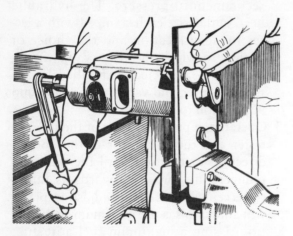

Fig 27.23 Tightening the transfer pump rotor
Courtesy of CAV

16 Carefully drive the transfer pump liner locating peg into the position in the pump end plate that corresponds to the pump's direction of rotation: position A-pump rotation anticlockwise, position C-pump rotation clockwise. Seat the piston retaining spring (or priming spring) (6) in the bottom of the regulating valve bore.

17 Fit a new seal washer (9) to the small diameter end of the regulating valve sleeve (8) and fit the piston (7) into the sleeve. Insert the regulating spring (10) and peg (11) into the large diameter end

of the sleeve, and place the transfer pressure adjuster (12) on the top of the sleeve. Fit the sleeve retaining spring (13) on to the pressure adjuster and pass the filter (14), small end leading, over the spring and on to the shoulder of the valve sleeve. Insert this assembly, valve sleeve first, into the bore of the end plate and fit the fuel inlet connection (15) and washer (16).

18 Place a new sealing ring (19) in its recess in the hydraulic head face, and fit the end plate to the head engaging the locating peg with the slot in the transfer pump liner. Tighten the end plate screws (3) and studs (4) to the torque figure given in the specifications, then tighten the fuel inlet connection (15) to the torque figure given.

19 Using the correct spanner (part no. 18G646), tighten the cam advance screw (39) to the torque figure given in the specifications and check the cam ring for freedom of rotation.

20 Fit new o-rings (116, 118) to the advance unit end plug (115) and spring cap (117), using a protection cap (part no. 18G640) to pass the rings over the threads. Screw the end plug finger tight into the end of the advance unit where the fuel duct enters the bore. Fit the piston (121) into the advance unit with its counter bored end at the open end of the housing and place the two springs (122, 123) in position in the piston. Place the shim washer inside the spring cap (117) and screw the cap finger tight into the housing. If the spring cap or end plug is renewed, ensure that the new part has the same identification letter as the component it replaces. Unmarked components should be used to replace unmarked components.

21 Fit a new o-ring (125) under the head of the hydraulic head locating bolt (124), using a protection cap (part no. 18G639). Position the non-return valve ball (128) in the side of the head locating bolt and fit the bolt to the advance unit. Using an assembly cap (part no. 18G647), fit a new

inner o-ring (126) to the shank of the locating bolt, and place the plain washer (127) on top of the o-ring.

22 Place a new advance unit joint gasket (111) on the pump housing with the straight side of the 'D'-shaped hole at the drive end of the pump; to ensure sealing, this joint washer should be fitted dry. Position the advance unit on the pump, fit a new aluminium and rubber washer to the stud and fit the cap nut (113).

23 Tighten the two hydraulic head locking screws, the hydraulic head locating bolt and the advance unit cap nut to the torque figures given in the specifications. Tighten the advance unit end plug and spring cap to the torque figures given in the specifications.

24 Insert the metering valve (55) into its bore in the hydraulic head.

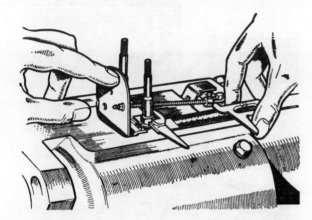

Fig 27.24   Setting the governor link length
Courtesy of CAV

25 Assemble the governor arm (50), control bracket (47) and governor arm spring (51), then fit the assembly to the pump housing, ensuring that the lower end of the governor arm engages the stepped plate of the thrust sleeve flange. Fit the keep plate (63) with its open end towards the shut-off bar (54) and fit new tab washers (65) with their pointed tabs towards the governor arm. Screw in the two control cover studs (64) to the

torque figure given in the specifications, and secure them with the pointed tabs.

26 Fit the small screw (48) and tab washer (49) to the metering valve end of the control bracket. Tighten the screw to the torque figure given in the specifications and lock it with the tab washer.

27 Assemble the spring retainer (57), spring (58) and linkage washer (59) on to the linkage hook (56). Pass the threaded end of the hook through the governor arm, fit the pivot ball washer (60) and backing washer (61) and screw on the linkage nut about three turns.

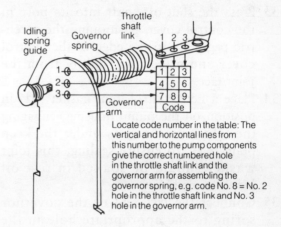

Fig 27.25   Application of the setting code
Courtesy of CAV

28 Press back the spring retainer and attach the linkage hook to the metering valve so that the hook end is turned towards the metering valve.

29 Press the governor arm lightly in the direction of the metering valve and, using a vernier gauge held parallel to the pump axis, set the governor link length (see Fig 27.24) to the dimension given in the specifications. This adjustment is made by slackening or tightening the linkage hook nut.

30 Locate the spring guide (53) in the correct hole in the governor arm and connect the governor spring to the guide. In many cases, a very light spring is fitted

over the spring guide. Refer to Fig 27.25 for the correct governor spring location in conjunction with the pump setting code discussed previously.

31 Insert the plain end of the shut-off bar (54) into the slot in the control bracket and position the shut-off bar under the tab of the control cover locking washer.

32 Using a protection cap (part no. 18G654), fit new lower o-rings to the shut-off and throttle shafts (68, 74). Fit a new upper o-ring to each shaft, using a protection cap (part no. 18G665) and pack the groove between the o-rings on each shaft with Shell Alvania no. 2 grease.

33 Press the shut-off shaft into its bore in the control cover, positioning the eccentric peg close to the edge of the control cover and projecting slightly from the joint face.

34 Place a new control joint gasket (91) in position on the pump housing, engaging the tabs with the slots under the keep plate (63). To ensure sealing, this joint washer should be soaked in test oil before assembly.

35 Connect the free end of the governor spring to the appropriate hole in the throttle shaft link (as per Fig 27.25), and press the throttle shaft into its bore in the control cover. Place the control cover in position on the studs, ensuring that the shut-off peg engages the shut-off bar. Pull the shut-off shaft fully home as the control cover is lowered onto the pump housing.

36 Fit new sealing washers (67) to the control cover studs and screw on the stud nuts to the torque figure in the specifications.

37 Place the dust caps (70, 76) on the throttle and shut-off shafts, fit the throttle arm (73) and shut-off lever (79) to their shafts and secure them in position with their nuts and washers.

38 Refit the inspection cover (106) to the side of the pump housing using a new gasket, and refit the quill shaft (105).

Testing and adjusting DPA pumps

After an overhaul, a DPA fuel injection pump must be tested and adjusted to specifications. While there are some slight variations, the tests and adjustments made fall into eight general categories:

1 transfer pump vacuum test;
2 transfer pump pressure test;
3 automatic advance test;
4 back-leakage test;
5 maximum fuel delivery test;
6 fuel cut-off test;
7 governor setting adjustment;
8 timing setting.

Fig 27.26 Hartridge series 2500 fuel pump test stand
Courtesy of CAV

To make the first seven tests, the pump should be set up on a power-driven test bench. A mounting plate to carry the pump is usually available for any particular test bench and bolts to the test bench table. The pump can then be driven directly by the test bench drive coupling.

Before setting up the pump on the test bench, it is essential to establish that the test bench is capable of providing an adequate fuel supply. Usually, a fuel supply of not less than 1 litre per minute is specified.

The pump should be set up on the test bench as follows:

1   Mount the pump on the test bench, ensure that the test bench is set to run in the direction of rotation indicated on the pump nameplate, and connect the pump drive.

2   Connect the hydraulic head outlet unions to the test bench test injectors by means of a set of matched injector lines. The usual specification is to use test injectors set to 175 atmospheres and injector lines 6 mm x 2 mm x 863.5 mm long.

3   Using transparent (where possible) flexible pipes, connect the injection pump to the test equipment as follows:

   a   Fit a suitable adaptor in place of the hydraulic head locking screw which does not have a vent screw, and connect a pressure gauge. The gauge should be capable of registering a maximum pressure slightly above the maximum transfer pressure. (The maximum transfer pressure should be quoted in the pump specifications.)

   b   Fit an end plate adjuster to the fuel inlet union. The adjuster provides both a means of connecting the supply pipe and of adjusting the transfer pressure. Use a 'T'-coupling in conjunction with the end plate adjuster and connect both the fuel supply and vacuum gauge.

   c   Connect the pump drain union to a measuring glass, and the measuring glass drain cock to the test bench return connection.

4   Once the pump has been connected to the test bench and gauges, etc., connect an automatic advance gauge to the advance unit spring cap in place of the small set screw and set the degree scale to give a zero reading.

5   Unscrew the idling and maximum speed stop screws to ensure that the throttle lever has its full range of movement.

6   Unscrew the pressure adjuster in the pump end plate (by means of the end plate adjuster) to the maximum extent, then screw it in approximately 1.5 turns.

7   Fill and prime the pump as follows:

   a   Turn on the fuel supply to the injection pump and open the pump air vent (or bleeder) screws.

   b   When test oil, free from air bubbles, flows from the hydraulic head vent screw, close the vent.

   c   When test oil, free from air bubbles, flows from the housing vent screw, close this vent also.

   d   Turn the pump drive in the direction of rotation for 90° and again open the hydraulic head vent. Close again when there are no air bubbles in the escaping test oil.

   e   Turn the pump drive a further 90° and again check both vents.

   f   Check that test oil is flowing from the pump drain connection.

   g   With the throttle fully open, run the test bench at 100 rpm. Loosen the injector lines at the injectors and retighten them when test oil, free from air bubbles, issues from the connections.

During testing, it is essential that the pump handles sufficient fuel to ensure lubrication of the rotor and hydraulic head assembly. For this reason, the pump must not be run for long periods at high speed with low fuel output, or run for long periods with the shut-off control in the closed position. Further to this, all test procedures should be carried out with the throttle and shut-off controls in the fully open position except where specifically stated otherwise.

Check the oil-tightness of all joint washers, oil seals and pipe connections while the pump is running and stationary.

Once items (1) to (7) have been completed, the pump may be adjusted. Unless otherwise stated, the test must be made with the throttle and shut-off controls in the full open position.

Transfer pump vacuum test

This test is designed to show the efficiency of the transfer pump and the presence of any faults on its inlet side.

The test is made by running the test bench at 100 rpm and turning off the test oil supply valve for a maximum time of 60 seconds. The vacuum gauge should reach 405 mm Hg in 60 seconds maximum. Because the test creates a shortage of test oil to lubricate the rotor, the pump must not be run for more than 60 seconds with the valve closed. After completion of the test, the pump must be bled again at the hydraulic head vent screw while the pump is running at 100 rpm.

Transfer pressure test

Because the transfer pressure exerts very considerable influence on the fuel delivery and controls the automatic advance, it is essential that the transfer pressure is kept within specifications through the pump operating speed range. Because of this, it is usual to check the transfer pressure at three or four different pump speeds.

Because the transfer pump connects directly to the hydraulic head-locating screw holes, the pressure gauge connected to one of these holes will directly read the transfer pressure. Provided the correct regulating spring and regulating sleeve have been fitted to the end plate, the transfer pressure should lie within limits at all specified speeds, the maximum pressure being adjusted by means of the end plate adjuster which is screwed in to increase the pressure.

Automatic advance test

The rate of automatic injection advance and the total advance vary from one pump application to the next, and are governed by two factors: the change in the transfer pressure and the spring(s) fitted to the automatic advance unit.

Like the transfer pump pressure test, readings are taken at a number of different pump speeds. Adjustment is made by shimming the automatic advance spring(s) to change the spring force opposing the force exerted on the advance piston by transfer pressure, but should only be attempted if the amount of advance is consistently above or below specifications. If the reading is low at one point and high at another, then some mechanical fault would seem to be indicated.

Back-leakage test

This test is designed to establish whether the amount of test oil leaking between the rotor and hydraulic head, past the pumping plungers and past the automatic advance piston is within desirable limits. Excessive back-leakage is a sign of worn components or a leak into the pump housing, while too little shows that there is probably insufficient test oil leaking past the pumping components for efficient lubrication.

The test specifications vary from one pump application to the next, but the back-leakage quantity is usually measured during 100 injections. The procedure is to run the pump at specified rpm, and use the measuring glass to measure the quantity of fuel that flows, during 100 injections, from the drain connection.

Maximum fuel delivery test

The specified maximum fuel pump output can be found by reference to the setting code on the pump typeplate as detailed in the beginning of 'DPA pump servicing', or to the pump test sheet.

The maximum fuel delivery is controlled by the maximum plunger movement and is adjusted by partial rotation of the adjusting plates. Although the roller-to-roller dimension is set during pump assembly, it is likely that a final adjustment will have to be made after checking the maximum fuel delivery on the test bench.

The normal procedure is to run the pump at specified rpm and measure the deliveries from the test injectors during 200 injections. There should be very little variation between injectors, since the same pumping element supplies all hydraulic head outlets, and the deliveries should lie within close specified limits. Before taking the readings, the test oil should be allowed to settle for fifteen seconds in the measuring glasses, and the glasses should be allowed to drain for 30 seconds before taking a second test.

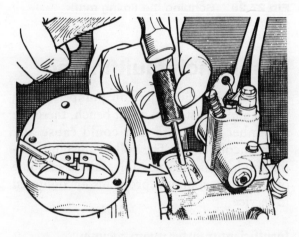

Fig 27.27 Adjusting the maximum fuel setting *Courtesy of CAV*

If the fuel delivery is incorrect, it must be adjusted at the adjusting plates. The fuel supply should first be turned off, the cover plate removed and the drive plate screws loosened. Adjustment is made by means of a probe engaged in the slot in the periphery of the top adjusting plate (see Fig 27.27), and the pump drive must be turned until the slot is accessible. Very little movement should be necessary, since the adjusting plates were adjusted closely when setting the roller-to-roller

dimension; clockwise rotation (from the drive end) will increase fuel delivery.

When an adjustment has been made, the drive plate screws must be retightened to the correct torque, using a torque wrench and adaptor. It is essential that the wrench and adaptor are kept in a straight line. Finally, the cover plate must be replaced, the fuel supply reconnected and air bled from the pump housing and the maximum fuel delivery checked again.

After adjusting the fuel delivery at the high specified pump speed, a second check is usually made at a lower speed. If this second test is less than the first by more than the specified figure, it indicates either an incorrect relationship between pump speed and transfer pump pressure or that pumping efficiency is failing with speed to a greater degree than it should.

Fuel cut-off test

One very important factor that must be checked during pump testing is that the engine can be stopped by means of the fuel shut-off control. Not only should the shut-off control be able to prevent all but a slight injection, but also the throttle should be able to reduce the injection rate to such a point that the engine stops.

Both of these can be checked by running the pump at low rpm with one control closed and the other fully open. A maximum delivery of 200 injections is usually quoted for each case.

Governor setting adjustment

The maximum engine speed is controlled by the governor, which should decrease fuel delivery once the corresponding maximum pump speed is exceeded. The pump is run on the test bench at specific rpm (above normal maximum), and the maximum speed screw adjusted to give the correct delivery from 200 shots, which is less than the maximum fuel setting adjusted previously.

Timing setting

This setting is made after all the foregoing tests and adjustments have been completed, with the pump removed from the test bench.

Because the plungers move outwards further as the fuel injection rate is increased, the commencement of injection changes with the fuel requirements of the engine and an invariable reference point must be found. The point used is the point at which the cam followers are in contact with both the cam ring and the plungers, with the plunger fully outwards in the maximum fuel position (i.e. the beginning of injection for no. 1 cylinder).

To locate the timing point, a special tool known as a timing flange is fitted to the pump drive, and the relief valve timing adaptor (as used for checking the roller-to-roller dimension) is used to connect two specified hydraulic head outlets to the injector tester. The timing flange incorporates a protractor and a scribing guide.

The protractor is fixed to the hub, which fits the pump drive, and the scribing guide can be rotated in relation to hub and protractor. For each pump application, a specified protractor reading must be aligned with a datum line on the scribing guide and the two components locked together.

To ensure that it is no. 1 injection, the relief valve timing adaptor is connected to specified hydraulic head outlets (they are identified by means of letters stamped adjacent to them), and the pump turned in the direction of normal rotation until a specified timing letter on the drive plate becomes visible through the pump inspection hole.

With the timing flange set and mounted on the pump, the correct timing letter visible through the inspection hole and the relief valve timing adaptor connected to the specified outlets, the injector tester is operated until a specified pressure is reached and the pump turned in the direction of rotation until resistance is felt. This resistance occurs when the cam rollers press on the plungers

to commence pressurising the fuel and this point must be commencement of injection. A scriber run through the scribing guide will mark the pump flange at the correct timing point (see Fig 27.28).

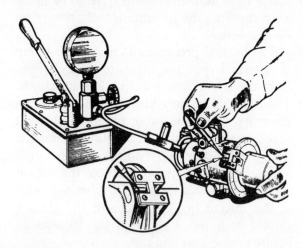

Fig 27.28 Scribing the timing mark
Courtesy of CAV

Test bench faultfinding

When a DPA fuel injection pump is being tested and adjusted on a test bench, there are a number of factors that could cause any fault encountered. The following faultfinding guide indicates possible causes of some of the more common problems encountered in service.

Insufficient transfer pump vacuum:
- damaged transfer pump o-ring seal;
- worn or damaged transfer pump vanes;
- loose or unevenly tightened end plate;
- transfer pump liner turning due to absence of locating dowel;
- incorrectly located transfer pump liner locating dowel;
- loose or damaged inlet or vacuum gauge connections;
- priming spring missing or broken;
- regulating spring missing or broken;
- damaged regulating sleeve gasket;
- regulating piston missing.

Low transfer pump pressure:
- incorrect adjustment;
- damaged transfer pump o-ring seal;
- worn or damaged transfer pump vanes;
- loose or unevenly tightened end plate;
- regulating spring missing or damaged;
- regulating piston missing;
- damaged regulating sleeve gasket;
- incorrect regulating sleeve or piston;
- fuel leakage at hydraulic head vent screws, pressure gauge connection or hydraulic head locating studs;
- fuel leakage at automatic advance unit.

High transfer pump pressure:
- incorrect adjustment;
- incorrect regulating sleeve and/or piston;
- sticking regulating piston;
- test bench test oil being supplied under pressure.

Low or fluctuating transfer pump pressure:
- one transfer pump vane chipped or broken;
- regulating sleeve inner seal faulty.

Low advance rate:
- advance unit incorrectly adjusted (too many shims fitted);
- incorrect advance spring(s) fitted;
- low transfer pump pressure;
- sticking advance piston;
- excessive clearance between the advance piston and the housing;
- sticking cam ring.

High advance rate:
- advance unit incorrectly adjusted (insufficient shims fitted);
- incorrect advance spring(s) fitted;
- high transfer pump pressure.

Incorrect maximum fuel delivery:
- air in the system;
- throttle not held fully open;
- fuel shut-off control not held fully open;
- incorrect maximum fuel setting;
- cam ring reversed;

- cam ring worn;
- governor link adjustment incorrect (mechanically governed pump);
- incorrect transfer pump pressure;
- sticking plungers or roller shoes;
- rotor plug loose or leaking;
- pumping components worn excessively;
- sticking metering valve.

Low fuel delivery at reduced rpm:
- low transfer pump pressure;
- plungers scored or worn;
- scoring in the region of the hydraulic head ports;
- excessive clearance between rotor and hydraulic head;
- scored metering valve;
- throttle not fully open;
- fuel leak at rotor sealing plug.

Difficulty in setting delivery with maximum speed screw:
- incorrect assembly of governor;
- sticking metering valve;
- sticking governor thrust sleeve (mechanical governor);
- incorrect transfer pump pressure (hydraulic governor).

Pump installation and timing

Since the procedure for timing and fitting is not standard for all engines, reference must be made to the engine manufacturer's handbook before carrying out this work. In an emergency, however, and if the timing marks are clearly marked on the engine and the pump mounting flange, most pumps can be fitted as follows:

1 Turn the pump drive shaft so that the master spline is in alignment with the master spline on the engine coupling.
2 Enter the drive shaft into the engine coupling as the pump is pushed on to the securing studs.

3 Push the pump hard against the mounting face and secure lightly with the three holding nuts.

4 Rotate the pump on the retaining studs until the timing mark scribed on the edge of the pump mounting flange is accurately aligned with the timing mark on the engine.

5 Tighten the retaining nuts. The pumps should now be correctly timed and all pipes, controls, etc. may be fitted and the air bled from the system.

Bleeding the DPA fuel system

Air will have to be bled from the DPA fuel system on installation of the pump and if the system should be drained by running out of fuel.

Before loosening any of the bleed screws, ensure that the surrounding area is thoroughly cleaned to prevent dirt and foreign matter getting into the system. Proceed as follows, carrying out operations (1) and (2) below while operating the fuel feed pump priming lever:

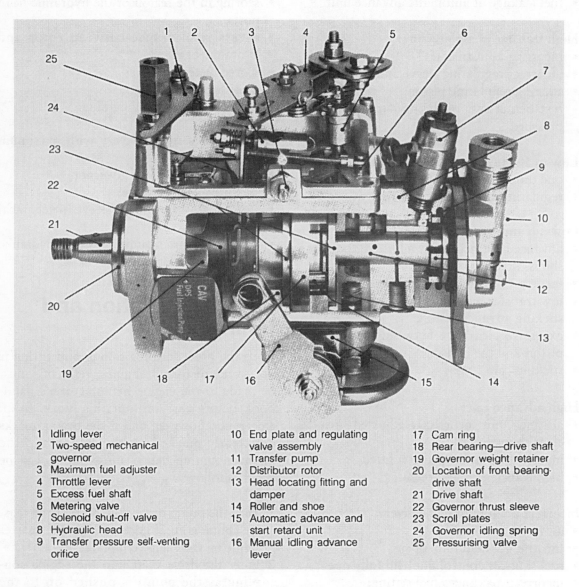

1	Idling lever	10	End plate and regulating valve assembly	17	Cam ring
2	Two-speed mechanical governor	11	Transfer pump	18	Rear bearing—drive shaft
3	Maximum fuel adjuster	12	Distributor rotor	19	Governor weight retainer
4	Throttle lever	13	Head locating fitting and damper	20	Location of front bearing-drive shaft
5	Excess fuel shaft	14	Roller and shoe	21	Drive shaft
6	Metering valve	15	Automatic advance and start retard unit	22	Governor thrust sleeve
7	Solenoid shut-off valve	16	Manual idling advance lever	23	Scroll plates
8	Hydraulic head			24	Governor idling spring
9	Transfer pressure self-venting orifice			25	Pressurising valve

Fig 27.29   Cut-away view of a DPS pump   *Courtesy of CAV*

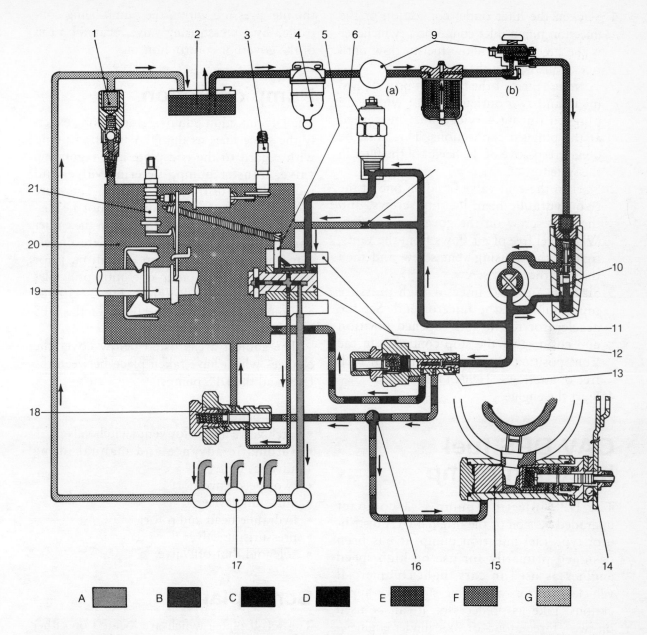

Fig 27.30 Diagramatic layout of the DPS fuel system   *Courtesy of CAV*

A Injection pressure
B Transfer pressure
C Metering pressure
D Differential pressure
E Feed pressure
F Cam box pressure
G Back leakage

1 Pressurising valve
2 Fuel tank
3 Throttle shaft

4 Sedimenter or water stop
5 Metering valve
6 Shut-off solenoid
7 Vent orifice
8 Filter
9 { (a) Feed pump (when fitted)
    or
    (b) Hand primer (when fitted)
10 Regulating valve
11 Transfer pump
12 Hydraulic head and rotor

13 Latch valve
14 Manual idle advance lever
15 Automatic advance and start retard unit
16 Head locating fitting
17 Injector
18 Rotor vent switch valve
19 Two-speed mechanical governor and control linkage assembly
20 Cam box
21 Idle shaft

1 Slacken the filter outlet connection or the injection pump inlet connection (whichever is the higher) and allow fuel to flow until free of air. Tighten the connection.

   Note: Filters of the type that provide two inlets and two outlets, two of which are plugged during service, must be vented at the plugged connections. This must be done irrespective of the height of the filter in the system.

2 Slacken the vent valve fitted on one of the two hydraulic head-locking screws, and the vent screw on the governor housing. When fuel free of air flows from the vents, tighten the housing vent screw and then the governor vent screw.

3 Slacken any two injector high-pressure pipe unions at the injector end. Set the accelerator to the fully opened position and ensure that the stop control is in the 'run' position. Turn the engine until fuel, free of air, flows. Tighten the unions.

4 Start the engine.

CAV DPS fuel injection pump

The DPS injection pump is a compact upgraded version of the original DPA distributor-type fuel injection pump. It has been designed primarily for use on high-speed engines as used in cars, light commercial vehicles, tractors and some stationary applications. Like its predecessor, it can be used on two-, three-, four- or six-cylinder engines.

The construction and operating principles of the DPS fuel injection pump are basically the same as those of the DPA pump, in that there are no ball or roller bearings, gears or highly stressed springs. There is also a single central pumping element, irrespective of the number of engine cylinders the pump is required to serve.

The pump is designed for flange mounting, and utilises a solid one-piece drive shaft. Pump lubrication is provided by diesel fuel, the fuel pressure within the pump being controlled by a pressurising valve located on top of the governor control housing.

Pump operation

The DPS injection pump operates along exactly the same lines as the DPA injection pump with regard to the end plate and regulating valve, transfer pump, metering valve, and pumping and distribution section. Therefore these sections of operation will not be discussed here but can be referred to in the earlier part of this chapter. For a complete understanding of the DPS pump operation, prior knowledge of DPA pump operation principles will be necessary. Refer to Fig 27.30 for a complete diagrammatic layout of the DPS fuel system.

The subject areas listed below cover the changes which have taken place between the DPA and the DPS pumps:

- scroll plates;
- latch valve and rotor vent switch valve;
- automatic advance and manual idling advance unit;
- two-speed governor;
- anti-stall device;
- hydraulic head and rotor;
- pressurising valve;
- solenoid shut-off valve.

Scroll plates

The scroll plates which are located on either side of the cam ring perform two functions: they provide automatic excess fuel delivery for quick engine starting under all operating conditions, and they adjust the maximum fuel delivery by controlling the outward movement of the pumping plungers. With reference to Fig 27.31, the scroll plates (9) are each provided with a slot in the outer rim to control their movement through a transversally mounted link plate (11), which slides into a slot in the governor control bracket.

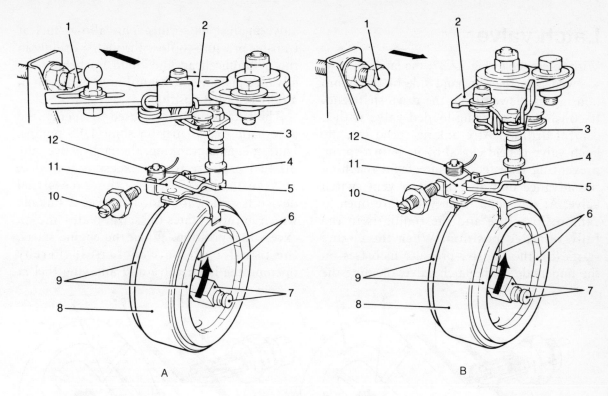

A Scroll plates in excess fuel position with throttle lever at 'idle' position

B Scroll plates in maximum fuel position with throttle lever open

1 Anti-stall stop
2 Throttle control—lever
3 Excess fuel linkage spring
4 Inner tongue—link plate
5 Excess fuel shaft and lever
6 Scroll profiles

7 Roller and shoe
8 Cam ring
9 Scroll plates
10 Maximum fuel adjuster screw
11 Link plate
12 Link plate spring

Fig 27.31   Schematic view of scroll plate mechanism   *Courtesy of CAV*

Movement of the link plate (11) is controlled in one direction by the excess fuel shaft (5) through spring linkage (3) connected to the throttle lever (2), and in the opposite direction by a link plate spring (12).

Excess fuel position

When the engine is to be started with the aid of excess fuel, the throttle lever is placed in the idling position, against the anti-stall screw (1). This moves the link plate (11) and scroll plates against the direction of pump rotation, compressing the link plate spring. The pumping plungers can now move further apart, allowing fuel in excess of normal maximum to be injected into the engine. At this point the cam ring is in the fully retarded

position for efficient starting. As the engine starts, the governor linkage turns the metering valve, thereby reducing the excess fuel quantity to that required for idle speed running.

Maximum fuel position

When the throttle is moved away from the anti-stall stop screw, the link plate spring moves the link plate and scroll plates transversally in the direction of pump rotation to the maximum fuelling position against a pre-set adjusting screw (10). In this position, the scroll plate profiles are now once again in a position to check the outward movement of the pump plungers, but this time to the maximum fuel quantity.

Latch valve

With reference to Fig 27.32, the latch valve is screwed into the left-hand side of the pump housing as viewed from the drive shaft end. It consists of a spring-loaded valve with a central drilling. At cranking speed (a), the latch valve is held closed by its return spring preventing transfer pressure from reaching the advance unit and the rotor vent switch valve. At this point, both valves are open to cambox pressure and the timing is in the fully retarded position. When the engine starts (b), the transfer pressure increases on the underside of the latch valve, opening the

valve against its spring. This allows fuel at transfer pressure to flow through a drilling in the hydraulic head and build up behind the advance piston, which until now had been in a fully retarded position.

The latch valve is also used to operate the automatic excess fuel on some DPS pumps. During engine cranking, the latch valve cuts off fuel pressure to the excess fuel device, as seen in Fig 27.33. As the excess fuel device is spring loaded, it moves a linkage which in turn rotates the scroll plates into an excess fuel position. When the engine starts, the transfer pressure increases, thereby opening the latch valve and allowing fuel at

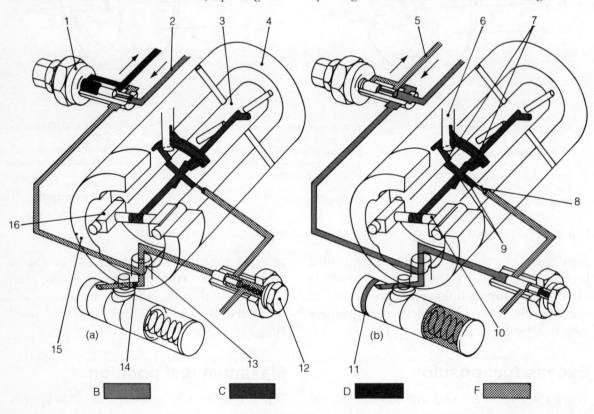

(a) Flow at engine cranking speeds
(b) Flow when engine starts

B Transfer pressure
C Metering pressure
D Differential pressure
F Cam box pressure

1 Latch valve
2 Inlet from transfer pump
3 Distributor rotor
4 Hydraulic head
5 Return to cam box
6 Metering valve
7 Filling ports—hydraulic head
8 Vent orifice

9   Rotor inlet ports
10 Pumping plunger
11 Pressure chamber auto-advance unit
12 Rotor vent switch valve
13 Head locating fitting
14 Ball valve
15 Cam ring
16 Roller and shoe

Fig 27.32   Diagrammatic layout of fuelling to latch valve and rotor vent switch valve
Courtesy of CAV

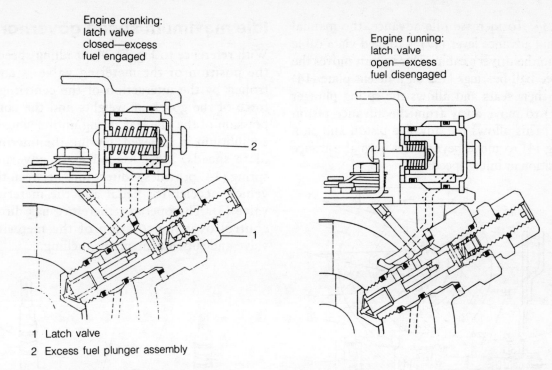

Engine cranking:
latch valve
closed—excess
fuel engaged

Engine running:
latch valve
open—excess
fuel disengaged

1 Latch valve
2 Excess fuel plunger assembly

Fig 27.33 Automatic excess fuel device   *Courtesy of CAV*

transfer pressure to build up behind the piston in the excess fuel plunger assembly. Increasing transfer pressure now moves the plunger and allows the spring-loaded scroll plates to be returned to the maximum fuel position.

Rotor vent switch valve

With reference to Fig 27.32, the rotor vent switch valve (12) is screwed into the right-hand side of the pump housing as viewed from the drive shaft end, and consists of a spring-loaded valve within a body.

The rotor vent switch valve also acts as a retaining bolt for the hydraulic head. Whenever the engine is being cranked over (a), the rotor (3) is being self-vented. This is due to the rotor vent switch valve being open and allowing the rotor to vent directly to the cambox housing. Self-venting of the rotor occurs every pump revolution when a vent orifice (8) in the hydraulic head communicates in turn with each of the rotor-inlet ports (9). Air and fuel are forced at metering

pressure past the orifice and travel through passages in the hydraulic head across the rotor vent switch valve to the cambox. When the engine starts (b), transfer pressure builds up and opens the latch valve, which in turn allows transfer pressure to act on the rotor vent switch valve, which then closes against its spring, thus isolating the venting passage from the cambox. Self-venting of the rotor now ceases.

Automatic advance and manual idling advance unit

The advance unit incorporates an automatic start retard function that operates at engine cranking speeds and progressively advances the start of injection as the engine speed increases.

Engines operating at low ambient temperatures may require additional injection advance to improve cold idling combustion stability and so prevent an engine misfire. An optional driver-operated manual advance device can be fitted to the advance unit as shown in Fig

27.34. To increase idle advance, the manual idling advance lever (17) is rotated via a cable from the driver's cabin. This in turn moves the three ball-bearings (15) on a detent plate (14) off their seats and allows the spring plunger (11) to move away from the advance piston (8). This allows the advance piston and cam ring (4) to move beyond the normal advance position at idling speed.

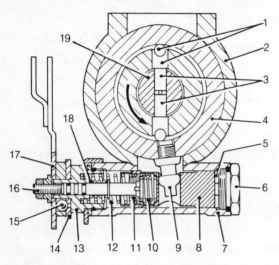

1	Roller and shoe	11	Spring plunger
2	Pump housing	12	Advance spring
3	Plungers	13	Advance spring end
4	Cam ring		cap
5	Transfer pressure	14	Detent plates
	chamber	15	Ball
6	Pressure end plug	16	Spindle
7	Auto-advance housing	17	Manual idling
8	Piston		advance lever
9	Cam advance screw	18	Spindle spring
10	1st stage (retard) spring	19	Distributor rotor

Fig 27.34 Sectioned view of auto-advanced and start retard unit with manual idlingadvance lever
Courtesy of CAV

Mechanical governor

Depending on the application of the DPS pump, two types of mechanical centrifugal governor can be used. For industrial use, a variable-speed governor is used. Its operation is the same as that of the DPA mechanical governor described previously. For automotive use, an idle maximum speed governor is used.

Idle maximum speed governor

With reference to Fig 27.34, at idling speeds, the position of the metering valve is controlled by the interaction of the centrifugal force of the governor weights and the compression of the idle leaf spring until a state of equilibrium is achieved. During the intermediate speeds, a pre-loaded main governor spring (14) provides a direct link between the vehicle accelerator pedal and the metering valve (3). The operator therefore has direct control over the rotation of the metering valve and subsequent engine fuelling.

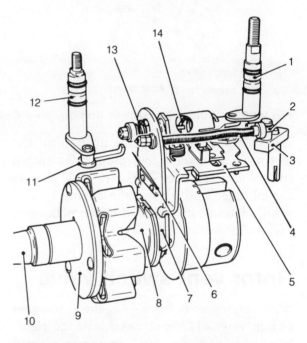

1	Throttle lever shaft	8	Thrust sleeve
2	Linkage hook	9	Governor flyweight
3	Metering valve		assembly
4	Governor link arm and	10	Drive shaft
	spring	11	Idle actuator
5	Control bracket	12	Idling lever shaft
6	Idling spring	13	Anti-stall device
7	Governor arm	14	Main governor spring

Fig 27.35 Schematic of the idle maximum speed mechanical governor
Courtesy of CAV

As the engine reaches its maximum speed, the centrifugal force of the governor flyweights (9) overcomes the pre-loaded tension of the main governor spring. The governor arm (7) now moves and rotates the metering valve to reduce the amount of fuel delivered, therefore controlling engine speed.

Anti-stall device

An anti-stall device is fitted to the DPS pump to prevent the engine stalling during deceleration. The anti-stall device shown in Fig 27.35 (13) is fitted between the governor arm (7) and the main governor spring (14) anchor point.

During deceleration, the main governor spring is released rapidly. This creates an imbalance between the centrifugal force of the governor weights and the governor spring, thus moving the governor arm and therefore the metering valve past the no-fuel delivery position. The anti-stall spring checks the movement of the governor arm during this phase of pump operation and ensures rapid reopening of the metering valve, thereby maintaining sufficient fuel delivery to prevent the engine from stalling at low rpm.

Hydraulic head and rotor

With reference to Fig 27.36, the hydraulic head and rotor are similar to the DPA head and rotor except on certain pumps. For pumps working under gravity fuel feed pressure, a self-venting orifice (1) removes any air bubbles from the fuel via a drilling (10) to the cambox before fuel flows to the pumping plungers. This helps in terms of a more efficient bleeding of air from the fuel injection pump during operation. It also enables an easy restart without bleeding whenever the engine runs out of fuel.

Some engines which require smooth idling characteristics have pumps fitted which have an equalisation groove (3) around the rotor shaft and by-pass holes in the delivery valves. The equalisation groove is cut around the majority of the circumference of the rotor on the same plane as the distribution outlet port (5). The delivery valves which have either a

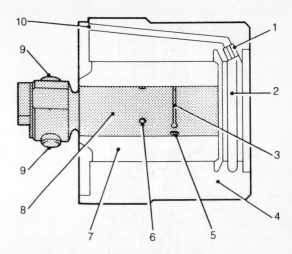

1 Vent orifice	6 Rotor filling port
2 Transfer pump recess	7 Sleeve
3 Equalisation groove	8 Distributor rotor
4 Barrel—hydraulic head	9 Plunger
5 Distributor outlet port	10 Drilling to cam box

Fig 27.36   Cut-away view of the hydraulic head and rotor
Courtesy of CAV

centrally drilled hole or a by-pass slot cut in them allow fuel to flow back into the equalisation groove at the end of injection. In operation, as an injector ceases to inject fuel and the delivery valve closes on its seat, residual fuel line pressure acts via the drilling in the delivery valve on the equalisation groove around the rotor. This achieves a constant residual line pressure in all the lines and improves line-to-line deliveries, particularly at idling speeds.

Pressurising valve

The pressurising valve is screwed into the top of the governor control cover, as shown in Fig 27.37. It consists of a spring-loaded ball and seat assembly. The lower spring is designed to act as a coarse filter to prevent anything from entering the valve and causing it to stick. Throughout the engine speed range, the fuel pressure in the cambox would fluctuate greatly if it were not for the pressurising valve, which eliminates pressure surges and controls cambox pressure to a

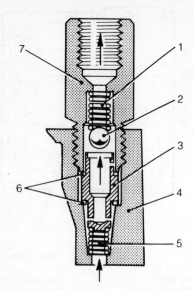

1	Upper spring	5	Lower spring
2	Ball valve	6	Copper washer
3	Valve seat	7	Valve holder
4	Governor control cover		

Fig 27.37 Section view of pressuring valve assembly in the relieving position
Courtesy of CAV

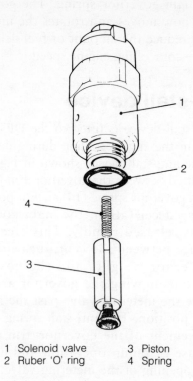

1	Solenoid valve	3	Piston
2	Ruber 'O' ring	4	Spring

Fig 27.38 Exploded view of solenoid-operated fuel shut-off valve
Courtesy of CAV

constant pre-set value. Back leakage fuel from the pressurising valve flows back to the fuel tank or filter housing.

Solenoid shut-off valve

An electrically operated fuel shut-off valve as seen in Fig 27.38 is screwed into the top of the hydraulic head and is used to stop the engine by cutting off the flow of fuel from the transfer pump to the metering valve. Being electrically operated, the device is readily operated by the stop–start key.

When the key is operated to start the engine, the solenoid is energised and lifts the piston against spring pressure, allowing fuel at transfer pressure to pass to the metering valve. When the engine is to be stopped, the power to the solenoid is switched off and a spring in the solenoid pushes the piston down, preventing fuel flow to the metering valve and rotor ports, thus stopping the engine.

Fuel pump testing

After an overhaul, a DPS fuel injection pump must be tested on a fuel injection test bench and adjusted to set specifications as per the DPS test plan. The procedure for testing and adjusting this pump should be carried out in accordance with the manufacturer's manual.

Pump timing

DPS pump timing is more involved and specialised than conventional DPA timing. A special timing tool is required, and the timing settings also alter due to the application of the pump. For this reason, a general timing explanation has not been included here. The relevant technical service information should be consulted prior to timing the pump.

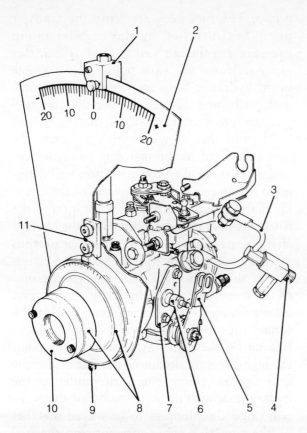

1 Clamp and pointer } tool part no.
2 Quadrant   } 7244-449
3 Timing adaptor assembly part no. 7144-262
4 Connection to nozzle test outfit
5 Manual idling lever in advanced position
6 Plunger timing tool, part no. 7244-448
7 Timing cover plate
8 Flange marking tool, part no. 7244-27
9 Locking screw
10 Insert
11 Securing bracket

Fig 27.39 Static timing tool attached to a
DPS pump
Courtesy of CAV

Pump-to-engine timing

There are two methods which can be used to
time a DPS pump to the engine.

The first method is to align the master
spline or key way of the pump drive shaft
with the mating spline on the engine drive
hub and then align the scribe mark on the
pump mounting flange. Finally, tighten the
mounting bolts and bleed the system.

The second method is by rotating the
engine in the direction of rotation until no. 1
piston is at the start of injection point on the
compression stroke. With the pump off the
engine and with reference to Fig 27.39,
rotate the pump drive shaft until the pump
timing tool (6) can be inserted into the pump
housing and locate the groove in the timing
disc. At this stage, the pump can be fitted to
the engine and secured in place. Following
this, bleed the fuel system.

The Roosa Master rotary injection pump

The Roosa Master DM and DB2 rotary distributor fuel injection pumps are similar in
construction and operation to the CAV DPA
fuel injection pumps. For this reason, only the
basic operation and fuel flow will be discussed.
However, the Roosa Master pump differs from
the DPA pump in its maximum fuel adjustment, its speed adjustment and its injection
pump timing to the engine. There are other
variations as well that will be mentioned
during the description of operation.

Basic pump operation

The transfer pump located at the rear of the
injection pump is driven via the distributor
pump drive shaft and rotor. It is a positive
displacement vane-type pump with four
vanes fitted to a rotor turning within a cam
ring. Transfer pressure is controlled by a regulating valve adjacent to the vane pump.

The distributor rotor has one or two
charging ports for efficient charging of the
pump plungers and one discharge port. The
distributor rotor also houses the two pumping plungers. High-pressure pumping is
achieved by the pump plungers being simultaneously forced towards each other by the
lobes on the cam ring via the cam rollers, the
number of cam lobes being the same for an

even number or double for an odd number of engine cylinders. The rotor rotates within very precise tolerances inside the hydraulic head, which houses the metering valve, the circular fuel passage, the discharge ports and discharge fittings. An injection advance device is mounted under the pump and automatically advances or retards injection timing, depending on engine speed.

The governor is of the mechanical flyweight design, incorporating the fundamentals of spring force and centrifugal force working in balance with one another to control the metering valve position.

Engine shutdown is achieved by moving the metering valve into a closed position by the operation of an external shut-off lever.

Charging and discharging cycles

By reference to Fig 27.41, it can be seen that fuel from the tank passes through the fuel filters and feed pump (if fitted) to the fuel inlet opening and screen to the vane type transfer pump. The fuel pressure from the transfer pump is controlled by the transfer pump pressure regulating valve. Fuel at transfer pressure leaves the vane pump via a passage in the hydraulic head and passes to the automatic advance device and the circular fuel passage surrounding the rotor shaft.

The fuel then flows through a port in the hydraulic head to the metering valve, which, under the control of the governor, will determine the amount of fuel flowing to the circular charging passage. With the rotation of the rotor, the inlet passage aligns with the circular charging passages in the hydraulic head, thus allowing fuel to flow into the pumping chamber, as shown in Fig 27.42. Further rotation of the rotor will move the charging port and inlet passages out of alignment and at the same time the plunger rollers will begin to ride up on the cam ring lobes. At this point the high-pressure discharge passage will come into alignment with one of the outlets in the hydraulic head. Further rotation of the rotor will cause the plungers to be forced together by the cam ring lobes, pressurising the fuel

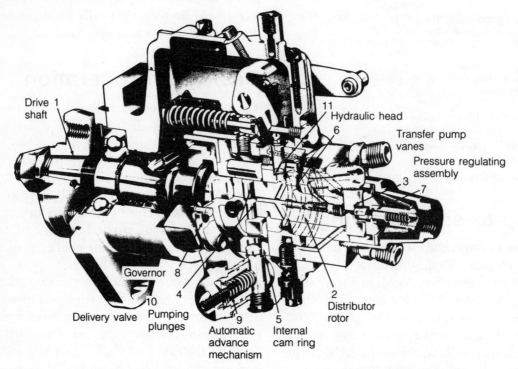

Fig 27.40   A Roosa Master DM fuel injection pump   *Courtesy of Stanadyne*

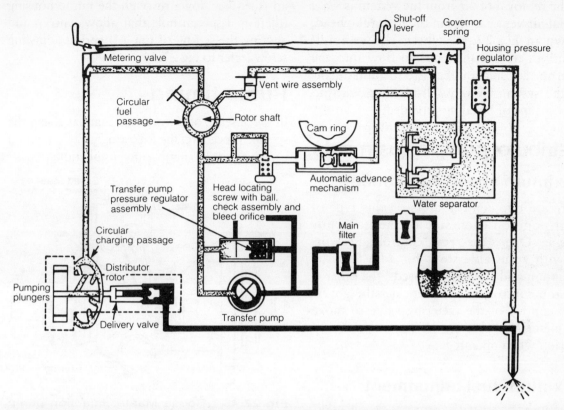

Fig 27.41 Roosa Master distributor pump fuel circuit *Courtesy of Stanadyne*

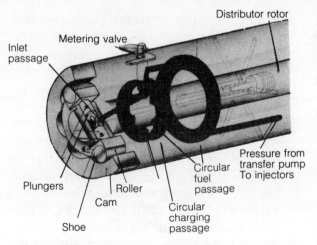

Fig 27.42 Charging cycle — Roosa Master DB fuel injection pump
Courtesy of Stanadyne

that is delivered to the outlet connections and on to the injectors (Fig 27.43).

During pump operation, when the plungers are not being intermittently charged with fuel at transfer pressure, the flow of fuel is diverted via slots in the rotor shaft for circulation through the pump housing for the purposes of lubrication, cooling and purging air that may have entered the system.

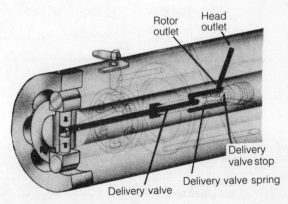

Fig 27.43 Discharge cycle — Roosa Master DB fuel injection pump
Courtesy of Stanadyne

The removal of air from the system is via a special air vent passage in the hydraulic head, shown in Fig 27.41, which allows small quantities of fuel (and air) to flow into the governor housing and back to the tank, making the system entirely self-bleeding with no other means of bleeding provided.

Distributor pump adjustments

Maximum speed adjustment

There are two control levers on this type of pump, one on each side of the governor housing. One is the speed control and is fitted with adjustable stops for adjusting the maximum and idle engine speeds; the other is the stop control, which over-rides the governor's control of the metering valve to move the metering valve to the no-fuel delivery position when operated.

Maximum fuel adjustment

This adjustment should only be made when the pump is on a test bench and the quantity of fuel delivered by the pump should always be within the manufacturer's specifications. The adjustments is carried out by first removing the top from the governor housing and inserting

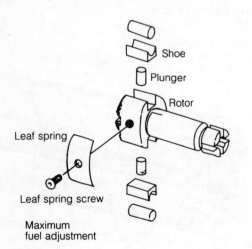

Fig 21.44 Rotor assembly showing leaf spring and screw fuel adjustment
Courtesy of Stanadyne

an Allen key down through the pump housing (there is a special hole that allows entry), and altering the setting of the leaf spring adjusting screw (refer to Fig 27.44).

Pump timing

In the absence of a workshop manual giving the specific procedure, the following general method can be applied to almost any installation:

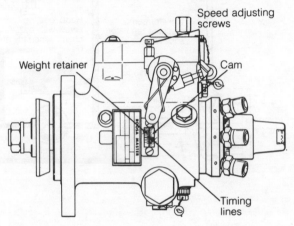

Fig 27.45 Roosa Master injection pump showing timing marks
Courtesy of Stanadyne

1 Rotate the engine crankshaft in the normal direction of rotation until no. 1 piston approaches TDC on the compression stroke. Continue to turn the crankshaft until the injection timing marks on the fan pulley or flywheel align.
2 Remove the small timing cover plate on the side of the pump housing and examine the timing marks for alignment (Fig 27.45). If the timing marks don't align, loosen the pump mounting bolts and rotate the pump until the marks align, then retighten mounting bolts.
3 Recheck the timing by rotating the engine forward for two revolutions and checking that the crankshaft timing marks and the pump timing marks align.

Pump service

Pump service — disassembly, inspection,

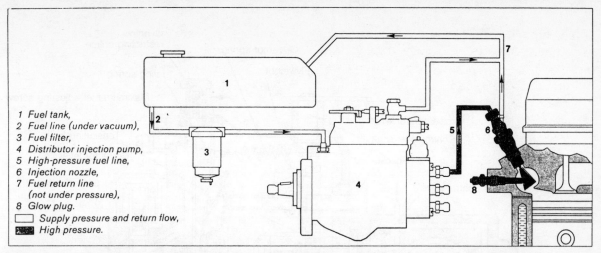

1 Fuel tank,
2 Fuel line (under vacuum),
3 Fuel filter,
4 Distributor injection pump,
5 High-pressure fuel line,
6 Injection nozzle,
7 Fuel return line
   (not under pressure),
8 Glow plug.
☐ Supply pressure and return flow,
▨ High pressure.

Fig 27.46   Fuel flow in a VE distributor fuel injection system
Courtesy of Robert Bosch BmbH

overhaul and adjusting — should be undertaken only with reference to Roosa Master Workshop Manuals and Service Data, using approved testing equipment.

The Bosch VE-type distributor pump

The VE-type distributor fuel injection pump is used on a wide variety of small to medium power diesel engines used in such applications as cars, commercial vehicles, small boats, earthmoving equipment and agricultural tractors. The VE injection pump is also manufactured under licence by other injection equipment manufacturers, such Nippon Denso and Zexel.

The VE type injection pump has a single high-pressure pumping chamber and plunger, regardless of the number of engine cylinders it has to serve. Fuel delivered from the high-pressure chamber is directed by means of a distributor groove in the plunger to a number of outlet ports corresponding to the number of engine cylinders. The pump is driven by a drive shaft, which is connected via a driving disc to a cam plate and plunger. The cam plate is designed with the same number of face cams as the engine has cylinders. As the cam plate rotates, it rides up and down a set of fixed rollers, causing the plunger to rotate

and reciprocate to provide both the pumping and distributing action.

Governing of the VE pump is accomplished by means of a mechanical governor incorporated in the pump housing.

To stop an engine fitted with a VE pump, a solenoid shut-off valve is used, which prevents the flow of fuel to charge the chamber, thereby preventing injection from taking place.

The pump also incorporates an automatic advance unit, which advances and retards the timing relative to the changing engine speed and load conditions.

As a starting aid in cold operating conditions, an optional manually or automatically controlled injection advance device can be fitted external to the pump to improve starting capabilities.

The pump is not only compact in size, but weighs about half as much as its in-line counterpart. The internal components are completely lubricated throughout by fuel and no special lubricating oil or system is required. The fuel continually circulates through the pump and back to the fuel tank, thereby continually cooling and purging air from the pump.

Construction and operation

The construction and operation of the pump may be followed by considering it to be composed of six individual working

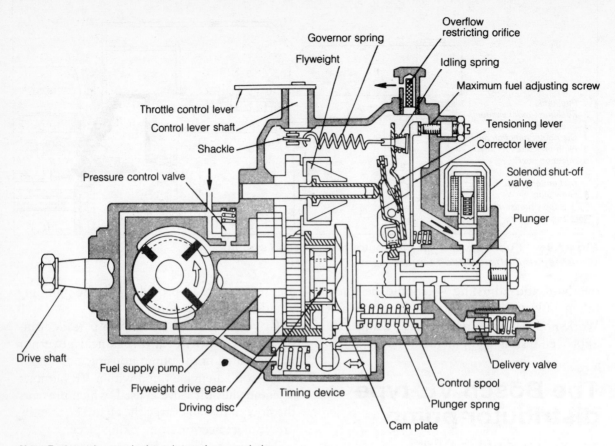

Note: Fuel-supply pump is shown in two views, one being a 90°-rotated view with the pump vanes and rotor in section and the other being a normal side view.
Timing device is shown as turned around by 90°

Fig 27.47   Schematic diagram of a VE fuel injection pump   *Courtesy of Robert Bosch GmbH*

modules, and examining each of those modules in turn:

1 fuel supply pump;
2 pumping and distribution section;
3 governing section;
4 solenoid shut-off valve;
5 automatic advance unit;
6 starting aids.

Fuel supply pump

Low-pressure charging of the pump housing is accomplished by a vane-type fuel supply pump situated at the drive end of the distributor pump. Fuel flow is from the fuel tank through the fuel filter and into the vane pump; from here, it enters the pump housing

at pressures that vary between 360 kPa and 810 kPa. Generally there is no fuel feed pump fitted to this fuel system, as the vane pump serves this purpose.

Being a constant displacement pump, the fuel supply pump can deliver several times the amount of fuel required for injection. Therefore, when the pump housing pressure reaches a predetermined level, excess fuel delivery is relieved via a pressure control valve and returned back to the inlet side of the fuel supply pump, as shown in Fig 27.48.

The pressure control valve is located beside the fuel supply pump and is of the spring-loaded piston type. This valve is pre-set on manufacture and requires no further adjustment.

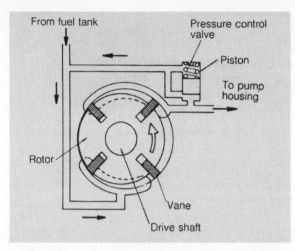

Fig 27.48 Arrangement of the fuel supply pump
Courtesy of Zexel

For the purpose of self-bleeding and cooling of the entire pump, fuel circulates through an overflow restricting orifice back to the fuel tank. The overflow restricting orifice is 0.6 mm in diameter and is situated in the banjo bolt in the fuel return line on top of the pump housing. While this orifice allows fuel to return to the fuel tank, it offers sufficient restriction to fuel flow from the fuel supply pump to cause the injection pump housing to be pressurised. Further, in conjunction with the fuel supply pump pressure control valve, the orifice is responsible for the pump housing fuel pressure necessary for the charging of the high-pressure chamber and the operation of the automatic injection advance unit.

A hand-operated plunger-type pump is incorporated into the body of the fuel filter housing for priming or bleeding the system. The hand pump is used to prime the system whenever the fuel filter is changed or the fuel pump housing is drained.

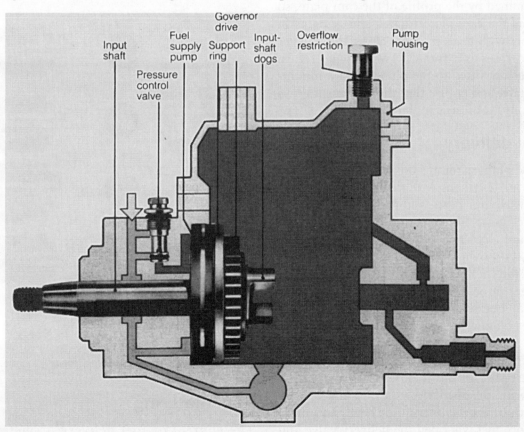

Fig 27.49   Layout of the pressure control valve and overflow restriction
Courtesy of Robert Bosch GmbH

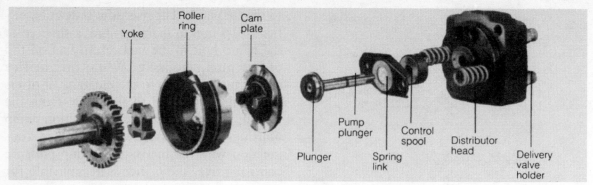

Fig 27.50 Exploded view of the high-pressure pumping assembly
Courtesy of Robert Bosch GmbH

Pumping and distribution section

The distributor pump drive shaft simultaneously drives the fuel supply pump, the cam plate and the pump plunger as shown in Fig 27.50. The plunger pumping stroke length is determined by the profile of the cam plate, so that as the cam plate rotates and remains in contact with the four cam rollers, the plunger reciprocates as it rotates. Two plunger return springs are fitted to the plunger via a mounting plate, and ensure that the plunger follows the contour of the cam face plate.

Fuel delivery

As the plunger rotates on its downstroke, the metering slit aligns with the intake passage in the distributor head, and fuel, under pressure in the pump housing, flows into the high-pressure chamber and drilling in the plunger body, as shown in Fig 27.51.

As the cam face runs up on the rollers, the plunger direction is reversed and the delivery stroke begins. The plunger rotates as it moves up and the intake passage is closed off early in the pumping stroke so that further upward movement of the plunger will raise the pressure of the fuel. Continued rotation will bring the distributor slit into line with an outlet port in the distributor head, and high-pressure fuel will open the delivery valve and flow into the injector line to be injected into the combustion chamber via the injector. The

delivery stroke is completed when the cut-off bore in the plunger moves past and out of the control spool, thus allowing the high-pressure fuel in the pumping chamber to discharge into the pump housing. The plunger then returns on its down-stroke to begin another charging stroke.

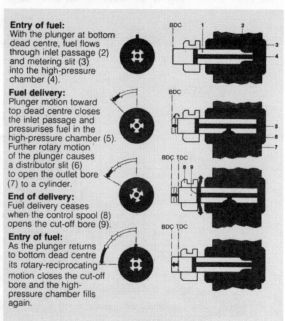

Entry of fuel:
With the plunger at bottom dead centre, fuel flows through inlet passage (2) and metering slit (3) into the high-pressure chamber (4).

Fuel delivery:
Plunger motion toward top dead centre closes the inlet passage and pressurises fuel in the high-pressure chamber (5). Further rotary motion of the plunger causes a distributor slit (6) to open the outlet bore (7) to a cylinder.

End of delivery:
Fuel delivery ceases when the control spool (8) opens the cut-off bore (9).

Entry of fuel:
As the plunger returns to bottom dead centre its rotary-reciprocating motion closes the cut-off bore and the high-pressure chamber fills again.

Fig 27.51 Pumping cycle of the VE fuel injection pump
Courtesy of Robert Bosch GmbH

Fuel metering

The control of fuel delivery or metering is carried out by the axial movement of the sliding control spool on the plunger, as shown

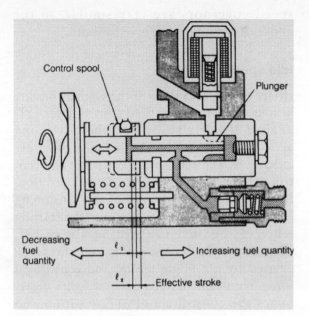

Fig 27.52 Spool control of effective pumping stroke and fuel delivery
Courtesy of Zexel

in Fig 27.52. Movement of the control spool to the left will decrease fuel delivery and conversely, when it is moved to the right, fuel delivery will increase.

Movement of the control spool to alter the effective pumping stroke during operation is done by the governor mechanism. If the maximum fuel delivery of the pump is to be altered, the maximum fuel adjusting screw (Fig 27.47) is provided for this purpose.

Note: Under no circumstances should the maximum fuel delivery of the fuel pump be altered unless it is by trained service personnel with appropriate testing equipment. Alteration of the fuel pump's output under any other conditions can lead to serious engine damage.

Delivery valve

The delivery valves in the VE-type injection pump perform the same functions as in other types of injection pumps; for more detailed explanation, refer to Chapter 26.

Governing section

Two types of governor are available for VE-type pumps to suit a range of engine applications. They are all mechanical flyweight governors, classified as follows:

- variable speed;
- idling and maximum speed.

The variable speed governor is designed to control the engine rpm at any selected speed, including idle and maximum no-load engine

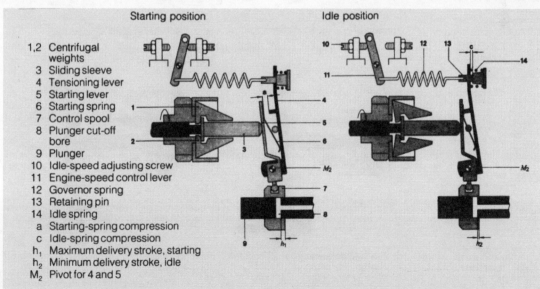

1,2	Centrifugal weights
3	Sliding sleeve
4	Tensioning lever
5	Starting lever
6	Starting spring
7	Control spool
8	Plunger cut-off bore
9	Plunger
10	Idle-speed adjusting screw
11	Engine-speed control lever
12	Governor spring
13	Retaining pin
14	Idle spring
a	Starting-spring compression
c	Idle-spring compression
h_1	Maximum delivery stroke, starting
h_2	Minimum delivery stroke, idle
M_2	Pivot for 4 and 5

Fig 27.53 Starting and idling positions of the variable speed governor mechanism
Courtesy of Robert Bosch GmbH

speeds. This governor is generally fitted to injection pumps used on industrial engines and tractors.

The idling and maximum speed governor is a typical automotive governor, controlling the engine rpm at idle and maximum speed only. The speed range between idle and maximum speed is controlled entirely by the operator. This governor is used in automotive applications.

Variable speed governor operation

Starting position

(**Refer to Fig 27.53**) With the centrifugal weights at rest and in a fully collapsed position, as the speed control lever is moved to the maximum speed position, the tension of the governor spring moves the tensioning lever (4) firmly to the left. As a result, the starting leaf spring (6) presses on the starting lever (5). The lever then pivots on its mounting point M2 and simultaneously moves the sliding sleeve (3) back to its extreme left position, and the control spool (7) to its maximum fuel position to facilitate easy starting.

Note: The starting positions for variable speed governors and idling and maximum speed governors are very similar, so the above description will serve for both.

Idle speed operation

(**Refer to Fig 27.53**) With the engine running at idle speed and the speed control lever (11) against the idle stop (10), the governing action is achieved by the balance of forces exerted by the idle spring (14) and the centrifugal governor flyweights. In this position, the idling spring (14) pushes the tensioning lever (4) to the left, which moves the starting lever (5) against the sliding sleeve (3). Therefore, the balance between the force exerted by the idling spring and centrifugal force acting on the governor weights determines the control spool's (7) position and relative fuel delivery for idle speed.

Higher speed operation

(**Refer to Fig 27.54**) When the speed control lever is turned from idle toward the maximum speed position, the governor spring (4) is tensioned, and the idle spring (5) is compressed until the shoulder of the idle spring guide contacts the tensioning lever (7). The tensioning lever then pivots on M2, compressing

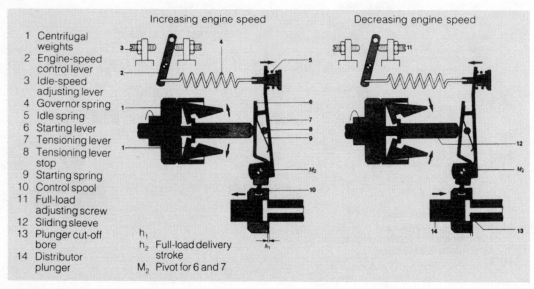

1 Centrifugal weights
2 Engine-speed control lever
3 Idle-speed adjusting lever
4 Governor spring
5 Idle spring
6 Starting lever
7 Tensioning lever
8 Tensioning lever stop
9 Starting spring
10 Control spool
11 Full-load adjusting screw
12 Sliding sleeve
13 Plunger cut-off bore
14 Distributor plunger
h_1
h_2 Full-load delivery stroke
M_2 Pivot for 6 and 7

Fig 27.54 Effect of engine speed changes — variable speed governor
Courtesy of Robert Bosch GmbH

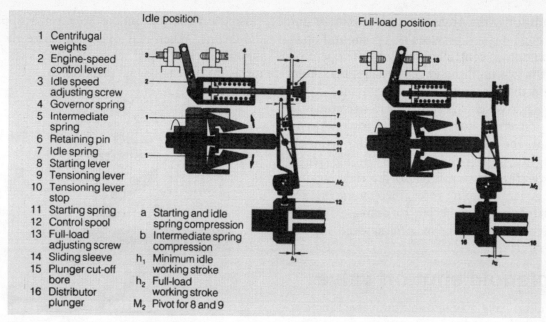

1 Centrifugal weights
2 Engine-speed control lever
3 Idle speed adjusting screw
4 Governor spring
5 Intermediate spring
6 Retaining pin
7 Idle spring
8 Starting lever
9 Tensioning lever
10 Tensioning lever stop
11 Starting spring
12 Control spool
13 Full-load adjusting screw
14 Sliding sleeve
15 Plunger cut-off bore
16 Distributor plunger

a Starting and idle spring compression
b Intermediate spring compression
h_1 Minimum idle working stroke
h_2 Full-load working stroke
M_2 Pivot for 8 and 9

Fig 27.55   Idle and full-load positions — idle and maximum speed governor
Courtesy of Robert Bosch GmbH

the starting spring (9) until the stop bears against the starting lever (6), which then also pivots on M2. The lower end of the starting lever moves the control spool (10) to the right, increasing the fuel delivery to the engine.

The engine speed increases due to the additional fuel delivery until the governor weight force, acting through the sliding sleeve against the starting lever, overcomes some of the initial governor spring force and pivots the starting lever on M2. This moves the control spool to the left to decrease the fuel delivery. Thus a balance is established between the governor spring force as determined by the speed control lever position, and the centrifugal force acting on the governor weights. A variation to either factor causes an immediate corrective change in the position of the control spool and subsequent engine fuelling. This action occurs at all selected speeds above idle.

Idle and maximum speed governor operation

Idle speed operation

(**Refer to Fig 27.55**) With the engine running at idle speed, the centrifugal force acting on the flyweights is applied via the sliding sleeve (14) to the starting lever (8), which reacts with the idle spring (7). Therefore the pre-set tension of the idle spring reacting and balancing with the governor weights' centrifugal force determines the control spool (12) position and subsequent idle speed.

Idle speed through to maximum speed operation

(**Refer to Fig 27.55**) When the engine speed is to be increased, the speed control lever (2) is moved to the right, collapsing the starting spring (11) and the idling spring (7), and leaving the force of the intermediate spring (5) balancing with the governor flyweight centrifugal force. The intermediate spring allows a gradual transition through the limited governed range to the operator-controlled engine speed range.

Further movement of the speed control lever to increase the engine speed fully collapses the intermediate spring, and the shoulder of the retaining pin (6) presses against the tensioning lever (9), giving a direct coupling between the engine speed control lever and the sliding control spool. Under these conditions, the governor is inoperative and the engine speed between this point and up to maximum is controlled solely by the operator.

It is not until the engine reaches maximum speed that the centrifugal force acting on the governor weights is sufficient to overcome the pre-tensioned governor spring force. At this point, the centrifugal force on the governor weights, acting through the sliding sleeve, moves the starting lever to the right against the governor spring force, thereby moving the control spool to the left to decrease the fuel delivery and limit the maximum speed.

Solenoid shut-off valve

An electrically operated shut-off valve is used to stop the engine by cutting off the flow of fuel from the fuel supply pump to the high-pressure chamber. Being electrically operated, the device is readily operated by the stop–start key.

When the key is operated to start the engine, the solenoid is energised and lifts the valve from its seat in the fuel intake passage, allowing fuel to flow into the high-pressure chamber. Conversely, when the engine is to be stopped, the power to the solenoid is switched off and a spring in the solenoid pushes the valve down,

closing off the fuel intake port and stopping the engine. When it is operating correctly, an audible click is heard when the start switch is turned to the engine 'on' position.

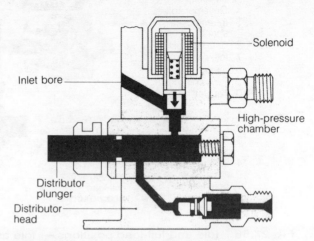

Fig 27.56   Solenoid shut-off

Automatic advance unit

The timing advance device (Fig 27.57) is designed to automatically adjust injection timing to suit changes in engine speed.

Operation

At low engine speed, the timer piston is held

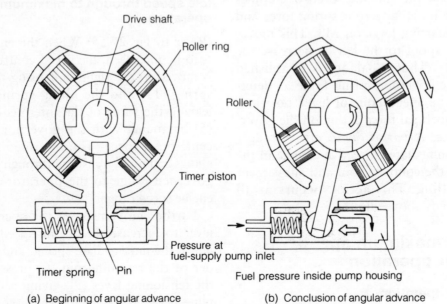

(a) Beginning of angular advance   (b) Conclusion of angular advance

Fig 27.57   Operation of the automatic advance unit   *Courtesy of Zexel*

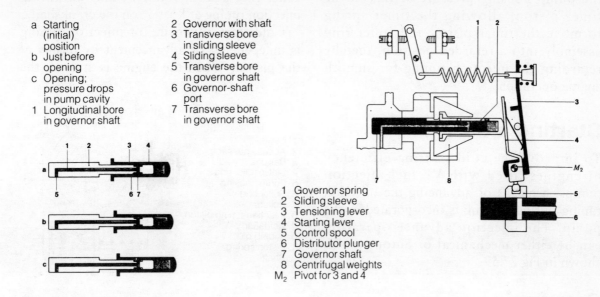

a Starting
  (initial)
  position
b Just before
  opening
c Opening;
  pressure drops
  in pump cavity
1 Longitudinal bore
  in governor shaft

2 Governor with shaft
3 Transverse bore
  in sliding sleeve
4 Sliding sleeve
5 Transverse bore
  in governor shaft
6 Governor-shaft
  port
7 Transverse bore
  in governor shaft

1 Governor spring
2 Sliding sleeve
3 Tensioning lever
4 Starting lever
5 Control spool
6 Distributor plunger
7 Governor shaft
8 Centrifugal weights
M_2 Pivot for 3 and 4

Fig 27.58   Governor assembly with load sensing advance/retard unit
Courtesy of Robert Bosch GmbH

against its stop (in a fully retarded position) by
a timer spring. As the speed of the engine
increases, the fuel supply pump pressure also
increases, progressively moving the timer piston
against the force exerted by the timer spring.
The timer piston's movement is transmitted via
a pin to the roller ring assembly, causing it to
rotate in a direction opposite to that of the
pump, thereby advancing injection timing.

Load sensing advance and retard unit

As loads vary on a diesel engine, the injection
timing must be advanced or retarded if opti-

mum engine performance is to be achieved.

With an engine operating in its normal
working load range, the automatic advance
unit would have moved the roller ring to its
maximum advanced position. If the load on
the engine decreases with the throttle position
unchanged, the engine speed will increase.

By reference to Fig 27.58b, it can be seen
that the resultant movement of the governor
weights will move the sliding sleeve (4) to
the right, until the port (3) in the sleeve
uncovers the drilling (7) in the governor
shaft, allowing fuel at supply pressure to
escape to the low-pressure side of the
fuel supply pump. This causes a drop in

1 Set screw
2 Cable
3 Stop
4 Coil spring
5 Advance lever

1 Temperature-
  sensitive
  control unit

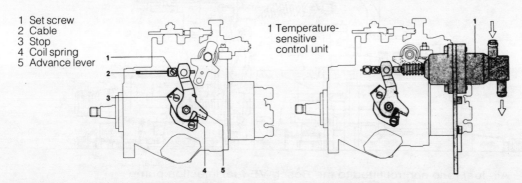

Fig 27.59   Cold-start injection advance devices   *Courtesy of Robert Bosch GmbH*

the pump housing pressure acting on the timer piston, allowing the timer spring to move the timer piston and roller ring assembly into a retarded position, thereby retarding the injection timing for smooth engine operation.

Starting aids

To improve the cold starting efficiency of engines fitted with VE fuel injection pumps, a means of advancing the injection timing during starting is incorporated in the pump. The injection advance operation can be either mechanical or automatic, as shown in Fig 27.59.

Operation

(Refer to Fig 27.60) In the manual system, when the cold-start cable is pulled, an advance lever (see previous diagram, Fig 27.59 (5)), turns a ball pin (3), to the roller ring (6). Turning this ball pin moves the

roller ring against rotation, thus advancing injection timing at least 5° on the crankshaft.

Cold-start advancing of injection timing is independent of advancement by means of the piston. When the engine is started, the

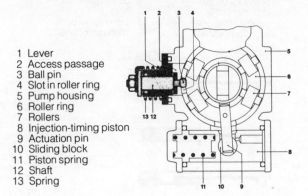

1 Lever
2 Access passage
3 Ball pin
4 Slot in roller ring
5 Pump housing
6 Roller ring
7 Rollers
8 Injection-timing piston
9 Actuation pin
10 Sliding block
11 Piston spring
12 Shaft
13 Spring

Fig 27.60 Operation of the mechanically operated cold start device
Courtesy of Robert Bosch GmbH

automatic (speed related) advance mechanism takes over without interference from the cold-start advance device.

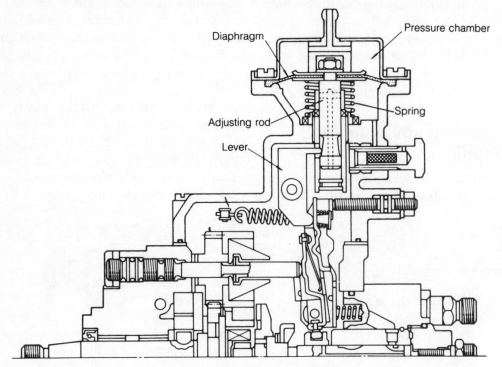

Fig 27.61 Air–fuel ratio control fitted to the Bosch VE fuel injection pump
Courtesy of Zexel

The automatic cold-starting system advances injection timing in the same way, except that the advance lever is operated by a temperature-sensitive bellows unit that reacts to changes in the water temperature of the engine. As the engine warms up, the advance unit becomes inoperative.

Air–fuel ratio control

The air–fuel ratio control unit is mounted on top of the fuel pump housing, as shown in Fig 27.61, and is used on fuel pumps fitted to turbocharged engines. When the turbocharger boost pressure is less than maximum, the device reduces fuel delivery accordingly so that the amount of fuel injected can be completely burned. If there were no set ratio between the maximum quantity of fuel injected and the quantity of air available, the turbocharged engine would be over-fuelled on acceleration, with resultant black smoke and poor fuel economy.

Operation

A pressure chamber on the top of the unit is connected to the engine inlet manifold by means of a flexible hose or pipe. Intake manifold boost pressure acts on the diaphragm (1) to oppose the force exerted by the spring (5) of the air–fuel ratio control. Therefore, when the engine and turbocharger increase in speed, boost pressure will also increase to act on the diaphragm and compress the spring.

Under low boost conditions, however, the spring holds the adjusting rod (2) in a higher position so that the larger diameter end of the control contour groove is in contact with the lever (3), which limits the leftward movement of the top of the tensioning lever, so limiting the maximum fuel delivery.

As boost pressure increases and the spring is compressed, the adjusting rod (2) moves down, causing the lever (3) to follow the contour of the adjusting rod, which allows the

tensioning lever to move the control spool towards the maximum fuel position.

Anti-reverse operation

Because of its design, the VE type injection pump will not inject fuel when turned in the direction opposite to that of normal rotation. This ensures that the engine will not fire under stall or roll-back conditions.

During normal operation, on the fuel intake stroke the intake port is open to allow fuel to flow into the high-pressure chamber, charging the system. By the start of the delivery stroke, the plunger has rotated so that the distributor slit is aligned with an outlet port in the distributor head. However, if the plunger is rotated in the reverse direction, the distributor slit will align with the intake port on the plunger upstroke, and fuel in the high-pressure chamber will be discharged back into the intake passage. As a result, injection cannot take place and the engine will not start.

VE injection pump timing

Injection pump timing is checked by measuring the plunger travel distance with the aid of a special adaption tool and dial indicator

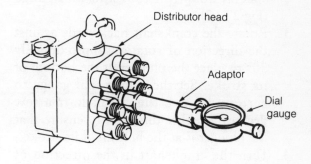

Fig 27.62 The timing dial gauge attached to the pump
Courtesy of Volvo

installed in the end of the distributor housing, as shown in Fig 27.62.

The timing procedure detailed below is common for engines fitted with VE-type fuel pumps, but the actual plunger travel distance used in the timing procedure will vary from engine to engine.

Timing procedure

1 Turn the engine in the direction of rotation until the valves in no. 4 cylinder (four-cylinder engine) or no. 6 cylinder (six-cylinder engine) are both rocking (valve overlap position). This will put no. 1 cylinder on TDC, between the compression and power strokes.

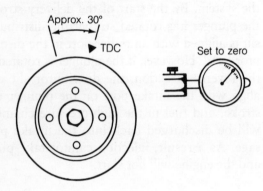

Fig 27.63   Zero setting the dial gauge
Courtesy of Volvo

2 Remove the small plug from the centre of the distributor head and install the special adaption tool and dial gauge (Fig 27.62).
3 Rotate the crankshaft backwards against the direction of rotation approximately 30° to place the plunger at the bottom of its stroke. Set the timing dial gauge to zero and move the crankshaft a few degrees in either direction to ensure that the plunger is at the bottom of its stroke.
4 Turn the crankshaft in the direction of rotation until the timing pointer on the flywheel or fan pulley aligns with the correct timing position — for example, TDC. With the engine in this position, read the dial indicator and refer to the manufacturer's specifications for the correct dimension.
5 If the dial gauge reading is not within the

correct range, loosen the two mounting bolts and mounting bracket and turn the pump body until the correct reading is obtained.
6 Tighten the mounting bolts and recheck the reading.
7 Disconnect the special measuring tool and refit the plug.
8 No bleeding is required as the pump is self-bleeding.
9 Start the engine.

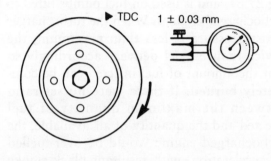

Fig 27.64   Checking the timing dimension
Courtesy of Volvo

Pump service

Pump service — disassembly, inspection, overhaul and adjusting — should be undertaken only with reference to VE Workshop Manuals and Service Data, using approved testing equipment.

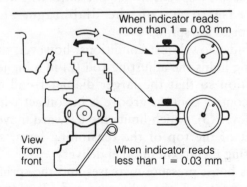

Fig 27.65   Adjusting the injection timing
Courtesy of Volvo

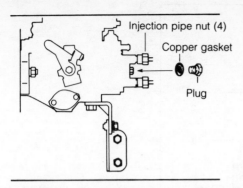

Fig 27.66   Refitting the access plug
Courtesy of Volvo

Electronic diesel control

Electronics are now being used on distributor type fuel injection systems to monitor engine operation and where necessary alter fuel metering and injection timing so as to achieve improved engine performance and fuel economy with minimal exhaust emissions. Electronic Diesel Control (EDC) replaces the centrifugal governor and with it comes a range of functional options which were never before available with a mechanical governed distributor-type fuel-injection pump.

EDC offers the following advantages:
- more accurate control over the start of injection and the quantity of fuel injected;
- more precise idle speed control;
- cruise control;
- temperature-compensated variations in fuel delivery;
- exhaust gas recirculation for improved emission control;
- electronic accelerator connected by closed loop circuitry to the injection pump for more sensitive governing;
- monitored engine operation and system self-diagnosis.

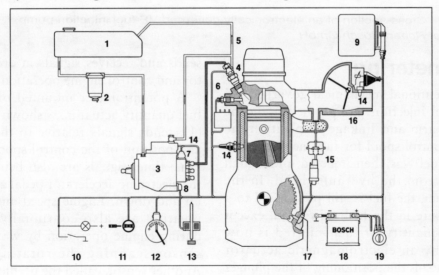

1	Fuel tank	11	Speed selector lever
2	Fuel filter	12	Accelerator-pedal sensor
3	VE pump	13	Road-speed sensor
4	Injection nozzle with needle-motion sensor	14	Temperature sensor (water, air, fuel)
5	Fuel return line	15	EGR valve
6	Sheathed-element glow plug, glow control unit	16	Air-flow sensor
7	Shut-off device	17	Engine-speed and TDC sensor
8	Solenoid valve	18	Battery
9	ECU (Electronic Control Unit)	19	Glow-plug and starter switch
10	Diagnosis indicator		

Fig 27.67   Schematic diagram of a fuel injection system with an electronically controlled VE fuel injection pump   *Courtesy of Robert Bosch GmbH*

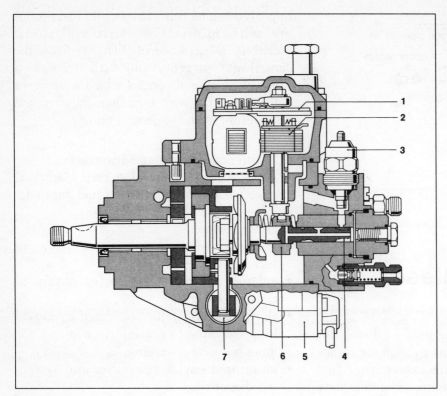

1 Control-collar position sensor

2 Injected fuel quantity actuator

3 Electromagnetic shut-off valve (ELAB)

4 Supply plunger

5 Solenoid valve for start of injection

6 Control spool

7 Timing device

Fig 27.68 Cross-section of an electronically governed VE fuel injection pump
Courtesy of Robert Bosch GmbH

Fuel metering

The conventional mechanical governed VE rotary fuel injection pump relied upon the governor arm and linkage to position the plunger control spool for fuel metering. The metered fuel was then injected under high pressure from the hydraulic head. In the EDC system, the fuel is still pressurised to a high pressure in the hydraulic head, except that the quantity of fuel injected is now metered by an electromagnetic actuator which controls the positioning of the plunger control spool.

Operational data acquisition

For the EDC system to operate efficiently, it must acquire and evaluate input data via sensors mounted on the injection pump, the engine and on the vehicle. Closed loop circuitry is the means by which the system sends and receives signals in order to monitor and control engine operation.

A potentiometer mounted on top of the fuel quantity actuator, as shown in Fig 27.68 (1), sends signals relative to the movement and position of the control spool (6). At the same time, signals are also being sent from the electronic accelerator pedal as it is moved up and down. Engine speed and crankshaft position are also continually monitored during engine operation by way of a speed sensor scanning the rotating flywheel. Another sensor, called the needle motion sensor, as shown in Fig 27.69, is located within the no. 1 cylinder injector and detects when injection commences.

Other inputs which are also continually fed into the EDC system during engine operation are:

- injection pump fuel temperature;
- engine coolant temperature;

- air intake temperature;
- manifold boost pressure;
- air intake quantity;
- vehicle speed;
- brake and clutch pedal position;
- the position of the cruise control operating switch.

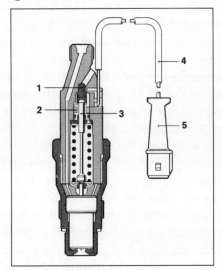

1	Adjusting pin	4	Cable
2	Sensor winding	5	Connector
3	Thrust pin		

Fig 27.69 **Injector nozzle assembly with needle motion sensor**
Courtesy of Robert Bosch GmbH

Closed loop circuitry

Closed loop circuits are used in electronic diesel control systems to provide an automatic accurate control of electronic processes. Engine and vehicle mounted sensors send data inputs to the electronic control unit which processes this information by comparing the input data received from the sensors with pre-programmed reference data in the control unit memory. The control unit then sends a compensating signal to output devices which adjust such things as quantity of fuel injected, injection timing and the amount of exhaust gas recirculated to the intake manifold. The resulting engine operation will change sensor output signal feedback to the control unit, thereby completing the cycle. This process, which takes place in a

fraction of a second, occurs continually during engine operation. In effect, the goal of the system is to control incoming data so that it conforms to the pre-set reference data programmed into the electronic control system memory.

The output devices, as mentioned previously, are used in the EDC system to perform mechanical operations within the fuel injection pump and on the engine. There are three output devices used in the system. They are as follows:

1 the solenoid valve mounted under the fuel injection pump, which is used to change injection timing;
2 the injected fuel quantity actuator mounted inside the injection pump, which is used to alter the position of the injector pump control spool;
3 the exhaust gas recirculation valve (EGR) mounted adjacent to the intake and exhaust manifolds, which is used to control the flow of exhaust gas into the intake manifold.

Operational data processing

On receiving feedback from the sensors, the EDC system uses this information to electronically control the quantity of fuel injected, the start of injection, exhaust gas recirculation rate and at the same time continually adapt the fuel delivered in accordance with the available boost air pressure in the intake manifold.

Engine governing

During engine operation, the signals received relative to the accelerator pedal position sensor and engine speed sensor are compared with the pre-set values programmed into the electronic control unit. Upon comparing the throttle position with that of the engine speed, the electronic control unit will determine whether or not a change in engine fuelling is necessary to bring engine speed in accordance with throttle position. This fuelling change is by way of the injected fuel quantity actuator (see Fig 27.68 (2)) moving the control spool until it has reached a fuel metered position which will bring engine speed to that set by the throttle lever position.

Governor operation will also ensure that the maximum speed of the engine is limited by the quantity of fuel injected. Any other information supplied to the EDC from vehicle- and engine-mounted sensors, such as coolant temperature, air temperature, boost air pressure, air quantity and clutch and brake position, are also taken into account to ensure efficient engine performance with minimal smoke emissions.

Start of injection

The point at which injection begins depends on the quantity of fuel to be injected, the speed and temperature of the engine and the boost air pressure if the engine is turbocharged. This information is recorded in the electronic control unit, shown in Fig 27.67 (9), which compares the actual commencement of injection measured by the needle motion sensor with the nominal start of injection as programmed into the EDC control system. Any necessary adjustment to the start of injection is then performed by a solenoid valve, shown in Fig 27.67 (8), which adjusts the pressure on the pressure side of the timing advance piston. Varying the pressure acting on the timing advance piston will in turn alter the injection advance position until such time as the nominal start of injection has been reached.

Exhaust gas recirculation

An exhaust gas recirculation system is being used on some diesel engines to dilute the air in the intake manifold with a small percentage of exhaust gas. During combustion, this exhaust gas does not burn, but absorbs some of the heat of combustion. This has the effect of lowering the temperature of the gas in the cylinder, thereby reducing nitrogen oxide emission.

A solenoid-operated EGR valve, as shown in Fig 27.67 (15), controls the flow of exhaust gas into the intake manifold. During engine starting and warmup, a blocking signal is sent from the electronic control unit to close the valve. As a result, exhaust gas recirculation does not take place. However, at all other times the valve is open, allowing the exhaust gas to be recirculated in response to the amount of fuel injected, the speed and temperature of the engine, and the rate of air flow entering the intake manifold.

Self-diagnosis

The EDC system has a built-in monitoring and self-diagnosis program which continually processes all sensor input information and compares this with pre-set programmed safe operating limits. If a problem arises, it is immediately stored as a fault code in the electronic control unit's memory and a warning is sent to the operator via a dash-mounted warning light. By activating the diagnostic mode in the system, a fault code can be displayed in the form of a flashing light sequence which will identify the particular problem area.

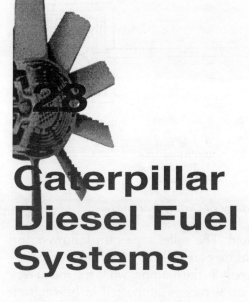

Caterpillar Diesel Fuel Systems

Caterpillar Inc. use three types of fuel system on their current production diesel engines:

1 compact pump fuel system;
2 new scroll fuel system;
3 unit injector fuel system.

The compact pump fuel system

The compact pump uses a constant-stroke, cam-operated, plunger-type injection pump of unique concept. The pumps follow the basic in-line pump principle of operation. They require no calibration and phasing as we know it, need no test bench for setting, and can have an individual pumping element changed without removing the pump from the engine. The plungers on Caterpillar pumps are similar to conventional plungers except that the helix on the plunger is called a scroll.

Operation

With reference to Fig 28.1, fuel flows from the tank through the primary fuel filter (10) and into the transfer pump (11). From the transfer pump, fuel continues to flow under low pressure through the priming pump (4) and into the secondary fuel filter (6). After leaving the secondary filter, the fuel flows via an anti-siphon block (2) and enters the injection pump housing (3), where it is pumped under high pressure through either precombustion type injection (PC) or direct injection (DI) into the cylinder.

During injection pump operation, a percentage of fuel is constantly sent back to the fuel tank via the anti-siphon block (2) so as to remove air from the system and help cool the injection pump. The orifices in the anti-siphon block are designed to control the amount of fuel that bypasses and flows through the injection pump housing. The transfer pump has a relief valve (13) and a check valve (12). The relief valve in the lower side of the pump housing controls the pressure of the supply fuel to a maximum of 200 kPa. The check valve on the upper side of the pump allows fuel to bypass the transfer pump gears whenever the system is being primed with the aid of the hand-operated priming pump (4).

The compact pump

With reference to Fig 28.2, the pump consists of a housing assembly made up of the housing, camshaft, cam followers, rack, etc. The pumping elements are retained in the housing by threaded bushings that screw into the housing above the elements.

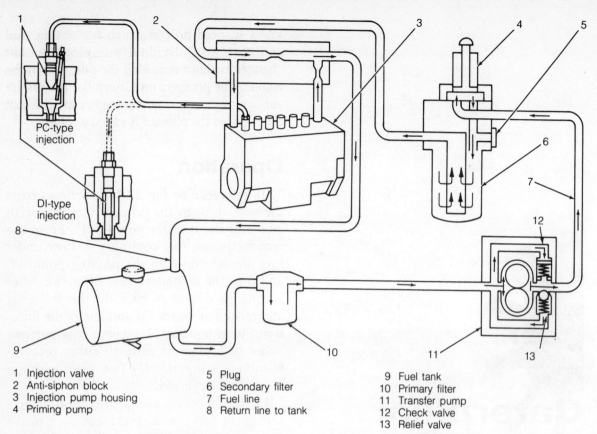

1 Injection valve
2 Anti-siphon block
3 Injection pump housing
4 Priming pump
5 Plug
6 Secondary filter
7 Fuel line
8 Return line to tank
9 Fuel tank
10 Primary filter
11 Transfer pump
12 Check valve
13 Relief valve

Fig 28.1   Schematic diagram of the fuel system   *Courtesy of Caterpillar Inc*

Pump element design

As shown in Figs 28.3 and 28.4, Caterpillar compact pumps feature a single port barrel (7), positively located in the pump housing by a dowel that engages in a slot in the barrel. Connected to the barrel by means of a clip (5) is the bonnet (2) which locates the check valve (4) and spring (3) and provides the connection for the injector line. The plunger (10) carries the gear segment (pinion) clamped to its lower end, and has a groove machined on its lower end to carry a washer (9). The washer provides the lower thrust face for the plunger return spring that lies between the dasher and the flanged upper end of the barrel.

The housing

A one-piece steel casting forms the pump housing, and also forms a part of the governor housing. The housing carries the camshaft in three plain bearings, the two end ones being pressure

lubricated. The roller type cam followers (or lifters, as they are called by Caterpillar) reciprocate directly in the housing, while the round section control rack is supported in bearings at each end of the pump housing.

Governors

Three types of governor are used on Caterpillar engines: **mechanical**, **hydra/mechanical** and **electronic**. The mechanical and hydraulic governor assemblies bolt to the pump housing and connect directly to the rack. An explanation of the operation of a hydra/mechanical variable-speed governor is provided in Chapter 31.

Automatic timing advance unit

On some engines the injection pump is driven through an advanced timing unit

move due to centrifugal force. As the speed of the engine increases, the weights move out against the force of the springs. The guide blocks, which must ride in the angled grooves, force a change in the angular relationship between the weights and flange assembly. This change in position alters the relationship of the injection pump camshaft to the drive gear, which results in a change in the point of injection. The amount of this change is proportional to the distance the weights move outwards from the static position — that is, the distance the weights move due to centrifugal force, which is proportional to the speed of rotation. Therefore the timing of the injection is controlled by the engine rpm.

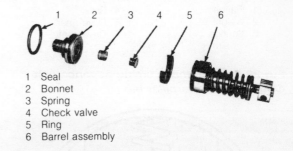

1 Seal
2 Bonnet
3 Spring
4 Check valve
5 Ring
6 Barrel assembly

Fig 28.3   Injection pump assembly
Courtesy of Caterpillar Inc

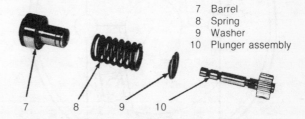

7 Barrel
8 Spring
9 Washer
10 Plunger assembly

Fig 28.4   Barrel assembly
Courtesy of Caterpillar Inc

Different automatic advance timing units are used for direct injected (DI) and pre-combustion (PC) chamber engines. The direct injection advance unit advances the timing two and a quarter degrees between low idle and 1100 rpm. The pre-combustion advance unit advances timing four degrees between low idle and 1100 rpm. There is no adjustment provided with these automatic advance units.

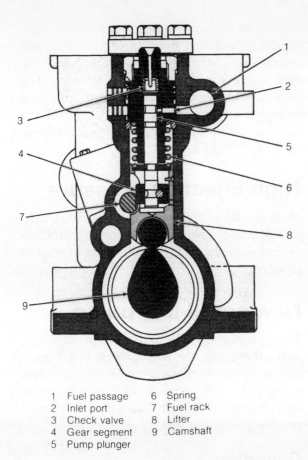

1	Fuel passage	6	Spring
2	Inlet port	7	Fuel rack
3	Check valve	8	Lifter
4	Gear segment	9	Camshaft
5	Pump plunger		

Fig 28.2   Compact fuel injection pump
Courtesy of Caterpillar Inc

which is mechanically actuated. This unit automatically advances the injection timing as the speed increases and retards it again as the speed decreases.

The advance timing unit shown in Fig 28.6 consists of two spring-loaded weights turning with the pump drive gear. These same weights drive a flange assembly through angled grooves in their surface, which engage with square guide blocks on the flange. The weights and springs are part of the carrier assembly, which is connected directly to the pump drive gear. The flange assembly drives the pump through a short splined shaft. The drive from carrier assembly to the flange assembly is entirely though the groove and guide block arrangement. This provides the means of automatic timing variation, as the weights

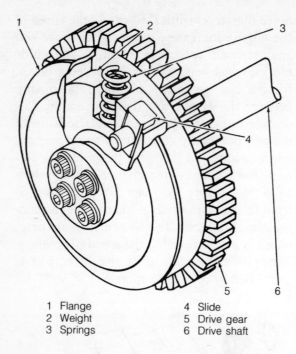

1 Flange	4 Slide
2 Weight	5 Drive gear
3 Springs	6 Drive shaft

Fig 28.5 Automatic timing advance unit
Courtesy of Caterpillar Inc

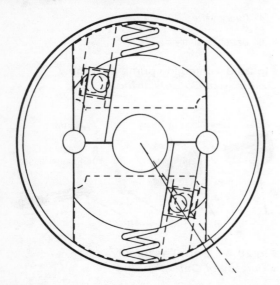

Fig 28.6 End view of the automatic timing advance unit showing an exaggerated angle of advance
Courtesy of Caterpillar Inc

The new scroll fuel system

The Caterpillar new scroll fuel system is very similar to the older compact fuel system with regard to system layout, component construction and fuel flow during priming and operation. The main difference between the two systems is the operating pressure. The new scroll pump can operate at injection pressures of up to 119 000 kPa, whilst the compact pump operates at injection pressures up to 55 000 kPa.

High injection pressure

High injection pressures are now being used as a means of improving the thermal efficiency and reducing exhaust pollutants of today's modern high-performance diesel engines.

New scroll fuel pump

The new scroll fuel pump is used on direct injected engines and is constructed and operates in a similar manner to the compact fuel pump except for a few modifications; namely, a different camshaft design and redesigned reverse flow check valve.

Operation

With reference to Fig 28.7, when the plunger (5) is at the bottom of its stroke, fuel at transfer pressure flows through the spill port (1) and bypass port (4) and fills the barrel area above the plunger. The plunger now rises until such time as the top of the plunger closes off ports (1) and (4) respectively. From this point on, pressure will start to rise and the check valve (2) opens, allowing fuel to flow into the injection line and to the fuel injection nozzle. The plunger continues to rise, injecting fuel into the engine. When the scroll (14) on the plunger uncovers the spill port (1), the fuel above the plunger escapes through a slot (15) down past the edge of the scroll and out the spill port back into the fuel gallery. This is the end of the injection stroke.

At the same time that the spill port uncovers the scroll on the plunger, the fuel injection nozzle closes and the spring (13) closes the check valve (delivery valve) (2) on to its seat.

With reference to Fig 28.8, the orificed reverse-flow check valve (11) now opens and allows fuel to flow through the orifice, therefore decreasing line pressure even further but at a slower rate than when the check valve was open. The reverse-flow check valve will remain open until injector line pressure falls to 6900 kPa, at which point the valve closes and holds injector line pressure constant.

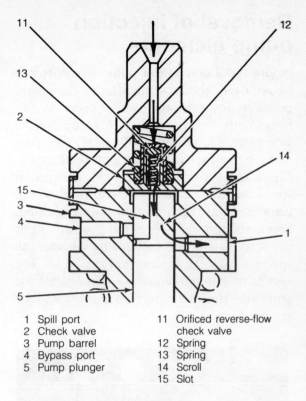

1 Spill port
2 Check valve
3 Pump barrel
4 Bypass port
5 Pump plunger
11 Orificed reverse-flow
   check valve
12 Spring
13 Spring
14 Scroll
15 Slot

Fig 28.8 Plunger and check valve assembly
Courtesy of Caterpillar Inc

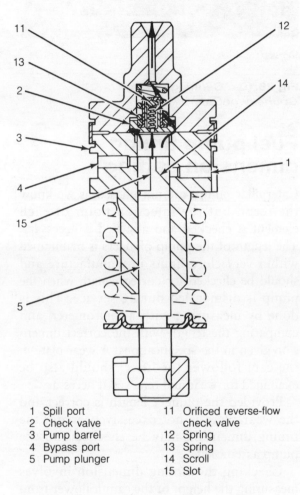

1 Spill port
2 Check valve
3 Pump barrel
4 Bypass port
5 Pump plunger
11 Orificed reverse-flow
   check valve
12 Spring
13 Spring
14 Scroll
15 Slot

Fig 28.7 Barrel and plunger assembly
Courtesy of Caterpillar Inc

The reverse-flow check valve is designed to reduce injector line pressure to such a level so as not to cause secondary injection or injector dribble. This valve will only operate below 8250 kPa and has no effect on line pressure above that point. On engine shutdown, the residual line pressure of 6900 kPa is gradually

released to the low pressure side of the fuel system through a small groove on the bottom face of the reverse-flow check valve.

Note: just after an engine shutdown, be careful when cracking the high-pressure fuel line nut, as fuel may squirt out and cause personal injury.

After the injection cycle, the pump camshaft rotates and its profile allows the plunger to move down ready for another charging cycle. The camshaft profile of the new scroll pump is different to that of the compact pump in that it incorporates an anti-backfire characteristic. For an explanation of an 'anti-backfire' camshaft, refer to Fig 26.6 in Chapter 26.

Servicing a compact pump

Because of their unique design, Caterpillar pump elements are not serviced in the same manner as other pump elements.

Removal of injection pump elements

Before the fuel injection pump elements can be removed, the rack must be in the centre position. To centre the rack, proceed as follows. With reference to Fig 28.9, remove the stop plate, spacer and both gaskets from the end of the fuel injection pump housing. Move the throttle lever to the maximum speed position or until the end of the rack protrudes past the injection pump housing. Secure the throttle lever in this position. Refit the stop plate on to the housing without the spacer or gaskets, as shown in Fig 28.10. The rack is now in the centre position against the stop and the fuel injection pumps can be removed.

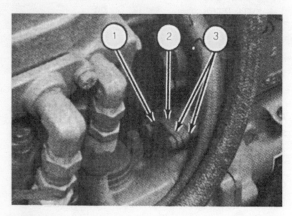

1 Stop
2 Spacer
3 Gaskets

Fig 28.9 Location of the governor rack stop
Courtesy of Caterpillar Inc

Fuel pump removal

To remove the pumps from the housing, proceed as follows:

1 Using the correct tool, remove the pump unit retaining bush.
2 Install an extractor on to the threads of the injection pump element and pull the pump straight up out of the housing.

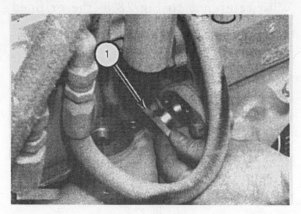

1 Stop

Fig 28.10 Centring the rack
Courtesy of Caterpillar Inc

Fuel pump timing dimension setting

Caterpillar pumps are not phased as we know the term, but the injection point of each element is checked and adjusted if necessary. The length of the pump plungers is maintained within very close limits in manufacture and should be checked for correct length when the pump is dismantled during service. This is done by measuring with a micrometer, and comparing the length with the correct dimension given in the specifications. A wear plate in the cam follower (or lifter) should also be examined for wear and renewed if necessary.

Provided the plunger length is correct and the wear plate is not excessively worn, the timing dimension may be checked and the pump assembled.

Checking the timing dimension involves measuring the height of the cam follower from the top of the housing at a particular point in camshaft rotation. Since the height of the cam follower governs the point of commencement of injection, if this height is correct then the timing for that element must be correct. If all elements are checked, and the heights are equal and correct when the camshaft has been turned through the correct number of degrees, then the pump is correctly phased.

The timing dimension is checked by fitting a special timing plate (or protractor) to the pump drive and a pointer assembly to the correct point on the housing (see Fig 28.11). The pump camshaft can then be turned by the timing plate until the specified degree line for the particular follower being checked

1 Plate
5 Washer
7 Bolt
A Depth micrometer and 10.`16 to 127.0mm rod
B Gauge

Fig 28.11 Protractor timing plate
Courtesy of Caterpillar Inc

aligns with the pointer. At this point, a gauge spacer is fitted to the top of the housing, and the timing dimension measured from the top of the gauge to the follower wear plate by means of a micrometer depth gauge (see Fig 28.12). Adjustment is made by changing the spacer under the barrel shoulder for one of a different thickness.

Refitting a pump element to the housing

To refit a pump element, proceed as follows:

1 Centre the fuel rack.
2 Install the correct adaptor (as used to remove the pump unit) on the pump element.

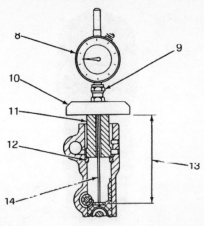

8 Indicator
9 Collet clamp
10 Base
11 Gauge—50.8mm long
12 Spacer
13 Timing dimension
14 Contact point—120.7mm long

Fig 28.12 Measuring timing dimension
Courtesy of Caterpillar Inc

3 Align the notches on the bonnet and barrel with the fourth tooth of the segment (pinion) gear.
4 Insert the injection pump element into the housing. When inserting the pump, the slot (Fig 28.13) must be aligned with the locating pin in the lifter, and the notches on the bonnet and barrel must align with the locating dowels in the pump housing. With the slot, pin, notches and dowels aligned, the fourth tooth of the segment gear will be aligned with the fourth groove of the rack. Do not try to force the pump into the injection pump housing as the locating pin can be damaged. When properly aligned, the pump can be installed without force.
5 After the plunger and barrel assembly are installed, place a new rubber sleeve over the bonnet, install the retainer bushing and tighten the bushing finger tight. If the bushing is not approximately flush with the top of the pump housing when tightened finger tight, the notch in the bonnet is not aligned with the dowel in the housing. Using the correct tool and a

Fig 28.13   Aligning the pump
Courtesy of Caterpillar Inc

torque wrench, tighten the retaining bushing to the torque specified in the manual specifications.

6 Install a new felt washer.

Timing the pump to the engine

Caterpillar pumps are timed to the engine by the use of timing pins, which ensure the correct positioning of the engine crankshaft and fuel injection pump camshaft.

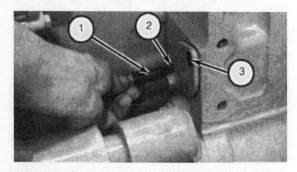

1   Timing bolt
2   Timing bolt location
3   Storage location

Fig 28.14   Locating TDC no. 1 cylinder with the aid of a timing bolt
Courtesy of Caterpillar Inc

The positioning of no. 1 piston on TDC compression stroke is the starting point for all timing procedures. To find this point, rotate the engine crankshaft in the correct direction of rotation until both the rocker levers on no. 1 cylinder are rocking. Continue rotating the crankshaft approximately one full turn until the timing bolt can be installed in the threaded hole in the flywheel. Note that the timing bolt is stored in the flywheel housing as seen in Fig 28.14.

The injection pump timing pin (service tool) can now be fitted into the injection pump housing. With reference to Fig 28.15, insert the timing pin through the hole in the pump housing and into the notch in the pump camshaft.

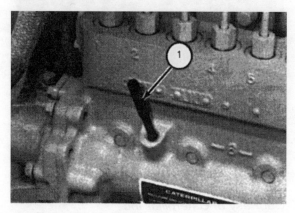

1   Timing pin

Fig 28.15   Timing pin installed
Courtesy of Caterpillar Inc

If the timing pin does not go into the notch in the pump camshaft, the automatic timing advance unit will have to be removed. With reference to Fig 28.16, the advance unit can be removed by first removing the four retaining bolts and then hitting the advance unit with a soft hammer. This should loosen the advance unit from its taper on the pump drive shaft. With the advanced unit removed from the pump drive shaft, insert two bolts back into the shaft. Use a lever to rotate the shaft until the timing pin fits into the notch on the pump camshaft. Refit the automatic timing advance unit and tension the bolts to the correct torque.

Remove the injection pump timing pin and the flywheel timing bolt. Rotate the crankshaft two revolutions and recheck to see that both timing pins can be inserted into their respective holes. If not, carry out the above procedure again.

Dynamic engine timing

Test instruments as seen in Fig 28.17 can be used to measure engine speed and injection timing throughout the entire engine operating range.

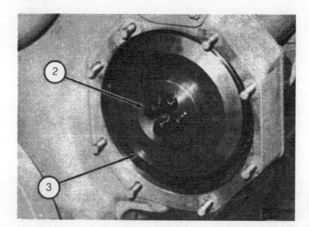

2   Bolts
3   Automatic timing advance unit

Fig 28.16   Automatic timing advance unit
Courtesy of Caterpillar Inc

The timing indicator uses transducers to determine engine speed and the rate of injection pump pulsations in the injection line. This recorded information is then displayed on a digital readout as the dynamic timing of the engine at a set speed. With reference to Figs 28.18 and 28.19, the fuel pressure transducer is fitted to the top of no. 1 pump element and the magnetic speed transducer is fitted into the engine flywheel housing.

Start the engine and bring it to correct operating temperature. With reference to the relevant timing charts, run the engine and check to see if timing and advance are as per specifications. If the engine timing is not correct, refer back to the static pin timing method.

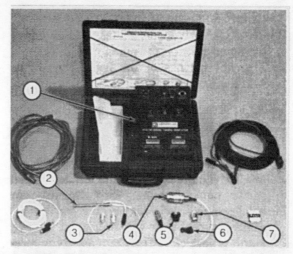

1   Engine timing indicator
2   TDC magnetic transducer
3   Pipe adapter
4   Injection transducer
5   Adapter
6   Tee adapter
7   Adapter

Fig 28.17   Dynamic timing indicator
Courtesy of Caterpillar Inc

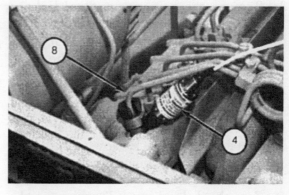

4   injection transducer
8   Fuel injection line for no. 1 cylinder

Fig 28.18   Transducer on no. 1 injector line
Courtesy of Caterpillar Inc

If the automatic advance timing is not in accordance with specifications, the advance unit should be dismantled and repaired.

Fuel rack adjustment

On Caterpillar engines, the fuel rack travel can be checked and adjusted with the fuel injection pump mounted on the engine. The testing and adjusting of rack travel is described below. This basic procedure can be used to test all scroll-type compact injection pumps.

2 TDC magnetic transducer

Fig 28.19 Transducer in flywheel housing
Courtesy of Caterpillar Inc

1   Remove the rack stop from the fuel injection pump housing, as shown in Fig 28.9.
2   Remove the governor control linkage from the governor control lever.
3   Fit the rack centring tool and dial gauge on to the pump housing, as shown in Fig 28.20.
4   With the governor control lever in the shut-off position, place the spacer (10) of the centring tool over the rod that makes contact with the rack. Now push the rod towards the fuel pump housing until it stops.
5   Zero the dial indicator. Then remove the spacer from the rod which contacts the rack.
6   Connect one end of a circuit tester to the brass terminal on the governor housing and the other to earth, as shown in Fig 28.21.
7   Rotate the governor lever to the full on position until the light in the tester just comes on. In this position, the rack stop collar (11) (see Fig 28.22) is just making contact with the torque spring or stop bar in the governor.

8   Observe the measurement on the dial indicator. Then refer to the specifications for the correct rack setting.
9   If an adjustment has to be made, remove the cover and air fuel ratio control (if fitted) from the rear of the governor.
10 To adjust the rack travel, loosen the lock nut and turn the adjusting screw to change the fuel rack setting. Refer Fig 28.22.
11 Finally, tighten the lock nut on the adjusting screw and replace the back governor cover.

1   Bracket group
3   Dial gauge
10 Spacer

Fig 28.20 Centring the fuel rack on the injection pump
Courtesy of Caterpillar Inc

1   Test light

Fig 28.21 Measuring fuel rack travel
Courtesy of Caterpillar Inc

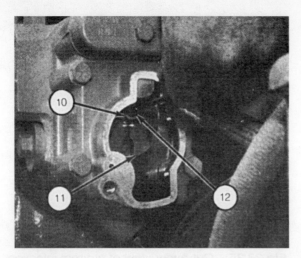

10 Locknut
11 Stop collar
12 Adjustment screw

Fig 28.22   Adjusting the rack travel
Courtesy of Caterpillar Inc

Priming the fuel system

Whenever the fuel system has been serviced or parts removed and replaced, the air will have to be bled out of the system.

Precombustion chamber engines

With the fuel pump control lever in the no-fuel position, loosen each injector line nut at the injector. Using the hand priming pump, pump fuel through the system until fuel with no air in it flows from the loose injector lines, then tighten the injector line nuts and start the engine.

Direct injected engines

Operate the hand primer and bleed all the air out of the fuel filters and fuel pump gallery, then secure the hand pump. With the fuel control lever in the run position, loosen all the injector lines at the injectors. Use the starter motor to turn the engine over until fuel without air flows from the loose injector lines, then tighten the injector line nuts and start the engine.

Injectors

Precombustion chamber injection

Owing to their precombustion chamber design, Caterpillar engines do not need the same degree of fuel atomisation as do most other engines. Because of this, Caterpillar injectors operate at lower than normal pressures and have one large-diameter spray hole.

The construction of the injector is completely different from all others. The injector assembly consists of three parts: a retaining nut, a valve body and a capsule-type nozzle assembly, as seen in Fig 28.23.

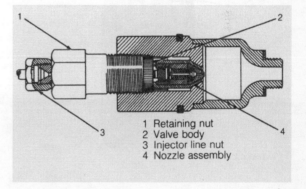

1 Retaining nut
2 Valve body
3 Injector line nut
4 Nozzle assembly

Fig 28.23   Precombustion chamber and nozzle assembly
Courtesy of Caterpillar Inc

Operation

Fuel is pumped from the injection pump through the fuel line and valve body to the nozzle. The fuel then passes through the nut assembly and through a stainless steel screen. This screen is the last filter the fuel must go through before injection. After the fuel passes through the screen, it enters the sleeve around the check valve, as shown in Fig 28.24. When the fuel pressure is high enough, the check valve moves outwards off its seat, allowing high pressure fuel past the check valve and out through a single orifice into the precombustion chamber. The check valve moves away from its seat whenever the fuel pressure is high enough to overcome the force of the spring and the compression in the cylinder. Conversely, a combination of these same two forces acting together in the nozzle holds the check valve tightly against its seat. Precombustion chamber nozzles operate on an injection line pressure of between 7000 and 17 500 kPa during engine operation. Because fuel flows in only one direction in this outward-opening nozzle, there is no back-leakage from the injector. Therefore, no return lines are fitted to precombustion chamber injectors.

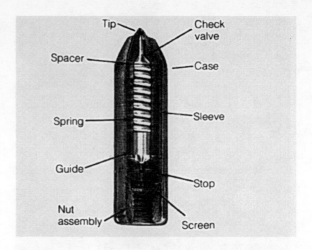

Fig 28.25 Cut-away view of a direct injection nozzle
Courtesy of Caterpillar Inc

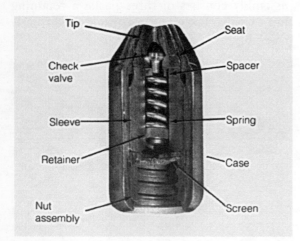

Fig 28.24 Cutaway view of a precombustion chamber nozzle
Courtesy of Caterpillar Inc

Direct injection

Fuel is pumped from the injection pump through the fuel line and valve body to the nozzle, as shown in Fig 28.25. The fuel then passes through a stainless steel screen. After the fuel passes through the screen, it goes into the sleeve area and down to the check valve. When fuel pressure is greater than spring pressure, the check valve will move away from its seat. Fuel will then pass through the multi-hole orifices of the nozzle and be injected into the combustion chamber.

During injection, fuel will pass up between the check valve and the guide, out a bleed hole in the case and into the trapped volume around the valve body (see Fig 28.26). After each injection, fuel under pressure in the trapped volume will return to the fuel line via a small orifice in the valve body. This flow of fuel through the nozzle and around the valve body lubricates the check valve and the guide. Because all back-leakage fuel from the nozzle returns to the injector line there is no need for any back-leakage return lines to the

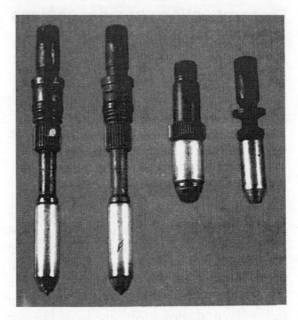

Fig 28.26 Capsule nozzles and valve bodies
Courtesy of Caterpillar Inc

fuel tank. Fuel line pressure in a direct injection system can reach as high as 69 000 kPa during operation.

New scroll fuel system injectors

In the new scroll system, high injection pressures are achieved by altering the design and operation of the injector. With reference to Fig 28.27, fuel enters the injector at (5), then goes through a filter screen and into passage (3) to the area below the diameter (8) of the valve (7). During previous operations of the injector, high pressure fuel has leaked past valve (7) and filled up the spring cavity area (9). For the injector to operate, valve (7) must move up and enter into the spring cavity area. To do this, system pressure must act on diameter (8) and rise significantly enough to first compress the spring (9) and secondly compress the trapped volume of fuel in the spring cavity area. High injection pressure is therefore determined by a combination of spring force and the force required to compress a liquid. Note that diesel fuel, being a liquid, is compressible to a slight degree when put under very high pressure. Injection line pressure in the new scroll fuel system can operate as high as 105 000 kPa.

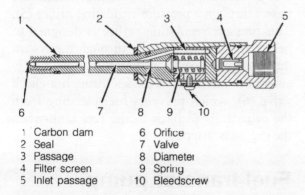

1 Carbon dam	6 Orifice
2 Seal	7 Valve
3 Passage	8 Diameter
4 Filter screen	9 Spring
5 Inlet passage	10 Bleedscrew

Fig 28.27 Fuel injection nozzle
Courtesy of Caterpillar Inc

The fuel injection nozzle is made as a one-piece unit which cannot be dismantled or adjusted in any way. If, when testing the nozzle, it does not operate according to specifications, it must be discarded and a new one fitted.

Pencil injector

Caterpillar also use pencil injectors in their direct-injected engines. For the construction and operation of the pencil injector, refer to Chapter 25.

Injector testing

To test capsule-type injector nozzles, use the following sequence:

1 pressure loss test;
2 valve opening pressure (VOP) test;
3 tip leakage test;
4 orifice restriction test;
5 bleedscrew leakage test (new scroll fuel system injectors only).

1 Nozzle assembly	F Gauge protector valve for gauge
A Line assembly	G Extention and fuel collector
B Adapter	H Gauge proctector valve for
C Tube assembly	gauge
D Gauge 0 to 34 500kPa	J Gauge protector valve (must be
E Gauge 0 to 6900 kPa	in the open position at all times)

Fig 28.28 Nozzle testing unit
Courtesy of Caterpillar Inc.

Pressure loss test

This test is designed to check the internal leakage past the guide pin inside direct injector nozzles. If the nozzle does not come up to set specifications on internal leakage, it is discarded.

Valve opening test

This test will indicate the pressure at which the injector will operate. If the VOP pressure is not within specifications, it is discarded.

Tip leakage test

This test will indicate whether or not the check valve in the nozzle is seating firmly. If the tip leakage rate is greater than specified it is discarded.

Orifice restriction test

This is a check of the spray and atomisation of the nozzle. Once again, if the nozzle does not spray from all holes and atomise as per specifications it is to be discarded.

Note: Do not use a drill or reamer to clean the single hole of the precombustion chamber nozzle. Also don't use a steel wire brush to clean the tip of the nozzle, as the orifice hole and check valve can be easily damaged.

New scroll fuel system injector testing

The test sequence for the nozzle used in this system is very similar to the previous test sequence. However, prior to testing this nozzle, the bleedscrew (see Fig 28.27(10)) in the nozzle body has to be screwed out by means of a special service tool. This prevents the over-pressurising of the testing equipment. Also, the final test in the sequence is the bleedscrew leakage test. The bleedscrew is now screwed back into the nozzle body and the nozzle pressurised to check for any external leaking around the bleedscrew seal.

This has been an overview on testing capsule nozzles. Because the test specifications for nozzles differ from engine to engine,

refer to the manufacturer's service manual for detailed information on the setting up and testing sequence for each type of nozzle assembly.

Unit injection fuel system

Caterpillar have introduced unit injection to a number of their engine categories. Unit injection has shown itself to be a reliable and efficient fuel injection system. With a tightening of emission controls and a need for a more fuel efficient engine, the high injection pressure obtainable from unit injection is becoming a necessity in the modern diesel engine.

Fuel system operation

With reference to Fig 28.29, fuel flows from the fuel tank through a primary filter screen (1) and into the fuel transfer pump (2). The fuel then flows under low pressure through the secondary filter (3) and into the fuel gallery in the cylinder head (4). The fuel gallery in the head is designed to run beside and around each unit injector. Fuel constantly flows around each injector and what is not used in charging the injector flows out the return fuel gallery. The unused fuel leaves the cylinder head and passes through a pressure-regulating orifice (5). This pressure-regulating orifice is designed to help maintain fuel pressure through the system during engine operation. Before the fuel finally enters the fuel tank, it passes through a check valve (6), which prevents fuel bleeding from the cylinder head back to the fuel tank when the engine is stopped.

Fuel transfer pump

The fuel transfer pump is of the plunger or piston type. With reference to Fig 28.29, whenever the piston is pushed down by the spring, fuel will flow through the inlet check valve and fill the cavity on the top side of the piston. When the cam turns around, the piston is raised up and begins to pressurise the fuel above it. This causes the inlet check valve to close and the check valve in the piston to open and allow fuel to transfer to the underside of it. On the downward stroke, the fuel under the piston forces the outlet check valve off its seat, allowing fuel to flow to the secondary filter.

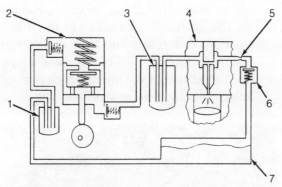

1 Screen
2 Fuel transfer pump (integral with governor)
3 Main filter
4 Cylinder head
5 Pressure regulating orifice
6 Check valve
7 Fuel tank

Fig 28.29 Schematic diagram of the unit injection fuel system
Courtesy of Caterpillar Inc

Governor

The governor used on unit injection engines can be either isochronous or variable speed. The isochronous governor is an electronic type and the variable speed governor is a mechanical fly-weight type. If required, the mechanical governor can be hydraulically assisted by means of a servo piston fitted to the side of the governor housing.

Unit injector

The unit injector, as shown in Fig 28.30, is a combined fuel injection pump and injector all in one. With the plunger at the top of its stroke, fuel from the fuel gallery enters the

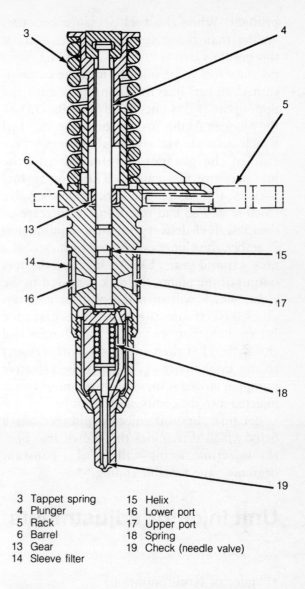

3	Tappet spring	15	Helix
4	Plunger	16	Lower port
5	Rack	17	Upper port
6	Barrel	18	Spring
13	Gear	19	Check (needle valve)
14	Sleeve filter		

Fig 28.30 Schematic diagram of a unit injector
Courtesy of Caterpillar Inc

injector around the edges of a sleeve filter (14). The fuel then fills the volume below the plunger (4). During the plunger's downward motion, the fuel beneath the plunger is initially displaced into the gallery through ports (16) and (17). As the upper port (17) is closed by the bottom edge of the plunger, fuel continues to be displaced through the lower port (16). When the lower port is closed off from the plunger, the effective pumping stroke begins. Fuel is now pressurised by the continued downward movement of the plunger. When the fuel pressure becomes greater than the spring force of the injector, the needle valve (19) opens, allowing high-pressure fuel to be injected into the combustion chamber. Injection continues until the upper port (17) is uncovered by helix (15) on the plunger. At this instant, high-pressure fuel which is sensed via a vertical channel on the side of the plunger is released into the low-pressure fuel gallery. The drop in fuel pressure thus causes the injector needle valve to close and so end injection. To increase or decrease fuel delivery into the combustion chamber, the plunger is rotated by means of a rack (5) and gear (13). To increase the fuel output of the pump, the rack is moved to the right, which will turn the plunger counter-clockwise (from the top). The distance between the bottom end of the plunger and the helix (15) then increases with respect to the upper port (17). Thus the effective pumping stroke is increased and more fuel is injected into the combustion chamber.

Because the unit injector plunger has a helix which determines the end of injection, the injection timing will be of a constant beginning and variable ending.

Unit injector adjustments

These are:

- injector synchronisation;
- fuel setting;
- fuel timing;
- valve clearances;
- fuel pressure;
- governor.

Injector synchronisation

In order that each injector gives the same amount of fuel to each cylinder, all injector racks must be synchronised to a reference position. This is done by setting each injector rack to the same position while the control linkage is in a fixed synchronising position.

The control linkage is at the synchronising position when the no. 1 injector is in the fuel shut-off position. Since the no. 1 injector is the reference point for all other injectors, no adjustments are made to it. Injector synchronisation should always be carried out whenever an injector has been removed and replaced, or at regular service intervals.

1 With the engine stopped and the electrical system shut off, pull out the centre rod (3) on the shut-off solenoid (1) until the solenoid is latched and held in the run position, (see Fig 28.31). This will allow free movement of the injector rack control linkage during injector synchronising.

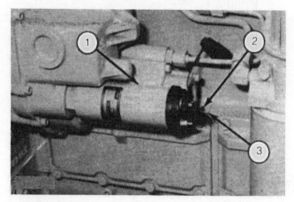

1 Solenoid
2 Ferrule
3 Centre rod

Fig 28.31 Fuel shut-off solenoid
Courtesy of Caterpillar Inc

2 Remove the rocker arm assembly from no. 1 cylinder.
3 With reference to Fig 28.32, install the injector spring compressor (6) to the cylinder head. This slightly compresses the injector spring, allowing free movement of the injector rack.
4 Now remove the rocker assembly from the cylinder where injector synchronisation is to take place.

Note: For convenience, all rocker assemblies can be removed at once. Install the injector spring compressor as shown in Fig 28.32.

6 Injector spring compressor

Fig 28.32 Injector spring compressor installer on no. 1 injector
Courtesy of Caterpillar Inc

5 Install the injector synchronising tool above the injector to be synchronised as shown in Figs 28.33 and 28.34.
6 With reference to Fig 28.35, firmly push the rack (11) towards the injector until it is fully home. The rack is now in the shut-off position.
7 With the rack held in the shut-off position, adjust the dial indicator to a zero position, then release the rack.

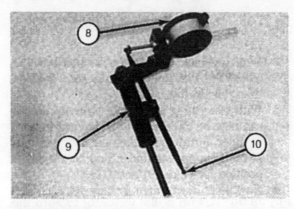

8 Dial indicator
9 Indicator group
10 Lever

Fig 28.33 Injector synchronisation tools
Courtesy of Caterpillar Inc

8 With everything set up, the synchronisation can now be checked with reference

8 Dial indicator
9 Indicator group

Fig 28.34 Injector synchronisation tooling installed
Courtesy of Caterpillar Inc

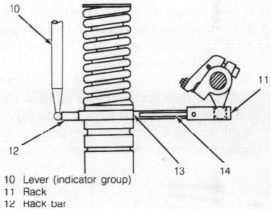

10 Lever (indicator group)
11 Rack
12 Rack bar
13 Injector base
14 Rack stop

Fig 28.35 Checking rack travel of injector
Courtesy of Caterpillar Inc

to no. 1 cylinder. Firmly push the rack to the shut-off position on no. 1 cylinder, and hold it in this position for steps (9) and (10).
9 Now push down, then quickly release, lever (16) of the injector being checked (see Fig 28.36). When the control linkage and rack come to rest, check the measurement on the dial indicator. It must indicate +.01 to +.05 mm.
Repeat the above two steps to confirm the reading is correct.

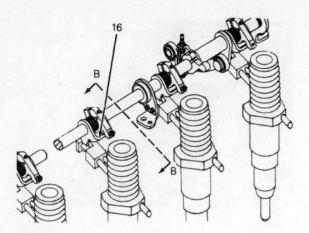

16 Lever (of injector being checked)

Fig 28.36 Injector rack control linkage
Courtesy of Caterpillar Inc

10 If the reading is correct, proceed to step (13).
11 If the dial indicator does not indicate the correct measurement, the control rod clamp will require adjustment.
12 With reference to Fig 28.37, loosen clamp (18) and turn screw (17), retighten the clamp and then repeat steps (8) and (9) until the dial indicator measurement is in accordance with specifications.

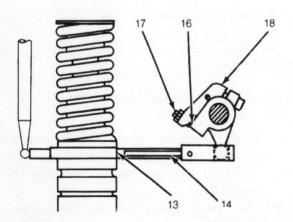

13 Injector base
14 Rack stop
16 Lever
17 Setscrew
18 Clamp

Fig 28.37 Injector in a synchronised position
Courtesy of Caterpillar Inc

13 Remove the dial indicator, mounting bracket and spring compressor and re-install the rocker assembly.
14 Synchronise all other injectors using no. 1 injector as a reference.
   Note: There is no adjustment for the control rod clamp on no. 1 injector.
15 With reference to Fig 28.31, pull the ferrule (2) by hand until the shut-down solenoid is unlatched. This now places the injector racks back in the fuel shut-off position.

Fuel setting

The maximum fuel setting of the engine is adjusted by a fuel setting screw located on the injector control linkage. The fuel setting screw determines the maximum travel distance of the no. 1 injector rack. Because all injectors are synchronised to no. 1 injector, they will deliver the same quantity of fuel as no. 1 injector. Before the fuel setting is checked, all injectors must be synchronised correctly.

2 Dial indicator
3 Indicator group

Fig 28.38 Using a dial indicator to zero the rack travel on no. 1 injector
Courtesy of Caterpillar Inc

1 With reference to injector synchronisation, over-ride the electrical shutdown solenoid and attach the dial indicator and indicator group to no. 1 injector as shown in Fig 28.38.

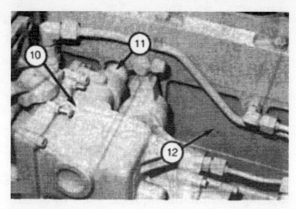

10 Governor
11 Sleeve
12 Cylinder head

Fig 28.39 Governor assembly
Courtesy of Caterpillar Inc

2 Push the rack to the shut-off position (fully in) and adjust the dial indicator to zero.

3 With reference to Fig 28.39, remove the clip and slide sleeve (11) out of the governor towards the cylinder head. Note that care must be taken not to damage the sleeve and seals, as oil retention in the cylinder head could be lost.

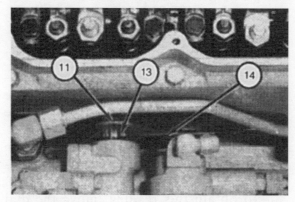

11 Sleeve
13 Link pin
14 Insertion tool

Fig 28.40 Fuel setting tools attached to governor housing
Courtesy of Caterpillar Inc

4 With reference to Fig 28.40, install the insertion tool (14) into the link pin (13) of the governor output shaft. When properly installed, equal lengths of the small

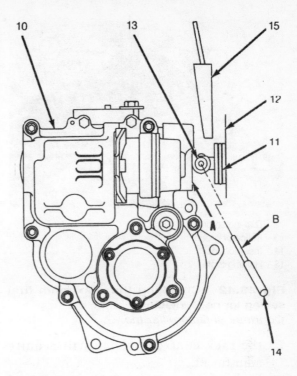

10 Governor
11 Sleeve
12 Cylinder head
13 Link pin
14 Insertion tool
15 Holding tool
A   Face of governor
B   Small diameter of tool

Fig 28.41 Installation of governor fuel setting tools
Courtesy of Caterpillar Inc

diameter of the tool (14) will extend from both ends of the link pin (13).

5 With reference to Fig 28.41, install the holding tool (15) between the sleeve (11) and small diameter (B) of the insertion tool (14). Now push the holding tool down until the small diameter (B) of the tool (14) contacts face (A) of the governor (10). The governor is now in a position to check the maximum fuel setting of no. 1 injector, as shown in Fig 28.42.

6 Now push down on the rack lever for no. 1 injector and quickly release it (see Fig 28.43). Read the dial indicator and check the rack travel with the specifications.

7 If the dial indicator reading is incorrect,

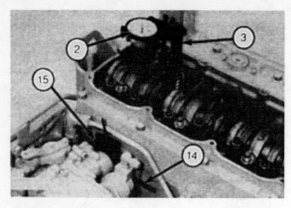

2 Dial indicator
3 Indicator group
14 Insertion tool
15 Holding tool

Fig 28.42 Checking the maximum fuel setting for no. 1 injector
Courtesy of Caterpillar Inc

the rack control linkage will require adjustment.

8 With reference to Fig 28.43, turn the fuel setting screw (16) counter-clockwise for more fuel or clockwise for less fuel. After the setting has been changed, flip the rack again and recheck the dial indicator reading. Repeat the above steps until the fuel setting is correct.

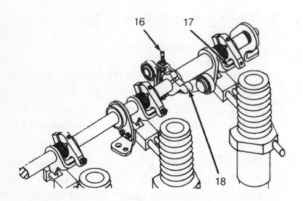

16 Fuel setting screw
17 Rack lever for no. 1 injector
18 Clamp

Fig 28.43 Rack control linkage
Courtesy of Caterpillar Inc

9 Remove the dial indicator and indicator group. Also pull the ferrule out on the shut-off solenoid until the solenoid is unlatched. This will put the racks back into the fuel shut-off position.

Injector timing

Injector timing is checked by placing a timing fixture over the injector and measuring dimension (D) as shown in Fig 28.44.

Prior to checking the timing dimension of the injector, the timing fixture has to be calibrated as shown in Fig 28.45.

1 Put the dial indicator and timing fixture on top of the timing block (3) and calibration fixture (4).
2 Make sure the long pin of the dial indicator is inserted into the hole in the centre of the timing block. The timing block is 62 mm long.
3 Now refer to the specifications for the correct timing dimension for the engine.
4 Subtract the fuel timing specification from the timing block dimension.

Example: length of injector

timing block	62.00
fuel timing specification	64.01
	−2.01 mm

The difference between the two dimensions is a minus (−) quantity. Therefore a minus sign is placed in front of the reading (−2.01).

5 The dial indicator will now have to be adjusted so that when it sits on the calibration fixture the dial reads −2.01 mm. To obtain this reading, move the dial indicator in the collet (B). The dial indicator is now calibrated for checking injector timing.
6 Rotate the engine crankshaft until no. 1 piston is at TDC compression. At this point the timing bolt can be inserted into the hole in the flywheel (see Fig 28.46). With no. 1 piston at TDC, refer to the settings in Fig 28.47 and determine which injectors are to be set

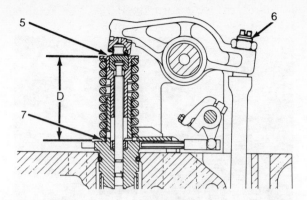

5 Tappet
6 Adjustment screw
7 Shoulder
D Fuel timing dimension

Fig 28.44 Injector timing dimension
Courtesy of Caterpillar Inc

with the no. 1 piston on compression stroke or exhaust stroke.

7 Now install the timing fixture over the injector which is to be checked and secure the timing fixture in place (see Fig 28.48).

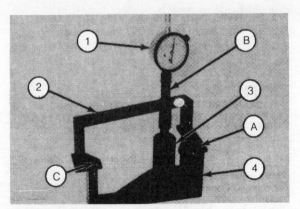

1 Dial indicator	A Bolt
2 Timing fixture	B Collet sleeve
3 Timing block	C Locating pin
4 Calibration fixture	

Fig 28.45 Calibrating the injector timing fixture
Courtesy of Caterpillar Inc

8 The dial indicator must now indicate a reading within 0.05 mm±.

9 If the dial reading is not within the manufacturer's tolerance, the injector rocker adjusting screw (6) will need to be

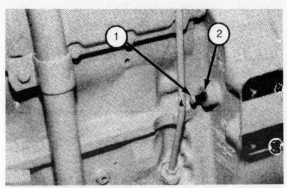

1 Timing bolt
2 Timing hole

Fig 28.46 Using a timing bolt to locate no. 1 piston TDC compressio
Courtesy of Caterpillar Inc

3114 Crankshaft Positions For Fuel Timing And Valve Clearance Setting	
SAE Standard (Counterclockwise) Rotation Engines As Viewed From The Flywheel End	
Check/Adjust with No. 1 Piston On	TC Compression Stroke*
Injectors	3–4
Intake Valves	1–2
Exhaust Valves	1–3
Check/Adjust With No. 1 Piston On	TC Exhaust Stroke*
Injectors	1–2
Intake Valves	3–4
Exhaust Valves	2–4
Firing Order	1–3–4–2

* Put No. 1 piston at top centre (TC) position and make identification for the correct stroke. Make reference to Finding Top Centre Position For No. 1 Piston. After top centre position for a particular stroke is found and adjustments are made for the correct cylinders, remove the timing bolt and turn the flywheel counterclockwise 360°. This will put No. 1 piston at top centre (TC) position on the other stroke. Install the timing bolt in the flywheel and complete the adjustments for the cylinders that remain.

Fig 28.47 Crankshaft positions for injector timing and valve settings
Courtesy of Caterpillar Inc

adjusted until the correct reading is obtained.

10 With the timing bolt installed in the flywheel, half the injectors can be checked. Then remove the timing bolt and rotate the flywheel 360°, insert the timing bolt and check the remaining cylinders.

1 Dial indicator
2 Timing fixture
6 Adjustment screw
8 Valve cover base

Fig 28.48 Using the timing fixture to check injector timing
Courtesy of Caterpillar Inc

11 After all the injectors have been checked and/or adjusted, remove the timing bolt and timing fixture from the engine.

Valve clearances

Whenever the rocker assemblies have been disturbed in any way, the valve clearances will have to be checked and, if necessary, reset. With reference to Fig 28.47, all the valves can be adjusted with the no. 1 piston on two different strokes, TDC compression and TDC exhaust.

Fuel pressure

The engine fuel pressure can be checked at two locations on the fuel filter housing. With reference to Fig 28.49, unfiltered fuel pressure can be checked at outlet (4) and filtered fuel pressure checked at outlet (5). The system fuel pressure in the cylinder head gallery at maximum engine speed should be between 200 and 400 kPa. At idle speed the fuel pressure should be a maximum of 50 kPa to the injectors.

4 Unfiltered fuel pressure tap
5 Filtered fuel pressure tap

Fig 28.49 Fuel pressure test points
Courtesy of Caterpillar Inc

Governor adjustment

The governor is so designed that the only on-engine adjustment that can be made is to the idle speed. All other governor adjustments and checks require the governor to be removed from the engine and run on a governor calibration bench.

Electronic engine controls

Caterpillar have developed electronic engine controls for use in their heavy duty truck engines. The introduction of electronics improves performance and fuel economy and reduces gaseous exhaust emissions. Programmable Electronic Engine Control (PEEC) is available for use on engines with the new scroll fuel system.

A change to electronic engine controls has also meant a change in engine fuel system components: the mechanical automatic timing advance unit has been replaced with an electronically actuated timing advance unit. An electronic rack actuator which includes a shut-down solenoid replaces the mechanical servo-assisted

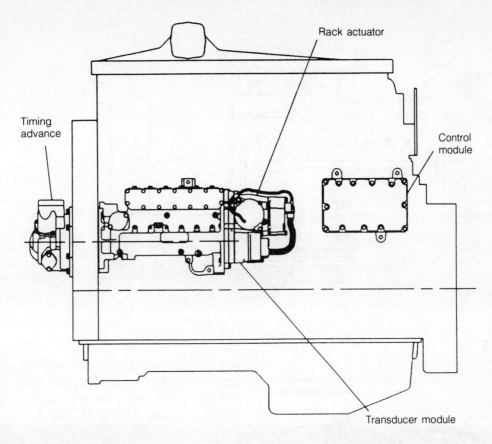

Fig 28.50   The location of electronic engine controls on the 3406B engine
Courtesy of Caterpillar Inc

governor. Also, a pressure transducer module that senses oil and boost air pressure is mounted on the fuel pump below the rack actuator. A control module which is engine mounted and cooled by diesel fuel connects via a wiring harness to the timing advance unit, rack actuator and transducer module.

Timing advance unit

The PEEC timing advance unit replaces the mechanical automatic timing advance unit drive. The springs and flyweights are replaced with an electronically actuated brushless torque motor. A brushless torque motor rotates and moves a spline carrier along the helical splines in the drive gear assembly, as shown in Fig 28.51. Any lateral movement of the drive

carrier will rotate it and the pump camshaft to an advanced position. A timing advance feedback sensor is incorporated into the timing advance housing and senses all injection advance changes (seeFig 28.52).

Rack actuator

The mechanical flyweight governor is replaced with an electronic actuator and transducer module. A double-acting hydraulic servo provides the mechanical muscle for moving the fuel rack and a linear potentiometer is used for closed loop control of the rack position. To shut the engine down, a brushless torque motor in conjunction with a shut-off solenoid is used to move the fuel rack to the shut-off position (see Fig 28.53).

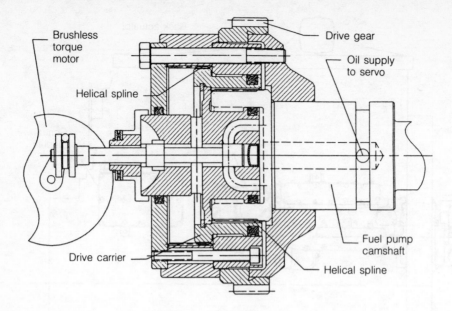

Fig 28.51 PEEC timing advance unit *Courtesy of Caterpillar Inc*

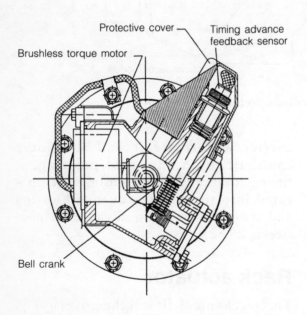

Fig 28.52 PEEC timing advance actuator and feedback sensor
Courtesy of Caterpillar Inc

Pressure transducer module

The sealed transducer module is mounted below the rack actuator. It contains an engine oil pressure sensor, a boost pressure sensor and protective signal conditioning circuitry. The oil pressure transducer is used to limit engine speed and power output if low oil pressure occurs (see Fig 28.54).

Control module

The control module consists of two major components: the main control and ratings personality module. The main control module contains an electrically erasable programmable read-only memory to store customer-specified parameters. The ratings personality module contains all the engine performance and certification information, along with the control software (see Fig 28.55).

The control module is cooled by fuel from the transfer pump. Fuel flows through the control module then on to the secondary fuel filter prior to entering the fuel injection pump.

PEEC functions

The following list of functions is performed by the PEEC system. The functions have been divided into the two major areas of engine- and vehicle-related functions.

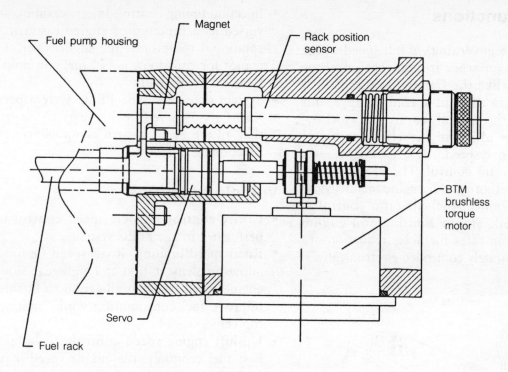

Fig 28.53   PEEC rack servo   *Courtesy of Caterpillar Inc*

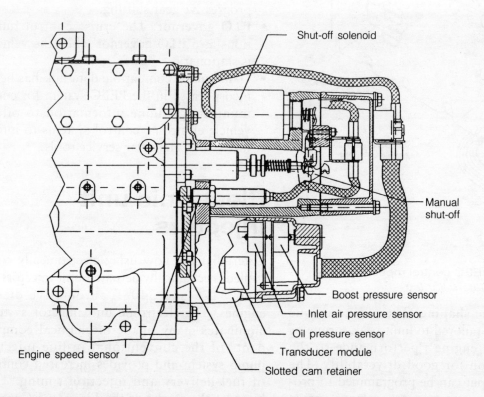

Fig 28.54   PEEC rack actuator and transducer module cross-section
Courtesy of Caterpillar Inc

Engine functions

- **Electronic governing**. A full-speed-range electronic governor is used. The governor functions like the Caterpillar mechanical governor in the mid-operating range, but includes the special features of isochronous low idle and the elimination of governor overspeed.
- **Fuel–air ratio control**. The PEEC system has full authority over engine fuel delivery. The mechanical fuel–air ratio control is eliminated. Smoke limiting and engine acceleration rates for noise reduction are more accurately controlled electronically.

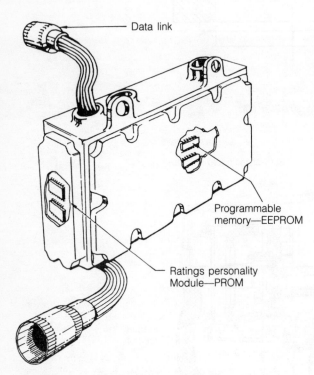

Fig 28.55   PEEC control module
Courtesy of Caterpillar Inc

- **Torque rise shaping**. The engine torque rise can be tailored to limit peak torque or match the engine's performance to the transmission for good driverability. The engine output can be programmed to provide constant power over a large engine speed range.

- **Injection timing control**. Injection timing is varied as a function of engine operating conditions to optimise the engine's performance for emissions, noise, fuel consumption and driverability.
- **System diagnosis**. The PEEC system performs its own self-health tests to insure that all the PEEC system components are functioning properly.

Vehicle functions

- **Cruise control**. Vehicle speed control is performed by the PEEC system.
- **Road speed limiting**. Road speed limiting allows implementation of a high-gear, slow engine speed truck specification to further improve fuel consumption while limiting top vehicle speed.
- **Upshift engine speed control**. To obtain best fuel economy, the engine speed may be limited to less than the top engine speed limit for certain vehicle speeds to promote progressive gear shifting.
- **PTO governor**. The cruise control functions as a PTO governor when the vehicle is stationary.
- **Data link**. A compatible data link has been incorporated in the PEEC system for communicating engine information to other vehicle electronic control systems to interface with Caterpillar service tools.

Electronic unit injectors

Caterpillar are now using electronically controlled mechanically actuated unit injectors in their 3176 and 3406E automotive diesel engines. The electronic unit injector system eliminates many of the mechanical components of the conventional in-line injector pump system and provides increased control of fuel delivery and injection timing. The heart of the system is the Electronic Control Module (ECM) which monitors the operation

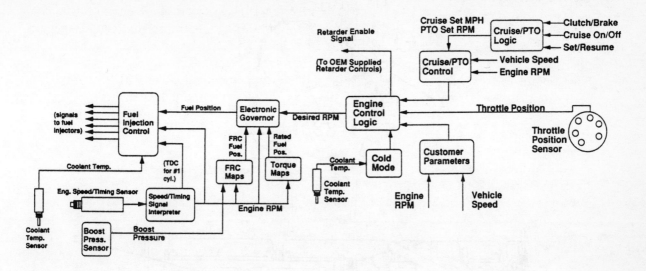

Fig 28.56   Schematic diagram of the electronic speed and governor controls on a 3176 diesel engine
Courtesy of Caterpillar Inc

of the engine and at the same time controls engine fuelling by sending an electrical signal to a solenoid mounted on each injector.

The following explanation of the electronically controlled fuel injection system relates to the 3176 unit injected diesel engine.

Electronic controls

The electronics controlling the engine consist of two main components: the Electronic Control Module and the Personality Module. The ECM is the microprocessor within the system and the Personality Module is the software containing the operating maps or instructions that define power, torque and engine speed control. The two work together (along with sensors to 'see' and solenoids/injectors to 'act') to control the operation of the engine.

Basically, the ECM determines actual engine speed based on signals sent from the throttle position sensor and the engine speed/timing sensor. In order to maintain a set engine speed, the ECM continually senses crankshaft speed and decides how much fuel to inject so as to achieve this desired speed.

Fuel injection

The ECM controls the amount of fuel delivered to the engine by varying the voltage signal sent to the electric solenoid mounted on each injector. The injector will only inject fuel if the injector solenoid is energised. During engine operation, the ECM sends a voltage signal to the solenoid to energise it. By controlling when the signal is sent and its duration, the ECM can control the injection timing and the amount of fuel injected into the engine.

The time duration of the signal sent to the injectors determines the quantity of fuel injected into the engine. For example, a short injector signal duration will be for idle and maximum no-load speed and a long signal duration will be for maximum torque output.

The ECM sets certain limits on the amount of fuel that can be injected. During engine acceleration there is a limit on the amount of fuel delivered relevant to the available intake boost air pressure which ensures correct air–fuel ratio for emission control purposes. Also controlled by the ECM is the rated or maximum fuel delivery,

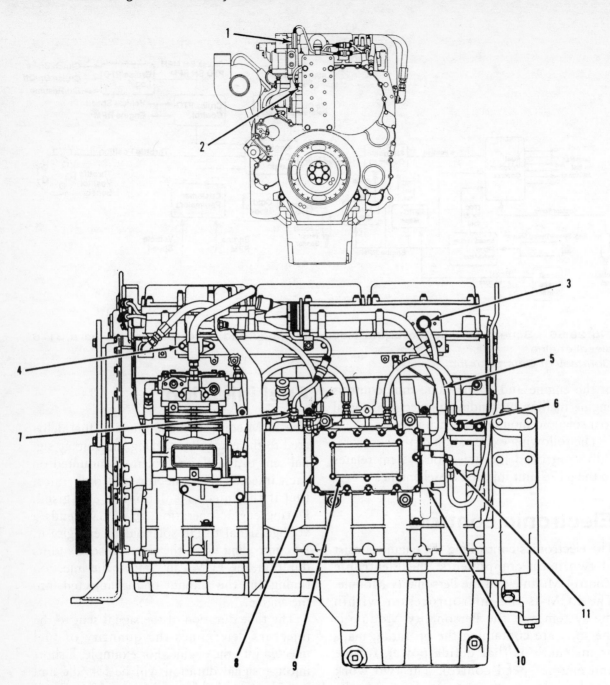

1	Coolant temperature sensor	7	Fuel pressure sensor
2	Speed/timing sensor	8	Electronic control module (ECM)
3	Injector enable circuit	9	Personality module
4	Fuel manifold	10	Transducer module
5	Engine wiring harness	11	Boost pressure inlet
6	Fuel transfer pump		

Fig 28.57   Electronic control system components on a 3176 engine
Courtesy of Caterpillar Inc

which is a set limit based on the power rating of the engine. It is similar to the rack stops and torque spring on a mechanically governed engine. Both of these limits are programmed by the factory into the Personality Module and are not programmable in the field. The ECM also has control over injection timing, which is determined by engine speed relevant to the varying loads placed on the engine. As the ECM knows where top dead centre for cylinder no. 1 is from the signal provided by the engine/timing sensor, it decides when injection should occur relative to top dead centre and provides the signal to the injector at the desired time.

Three-cylinder cutout

Under certain operating conditions, the engine may operate on just three cylinders. This feature is called **three-cylinder cutout** and occurs when the engine is operated under no load at high speed (when signals to the injectors are of very short duration). Under these conditions, the ECM does not allow fuel to be injected into cylinders 4, 5 and 6, but instead allows for more precise fuel metering to cylinders 1, 2 and 3. The accompanying change in feel and sound of the engine should not be misdiagnosed as an engine problem. When more engine power is needed, all six cylinders will be fuelled and full power delivered.

Programmable parameters

Certain operational parameters that affect engine operation may be changed through the use of electronic service tools such as the Electronic Control Analyser Programmer (ECAP) or the Digital Diagnostic Tool (DDT). The system parameters which are stored in the ECM are protected by passwords which prevent unauthorised changes within the system.

Password protected parameters are either System Configuration Parameters or Customer Specified Parameters. System Configuration Parameters are set at the factory and affect emissions and power ratings within a family of engines and would normally never need to be changed through the life of the engine. Customer Specified Parameters allow a customer to restrict how a driver operates the vehicle. These parameters are variable and can be changed to affect such things as the cruise control speed, vehicle speed limits, engine speed and power ratings within limits set by the factory.

Starting the engine

Electronic engine controls not only control the engine when it is operating, but also when it is to be started. The moment the vehicle ignition is turned on, the ECM will automatically signal the injector solenoids to provide the correct amount of fuel to start the engine and at no time should the throttle be depressed during engine cranking.

Cold-mode operation

The engine control system performs a cold-start strategy for the correct warmup time after a cold engine start. Once activated, this cold-start strategy, known as **cold mode**, will increase the idle speed to 1000 rpm until the engine temperature rises above 20°C, or until the engine has been running for twelve minutes. During this cold-start mode, fuel injection quantity and timing will vary for improved startup performance and white smoke control.

Progressive gear shifting

Progressive gear shifting refers to the quick shifting of gears through the lower speed ranges of the transmission so as to prevent the engine winding up to a high speed. Gear shifts

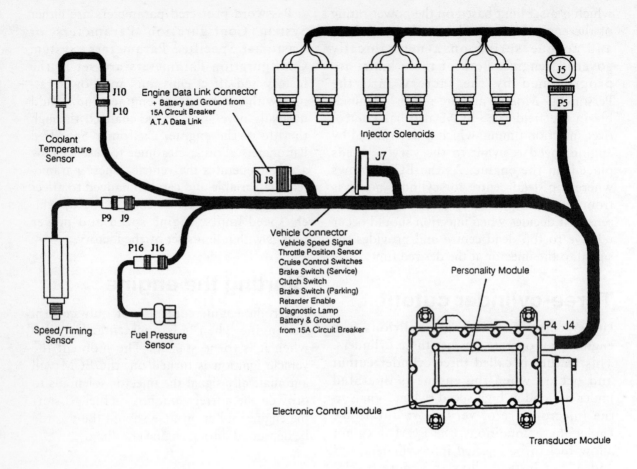

Fig 28.58 Engine wiring harness and system components
Courtesy of Caterpillar Inc

are designed to be carried out above peak torque speed, but below the maximum speed of the engine. Taking the engine to its maximum speed during each gear shift before shifting to the next gear wastes fuel and fails to take advantage of the torque characteristics of the engine.

Electronic control system components

The major components of the electronic control system, as shown in Fig 28.57, are: (1) coolant temperature sensor (located in the water temperature regulator housing); (2) speed/timing sensor (in the right side of the front housing); (3) injector enable circuit (provides a signal to the fuel injection pump group solenoids); (4) fuel manifold; (5) engine wiring harness; (6) fuel transfer pump; (7) fuel pressure sensor; (8) Electronic Control Module; (9) Personality Module; (10) Transducer Module and a throttle position sensor (remote mounted in the vehicle cabin); (11) Boost sensor (located in the transducer module (10)).

Electronic control system

The electronic control system is integrally designed into the engine's fuel system and air inlet and exhaust system to electronically monitor and control fuel delivery and injection timing. Injection timing is achieved by precise control of when fuel is injected and engine speed is controlled by adjusting the duration of fuel injection. The ECM energisers the fuel injection pump solenoids to start injection of fuel, and de-energises the fuel injection pump solenoids to stop the injection of fuel into the engine.

Within the electronic engine control system there are three types of electronic components: input, control and output.

An **input** component (generally a switch or engine/vehicle mounted sensor) is one that sends an electrical signal to the ECM. The signal sent varies in either voltage or frequency in response to change in some specific system of the vehicle.

The input sensors monitor engine speed and timing, throttle position, coolant temperature, fuel pressure, boost pressure, vehicle speed, cruise switches status (on/off and set/resume), clutch switch, brake switch and parking switch.

The ECM acting as the **control** component in the system sees the input from each sensor signal as information about the condition, environment or operation of the engine/vehicle. This information is processed and compared against pre-programmed operating parameters within the ECM and, if necessary, appropriate signals are sent to operate the fuel injector pump solenoids or the diagnostic warning light in response to data received.

An **output** component is one that is operated by the ECM. The component receives electrical signals from the control group and uses these signals to either:

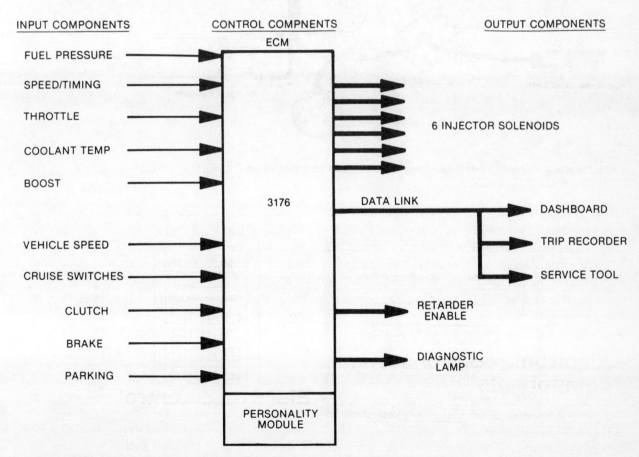

Fig 28.59   Input, control and output components on the 3176 electronic engine control system
Courtesy of Caterpillar Inc

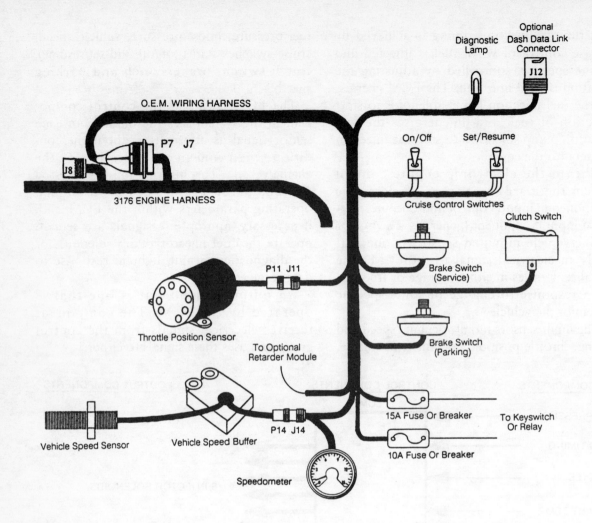

Fig 28.60   Vehicle wiring harness and system components   *Courtesy of Caterpillar Inc.*

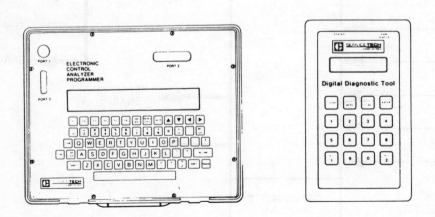

Fig 28.61   Electronic service tools used to interface with the on-board system computer
Courtesy of Caterpillar Inc

1 perform work (such as moving a solenoid plunger) and thereby take an active part in regulating the fuel delivered to the engine;

2 give information or warning (such as a light or an alarm) to the operator of the vehicle or service person.

Data link

The electronic system incorporates a data link which is an output component used to communicate engine information to other electronic vehicle control systems and to interface with Caterpillar service tools such as the Electronic Control Analyser and Programmer and the Digital Diagnostic Tool as shown in Fig 28.61.

Retarder enable

If the engine is equipped with a Jacobs Engine Brake, it can be operated through the retarder enable output. The retarder operation is determined by the following inputs: a dash switch, a clutch switch, throttle position, a cruise switch and engine speed.

System diagnostics

The engine has built-in diagnostics to ensure that all components are operating properly. In the event of a system malfunction, such as engine overheating, or component failure, such as a throttle position sensor fault, the operator will be alerted to the fault via a dash-mounted check engine light. Such faults detected within the system are labelled as **active diagnostic codes**.

An active diagnostic code represents a problem that should be investigated and corrected as soon as possible. Repairing the fault that caused the active code to register will cause the code to be cleared from the system.

When an active code is generated, the check engine light will turn on and remain on, blinking every five seconds. When the ECM generates an active diagnostic code due to a fault in the system, it also logs the code in permanent memory where an internal diagnostic clock records the hour of the first fault code occurrence, the hour of the last occurrence and the number of occurrences of the fault code. Logged codes which have accrued in the ECM memory should be investigated on a regular basis and then cleared from the ECM memory so as to make way for future codes.

Fault code	Description
01	Override of idle shutdown throttle
25	Boost pressure sensor fault
27	Coolant temperature sensor fault
28	Check throttle sensor adjustment
31	Loss of vehicle speed signal
32	Throttle position sensor fault
34	Loss of engine RPM signal
35	Engine overspeed warning
36	Vehicle speed signal out of range
37	Fuel pressor sensor fault
41	Vehicle overspeed warning
42	Check sensor calibrations
47	Idle shutdown timed out
51	Intermittant battery power to ECM
52	ECM or personality module fault
53	ECM fault
55	No detected faults
56	Check customer or system parameters
57	Parking brake switch fault
63	Low fuel pressure warning
72	Cylinder 1 or cylinder 2 fault
73	Cylinder 3 or cylinder 4 fault
74	Cylinder 5 or cylinder 6 fault

Table 28.1 The system fault codes relating to a 3176 engine
Courtesy of Caterpillar Inc

Active codes may be viewed using either of the electronic service tools (ECAP or DDT), or by using the cruise control switches. Logged codes in the ECM memory can only be retrieved or erased using the ECAP or DDT service tools. One of the simplest ways of retrieving a fault code is to use the cruise control switches to flash the code on the dash-mounted check engine light. With the ignition switch on and the cruise control switch off, move the cruise control set/resume switch to the resume position. The diagnostic lamp will then flash to indicate a two-digit fault code. The sequence of flashes represents the system diagnostic message. The first sequence of flashes adds up to the first digit of the fault code. After a two-second pause, a second sequence of flashes will occur, representing the second digit of the fault code. Any additional fault codes will follow, after a pause, and will be displayed in the same manner. Table 28.1 shows the full list of fault codes for the 3176 electronically controlled engine.

Electronic Control Module (ECM), Personality Module and Transducer Module

The engine uses a microprocessor-based Electronic Control Module which is isolation mounted on the rear left side of the cylinder block, as shown in Fig 28.62. The ECM is cooled by fuel as it circulates through a manifold between two circuit boards in the control module housing.

One function that the ECM performs is that of a full-range speed governor. This electronic governor functions like a mechanical governor in the mid range. That is, there is droop to provide the driver with a feel for engine load. The throttle actuation characteristics are better than those of the mechanical governor, since the linkage to the engine has been eliminated. The electronic governor includes the special features of programmable isochronous idle and the elimination of governor overspeed. Isochronous idle control (constant engine rpm) is accomplished regardless of the load on the engine at idle speed.

All inputs and outputs to the ECM are designed to tolerate short circuits to battery voltage or ground without damage to the ECM. The ECM power supply provides electrical power to all engine-mounted sensors

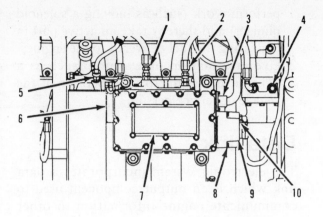

1	Fuel outlet	6	ECM
2	Fuel inlet	7	Personality module
3	Engine wiring harness	8	Transducer module
4	Fuel transfer pump	9	Air inlet port
5	Fuel pressure sensor	10	Boost pressure inlet

Fig 28.62   Electronic Control Module (ECM) *Courtesy of Caterpillar Inc*

and actuators. Reverse voltage polarity protection and resistance to vehicle power voltage swings or surges due to changing alternator load have also been designed into the ECM.

The **Personality Module** which is part of the ECM contains all of the software or instructions for the ECM to do its job. It also contains the performance maps which define fuel rate, timing, etc. so the engine can produce its specified power outputs.

The **Transducer Module**, which includes a boost pressure sensor, is mounted directly to the ECM and uses air lines to connect to the intake plumbing so as to monitor the air pressure before and after the turbocharger. The transducer module is designed to evaluate the pressure difference between the air entering the engine and the boost air in the intake manifold. This pressure difference is converted into an electrical signal which is sent to the ECM for the purpose of controlling fuel delivery during engine acceleration. This component replaces the air–fuel control unit on previous mechanically controlled engines.

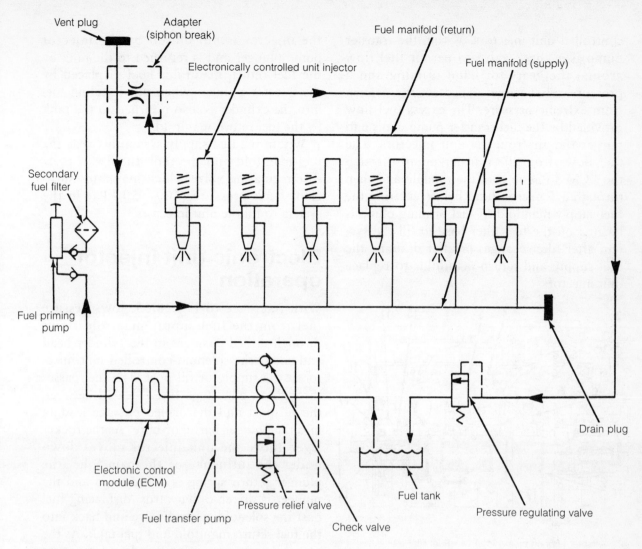

Fig 28.63 Schematic diagram of the fuel system for a 3176 engine
Courtesy of Caterpillar Inc

Idle shutdown timer

The idle shutdown timer is a feature of the electronic control system that can be selected by the customer. The timer, which can be programmed by the ECAP service tool, can shut the engine down after a time period of between three minutes and 60 minutes and can be adjusted in increments of one minute.

Throttle position sensor

A cab-mounted throttle position sensor is used to eliminate the mechanical linkage between the engine and the operator's foot pedal. The throttle position sensor is a rotary position sensor which monitors the position of the throttle pedal and in so doing sends an electrical signal to the ECM, which interprets the information and fuels the engine accordingly.

Fuel system

The fuel supply circuit, as shown in Fig 28.63, is a conventional design for unit-injected engines, in that it uses a gear type fuel transfer pump to draw fuel from the fuel tank and deliver it to the electronically controlled unit injectors. Within the transfer pump is a check valve to permit fuel flow around the gears for hand priming and a pressure relief valve to protect the system from extreme pressure. The excess fuel flow provided by the fuel transfer pump cools and purges the air from the unit injectors. The fuel flows from the transfer pump through the ECM so as to cool the module and then through a 5 micron filter before entering the fuel supply manifold. A fuel priming pump is located on the fuel filter base to fill the system after filter changes or after draining the fuel supply and return manifolds to replace unit injectors.

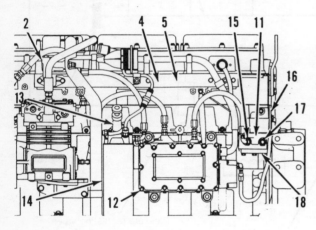

2	Adapter (siphon break)	14	Fuel filter
4	Fuel return	15	Fuel outlet (to ECM)
5	Fuel supply	16	Spacer
11	Fuel transfer pump	17	Fuel inlet (from tank)
12	ECM	18	Cover assembly
13	Fuel priming pump		

Fig 28.64 Fuel system components on a 3176 engine
Courtesy of Caterpillar Inc

The fuel to and from the unit injectors passes through an adapter (siphon break) mounted on the supply and return manifold. The adapter is designed to prevent fuel siphoning back to the tank when the engine is not running. The fuel flows continuously from the fuel supply manifold through the unit injectors when the supply or fill port in the injector is not closed by the injector pump plunger and is returned to the tank by the fuel return manifold. Fuel displaced by the injector plunger when not injecting fuel into the cylinder is also returned to the tank by the fuel return manifold.

Within the fuel supply system between the fuel manifold and the tank there is a pressure-regulating valve which maintains sufficient back pressure (400–550 kPa) in the system to fill the unit injectors.

Electronic unit injector operation

With reference to Fig 28.65, low-pressure fuel from the fuel supply manifold flows through drilled passages in the cylinder head and enters the solenoid-controlled unit injector at the supply or fill port. The fuel passes through an edge type filter located between the fill port and the drilled passage leading into the plunger barrel or bore. As the rocker lever above the unit injector moves down under the influence of the cam lobe, the plunger return spring is compressed and the plunger is driven downwards, displacing fuel past the solenoid control valve and back into the fuel return manifold and fuel tank. As the plunger continues to travel down it covers the fill port. Therefore the fuel below the plunger is now forced down around the injector nozzle and back up past the open solenoid control valve. After the fuel passes the open solenoid control valve, it flows through a passage in the injector body and returns to the tank via the spill port and fuel return manifold. Injection will commence when the electric solenoid is energised, lifting the solenoid control valve up and cutting off the fuel flow past the valve. The actual start of injection is controlled by the engine speed/timing sensor in conjunction with injection timing requirements programmed into the ECM.

With the solenoid valve now closed, the downward movement of the injector plunger

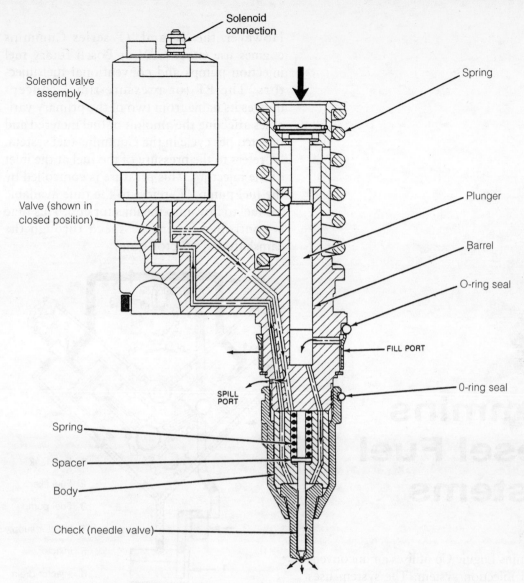

Fig 28.65   Cross-sectioned diagram of an electronically controlled unit injector
Courtesy of Caterpillar Inc

causes the fuel pressure to rise in the injector nozzle area. As the pressure rises, it overcomes the injector spring tension and lifts the injector needle valve or check off its seat, allowing fuel to spray into the combustion chamber. After the correct amount of fuel has been injected into the cylinder, the ECM signals to de-energise the injector solenoid, thereby opening the solenoid control valve. At this point the high-pressure fuel within the injector is dumped through the spill port to the fuel return manifold and tank. The needle

valve in the injector will also return to its seat as injection ends.

As the injector plunger completes its downward travel, it begins to rise under the influence of the unit injector plunger return spring. As the plunger returns to its full up position, the fill port in the injector body is again uncovered, allowing fuel to refill the plunger bore.

Low-pressure fuel then circulates through the injector body and out the spill port until the solenoid valve assembly is again energised.

However, the 'B' and 'C' series Cummins engines use either CAV or Bosch rotary fuel injection pumps and conventional fuel injectors. The PT (or pressure-time) concept derives its name from two of the primary variables affecting the amount of fuel metered and injected per cycle in the Cummins fuel system. 'P' refers to the pressure of the fuel at the inlet of the injectors. This pressure is controlled by the fuel pump. 'T' refers to the time available for fuel to flow into the injector cup. This time is controlled by engine speed through the camshaft and injector train.

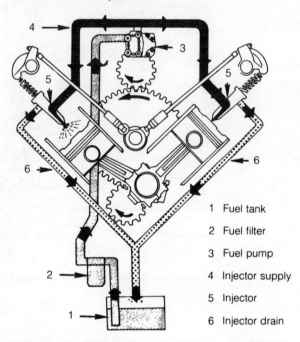

1 Fuel tank

2 Fuel filter

3 Fuel pump

4 Injector supply

5 Injector

6 Injector drain

Fig 29.1 Schematic diagram of fuel flow and mechanical linkage in the Cummins PT fuel system

Metering of fuel in the system is based on the principle that the volume of liquid that will pass through an orifice is proportional to the pressure of the liquid, the time of flow and the orifice size.

In basic terms, the PT fuel system utilises simple mechanically operated injectors through which fuel continually circulates. In each injector, a fixed metering orifice leads fuel into a pressure chamber below a reciprocating plunger. As the plunger descends, fuel

Cummins Diesel Fuel Systems

The Cummins Engine Co utilises an unconventional fuel injection system. The system uses the existing engine camshaft to operate unit injectors mounted in the cylinder head. During injection, the fuel is raised to injection pressure by the unit injectors and then sprayed directly into the combustion chamber. The Cummins system may also be considered mechanical, since there is no injector valve to be opened hydraulically by fuel pressure.

The Cummins PT fuel injection system

The Cummins PT fuel injection system is used on the majority of Cummins engines.

in this chamber is forced through multiple spray holes into the combustion chamber. The injector plunger is operated from the engine camshaft via a pushrod and rocker lever. Fuel can flow through the metering orifice into the

pressure chamber only during the upper part of the plunger's stroke. Hence the metering time is related directly to engine speed.

Fuel is supplied to the injectors through a fuel line from the fuel pump — an assembly

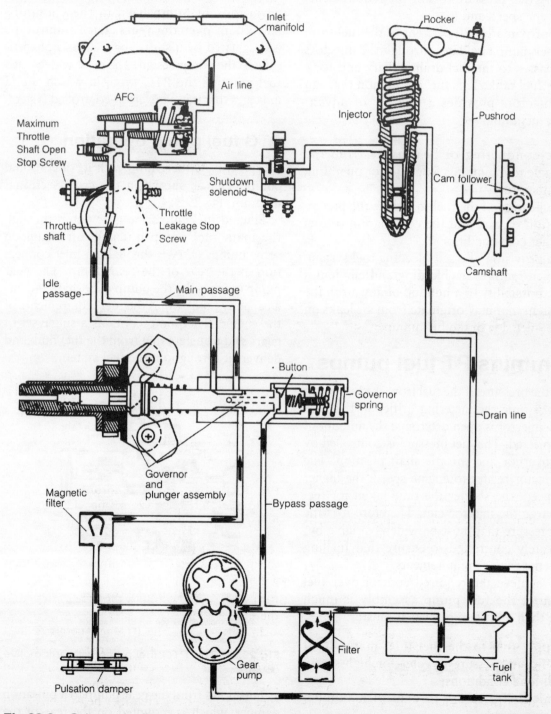

Fig 29.2   Schematic diagram of the complete Cummins PT fuel system (with AFC fitted)

incorporating not only a gear pump to raise the fuel pressure to an intermediate level and supply it to the fuel gallery in the engine cylinder head, but also the throttle, governor and air fuel control (AFC) (when fitted), which modify fuel pressure to suit the requirements of engine speed and load.

Approximately 70 per cent of the fuel from the fuel pump circulates through the injectors and passes to the fuel drain gallery and back to the fuel tank. This fuel circulation through the injectors provides a number of advantages, including:

- the conducting of heat away from the nozzle to maintain a safe injector operating temperature;
- the heating of the fuel to reduce the precipitation of wax and the coagulation of fuel under cold conditions;
- the provision of a self-bleeding fuel system, which requires no bleeding and eliminates the possibility of a buildup of any air in the system that may originate from air leaks on the inlet side of the fuel pump.

Cummins PT fuel pumps

Both the pressure of the fuel from the fuel pump and the time the metering orifice in the base of the injector is open determine the amount of fuel injected. The fuel pressure is controlled by the governor and throttle shaft position. The time factor relates to engine speed: the higher the speed, the shorter the time taken for fuel to charge the injector cup. Therefore it is the fuel pressure that must be widely variable but accurately controlled to ensure that fuelling meets the engine's requirements.

To achieve the required control over fuel pressure, the fuel pump assembly is much more than a lift pump, since it must:

- supply fuel to the fuel inlet manifold at sufficient pressure to cater for high-speed, full-load conditions;
- limit fuel pressure to control maximum engine speed;
- regulate fuel pressure between idle and maximum speed;
- provide a manual method (the throttle shaft) to control fuel flow.

There have been a number of types or variations of pump used in the Cummins PT system over the years. Each pump type is designated by a suffix that relates alphabetically to the pump design. The most widely used fuel pump is the PTG type, in which the G indicates that it is a governor-controlled system.

PTG fuel pump operation

A typical PTG fuel pump with its operational components is shown in the cross-sectional diagram, Fig 29.3.

Filtered fuel enters the gear pump through the main fuel pump housing, although on some pumps entry is through an inlet connection at the rear of the gear pump. The gear pump is driven by the pump mainshaft and has a capacity many times the fuel requirements of the engine. The pump contains a single set of gears and transfers fuel from the fuel tank and delivers it throughout the fuel system.

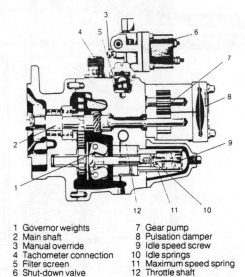

1 Governor weights	7 Gear pump
2 Main shaft	8 Pulsation damper
3 Manual override	9 Idle speed screw
4 Tachometer connection	10 Idle springs
5 Filter screen	11 Maximum speed spring
6 Shut-down valve	12 Throttle shaft

Fig 29.3 The PTG fuel pump with automotive governor

Fuel flows from the gear pump to a pulsation damper, which is mounted on the rear of the

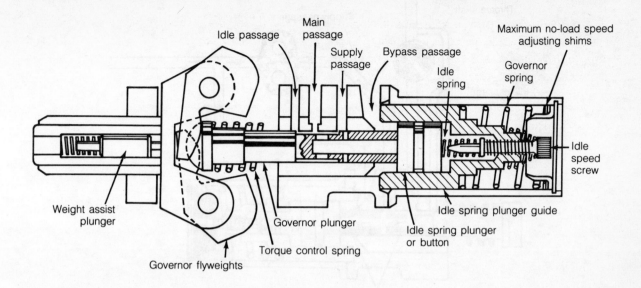

Fig 29.4   Sectional view of the PTG governor assembly

gear pump. It contains a flexible steel diaphragm, which flexes back and forth to absorb fuel flow pulsations and so stabilise the fuel pressure. From the gear pump, fuel also flows through a wire gauze magnetic filter and on to the governor assembly.

Essentially, the governor consists of seven parts:

1 a governor weight assembly;
2 a governor plunger;
3 a ported control sleeve;
4 an idle spring plunger (or button);
5 an idle plunger guide;
6 an idle spring;
7 a (main) governor spring.

The governor plunger moves axially in the ported sleeve, under the influence of the centrifugal force on the flyweights from the one end and the force exerted by the governor springs from the other.

The plunger may be likened to a spool valve, with a 'waist' between two control lands. A radial drilling leads from this area to an axial bore emerging at the spring end of the plunger.

The ported sleeve contains four ports:

1 a supply passage located to supply fuel to the area between the plunger lands;

2 a main passage leading to the throttle shaft;
3 an idle passage leading directly to the injector supply gallery;
4 a bypass passage leading fuel back to the gear pump inlet.

The pre-tensioned governor spring acts against the idle plunger guide to hold it firmly against a shoulder in the housing. The idle spring, located inside the idle plunger guide, acts against the button, which is, in turn, held against the end of the governor plunger.

When the engine is cranked, fuel from the gear pump enters the governor plunger through the supply passage and fills both the bore and the waist. Fuel is able to flow through the idle passage, which is fully open to the injectors.

As soon as the engine starts, centrifugal force acting on the flyweights is transferred to the plunger, moving it against the idle spring, so that the control edge of the plunger land partly covers the idle passage, restricting fuel flow and pressure to the injectors. This movement is opposed by the idle spring and a balance is reached between centrifugal force and idle spring force. Engine speed is controlled by the fuel pressure, which in turn is controlled by the flow through the idle passage. During idle, the throttle shaft remains closed.

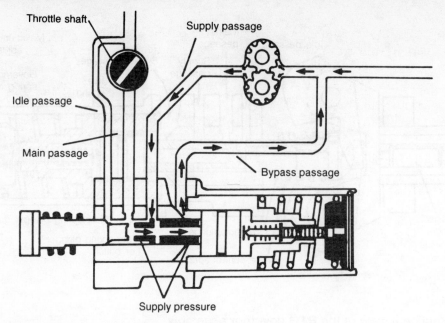

Fig 29.5 Schematic diagram of governor fuel pressure control

At the same time, gear pump supply pressure is controlled as the button is forced from its seat against the end on the governor plunger to dump excess fuel back to the gear pump inlet through the bypass passage.

When the throttle is opened to increase the speed of the engine, fuel passes at supply pressure through the throttle shaft to the injectors to increase the rate of fuel injection. The engine speed increases and the flyweight centrifugal force acts on the governor plunger to force the plunger against the button in the idle spring guide. When the force created by the fuel pressure acting on the button exceeds the force holding the plunger and button together, the button is unseated and fuel is bypassed to the inlet side of the gear pump. This is shown in Fig 29.5. The bypass regulator therefore maintains the correct supply by unseating the button at the designated pressure and bypassing the excess fuel.

The size of the recess in the button controls

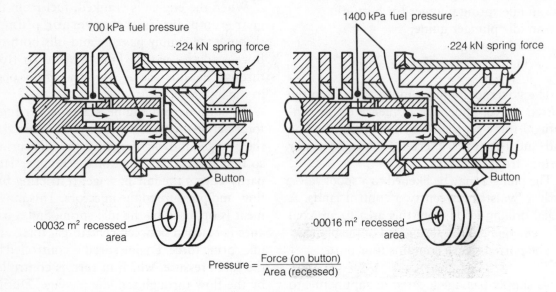

$$\text{Pressure} = \frac{\text{Force (on button)}}{\text{Area (recessed)}}$$

Fig 29.6 Use of a 'button' to vary the fuel system pressure

the fuel pressure to the injectors, and a range of buttons is available to enable the fuel pressure to be set as specified (Fig 29.6). Varying the pressure will alter the torque and power ratings of the engine, and should only be done within the limits of the manufacturer's recommendations.

Further, at maximum governed speed, the centrifugal force acting on the governor fly-weights is sufficient to compress the governor spring, allowing the plunger to partly restrict the main passage, so controlling the fuel pressure to the throttle shaft.

Thus, at idle speed, governing is achieved by a balance between centrifugal force and idle spring force, and at maximum speed, governing is achieved by a balance between centrifugal force and (main) governor spring force.

The now-regulated manifold fuel pressure leaves the governor and flows up to the throttle shaft (Fig 29.7). The throttle shaft has a transverse hole drilled through it, and partially rotates in a ported sleeve pressed into the fuel pump housing. The shaft allows the operator to alter the system fuel pressure between idle and maximum engine speeds, thereby controlling the torque and power output during this operating range.

The transverse drilling in the throttle shaft functions as a variable orifice to control the amount of fuel flow to the injectors. The drilling itself can be altered in size by an adjusting screw located inside the throttle shaft. This screw is used to adjust system pressure during calibration of the pump and should only be altered by trained personnel.

The transverse drilling in the throttle shaft carries fuel at engine speeds above idle. However, during idle speed, fuel flow is via an idle passage, as shown in Fig 29.7. With increasing engine speed and governor action, a taper on the governor plunger gradually closes off the idle passage, allowing fuel flow through the main passage.

The throttle shaft operates between two stop screws: one limits maximum rotation of the shaft and the other is the throttle leakage screw (Fig 29.7).

The maximum travel screw prevents the throttle shaft from rotating beyond the full open position, and allowing unrestricted fuel flow through the transverse drilling.

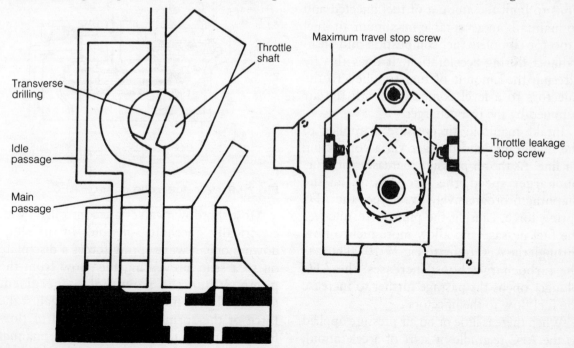

Fig 29.7   Throttle shaft and stop screws (schematic)

Note: This screw does not adjust the maximum engine speed; in this system, the maximum engine speed is adjusted by the governor spring tension.

The throttle leakage screw is designed so that when the throttle shaft is closed, there is always a small amount of fuel flowing through the throttle shaft, as shown in Fig 29.8. This is defined as throttle leakage and is required to keep the fuel lines filled with fuel to cool and lubricate the injectors when the throttle is closed. Throttle leakage is an important setting on the fuel pump. If it is set too high, it can result in slow acceleration and excessive carboning of the injectors. If it is set too low, it causes a hesitation in engine response when the throttle is reopened after a downhill run, and leads to injector plunger and barrel damage.

It can now be seen that there are two main components controlling system fuel pressure in the PTG pump: the governor and the throttle shaft.

From the throttle shaft, fuel flows to the air–fuel control (or AFC) section of the pump, if fitted (refer to Fig 29.9). The AFC assembly is necessary on turbocharged engine applications to limit the amount of fuel injected and so maintain an acceptable maximum air–fuel ratio for complete fuel combustion and clean exhaust during acceleration. It does this by altering the amount of fuel supplied to the injectors to a level compatible with the air supplied by the turbocharger.

Intake manifold air pressure is applied to the diaphragm and plunger via a connecting air line. As the air pressure increases with turbocharger speed, the force acting on the diaphragm progressively overcomes the AFC spring force, causing the plunger to uncover the fuel passage and allow more fuel to flow through the AFC (refer to Fig 29.10). Thus, as the turbocharger boost increases, the AFC plunger opens the passage further to increase the fuel flow to the injectors.

When there is little or no air pressure applied to the AFC (e.g. idle or start of acceleration), the flow of fuel around the AFC plunger is blocked off. Under these conditions, all fuel flows around the 'no air' adjusting screw, as shown in Fig 29.10.

From the AFC, the fuel finally flows to the shutdown valve (see Fig 29.11), before passing to the fuel gallery and the injectors.

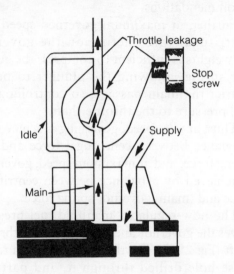

Fig 29.8 Throttle shaft in throttle leakage position (schematic)

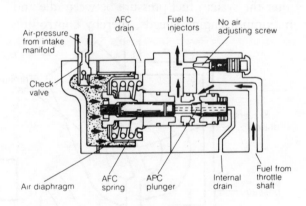

Fig 29.9 Air–fuel ratio control (AFC)

Most shutdown valves are controlled by an electrically operated solenoid. In the shutdown mode, a wave spring forces a disc plate on to a seat, preventing fuel flow from the pump. When the solenoid is energised, the disc plate is lifted from its seat against the force of the spring, permitting fuel to flow from the pump to the injectors. The manual over-ride, designed to over-ride the solenoid

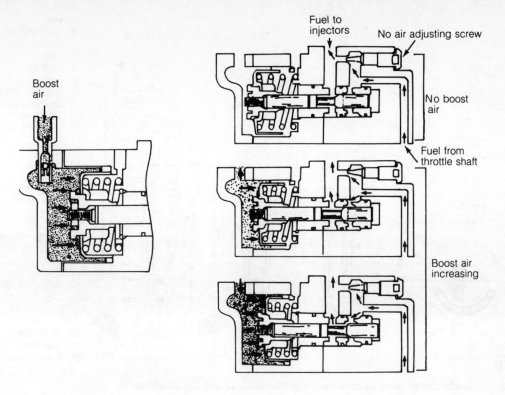

Fig 29.10   Operation of air–fuel control (AFC)

and open the valve manually in case of a solenoid or electrical malfunction, is also incorporated in the system.

The PT system injectors

The PT injector is a simple mechanical unit that receives fuel under varying pressures from the fuel pump assembly, and meters, injects and atomises it through fine spray holes into the combustion chamber.

All injector types are similar in that they feature a plunger reciprocating in the injector body under the influence of the camshaft–pushrod–rocker combination and a return spring. All feature continuous fuel

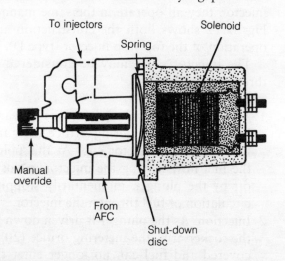
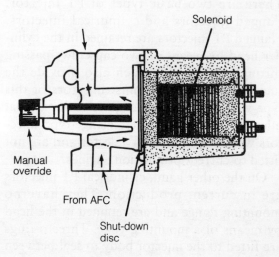

Fig 29.11   Shutdown valve operation

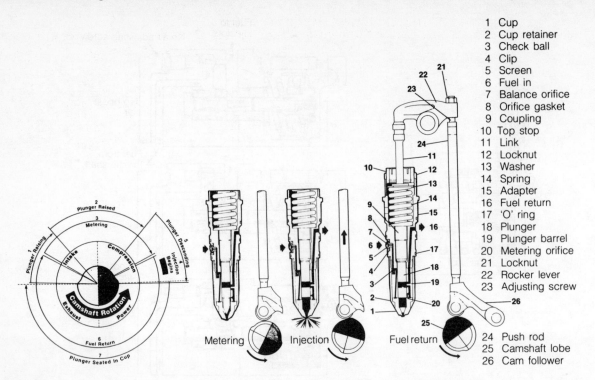

1 Cup
2 Cup retainer
3 Check ball
4 Clip
5 Screen
6 Fuel in
7 Balance orifice
8 Orifice gasket
9 Coupling
10 Top stop
11 Link
12 Locknut
13 Washer
14 Spring
15 Adapter
16 Fuel return
17 'O' ring
18 Plunger
19 Plunger barrel
20 Metering orifice
21 Locknut
22 Rocker lever
23 Adjusting screw
24 Push rod
25 Camshaft lobe
26 Cam follower

Metering   Injection   Fuel return

Fig 29.12   Construction and operation of a top stop (type D) injector

circulation, so every type has both a fuel inlet and an outlet — an outlet apart from the spray holes, that is. However, there are some considerable constructional differences and improvements in the more recently developed types, which are also a little different in operation from earlier designs.

PT injector types

There are two basic types of PT injector: flanged injectors and cylindrical injectors. Flanged PT injectors are retained in the cylinder head by means of two capscrews passing through the flange, which also provide the fuel line connection points. Injectors of this type would be used on engines with external inlet and drain fuel pipes. Flange-type injectors were the original PT injector and are not fitted to current-production engines.

On the other hand, cylindrical PT injectors are in current production. They have no mounting flange and are retained in the head by means of a mounting yoke. Three o-rings are fitted to the injector body to seal between the fuel inlet and outlet galleries in the cylinder head. The common cylindrical injectors in use today are the PTC, PTD and PTD 'top stop' types.

Operation of cylindrical PT injectors

Although there are a number of constructional differences between different types of PT injector, they all operate in the same manner. Fig 29.12 shows both the construction and operation of the top stop injector (type D).

The injector cycle may be considered in three stages:

1 **Metering.** As the plunger moves upward, it uncovers the metering orifice (20) and fuel enters the injector cup. At this point, the fuel flow leaving the injector is closed off by the plunger, momentarily stopping circulation of fuel through the injector.
2 **Injection.** As the plunger is driven down by the rocker arm, the metering orifice (20) is covered and fuel can no longer enter the

cup, nor can it escape except through the spray holes. With further downward movement, the plunger contacts the trapped fuel and forces it through the spray holes into the combustion chamber.

3 **Fuel return**. After injection is completed and the plunger is seated in the cup, the plunger remains seated until it begins to rise to start the injection cycle again. Fuel again circulates freely through injector, providing cooling and lubrication.

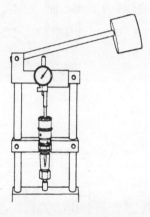

Fig 29.13   The top stop injector plunger travel adjusting fixture

Top stop injector

This is the later type Cummins injector, so called because it features a splined locknut and stop mechanism (10) in the top of the injector body, which limits the upward movement of the injector plunger (Fig 29.12). The plunger travel for top stop injectors cannot be set with the injectors in the engine. A special top stop adjustment fixture, shown in Fig 29.13, is required. The injector spring is pre-loaded by means of a weighted handle at a prescribed travel as shown by the dial indicator. The plunger travel is changed by turning the adjusting nut (10, Fig 29.12). Plunger travel is pre-set in manufacture or on reconditioning.

Most of the time during engine operation, the plunger spring force reacts against the stop in the top of the injector and not against the camshaft, which in previous designs carried this load at all times. Therefore the injector mechanical drive train is greatly relieved of this continuous loading, which in turn allows improved lubrication of the camshaft lobes and cam followers, extending the life of the drive train.

Automatic timing control system

As a means of controlling pollution and increasing engine performance, Cummins have introduced an automatic device to control injection timing. The step timing control (STC) system is designed to change the fuel injection timing according to engine load and speed conditions.

STC injection

Refer to Fig 29.14. The STC system consists of special top stop injectors with a hydraulic tappet between the injector rocker lever and the plunger, and with an STC control valve mounted separately on the engine. STC has two stages of injection timing: the engine operates with advanced timing during starting and light engine load conditions, and at normal timing during medium to high engine load conditions.

The hydraulic tappet consists of an inner piston and an outer piston sleeve which reciprocates in a housing. Also incorporated in the hydraulic tappet is an inlet check ball and a load cell check ball.

Advanced timing

When system fuel pressure is less than 221 kPa (starting and low speed), the STC control valve opens to allow oil from the engine lubricating system to charge the hydraulic tappet. As the cam follower begins to ride up the cam injection ramp, the injector lever begins to force the inner piston downwards. Since the

Advanced timing

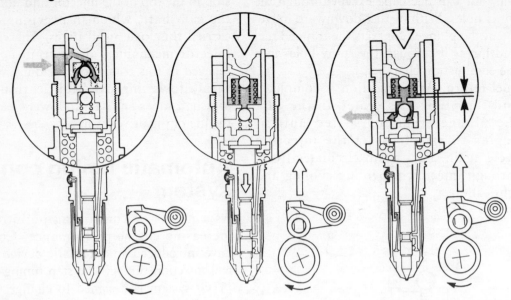

Normal timing

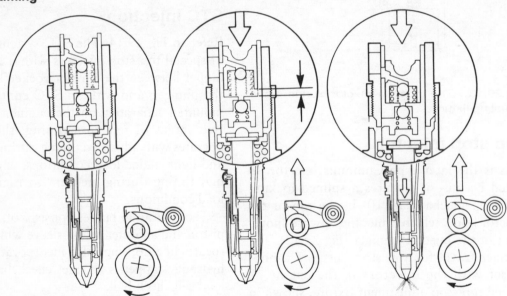

Fig 29.14 An STC injector showing advanced and normal timing positions

oil between the inner and outer piston now forms a solid link, the downward force is immediately transmitted to the outer piston, and the injector plunger now travels down earlier than it does under normal timing. At the end of the injection stroke, when the plunger bottoms in the cup, the oil pressure increases in the tappet until it causes the load-

check valve to open and dump the oil out of the injector, which then drains back to the engine sump.

Normal timing

When fuel pressure is greater than 221 kPa (mid-range speed), the STC control valve prevents oil entry to the hydraulic tappet;

therefore, with no oil in the tappet, as the camfollower begins to ride up the cam injection ramp, the injector rocker lever will force the inner piston downwards. Due to the fact that there is no oil in the hydraulic tappet, the inner piston must travel further to make direct contact with the outer piston before the injector plunger can begin its downward travel, which causes injection to occur later.

Several advantages are claimed for the STC system. During advanced injection timing, it improves cold weather idling characteristics, reduces white smoke, improves light-load fuel economy and reduces injector carboning.

During normal injection timing, it controls cylinder pressures and reduces nitrogen oxide emissions.

Servicing the PT fuel system

Like all fuel systems, the PT system needs periodic maintenance checks and adjustments. These include checking (and perhaps making adjustments to) the fuel system pressures and governor adjustments and, since there is a large range of Cummins engines, each with a number of power ratings and governors to suit the diversity of applications to which these engines are put, these checks and adjustments can only be undertaken if the relevant service data are available. In the absence of relevant service data, the following adjustments may be helpful.

Refitting the fuel pump

No pump timing is required when refitting a PTG fuel pump to the engine, since injection timing is controlled by the position of the engine camshaft, which ultimately drives the injector plunger. Once fitted, the fuel pump housing must be primed with clean diesel fuel. This can be done by removing a plug from the top of the housing and filling the pump housing with diesel fuel. After refitting the plug, the engine should be cranked over with the

starter motor until it starts. No bleeding of the injectors or fuel pump is necessary as it is a 'tank-to-tank' fuel system.

Refitting injectors

When injectors are to be refitted into the cylinder head, a number of steps should be followed. The injector hole in the cylinder head should be cleaned out, and new o-rings fitted to the injectors, with care being taken to ensure that they are not twisted. The o-rings should be lubricated with engine oil and the injectors inserted in the cylinder head so positioned that the injector fuel inlet orifice (balancing orifice) is adjacent to the exhaust manifold on in-line engines and to the valley on 'V' engines. Finally, the injectors should be pushed home to their seating position and the retaining clamp correctly tensioned.

Injector adjustments

The injector adjustment must be correct. Apart from the danger of damage to the injector, an over-adjusted injector will not deliver sufficient fuel, could bend an injector pushrod and will advance injection timing. An injector set too loose will cause increased fuel delivery, retarded injection timing and carboning up of the injector spray holes.

In practice, this is a very simple operation, with two methods being employed: the torque method and the dial indicator method.

The torque method (as applied to a six-cylinder engine)

1   Rotate the crankshaft in the direction of engine rotation. On the front accessory drive pulley or crankshaft pulley there are a series of three VS (valve set) marks, such as A or 1-6VS, B or 2-5VS, C or 3-4VS, as shown in Fig 29.15. Align one of these marks with the pointer on the timing gear cover, then check both cylinders indicated on the pulley to see which valve rocker levers are loose. Adjust the injector of the cylinder in which the rocker levers are

loose. The alternative cylinder in the VS number will be ready for adjustment one turn of the crankshaft later.

2   Loosen the injector adjusting screw locknut. Then tighten the adjusting screw until the injector plunger is at the bottom of its travel. Then tighten the adjusting screw a further 15 degrees to squeeze oil from the cup. Loosen the adjusting screw one full turn.

3   Then, using a suitable torque wrench, tighten the adjusting screw to the cold setting specified, as seen in Fig 29.16, and tension the locknut.

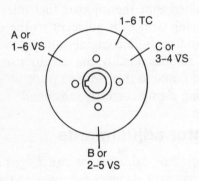

Fig 29.15   Timing marks on the accessory drive pulley

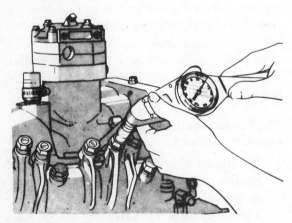

Fig 29.16   Adjusting the injector plunger by the torque method

With the torque method, after the injector has been set, the valve crossheads and valve clearances can be adjusted on the same cylinder. Refer to the manual for the adjustment procedure and clearances.

The dial indicator method (applied to a six-cylinder engine)

Cummins have now introduced a more refined method of injector adjustment. With this method, the injector plunger travel is measured by a dial indicator, which requires the injectors and valves to be set on separate cylinders. The injector is set with the piston at the beginning of the compression stroke and valves on the corresponding cylinders at the end of the same stroke.

Right-hand rotation engine

Bar in direction	Pulley position	Set cylinder Injector	Valve
Start	A or 1–6 VS	3	5
Adv. To	B or 2–5 VS	6	3
Adv. To	C or 3–4 VS	2	6
Adv. To	A or 1–6 VS	4	2
Adv. To	B or 2–5 VS	1	4
Adv. To	C or 3–4 VS	5	1

Note: This table is to be used for dial indicator setting only.

Fig 29.17   Injector-valve setting table

Fig 29.18   Dial indicator set up to measure plunger travel

1   Rotate the engine crankshaft in the direction of rotation. Align the A or 1–6VS mark on the accessory drive pulley or crankshaft pulley with the pointer on the timing gear cover.

2   When the A or 1–6VS mark is aligned with the pointer, the inlet and exhaust valves for cylinder no. 5 will be in the closed

position. Also the injector plunger for cylinder no. 3 will be at the top of its travel. If the valves on no. 5 cylinder are not closed — that is, the rockers are loose — refer to the alternative A or 1-6VS in the table and check valves on cylinder no. 2 and injector on cylinder no. 4.

Note: The instructions using cylinder no. 3 to begin injector adjustment are for illustration purposes only. It is possible to start with any cylinder for injector adjustment provided that the crankshaft and camshaft positions are in accordance with the tune-up table (Fig. 29.17).

3 Use the injector adjustment kit to check the travel of the injector plunger. Install

Fig 29.19 Actuating the rocker lever to check plunger travel with the dial indicator

the dial indicator and support so that the extension for the dial indicator is against the injector plunger, as shown in Fig 29.18.

4 Actuate the rocker lever to push the injector plunger to the bottom of its travel, using the rocker lever actuator from the adjustment kit, as illustrated in Fig 29.19. Let the plunger rise to the top of its travel. Actuate the lever again and set the dial indicator to zero, while holding the plunger at the bottom of its travel seated in its cup.

5 Tighten the rocker lever adjusting screw until the injector plunger has the correct travel, as per specifications.

6 Hold the adjusting screw in position and tighten the locknut to the specified torque. Actuate the rocker lever two or three times to check that the adjustment is correct.

7 After the plunger travel has been adjusted, the crossheads and valves must be adjusted for the cylinder shown in the table in Fig 29.17 before the crankshaft is rotated to the next valve set mark.

Adjustment of top stop injectors

1 Rotate the crankshaft in the direction of engine rotation and align the A or 1-6VS mark on the accessory drive or crankshaft pulley with the pointer on the timing gear cover. Refer to the table (Fig 29.17) for the location of the injector and valve adjustments.

2 Loosen the locknut for the rocker lever adjusting screw and tighten the adjusting screw until all the clearance is removed from between the rocker lever and injector link. Further tighten the adjusting screw one additional turn.

3 Back off the adjusting screw until the spring washer is against the stop of the injector, as shown in Fig 29.20.

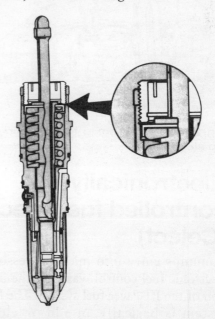

Fig 29.20 The top stop injector with washer and spring against the stop

4 Tighten the adjusting screw to 0.56–0.68 Nm (5–6 lb), using a torque wrench (Fig 29.21). If a torque wrench is not available, tighten the screw until there is light pressure against the injector link. The link must be free enough so that it can be rotated by hand. Finally, hold the adjusting screw and tension the locknut.

   Note: The figure quoted above is included as a typical figure only. Refer to the workshop manual for the correct setting for any required application.

5 After the injector plunger has been adjusted, the crossheads and valves must be adjusted for the cylinder shown in the table before rotation of the crankshaft to the next valve set mark.

   Note: Top stop injectors need two adjustments. The first, as mentioned earlier in the chapter, is the plunger travel distance, which is set at the factory or after reconditioning, and the second is as mentioned above.

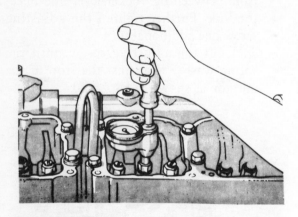

Fig 29.21 Tensioning the adjusting screw-top stop injector

Electronically controlled fuel injection (Celect)

Cummins entry into microprocessor based electronic fuel control was with the introduction of the PT-Pacer fuel system. The PT-Pacer system is basically an add-on electronic control device to the existing PT fuel system.

An electronic fuel control valve is mounted on top of the PT fuel pump housing and in conjunction with an electronic control module regulates the fuel delivered to the conventional PT injectors. Cummins have further developed electronic engine controls and have now introduced a full electronically controlled injection and governing system. The new electronic system is called Celect and is fitted to L10 and N14 automotive truck engines.

In the Celect system, Cummins have replaced the PT fuel pump with a simple gear pump which is used to draw fuel from the fuel tank and deliver it to the electronically controlled injectors mounted in the cylinder head. The Celect injector is an all-new top stop design injector and is operated in the same way as the mechanical PT injector by way of the camshaft and injector pushrod in order to develop the high pressure necessary for injection. The metering and timing of the fuel are now accomplished by the actuation of an electric solenoid-operated control valve which is mounted on the top of each injector assembly. During engine operation, the ECM (electronic control module) which is the heart of the system sends signals to the injector solenoids in order to control fuel metering and timing relative to engine operating conditions.

By using electronics to control fuel metering and timing functions on the engine, the combustion process can now be precisely controlled, resulting in improved fuel economy and reduced exhaust emissions.

The Celect system offers a number of advantages over the conventional mechanically controlled fuel injection system in that it provides:

- electronic control of vehicle performance and speed (speed limited);
- engine protection;
- tamper resistance;
- system self-diagnosis;
- customer selected features

Each of the above advantages is now explained in greater detail.

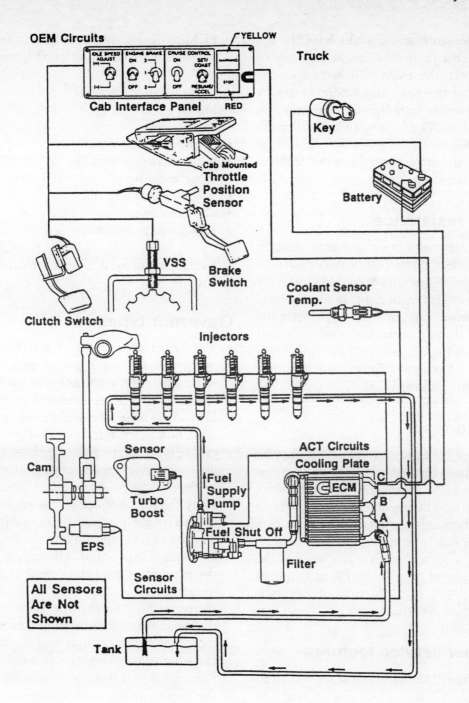

OEM Circuits

Cab Interface Panel

IDLE SPEED ADJUST (+) (−)

ENGINE BRAKE ON 3 OFF 2

CRUISE CONTROL ON OFF SET/ COAST RESUME/ ACCEL

YELLOW WARNING

STOP RED

Truck

Key

Battery

Cab Mounted **Throttle Position Sensor**

VSS

Brake Switch

Coolant Sensor Temp.

Clutch Switch

Injectors

Cam

Sensor

Turbo Boost

EPS

Fuel Supply Pump

Fuel Shut Off

ACT Circuits

Cooling Plate

ECM

C B A

Filter

Sensor Circuits

All Sensors Are Not Shown

Tank

Fig 29.22 Schematic diagram of the Celect electronically controlled fuel injection system

Speed limited

- As the engine performance and vehicle speed are continually monitored and controlled by the ECM, the maximum attainable vehicle speed can now be set by the vehicle owner in accordance with the particular government road speed regulations.

Engine protection

- Celect provides an engine protection system which continually monitors such things as coolant temperature, oil pressure, oil temperature and coolant level. In the event that a fault develops in any one of these areas, the ECM will determine the severity of the fault and where necessary derate engine speed/power or shut the engine down. The fault will also turn on the dash-mounted warning or stop engine light so as to inform the operator of the problem in the system.

Tamper resistance

- Tamper resistance is an important feature of the Celect system, with two measures being used to discourage people tampering with the system in an effort to alter vehicle performance. One of these is to limit the speed of the engine when the vehicle speed sensor has been interfered with. Another is the use of passwords to gain entry to Compulink and the ECM.

Self-diagnosis

- Built-in self-diagnostics is another feature which comes as standard with the Celect system. The ECM continually runs self-checks on all electronic components in the system as well as checking the engine sub-systems such as the cooling system, etc. If a fault is detected in the system, the driver is advised of the fault by way of the illumination of an amber warning light or a red stop engine light mounted on the vehicle dash.

Customer service features

- Apart from the standard features listed previously, Cummins also offer a range of customer selected features which can be programmed into the ECM by using Compulink. Compulink is a portable service tool which can be easily connected to the ECM via the data link connector and is used by Cummins service personal to diagnose system faults. Changes to the vehicle operating parameters and calibration of the

ECM to obtain the required engine performance can also be done using Compulink.

The customer-selected features are as follows:

- engine governor type;
- progressive gear shifting;
- cruise control;
- idle adjust switch;
- idle shutdown;
- gear-down protection.

Each feature will now be examined in greater detail.

Governor types

- The Celect system can be programmed to operate under two types of engine governor, namely the automotive or the variable speed type. The automotive governor is also known as an idle/maximum speed governor. With reference to Fig 29.23, it can be seen that engine speed within the idle maximum speed range is determined by the throttle position sensor input as well as by the load applied to the engine. Since the throttle position determines the amount of fuel injected into the engine, the resultant engine speed is directly related to the amount of load the engine is required to carry. That is, if the load on the engine is increased but the throttle position is left the same, the engine speed will drop due to there not being enough fuel injected into the engine to carry the increased load. Remember that this governor only governs the engine at idle and maximum no-load speeds; therefore there is no governor response to changing engine load speed between these two speed ranges. Figure 29.23 illustrates what happens to the engine speed of a vehicle with an automotive type governor when the vehicle load is increased without a corresponding increase in throttle position.

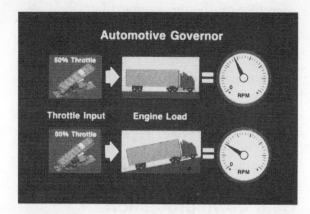

Fig 29.23   Operation of the automotive-type governor

The variable speed governor, on the other hand, will govern the engine at all speeds between idle and maximum. During engine operation, the governor will attempt to maintain a pre-set constant speed under varying engine load conditions, as shown in Figure 29.24. Therefore, any variation in engine speed is solely based on input from the throttle position sensor. That is, the governor continually senses engine speed and if, at any time, the engine speed decreases due to increased load conditions, the governor will automatically increase engine fuelling to carry the increased load at the same engine speed. If, however, the load on the engine increases to such an extent that the governor can no longer

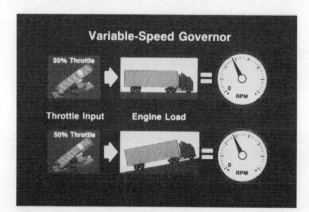

Fig 29.24   Operation of the variable speed-type governor

provide enough fuel to sustain the current speed, the engine speed will drop according to the amount of load placed on it. Figure 29.24 shows what happens to the engine speed of a vehicle with a variable speed governor when the vehicle load is increased without a corresponding increase in throttle position.

Progressive gear shifting

- Progressive gear shifting can be programmed into the Celect system so as to promote fuel economy in operations where the greater percentage of driving is in the lower gears — for example, in city driving conditions. When the vehicle is operated in the lower gears, progressive gear shifting limits the rate at which the engine will accelerate beyond a set engine speed, as shown in Fig 29.25. Essentially the driver can accelerate freely up to a certain engine speed (progressive shift speed); beyond this speed, engine acceleration is at a slower rate. Although the engine acceleration is slower above the progressive shift speed point, the engine is still capable of reaching maximum governed speed. Therefore, the progressive shift feature does not reduce engine performance, it simply discourages vehicle drivers from taking engine speed to the governed limit during each gear change in the lower gears. In this way, engine wear is reduced and fuel economy is improved as a result of controlled engine speed during gear changing. The graphs in Fig 29.25 illustrate the progressive gear shift feature which determines the rate of engine acceleration during gear changing in the lower transmission gear ranges.

Cruise control

- Cruise control is available on all Cummins Celect engines. A toggle switch mounted on the vehicle dash allows cruise control to be activated. An accompanying cruise control position select switch can be used by the driver to set and adjust the cruise control speed while driving. The cruise control switches operate in a similar manner to those found on some passenger cars, which are equipped with cruise control. The same switches which operate the cruise control are used to vary the speed of the PTO (power take off) whenever the vehicle is moving at 10 km/hour or less.

Idle adjust switch

- Celect now offers the vehicle operator the advantage of adjusting the idle speed to suit varying operating conditions. This can be done by flicking a toggle switch mounted on the vehicle dash to either increase or decrease idle speed.

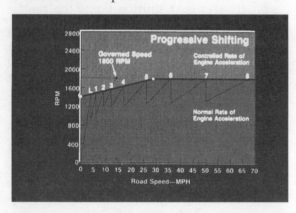

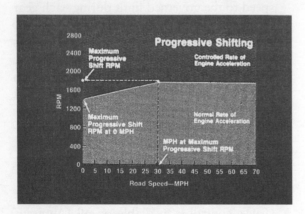

Fig 29.25 Progressive shift curve

Idle shutdown

- In an effort to reduce the period of time an engine is allowed to idle, an idle shutdown feature can be programmed into the Celect system. This feature will automatically stop the engine after a pre-set idle period. The idle period can be anywhere from three minutes to one hour and is programmable within these limits by using Compulink. This feature will eliminate the many hours of wasted engine running time which are clocked up due to operators allowing engines to idle while they have their meal breaks or load their vehicles.

Gear down protection

- Gear down protection can be programmed into the Celect system to prevent the vehicle being driven at maximum road speed while operating in one gear below top gear. This prevents the engine from operating at unnecessary high speed, thus promoting good fuel economy.

Variable performance ratings with ESP

Cummins have designed into certain N14 Celect engine models improved driveability performance whenever the vehicle is operated in hilly terrain. The ESP mode, as it is known, has been programmed into the ECM to operate the engine at variable power and torque outputs that adapt to different road conditions. Under normal road driving conditions, the N14 ESP engine will operate at base performance ratings. Once in the hills, however, when the vehicle road speed falls below a certain limit with wide open throttle, the ESP mode switches to higher performance outputs so as to maintain vehicle speed.

The ECM continuously monitors a variety of parameters such as vehicle speed, throttle position and transmission gearing so as to learn the average speed the driver is trying to maintain under normal flat road conditions. This speed is registered as the vehicle's 'learned speed', which then becomes a reference point as to when to switch to ESP mode. Therefore, whenever the vehicle is driven up steep grades or hills with wide open throttle, the ECM detects a drop in vehicle speed as compared to the recorded 'learned speed'. Once there is a mismatch between these two readings, the ECM instructs the injectors to inject more fuel into the engine in order to try to maintain vehicle speed.

The ESP control logic monitors vehicle speed and performance continually and will operate in either manual throttle control or cruise control. ESP mode offers improved driveability in hilly terrain, resulting in more consistent road speed and less downshifting.

Components of the Celect system

The Electronic Control Module (ECM) consists of:

- memory elements or pre-programmed operating instructions;
- an engine control microprocessor;
- a fault code microprocessor; and
- solenoid driver circuitry

as shown in Fig 29.26.

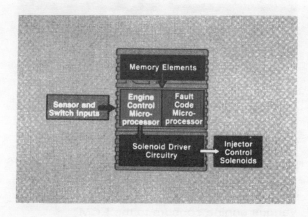

Fig 29.26 Breakdown of the electronic component sections in the Electronic Control Module (ECM)

Each feature of the ECM will now be examined in greater detail.

Programmed instructions

- Memory elements are the pre-programmed instructions or software that tell the Celect system what to do and how to do it. Such

instructions can be changed, updated and expanded in order to suit the operational conditions of the particular vehicle.

Engine control microprocessor

- The engine control microprocessor receives signals or inputs from sensors and switches located on the engine and vehicle and compares this information with that programmed into the memory elements. Based on this processed information, the engine control microprocessor sends fuelling and timing signals or outputs to the solenoid driver circuitry. The solenoid drivers then send current impulses to operate each injector control solenoid, as shown in Fig 29.27. The supplied current operates each solenoid, which in turn operates the solenoid control valve that determinies the amount of engine fuelling and the commencement of injection.

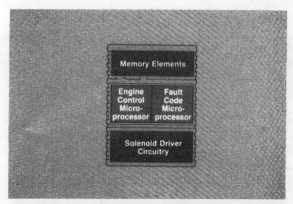

Fig 29.27 The ECM evaluates sensor inputs in conjunction with pre-programmed operational data then signals the solenoid driver to operate the injector control solenoids

Fault code microprocessor

- The fault code microprocessor receives and processes information from the sensors and switches fitted to the engine and vehicle. Whenever a signal received from a sensor is outside set operating parameters the ECM must regard it as being suspect. As there can be fluctuations in signals sent from sensors, the ECM will monitor any out of range signal for a short period of time to verify that the signal is continuously out of range and that it is not simply a normal fluctuation in signal transmission. If the out of range signal continues, then the ECM assumes a system malfunction has occurred. The fault code microprocessor will then communicate to the engine control microprocessor that the particular signal can no longer be used in any of its control calculations. In such a case, the engine control microprocessor will use a default value instead of the out of range signal value coming from the faulty sensor or sub-system. This default value is an average of the signals that usually come from the sensor under normal operating conditions. By using this value, the ECM can continue its normal workings without the benefit of the failed sensor information. Engine performance may remain the same in such circumstances or be derated depending on the severity of the system fault. At the same time the ECM performs the above operations, it also broadcasts a fault code signal (as shown in Fig 29.28) to the vehicle driver via the dash-mounted warning lights. The fault code is also recorded in the memory of the ECM and can be retrieved at a later date during vehicle servicing.

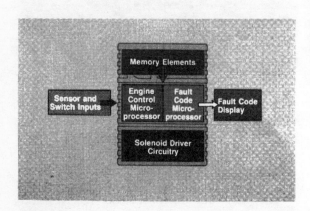

Fig 29.28 The ECM evaluates sensor inputs and performs self-diagnosic functions such as broadcasting fault code information

Engine protection shutdown can be programmed into the Celect system which allows the customer to choose engine shutdown or engine speed/power derate while an engine protection fault is active. If the engine shutdown feature is programmed into the ECM the engine will shut down after the fault has been active for 30 seconds.

Solenoid driver circuitry

• The solenoid driver circuitry receives fuelling and timing commands from the engine control microprocessor and in turn provides the power necessary to operate each injector control solenoid to carry out these fuelling and timing requests.

Electrical sub-system components

Three major wiring harnesses connect the Celect electrical sub-system components to the ECM:

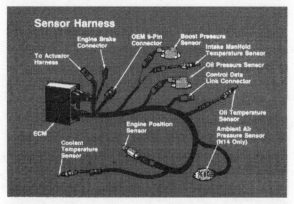

Fig 29.29 The sensor harness connects the various engine sensors to the ECM

1 the sensor harness;
2 the OEM (original equipment manufacturer) harness;
3 the actuator harness.

Sensor harness

The sensor harness, as shown in Fig 29.29, connects the various engine sensors to the ECM. A description of each sensor is as follows.

- **The coolant temperature sensor** is mounted in the thermostat housing as shown in Fig 29.30 and monitors the temperature of the engine coolant. This sensor uses an electronic sensing device which changes its internal resistance when exposed to changes in temperature. As the sensor's resistance changes so to does the voltage signal sent from the sensor back to the ECM. By converting these input voltage signals into temperature information, the ECM can determine the temperature of the engine coolant.

Input from this sensor is also required to control engine timing during startup and normal engine operation. In addition, this sensor provides input information to the engine protection system and may also control the operation of the fan clutch if fitted.

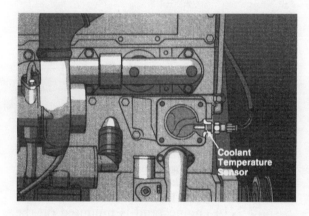

Fig 29.30 Coolant temperature sensor mounted in the thermostat housing

- **The engine position sensor (EPS)** is mounted on the back of the engine timing cover and is used to determine engine speed and injection timing. The EPS sensor reacts to changes in a magnetic field by producing a voltage pulse. The tip of the sensor is mounted very close to, but not touching, the camshaft gear. Machined into the camshaft gear are 24 specially machined surfaces with one unique tooth indicating to the ECM no. 1 cylinder at top dead centre compression stroke as shown in Fig 29.31. As the cam gear turns, the notches on the cam gear pass by the sen-

sor's tip. With the passing of each notch, the EPS sensor produces a voltage pulse. By counting the number of pulses over a period of time, the ECM can determine how fast the camshaft is turning. From this input information, the correct time of injection can then be determined.

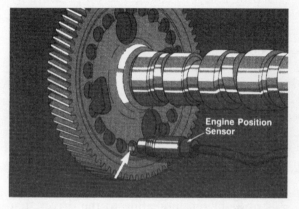

Fig 29.31 Engine speed and position sensor mounted behind the camshaft gear

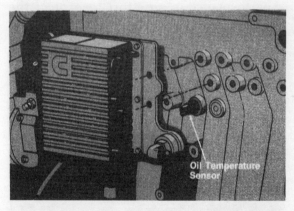

Fig 29.32 Oil temperature sensor located in the side of the cylinder block (L10 engine)

- **The oil temperature sensor,** as shown in Fig 29.32, is fitted into the main engine oil gallery on the L10 and in the oil pump on the N14 engines. Like the coolant temperature sensor, this sensor uses an electronic sensing device to sense temperature. The signals from this sensor are used to advise the ECM of the engine oil temperature. This sensor also provides input data to the engine protection system and if oil temperature should rise to an abnormal level, the ECM will warn the driver of a system fault through the dash-mounted warning or stop engine light.

- **The oil pressure sensor**, as shown in Fig 29.33, is fitted to the main oil gallery. This sensor reacts to changes in oil pressure by changing its internal resistance. As there is a voltage signal continually being sent between the ECM and the oil pressure sensor, the changing resistance within the sensor alters the voltage signal sent from the sensor back to the ECM. The ECM continually compares this input voltage from the sensor with a set voltage level that indicates safe engine oil pressure. If the input voltage is below the programmed safe voltage level, the ECM turns the engine stop light on, indicating to the driver that an engine-damaging condition is apparent. At the same time the stop engine light comes on, the ECM also reduces engine performance in an effort to protect the engine from unnecessary damage.

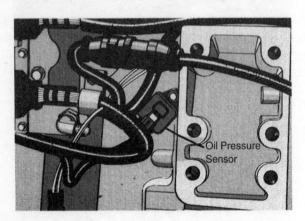

Fig 29.33 Oil pressure sensor mounted in the main engine oil gallery

- **The coolant level sensor** is mounted in the top tank of the radiator. This sensor operates like an on–off switch. When the coolant covers the sensor, it completes a circuit — that is, it turns on the switch within the sensor, allowing it to conduct current flow. The ECM interprets this current flow

as a signal indicating that the coolant is at a safe operating level. Whenever the coolant level drops and the sensor is uncovered, the sensor switches off and no longer conducts current flow. The ECM sees this change in current flow from the sensor as an indication of loss of coolant in the cooling system. In response, the ECM immediately turns on the stop engine light, indicating to the driver that an engine-damaging condition is apparent. As a further level of protection, the ECM will also derate engine performance in an effort to protect the engine from unnecessary damage.

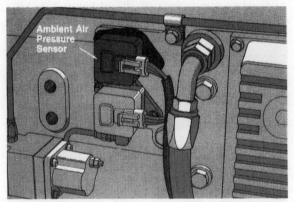

Fig 29.34 Ambient air pressure sensor mounted on the side of the cylinder block

- **The ambient air pressure sensor** is fitted to some N14 engines and is mounted on the side of the cylinder block, as shown in Fig 29.34. This sensor reacts to the changes in ambient air pressure by changing its internal resistance. The resistance of the sensor will in turn determine the voltage signal sent to the ECM. The ECM is programmed to recognise that different voltage levels represent different levels of ambient air pressure. Therefore it compares the input voltage from the sensor and determines the pressure of the ambient air. If at any time the engine is operated at abnormally high altitudes, the sensor detects the change in air pressure and signals the ECM to reduce engine fuelling relevant to the intake air pressure at that altitude.

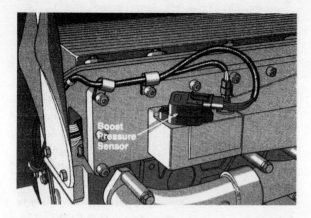

Fig 29.35 Turbocharger boost air pressure sensor mounted on the intake manifold

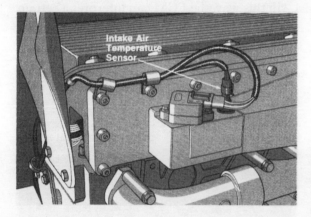

Fig 29.36 Intake air temperature sensor mounted on the intake manifold

- The **turbocharger boost pressure sensor** is mounted on the side of the intake manifold, as shown in Fig 29.35, and like the ambient air pressure sensor, reacts to changes in turbocharger boost pressure by changing its internal resistance. The resistance of the sensor will in turn determine the voltage signal sent to the ECM. The ECM is programmed to recognise that different voltage levels represent different levels of boost air pressure; therefore it compares the input voltage from the sensor and determines the pressure of the boost air. The input from this sensor is crucial in determining the precise control of fuel metering during engine acceleration and normal running. This electronic sensor

component, in conjunction with the ECM, has eliminated the use of the AFC (air–fuel control) as fitted to the conventional PT fuel pump system.

- The **intake air temperature sensor,** as shown in Fig 29.36, is mounted on the rear of the intake manifold. Like the coolant and oil temperature sensors, this sensor also uses an electronic sensing device to sense temperature. The signals from this sensor are used to advise the ECM of the engine air intake temperature for the purpose of engine control and also provides input data to the engine protection system.

Original equipment manufacturer (OEM) harness

The OEM harness, as shown in Fig 29.37, connects a number of OEM-installed components to the ECM. A description of each component is as follows.

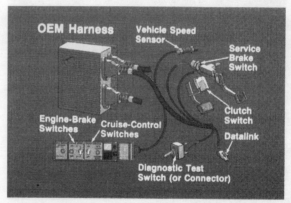

Fig 29.37 Electrical wiring harness fitted by the original equipment manufacturer connects vehicle sensors and switches to the ECM

- The **service brake pressure switch** is mounted in the service brake air pressure circuit and sends signals to the ECM to disengage the cruise control, engine brakes or power take-off whenever the brakes are applied.
- The **clutch pedal switch** is mounted beside the clutch pedal and has a probe in contact with the pedal lever. This switch is active during cruise control mode and sends a

signal to the ECM to deactivate cruise control whenever the clutch is disengaged. Clutch pedal movement will also deactivate the engine brake and power takeoff if the vehicle is so fitted.

- **The idle/diagnostic test switch**, as shown in Fig 29.38, is a dash-mounted three-position toggle switch which has a dual purpose of adjusting idle speed and providing access to diagnostic fault codes whenever the system fault warning lights are illuminated. Engine idle speed can be adjusted in increments of 25 rpm within the range of 650 to 800 rpm. Moving idle speed adjust switch to the (+) position increases idle speed and to the (−) reduces idle speed.

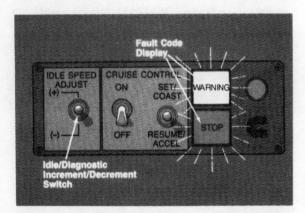

Fig 29.38 Dash interface panel comprising idle/diagnostic switch, cruise control switches and fault warning and stop engine lights

- **The cruise control switches**, as shown in Fig 29.38, are dash mounted, with one switch being used to engage cruise control and the other to be used by the driver to alter vehicle speed while in cruise control mode.
- **The vehicle speed sensor** is mounted on the transmission output shaft housing. This sensor is similar in operation to the engine speed sensor in that it detects the passing of gear teeth from a gear attached to the vehicle transmission output shaft. As each gear tooth passes the tip of the sensor, a voltage pulse is sent to the ECM. The ECM uses this sensor signal in conjunction with preprogrammed vehicle tyre size and trans-

mission/axle gearing ratios to adjust the engine speed so as to control road speed governing or cruise control.

- **The throttle pedal assembly** consists of a throttle pedal with an idle validation switch and a rotary potentiometer mounted beneath it, as shown in Fig 29.39. The idle validation switch informs the ECM whenever the throttle pedal is 'on idle' and 'off idle'. The rotary potentiometer senses throttle pedal movement from the idle to the maximum speed position and sends variable voltage signals to the ECM. The voltage signals from the potentiometer are directly proportional to the pedal position. In this way, the ECM can interpret a certain input voltage against a certain angular throttle pedal position.

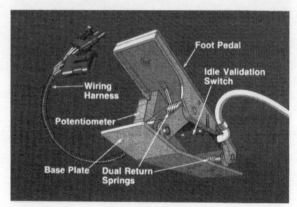

Fig 29.39 Electronic throttle pedal assembly

Actuator harness

This electrical wiring harness connects the ECM to the injectors and the fuel shut off solenoid, as shown in Fig 29.40. The Celect injector is different from the PT injector in that the fuel metering and timing functions are now performed by a solenoid mounted near the top of the injector. The wiring harness to each injector solenoid consists of a supply and return wire. The return wire provides a more effective ground than would the electrical path through the cylinder block.

The fuel shutoff solenoid is similar in

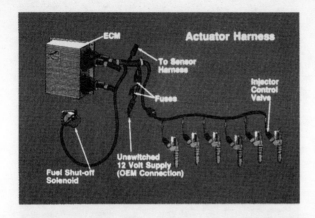

Fig 29.40 Actuator harness connects the injector solenoid control valves and fuel shut-off solenoid to the ECM

construction to the PT type, except that it is now controlled by the ECM and not the ignition key. This enables the ECM to have control over the engine in case of emergency shutdown. As the ECM has total control over the fuel shutoff solenoid, the familiar manual over-ride screw as used on the PT system is no longer fitted.

Celect system operation

Fuel flow

With reference to Fig 29.41, fuel is drawn from the fuel tank and passes through a cooling plate mounted on the back of the ECM. The cooling plate helps in dissipating heat generated by electrical current flow through the ECM electronic circuits. The fuel then flows to the fuel filter where it is filtered. The filtered fuel is drawn into the fuel supply pump which is a gear type driven through the engine accessory drive. Within the fuel pump there is a regulating valve, as shown in Fig 29.42, which regulates the fuel pressure in the system to a maximum of 1050 kPa. The fuel under pressure leaves the fuel supply pump and flows via an external fuel line to a fuel gallery in the cylinder head. The fuel flows along this gallery in the head and is distributed to the inlet of each injector as shown in Fig 29.43.

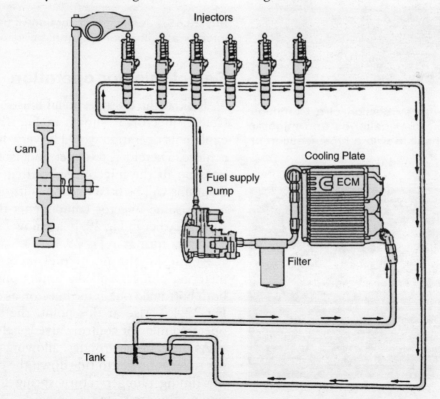

Fig 29.41 Fuel flow through the Celect system

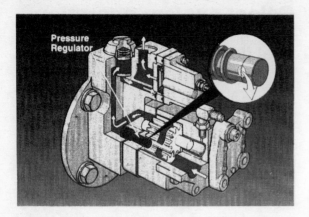

Fig 29.42 Diagram showing the location of the pressure regulator and fuel flow through the Celect system fuel pump

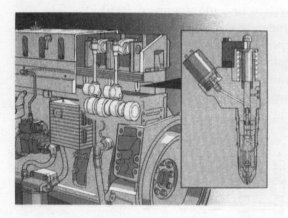

Fig 29.43 Cutaway section of a Cummins engine showing fuel galleries and injector operating mechanism with a cross-section of a Celect injector

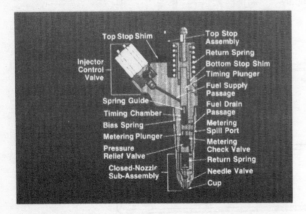

Fig 29.44 A cross-sectional view of a Celect injector with all components identified

As the fuel enters the injector, the solenoid control valve, under the influence of the ECM, determines the quantity and the time that the fuel is injected into the engine. The only fuel which returns to the fuel tank is the fuel which is emptied from the timing chamber along the timing spill port at the end of injection. The actual pressurisation of the fuel for injection is still achieved mechanically via the cam lobe, push rod and rocker lever assembly.

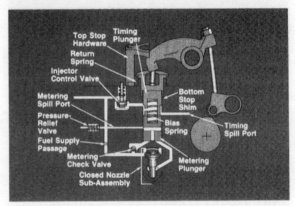

Fig 29.45 A simplified version of the Celect injector and its operating mechanism

Celect injector operation

To look at the cross-sectional illustration of a Celect injector as shown in Fig 29.44 and explain its operation would be very difficult to achieve. Therefore, to better understand what goes on in the injector, simplified text and diagrams will be used to explain its operation.

The same injector components that were shown earlier in Fig 29.44 are now laid out in a simpler format in Fig 29.45.

At the beginning of fuel metering, the metering plunger and the timing plunger are both bottomed out in the injector, as shown in Fig 29.45. Also at this point, the solenoid-operated injector control valve is held closed.

As the camshaft rotates, allowing the injector roller follower to ride down the cam lobe, the timing plunger return spring forces the timing plunger to move upwards. When this happens, fuel at pump pressure will unseat the metering check ball and flow into the metering chamber, pushing the metering plunger against the timing plunger, as shown in Fig 29.46. The fuel will continue to flow into the metering chamber while the timing plunger moves upwards and the injector control valve is held closed.

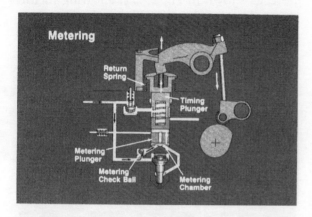

Fig 29.46 Fuel entering the Celect injector during the metering phase

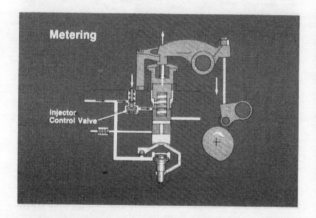

Fig 29.47 Metering ends as the injector control valve is opened

When the ECM de-energises the injector control valve, it opens. Pressurised fuel will flow past the open control valve and fill up the timing chamber, thereby stopping any further upward movement of the metering plunger. The metering cycle has now ended, as shown in Fig 29.47. During this time, the combined pressurised fuel and bias spring ensure that the metering plunger remains

stationary while the timing plunger continues to rise. This same fuel pressure which keeps the metering plunger stationary is also sufficient to maintain adequate pressure below the metering plunger so as to keep the metering check ball on its seat.

The above sequence of events will ensure that an accurately metered quantity of fuel is trapped in the metering chamber. In fact, this is the actual quantity of fuel which will be injected during the oncoming injection cycle.

As the camshaft rotates, the timing plunger is moved further upwards by its return spring, allowing the timing chamber to continue to fill with fuel. Further rotation of the camshaft will see the injector cam lobe begin to lift the cam follower and pushrod, which in turn starts to push the injector rocker and timing plunger downwards. As the timing plunger moves down, some of the fuel in the timing chamber is forced out past the injector control valve and into the fuel supply passage, as shown in Fig 29.48.

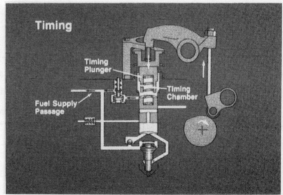

Fig 29.48 The timing plunger begins its downward travel, signalling the start of the injector timing process

When the ECM determines the start of injection, the injector solenoid is energised, thereby closing the injector control valve and trapping the fuel in the timing chamber. This trapped fuel will act as a solid hydraulic link between the timing plunger and the metering plunger. Therefore, the metering plunger is forced to move down under the influence of the descending timing plunger. As the metering plunger descends, the trapped fuel in the metering chamber experiences a rapid rise in pressure. As the pressure rises to approximately 35 000 kPa, the needle valve in the injector tip will rise up against the compression of the return spring, allowing fuel to flow through the injector spray holes and into the combustion chamber, as shown in Fig 29.49.

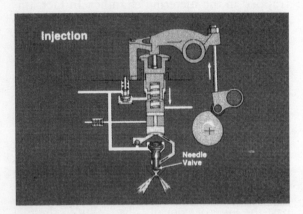

Fig 29.49   The injector control valve closes, signalling the start of injection

Injection will continue until the metering plunger uncovers the metering spill port, as shown in Fig 29.50. When this happens, the fuel pressure within the metering chamber falls rapidly, allowing the needle valve in the tip of the injector to be forced on to its seat by its return spring. At this point, injection ceases.

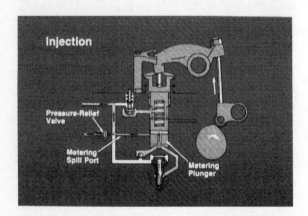

Fig 29.50   Injection ends when the metering plunger uncovers the metering spill port releasing pressure in the metering chamber

At the same time as injection ends, the pressure relief valve adjacent to the metering spill port is forced off its seat, thereby eliminating any high-pressure spike which may develop in the system. Immediately after the metering spill port has been uncovered, the top edge of the metering plunger uncovers the timing spill port, as shown in Fig 29.51, allowing fuel in the timing chamber to spill to a drain passage as the timing plunger continues its downward movement. Injection is now completed and the camshaft continues to rotate for the next injection cycle.

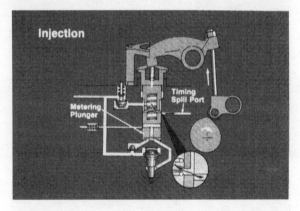

Fig 29.51   The timing spill port opens immediately after the end of injection to release fuel pressure in the timing plunger chamber

Celect self-diagnosis

If any faults, such as electronic system malfunctions or abnormal engine operating conditions, should occur in the Celect system during engine/vehicle operation, they will be recorded in the ECM memory as active fault codes. The ECM will assess this input information and determine whether the fault is of a minor or serious nature. At this point, the vehicle driver is informed of the active or current fault in the system by way of the illumination of the warning or stop engine lights mounted on the vehicle dash, as shown in Fig 29.52.

If the warning light is illuminated, then a minor system problem has occurred and the vehicle can still be operated until such time as it is practical to have the fault rectified. However, whenever the stop engine light illuminates, there is a serious problem in the system which could result in an engine-damaging situation should the engine continue operating. Such a problem could be low coolant level, high coolant temperature or low oil pressure. In this situation, the vehicle should be stopped in a safe place and the engine shut down as soon as possible.

Fig 29.52 Warning and stop engine light used to indicate minor or serious problems in the Celect electronic system

In order to identify the system problem, the fault code must be retrieved from the ECM memory. This can be carried out by activating a simple flashing light sequence or by directly accessing the ECM fault code information by using service tools such as Compulink or Echeck (electronic check).

To activate the flashing light sequence, the driver has to move the idle/ diagnostic switch to the (+) position. Whichever fault light is currently illuminated will then flash a specific three-digit code sequence that indicates a given fault code number. For example, the flash sequence for fault code 244 will be two flashes, a pause, four flashes, a pause, then another four flashes. If there is more than one active code, there will be a pause after the first code then the next code will be flashed out. If there is only one active fault code, then the display will simply repeat itself.

Active codes can be removed from the

system by eliminating the cause of the fault. An example would be a fault code indicating loss of coolant below the level of the coolant sensor. After inspecting the system for leaks and then refilling the radiator with coolant, the sensor would be recovered, thereby turning off the active code and subsequent dash warning light. However, the fact that the fault has occurred is now recorded in the ECM memory and can only be erased by using Compulink or Echeck service tools.

As fault light operation is important in the prevention of engine and electronic component damage, the warning and stop engine lights will be illuminated for approximately two seconds as a bulb and system check whenever the ignition key is turned on.

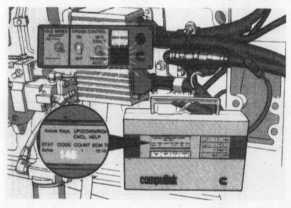

Fig 29.53 Cummins Compulink service tool being used to identify a system fault code which caused the stop engine light to illuminate

Compulink or Echeck can also be used to access the ECM in order to retrieve fault codes. Compulink connects to the ECM via the data link connection, as shown in Fig 29.53. As stated earlier, it is a diagnostic service tool which can be used to diagnose Celect system problems as well as reprogram customer-selected features and engine calibration parameters in the ECM. Apart from retrieving fault codes, Compulink also provides troubleshooting procedures which can be used to ascertain more information about system faults.

Echeck is a hand-held diagnostic tool, as shown in Fig 29.54, which can be plugged into the ECM and is capable of giving more explicit information about fault codes beyond a simple flashed code from a fault light. Echeck can be used for accessing information within the ECM, and with the addition of a programming cartridge can be used to reprogram the ECM.

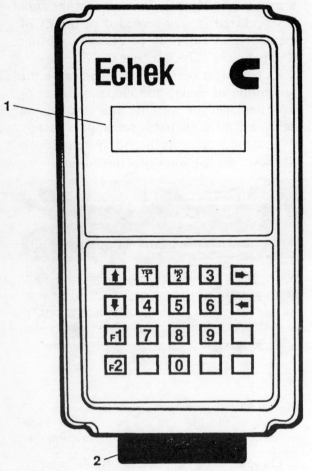

1 **Display window**– shows data and messages to the user.
2 **Memory cartridge**– contains the software necessary to test Cummins systems.

Fig 29.54 Hand-held Echeck reader which is used to gain access to the ECM so as to identify fault codes

Inactive fault codes which were originally filed in the ECM memory as active fault codes can also be retrieved by Compulink or Echeck for evaluation by service personal. An inactive fault is a fault that was once present in the system as an active fault but has since been rectified. The fault code remains inactive

simply to inform service personal of the recent operational history of the vehicle. Inactive fault codes can be erased from the ECM by using Compulink or Echeck.

Injector and valve-setting procedure for Celect engines

Manually rotate the engine crankshaft in the correct direction of rotation and align the 'A' or '1-6' mark on the accessory drive pulley with the pointer on the gear cover, as shown in Fig 29.55. When the timing mark is aligned with the pointer, the intake and exhaust valves for no. 1 cylinder must be closed (both rocker levers loose). At the same time, the injector plunger for the same cylinder (no. 1) must be at the bottom of its stroke. No. 1 cylinder is now ready to have its injector adjusted.

If these two conditions do not occur on no. 1 cylinder, then no. 6 cylinder will be ready to adjust.

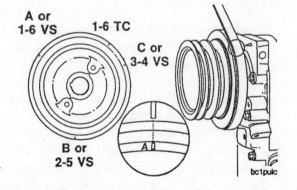

Fig 29.55 Alignment of the valve set marks on the accessory drive gear with the pointer on the timing gear cover

Starting with no. 1 cylinder timing marks aligned and with both the intake and exhaust valve rockers loose, loosen the injector-adjusting screw lock nut. Bottom out the injector plunger by screwing the injector-adjusting screw in as shown in Fig 29.56 so as to remove any fuel still in the injector and then back off the injector-adjusting screw. Now turn the injector-adjusting screw carefully until the injector timing plunger just touches bottom. Back the adjusting screw out two flats (or 120°) then hold the adjusting screw and tighten the lock nut to the specified torque as per the workshop manual. This will now provide a clearance between the rocker lever and the injector push rod of 0.56 mm on N14 engines and 0.66 mm on L10 engines.

Note: It is important that the injector plunger is not placed under any compression force once

it is bottomed out. Further tightening of the adjusting screw will increase the crush applied to the injector timing plunger, resulting in an abnormal injector train wear and damage to the internals of the injector.

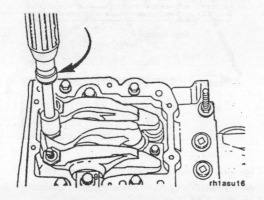

Fig 29.56 Screwing injector adjusting screw down so as to remove fuel from the injector prior to adjusting it

Injector and Valve Adjustment Sequence		
Bar Engine In Direction of Rotation	Pulley Position	Set Cylinder Inj. and Valves
Start	A	1
Advance to	B	5
Advance to	C	3
Advance to	A	6
Advance to	B	2
Advance to	C	4
Firing Order: 1-5-3-6-2-4		

Fig 29.57 Injector and valve-setting sequence for Celect engines

After the injector has been set on no. 1 cylinder, the valves for that cylinder can be set also. On completion of the injector and valve lash adjustment for no. 1 cylinder, refer to the injector and valve adjustment sequence chart as shown in Fig 29.57 and adjust the remaining cylinders in the correct firing order sequence.

fuel injectors are basically fuel pump–injector combinations, and are operated from the engine camshaft via a pushrod and rocker system. This necessitates the injectors being located under the rocker cover, together with a supply and a return line to each and an injector control tube (or shaft) which links to each injector's rack.

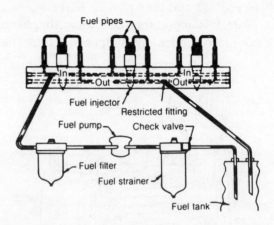

Fig 30.1 Schematic diagram of a typical fuel system
Courtesy of Detroit Diesel Corp

The fuel pump is a constant displacement gear pump — a lift pump — which circulates fuel at (relatively) low pressure through the system. The filter between the fuel tank and the pump is termed a fuel strainer; in other instances it would be known as a primary filter.

The fuel manifolds (or fuel galleries, perhaps) run the length of the cylinder head, and each injector connects to both. A restricting elbow is fitted at the end of the outlet manifold to maintain pressure in the system, particularly in the injectors. In installations in which the engine stands without running for some time, the fuel could drain back into the tank, causing starting difficulties; a check valve may be fitted between the fuel strainer and the tank to prevent this.

Fuel passes from the supply tank through the fuel strainer, then enters the gear-type fuel pump, which raises the fuel pressure to an intermediate level, which changes with

30
Detroit
Diesel Fuel
Systems

The Detroit Diesel system features camshaft-operated unit injectors mounted directly in the cylinder head. The unit injectors raise the fuel to injection pressure and spray it directly into the combustion chamber. The Detroit system may seem unconventional; however, it consists essentially of a combined plunger-type injection pump and hydraulically operated injector.

The fuel injection system used on Detroit Diesels features a simple layout, which has some considerable advantages. As can be seen by reference to Fig 30.1, the system consists of the fuel injectors, the fuel manifolds, the fuel pump, the fuel strainer, the fuel filter and the necessary connecting fuel lines. The

engine speed but is somewhat below 500 kPa. From the fuel pump, fuel flows through the fuel filter into the fuel inlet manifold, then through the fuel pipes to the injectors, where the fuel required is metered, has its pressure raised to injection pressure, and is passed into each engine cylinder at exactly the required point in the engine operating cycle. Surplus fuel returns from the outlet side of the injectors, through the outlet pipes into the outlet manifold, and then returns to the fuel tank via a return line.

The continuous flow of fuel through the injectors prevents the buildup of air pockets in the fuel system, and cools those injector parts subject to high combustion temperatures.

The unit fuel injector

While it is simply known as a 'fuel injector', the Detroit Diesel fuel injector does much more than the typical injector described in Chapter 25 — it combines a complete pumping element and a closed injector in one compact,

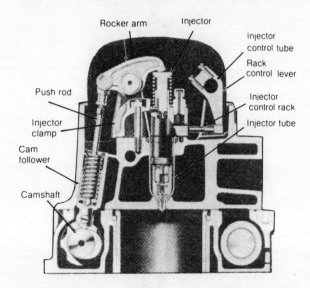

Fig 30.2 Fuel injector mounted in the cylinder head
Courtesy of Detroit Diesel Corp

pushrod-operated unit. There are two types: the early 'crown valve' type and the later

model known as a 'needle valve' injector. All current Detroit unit injectors are of the needle valve design. The crown valve-type unit injector is a non-current production injector and will not be discussed in this chapter.

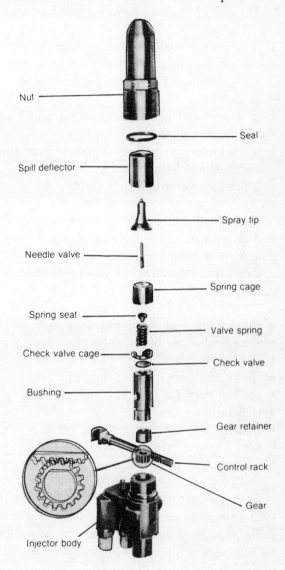

Fig 30.3 Exploded view of the lower components in a needle valve injector
Courtesy of Detroit Diesel Corp

The Detroit Diesel unit fuel injector is a lightweight, compact unit, which combines with an open-type combustion chamber to give quick, easy starting without the need for cold starting aids. The design and operation of the unit injector permits the use of simplified controls and uncomplicated adjustments, while eliminating the need for high-pressure fuel lines with their inherent problems associated with fuel compressibility and pressure waves.

The unit fuel injector performs four functions:

1 It raises the fuel pressure to that required for efficient injection, the maximum pressure reaching 150 MPa at full load in some cases.
2 It meters and injects the exact amount of fuel for the engine load.
3 It atomises the fuel as it passes into the combustion chamber.
4 It permits continuous fuel flow.

To fulfil the dual role of both fuel pump and injector, this injector assembly has to be a little more complex than a simple injector. Essentially, it consists of the following parts:

- the injector body and (retaining) nut;
- the plunger and bushing;
- the nozzle assembly;
- the check valve, valve spring, cage, etc.;
- the follower and spring;
- the control rack;
- numerous lesser components, including the filter caps (or inlet and outlet unions), filters and springs, spill deflector, stop pin, etc.

The injector body is, of course, just what its name implies. It carries the necessary drillings to carry fuel both from the fuel inlet — one of the filter caps — and to the fuel outlet — the other filter cap. It houses the two filters, and is threaded on its lower end to accept the nut. Further, the body is drilled to carry the control rack, formed to accept a mounting clamp, and provides the guide in which the follower reciprocates.

The plunger and bushing may well be likened to an in-line element, for there is similarity in both design and function. The bushing is located so that its lower end, carrying two funnel-shaped ports, lies within a fuel supply chamber. Two helices are milled on the plunger, creating an area of considerably reduced diameter a small distance up from its lower end. This area, with a helix at each end, is known as the metering recess.

A number of components are located between the lower end of the bushing and the spray tip, and are locked together to form a fuel-tight seal when the nut screwed on to the injector body is tightened during assembly. The check valve cage is located immediately against the bushing, with the spring cage between the check valve cage and the spray tip. The check valve has limited movement between the bottom of its recess in the cage and the bushing.

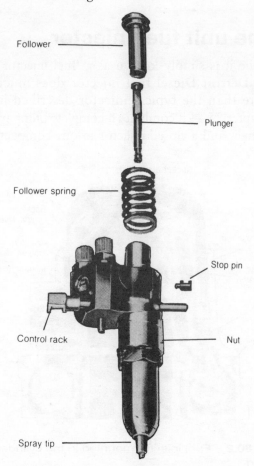

Fig 30.4 Exploded view of the upper components in a needle valve injector
Courtesy of Detroit Diesel Corp

The (needle) valve spring lies within a cylindrical spring cage, with a spring seat at its lower end which bears against the end of the needle valve. The needle valve spigot passes through a central drilling in the spring cage to contact the spring seat. As in a conventional injector, spring force is applied to the needle valve to hold it against its seat.

The spray tip design is similar to the conventional multi-hole nozzle with an inward-opening needle.

The upper end of the plunger carries the gear (or pinion) which has a 'D' shaped axial hole to correspond with the 'D' section upper end of the plunger. This arrangement allows the plunger to reciprocate in the gear (and in the bushing), but causes the plunger to be rotated in the bushing should the gear be turned by the control rack under governor action.

The follower, somewhat like a mushroom-type tappet in appearance, reciprocates in the injector housing, and is so designed on the lower end to engage positively with the top of the plunger so that they reciprocate as one.

A round-ended keyway is cut vertically on the body of the follower. It is engaged by the spigot end of a pin (the stop pin) to prevent rotation of the follower and, since the keyway does not extend to the lower end of the follower, retains the follower in the assembly prior to installation in the engine.

The follower spring — a standard type of compression spring — seats on the injector housing and against the follower flange.

The control rack is basically round in cross-section, with a flat side where the gear teeth are cut, and a square 'U'-end at right angles to its axis. The rack is fitted directly to the injector housing in mesh with the plunger gear. It is moved axially to turn the plunger by the injector rack control lever on the injector control tube, which engages with the 'U'-end.

Of the small parts, most have been mentioned previously — the filters, filter caps, stop pin, etc. The stop pin retains the follower in the injector body, and is itself simply retained by the lowest coil of the follower

spring engaging with a flat or groove on the body of the pin.

The drilling in which the pin is housed is so positioned that, with the flat of the pin uppermost, it lies flush with the shoulder of the injector against which the spring seats.

The spill deflector is simply a sacrificial tube surrounding the bushing to prevent erosion of the injector body resulting from the high-velocity escape of fuel from the bushing ports during the end of injection.

Operation of the unit fuel injectors

Fuel from the fuel pump enters each injector at the inlet side, passing through the filter cap and filter element. From this filter, the fuel passes through a drilling into the supply chamber — that is, the area between the plunger bushing and the spill deflector. All the fuel entering the injector moves towards the outlet connection until the plunger rises to open the bushing ports to the supply chamber, when fuel can flow into the bushing.

As the plunger begins its downward stroke, some of the fuel under the plunger is displaced back into the supply chamber through the lower port until that port is closed off by the lower end of the descending plunger. Some of the remaining fuel trapped below the plunger then passes up through the central passage in the end of the plunger and into the metering recess. This fuel continues to escape into the supply chamber through the upper bushing port until this port is closed off by the edge of the upper helix as the plunger descends and the fuel remaining under the plunger is trapped. **Thus it is the upper helix covering the upper port that establishes the beginning of injection.**

Once the fuel is trapped in the bushing, and with the plunger descending, it must escape. As the fuel pressure rises, the non-return (or check) valve opens and fuel pressure builds up as far as the needle valve seat. As in a conventional injector, the needle valve

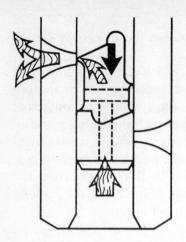 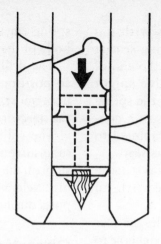 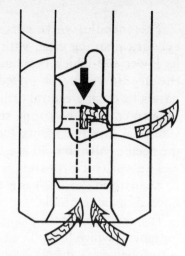

Injector operation: The plunger descends, first closing off the lower port and then the upper. Before the upper port is shut off, fuel being displaced by the descending plunger may flow up through the 'T' drilled hole in the plunger and escape through the upper port.

After the upper port has been shut off, fuel can no longer escape and is forced down by the plunger and sprays out the tip.

As the plunger continues to descend, it uncovers the lower port, so that fuel escapes and injection stops. Then the plunger returns to its original position and awaits the next injection cycle.

Fig 30.5 Plunger and bushing — design and operation *Courtesy of Detroit Diesel Corp*

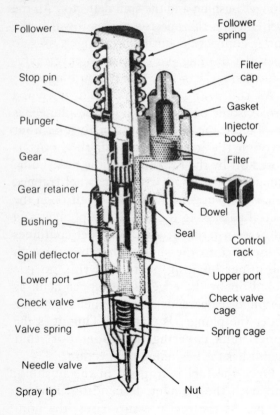

Fig 30.6 Needle valve injector
Courtesy of Detroit Diesel Corp

lifts from its seat, against spring pressure, when fuel pressure builds up sufficiently, and fuel passes through the spray holes into the combustion chamber. As soon as the lower bushing port is uncovered and fuel pressure is relieved, the valve spring snaps the needle on to its seat, positively ending injection (see Fig 30.5).

Hence it is the uncovering of the lower bushing port as the plunger descends that determines the end of injection. As in a conventional nozzle, some fuel escapes between the needle valve and nozzle body and a pressure relief drilling is provided in the spring cage to allow this fuel to escape back into the low-pressure fuel system. The check valve is provided to prevent gas leakage into the injector and fuel injection system should the needle valve fail to seat correctly.

The plunger is returned to its uppermost position, after completing its downstroke, by the follower spring. Thus the operating cycle begins again as the plunger rises and fuel passes into the bushing from the supply chamber through the bushing ports.

As in most other systems, the quantity

of fuel delivered is related directly to the amount of time for delivery. For increased fuel delivery, the period of injection is extended, and vice versa. In this instance, injection begins when the upper port is covered, and ends when the lower port is uncovered. Since the upper port is covered by a helical shoulder, as the plunger is rotated to provide more fuel, so the upper port is covered sooner and injection is advanced.

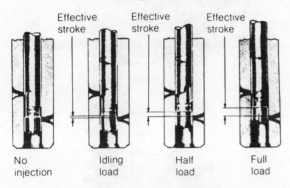

Effective stroke   Effective stroke   Effective stroke

No injection   Idling load   Half load   Full load

Fig 30.7   Fuel metering from no load to full load
Courtesy of Detroit Diesel Corp

In some instances, the lower helix is not a true helix, but is a shoulder, square to the plunger. In such a case, the instant at which injection ceases does not vary as the plunger is rotated, and increased fuelling simply means that injection starts earlier but ends at the same time. However, in other instances a true helix is used, and increased fuelling is associated with an earlier start and a later finish to injection.

Those plungers designed to delay the completion of injection as fuelling is increased are known as variable — or retarded — ending plungers. A typical design is shown in Fig 30.8. These plungers are used in modern Detroit Diesel engines to give better control of combustion, ensuring more complete burning of the fuel with resultant reduced exhaust emissions.

To stop the engine, the control rack is moved fully out to the 'no-fuel' position, rotating the plunger to the point where the upper port is not closed by the plunger during its downward movement until after the lower   port is uncovered by the edge of the lower helix. Thus at no stage is fuel trapped in the bushing, and no injection occurs.

For maximum fuel delivery, the plunger is rotated away from the 'no-fuel' position to a point where the upper port is closed immediately after the lower port. This produces the longest possible stroke before the lower port is uncovered to release the trapped fuel, so producing maximum fuel injection.

As the plunger is rotated from the no-fuel position to the maximum fuel position, the contour of the upper helix advances the closing of the upper port, and hence advances the beginning of injection.

The power output of a Detroit Diesel engine can be varied, within limits, by the use of injectors having different fuel output capacities. The fuel output of the various injectors is

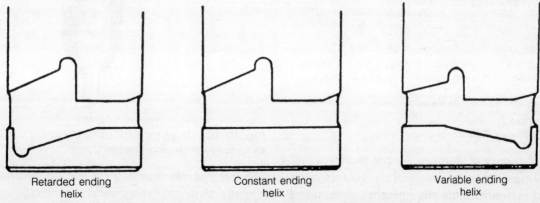

Retarded ending helix   Constant ending helix   Variable ending helix

Fig 30.8   Types of injector plunger   *Courtesy of Detroit Diesel Corp*

plunger and the type of spray tip used. Each fuel injector has a circular disc pressed into a recess on the side of the body for identification purposes — this can be seen in Fig 30.9. The number on the disc indicates the nominal output of the injector in cubic millimetres.

Diesel plungers and bushings are supplied as mated pairs, but additionally are marked with corresponding numbers for ease of identification. Of course these components must never be intermixed with others, or be replaced as anything but an assembly.

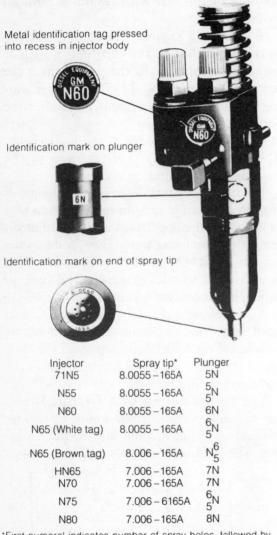

Metal identification tag pressed into recess in injector body

Identification mark on plunger

Identification mark on end of spray tip

Injector	Spray tip*	Plunger
71N5	8.0055 – 165A	5N
N55	8.0055 – 165A	$\frac{5}{5}$N
N60	8.0055 – 165A	6N
N65 (White tag)	8.0055 – 165A	$\frac{6}{5}$N
N65 (Brown tag)	8.006 – 165A	N$\frac{6}{5}$
HN65	7.006 – 165A	7N
N70	7.006 – 165A	7N
N75	7.006 – 6165A	$\frac{6}{5}$N
N80	7.006 – 165A	8N

*First numeral indicates number of spray holes, followed by size of holes and angle formed by spray from holes

Fig 30.9 Needle valve injector identification markings
Courtesy of Detroit Diesel Corp

The numbers stamped on the plungers and spray tips aid in assembly of the correct parts when reconditioning the injectors. As is usual with pumping plungers and barrels, Detroit

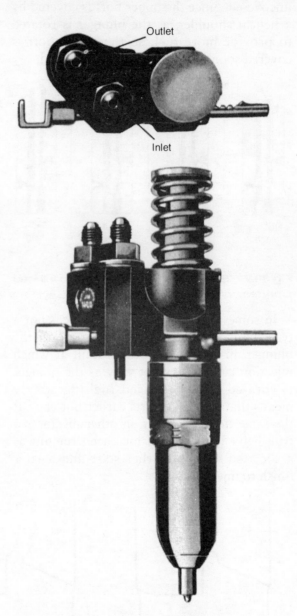

Outlet

Inlet

Fig 30.10 Injector with offset body
Courtesy of Detroit Diesel Corp

Since the plunger helix angle controls the output and operating characteristics of a particular type of injector (while the injectors

type of injector (while the injectors are external-ly similar), care must be taken to ensure that the correct injectors are used for each engine appli-cation. If injectors of different types are used in the same engine, erratic operation will result and serious damage may be caused to the equip-ment that it powers. Further, it is important not to mix needle valve injectors and (early model) crown valve injectors in the same engine.

When space is restricted around the exhaust valve mechanism in engines with a four-valve-per-cylinder cylinder head, an injector with an offset injector body is used (see Fig 30.10). A narrower injector clamp is required with the offset injector body, but may be used with standard injectors.

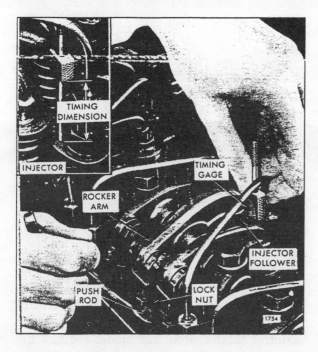

Fig 30.11   Timing the unit injector
Courtesy of Detroit Diesel Corp

Service requirements of the Detroit Diesel fuel system

Like any other fuel injection system, the Detroit Diesel system components require ser-vice periodically. The service procedures are not difficult to follow, and can readily be

undertaken if the necessary special equipment is available. However, it is not likely that this equipment will be available — except, of course, in workshops engaged in Detroit Diesel sales and service. In such workshops, the required manufacturer's manuals are sure to be available, and so no advantage can be gained by pursuing detailed service procedures here.

There are, however, two service proce-dures on the conventional system that can be performed with little special equipment — setting the injector timing and adjusting the control racks — that will allow the general serviceperson to fit exchange injectors.

Timing unit injectors

Each injector is timed by setting the injector follower to a specified height in relation to the injector body, with a special tool, a **tim-ing gauge**, being used to measure this height. Adjustment is made by rotating the threaded pushrod, which is screwed into a clevis (or yoke) attached to a rocker arm. The effect of this adjustment may be likened to adjusting the cam followers in an in-line pump.

Fig 30.12   Adjusting no. 1 injector rack control lever
Courtesy of Detroit Diesel Corp

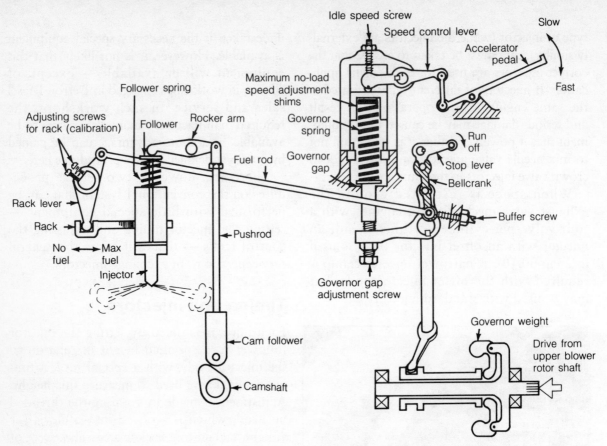

Fig 30.13 Detroit Diesel variable speed governor and injector (schematic)

The adjustment is made with the governor control lever in the no-fuel position. The crankshaft must be rotated in the direction of rotation until the exhaust valves of the cylinder being timed are fully open. **Left-hand turning engines should not be turned in the direction of rotation by means of a spanner on the crankshaft bolt.** With the spigot of the timing gauge located in the hole provided in the top of the injector body, the pushrod is adjusted until the shoulder of the gauge will **just** pass over the top of the injector follower.

Note: Because different engines have standard or advanced camshaft timing, care must be taken to ensure that the gauge used is correct for the particular application.

Adjusting the control racks

Accurate adjustment of the injector control rack levers is necessary to ensure equality of fuel deliveries and correct relationship between the governor and the fuel deliveries. Alteration of the control lever settings is quite simple, as each is located and locked on the injector control tube by either one or two lock screws. Older engines have two screws on the control levers and if one screw is released and the other tightened, the control lever will turn, within limits in relation to the control tube. On current model engines, the control levers have only one screw adjuster, as shown in Fig 30.12, which works in conjuction with a spring to move the control lever and injector rack in or out whenever the screw is turned. This one screw adjustment now prevents all the control levers being held in the fuel injection position in the event that one unit injector may seize, thereby preventing the remaining injectors from being moved to the no-fuel position.

Although the actual adjustment is very

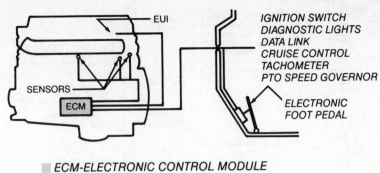

ECM-ELECTRONIC CONTROL MODULE
EUI-ELECTRONIC UNIT INJECTORS

Fig 30.14   Main components of Detroit Diesel Electronic Control system
Courtesy of Detroit Diesel Corp

Although the actual adjustment is very simple, some variation in approach and sequence is necessary over the range of governor systems, and the workshop manual, which covers all governor systems individually, should be consulted.

Basically, in the method generally employed, the governor-fuel system is set in the full-load position — with the engine stopped, of course. All rack control levers are first loosened on the control tube, and the engine speed control lever is moved to the maximum speed position. The governor reacts to the selection of maximum speed by moving the injector control tube to the maximum fuel position, and the control levers are adjusted so that the racks reach the full-fuel position

Locating a faulty injector

A faulty injector can be located on the engine by isolating it from the remaining injectors. Prior to testing the injectors, the engine should be at operating temperature and the rocker cover removed.

With the engine at idling speed, use a large screwdriver to hold down the injector follower which will prevent the injector from operating. If the injector is faulty, there will be no change in the sound of the engine and no change in engine speed. If the injector is operating correctly, the engine sound will change and its speed decrease. The remaining injectors are checked in the same way until the faulty injector is found.

Electronic engine controls

Advanced technology in the internal combustion engine field has brought about electronic control of the operation and performance of today's high-speed diesel engines. More than just a governor, the benefits gained through the use of electronic controls include decreased fuel consumption, reduced exhaust emissions, improved driveability, self-diagnosis and engine protection.

The Detroit Diesel Electronic Control (DDEC) is a microprocessor-controlled unit injector fuel system. The major components are the electronic control module (ECM), the electronic unit injectors (EUI), and the engine-mounted sensors, as shown in Fig 30.14. The basic system revolves around the electronic unit injectors, which are solenoid controlled and cam driven for mechanical pressurisation of the fuel into the combustion chamber.

Detroit Diesel's initial entry into electronic engine controls was with DDEC I, which has since been refined and improved upon with the introduction of DDEC II, described below.

The ECM is the 'brain' of the system, receiving electronic inputs from the operator as well as from the engine and vehicle mounted sensors. This input information is used to precisely control engine fuelling, and to provide feedback to the operator and mainte-

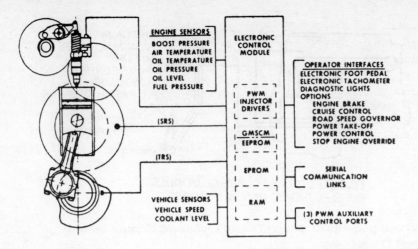

Fig 30.15 Schematic diagram of the Detroit Diesel Electronic Control System
Courtesy of Detroit Diesel Corp

nance monitor as to the operating condition of both the DDEC system and engine subsystems, such as the cooling system, etc.

Within the electronic control module there is an electrically erasable programmable read-only memory (EEPROM). The EEPROM controls the basic engine functions such as rated speed and power, injection timing, engine governing, torque shaping, cold start logic, self-diagnostics and engine protection.

An explanation of some of the more unusual control functions mentioned above is as follows.

- **Torque shaping** is basically the scheduling (or controlling) of fuel injection quantities relative to engine speed, at full throttle position.
- **Idle speed variation** due to accessory operation can now be controlled at a set constant speed irrespective of changing accessory loads. Also an improved feature of the limiting speed governor is the calibration of speed droop. Speed droop can be calibrated from zero to 150 rpm to gain optimum co-ordination between engine speed and vehicle gearing, to obtain the best performance for the application.
- **Cold starting logic** is the term used to describe the electronic system's ability to meter and time fuel injection relative to the engine operating temperature. To improve

engine cold starting, as opposed to hot starting, the timing and quantity of fuel injected is changed during cold engine cranking. A typical program would be retarded injection timing and increased fuel delivery.

However, once the engine starts, the exhaust emissions (white smoke) and engine vibrations would increase under such metering and timing conditions. Therefore the electronic control module reprograms the fuel injection system to an advanced injection timing position at a faster idle speed, thus eliminating the white smoke and providing a quick engine warmup. After the engine attains correct operating temperature, the timing is retarded and idle speed is slowed down, thus reducing fuel consumption, exhaust emissions and combustion noise.

Electronic Control Module

The ECM determines the amount of fuel and when it is to be injected into the engine. It then transmits this information by command signals through high current switching units (pulse width modulators (PWM)) to the electronic unit injector solenoids. The high current switching units generate electrical signals to

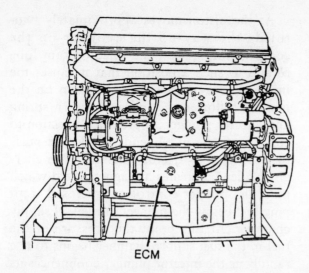

Fig 30.16   Electronic control module mounted on the side of a Series 60 cylinder block
Courtesy of Detroit Diesel Corp

control the opening and closing (pulse width) of the unit injector solenoids, which in turn determine the quantity of fuel injected into the engine. The system also monitors several engine functions using electrical sensors which send signals to the electronic control module. The ECM computes this incoming data and determines the correct fuel output and timing for optimum power, fuel economy and exhaust emissions. The ECM also has the ability to display system and engine fault warnings as well as shut down the engine completely in the case of a damaging engine condition, such as low oil pressure, low coolant level, or high oil and coolant temperatures.

The DDEC system is self-diagnostic — that is, it can identify faulty components and other engine-related problems by providing the technician with a diagnostic code which is explained in detail later on in this chapter. Figure 30.15 shows a schematic diagram of the complete DDEC system.

The ECM is mounted in a die-cast aluminium housing which is attached by anti-vibration mounts to the side of the cylinder block. Heat generated by the ECM during engine operation is absorbed by either air flow past the ECM housing or by fuel circulating through a cold plate mounted on the back of

the ECM. After the fuel passes through the cold plate, it then passes through the secondary filter and finally to the engine for use by the injectors. Engine type and application will determine the most efficient method of cooling the ECM.

Electronic unit injectors

The electronic unit injectors used with the DDEC system operate on the same basic principle as the unit injectors which have been used in Detroit Diesel engines for over 50 years. Like the mechanical injector, the electronic injector is operated by the engine camshaft and rocker arm. The main difference between the two injectors is that the fuel metering and injection timing functions in the electronic injector are controlled by a solenoid-operated poppet control valve under command from the ECM.

By contrast, helices and ports machined into the plunger and bushing perform metering and timing function on the mechanical unit injector.

The electronic unit injector performs four functions:

1 It creates high fuel injection pressure required for efficient combustion.
2 It accurately meters fuel injection quantities and varies injection timing to suit engine load and speed conditions.
3 It atomises the fuel for mixing with the air in the combustion chamber.
4 It permits continuous fuel flow for component cooling.

Injector operation

Fuel enters the injector through two fuel inlet filter screens located around the injector body. The filter screens, as shown in Fig 30.17, are used to prevent relatively coarse foreign material from entering the injector. The fuel return opening shown in the same diagram allows excess fuel to return to the fuel gallery and then back to the tank. On DDEC engines, the fuel pressure within the cylinder head gallery is created

As the piston moves approximately two-thirds the way up the cylinder on the compression stroke, the injector cam lobe rotates to such a position that it causes the injector rocker arm to push down on the injector follower, the follower return spring and injector plunger. In order for injection to commence, the ECM sends an electric pulse to activate the injector solenoid. The energised solenoid creates a magnetic field which pulls the poppet control valve closed trapping fuel below the plunger in the fuel supply chamber. At this point the pressure of the fuel in the fuel supply chamber begins to rise rapidly as the injector plunger commences its downward stroke.

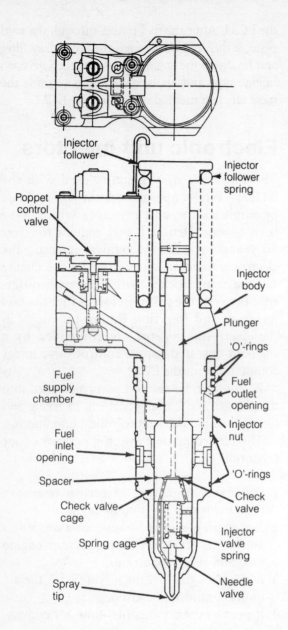

Fig 30.17 Cross-section of an electronic unit injector
Courtesy of Detroit Diesel Corp

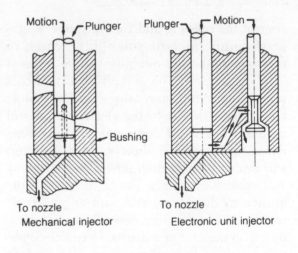

Fig 30.18 Helix-port injection control — mechanical injector (left); Poppet-valve injection control — electronic injector (right)
Courtesy of Detroit Diesel Corp

in the same way as in the conventional mechanical unit injection by way of a restrictor installed in the fuel return line out of the cylinder head.

After entering the injector body, the fuel passes through a drilled passage into the poppet control valve area and the fuel supply chamber, as shown in Fig 30.18.

The rising fuel pressure within the injector acts on the needle valve until such time as it overcomes the needle valve spring force, allowing the valve to open and fuel be injected in a finely atomised form into the combustion chamber.

Injection ends when the ECM switches off the electric pulse to the injector solenoid, thereby allowing a return spring within the solenoid housing to open the poppet valve, permitting the trapped fuel in the fuel supply chamber to escape to the tank return line. The amount of fuel injected into the engine is determined by the 'pulse width'. This is the amount of time for which the injector solenoid is energised, thereby holding the poppet control valve closed. The greater the 'pulse width', the more fuel there is injected into the engine.

Within the injector, there is a check valve situated between the fuel supply chamber and the injector spray tip, as shown in Fig 30.17. This check valve normally has no effect on the injection process but will function to prevent combustion gases from flowing back into the injector and fuel system if a particle of debris should become lodged between the needle and injector nozzle seat.

When the injector rocker arm has completed its downward travel, the injector follower spring returns the follower to the fully raised position. As the injector plunger moves up, fuel enters the fuel supply chamber for the start of another injection cycle. The constant circulation of fuel through the electronic injector and cylinder head replenishes the fuel in the fuel supply chamber as well as cooling and purging air from the injector.

Sensors

A number of engine- and vehicle-mounted sensors are used with the DDEC system to provide information to the ECM regarding engine and vehicle operation. This information is continually monitored by the ECM and checked against known safe operating system paramaters in order to detect faults which may occur in the vehicle and DDEC system.

- The **Electronic Foot Pedal Assembly (EFPA)**, as shown in Fig 30.19, replaces the mechanical linkage between the foot pedal.

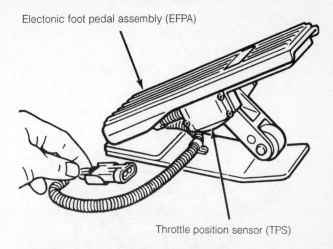

Electonic foot pedal assembly (EFPA)

Throttle position sensor (TPS)

Fig 30.19   Electronic foot pedal assembly
Courtesy of Detroit Diesel Corp

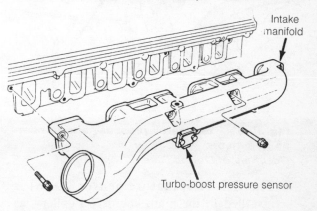

Intake manifold

Turbo-boost pressure sensor

Fig 30.20   Turbo boost sensor mounted on the intake manifold
Courtesy of Detroit Diesel Corp

and the fuel injection pump throttle lever. This sensor is in the form of a variable resistor that sends variable voltage signals to the ECM as the throttle pedal is depressed. •

The **Turbo Boost Pressure Sensor (TBS)** is mounted on the intake manifold as shown in Fig 30.20 and monitors turbocharger boost pressure. This sensor provides data to the ECM for smoke control during engine acceleration. In addition to this, the sensor can be used to troubleshoot air system problems.

- The **Oil Pressure Sensor (OPS)** is installed into the main engine oil gallery, as shown in Fig 30.21. The OPS sends an electrical signal to the ECM telling it what the engine oil pressure is at any given engine speed. A low oil pressure signal exceeding seven seconds will cause the ECM to activate the 'warning' and 'stop' engine functions.

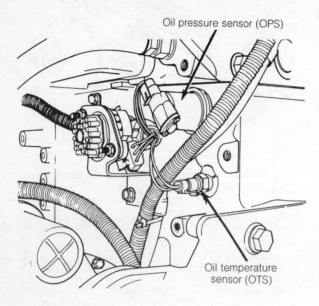

Fig 30.21 Engine oil pressure and temperature sensors
Courtesy of Detroit Diesel Corp

- The **Oil Temperature Sensor (OTS)** is installed in the main engine oil gallery, as shown in Fig 30.21. The OTS sends an electrical signal to the ECM, indicating engine oil temperature. The ECM uses this information to modify engine speed for better cold weather starting and faster engine warmup. Oil temperatures exceeding specification for two seconds or more will activate the 'warning' and 'stop' engine functions. In some engine applications, the OTS is used to monitor the overall engine operating temperature as per the engine temperature gauge. Alternatively, engine temperature can be monitored through the engine coolant.
- The **Synchronous Reference Sensor (SRS)** is mounted on the rear of the engine timing cover and is used by the ECM to determine the speed of the engine. The sensor portion of the SRS extends through

a hole in the timing gear case and is positioned just behind one of the engine timing gears, as shown in Fig 30.22. A raised metal pin which is mounted into the back of the timing gear passes the SRS, generating a signal which is sent to the ECM. The frequency of the SRS signals is thereby used to calculate engine speed.

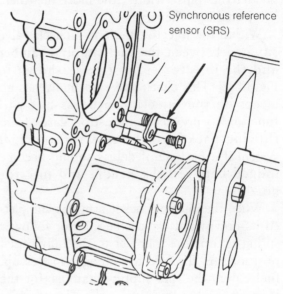

Fig 30.22 Synchronous reference sensor mounted on the back of the front timing cover
Courtesy of Detroit Diesel Corp

- The **Timing Reference Sensor (TRS)** is mounted on the side of the timing gear cover adjacent to the crankshaft timing gear and is used by the ECM to determine the crankshaft position for injection timing purposes. The sensor portion of the TRS extends through an opening in the gear case and is positioned near the teeth of the crankshaft timing gear, as shown in Fig 30.23. As the crankshaft gear rotates, a specially machined gear tooth passes the TRS as each piston approaches 10° before top dead centre. Each time the special tooth passes the TRS, a signal is sent to the ECM, which uses this information to determine when the injector solenoids are to operate — hence the commencement of injection.

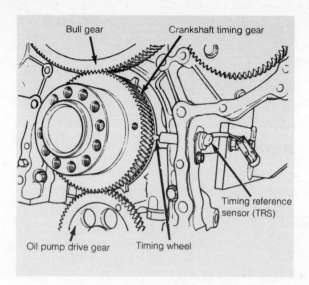

Fig 30.23 Timing reference sensor installed on the side of the timing gear housing
Courtesy of Detroit Diesel Corp

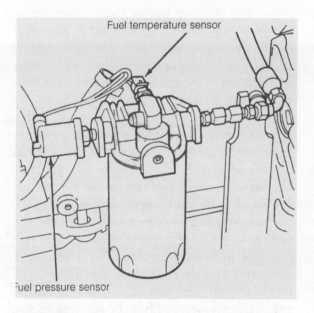

Fig 30.24 Fuel pressure and temperature sensors
Courtesy of Detroit Diesel Corp

- The **Fuel Pressure Sensor (FPS)** is installed into the secondary fuel filter, as shown in Fig 30.24. The FPS sends an electrical signal to the ECM, telling it what the engine fuel pressure is at any given engine speed.

- The **Fuel Temperature Sensor (FTS)** as shown in Fig 30.24, povides a signal to the ECM so it can monitor fuel temperature and assist in calculating engine fuel consumption data. The ECM utilises the fuel temperature signal to adjust the fuel consumption rate calculations whenever there are changes in fuel density due to variations in the fuel temperature.

- The **Coolant Level Sensor (CLS)** is mounted in the coolant top tank or overfill tank. The sensor module sends an electrical signal to the ECM to indicate that the coolant is at the correct level. Low coolant level will uncover the level sensor which in turn will activate the 'warning' and 'stop' engine functions.

On-board diagnosis

As mentioned earlier, the DDEC system has been programmed to run self-diagnosis checks whenever the engine is running. This program checks the condition of the electrical wiring, the operation of the sensors themselves and the relevant engine-operating conditions. The self-diagnosis program also incorporates special tests through which the engine can be run in order to determine individual cylinder operating condition. As well as monitoring the different sensors located on the engine, the self-diagnosis program will also check the operation of the on-board computer.

In the DDEC II system, there are two basic ways of obtaining the results of the on-board diagnosis. One is **ongoing diagnosis**, which performs diagnostic checks repeatedly while the engine is running. The other is **demand diagnosis**, which diagnoses only on demand from an outside control, such as a diagnostic data reader (DDR), as shown in Fig 30.25.

Ongoing diagnosis

With the ongoing diagnosis system, any problems which occur in the system are signalled to the driver by the illumination of the amber **engine warning light** or the red **engine stop**

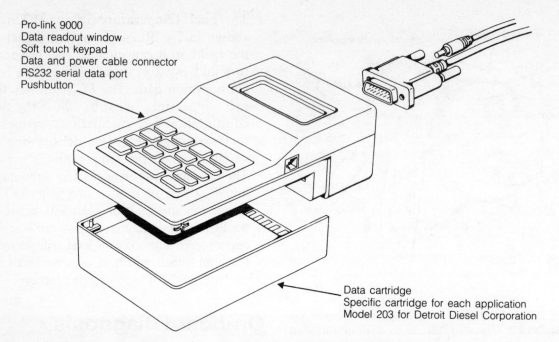

Pro-link 9000
Data readout window
Soft touch keypad
Data and power cable connector
RS232 serial data port
Pushbutton

Data cartridge
Specific cartridge for each application
Model 203 for Detroit Diesel Corporation

Fig 30.25   Diagnostic data reader   *Courtesy of Detroit Diesel Corp*

light mounted on the dash. Prior to starting the engine and with the ignition switch turned on, the engine warning light and the engine stop light will come on for about five seconds as a light bulb check and an initial system check.

If a problem occurs in the engine during operation and is outside its safe operating parameters, it is diagnosed by the ECM and signals the driver through the illumination of, firstly, the engine warning light and then the engine stop light. If the problem is of a minor nature, the engine warning light will come on, indicating to the driver that a fault has occurred in the system. If the driver wants to identify the fault, he or she can press the toggle switch incorporated in the engine warning light and the light will flash a number of times, indicating the error code number relevant to the diagnostic codes chart, as shown in Fig 30.26.

Example

Error code 45 (low oil pressure). The engine warning light will flash four times then pause then flash five times and pause, after which it will repeat the same code or another code as long as the toggle switch is depressed.

Whenever the stop engine light comes on, it is a warning to the driver that a potential engine-damaging condition has been detected, such as low oil pressure, low coolant level or high oil temperature. In addition, the ECM immediately cuts power back to 80 per cent of the current throttle setting. After approximately seventeen seconds, power is again cut back to 40 per cent of the original throttle setting. Thirty seconds after the fault has been detected, fuelling to the injectors is cut off, thereby stopping the engine.

However, the operator can over-ride the system so as to move the vehicle to a safe location at reduced power. To over-ride a potential engine shutdown condition, the toggle switch incorporated in the stop engine light is depressed (within 30 seconds of the stop engine light coming on), which will allow the engine to continue running for another 30 seconds (starting again at 80 per cent of original throttle) before being shut down. The stop engine over-ride can be activated a number of times, depending on engine application, before the ECM takes over completely and shuts the engine down.

Whenever either of the two engine warning lights on the dash come on, the fault is logged and stored in the ECM. Even though the driver may rectify the fault (e.g. error code 43 — low coolant level: filling the radiator with water), which as a result switches off the engine warning light, this does not erase the logged fault in the ECM. This fault is now stored as an historical code (02) and can be displayed later on during servicing with the aid of a diagnostic data reader.

Demand diagnosis

Whenever an engine fitted with a DDEC system is to be serviced, diagnostic information can be requested on demand by using a DDR. The DDR is a hand-held device incorporating a key pad and a monitor which resembles the display of a personal computer as shown in Fig 30.25. It is connected into the ECM by means of an interface cable.

Diagnostic data reader (DDR)

Operation

With the reader plugged in and the ignition turned on, the reader will display the menu for either the DDEC I or DDEC II, depending on which is selected.

Note: Only the more relevant functions from the list of menu selections in Fig 30.27 have been described here.

Diagnostic functions

- **01 Active codes.** Requesting this will display all codes which are currently turning on the engine warning light. Each code is defined beside its number on the display. An example would be the previously mentioned error code 43 (low coolant level 01)
- **02 Historical codes.** This recalls all codes logged since the memory was last cleared. An example would be the error code 43

Detroit Diesel electronic controls

Diagnostic connector

To read codes: Use diagnostic data reader or short pin A to pin M. The latter method will flash codes at the CEL

Error code#	Description	Error code	Description
11	Power take-off sensor lo volt	43	Low coolant level
12	Power take-off sensor hi volt	44	Engine overtemperature
13	Coolant sensor lo volt	45	Low oil pressure
14	Eng temp sensor hi volt	46	Low battery voltage
15	Eng temp sensor lo volt	47	Hi fuel pressure
16	Coolant sensor hi volt	48	Lo fuel pressure
21	Throttle pos sensor hi volt	51	EEPROM error
22	Throttle pos sensor lo volt	53	ECM—A/D fail
23	Fuel temp sensor hi volt	54	EEPROM memory failure
24	Fuel temp sensor lo volt	55	Vehicle speed sensor
25	No codes	56	Proprietory comm. link
26	Power control enabled	58	ECM—A/D fail
31	Fault on auxiliary output	61–68	Cruise ctl/press gov ctl switch
32	ECM backup system fail	71–78	Inj response time long
33	Turbo bst sensor hi volt	81	Inj response time short
34	Turbo bst sensor lo volt	82	Crankcase monitor—hi volt
35	Oil prs sensor hi volt	84	Crankcase monitor—lo volt
36	Oil prs sensor lo volt	85	Crankcase pressure hi
37	Fuel prs sensor hi volt	86	Engine overspeed
38	Fuel prs sensor lo volt	87	Press gov ctl—hi volt
41	Timing reference sensor		Press gov ctl—lo volt
42	Synchronous ref sensor		

Fig 30.26 DDEC II diagnostic error codes
Courtesy of Detroit Diesel Corp

again. Although this is also an active code at present, when it is corrected (i.e. the radiator is filled with water), the code would be erased from the active codes but still remain in the historical codes. On completion of viewing the historical codes they can be erased by selecting code 40 (code erase). This should always be carried out so as not to become confused with the codes which will be logged in the future.

- **03   Prom ID** (Program identification). This should only be requested when the engine is not running because the ECM will only send out part of the Prom ID information if requested while the engine is running.
- **04   Engine RPM.** Engine RPM is calculated from the timing reference sensor, mounted on the back of the engine timing gear cover (Series 60 and 50) or behind the cam pulley on two-stroke cycle engines.
- **05   ECM input volt.** The ECM voltage reading is the voltage that the ECM is receiving from the battery. This voltage should always be in the following range:
  - ignition on, engine off — greater than 10.0 volts;
  - engine cranking — greater than 6.0 volts;
  - engine running — greater than 10.0 volts.
- **06   % engine load.** A percentage calculated by engine speed and torque; used with engine management systems. The range is 0 to 100 per cent.
- **07   Throttle sensor.** The throttle position sensor is part of the electronic foot pedal assembly, which replaces the accelerator pedal and mechanical linkage to the engine. Its movement is recorded as throttle counts and throttle per cent, which are displayed on the DDR screen. The range of values to expect from this sensor is:
  - throttle counts — 20 to 242;
  - throttle per cent — 0 to 100 per cent.

  Throttle counts is the digital representation of the throttle position sensor output voltage where:
  - 0 throttle counts = 0 volts;
  - 225 throttle counts = 5 volts.

  A properly calibrated throttle position sensor should read 20 to 30 counts at no throttle.

- **08   Pulse width (PW).** The amount of time in crank degrees that the ECM is requesting the injectors be turned on. This is directly related to the amount of fuel being injected. The values for pulse width range from 0 to 25.5 crank degrees BTDC. If the engine is in 'smoke control', S will appear on the DDR display.
- **09   Beg of injection (BOI).** Indicates when the ECM is requesting that the injectors begin turning on. The range of values for BOI is 0 to 20.5 crank degrees BTDC. If the engine is in 'smoke control', S will appear on the DDR display.
- **10   Inj resp times (injector response times).** Identifies a specific injector and shows the time it takes after the ECM has requested the injector solenoid be turned on to when the injector solenoid poppet valve closes (recorded in milliseconds). This display will cycle through all injectors, showing the response time of each one. The range of values to be expected under warm engine conditions is 0.8 to 1.60 ms.

  Injector response times vary from injector to injector at a given RPM. Each individual injector's response time should remain relatively consistent from one firing to the next.

- **11   Cyl cutout req (cylinder cutout request).** This selection will selectively disable individual injectors to determine their power contribution. This feature works with the engine at idle, rated speed or at an RPM set by the DDR. Under these conditions, DDEC II will try to maintain a constant engine speed. When an injector at a good cylinder is cut out, DDEC II will attempt to compensate for it by giving more fuel to the other injectors. Thus, if the pulse width does not increase when a cylinder is cut out, that cylinder was not contributing in the first place (pulse width = the amount of fuelling). An example of a cylinder cutout test is as follows.

MPSI READER MENU SELECTIONS
ECM DATA (Model 203 Cartridge)

01 Active Codes (Yes/No)	20 Idle Speed
02 Historical Codes (Yes/No)	21 PTO Counts
04 Engine RPM	22 PTO RPM
05 ECM Input Voltage	23 Cruise Switches
06 % Engine Load	24 Spd Sensor Diag
07 Throttle Sensor	25 Vehicle Speed
08 Pulsewidth	26 Act Driver 1%
09 BOI	27 Act Driver 2%
12 Coolant Level	28 Act Driver 3%
13 Coolant Temp	29 Misc Switches
14 Fuel Pressure	30 Misc Outputs
15 Fuel Temp	31 Misc Status
16 Oil Level	36 Two ECMs
17 Oil Pressure	37 # of EEPROM Chgs
18 Oil Temp	47 By-Pass Valve
19 Turbo Boost/Baro	48 External Pump PSI
	49 Air Inlet Rest

[ENGINE] ◄─── FUNCTION SELECTIONS ───► PRO-LINK

DIAGNOSTIC CODES	**41 SPECIAL TESTS**
01 Active Codes	**RS-232 SERIAL PORT**
02 Hist Codes	
40 Code Erase	PRINTER OUTPUT
Code Options	ECM Data
	Diagnostic Codes
03 **PROM ID**	PROM ID
10 **INJ. RESPONSE TIMES**	CCO Test Results
11 **CYL. CUTOUT REQUEST**	Snapshot Data
MID MSGS BEING RECVD.	Inj. Response Times
	Engine Trip Data
34 **VAR CHAR REQUEST**	EEPROM Data
	Special Test Results
ENGINE TRIP DATA	
	TERMINAL OUTPUT
35 Fuel GPH	P.C. INTERFACE
35 Total Gallons	PORT SETUP
38 Engine Hours	
39 PTO Hours	**CUSTOM DATA LIST**
43 Instantaneous MPG	Display Standard
44 Average Trip MPG	Display Custom
45 Trip Miles	Edit Custom
46 Trip Gallons	Reset Custom
37 **REPROGRAM EEPROM**	
Cruise Control Calc	**CONTRAST**
	ADJUST
Reprogram EEPROM	**ENGLISH/METRIC**
Change Password	**SNAPSHOT**
	RESTART

Fig 30.27   DDR menu selections
Courtesy of Detroit Diesel Corp

The first line of the results display will show the average pulse width when no injectors were cut out. The next lines will show the pulse width for injectors operating with one injector in the engine disabled. For example, a display for an 8v-92 might look something like this:

No cutout pw = 4.3
1L cutout pw = 4.7
3R cutout pw = 4.8
3L cutout pw = 4.7
4R cutout pw = 4.7
4L cutout pw = 4.3
2R cutout pw = 4.8
2L cutout pw = 4.8
1R cutout pw = 4.7

In this example, injector 4L is suspect, since no additional pulse width was required to maintain 1000 RPM once that injector was cut out.

- **12   Coolant level.** This is part of the engine protection system and detects the presence or absence of coolant. Low coolant will log code 43 and will indicate 0 per cent (100 per cent = full). When the sensor probe is in the coolant, the output voltage is less than 2.2 volts. When out of the coolant, the output voltage is greater than 2.5 volts. These voltages are measured with the sensor connected to the wiring harness. If the engine shutdown option is installed, error code 43 will shut down the engine. Two additional codes may be logged: error code 13 = signal voltage low and error code 16 = signal voltage high.

- **13   Coolant temp.** The DDEC II system monitors coolant temperature instead of oil temperature on some engines. The engine protection system is triggered whenever the coolant temperature is greater than 105°C. This will shut down the engine if the shutdown option is installed. Only the engine warning light comes on at 102°C. Either of these conditions will log an error code 44 (engine over-temperature). Two additional codes may be logged due to the coolant temperature sensor circuit: error code 14 (signal voltage high) and error code 15 (signal voltage low). If error codes 14 or 15 are active, a blank display for coolant temperature will appear.

- **14   Fuel pressure.** Engine fuel pressure can be checked during engine operation by using ECM Data code 14.
- **15   Fuel temperature.** DDEC II uses this sensor during its fuel economy calculations to compensate for fuel temperature. (Fuel consumption can be displayed using code 35.) Two possible codes may be logged due to the fuel temperature sensor circuit: error code 23 (signal voltage high) and error code 24 (signal voltage low).

  If either of these codes is active, a default value of 38°C for fuel temperature will appear. Use ECM Data code 15 to display fuel temperature data.
- **16   Oil level.** Not currently used. Should an oil level sensor become available, use ECM data code 16 to display data.
- **17   Oil pressure.** This engine protection system is triggered whenever oil pressure falls below a given value dependent on RPM. The sensor failure codes are error code 35 (oil pressure sensor high), error code 36 (oil pressure sensor low) and error code 45 (low oil pressure).

  If the shutdown option is installed, error code 45 will shut down the engine. If either error code 35 or 36 is active, a default value of 305 kPa for oil pressure will appear.
- **18   Oil temperature.** The DDEC II system monitors oil temperature instead of coolant temperature on some engines. The engine protection system is triggered whenever the oil temperature is greater than 127°C. This will shut down the engine if the shutdown option is installed. Only the engine warning light comes on at 121°C. Either of these conditions will log an error code 44 (engine over-temperature).

  Two additional codes may be logged due to the oil temperature sensor circuit: error code 14 (signal voltage high) and error code 15 (signal voltage low). If error codes 14 or 15 are active, a default value of 80°C for oil temperature will appear.
- **19   Turbo boost/baro (turbocharger boost (gauge) and barometric pressure).** The turbo boost pressure sensor is a two-part display. One reading is the ambient barometric air pressure when the engine is off idling. The other number is the pressure measurement from the sensor monitor. The ECM uses the TBS reading along with engine RPM to calculate air flow. If the air flow drops below a predetermined (calibration) level (e.g. during sudden acceleration), the fuel will be limited to prevent smoke. Two diagnostic codes may be logged due to the turbo boost pressure sensor, they are error code 33 (signal voltage high) and error code 34 (signal voltage low).
- **20   Idle speed.** This readout indicates the RPM at which the engine should be idling, based on the oil or coolant temperature. Most DDEC II applications are set up to idle at a higher RPM under cold temperature conditions.
- **35   Fuel consumption.** This shows two lines of data:
  1 instantaneous litres/hour fuel consumption;
  2 total fuel consumed (since the engine was released from assembly).
- **38   Engine hours.** The total number of hours the engine has run since being built. This does not include time where the ignition key is on but the engine is not running.
- **39   PTO hours.** The total number of hours that the engine has run at idle on the power takeoff and on the fast idle switch.
- **40   Code erase.** Clears historical codes. If a code is currently active, it would be relogged after clearing.

  Note: Removing battery cables or pulling the ECM fuses will no longer clear codes as it did with DDEC I. Refer to the DDEC II Troubleshooting Guide for details.
- **41   Special tests.** This mode is sometimes referred to as the flight recorder option, since it allows for recording and playback of information during actual engine operation. It is useful for testing how a parameter (such as a sensor output) responds in

any one of three situations:

1 when cylinders are cut out (disabled) (e.g. pulse width or RPM response when a cylinder is disabled);
2 at different engine speeds (e.g. turbo boost or oil pressure at different RPM's);
3 for a given time period (about fifteen seconds) (e.g. can be used as an aid to diagnosis of an intermittent problem by capturing sensor data during the occurrence of an intermittent fault). Once Code 41 is selected, the DDR screen will display the following:

> Special Tests 41
> Value vs Cyl Cutout
> Value vs RPM
> Value vs Time

Once one of these is selected, the DDR will display a list of available data modes which can be logged. The list is as follows:

> Y Value 41
> Engine RPM
> ECM Input Volt
> % Engine Load
> Throttle Sensor
> Pulse Width
> Beg of Injection
> Inj Resp Times
> Coolant Level
> Coolant Temp
> Fuel Pressure
> Fuel Temperature
> Oil Level
> Oil Pressure
> Oil Temperature
> Turbo Boost
> Idle Speed
> PTO Counts
> PTO RPM
> Vehicle Speed

Only one data mode can be selected at a time. As an example, if the Value vs Time option is selected, the DDR will display:

> RPM Control
> Auto RPM Control
> Used RPM Control

If Auto RPM Control is chosen, the DDR will request DDEC to begin at idle speed and log the parameter. Speed is then increased by 25 RPM, and the parameter is logged again. This process continues automatically until either no-load speed or 2200 RPM is achieved. The results are displayed once the test is complete.

Example: If the engine tested idles at 500 RPM, has a rated speed of 1800 with 0 droop and oil pressure was being monitored, then the results might look something like the following:

RPM	Oil Pressure (kPa)
500	105
525	107
550	108
575	110
600	113
625	117
650	125
-	-
-	-
-	-
1775	381
1800	381
1725	381
1750	381

(*Note:* Middle RPM — values not shown in 1700 381 example.)

Note: This chart is not intended as any guideline on acceptable oil pressures. It is only being used for illustrative purposes.

31
Governors

Any device that automatically exerts control over engine speed may be termed a governor. As this broad statement indicates, governors take many forms and exert their control in many different ways.

The obsolete 'hit-and-miss' governor, which cut off the fuel supply and operated a decompressor when engine speed reached a predetermined point, then reversed the procedure when the engine speed fell to a certain point, represented one of the cruder governors. At the other end of the scale are the sensitive hydraulic governors, which exercise a delicate control over the quantity of fuel injected, increasing or decreasing it as required to maintain the engine speed at

the required level, and electronic governors, which react to other variables such as ambient temperature, turbocharger boost, fuel temperature and many other factors to maintain precise speed control and low emission operation.

In this chapter, governor principles will be considered together with examples of various types of governor as fitted to in-line injection pumps. Generally, governors that are specific to, or are an integral part of, other fuel injection systems will be discussed in the relevant chapters. Electronic governing systems are now being extensively used on modern automotive truck engines and as there are various systems, each system will be discussed under the particular injection system it is fitted to.

While governors are desirable on petrol engines in many applications, the inherent characteristics of the diesel fuel injection pump dictate that a governor must be used on all diesel engines. At a fixed control rack setting, the fuel delivery increases as the engine (and pump) speed increases. Should the engine load be lightened in some way, the engine speed will increase and the quantity of fuel injected will increase as the engine speed climbs. This increase in the quantity of fuel injected as the pump speed increases is known as the **rising characteristic** of the injection system and, unless some governing device is fitted to the engine, overspeeding must result.

On the other hand, if the rack is moved to the idle position, the engine speed will slacken and the quantity of fuel injected will fall off with engine speed. This action will cause the engine speed (and injection rate) to progressively fall until the engine stops through lack of fuel. Again, a governing device is necessary to prevent this from happening.

In certain applications, a constant speed is required from the engine. Without a governor, but with the throttle set, the load will either be heavy enough to cause the engine to lose speed, or too light and the engine will gain speed. Should the engine start to lose speed because of the load, it will continue to lose speed because of the injection pump characteristics. For the same reason, if the engine speed increases due to lack of load, it will continue to increase.

From the above it should be obvious that a governor is required on a diesel engine to:

- prevent stalling and overspeeding; and/or
- maintain engine speed relatively constant regardless of load variations.

A third governor function is often associated with the first one. This is to maintain engine speed relatively constant at any speed selected by the operator and set by means of a throttle control.

The governors generally employed are classified by the function or functions they fulfil as:

- constant-speed governors;
- variable or all-speed governors;
- limiting or idling and maximum speed governors.

Apart from their governing characteristics, governors may further be classified by the principle on which they operate as:

- mechanical (or centrifugal);
- pneumatic;
- hydraulic;
- electronic;

In addition, some manufacturers make governors that operate on a combination of two of the above principles — for example, mechanical-hydraulic and pneumatic-mechanical governors.

Governor terminology

Before examining the operation of the various types of governor, there are a number of terms, peculiar to governors and their operation, that should be defined.

- **Maximum no-load speed.** The maximum speed an engine can run at without carrying any load apart from engine components. However, there is not a uniform standard for expressing the maximum speed of an engine and some manufacturers use the term **high idle** when referring to the maximum no-load speed of their engines (see Fig 31.1).
- **Rated speed.** This is the speed at which the engine produces its rated power. Depending on the application of the engine, rated power is generally produced anywhere from 0 to 300 rpm below the maximum no-load speed. Rated speed is also referred to as **full load speed** by some engine manufacturers.
- **Torque rise.** The rise in engine torque from what is produced at rated speed to what is produced at maximum torque speed. It is usually expressed as a percentage of the torque produced at rated or full load speed.
- **Power band.** The varying power produced by the engine within the speed range of rated speed and maximum torque speed.
- **Speed droop.** A very basic fact concerning governors is that they operate when a change in the engine speed occurs. The change in speed necessary to bring about the governor's automatic action may be temporary, lasting only until the governor makes the necessary corrections and restores the engine speed, or it may be permanent, the governor action allowing a small speed change only.

A change in engine speed will occur when a load is applied to an unladen engine running with a fixed throttle or when the load is removed from a loaded engine that also has its throttle set. The change in speed will depend on the governor — some governors react to a small speed change, while some require a considerable change. The

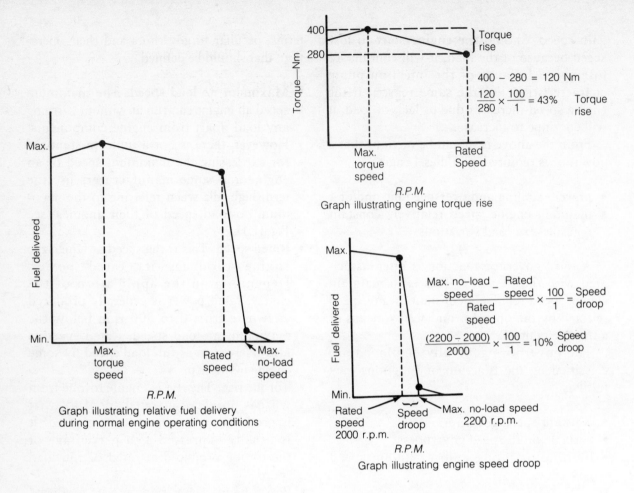

Fig 31.1 Graphs depicting governor control of engine fuelling and speed

change in engine speed necessary to cause the governor to operate is termed **speed droop**, and is usually related to full throttle operation.

The speed droop of a particular governor is usually specified as a percentage calculated from the following formula:

speed drop (%) =

$$\frac{(\text{max no load speed-rated speed}) \times 100}{\text{rated speed}}$$

Speed droop is a measure of the efficiency of operation of a governor — the smaller the speed variation, the more exacting the control exerted by the governor. The speed variation cannot be eliminated completely in any governor, however, since it is the speed variation that brings about governor action in the first place, but it can be only a temporary speed change, which is quickly corrected.

For general applications, the governors employed have a characteristic permanent speed droop. For tractors, this may lie between 8 and 13 per cent; for general industrial and automotive applications, 5–10 per cent is satisfactory, but for engines driving AC generators a temporary speed droop of +0.5–+1.5 per cent is generally specified.

- **Hunting.** When a governor exhibits an overcorrective tendency and causes the engine speed to continually increase and decrease about the mean governed speed, the engine is said to 'hunt'. Sensitive governors are more inclined to promote hunting than the less sensitive ones.
- **Sensitivity.** This term refers to the smallest

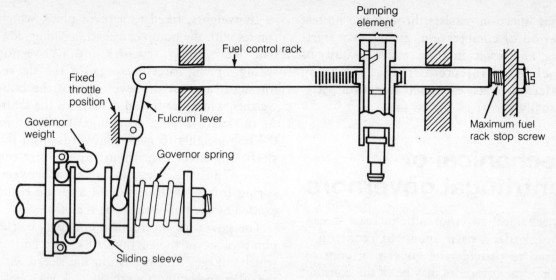

Fig 31.2 A simple constant speed governor

change in speed necessary to cause the governor to produce corrective movement of the fuel control mechanism, and is expressed as a percentage of the governed speed.

- **Deadband.** This is the narrow speed variation during which no measurable correction is made by the governor.
- **Isochronous.** An isochronous governor is one that is capable of maintaining a constant engine speed for any load between no load and full load without any alteration being necessary to the control setting. With a governor of this type, the speed droop is only temporary.
- **Stability.** The stability of a governor is its ability to maintain a definite engine speed under constant or varying load conditions, without hunting. After a sudden load change, a governor showing good stability will attain a steady speed very quickly.
- **Torque control.** In certain applications, the injection rate, as determined by the governor and maximum fuel stop, is not sufficient over the operating range to allow for sudden load increases. To provide sufficient engine torque to cater for such overload conditions, the maximum fuel delivery is not fixed, but is varied as a function of engine speed to give maximum injection rate at less than full speed. It is

usual for such governors to produce maximum engine torque at 55–65 per cent of rated engine speed, thereby giving a very useful reserve of torque to overcome the temporary overload conditions that cause the engine speed to continue to drop, irrespective of corrective governor action.

If the rack stop were set to the maximum amount of fuel that could be burned efficiently in a naturally aspirated engine, the engine would exhaust excessive smoke and give high fuel consumption at high speeds. This is brought about by two factors: as the engine speed increases, so the amount of fuel that can be burned falls slightly due to the fall in volumetric efficiency of the engine; and there is a tendency for the amount of fuel delivered by the injection pump at a fixed rack setting to increase slightly with the pump speed. Torque control devices automatically adjust the maximum fuel delivery when the throttle is fully open to suit the engine rpm.

- **Run-up speed.** This is the name often given to the increase in engine speed between full load and no load.
- **Excess fuel.** To aid starting under cold conditions, injection is allowed to continue for a longer than normal period when the 'cold start' device is operated. This ensures

that injection persists through the hottest period of compression, giving easy starting, and results in an excessive quantity of fuel being injected. Instead of being referred to as 'extended injection', it is usually known as 'excess fuel'.

Mechanical or centrifugal governors

In mechanical governors, the increase in centrifugal force with speed of rotation is utilised to provide the governing control. Mechanical governors may be of the constant speed, all speed or limiting speed types.

Simple constant speed governor

Constant speed governors are fitted to engines that are required to run at a set or constant speed, and are governed to this set speed. Applications include engines that power alternator sets, water pumps, conveyors, etc.

The simple constant speed governor (Fig 31.2) consists of two pivoted bob-weights or fly-weights, fixed to a pivot plate, which rotates with the pump camshaft, a sliding control sleeve, a pivoted fork and a governor spring. Spring force acts against the sleeve, forcing it against the lever arm of the bob-weights, which are forced in towards the shaft. As the shaft rotates, centrifugal force causes the bob-weights to move outwards from the shaft, the lever arm thrusting against the sleeve. Thus the sleeve is balanced between spring force on the one end and the force exerted by the bob-weights on the other.

The governor mechanism connects to the pump rack via the pivoted fork, one end of which engages in a groove in the sleeve with the other end connecting to the rack via a link.

Should the engine speed drop due to an increase in engine load, the centrifugal force acting on the weights will decrease, allowing the spring to push the sleeve along the shaft. This movement will move the rack, via the pivoted fork, to increase the fuel supply to the engine.

On the other hand, should the engine speed increase due to a lightening of the load, the subsequent increase in centrifugal force will fling the bob-weights outwards and the lever arms will force the sleeve along the

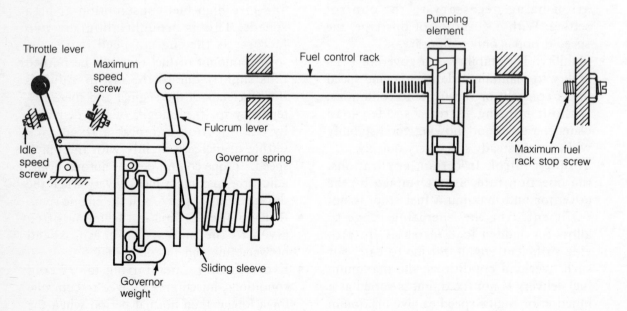

Fig 31.3 A simple variable speed governor

shaft against the spring. Movement in this direction will move the rack to reduce the fuel delivery from the pump.

Thus any change in the engine speed will cause an immediate change in the quantity of fuel injected, which will compensate for (or at least tend to compensate for) the speed change.

Simple variable speed governor

In applications where engines may be required to operate at any selected speed, variable speed governors are used. These governors govern the engine at any set engine speed, from idle to maximum. Governors of this type are used extensively in engines for earthmoving equipment and farm tractors.

The simple constant speed governor can readily be adapted to illustrate the principle of the variable speed governor. The governor shown in Fig 31.3, like the constant speed governor, features pivoted bob-weights, a sliding sleeve and a pivoted fork, but utilises a floating control fork pivot, the position of which is determined by the throttle setting.

When the throttle is moved to increase engine speed, the floating pivot is moved to the right (Fig 31.3), and the fork pivots about its lower end located in the sliding sleeve. Quite a small amount of throttle control movement will move the rack to the full-fuel position, and provision is provided for further throttle movement by the spring in the linkage, which simply compresses.

As the engine (and governor) speed increases, the increasing centrifugal force will cause the bob-weights to move outwards and force the sliding sleeve along the shaft against the governor spring. This will move the lower end of the control fork to the right and the spring in the throttle linkage will extend to its full length. After this point in the operation, any further movement of the sleeve to the right will cause the control fork to turn on its floating pivot and move the control

rack towards the no-fuel position, reducing the fuel delivery to the engine.

Once the throttle has been set, the governor will function as a constant speed governor, the engine's speed being controlled by the position of the floating pivot.

Simple idling and maximum speed governor

Idle and maximum speed governors are used on engines that need governing at idle and maximum speeds only. The speed range between these two extremities is entirely controlled and governed by the operator. Governors of this type are used solely for road transport vehicles, and are often referred to as **automotive governors**.

When a diesel engine is used for automotive applications, it is desirable that the driver retain a complete control of the engine fuel supply over the operating speed range. However, the engine must be protected against its tendency to overspeed once high speed is reached, and it is highly desirable that the tendency to stall at idle is eliminated. For these reasons, a governor that controls the maximum speed and idling speed, but allows full driver control in between, was developed.

The principle of the idling and maximum speed governor is clearly seen in the modified simple constant speed governor shown in Fig 31.4. The governor features the usual pivoted bob-weights and sliding control sleeve, but utilises two governor springs — a light idling spring and a heavy maximum speed spring — and a rack control fork with a throttle-controlled floating pivot.

At idle, the control sleeve is held in a balance between the centrifugal force acting indirectly on it via the bob-weights and the force exerted by the light idling spring. The heavy spring does not contact the sleeve and the unit acts as a constant speed governor.

As the throttle is opened, the fork pivots on the sleeve and moves the rack towards the

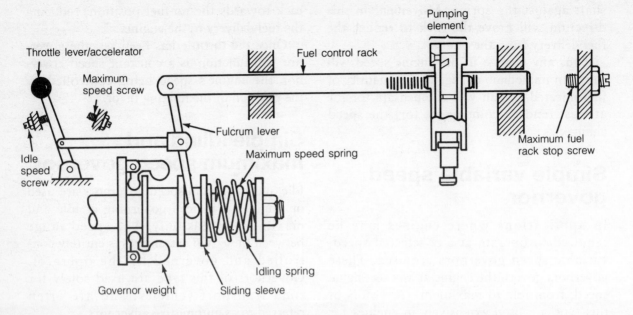

Fig 31.4   A simple idling and maximum speed governor

maximum fuel position. As soon as the engine speed increases, the sleeve is moved against the heavy maximum speed spring by the bob-weights. However, until the governed maximum speed is reached, the centrifugal force acting on the bob-weights is not sufficient to compress the heavy spring, and the rack remains in the position dictated by the throttle.

When the maximum governed speed is reached, the unit acts once more as a constant speed governor. The force acting on the bob-weights is sufficient to compress the heavy spring and the sleeve is once more held in balance. As the engine speed builds up, so the sleeve moves towards the spring, causing the fork to turn on its floating pivot to move the rack and reduce fuel delivery. Thus the maximum speed the engine achieves is limited.

Typical variable speed governor

CAV Minimec injection pumps feature a variable speed governor built into the pump housing.

The governor (Fig 31.5) consists essentially

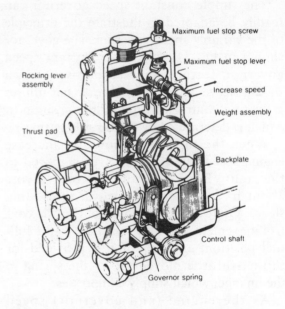

Fig 31.5   Minimec centrifugal governor

of a weight assembly, which is a sliding fit on the camshaft and supports two pairs of sliding weights. Each pair of weights is linked by a pin that locates in two slots inclined to the camshaft axis. At the centre of each pin is a slipper, which slides on an inclined plane parallel to the slots. The complete weight assembly is forced to rotate by the backplate, which is bolted to the camshaft and which surrounds the weights. A governor spring, controlled by the control shaft and control lever, acts through a thrust pad and presses the weight assembly against the backplate. A groove in the thrust plate engages with two pins of a rocking lever fitted over the control shaft, and transmits the axial movement of the thrust pads and weight assembly to the control rod.

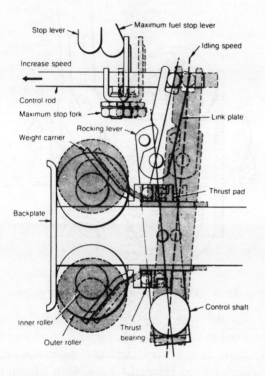

Fig 31.6 Operation of the Minimec governor

When the camshaft rotates, the weights of the governor will tend to be thrown outwards, and the centrifugal force will be transmitted as an axial force to the thrust pad by the action of the slippers on the inclined planes. The resultant deflection of the governor spring is used to control the unit. If the engine is initially running at idling speed, for example, and the control lever is turned to the maximum speed position, the governor spring will be wound up against the thrust pad and the weight assembly will be pressed hard against the backplate as shown

unshaded in Fig 31.6. The resultant forward motion of the rocking lever assembly is transmitted to the control rod, and the control rod moves to the maximum fuel position. The engine speed will now increase until the centrifugal force is great enough for the weights to push the weight assembly back to an equilibrium position in which the amount of fuel supplied is just sufficient to maintain the maximum speed. Similarly, if the control lever is set to the idling position, the pressure of the governor spring will be sufficient for the action of the weights to push the weight assembly away from the backplate against the spring and the governor will take up the position shown shaded in Fig 31.6.

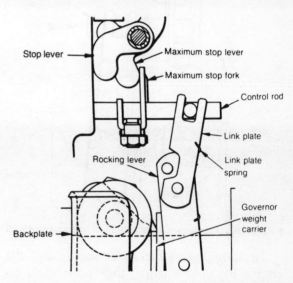

Fig 31.7 Maximum fuel position of the control rod

At any other speed between idling and maximum, the governor will take up an appropriate intermediate position.

The travel of the control rod in the maximum fuel direction is limited by a maximum stop fork on the control rod, which engages with a maximum fuel stop lever mounted on the excess shaft supported by the pump unit housing (Fig 31.7). The maximum fuel stop lever is basically a bell crank lever, one arm of which is positioned by the maximum fuel stop screw while the other limits the forward travel of the control rod by contacting the stop fork attached to it. The maximum fuel stop screw projects through the top of the pump housing and is adjusted externally.

The external stop control lever is mounted on a hub that fits over the excess shaft but is not attached to it, and terminates in an internal stop lever butting against the maximum stop fork. When the stop lever is turned towards the stop position, the control rod is pushed back and the fuel is cut off.

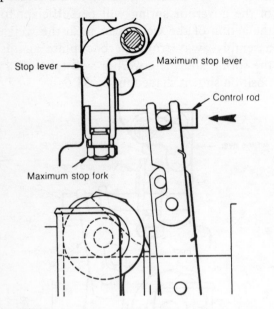

Fig 31.8   Excess fuel position of the control rod

To allow excess fuel to be supplied to the engine for cold starting, the excess shaft on which the maximum stop lever is mounted is spring loaded and can be pressed inwards. When this is done, the maximum stop lever moves inwards away from the maximum stop fork, allowing the control rod to move to a position of greater than normal fuel supply if the control lever is turned to the maximum speed position (Fig 31.8). The stop lever then butts against the pump unit housing and limits the travel of the control rod. As soon as the engine starts, the governor moves the control rod to a position of lower fuel supply and the maximum stop lever springs back into position, thus disengaging the excess fuel position automatically. Furthermore, if the excess

shaft continues to be pressed inwards after the engine has started, a baulking spring on the maximum stop fork will contact the maximum stop lever, restricting the engine speed until the excess shaft is released.

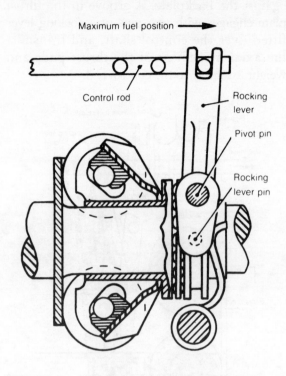

Fig 31.9   Governor with reverse linkage

An alternative variable speed governor may be used in CAV Minimec fuel injection pumps. Known as a **reverse linkage governor**, it is designed to prevent the possibility of stalling the vehicle engine by the sudden application of the brakes in emergency stopping.

If a vehicle fitted with the normal type of Minimec governor (Fig 31.5) is stopped abruptly by severe application of the brakes, the control rod can be carried by its own momentum (in the direction of vehicle motion) towards the no-fuel position. If there is no pressure on the governor spring (i.e. no pressure on the accelerator pedal) and the momentum is sufficiently great, this movement of the control rod could shut off the fuel supply and stop the engine.

In the reverse linkage arrangement of the governor, the rocking lever is pivoted as shown in Fig 31.9 so that the control rod operates in the opposite direction for the minimum and maximum fuel positions. In this manner, the control rod linkage is counterbalanced. Thus, in the event of sudden application of the brakes in similar circumstances, the control rod is not affected by momentum and the fuel supply is maintained under control by the governor.

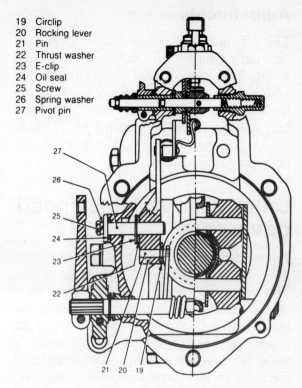

19 Circlip
20 Rocking lever
21 Pin
22 Thrust washer
23 E-clip
24 Oil seal
25 Screw
26 Spring washer
27 Pivot pin

Fig 31.11   Sectioned end view of the rocking lever assembly

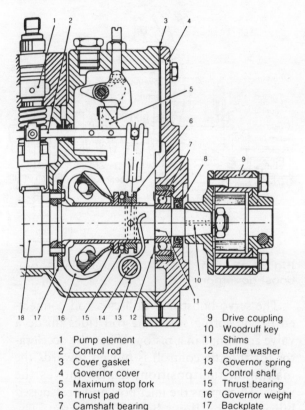

1 Pump element	9 Drive coupling
	10 Woodruff key
	11 Shims
2 Control rod	12 Baffle washer
3 Cover gasket	13 Governor spring
4 Governor cover	14 Control shaft
5 Maximum stop fork	15 Thrust bearing
6 Thrust pad	16 Governor weight
7 Camshaft bearing	17 Backplate
8 Oil seal	18 Camshaft

Fig 31.10   Sectioned view of the governor assembly

A typical reverse linkage arrangement is shown in Fig 31.10 and Fig 31.11. The governor and the governor spring (coiled type or leaf type) are the same as those used with the normal form of linkage, but the rocking lever is of different design.

The rocking lever is a straight form of lever without a link plate, and pivots on a pin mounted on the side of the pump unit housing. The rocking lever and pivot pin are shown in Fig 31.12.

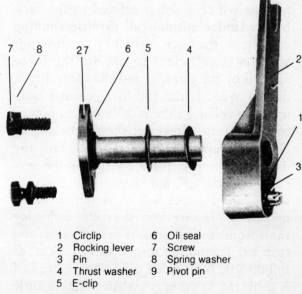

1 Circlip	6 Oil seal
2 Rocking lever	7 Screw
3 Pin	8 Spring washer
4 Thrust washer	9 Pivot pin
5 E-clip	

Fig 31.12 Rocking lever and pivot pin

Adjustments

The Minimec governors feature standard externally adjusted idle and maximum speed stops, but make use of a maximum fuel adjustment, which screws vertically down from the top of the governor housing to contact the maximum fuel stop lever. This in turn limits the rack movement towards the maximum fuel position.

Caterpillar variable speed governors

The mechanical variable speed governor used on Caterpillar engines is of a simple design. The governor weight carrier is driven by a gear on the pump camshaft and carries the two fly-weights, the inner ends of which act against a thrust bearing. As the governor weights move outwards under centrifugal force, the thrust bearing compresses the governor spring. The throttle lever acts against the governor spring, increasing the force applied to restrain the governor weights as the throttle is moved towards the high-speed position.

A simple torque control device is fitted to this governor. It consists of a leaf spring against which a collar affixed to the rack bears. Under normal full throttle running conditions, the force exerted by the governor weights is sufficient to oppose the force applied by the throttle, and the control rack moves towards the full-fuel position only until the collar on the rack bears against the torque spring. However, should the engine become overloaded and its speed fall, the decreased centrifugal force acting on the governor weights will not restrain the governor spring, and the rack will move further in the maximum fuel direction, the collar deflecting the torque spring until it rests against the stop bar behind the torque spring. Thus, at full throttle overloaded conditions, more fuel is delivered to the engine than at full throttle normal load conditions, giving increased torque when required.

Obviously, considerable force would be required to increase the engine speed by increasing governor spring force. In applications where the throttle is set, this provides no problem, but in applications where the throttle needs to be continually altered, operator fatigue may result. To overcome the problem, the throttle is servo-assisted.

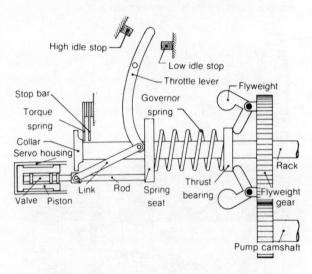

Fig 31.13 Layout of the Caterpillar servo-boost governor

The servo-boost unit utilises a rod connected to the spring seat. The rod rides inside a valve contained in a piston. When the accelerator (or throttle control) is moved towards the maximum fuel position, it also moves the valve. This opens the inlet port and pressurised lubricating oil flows behind the piston. The piston then pushes against the rod and helps to compress the governor spring. When the accelerator movement stops, the oil pressure forces the piston slightly further, permitting the pressure behind the piston to escape.

Adjustments

Caterpillar governors have two adjustments: high idle and low idle (maximum speed and idle speed). These are readily accessible by the removal of a retainer/cover. These are adjusted on the engine to give the required governed speeds.

The maximum fuel delivery is controlled by the maximum rack movement towards the full-fuel position. It may be adjusted on or off the engine according to the workshop manual, to give the correct rack movement, which is measured by means of a dial gauge.

Typical idling and maximum speed governor

The CAV LW governor shown in Fig 31.14 is a typical example of an idling and maximum speed governor. The two spring-loaded fly-weights (15) are carried on a sleeve fitted to the injection pump camshaft (14), and move outwards under centrifugal force as the camshaft rotates. Bell crank levers (17) trans-mit the centrifugal action of the weights to

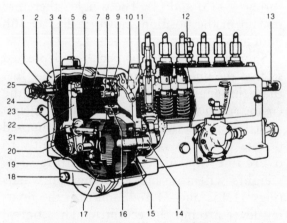

the lever is conveyed to the injection pump control rod (11) by the link screw (4) through the link block (8). The position of the control rod is thus adjusted to increase or decrease the quantity of fuel delivered by the injection pump elements.

The accelerator pedal is connected to the control lever (23), which is clamped to the shaft (20). When the shaft is turned by move-ment of the accelerator pedal, the eccentric — an integral part of the shaft — moves the floating lever and the control rod indepen-dently of the weight mechanism.

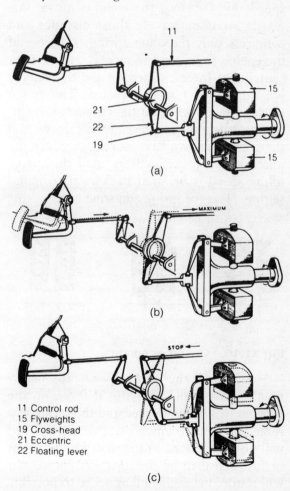

1	Auxiliary idling stop locknut	14	Camshaft
2	Cover	15	Flyweights
3	Auxiliary idling stop valve	16	Spring adjusting nut
4	Link screw	17	Bell crank levers
5	Air breather	18	Drain plug
6	Lever link	19	Cross-head
7	Link springs	20	Shaft
8	Link block	21	Eccentric
9	Stop pawl	22	Floating lever
10	Stopping control lever	23	Control lever
11	Control rod	24	Auxiliary idling stop spring
12	Fuel inlet	25	Auxiliary idling stop sleeve
13	Control rod stop		

Fig 31.14 CAV injection pump with an LW governor

11	Control rod
15	Flyweights
19	Cross-head
21	Eccentric
22	Floating lever

Fig 31.15 Governor operation

the link pin and crosshead assembly (19) as a longitudinal movement. The crosshead turns the floating lever (22) about the eccentric (21), and the movement of the upper end of

Operation of the idling and maximum speed governor is shown diagrammatically in Fig 31.15 (components numbered as for Fig 31.14). While the mechanism is at rest, the flyweights (15) lie close to the camshaft sleeve, and the injection pump control rod (11) is held towards the maximum fuel position.

Before the starter motor is engaged with the engine flywheel ring, the accelerator pedal should be fully depressed. After the engine fires and runs up to speed, the accelerator pedal should be steadily released and the governor will then come into operation to control the speed engine at the predetermined idling speed (Fig 31.15a).

Movement of the flyweights is governed by two sets of springs (see Fig 31.16). At idling speed (Fig 31.16a), the weights move outwards a comparatively short distance and compress only the outer springs (2). Should the engine speed tend to increase, the greater centrifugal force exerted on the fly-weights will move them further outwards. This action of the weights will pull the crosshead assembly inwards, towards the camshaft sleeve, and the control rod will be moved to reduce the injection pump fuel delivery until the engine idling speed is brought back to its original setting. (1) is the spring adjusting nut.

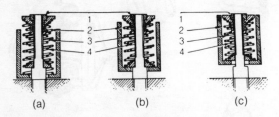

(a) (b) (c)

Fig 31.16 Governor springs

Similarly, if the idling speed falls below that required, the centrifugal force on the weights will be diminished and the spring will force the weights inwards. The control rod will now be moved to increase the quantities of fuel delivered by the injection pump, and will restore the engine idling speed to normal.

Movement of the flyweights is extremely small and the idling speed is therefore maintained at a reasonably constant level.

Engine speeds between the predetermined idling and maximum limits are controlled by movement of the accelerator pedal (see Fig 31.15b). This ungoverned condition is achieved by providing the floating lever (22) with two pivot points. Under governor control, the floating lever is moved around the eccentric (21), while movement of the accelerator pedal turns the shaft and the eccentric as a whole, thus pivoting the floating lever about the crosshead arms (19).

When the accelerator pedal is depressed to increase engine speed, the shaft and the eccentric will turn the floating lever and move the control rod towards the maximum fuel position, irrespective of the position of the governor weights.

Throughout the intermediate speed range of the engine, the governor flyweights compress the outer idling springs — (2) in Fig 31.16 — but are prevented from further outward movement by the heavier inner springs — (3) and (4). The weights therefore remain in the position shown in Fig 31.16b until maximum speed is reached.

Should the accelerator pedal be depressed so that the injection pump delivers more fuel than the engine requires for the load, the engine speed will tend to exceed the predetermined limit and the centrifugal force imposed on the weights will increase sufficiently to overcome the inner spring loading. The weights will now move further outwards (Figs 31.15c and 31.16c) and turn the floating lever around the eccentric. The control rod is thereby drawn back to a position of reduced fuel delivery, despite the over-depressed position of the accelerator pedal.

Adjustments

In an idling and maximum speed governor of this type, the governor weights and springs combine to determine the speeds at which governor action takes place. However, the effect of any governor action to alter fuelling could be cancelled out by a compensating movement of the eccentric shaft. Therefore the maximum movement of the eccentric shaft and control lever in the full speed direction must be limited to prevent extra throttle movement being applied to hold the control rack against the rack stop, despite any governor action to reduce fuelling. There are two such stops incorporated in these governors, and these are termed maximum fuel stops.

Equally it is true that excessive eccentric movement in the idle speed direction could overcome corrective governor action at idle speed, so causing the engine to stop. An idle fuel stop is included to limit this movement.

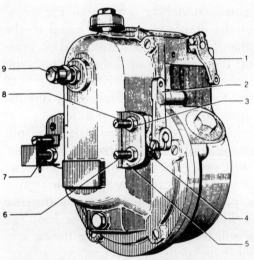

1 Stop control lever   6 Unsealed maximum fuel stop
2 Control lever   7 Sealed maximum fuel stop
3 Idling stop locknut   8 Idling speed stop
4 Pawl on control shaft   9 Auxiliary idling stop
5 Flange

Fig 31.17   Arrangement of governor stops

By reference to Fig 31.17, it can readily be seen that the governor carries two maximum fuel stops, one (7) covered to prevent unauthorised tampering, which is set on the test bench, and a second (6) which can readily be altered on the engine. An adjustable idle fuel stop (8) and an idle buffer (9) are also incorporated in the governor housing, while a rack stop (including, perhaps, an excess fuel device) will certainly be incorporated on the other end of any injection pump to which the governor is fitted.

Between the governor speed limits, no difficulty would arise during calibration in holding the control rack at the desired

position. However, if the pump were to be run at or near either governed speed, the governor would function and attempt to alter the rack position. All interference can be eliminated by removing the governor cross-shaft, and it is recommended that this be done before calibrating the pump. During calibration, and until it is to be set, the rack stop should be removed or adjusted well clear of the rack.

Once the pump has been calibrated, the governor shaft should be refitted, the stops adjusted and the governor action checked. The master stop (7) should be adjusted while running the pump at a specified speed with the control lever held against the stop by a spring to give either a specific fuel delivery or rack position. (This will only be correctly set if the governor link has been adjusted to its correct length during reassembly.)

The maximum speed governor action can be checked by running the pump at a specified speed at or near maximum speed and checking the fuel delivery (or rack position) against the specifications, then increasing the pump speed to a second point and rechecking the fuel delivery (or rack position). At the second (higher) speed, the fuel delivery will have dropped to a lower specified figure (or the rack will have moved back to a new specified position) if the governor is functioning correctly. Some slight adjustment is allowable at the governor springs but will not be necessary if the springs were set up correctly during assembly.

The idling stop (8) is adjusted and the governor checked at idle speed in a similar way to the maximum fuel stop (7), but with the control lever held back in the engine idle position. Again two speeds and associated fuel deliveries (or rack positions) will be given in the test sheet for the pump.

The idle stop (8) and the second maximum fuel stop (6) may both be adjusted to give a certain fuel delivery, but this may have to be adjusted on the engine to give the required engine idle and the maximum power with a satisfactory clean exhaust.

The rack stop must be adjusted after setting the maximum fuel stop (7) to allow the rack to move at least as far as the maximum fuel stop allows. If the rack stop restricted rack movement before stop (7) limited the control lever movement, straining of the governor linkages would result. The rack stop should be adjusted according to the test sheet.

The idle buffer (9) is best adjusted on the engine to prevent stalling when the engine speed is suddenly cut to idle, but not far enough in to start the engine surging or the idle speed increasing.

Pneumatic governors

Pneumatic governors utilise the changing inlet manifold depression to control the fuel pump delivery. They consist of two separate sections — the governor unit, which is fitted to the injection pump, and the venturi or throttle unit, which is fitted to the inlet manifold — which are connected by a pipe or pipes.

A simple pneumatic variable speed governor

The simple pneumatic governor (Fig 31.18) shows the basic construction of the two sections. The governor unit consists of its housing, a flexible diaphragm and a spring.

The diaphragm connects to the pump rack, and the spring forces the diaphragm and rack towards the maximum fuel delivery position. The throttle unit consists of a butterfly, which is controlled by the operator's throttle control. The unit is fitted to the inlet manifold so that all air passing to the engine must pass through it. The two sections are connected by a pipe.

At idle, the butterfly is almost closed, and the depression on the engine side of the butterfly is high. The governor unit is directly connected to the engine side of the butterfly by the pipe, so that the pressure on the spring side of the diaphragm will be equal to the inlet manifold pressure. Atmospheric pressure on the rack side of the diaphragm will force the diaphragm towards the spring until a point of equilibrium is reached, moving the rack to the low-fuel delivery position.

As the throttle is opened, the manifold depression will become progressively less. This will cause the pressure on the spring side of the diaphragm to approach atmospheric pressure and the pressure difference across the diaphragm will become less. The spring will then be able to force the rack in the higher fuel delivery direction.

Once the throttle is set and the diaphragm moves the rack to the required position, the engine will run at a steady speed. Should extra load be applied so that the engine speed falls, the manifold depression will also fall — the pressure will rise closer to atmospheric —

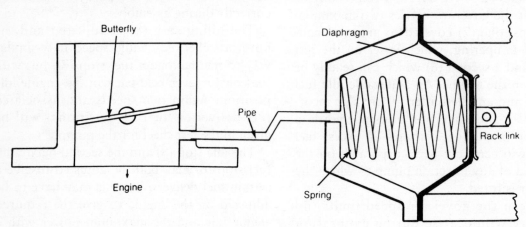

Fig 31.18 A simple pneumatic governor

and the spring will force the diaphragm and rack towards the maximum fuel direction, where it will stay until the manifold depression returns to its original point.

If the engine load becomes lessened and the engine speed increases, the manifold depression will climb correspondingly — the pressure will become less. The atmospheric pressure will be more effective with less pressure opposing it and the diaphragm will move to compress the spring slightly, cutting down the fuel delivery. The fuel delivery will remain at this reduced level until the manifold depression returns to its original level.

A typical pneumatic governor

While the throttle unit shown in Fig 31.18 is sufficient to illustrate the basic principle of the pneumatic governor, in most cases this component is much more correctly termed a **venturi unit**.

A venturi is a tube tapered internally from both ends, the arrangement giving a minimum internal diameter somewhere along the tube. Should a fluid be caused to flow through a venturi, the pressure will change along its length, the point of lowest pressure being the point of minimum diameter. How low the pressure drops is dependent on the fluid's speed through the venturi — the greater the speed, the lower the pressure.

The venturi unit shown in Fig 31.19 is a typical example. A small auxiliary venturi is situated within the main venturi, the butterfly being cut out where necessary. Depending on the position of the butterfly (i.e. how far it is open), varying proportions of the engine's air supply must pass through the auxiliary venturi. Hence, when the engine is running, the velocity of the air passing through the auxiliary venturi (and the subsequent pressure at the smallest diameter) is dependent on the butterfly position and the engine's speed. It is to the auxiliary venturi that the vacuum pipe connects.

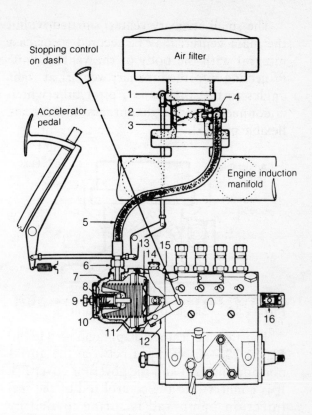

Fig 31.19   CAV fuel pump with pneumatic governor and single-pitot venturi unit

The CAV pneumatic governor shown in Fig 31.19 consists of a venturi flow control (venturi unit) located between the engine intake manifold and the air cleaner, and a diaphragm unit mounted directly on the fuel injection pump.

Reference to the diagram will show that the body of the venturi unit is flanged at one end so that it can be secured to the intake manifold, and is spigoted at the other to accommodate the air cleaner. The diameter of the throat must be selected to suit the capacity of the engine to which it is fitted.

Airflow through the throat of the venturi is regulated by a butterfly (2), which is mounted on a spindle carried in bushes pressed into the venturi body. The control lever (1) is secured to the butterfly spindle and is connected by a suitable control linkage to the accelerator pedal. Maximum speed and idling stops (Fig 31.20) provide means of adjusting the limits of movement of the butterfly.

The small auxiliary venturi situated within the main venturi may be secured to or cast integral with the body of the venturi unit. Projecting into the auxiliary venturi at right angles to the airflow is a pitot tube which is connected to the diaphragm unit by the flexible pipe (5).

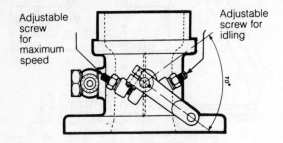

Adjustable screw for maximum speed

Adjustable screw for idling

Fig 31.20   Single-pitot venturi unit

The flexible leather diaphragm — (13) in Fig 31.19 — is clamped between the governor housing (15) and the governor cover (7). It is connected to the control rod of the fuel injection pump and is spring loaded by the governor spring (11). Pressure exerted on the diaphragm by the spring tends to move the diaphragm and control rod towards the maximum fuel stop (16).

Control rod movement is limited by adjustable stops. Auxiliary idling stops (one type is shown in Fig 31.19) may be fitted to governors with single-pitot venturi units. That illustrated in Fig 31.19 consists of a plunger (10), which is spring loaded by the spring (8). The adjusting screw (9) permits adjustment of the spring force acting on the plunger.

Maximum fuel stops are normally fitted at the end of the pump housing remote from the governor. They provide the means of adjusting the maximum fuelling and may be sealed after setting to prevent unauthorised adjustment.

The operation of a governor fitted with a single-pitot venturi unit may be followed by reference to Fig 31.19. As the throttle is advanced and the butterfly opens, the rate of airflow through the auxiliary venturi changes from a maximum at closed throttle to a minimum at full throttle. Should the throttle be abruptly closed while the engine is running at high speed, the air velocity through the venturi will immediately become very high, but will drop as the engine slows down. Again, should an engine's speed fall while the throttle is fixed, the air velocity will also fall due to the engine requiring less air. Associated with these changes in air velocity are corresponding changes in the depression within the venturi.

A pitot tube projects into the auxiliary venturi, and is connected to a flexible pipe (5). The flexible pipe and the pitot tube interconnect the venturi and the airtight chamber in the diaphragm unit so that the depression in the venturi and the airtight chamber are maintained at the same level. Thus, while atmospheric pressure acts on the pump side of the diaphragm (13), air only at the same pressure as that in the venturi acts on the other. The resultant force tends to move the diaphragm away from the pump housing. Because the diaphragm is connected to the control rod, this movement of the diaphragm reduces the fuel injection rate.

The governor spring (11) exerts pressure on the diaphragm in opposition to the force created by the pressure differential and, in consequence, the diaphragm will assume a position where the two forces acting on it are in equilibrium. It follows, therefore, that any change in the value of the depression will cause the diaphragm to move and, since the diaphragm is connected to the control rod of the fuel injection pump, a change of fuelling will occur.

Force exerted on the diaphragm due to the pressure differential tends to move the control rod towards the auxiliary idling stop, while that exerted by the governor spring tends to move the control rod towards the maximum fuel stop (16). When the engine is running at a fixed throttle setting, the control rod assumes a position where the forces acting on the diaphragm are in equilibrium. Fluctuations in engine speed resulting from changes of engine loading will result in corresponding changes of the depression. The increase in the depression that occurs when the engine exceeds the selected speed will cause the control rod to move towards the auxiliary idling stop. The output of the fuel injection pump will then be reduced and engine speed will fall until the selected engine speed is restored. Similarly, a fall in engine speed resulting from increased engine loading will cause the control rod to move towards the maximum fuel stop under influence of the spring (11), thus increasing the output of the fuel injection pump and increasing the engine speed until the selected running speed has been regained.

Any selected engine speed will therefore be maintained within close limits, since any speed change is accompanied by a compensating change in the output of the fuel injection pump.

When the engine is stationary, the control rod is held against the maximum fuel stop by the force exerted on the diaphragm by the governor spring. Although the control rod is in the correct position for starting the engine, the accelerator pedal is usually depressed during this operation. After the engine has started, it may be idled by releasing the accelerator and thus closing the butterfly valve in the flow control unit. Restriction of the main venturi will cause an immediate increase in the velocity of the airflow and the resulting increase in the depression will move the control rod to the idling position. Speed control is maintained at idling in the same manner as at intermediate throttle settings. Violent movement of the control rod is prevented, however, by the spring-loaded auxiliary idling stop. An increased depression caused by any increase in engine speed will move the diaphragm against the stop and overcome the force exerted on the plunger by the spring (8).

When difficulty is experienced in obtaining even running at idling without exceeding the maximum idling speed or the maximum no-load over-run, the use of a pneumatic governor incorporating a cam-operated idling stop is recommended (Fig 31.21). The cam is rotated by movement of the control lever, which is connected by suitable control linkage to the accelerator pedal. The linkage is so arranged that the spring is compressed when the accelerator pedal is released.

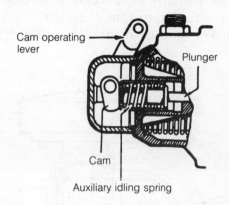

Fig 31.21   Cam-operated idling spring

The operation of governors fitted with double-pitot venturi units (Fig 31.22) is basically the same as that of governors with single-pitot venturi units, movement of the diaphragm and control rod being governed by the velocity of the airflow through the auxiliary venturi (3).

A pitot tube projecting into the second auxiliary venturi (1) is connected by a flexible pipe to an air valve (5), which is fitted in place of an auxiliary idling stop. The butterfly valve is not cut away to permit the passage of air through the auxiliary venturi (1) when the valve is closed, so that at idling speeds there is no airflow through the second auxiliary venturi and if the air valve (5) opens, it opens to atmospheric pressure. When the butterfly valve is open, the velocity of the airflow through both auxiliary venturi is the same and the air valve (5) opens to a depression equal to that in the diaphragm chamber (4).

When the engine is idling, the metal centre of the diaphragm is in contact with the air valve (5). An increase in engine speed will cause an increase in the depression in the diaphragm chamber (4) and the diaphragm and control rod will move towards the no-fuel position. Movement in this direction beyond the normal idling position will reduce the output of the fuel injection pump and at the same time open the air valve (5). Since the air valve opens to atmospheric pressure when the butterfly valve is closed, the depression in the diaphragm chamber (4) will be relieved and the diaphragm and control

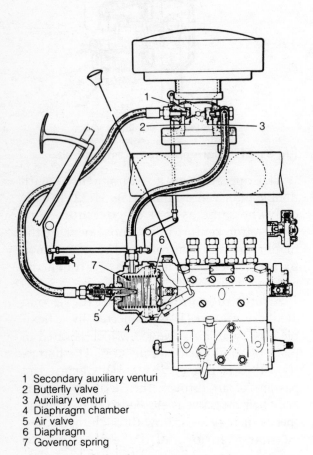

1 Secondary auxiliary venturi
2 Butterfly valve
3 Auxiliary venturi
4 Diaphragm chamber
5 Air valve
6 Diaphragm
7 Governor spring

Fig 31.22 CAV pump with pneumatic governor and double-pitot venturi unit

rod will move towards the maximum fuel position. This movement will be arrested, however, when the diaphragm reaches the normal idling position, at which point the air valve will be closed and the depression in the diaphragm chamber restored. This interference with normal governor action serves to prevent violent movement of the control rod

at idling speeds, but does not interfere at high speeds when the velocity of the airflow through both auxiliary venturis is equal.

Adjustments

Adjustments are provided for maximum fuel delivery, absolute maximum engine speed and idle. The maximum fuel stop is normally adjusted during calibration to specifications and then sealed to prevent unauthorised adjustment. Any adjustment that may be deemed necessary during service may be effected by removing the cap or cover, removing or releasing the locking device and screwing the adjusting screw outwards to increase the maximum fuel setting, and inwards to reduce it.

Alteration of the setting of the maximum fuel stop will change the power output of the engine and the fuel consumption. An excessive increase of the maximum fuelling will result in a smoky exhaust and increased fuel consumption. When adjustment is made, a compromise should be sought between power output, exhaust colour and fuel consumption.

Absolute maximum speed is governed by the throat diameter of the venturi. The maximum speed of the engine can be adjusted to speeds below this figure by limiting the movement of the butterfly valve in the venturi unit. Adjustment is made by movement of the stop screw shown in Fig 31.20.

When single-pitot venturi units are fitted, the idling speed is adjusted by movement of the idling stop (Fig 31.20). Adjustment of the auxiliary idling stop in the governor housing should only be made when hunting occurs at the correct idling speed. If hunting does occur, ensure that it is not attributable to engine faults (such as faulty injectors) before making adjustments.

When double-pitot venturi units are fitted, the positions of the idling stop on the venturi unit and of the air valve assembly in the diaphragm unit must be adjusted at the same time. Adjustment of either will affect the idling speed, and it is only by adjusting both settings simultaneously that a setting can be achieved where even running is obtained at the correct idling speed.

Combined pneumatic-mechanical governors

The combined governor consists of a pneumatic and a mechanical governing assembly, combined together to act as a unit and designed to give accurate control of engine speed throughout the entire speed range. A schematic diagram of a typical design is shown in Fig 31.23.

In terms of overall performance, pneumatic governors are the least accurate of all modern governors, especially in the high-speed range. However, in the low-speed, light-load range, their ability to maintain close speed regulation is good, due to the large operating depression with the partly open butterfly.

In the high-speed range, the operating depression is small — the butterfly is wide

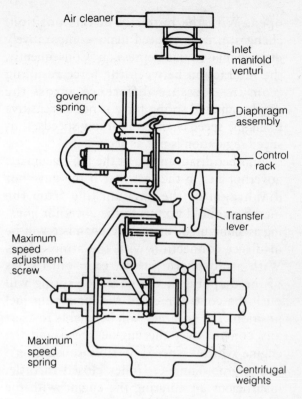

Idle speed—pneumatic governing

(a)

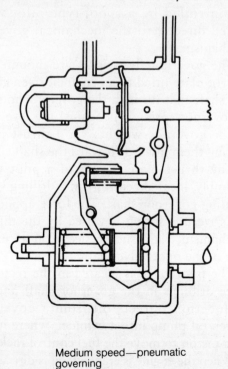

Medium speed—pneumatic governing

(b)

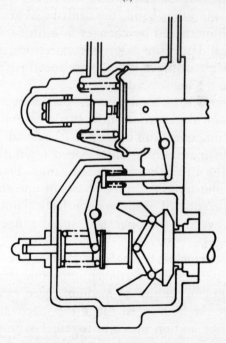

Maximum speed—combined pneumatic and mechanical governing

(c)

Fig 31.23   Operation of the combined pneumatic-mechanical governor

open. With the butterfly in this position, changes in engine speed make comparatively little change to this depression. Consequently, the interaction between the force resulting from the pressure difference across the diaphragm and spring force is not as sensitive to engine speed changes as at low speeds, thus speed regulation is not as accurate.

Another disadvantage of the full pneumatic governor lies in the fact that if the governor diaphragm or the vacuum line from the intake manifold venturi to the governor housing is punctured, the spring chamber will be in direct connection with the atmosphere. With atmospheric pressure on both sides of the diaphragm, the governor spring will push the control rack to the maximum fuel position. The governor will be unable to exert any control over the engine speed and the engine will overspeed, possibly causing serious engine damage. Under closed throttle, insufficient air entering the engine with the butterfly closed will limit the engine speed, but excessive exhaust smoke will result.

On the other hand, the centrifugal governor is unaffected by changes in altitude and physical damage to external connections, and is capable of maintaining close speed regulation in the high-speed range.

Therefore, by combining the pneumatic and mechanical governors in a single assembly, each component can be used to its best advantage in maintaining close speed regulation over the full operating speed range. Figure 31.23 illustrates the three phases of operation of the combined pneumatic-mechanical governor, covering the operating speed range of the engine.

In conclusion, the pneumatic governor section operates like a conventional pneumatic governor in the low-to-medium speed range, and at the high-speed range the mechanical governor section operates together with the pneumatic governor section, thereby eliminating the influence of altitude changes to the governing effect.

Combined mechanical-hydraulic governors

Some manufacturers utilise the sensitivity of mechanical speed sensing in combination with an hydraulic servo system to provide a combined or hydra-mechanical governor. If the source of hydraulic fluid is the engine lubrication system, a further advantage is created in the automatic engine shutdown that occurs should the engine oil pressure fail.

A simple hydra-mechanical governor

The simple variable speed hydra-mechanical governor (Fig 31.24) senses engine speed mechanically through a simple pair of pivoted fly-weights balanced by a governor spring, and controls the engine fuelling by an hydraulic servo system. The hydraulic servo is controlled by a spool-type pilot valve linked directly to the mechanical governor mechanism.

The governor fly-weights are mounted on a pivot plate fitted to an engine-driven governor shaft that turns in the governor housing. A governor spring acts against the lever arm of the governor weights via a thrust plate, forcing them inwards toward the shaft.

The thrust plate is part of a pilot valve assembly, located centrally in a drilling in the rotating governor shaft. The force applied by the governor spring is varied by the throttle mechanism, via a sliding sleeve on an extension of the pilot valve shaft.

The pilot valve is located in the region of three drillings in the governor shaft and, by its location, directs oil from a governor-driven oil pump into a cylinder, where it acts on a piston to move the fuel control rack.

When the engine is cranked, oil is directed by the spool valve into the cylinder, where it acts

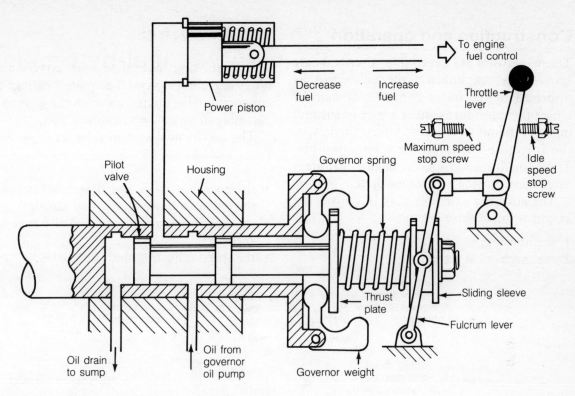

Fig 31.24   A simple hydra-mechanical governor

on the piston to move the rack toward the full fuel position. As the engine speed approaches selected speed, the flyweights overcome the governor spring force and begin moving the spool valve to seal off the port leading to the cylinder.

If the engine exceeds the selected speed, the fly-weights move the spool valve beyond the point where the port is sealed, and oil is dumped through the open dump port, allowing the piston to move back into the cylinder, moving the fuel rack to decrease the engine fuelling.

Should the engine speed fall below selected speed, the fly-weights will move inwards under the influence of the governor spring, allowing the spool valve to open the port to the cylinder. Oil flow into the cylinder causes the piston to increase the fuelling.

When a change of engine speed is desired, the operator simply alters the governor spring force with the throttle lever and the fly-weights react to the change and move the spool valve to either dump oil from the

cylinder to lower the speed, or allow oil flow into the cylinder to increase engine speed.

Woodward SG hydra-mechanical governor

Like the simple mechanical-hydraulic governor, the Woodward SG governor senses engine speed mechanically, and uses an internal hydraulic system to adjust the engine's fuel setting. Except for Cummins PT system applications, where the governor controls fuel pressure in the system, the governor is connected to the engine's fuel injection rack via a mechanical linkage. The governor controls the amount of fuel injected into the engine to compensate for varying engine load conditions.

The SG governor can be used as a variable speed governor, or as a constant speed governor, depending on the application required. Because of its adjustable speed droop feature, it is suitable for a variety of applications where isochronous governor control is not required.

Construction and operation

The Woodward SG governor is a separate, or stand-alone, unit linked to the fuel system, as opposed to the more common system in which the governor is either a part of the fuel injection pump or is a unit bolted directly to the injection pump to form an assembly. Thus, for this governor, the engine manufacturer must provide a governor drive.

The governor assembly may be considered as consisting of three sections:

1 the housing;
2 the mechanical system;

3 the hydraulic system.

The **housing**, complete with covers and adjusting screws, as well as plain bearings to support moving shafts, encloses the governor assembly in a clean environment.

The **mechanical system** consists of several parts, including:

- the governor shaft and flyweights (termed the ballhead bushing and ball arms);
- the governor spring (termed the speeder spring);
- the speed-adjusting shaft (and lever);

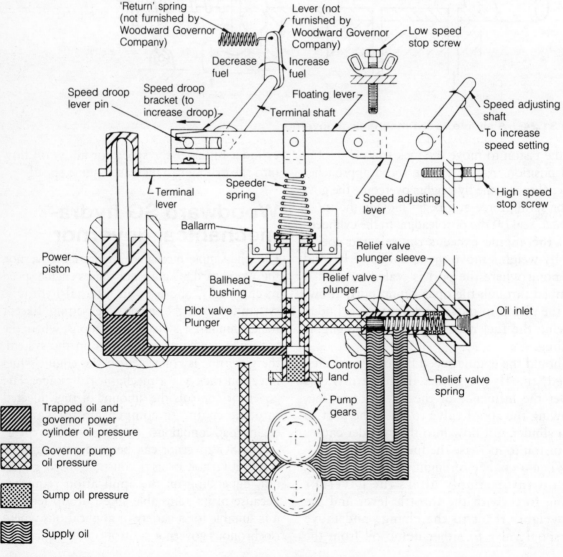

Fig 31.25 Schematic diagram of a Woodward SG governor

- the terminal shaft (with terminal lever and speed droop bracket); and
- the floating lever.

The governor shaft, the driven part of the governor, turns in the governor housing. Termed the ball head bushing by the manufacturer, it consists of a hollow shaft with radial ports or drillings, externally splined at one end to accept the drive from the engine (and in turn to drive the oil pump), and carrying the governor weights in a 'T' crossarm at the other.

The governor weights pivot in the crossarm, and act against a flange on the pilot valve (see the hydraulic system) via a thrust bearing. (The pilot valve is located in the axial drilling in the ball head shaft.)

The governor spring (the speeder spring) also acts on the pilot valve flange to balance any force exerted by the governor weights. This is a tapered spring in that the diameter of the coils increases from one end to the other.

The speed-adjusting shaft, carrying a speed-adjusting lever within the governor housing, runs across the governor and is free to be rotated, within limits, to select engine speed.

The terminal shaft (usually fitted with an external lever for connection to the fuel system) lies parallel to the speed-adjusting shaft, and carries an internal arm — the terminal lever — which links to the hydraulic system piston via a pushrod.

The terminal lever shaft carries the speed droop bracket, which can be adjusted along the terminal lever to adjust the governor's speed droop characteristics.

The floating lever links the speed-adjusting lever and the terminal lever via the speed droop bracket, and carries a fork along its length to engage the governor spring. The lever is slotted on one end to engage a protruding pin on the speed droop bracket; the other end is joined by a pivot pin to the speed adjusting lever.

By this arrangement, partial rotation of the speed-adjusting shaft moves one end of the floating lever via the speed-adjusting lever. The floating lever pivots on the speed droop bracket pin, and the resultant movement at the spring fork changes the force applied to the governor spring.

Adjusting the speed droop lever along the terminal lever effectively varies the length of the floating lever, by changing the point at which it pivots.

The **hydraulic system** of the governor also consists of several parts;

- the governor oil pump;
- the pressure relief valve;
- the pilot valve;
- the power piston; and
- the ports and drillings to carry the hydraulic fluid.

The oil pump is a conventional gear-type pump, turning directly in the recess machined in the governor housing. Drive is provided by the governor shaft (the ball head), which is externally splined to match the internal splines in one of the oil pump gears.

The pressure relief valve lies in the governor housing, and consists of a simple spring-loaded plunger in a ported sleeve.

The pilot valve consists of an extended spool valve which operates in the axial drilling in the governor shaft. The extended end carries a flange against which the flyweights and governor act.

The power piston lies in a cylinder machined in the governor housing, where it moves axially due to the force generated by hydraulic pressure.

The ports and drillings in the governor housing allow connection to the engine's lubrication system, and provide the path for oil flow to the gear pump, and on to the pilot valve and pressure relief valve.

The pilot valve either directs oil through drillings into the power cylinder and seals the power cylinder to prevent the escape of oil, or provides a dump circuit to allow oil to drain from the power cylinder.

When the engine (and governor) is at rest, the governor spring acts through the pilot valve flange and thrust bearing on to the lever arms of the governor weights which lie at their innermost position. At this position, the pilot valve is positioned to provide an unrestricted oil flow into the power piston cylinder.

However, it would take considerable cranking time for sufficient oil flow to be generated to move the power piston to fuel the engine. This delay can minimised by pushing a button mounted externally on the governor housing which turns the terminal shaft toward the full-fuel position, over-riding the governor until the engine starts.

Operation

Once the engine starts, oil from the engine lubricating system enters the governor oil pump in the governor housing. The oil pump raises the pressure of the oil to a pre-set value controlled by the spring-loaded relief valve. The oil under pressure is contained in the space between the two control lands of the pilot valve plunger, and is directed through the open supply port into the power piston cylinder. The resulting piston movement acts on the terminal lever through the pushrod to establish governor control of engine fuelling.

When a change of engine speed occurs, the resultant change in the centrifugal force acting on the governor weights allows the pilot valve to move — either to dump oil from behind the power piston or to direct oil into the cylinder.

When the engine load is increased, the engine speed will drop, and the centrifugal force acting on the governor weights will decrease. With reduced centrifugal force opposing it, the governor spring will force the pilot valve down, and the governor weights inwards.

As the pilot valve plunger moves down, it will uncover the lower port of the governor shaft. With this port uncovered, oil under pressure from the governor pump will be admitted to the power cylinder below the piston, and will force the piston upwards.

This upward movement of the power piston will be transmitted to the terminal lever via the pushrod, and will rotate the terminal shaft to increase engine fuelling.

Because one end of the floating lever is linked to the speed droop bracket on the terminal lever, that end of the floating lever will also rise as the terminal shaft rotates, reducing the force exerted on the governor spring.

As a result of this reduced spring force, the governor fly-weights will move out as the pilot valve rises, until the control land on the pilot valve covers the port in the governor shaft. This will trap oil under the power piston. With the power piston held in this new position by the trapped oil, the engine will carry the increased load at a slightly reduced speed.

When the engine load is decreased, the engine speed will increase and the governor weights will be forced outwards by centrifugal force. This will force the pilot valve to move up and allow the oil trapped under the power piston to escape into the engine sump. The power piston now begins to move downwards, allowing the terminal lever and terminal shaft to rotate to a decreasing engine fuelling position. At the same time the floating lever starts to move down, placing an increased force on the speeder spring which pushes the pilot valve plunger down, closing off the lower port to the power piston. With the power piston now held in this new position by the trapped oil, the engine will rise in speed back up to the original speed setting prior to the engine being loaded. This sequence of events takes place in a very short period of time, making the SG governor very sensitive to engine load changes.

Speed droop

The SG governor has a speed droop adjustment built into the governor mechanism to meet a range of applications. With the speed droop bracket adjusted as far from the speeder spring as possible, any movement of the terminal lever will change the position of the floating lever and thus alter the force exerted by the speeder spring. The amount of movement in the floating lever is greatest when the speed droop bracket is adjusted away from the speeder spring and least when the bracket is moved towards the speeder spring. Therefore, the greater the movement of the floating lever, the less will be the force exerted by the speeder spring on the governor weights and pilot valve, which results in slower reaction time by the governor in fuelling the engine.

Speed adjustment

The speed-adjusting shaft is turned by a mechanism on the engine to set the governor for the desired running speed. A high-speed stop screw is provided on the side of the governor housing to limit the maximum engine speed for variable speed operation. If the

engine is to be operated at a constant speed setting, stop screws may be used to lock the position of the speed-adjusting shaft. Shutdown of a variable speed governed engine can be accomplished by turning the speed-adjusting shaft below the idle speed setting. In constant-speed applications with a locked throttle shaft, an electric fuel shut-off solenoid is used to stop the engine.

Automatic engine shutdown

The SG governor hydraulic circuit is supplied with and operates on engine lubricating oil. If at any time engine oil is not supplied to the governor due to an engine malfunction, the terminal shaft return spring will force the power piston into its cylinder and move the terminal shaft and fuel control to the no-fuel position, thereby shutting down the engine.

32

Electronic Engine Control System Diagnostics

All electronic engine control systems contain some sort of central processing unit such as an Electronic Control Module (ECM) which has control over all aspects of engine operation. The ECM contains a variety of standard integrated software packages which allow for detection, logging and retrieval of diagnostic information about the electronic engine control system. The diagnostic software is an integral part of the electronic system software which continually performs the task of plausibility testing and validity checking on all system inputs. The purpose of the diagnostic software is to aid in troubleshooting the electronic system components and at the same time provide constant monitoring of the engine sub-systems such as the cooling and lubricating systems.

The diagnostic software performs the task of monitoring all the inputs from sensors and detects cases where the input is out of the allowable signal range (e.g. signal volts too high or low) or in an invalid state (e.g. too low oil pressure or water level). Upon the detection of an unusual condition within the system, the software contained within the ECM starts a timer which measures how long it takes for this input/sensor to revert back to a normal state. If this condition does not clear within a certain period of time, then a fault will be assumed. These time periods have been specified in the system so as not to detect false faults which can occur due to intermittent power surges within the system. Faults detected within the electronic engine control system are called active faults — that is, they are presently active within the electronic system.

After a failure is detected, the diagnostic software performs the following functions.

1 The electronic malfunction light located on the vehicle dashboard will come on. This light will remain on for an active fault, and go off once the active fault has been repaired. The electronic system can also be designed to activate an alarm as well as the malfunction or fault light if the system fault relates to low oil pressure, low coolant level or high coolant temperature.
2 A fault message will be sent on the output data line to alert other devices of this failure. A similar message will be transmitted when the failure is cleared.
3 The normal electrical signal on the output data line for this sensor will be replaced with a 'bad data' indicator. This signals the other devices on the data line to ignore the data from this sensor.

4 The ECM registers the fault code in its internal memory fault table. This fault table contains an occurrence count of when and how many times the failure occurred. This occurrence count is limited to a certain number — for example, fifteen. The stored codes will remain in the ECM memory until cleared by an off-board diagnostic computer.

5 A default value will be assumed for a sensor with an out-of-range input signal. This default value provides a means of allowing the engine/vehicle to operate in a safe mode even though the ECM does not have any information from that particular sensor. In some engine control systems where the fault can result in an engine damaging situation such as loss of oil pressure or coolant, the ECM will derate the engine speed and power and, if necessary, shut the engine down.

All the failures in the electronic system are recoverable. This means that if the out-of-range signal from a sensor changes back to normal for a continuous period of time, then the fault will be cleared and the fault light will go off. However, the fault occurrence count will be kept in the ECM memory table in order to allow for later troubleshooting of this now inactive fault. An inactive fault is a fault which has occurred in the system originally as an active fault and has since been rectified. The fault code simply remains in the ECM memory so as to provide service personnel with a record of all the faults which have occurred in the system since the last service interval.

The ECM diagnostic software is directly tied to the output data link connection which is mounted under the vehicle dashboard. This connection provides an easy means of troubleshooting the system, since a complete fault history can be retrieved from the data link with a diagnostic tool as described below.

To utilise the diagnostic capabilities of the electronically controlled fuel injection system, several diagnostic tools are available. These tools are listed below.

Pro-Link 9000

The Pro-Link 9000 is a hand-held device which connects to the output data link connection located under the dashboard of the vehicle. This unit displays all active faults, all occurrences of inactive faults and allows monitoring of selected system parameters. This unit also allows stored inactive fault codes to be cleared, resetting of idle speed and customer data reprogramming. This tool can be used to access a number of electronic engine control systems provided the relevant software package is inserted into the back of the unit.

Fig 32.1 Hand held diagnostic data tool
Courtesy of Mack Trucks Inc

Diagnostic computer

The diagnostic computer is the most advanced of the diagnostic tools available for troubleshooting electronically controlled fuel injection systems. In addition to performing all the functions of the hand-held diagnostic tool, this unit will allow for enhanced diagnostics of the system, and also reprogramming of factory-set data. Once again, the diagnostic computer can be used to access a number of electronic engine control systems provided the computer has been programmed using the relevant system software.

Fig 32.2   Diagnostic Computer
Courtesy of Mack Trucks Inc

Digital multimeter

The digital multimeter is used to perform specific tests in the diagnostic testing procedures. These tests include measuring voltage and resistance, and checks for short circuits.

For consistent, successful results in the diagnostic tests, an understanding of the following terms is essential.

- **Voltage (volts)** is the electric potential or potential difference expressed in volts.
- **Resistance (ohms)** is the opposition offered by a component to the passage through it of a steady electric current, expressed in ohms.
- **Current (amps)** is the term for the strength of the flow of electricity, expressed in amps.
- **Short circuit (short)** is a connection of comparatively low resistance accidentally of intentionally made between points on a circuit between which the resistance is normally much greater.
- **Open circuit (open)** is any situation where the normally closed or continuous flow

of electricity has been interrupted — for example, a broken wire in the wiring harness.

Since there are many various types of digital multimeter available, specific instructions are not given here. Knowledge of the operation of the multimeter is assumed.

Fig 32.3   Digital multimeter being used to test a sensor within the electronic fuel injection system
Courtesy of Mack Trucks Inc

Diagnostic blink codes

The ECM is capable of blinking a two- or three- digit blink code for each of the detected active faults in the electronic system. These codes are displayed on the electronic malfunction light which is located on the vehicle dashboard. The primary reason for the blink code is to allow for a quick diagnosis of an active fault in the system without requiring an expensive troubleshooting tool. The blink codes can be used for isolating and troubleshooting any active faults in the electronic system.

A general description on how to use the blink codes so as to retrieve information from the ECM is provided below.

1 Turn the ignition key on and wait until the electronic fault light illuminates as the

system goes through a bulb and system check. If there are no faults in the system, the light will go out after a few seconds.

2 If there is an active fault in the system, the fault light will stay on after the system check.

Active fault blink code No. 1	No. 2	Component	Failure
1	1	Engine oil pressure sensor	Open/low voltage
1	2	Engine oil pressure sensor	High voltage
1	7	Coolant level sensor	Open/high voltage
2	1	Coolant temperature sensor	Low voltage
2	2	Coolant temperature sensor	Open/high voltage
2	3	Intake manifold air temp. sensor	Low voltage
2	4	Intake manifold air temp. sensor	Open/ high voltage
3	1	Buffered RPM (tachometer signal)	No signal
3	2	RPM/TDC (engine position) sensor	No signal
3	3	Injection pump RPM (eng. speed) sensor	No signal
3	4	Timing event marker	No signal
3	5	Timing actuator	Not responding properly
4	1	MPH sensor	Low voltage
4	2	MPH sensor	Open/high voltage
4	3	MPH sensor	Inactive
4	4	Rack position sensor	Mechanical misadjustment
4	5	Rack position sensor	Electrical failure
5	1	Throttle position sensor	High voltage
5	2	Throttle position sensor	High voltage
5	4	Fuel control actuator	Not responding properly
6	1	Fuel request line	No signal
6	2	Data line input (proprietary)	No signal
6	3	SAE/ATA J1708 serial line	No signal
7	2	Parking brake switch	High voltage
7	4	Shutdown over-ride switch	High voltage

Active fault	Sub-system	Failure
Red light and alarm	Engine coolant temp	Data valid but above normal operating range
Red light and alarm	Engine oil pressure	Data valid but below normal operating range
Red light and alarm	Engine coolant level	Voltage above normal or shorted high

Table 32.1 Active fault blink codes used in the V-Mac electronic engine control system
Courtesy of Mack Trucks Inc

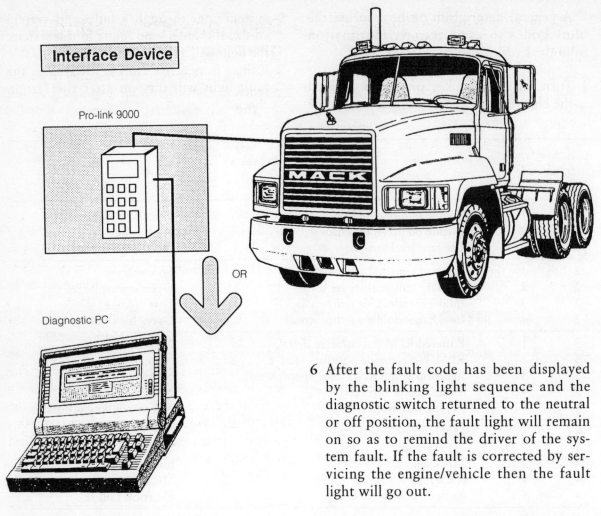

Interface Device

Pro-link 9000

OR

Diagnostic PC

Fig 32.4 Diagnostic tools being used to interface with the on-board computer
Courtesy of Mack Trucks Inc

3 To activate the fault code, the cruise control resume/accel switch or a separate diagnostic switch has to be pressed in order to make the fault light blink out the fault code.

4 On activating the diagnostic switch, the ECM will begin to flash a two- or three-digit code. The first sequence of flashes adds up to the first digit of the fault code. After a two-second pause, a second sequence of flashes will occur which represents the second digit of the fault code.

5 Any additional fault codes in the system will follow after a pause and will be displayed in the same manner.

6 After the fault code has been displayed by the blinking light sequence and the diagnostic switch returned to the neutral or off position, the fault light will remain on so as to remind the driver of the system fault. If the fault is corrected by servicing the engine/vehicle then the fault light will go out.

An active fault represents a fault in the system that should be investigated and repaired as soon as possible. Active faults which occur in the system are also recorded as logged or inactive faults in the ECM memory table. Inactive faults can only be retrieved from the ECM memory by the use of electronic service tools. These same service tools must also be used to wipe the inactive code from the ECM memory bank.

Diagnostic test procedures

Before beginning any troubleshooting procedure, it is imperative to make certain that a problem actually exists. If possible, talk to the driver of the vehicle and try to obtain as much information as possible about the problem. Verify that the complaint is not due to normal engine operation.

Once a fault has been determined, whether active or inactive, the testing procedure to locate the fault must be in accordance with that laid down by the engine manufacturer.

Before beginning the test sequence, check the condition of the wires and connectors. Check the batteries for correct voltage. Many electrical problems are caused by dirty, loose or disconnected connectors. Examine the wiring harnesses for places where sharp metal edges may have cut through the wiring. Check for damaged connectors or wires which may have pulled out of connector terminals. Intermittent problems are usually an indication of a loose or poor connection, or marginal adjustment on a particular component. After the wiring and connectors, the next most likely component to fail is a sensor or switch. The least likely component to fail is the ECM.

Beginning the testing procedures

After determining the fault code from the diagnostic blink procedure explained earlier, use the manufacturer's workshop manual which explains the test procedures to follow in order to find the fault. The test sequences are set up in a step-by-step method which will allow you to logically find a solution to the problem. Follow the tests exactly as they are outlined. Start at the beginning of each sequence and perform each test in the order in which they are given. The following diagrams are examples of the testing procedure used to check the electrical connections in an electronic engine control system.

As there are many and varied test procedures between one electronic system and the next, they cannot all be explained here in the same exacting detail as that of the manufacturer's service manual. Therefore, in order to be successful at fault finding in the electronic system, always use the recommended service tools and test procedures laid down for that system.

Test 1 (Checking for proper voltage on the voltage reference PLUS(+) line)

1. Disconnect the harness from the oil pressure sensor.

2. Turn the ignition key to the ON position.

3. Measure the voltage from the voltage reference PLUS(+) line(pin B) at the sensor end of the harness connector to a good ground.

If the voltage is between 4.75 and 5.25 volts, proceed to test 2.

If the voltage is NOT between 4.75 and 5.25 volts, proceed to test 3.

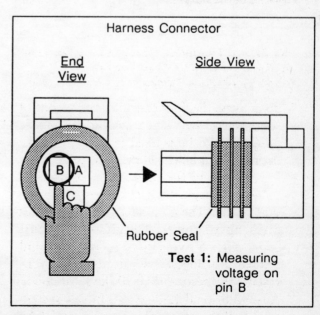

Fig 32.5   Checking the oil pressure sensor for correct voltage   *Courtesy of Mack Trucks Inc*

Test 2 (Checking for stray voltage on the signal line)

1. Measure the voltage from the oil pressure signal line (pin C) at the sensor end of the harness connector to a good ground.

If there are more than 0.5 volts present, proceed to test 4.

If less than 0.5 volts present, proceed to Test 5.

Test 3 (Checking the voltage reference PLUS(+) line high or low)

If the voltage in test one was greater than 5.25 volts, proceed to test 6.

If the voltage in test one was less than 4.75 volts, proceed to test 7.

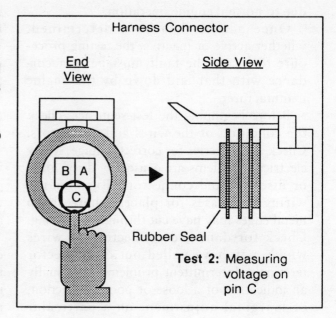

Harness Connector

End View

Side View

B A

C

Rubber Seal

Test 2: Measuring voltage on pin C

Fig 32.6 Checking the oil pressure sensor for stray voltage *Courtesy of Mack Trucks Inc*

33
Engine Emission Controls

The environmental requirements for diesel engines cover two entirely different subjects: air pollution problems and noise abatement.

The air pollution problem

Air pollution is a very complicated problem. There has always been a continuous cycle of adding to and extracting from the atmosphere. Humankind has increased the amount of substances added to the atmosphere but has done little about removing them. The most serious emissions of air pollution take place within the 30th and 60th parallels of the Northern Hemisphere, a belt in which the industrial areas of the world are concentrated.

Motor vehicles account for only a small proportion of the total amount of emission; diesel powered trucks account for less than 2 per cent. In principle, diesel exhaust gases are no problem on the highways where the engine is operating under suitable conditions and where the resulting exhaust gases are quickly thinned out by the air. However, the situation is entirely different in urban areas. Here there are many more vehicles and many of the engines are operating at idling speed or under other conditions conducive to poor combustion. Furthermore, these gases are emitted in the immediate vicinity of people.

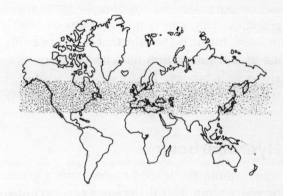

Fig 33.1   Zone of greatest air pollution (shaded)

Diesel exhaust gases

When discussing diesel exhaust gases, a distinction is made between the particle content of the emissions and the gas content.

The particle content — or soot, as it is generally described — consists of particles of carbon. The toxic gases of significance in exhaust gases are hydrocarbons (HC), nitrogen oxides NO_x and, to a certain extent, carbon monoxide. The greatest proportion of the exhaust gases consists of carbon dioxide and water.

Soot

Soot consists of particles of carbon that have not been completely burnt. The injection of fuel into the combustion chamber of an engine mixes it with air, but the mixture is not complete in all areas, which means there are local surpluses of fuel, and high temperature. Due to the lack of oxygen (rich mixture), dry distillation of the hydrocarbons in the fuel takes place and, due to the separation of hydrogen, the result is carbon. As combustion continues, this carbon mixes with oxygen to form carbon monoxide if there is sufficient oxygen and if the temperature is not below 1000°C.

If the supply of oxygen is poor and/or the temperature is too low, the particles of carbon remain in particle form and are seen in the exhaust gases as black smoke.

The particles join together to form small granules. This soot is not injurious to health in itself, but it is thought that it can possibly act as a condensation nucleus for more injurious substances. However, the soot is a source of irritation, since it reduces visibility and blackens the surroundings.

Hydrocarbons

The formula HC is used to designate a group of more than 100 different hydrocarbons. The hydrocarbon content in exhaust gases produced by motor vehicles is primarily the result of incomplete fuel combustion as well as of fuel that has evaporated from the fuel system. The greater proportion of HC emissions are not injurious to health, but some of them smell foul and others irritate the eyes and throat.

The amount of HC in exhaust gases is dependent on a number of factors related to the combustion process. High temperature, for example, gives a low HC content. One of the measures taken to combat HC emissions is therefore to design the engine to give a higher temperature during the combustion process under conditions of low load. The HC content of direct-injection diesels is also directly dependent on the so-called sack volume of the nozzle.

Hydrocarbon emissions are undergoing special study in the United States because they contribute to the formation of photochemical smog. Smog is the result of various reactions in the atmosphere started by the ultraviolet radiation of the sun. These reactions produce substances that, among other things, reduce visibility, irritate the eyes and damage vegetation. Smog can also form where there is a combination of heavy exhaust emissions, poor circulation and strong sunlight. Smog conditions occurred first in Los Angeles, but can now be found in most of the larger cities of the United States. In fact, there was smog in Los Angeles long before the motor vehicle, due to air pollution from natural sources.

Nitrogen oxides

NO_x is the collective term used for nitrogen oxides. The oxides present to any extent in diesel exhaust gases are nitric oxide (NO) and nitrogen dioxide (NO_2).

NO is colourless and without smell. In air, NO oxidises to NO_2, which is brownish-red and has a pungent, irritating smell. Excessively high concentrations of NO_2 are injurious to the lungs. Furthermore, NO_2 combines easily with the haemoglobin of the blood, preventing the blood from absorbing and transporting oxygen from the lungs and through the body. As with carbon monoxide poisoning, the ultimate consequence of this is suffocation.

The nitrogen oxides in exhaust gases are formed through the reaction between nitrogen and oxygen. This reaction is affected by the conditions prevailing in the combustion chamber, thus high temperature, high pressure and a good supply of oxygen give a high NO_x content.

Carbon monoxide

Carbon monoxide (CO) has no smell and is colourless. Carbon monoxide is poisonous because it can easily combine with the haemoglobin of the blood, preventing the blood from absorbing and transporting oxygen through our bodies. Again, the ultimate consequence of this is suffocation.

CO is formed during an intermediary stage of combustion. It later combines with oxygen to form the non-toxic carbon dioxide, CO_2. CO only occurs in exhaust gases if the supply of oxygen is insufficient. Since diesel engines work with a considerable surplus of air, the content of CO in diesel exhaust gases is low.

Exhaust emission controls

There is no single, simple solution to the complicated problem of air pollution by engine exhaust emissions. However, engine and fuel injection manufacturers have developed some effective methods of reducing the exhaust emissions from diesel engines.

Turbocharging

One of the many benefits of turbocharging is that it provides a greater surplus of air for combustion than is possible in a naturally aspirated engine. This increased air available in the cylinders ensures more complete combustion overall, with resultant reduced concentrations of hydrocarbons, soot and carbon monoxide in the exhaust emissions. However, during acceleration of a turbocharged engine from low speeds, low initial turbocharger boost causes the fuel-to-air ratio to be much higher than under normal operating conditions. As a result, incomplete combustion, caused by more fuel being injected than can be burned with the available air, produces dense black exhaust smoke.

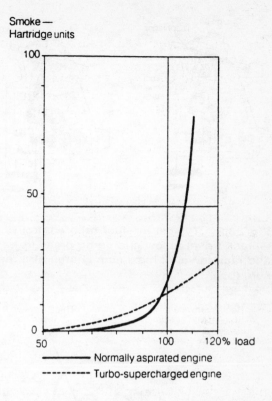

Fig 33.2 Exhaust smoke comparison — turbocharged and naturally aspirated engine

This incomplete combustion is only of short duration for, as the engine gains speed and exhaust gas energy increase, turbocharger output also increases, resulting in a suitable fuel-to-air ratio for efficient combustion.

Manufacturers have overcome this acceleration smoke problem by fitting an air–fuel ratio control, such as the typical example shown in Fig 33.3, to the injection pump. This device limits the quantity of fuel injected during acceleration relative to the turbocharger boost pressure to ensure that there is always enough air available for complete combustion of the fuel charge.

Another alternative that has been used is the throttle delay cylinder, something like a shock absorber, which allows the fuelling control mechanism to move toward maximum at a controlled (slow) rate, irrespective of how fast the throttle is being opened.

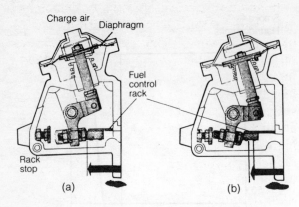

Fig 33.3 Typical air–fuel ratio control unit — rack travel at low charge air pressure (a), and rack travel at maximum charge air pressure (b)

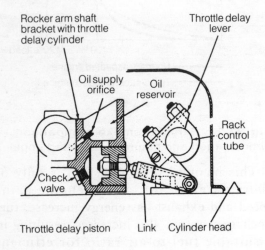

Fig 33.4 Throttle delay cylinder as fitted to a Detroit Diesel engine

Injector nozzle design

The multi-hole injection nozzle is designed so that the spray holes open into a cavity beneath the point of the needle valve called the dome cavity or sack, as shown in Fig 33.5. When the needle valve closes, a small amount of fuel remains in the sack and enters the combustion chamber, too late for efficient combustion. Experiments have shown that the volume of this sack is directly related to the unburned hydrocarbon content of the exhaust gas. To minimise this effect, injection

equipment manufacturers have designed the needle and seat angles and the positioning so that the needle travels as far down into the sack as possible, thereby reducing the sack volume to a minimum.

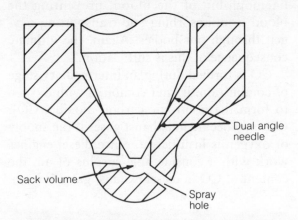

Fig 33.5 Emission control nozzle tip featuring a dual-angle needle and reduced sack volume

Electronic engine control systems

With the advent of electronics to monitor and control engine performance, manufacturers are now able to precisely control fuel metering, the duration of injection and the timing of injection relative to changing engine load and speed conditions. By using an electronic engine management system, the quantity of fuel injected is always accurately matched to the available air for efficient combustion throughout the entire engine operating range. Thus, by using electronics to manage the performance of the diesel engines, exhaust emissions that have previously been high in the low-to-medium speed range with conventionally governed engines are now as low as when the engine operates under optimal conditions.

Combustion chamber design

In the two-stage combustion system designed by Deutz Engines, fuel is injected into a swirl chamber containing about half the volume of hot compressed air for combustion. This low air-to-fuel ratio existing at the beginning of the combustion phase limits the formation of oxides of nitrogen, thereby reducing the hazardous exhaust emissions. As combustion continues (see Fig 33.6), the rising pressure pushes the partly burned combustion products into the double-swirl combustion chamber recessed in the piston crown, where the after-burning process takes place in the presence of excess air, under relatively low temperature and high turbulence conditions. These conditions again limit the formation of oxides of nitrogen, and minimise the output of hydrocarbon emissions into the environment.

Fig 33.6 Deutz dual-stage combustion chamber

Future emission control

In summary, the greatest formation of NO_x is when combustion temperature is at its highest and for a long duration, as would occur when an engine is operating at maximum torque. The formation of HC, on the other hand, is greatest when combustion is at a low temperature and of short duration, as would occur at low load and high speed — a situation in which low temperature and reduced time availability results in incomplete combustion and particle emission.

In an effort to clean up exhaust emissions and reduce atmospheric pollution, nitric oxides and particle emission are the prime target areas which will need to be looked into. Diesel engine research and development today is largely focused on reducing such exhaust emissions. The way to go about reducing these emissions is by lowering the temperature of the intake air which reduces combustion temperature and also by retarding injection timing. However, as soon as injection timing is retarded, combustion efficiency is lowered with a reduction of NO_x and a corresponding increase in fuel consumption. Also, with retarded injection timing, full combustion cannot be achieved within the cylinder with a resultant increase in exhaust gas temperature.

The general conclusion is that it is difficult to simultaneously achieve good fuel consumption, small particle amounts and low NO_x emission. Therefore, an acceptable compromise must be found. To find this balance, a carefully controlled combustion process with ample air supply at a low temperature must be developed. Combustion must be optimised, to delay heat release and limit combustion temperature. As mentioned earlier, the way to achieve this is to cool the intake air before it enters the engine and retard the injection timing. At full load, the temperature of the air entering an engine without boost air cooling may be as high as 150°C. By passing the air through an aftercooler, the temperature will drop to about 20°C above that of the ambient air at high load, and very close to this temperature at low load, ensuring that combustion occurs at a lower temperature.

Retarding injection timing under full load conditions is beneficial in reducing the NO_x content, but the same retarded timing on an engine under light load with low intake air temperature can result in poor combustion, with resulting higher amounts of unburnt fuel (HC) in the exhaust.

In an effort to reduce emissions over the complete engine operating range, injection can be timed to occur at a more suitable moment — that is, retarded in the working range, where the formation of nitric oxides is greatest, and advanced where the formation of unburnt hydrocarbons dominates. This requires a device that adjusts the start of injection according to engine speed and load.

Such a device is an **electronics engine management system**, which can be programmed to alter the injection timing relevant to changing engine speed and load conditions.

In conclusion, future reduction of NO_x will force injecting timing to be further retarded, with even greater increases in exhaust temperature. With exhaust temperature on the increase, the level of heat energy in the exhaust system will also increase. This higher-than-normal heat energy has the capability of driving not only the turbocharger, but also a turbine which is geared to the flywheel. Turbocompounding, as it is called, uses the exhaust gas to drive a turbine which is geared down and drives through a special coupling on to the engine flywheel. In this way, the unwanted heat now being produced in the exhaust system can be used to advantage in helping to operate the engine. This in turn will make the engine more efficient, as its own by-products will help to drive it with the end result of reduced fuel consumption and decreased exhaust emissions.

Noise control

Diesel engine manufacturers in recent years have made determined efforts to control and even lower the noise levels of their engines.

A rigid, strongly built basic engine, with castings made largely from cast iron, appears to be an effective first design step for quiet running. The ribbed convex surfaces of the engine blocks are examples of this design, as are timing covers that have slightly convex surfaces and are stiffened by an irregular network of ribs. As a further noise reduction measure, engine sumps have been strengthened in material and construction to prevent unnecessary vibration.

It would seem reasonable to assume that a turbocharged diesel engine would be noisier than a naturally aspirated model, since it provides greater power output and higher peak operating pressures. However, in practice, the turbocharged engine is much quieter than its naturally aspirated counterpart. There are a number of reasons for this. The typical diesel knock of an engine is due to

Non-toxic content (in concentrations present)	Direct injection	Indirect injection
Nitrogen gas (N_2)	76%	74%
Carbon dioxide (CO_2)	9%	11%
Water vapour (H_2O)	9%	11%
Oxygen (O_2)	6%	4%
Toxic contents		
Carbon monoxide (CO)	0.10%	0.05%
Nitrogen oxide (NO)	0.12%	0.10%
Nitrogen dioxide (NO_2)	0.02%	0.01%
Hydro carbons (HC)	0.02%	0.01%

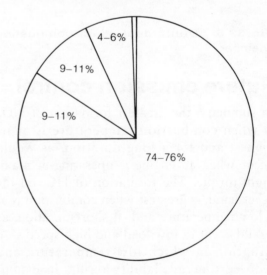

Fig 33.7 Exhaust emissions of a turbo-charged engine operating under load (by volume)

uncontrolled combustion resulting from the fuel injection continuing through the delay period, as described in Chapter 5. In a turbocharged engine, the air enters the cylinders at a higher temperature and pressure, which greatly reduces the delay period, thereby reducing the intensity of the uncontrolled combustion and its subsequent audible noise.

Furthermore, induction noise arises when the inlet valve opens during valve overlap and residual cylinder pressure is released into the intake manifold and air cleaner. This oscillating pressure surge is effectively dampened by the compressor part of the turbocharger. Exhaust noise is dampened in a similar manner. The pressure pulses that

occur when the exhaust valves open are modulated within the turbine housing of the turbocharger to the extent that some engines can be operated without the aid of a silencer.

Another factor is that the turbocharged engine is smaller in size than a naturally aspirated engine of comparable output. Being more compact, the turbocharged engine has smaller noise-emitting surfaces.

Noise control has also been improved by redesigning the engine cooling system to enclose the cooling fan and its ducting. Further, by increasing the size of the fan and attaching it directly to the front of the crankshaft, it operates at slower speeds and at reduced noise levels.

34

Alternative Fuels

Today, the majority of internal combustion (IC) engines operate on either the compression ignition or spark ignition principle. In both cases, suitable fuels have been developed in parallel with the development and improvement of the engines — petrol for use in spark ignition engines and diesel fuels (Chapter 15) for compression ignition engines.

These fuels are subject to exacting standards to ensure constant quality for the consumer. A vast network of distribution points throughout the world ensures the supply of both petrol and diesel fuel. Both situations are important when considering fuel alternatives.

However, with the shortage of fossil fuels predicted during the past decade, together with rising fuel costs, research has been undertaken worldwide into fuel alternatives for existing engines.

Fuels today, both proven and experimental, are either liquid or gaseous.

The liquid fuel options include:

- the diesel fuels — automotive distillate and industrial diesel fuel;
- petrol;
- alcohols (methanol, ethanol), vegetable oils and vegetable oil derivatives.

Gaseous fuels that are either in use or are considered to have potential include:

- liquified petroleum gas, LPG (propane butane);
- natural gas (primarily methane);
- biogas.

Liquid fuels

At the present time, the main fuels used for internal combustion engines are the diesel fuels and petrol. As both have a high energy content and are easy to store in non-pressurised tanks, these fuels are most suitable for mobile application. Liquid fuels that are considered as alternatives are the alcohol fuels (methanol ethanol) and vegetable oils.

Diesel fuels

Diesel fuels are mixtures of various hydrocarbons and are produced by distillation of mineral oil and/or by 'cracking' and hydrogenation of the residual products of the distillation process. Future diesel fuels are predicted to have a higher density and viscosity than present-day fuels, as well as a lower cetane number. This will be the result of production by a secondary refining process, which basically converts the heavy oil residuals left behind after the initial refining into usable diesel fuel. However, the secondary refining process does result in some degradation of the quality of the diesel fuel produced, although it still can be used in the more efficient diesel engines. Fuel produced by the secondary refining process usually has a lower cetane number and consequently a reduced readiness to burn. Automotive distillate is produced by either distillation or cracking. Its properties have been defined in Chapter 15.

Industrial diesel fuel is to a great extent produced from residues obtained during the oil refining process. It is cheaper than the more refined fuel, but requires higher investment and operating costs regarding storage, pre-heating and preparation. The higher percentage of ash, sulphur, sodium, vanadium, asphaltenes and carbon residues in this diesel fuel results in combustion products with corrosive and abrasive action, which increase the rate of engine wear. Despite this, it is used for large engines, particularly for marine propulsion, since the low price makes it economical to use, regardless of any initial high expenditure and increased rates of engine wear. Industrial diesel fuel must not be used in high-speed diesel engines.

Petrol

Petrol is also produced from mineral oil and is almost entirely used as fuel for spark ignition engines.

Alcohols

Alcohol fuels, especially methanol and ethanol, have been shown to have some potential as alternative fuels. Methanol (methyl alcohol) can be produced from brown coal, bituminous coal, wood and natural gas. Ethanol (ethyl alcohol) is formed by alcoholic fermentation of plant materials

with a high sugar or starch content. As the properties of ethanol are similar to those of methanol, engines suitable for methanol operation can also be operated on ethanol. Due to its higher calorific value (1.36 times that of methanol), the consumption of ethanol is lower than that of methanol.

However, both alcohols have a calorific value roughly half that of the petroleum-based fuels, thus necessitating approximately double the rate of fuel admission for similar engine performance, and increased fuel tank capacity. On the positive side, the exhaust gases emitted have a relatively small percentage of pollutants and a low concentration of nitrogen oxides (NO_x), and are free from black smoke. Both fuels have a high octane rating (which would suit a petrol engine), but a low cetane rating.

Alcohol fuels can be used in a diesel engine by using a dual fuel injection system. In the system shown in Fig 34.1, immediately prior to the injection of the alcohol fuel, a small amount of diesel fuel is injected, via a second spray nozzle, into the cylinder, where it is ignited normally by the heat of compression. During this combustion, the alcohol is injected into the combustion chamber and is ignited by the burning diesel fuel.

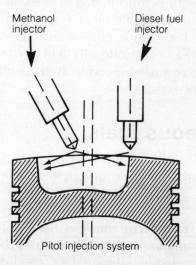

Methanol injector   Diesel fuel injector

Pitot injection system

Fig 34.1   Dual-fuel injection system

When the alcohol fuels are used in petrol engines, it is desirable to increase the compression ratio to gain comparable power, and to change synthetic fuel system components. However, the major modifications necessary involve increasing the fuelling rate and overcoming the inherent cold starting difficulties.

Vegetable oils

Vegetable oils are not clearly defined chemically. Not only are there differences between oils of the same species, but also of different plants and origins. As the ignition quality and the calorific value of vegetable oils are generally similar to those of commercial diesel fuels, they would seem to provide the alternative. Indeed, some tests have proved similar fuel consumption and engine power.

However, although vegetable oils are all virtually sulphur-free, they create other problems in that they are generally too viscous, often acidic, they choke injector nozzles with carbon and leave a high carbon residue on burning. In addition, the unburned residues form lacquer, leading to ring stick. These problems manifest themselves in long-term use and have yet to be solved. However, a great deal of research has been done into blends with petroleum-derived fuel, and into the use of vegetable oil esters — chemically modified vegetable oils — and there is no doubt that vegetable oils will provide an alternative fuel source for diesel engines in the years to come.

Gaseous fuels

Generally, all combustible gases can be used in internal combustion engines. The most popular gases are:

- **Liquified petroleum gas (LPG)**. This is predominantly propane and is produced from petroleum during the normal distillation process. Depending on the ambient temperature, it is stored in a liquefied state at pressures between 511 kPa and 1540 kPa. In this physical state it has an energy content slightly lower than that of liquid fuels. LPG is easier to handle and store as a liquid, but for mixture formation and combustion within the engine, it must be transformed into a gaseous state.
- **Natural gas**. This is a petroleum-related gas, which occurs naturally in underground gas fields. Although it is most widely used as a domestic fuel, it is also used as an engine fuel.
- **Biogas**. This gas, which is often referred to as methane, is produced in biogas systems during the decomposition of biomass materials such as plants, liquid manure and manure in the absence of air and preferably at constant temperature levels. Its composition is principally methane, with hydrogen sulphide and carbon dioxide the major impurities.

Gas ignition systems

Gases readily mix with air to produce a homogeneous mixture and, provided that the gases are relatively free of impurities, burn evenly with almost no black smoke emission. As the energy content of gases, even in a compressed state, is lower than that of liquid fuels, the specific fuel consumption of a standard engine is higher. However, with LPG this can be offset to some extent in petrol engines by increased compression ratios.

In the engine (whether it be a former petrol or a diesel engine designed to run on gas), an ignitable mixture is produced in a gas–air mixing carburettor, and led via the intake manifold into the combustion chamber, where it is compressed and ignited.

Ignition of the gas–air mixture is by an electric spark at a spark plug. This ensures reliable ignition of the mixture with all types of gas. The main disadvantage of gas as an alternative fuel for diesel engines lies in the cost of conversion.

Index